GW00835897

Time To Reflect

TIME
TO
REFLECT

An anthology
of
British Verse

William H. Sydenham
Publisher and Managing Editor

Editor
Vanessa Sydenham

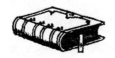

ISBN 0-9528964-1-9

Published by
Poetry In Print
PO Box 106
Huntingdon, Cambs.
PE17 5BS

Printed in England
by MPG Books Ltd., Bodmin

iv

INTRODUCTION

This is our second anthology of British verse. It follows our highly successful 1997 National Open Poetry Competition, which was open to all poets without regard to age, gender or experience. As will be evident from the following pages, we received numerous fine poems, many of which are outstanding. We congratulate all of our poets, young and not so young, many of whom have achieved recognition for the very first time.

The selection committee approached their difficult task with open minds. They have not allowed themselves to be influenced by any theory of what a poem should be, except that which requires that the poem should be interesting and within the bounds of poetry. The wide variety of poems chosen are designed to appeal to the general reader and to give pleasure to all who enjoy poetry for its own sake.

The judges were placed in the unenviable position of having to select a few winners from so many fine entries. It took many hours of dedicated deliberation to reach a conclusion and we thank them very sincerely for it.

Finally, we offer our sincere apologies to Jenny Joseph. Unbeknown to us a poem published in our last anthology, written by Jenny, was submitted with a new title. The poet concerned has written in person to Jenny. It was an error and all concerned have accepted the explanation given. Although we published this poem in good faith, we nonetheless apologise unreservedly.

CONTENTS

ACKNOWLEDGEMENTS

The publishers and editors are grateful for the efforts of the following
individuals in making this anthology possible:

Natasha Sydenham, Steven Westbury, Sandra Hunt,
Charlotte Osborne, Lisa Hunt, Sam Weller and Paul Jackson

Grand Prize Winner

Linda Bodicoat, Leics

Second Prize Winners

Rosemary Atherton, Gwent
Jim Henderson, Flint

P. Frost, Suffolk
Jackie Johnson, Suffolk

Third Prize Winners

Patricia Atkin, Notts
Margaret Brown, France
Carole Hall, West Yorks

Elizabeth Amery, N. Lincs
J. Button, Warks
Bradley Jacob, Essex

Fourth Prize Winners

Joyce Ayland, Hants
Elizabeth Aitken, Kent
Constance Burrows, E. Sussex
Richard Copeland, West Midlands
J.J. Clare, West Midlands
Marion Cook, West Yorks
Chris Davies, West Midlands
Denise Dye, South Yorks
Norman Dallen, Surrey
Kenneth Edwards, Conwy
Fran Merrett, North Lincs
K. McQueen, Leics
Margaret Ramsden, Cheshire

Charlotte Allum, Suffolk
Brenda Barber, Leics
Anne Brown, Cambs
Janet Cullup, Cambs
June Cameron, Tyne & Wear
Marina Davey, Hants
Audrey Donoghue, Gwent
Magda Dyson, West Yorks
Pauletta Edwards, Avon
Lorraine Meredith, Wrexham
Patricia McGowan, W. Mids
Joanne Reeder, South Yorks

Junior Awards

**Best Poem 10 and under,
Runner Up**

George O'Donnell, Kent
Carrie-Ann Turner, S. Yorks

**Best Poem 11 to 15 years,
Runner Up**

Kathryn Cullen, Kent
Jennifer Copestake, S. Yorks

Congratulations also to our Awards of Excellence winners

Illustration: Myles Birket Foster

We look before and after,
And pine for what is not:
Our sincerest laughter
With some pain in fraught;
Our sweetest songs are those that tell of saddest thought.

P. B. SHELLEY

Grand Prize Winner

Street Child

In the stillness of the morning,
See the sadness in her eyes.
As the world looks on in silence
On the child that cannot cry.
She's the victim of the tourist;
Sells her body, just to eat.
All her clothes are torn and dirty,
She has blisters on her feet.

If we bow our heads in sorrow
But then turn and walk away.
We deny her precious childhood,
Steal her innocence, her play.
See the child that is within her,
See the crime that should appal.
She's the child the world's forgotten,
She's the daughter of us all.

Help her face a new tomorrow,
Give her hope and happiness.
Help to save her from defilement,
All her suffering and distress.
If we speak aloud, condemning
All the evil that we see.
Give our wealth and our compassion,
Give her love and set her free.

Linda J. Bodicoat

9

Second Prize Winners

Street Dreams

Walking through the city streets, young girl so alone.
Circumstances led to this: No friends, no job, no home.
Close to tears, she looked around to seek a friendly face.
Folk, heads down, ignored her plight, just speeded up their pace.
Fatigue set in, she chose her patch, outside a high street store
Blanket old and pavement cold. She couldn't take much more.
Sitting there - did no-one care? - she let her mind go back
To happier times, to childhood days - to Dad and Mum and Jack.
The special days, the holidays, her parents, good and kind.
A teardrop fell as she realised just what she'd left behind.
The birthdays past when plans were made to give her a surprise:
On waking in the family home, the sight that met her eyes.
Balloons and streamers, gifts galore, were scattered all around.
"Happy Birthday, Suzy dear", was the cheerful sound . . . . .
Suzy, sad girl. Wiser now. Why did she scream and shout? . . . . .
Perhaps, if apologies were made, they could work it out . . . .
Searching through her bag, she found her one and only coin:
Getting up, she walked along and reached the nearest 'phone
Fingers trembling: voice a whisper: Mum could barely hear.
Soon to rejoice, Mum's tearful voice, "Happy Birthday, Dear".

Rosemary Atherton

Death Of The Titanic

Guaranteed unsinkable, this Lady would prevail,
O're stormy seas with thrashing waves and unrelenting gales.
Boasting her stability, they did not speculate,
Cocooned in their complacency they might be tempting fate.

The icy smooth Atlantic upheld the regal maid,
Her portholes lending shafts of light to ease the inky shade.
Fragmented crystals glittered from the dark encasing sky,
Creating false security to hoodwink and belie.

Thrust by her engines forward she glided neath the moon,
Accommodating those within, oblivious of their doom.
The Band was playing Ragtime, the party aura spread,
Then shattered by that fateful cry, "Iceberg right ahead".

Unheeded warnings might have saved the Maiden from her fate,
Too fast to swing her bows to stern, alas too fast! too late!
Looming from the briny deep the monstrous giant towered.
Then scraped along the starboard side, as awestruck mortals cowered.

Too soon invading waters caused the mighty bows to dip,
For the Berg had gauged a fatal wound along this noble ship.
Resigned, the maid with dignity, sent forth a rumbling boom,
Then slipped beneath her conqueror to meet her glassy tomb.

The perished now sleep peacefully, the rescued came to terms,
Mourning for their loved ones as fearful memories burn.
The souls they lost were Heavens gain, their former host lays maimed,
For man's design prevaileth not, but Heaven and Earth remain.

P. Frost

Homeless

She came and went like a ship in the night,
Arrived in the darkness, left in the light.
We gave her shelter, provided a bed,
Also made sure that she had been fed.

My son brought her home from the College that day
Said that she needed somewhere to stay,
We told him that she could stay for one night
But did not know if we were doing right.

Her family disowned her, they cast her out,
I don't know the facts, of what it's about,
The main thing was, she needed a place,
After all she is part of the human race.

She could have robbed us for all that we knew,
When we did not know her, did not have a clue,
But our consciences told us we must take her in
With the temperature freezing, wind a bit thin.

I did not see her, never met her at all,
Though my Wife had spoken to her in the hall,
Said she was pleasant, not badly dressed,
The Girl then departed upstairs to rest.

Looking back now I know we did right,
She came and went like a Ship in the night.

Jim Henderson

12

To My Autistic Son

What war are you fighting while in your sleep
What nightmares intrude to make you weep
Your body fights an imaginary foe
Your voice cries out in pain and woe

I talk to you, can you hear me son?
Is your mind with me or is it gone?
Let me into your secret world
Let me see your brow unfurled

You act out a play on your own secret stage
The delight, the misery and the rage
I am the audience but cannot see
What the plot or the ending will be

Your inner pain has torn me apart
I want to soothe the ache in your heart
I want the terror to disappear
Listen son, is it me that you hear?

I try to put myself inside your skin
But can't imagine the torment you're in
If I could I'd take your place
And let you join the human race

They say that one day out of the blue
Your love for me will come shining through
So I'll keep trying to turn the key
To open the door that keeps you from me

Jackie Johnson

Third Prize Winners

Sentimental Journey

I paid a visit yesterday to Wensor Castle Farm,
It hadn't lost its stateliness, it hadn't lost its charm,
Its ageing walls more weathered now than those we used to know
When we were pleased to call it 'home' so many years ago.

I didn't try to enter even though the door stood wide,
But through the iron gateway I stole a peep inside.
That love and care was lavished there was obvious to see
And I was glad for this old house had cared for you and me.

My memory took a backward leap of twenty years or more,
Our wedding day a week away, we stood before that door.
The Autumn dusk was falling as the Agent made to show
The rooms of this old mansion built a century ago.

One could almost see the ghosts of bygone ages in the hall
And hear the strains of music from a long-ago hunt ball.
The lords and ladies dancing in their crinoline and lace
Curtsying and bowing in an age of matchless grace.

If only these old walls could speak I wonder what they'd say
About the scores of people that had paused here on their way,
That had filled the rooms with laughter, joy and sadness, pain and tears
And shared their dreams and hopes with this old house throughout the years.

We'd felt the house was filled with warmth when we had sheltered here,
We'd talked of hopes and dreams and of the future we would share . . . .
And as I took a final look and turned to go my way
I knew I was the richer for my visit yesterday.

Patricia Atkin

14

Time

Turn to the man beside you, take his hand and say -
don't worry friend, I have the time,
I'll help you find the way.

I have no wealth to offer, money none to spare -
but time I have and plenty,
it's mine to give and share.

I've time to sit and listen, comfort, calm and heal -
to hold your hand, stroke your brow
and soothe the pain you feel.

I've time to give you all the space to cry, and speak your fears -
and when you're through I'll still be here
to wipe away the tears.

I've time to be there with you, waiting for relief -
that comes too late to save the child,
then I'll share your grief.

I've time to hear your anger and try to help you cope -
but most of all I have the time
to show that there is hope.

Help's not simply giving cash, it's reaching out a hand -
having time to show you care
and time to understand.

Margaret J. Brown

Request For A Transfer

It's hard to have the soul of a poet
And live on a council estate.
To look at the dirt and graffiti,
To see beauty and fight back the hate.

When each day becomes a new battle
Which the vandals look certain to win
It's so hard to keep your mind open
To the goodness that life holds within.

You can lock your front door, so the old saying goes,
Just shut yourself in there and hide
But life's not within a council flat's walls -
It's throbbing and churning outside.

So you pick your way out through the torn refuse sacks
Which lie by the paint-spattered wall
And you don't see the four letter words on your door -
You pretend that you're not there at all.

Carole Hall

A Whisper Of Time

Delicate as wings
On a butterfly
That flutters past
In the wink of an eye
Before we realise it
Time has flown
Here we are left
Distant and dreaming
Deep in contemplation
In a world of our own

Elizabeth Amery

16

Last Of The Summer Wine

Last of the summer wine are we, we take our dogs a walk
Around the local park each day and stop and stand and talk
We'd sit if there were any seats but local yobs have been
And vandalised them one by one, destruction is their scene
There's problems too with motor bikes that tear around the park
They'll maim someone one of these days and treat it as a lark
We talk about the good old days when we were in our prime
We safely walked the streets at night and very little crime
Our school days seemed to pass so slow but middle years went fast
As we grow older every year goes quicker than the last
We love to reminisce at length the life we used to lead
A good night out cost us five bob, including a good feed
A tanner bought a pint of ale, with cigs fourpence for ten
Although it's good to reminisce, we wouldn't change now for then
We dwell upon the happy times, not rigours of the day
When we worked sixty hours a week with very little pay
The mills closed down one week a year, that week we got no pay
We saved our money week by week for our 'wakes' holiday
When we were ill in good old days we got a doctor's bill
The good old days meant keeping fit, they were bad old days when ill
Our pension now buys all we need, prescriptions, doctor, free
We're thankfull for the welfare state, and now just one more plea
Let's have more seats around the park, get motorcycles banned
Then we can safely walk our dogs and sit instead of stand

J. Button

17

Losing The Battle, Winning The War

A poem of love, a rhyme from the heart,
But where to begin? A suitable start;
When all hope has left you, it just can't get worse,
Creatively put, your feelings in verse.

Love seems a saviour, in a world full of fears,
Sadness is no crime, but cry joyful tears.
In life; defeat pain, stand strong in the crowd,
Smile if you're happy, be vibrant and loud.

It's easy to say, that life seems unfair,
But it just won't suffice, to relinquish the care.
There's plenty of hope, there's plenty of dreams,
It's hard when you're hurt, and life's torn at the seams.

So try believing in love, when all seems decayed,
Hold onto your hopes, and don't be afraid,
Think to the future, hold onto the past,
So cherish your memories, and then they will last.

For lovers and romance, a tale to be told,
Our love is the answer, it's as precious as gold,
Our world tries to tempt us, our trust is unsure,
We're losing the battle,
But winning the war.

Bradley Jacob

18

Junior Awards

Thoughts

Sometimes when I'm lying in bed,
I think of the world,
All the lives that are led,
I think of people that I've never met,
Those less fortunate,
Those we forget.
A million lives that I'll never know,
A million emotions that I'll never show.

I think of places that I've never been,
The world around me remains unseen.
I think of war, of fighting and peace,
For man's selfish needs, someone's life must cease.
A million voices that I'll never hear,
A million people that live in fear.
Everyone's life has a different theme.
We never see reality, only the dream.

Kathryn Cullen (Age 15)

The Shell Cocoon

Enfolded in the beauty of silken movement,
Touched by the colours of mother pearl,
Trapped in a heartstirring moment,
Waiting for the shell to shatter,
Your wings to unfurl.

A butterfly in a shell of feelings,
Cocooning through a magnificent phase,
Starting as a heartless being,
Ending as an intricate maze.

A maze of sweet feelings,
A maze of emotions,
With fast colours swirling,
And musical motions.
A maze free of violence,
With tendrils of beauty,
A lake of pure silence . . .

. . . It means so much to me

Jennifer Copestake (Age 13)

The Rainbow

I can sit and wonder why
How the rainbow lights the sky
Does it fly does it climb
I can sit and wonder all the time
Underneath this splendid tree
The twinkling colours shine on me
There's a colour I can see
Can you too
It's blue!

George O'Donnell (Age 6)

My Imaginary Friend Jim

Jim gets me into trouble
By blowing bubble-gum bubbles.
He spikes his hair with my dad's gel
Jim leaves a mess you can tell
So all my dad does is yell.
Jim paints my face as Coco the clown
All my mum does is frown.
He makes mud pies in my mum's best china
Then puts mud on my face so I'm as black as a miner.
We jump on my bed spread
So my parents shout "Go to bed!"
Jim and I went to my sister's wedding
And he split her bedding.
Jim once dressed me up as a punk
Then he drowned my dad's prize chipmunk.
He cuts my doll's hair
Most of them are old and rare.
If you can't believe this poem
Perhaps you'd rather not know him.

Carrie-Ann Turner (Age 10)

Of The Heart

Oh vast fair country situate so far across the sea
My mind is with you often, great love I feel for thee
Is the farm still in Irene, can you walk up Jan Smuts Hill?
Is the churchyard full of blossom, is life a pleasure still?

I well recall my favourite spot, they call it Paarl you know
And pearl it is amongst the hills and grapevines - you can go
To Stellenbosh and Franschhoek, then to the ostrich farm
And then back home to Rosenberg to dine in peace and calm

I think of red hot summer days, of braais by garden pool
Of getting high on good champagne - then jumping in to cool!
I remember cold bright mornings - the early morning sun -
The sky a myriad of stars each night when day is done

The creatures in the Kruger, giraffes, baboons and deer
The brightly multicoloured birds - their calls upon the air
I saw a monstrous elephant acoming o'er the hill
And rhinos at the waterhole - what next my eyes to thrill!

I planted a brunfelsia beside the back door stoep
(Yesterday-today-tomorrow) - what can you do but hope?
Deep purple, mauve and then white, it's highly perfumed too -
Can it know of tomorrow and what it means for you?

A world within one country, I know this to be true
The mountains, deserts, plains and hills and seas of azure blue
Oh dear, belovèd country - what is to be will be
For now your heart lies bleeding - and you've stolen mine from me

Charlotte Allum

To

To be in the light when you stand in the dark
To touch with the eye what the hand can't reach
When you feel you are falling a hand there to grip
Not to feel lonely when you know you're alone
To find extra strength when you feel you are weak
To find all these strengths is a blessing indeed.

M. Anderson

The Owl

The owl comes out at night
Looking so lovely when in flight,
Hovering and diving on its way,
Searching the ground for its prey.

It moves along in silent flight
Relying on its perfect sight.
If anything moves or even blinks
You can bet its life is soon extinct.

Oh, what a bird of renown,
Hunts in the country or a town,
Lives in a barn or any old tree
Well out of sight of you and me.

In haunting films it's in them all
With its spooky, hooting call.
When a full moon is in the sky
A hooting owl is nearby.

This little owl has done no harm;
It helps them all on the farm
To keep the vermin numbers down
And stop them spreading into town.

So you lovely bird go your way,
Hunt by night, sleep by day.
As we sleep you do your rounds;
Thank you for keeping the vermin down.

Francis Allen

Autumntide

Autumn leaves a'falling,
Stormcock a'calling.
Chill of Autumn air,
Michaelmas Fair.
Days a'shortening,
Seasons a'changing,
Winter draws on.

Swallows long away,
Storminess the day.
Bonfires a sight,
Fireworks night.
Frosty the morning,
Seasons a'changing,
Winter draws on.

Chestnuts a'roasting,
Cold hands a'toasting.
October, November,
Always remember;
God ordaining,
Seasons a'changing
Winter draws on.

Malcolm Arnott

Untitled

She sees not the moon by night
Nor the sun that gives us warmth and light
She has only sightless eyes
And delicate fingers to trace the lies
Hidden on faces she knows so well
An inflexion of the voice will also tell.
Sounds are enormous in her small ears
She's learnt it all over the years
But colours are a mystery still
And she finds this a bitter pill.
What is green and red and blue
What are these colours of different hue.
She can feel the trees and flowers that grow
Feel the rain and feel the snow
But she's happy with me by her side
For I am the dog who is her guide.

J. Ahmadi

23

Potatoes Were Only A Penny

When things were rationed years ago, we were all quite poor,
We didn't know what carpet was, just lino on the floor.
Walls were stippled green and brown, it was the quite 'in thing',
An old gas stove, mantle shelf, and a bath that was made of tin.

Potatoes were a penny a pound, bread was twopence more,
We didn't have oranges very much, everyone was poor.
Bread and dripping for my dear old dad, he did enjoy it so,
He would ride his bike each day, even in the snow.

There was a shop just down the road, it was my favourite place,
Lots of sweets in the jars, and Mr Clarke's smiling face.
We'd take jam jars into his shop, and he would give us a sweet;
This was great fun for all the kids, who lived along the street.

The milkman's horse would come along, and stop for quite a while,
Ruthie's mum would come along, and pick up a huge big pile!
This was for tomatoes that she grew, in her little back yard,
Make do or mend, that's what we'd do, times were really hard.

The winkle man would come along, each Sunday afternoon,
Crying 'cockles and mussels' for everyone, he couldn't come too soon!
There was a tramp near by that came along, and sang as loud as can be,
We'd give him a penny, a piece of bread, and sometimes a cup of tea.

Oh those days of long ago, they really weren't so bad,
We'd make ends meet all the time, it made us feel real glad.
There wasn't a rat race in those days, we all helped each other,
I came through these challenging years, with the help of mother.

Joyce Ayland

Heaven Scent

The depth of dependence
To know I belong,
My passion in alto -
Her sorrowful song,
Douse doubt away
To a land far gone;
Never saw an angel before she came along

Eloise Arnold

24

Pearl Reflections

Since first we were married, thirty years to the day,
Our love has been tested in so many ways.
There's been sunshine and showers as we travelled along
The pathway of life, so winding and long.

We've walked close together up hill and down dale
Trusting in God that our love would not fail.
Climbed mountains not knowing if we'd reach the top
But always we made it, with love as the prop.

On reaching the summit what beauty we found
Blue skies and green fields, rippling streams o'er the ground.
Mother nature reflecting the tapestry of life
Woven with love, by a man and his wife.

God willing, together, for many years more
We'll add colours and textures that life holds in store.
Not always the pattern designed long ago
But then, who are we, our future to know?

We trust the next THIRTY have days filled with joy,
Love and contentment as in years gone by.
Days of sunshine and laughter we can happily share
Then our love will grow deeper, year after year.

Audrey V. Anderson

Passing By

I have a friend whose name is Joe
He seems to be always on the go
Chirpy and cheery just like a bird
Knowing everyone, with never a bad word
After talking to him you've got to keep smiling

No need to look sad, forlorn and beguiling
He's had his troubles and sorrows too
But he comes up trumps just for you
If you're feeling down hearted just talk to Joe
He'll put you on the right road smiling as you go
How he does it, I don't really know

But he keeps the same, rain, snow or blow
A lesson to learn in all these things
Live for each day and what it brings
A cheery word goes a long long way
And it doesn't cost a thing as you go on your way

Lilian Attley

Death

Life is an endless highway it seems
An inevitable end we only can dream
Death a confused and curious question
On our lips we decline to mention

Eerie mists which hang in the air
Hover over ground so low so bare
Whispering spirits of lives once lived
Drifting towards the realm of the dead

Dark headstones on curious slopes stand silent
Stone angels rising tall decay shows their face
The journey of life has lost its place
Another sleeper in the quiet earth

Death is not the end?

Kerry L. Armitage

Sharon

Thick tense under pressure
The air envelopes a body.
From the gloom
A solitary figure
Takes up the struggle.
Dispatched by Satan
A menacing personna
Stalks overhead.
Dressed in red and black
Armed with flimsy framed fabric
She battles forward.
The beast slavering
Strides the skies
Spitting shards of phlegm
Electric tongue flicking
Guttural rumblings
Fill the heavens with invections.

Edward Alexander

Jesus Wept

"Jesus Wept"! Did he never laugh?
Did he never lie on his mother's knee
Chortling and chuckling full of glee,
Clapping his hands delightedly
And cooing to birds in a nearby tree?
Did he see just the darker half?

"Jesus Wept"! Did he never sing?
Did he never jump and dance with joy,
Or run and play with a favourite toy,
Create a noise just to annoy
When he was a very tiny boy?
Did his voice never rise and ring?

"Jesus Wept"! Never full of fun?
Do you tell me he never did chase a cat,
Or tease it 'til it turned and spat,
Nor climbed the trees, nor fell down flat,
And fingers meddling with this and that?
Did he never laugh at a pun?

Why God himself must have laughed when
He'd made the elephant's trailing nose
And the camel that never did smell like a rose;
The giraffe that needs not to stand on its toes,
And the hippo that under the water blows.
He certainly did laugh then!

Margery Harrington Allan

A Casualty Of War

A Trooper was Tom Cammock, in the Royal Horse Artillery
Who faced the Boer and German, far across the sea
Riding on the lead horse, with cannon behind the team
A little man fulfilling, everyones heroic dream

Bullet, shell or sabre, never found this Ulster son
It was the germ Malaria, that took him from his gun
Having fought in Africa and managed to survive
Was years after sent to France and still remained alive

But there the Foeman got him, by devious means alas
Using the putrid killer, know as Mustard Gas
With bandaged eyes he left, that bloody battlefield
A half blinded future, fate for him had sealed

As a boy I watched him, shuffling along by the Gasworks wall
That unsung little Hero, who one time rode so tall
Shoulders raised to take more air, in lungs seared long before
He'd seen his days of glory and drove the horse no more

He dwelt for thirty years and more, at his Belfast abode
In the Street of Havelock, just off the Ormeau Road
With his wounds he suffered, the years filled with pain
Until the Lord called him home, a life not lived in vain

Viewing those marching Veterans and on hearing the bugle call
I see Trooper Cammock on the lead horse, mounted proud and tall
In conflict as a youth and man, on a foreign field
Emblazoned in his nature, to not give way or yield

Monty Alexander

Vandals

There's a tree at the end of the road,
Old and gnarled and free.
The youngsters who carve and swing on it
Don't see the history.

An old lady lives at the end of the road,
Old and gnarled like the tree.
The youths who swing on her gate and abuse her
Don't see the history.

A bulldozer waits at the end of the road,
Ready for house and tree.
The vandals in the Town Hall
Don't see the history.

J. Alexander

My True Love

In Scarborough looking at a seaside view
That was the place I fell in love with you.
In amongst the sea and golden sand,
You looked at me and I took your hand.

We've been going out ever so long,
Because our love is ever so strong.
We've been through so much together,
Because I want our love to last forever.

I think of you all the time but that's cool,
Because my love for you is a bottomless pool.
You're constantly on my mind because I care,
As long as there's a me and you I want you there.

You are the only one on earth for me,
My heart's all yours, you hold the key.
Your kiss sends shivers down my spine
A cuddle makes me glad your mine.

Helen Abel

To The Robin

Dear Robin Redbreast, sweet little thing,
Symbol of Winter, messenger of Spring.
How elegantly you stand amid Winter's snow
With your cocky little head and your red breast aglow.

We see you about us all the year long;
You never desert, and regale us with song.
How jealously you guard your little domain
From fellow robins who would it attain.

Little ball of fluff with a twinkling eye,
You fly down to earth to gather crumbs which we shy,
Then fly off again, just out of our sight
Like a beautiful dream that is gone with the night.

That's as it should be for man being man
Would harm you for sure as only man can.
To lose you would cause sorrow and despair;
You flit through our lives like a breath of fresh air.

It is said that a thorn from the crown of our Lord
Pierced your body and out the blood poured.
If that is so, you are truly most blest
Bird amongst birds, above all the rest.

Marlene Ann Allen

Wearing The Bottoms Of Your Trousers Rolled

summer's long gone - yet
seeing flowing hair, slim hips moving,
'Indian Summer' blossoms

stinging shower:
under the soap-wrinkled skin
young again

clouds on the horizon
looking away for a moment,
suddenly vanish

yet lost - through
a mind like a sieve
small memories

strolling on this path:
I grow lonelier, happiness
and hair falling out

growing old;
fly front undone -
again - no one noticed!

so much complex
organisation,
civilised death

Paul Amphlett

Sunset

Fire!
Like the Serengeti roof could not aspire
Nor the hellish torch attain
The sky, luminescent orange
Shot with shimmering opalescent spray

Melting the statue on the hill
It's stone arms slip in molten stream
The birds, in drugged hypnotic flight
Drift as to the sun-god's sacrifice

Resisting the final deathly throws
It's weakening labours cast a burnished gold
Fading orange sinks to deepest blue
And breathing darkness holds all at it's will

Leona Aitken

Majestyx

You are the keeper
A dealer in forbidden keys

But as your magic
Becomes familiar

You taint our faith

And eclipse our perspective
With your black crown

Paul Austin

29

Mother

She sits alone in her old armchair,
Someone must love her someone must care,
She's almost eighty - has no friend
Will she suffer thus - until the end?
Her memories, her life - all those dreams
Are filled with darkness; almost screams!
If only someone would hear her plea,
Befriend her and find her family.
She lives in hope, the days pass by
Life is cruel and hopes to die,
But every day brings a new hope
And that's the reason she can cope!
So is this your mother sitting there
Give it some thought and show you care,
The mother, who did so much for you
Showed you love, which was pure and true.
So travel by car, train or bus
Show you love her and make a fuss,
Make her happy, make her dreams come true
She's your mother - give the love she's due!

N.W. Addison

Salute To A Black Bird

The blackbird is singing,
a sure sign of Spring.
Of all the bird family,
to me he his king.
His message of hope rings
clear from the trees.
Being carried along, to all,
on the breeze.
He makes me so humble,
this beautiful bird.
In all kinds of weather,
his song can be heard.
He sings of the joy of being alive.
I bow to his wisdom
His beauty His drive.

Heather Agius

Brian's Lot
(Inspired by Brian Cooke)

Brian worked hard at his steady job
Delivering goods in his company van.
But today looked like being one of those days
As nothing was going according to plan.

He was driving too fast, to make up lost time
Bouncing off speed ramps placed in the road.
Not hearing the crashes, the scraping of metal
From goods that fell as he shed his load.

He passed two old ladies walking their dogs
Gave them a smile as they looked up amazed
A vacuum cleaner landed beside them
Leaving them shaken and clearly dazed.

When glancing in his rear view mirror
Brian felt panic at the problem he'd caused
Reversing, he reloaded his battered goods
But on reaching the ladies he suddenly paused.

The old dears were trying to abscond with the cleaner
The dogs were barking but Brian was cross.
He chased them and slipped in something nasty
How was he going to explain to his Boss?

Christine Ash-Smith

Lost For Words

He leans against the sofa in a comfortable pose;
A writing pad beside him, his glasses on his nose,
A pencil at the ready - and yet he wonders why
Another unproductive day goes by.

He keeps a second notebook and pencil by his bed
To trap the fleeing phrases that mutter in his head.
His mind is over-active, and yet he heaves a sigh -
Another unrecorded day goes by.

Inspiration hovers like an uncompleted sneeze,
But putting pen to paper no longer comes with ease.
Although he seeks intently assistance from the sky,
Another uneventful day goes by.

He gazes in frustration at works he's penned before,
Knowing that inside him there's material for more.
To friends he wails in anguish: "However hard I try
Another unsuccessful day goes by."

In short, through seven seasons things move from bad to worse
Until he has the notion of putting it in verse.
At last the deadlock's broken; he no longer has to cry:
"Another uncreative day goes by."

Elizabeth Aitken

Spring & Summer In Suffolk

Soon it will be Spring
To see the leaves again on the trees
And to hear the birds sing
All God's creation alive again

To us that can see
What a joy nature is
To see again Spring flowers in bloom
The golden daffodil, tulips and hyacinths
Which sadly are gone too soon

Then comes the beautiful summer flowers
What a joy to behold
Are the roses that grow here in Suffolk
The wild poppy too
That grows in the fields and by the wayside
That bring happy thoughts untold

Of days when young
Of delightful walks in the fields
And lovely countryside
And to watch at Harvest time
And to see the men bring in their yield

Alice E. Adams

Old Jake

Jake, stalwart oak of a man,
craggily handsome, proud.
Strength, life's pressures gave,
'till aged and bowed,
this woodman sleeps -
in the old oak chair.

Marianne Atkinson

Spain

There was a young fellow from Spain
He always made it rain,
He took off his top,
Then he drank some pop,
And then he got a pain.

David Armstrong (Age 9)

31

Traces

Just imagine if I were to disappear,
to leave all you marionettes stringless?
You could wander about my halls in great despair,
echoing voices in harsh retreat, where, oh where?

My old, half-empty, sipped wine glasses are still there,
and you could touch them, sounding notes and dust.
The records are still playing Stones and Monk and you try to sing along
but you flounder and trip for you don't know the words to my own complex songs.

Then you trail your fingers like cobwebs across my dresses
and smiling, you all think of me and my eyes and my hair.
And again you cry where, oh where? And why, oh why?
But all you can see are my books and my thoughts and my empty wineglasses, almost dry.

Then you look at the door which is still ajar
and the trail of prints that I have left behind.
But I am long gone, and you're ten years too slow.
Couldn't you hear the goodbyes when I said hello?

Alexandra Ault

Friday Night

My clean shirt and mi new tie
Mi best suit and mi shoes.
It's Friday night, ter local pub
To drink away mi blues.
That first pint's always lovely
And my, it tastes good.
The barmaid - she's a looker
She knows I would if I could.
I'm not a bad dart thrower.
I'm also good at pool.
I'm handy at all card games
'Cos I knows all the rules.
The night it passes quickly
The landlord shouts "It's time.
Come on lads with the glasses
It'll soon be closing time".
The doors they close behind us
It's off back home I go
Ter sleep it off, 'til next week
And Friday night once more.

David Atkinson

Katherine's Toys

It's evening now and all is quiet;
My Angel sleeps upstairs,
Surrounded by her toys and dolls
And lots of cuddly bears.

Whilst down below, all's a mess:
Toys are strewn around,
Upon the chairs, upon the floor,
Some will not be found.

And now each silent object
Becomes sacred to me;
Katherine left them where they are -
I want to let them be.

And yet I must clear up the mess
Ready for next day,
When sunshine skips back down our stairs:
My daughter's come to play!

Jennifer Ashby

If Cowards Die Many Times Before Their Death -

I am a living ghost.
If you would be my letter
I would privatise your post.

And have all your mail redirected
To the address that is my heart;
But I am a timid spirit
And we live in words, apart.

The pilot has a cage of steel,
The sailor has his ship,
The gambler has a spinning wheel,
And the junkie has his trip:

But I only have my bright despair,
And a silent golden tongue.
And I am old and bitter -
You are sweet and young

Robert Arnold

Who Are You?

At night you dance for me alone, in my mind ballet.
I look close, you poise motionless, Arabesque, Attitude Croisee.
Slender arms holding your crystal ribbon high.
Body refracting street light and moons radiance.
Faceless, on whom do you model? Fontyen, Markova,
Or none? A whim of your creator?
Who will you dance for me tonight?
Giselle, country girl, alive and free.
La Sylphide, fairy, inviting, enigmatic, will-o-the-wisp.
Yours is the aura of romance
To be beautiful to dance the evil parts.
I present you with no Grimm's Fairy Tale.
Your stance is full of life and zest.
Dangerously you perform on silver points.
Sensual long limbs, shapely thighs, petite breasts, you dance naked!
Pony tail held high! Defiant flag to modesty?
Is your name Issadora?
I see through you, know your game.
You tempt men's souls, fantasise their dreams,
Create imagination. Oh where is your reality?
Who are you dancer? What dance for me tonight?
Will you always remain another artists dream, his fantasy?
A nymph, a sprite, a wish captured in crystal glass.

Keith Andrews

Musings On The Millennium

Can we look forward to the thousand years ahead?
Do we rejoice - or are they years we dread.
The thousand years gone past, dark shadows there,
But light and sweetness too, were ours to share.
Innocence and purity - those lovely words,
Now strictly for the birds.
When air was pure, and water, and maidens' thoughts, perchance,
Today its porn and condoms, - what happened to romance?
Unborn babes - once gifts from God - now don't see light of day.
Accidents - unwanted - torn from life and cast away.
Yes, there were wars, men fought and died, but bravely face to face
Now a switch is thrown and far away,
A mushroom cloud burns up the human race.
Juices flowed for wholesome food enjoyed so heartily.
A shadow now blunts appetite - the monster B.S.E.
So are we looking forward to the thousand years ahead?
Of course we do, for still the human spirit is not dead.
Children' cheeks are rosy still, grass is green, fish leap in streams.
On dark horizons hope will shine and still we'll dream our dreams.

Olive Adams

Numbness

It's cold outside,
But our love will melt the snow away . . . .
          It's cold outside,
Will your love freeze day by day?
It's cold outside,
          Break my heart . . . . and you'll pay . . . .

Truth is out, the truth is out!! . . . .
The ice is on fire!! . . . .
          The truth is out, the truth is out!! . . . .
You sang my death wish in the choir . . . .
Truth is out, the truth is out!! . . . .
          You always were a liar . . .

My heart has broken . . . you threw me away . . . .
Without feeling . . . you pushed me from a height . . . .
          My heart has broken, you threw me away . . . .
How will I cope, when your thought haunts at night?
My heart has broken . . . you threw me away . . . .
          Laughed at my love . . . believe me . . I WILL BITE . . . .

Noreen Akram

Tomorrow's World Today

Nowadays words have double meanings
Windows are not just for looking through
They are a useful addition to the computer.

A mouse is not just a little furry animal
It is a part of the equipment necessary
In the use of your computer.

A megabyte might have been a large bite out of something
It isn't, it is a part of the computer
An 'E' Mail is not an elegant male
It is instead, of using the post.

An internet is not a web, it is another means of
Communicating with people all over the world
As you go to your bank it's a miracle how your money
Appears magically from a hole in the wall.

A dish as well as putting your food on
You can put it on the wall outside your house
To receive pictures through your television
Instantly from all over the world.

A microwave in early days could have been
A new style for your hair it is not
It is a wonderful invention for making meals hot.

OH! what a wonderful world we live in today.

Audrey Allott

Mother Of Mine

You're my pride and joy, you mean to me,
What I can't put in words,
You kept me warm, you blew my nose,
Your sweetest words I heard,
You helped me grow up strong and sturdy,
Ready for the world, you cared for me, you gave me love,
Your special little girl,
I love you Mum, you're really great,
And you deserve the best,
Of all the people that I've met,
You're the best of all the rest,
You're special Mum, you're all I need,
To help me through the day,
And nothing you can say or do,
Can take my love away.

Julie Atherton

35

On The Way to Heaven

Growth was single reached
to ape the level of flat earth,
edges from this fallen tree
were loaded on the barrow.

On the journey,
some fell out and
found themselves returned,
the first to arrive.
Rejoined the loam
that gave them life.

Some of the logs
from trunk and branches
slowly burned in fire,
though the saw was
slow to condemn,
conscious of sorrowful cuts.

Wrenched twigs, severed leaves
came loose and went to ground,
ghost reminders left behind
were scattered all around.

Chris Antcliff

Untitled

Lying here, warm in my den,
My tail curled round my ears,
What's that I hear? I jump in fright
The sounds are coming near.

I prick my ears, hold up my head,
My tail, erect and straight
I'll have to run for all I'm worth,
Before I am too late.

I slowly walk, I take great care
To the entrance of my den,
Look left, look right and take my chance
Beware of dogs and men!

And now I run, I mustn't stop
I've got to keep my head,
And if I stop I know full well,
For sure I will be dead.

The bugles sound the dogs all bark,
The men shout "Tally-Ho"!
I've got to keep on running fast
Lord please just let me go.

At last a place that could be safe
And down I quietly lay,
The sounds of dogs and men go past
I'll see another day.

Jaki Acock

Man Of The Road

With great concentration and without an utter,
He searches for fag-ends in the gutter.
Finding one, picks it up and lights it for all to see,
A filthy habit to most, but he wouldn't agree.

Has a face so rugged and deeply lined,
Seen fair battle with the weather, in its time.
Carries a slight stoop but his steps never falter,
Hardly ever speaks, only to beg for food and water.

His only possessions are shabby clothes,
And a tattered bag.
No money has he! but that doesn't make him sad.
Who knows where he comes from or where he goes?
A great mystery to all, is our 'man of the road'

Patricia Joan Abbott

A Downward Slide

I look downwards and feel queasy.
Your great height had not made the decision simple.
I sit on the perimeter, a position taken up many times before.
My hands tightly grip the edges,
Clinging on to the feelings of despair and hopelessness,
Unable and afraid to leave.

My fingers unclasp the cold unfeeling sides.
I start the journey downwards without realising it.
I feel the wind blowing gently on my face,
Cooling the angry flames inside.
Once again I feel free, unburdened
Able to enjoy the excitement of what is yet to come.

Suddenly my hands begin to feel warm,
Too warm. My body is alight.
The once reassuring breeze fans the growing flames,
I try to halt the descent.
The jagged metal pierces my skin,
The blood oozes out like the breath from my lungs.

I twirl around going down, down,
The pain rips through me.
The speed is too great to stop.
I must ride to the end.

Joy Aldridge

The Priceless Gift

The stable was cold and draughty but the hay was clean and sweet
The babe was gently sleeping with wise men at his feet.
The shepherds they were kneeling on the floor so rude and bare
Whilst angel voices echoed in the cold keen air.

Three kings then came to join them, bearing gifts so grand
Soon the news went winging out across the land
Tonight is born a saviour, in a humble stall
Come let us rejoice then and praise Him, one and all.

For He has brought salvation, His is the gift of love
Sent by a loving father watching from above.
That tiny little baby lying there so calm
Will lift up all our burdens and offer healing balm.

We only have to trust him and accept his gift so dear
Come let us kneel together and offer up a prayer,
We pray that all who know Him will spread the message wide
So all the earth may love Him and not just for Christmastide.

Jennifer Ashman

Holy Mary Fridge Magnet

Glow in the dark,
Blessed Virgin Mary fridge magnet,
Surrounded by a slice of watermelon,
Bite out of it,
And a, press to moo, Fresian cow.

Holy water, for pouring in the fountain at the front door,
Respectfully replacing Powers' in a half bottle,
And, this is an object of respect,
Fresh for a bless-me,
Hoping it doesn't hiss as I dab it on my forehead with my finer.

Peter Albert

Futility

Why is it that experience takes so long?
Wisdom an affliction for the old!
When our lives are but a passing heartbeat
For this age old world.

Why is it that the lust for life
Is strongest when we grow?
But when we appreciate what's ours
Our bodies tell us "time to go!"

It is a lucky man who finds himself
To be strong in body and yet wise.
To know the truth before it's too late
Is surely the greatest prize.

A. Armes

The Oak

Standing magnificent, defiant,
Soaring into the sky.
Tremendous girth, unbelievable
Roots, spearing down into the soil,
Unrepentant why!
Born from an acorn, hundred years ago or more.
Ignored by many as expected.
Scenery, scorn.
Cherished by those as being there
As nature chose to adorn

John Astell

Diet Through The Months

After all the festive fun, many diets have now begun,
They start a week then alas, new years parties you let pass,
Going strong now doing well, until you're under cupid's spell,
Valentines Day chocolates and wine, a dinner for two that's just fine.
Start again until Easter bunny hops, chocolate and sweeties in all the shops,
Easter eggs and hot cross buns, oh I bet I've put on tons,
April showers as I jump on the scales, they must be wrong I haven't failed?
May Day at the seaside great, the smell of the fish shop just my fate,
June's the month of my holiday, will I fit into my bikini (no way!)
I start now on a real fast plan, loose two stone in a week if I can.
On the beach the Baywatch tottie, as a baggy t-shirt hides my botty.
In July I try one more time, weddings to attend and I must shine,
How I long for a lovely treat, as I pick on my salad and bit of cooked meat,
I buy an exercise bike, video and all trendy gear, but after that sweating I just need a beer.
I look in my wardrobe with nothing to wear, I try to pretend that I don't care,
The fair arrives in town and so does the food, I try to diet but I'm not in the mood,
All the smells and the thrills calories galore, I'll have to starve myself once more.
Halloween toffee apples, Guy Fawkes hot dogs,
I'm sure these occasions are just made for hogs.
Birthday cake, nights out to name but a few, what harm can these do?
Christmas is coming and I have to impress, as I try and squeeze into my little black dress
Another quick miracle is what I need, I'll have to chop off my belly if I'm to succeed,
Turkey, mince pies and Christmas pud, as I sink in the chair with one heavy thud,
Jump on the scales as I scream with fear, oh what the heck I'll try again next year!

Debbie Blackburn

The Metal Girder

They built a new bridge
It was made from silver metal girders.
In July I crossed the bridge
And I noticed how bare the girders were
They were new and completely untouched.
I wrote his name on a girder, above mine
And drew a big heart around them both.
Then stood back and admired the evidence.

In December I walked over the bridge again
But it was different now everything had changed.
It was cold and the girders were grey and dull.
I did not feel the same as before.
I searched every inch of the bridge, every girder
But it was gone, completely erased.
How I wish I could forget him
As easily as that girder could.

Karen Allen

Friendship

You're a friend in a million
You're a friend in a billion
I never can bear to lose
My friendship with you
If I ever do, that
Will be a nightmare come true

A friend is someone like you
Caring and friendly as you
A friend you can turn to
Whenever you need to

Shumi Begum (Age 12)

A Promise

I promised to write you a poem
Though I'm sure I don't know what to say
I could say that I'll always love you
But I tell you so often each day

I could say you're my only ambition
That in you my every hope lies
But I know that those words are not needed
You can see all these things in my eyes.

I could say how time drags 'till I'm with you
Then how it flies when you're near
Perhaps I should say how I'm longing
To hold you forever my dear.

I should tell you how I never knew love
'till you came and opened the door
But what is the use when I'm certain
You knew all about this before.

I promised to write you a poem
But try as hard as I may
To find words to express my emotions
You know everything I could say.

So I'd better give up the idea
Of writing my feeling in rhyme
I'll just have to say that I'm sorry
And admit that I'm beaten this time.

F.N. Barton

It's No Secret

Skylark on the wing
Your notes ring loud and clear
Out across the valley
A pleasure to my ears

Sky lark on the wing
Tell me what you see
High among the clouds
Singing songs for free

If I was to tell you
The truth, would you believe,
And never speak a word,
But keep it secretly

I look down on a world
Where nature's built a dream,
Where man has never walked,
And greed is never seen.

Where creatures of the earth,
Live in harmony,
And freedom is for living,
And living is for free.

And only those who've known,
The happiness it brings,
Can ever know the reason,
Why a skylark - sings.

Bakewell Burt

Bubble Bath

September sunshine spreads its golden warmth into the room
Enfolding me in a lover's embrace
And scatters dancing patterns overhead
Lazily content, I lie beneath a veil of perfumed bubbles
And from under dipping lashes
Watch the line of beads slide over my skin
To leave pale tattoos
Tiny rainbows glisten in droplets to collect at my fingertips
And wait their turn to shimmer into the silken pool
The water swirls and eddies, and then is still again
And all the while smug decadence sprawls around.

Phyllis Bevan

A Lucky Old Man

Where have all the years gone?
It was only yesterday I was twenty one

What happened to the lad that would run ten mile
Then cross the finish line with a beaming smile

Now today is the day I collect an old age pension
My aches and pains I care not to mention

When suddenly I hear the voice of a tiny tot
It's worked a miracle all my pain is forgot

These few words are a miracle for sure
Just for one day the perfect cure

Come on Grandad let's go out and play
I am smiling again it's my lucky day

T.R. Billingham

The Spirit Of A True Friendship

Friends bound like sisters
We could of bore 'neath
The same bright star
Understanding one another's sorrows
Shows how alike we both are
Discussing our differences
Shows a deeper friendship by far

Whenever I have been down
You're there to bring me round
I would like to thank you
For a gift of sisterhood
That you have shown me
And the kindness of the friendship
You have given me

You have always been there
A true friend from the start
So now I'd like to thank you . . . Angie
From deep within my heart
My thoughts are today of thanks
My heart is today filled with joy

Jane Marie Binks

Threat Of Love

You threaten my existence
Whisper sounds of love
That penetrate my being
Until I can hardly move,
Transfixed by raw emotion
Until fear comes closing in.

You enter my lonely world
Of invisible torment and pain
Invade night-time dreams
Of raging unspent passion
Gripped by trembling fear
Until stillness comes again.

You struggle in my chaos
With knowledge in your eyes,
Reach undiscovered places
And creep inside my skin.
And as I look into your eyes
And feel your hands on mine
I try to hide the feelings
As fear comes creeping in.

Grace Bigmore

Murder As You Eat

In school dinners the gravy is acid,
The potatoes are bits of gutter,
If you eat it, you'd be a nutter.
It's all supposed to be nice,
But the burgers are full of lice!
The rice puds are maggots -
All slimy and white.
You've got to have a lot of might,
To eat the stone pies.
They say it's nice,
They're all lies,
The meat's just horrid
They say it's treats
The spaghetti bolognaise is dirt and worms
Our jacket potatoes are bombs
One bite and your guts fly the room
The next on the list
Is the TOMB.
Yet when I leave some
The teachers all say it's YUM.
But just to say
It doesn't suit my TUM.

David Berrie (Age 7)

Ready To Go

A weary body
Tired and old
Aching bones
Especially in cold
Yes, worse in winter
But even in heat
Can't get about
Anymore on these feet.

Hearing is going
Eyes on their way
Muscles are fading
Hair going grey.

I can't enjoy this world
My times up I know
But I've had a good life
And I'm ready to go.

Kathleen Jane Barton

For Susan Lesley
(Part of our family since the death of her mother)

As she says "What Wyn" for the hundredth time,
I reflect upon the life of this charge of mine.
I think of her mother,
When she knew she must soon this earth leave.
Did she worry, or fret, and anxiously grieve
For her child, whom she had watched grow in body,
But not in mind,
Thinking of the happiness she may never find.
Did this mother wonder how her daughter would fare
Without the bond they had come to share?
She who had picked up her child when she fell,
Too close, maybe, to be aware of the protective shell
Given to protect those chosen few,
They who see life with a different view.
Happy with the true basics in life,
Endowed with a mind forever free from strife.
Rest in peace, Susan's mother, and with the angels smile,
For every step she has taken has been worthwhile.
Each new day she will some new pleasure find,
Content in life and with untroubled mind.

Evelyn Blackshaw

The Other Woman

I can't believe I'm hearing this, I won't listen to what you say,
You always knew there was a chance she might find out one day.
You say that she's suspicious, so we'll have to be discreet,
And pretend that we are strangers when we're passing on the street.

You want me to forget the many times you've held me tight,
And all the whispered promises you made me in the night.
The ways you made me come alive, responding to your touch,
And how you made me realise it was you I loved so much.

That just to think about you now, wherever I might be,
Will bring your image to my mind and recall your voice to me.
Life only has a meaning because I know you're there,
I think, I feel, I function, I see beauty everywhere.

You awakened all my senses and showed to me love's power,
I am with you every second, every minute, every hour.
So how can I forget you now, pretend you don't exist,
Forget you ever loved me, pretend we never kissed.

You might as well command the stars to fall down with the rain,
And tell the sun to hide its face and never shine again.
There is no anaesthetic that could ever dull the pain,
And no sort of amputation could make me whole again.

And even if you murdered me I never could be free -
Because darling, I belong to you and you belong to me.

G.R. Bennett

Life's A Stage

As you step upon the dusty boards,
And the curtains swirl apart,
A thousand faces all stare back,
To the Silence of your heart.

Reciting words of a different life,
In a character not your own,
Something missing from our soul,
Like a king without his throne

Perhaps we're trying to believe,
That there's something more to see,
For life's a stage we're all stood on,
And you too are just like me.

Gary Blow

Conflict

A young fawn grazes calmly,
Suddenly, it runs and leaps
Like a ballet dancer performing
A wild, impossible feat.
A sleek car, engine purring,
Moves swiftly, purposefully
Along the tarmacadam ribbon
Like a missile homing in;
And, beautiful bodies wrecked, they meet
In a tangled, mangled carnage,
Of soft sensitive, sensuous flesh
And hard, sharp, streamlined metal
Each destroying the other,
In a bloody crumpled mess.

J.M. Bint

Nothing But The Grave

I challenge you to a duel
Of words and phrases
On empty pages
Of images conjured
And memory banks plundered
Of long forgotten dreams

My restless wandering imagination
Carves its way
Through rocks of resistance
Its meandering power
Only adds to its strength

Breaking down the barriers
Of dulled emotions and senses
To escape the valley of desolation
Onto the planes of creation
Through the caverns of the mind
Through planes of thought
Unchained by time

I challenge the unbelievers
Whose falling footsteps crush the flower
Whose angry words pull down the tower
Who would destroy all that is made
Who see beauty in nothing but the grave
I challenge you to a duel

Ian Barton

Goodnight, Sleep Tight

As the stars twinkle
up in the skies
children rest you
droopy eyes.
Tucked up cosily
under the covers
with a kiss on the cheek
from each of your mothers.
Now let your thoughts
turn to dreams,
in a land where nothing's
quite as it seems.
A lullaby is softly sung,
those goodnight bells are softly rung,
teddy sits just by your bed
now rest your tiny, sleepy head.

Clare Baxter

When Summer Comes To An End

When Summer comes to an end,
I'll surely miss
The fervent bliss
Of my golden glowing friend.

Days will change from bright to grey
Until our distant month of May
And down will fall the sleet and snow,
The reign of Winter as we know.

When Summer comes to an end,
What will become
Of my fiery sun?
Who shall replace my friend?

Who will love me warm and tender?
Who will shine uplifting splendour?
Who will give me days so bright?
Who will be my strength and light?

When Summer comes to an end,
The rain will pour
And winds will roar
Like the threat of an awful fiend.

My heart will yearn
For the precious return
Of my radiant, glorious friend;
When Summer comes to an end.

Helen Deborah Bennett

A Winter Sunday

On Sundays I feel so tired
I just don't want to get up out of bed.
With frost-bitten leafless trees.
Everywhere's white and the air is crisp.
A piece of fluffy undisturbed snow,
Soon to be trampled on by big black boots.
A little robin sings his faithful song.
When all the snow has eventually gone.

Danny Bark (Age 13)

My Teeth

If I want to keep my teeth all white,
I have to brush them every night.

I have to keep my gums all pink,
And wash my mouth out at the sink

If my teeth had stuck right out
I would close my mouth as I walked about.

My teeth are white and shiny bright,
And sparkle when its dark at night.

I clean my teeth on top and beneath,
Then I get my thumb and scrub my gum.

So keep out the plaque,
Don't get an attack,
And don't make all your teeth go black!

Carla Bird (Age 10)

The Softest Days

A panorama of beauty lies
Upon the opening of my eyes
As I lay beneath the blue
And taste the air that helps renew

The softest days meandering by
Do not disturb me as I lie
Pondering clear crystal views
That hold one's breath in every hue

The caressing breeze to pacify
A living sun to beautify
Nature's bounty to subdue
And feed the soul as morning dew

So is it my fate to wonder why
There is no will in me to try
To take the gold that's my due
But search for greater goals anew

John Batt

Time

Where have all the years gone?
The things I've said and done
So much to look back and say
I remember as if it was yesterday
Poor but loving were my childhood years
Proud was my father, not one to fear
So many memories, school days and teens
A young girl living out all her dreams
Then comes love stirring feelings inside
Two of us together now side by side
A family now we have of our own
No turning back the seeds have been sown
Where did the patience go, I thought I had
It would be much needed, so said my dad
Children can take up such a lot of time
Sometimes I remember we didn't have a dime
But childhood should be special it's true
That's when your real self grows inside of you
Children grown up now, how fast the time did fly
Grandchildren asking now, how long before you die?
But as I look back now, the years have been kind
The happy times I'll not forget, the bad, distant in my mind
So where have all those years gone?
Rolled over one by one
Too fast I say for I've not done, my life has just begun.

Barbara Barnes

45

Today

Drink and drugs are all of the rage
For youths and youngsters in this day and age
They try it just once
But are tempted for more
As they watch each other drop to the floor
One too many they'll take one day
Then there will be no more play
So sorry they are
They're in trouble and strife
But still take drugs and waste their life
Young and free will their life carry on
How many young have already gone
So healthy and strong
And so full of cheer
Some of those kids are no longer here
No lessons learnt by mates being ill
In their mouth with one more pill
Washed down with a drink
Of vodka or stout
Back to casualty to be pumped out
Pills and drink they take all the time
To pay for their habits they turn to crime
The young and the old
Are beaten up so bad
Just to pay for their pills it's really sad

Linda Blything

I Don't Want Toys For Christmas

Grandad would often call for me,
And off for walks we'd go,
With his walking stick in one hand,
And his hair as white as snow.

We'd stroll across the country-side,
By pine trees tall and straight,
Then down across by bluebell wood,
And o'er the wooden gate.

He took me to the sea-side,
So that I should see the sea,
Then he made a castle out of sand,
And said that's just for thee.

The stories that he told me,
Made me look at him in awe,
My dear old lovely Grandad,
Was my bestest friend of all.

I don't want toys for Christmas
Or a great big cuddly bear,
All I want is my Grandad back,
So that Christmas we could share.

John Bendle

The Vixen

All is bright beneath a big full moon,
As the stars all dance to a heavenly tune.
There in the grass the vixen sits still,
Adjusting her body to the late night chill.

Her ears prick up when she hears a sound,
As closely she huddles low to the ground.
Always aware that danger is near,
She waits for the moment the coast is clear.

With a motherly cry she calls her brood,
And tentatively teaches how to look for food,
Scratching and digging they rummage around,
Eating wiggley worms they pull from the ground.

The moon descends as the warm sun appears,
And the family hide as the darkness clears.
They snuggle up close to their mothers warm fur,
Now safe and sound from the trappers lure.

Sandra Balfour

A Summer's Message

Burning rays from the brilliant sun
Drying the earth, touching everyone.
Cloudless skies, this summer weather
Spells like this never last forever.
Tossing and turning on beds like fire
Drinking cold water to quench our desire.
So sticky and hot is our plight
Trying to sleep through a sultry night.

Scenes will change and dark clouds appear
Bliss at last, the air will clear.
The sky erupts with ferocity
Like a message of calamity.
Dazzling lightening and roars of thunder
The Lord is angry, can you wonder.
Perhaps he is with the world we know
Many people ready to strike the next blow.

Take note, look up and see the sight
The heavens alight with all its might.
Countless are frightened of the unknown
They cower in corners, or hate being alone.
We cannot control the clouds in the sky
Rolling and swirling passing us by
It's natures way to refresh the air
This wonderful world, we should all take care.

Ivy Baker

Indelible Stain

A drop of wine upon the floor,
The stain on the carpet leaves a trace,
That somebody was here before.

The drop of wine,
Leaves a memory,
Of somebody's life,
Every stain, mark and scratch,
Leaves a story behind
That has embedded its self,
Into the universes history.

Kim Bickley (Age 16)

Freedom

How lovely it is to be free,
Instead of working from nine until three
I have time to stop and have a chat
To everyone about this and that
And then the nicest
Thing of all is not
Being at everyone's beck and call

Diana R. Best

47

A Battlefield Lament

All love, all joy, all hate;
Every tear that has fallen,
That is falling now,
That has still to fall;
Every last kiss, every fear and heartfelt wish;
Every lost hope of every life,
All these and more lie motionless in heaps and rows
Or isolated sprawls,
In various attitudes of death.

No sunlight, wind or rain;
No shadowed night,
None of these things
Will bother them again;
Pale, lifeless forms in fullest bloom cut down.
Only the flies bear interest now,
Yet, in the Spring, ironically, fresh flowers
Will cover their remains;
New life born out of old.

Peter P. Balshaw

Miss Toogood

She attires herself with scorn at the dawn of each new day,
easing it over her waking soul like a favourite, well-fitting kid glove.
Scorn arches an eyebrow across the All-Bran
as the wireless recites rising unemployment figures
(they should pull up their socks, get on their bikes)
and scoffs at her cousin's postcard from Sydney Opera House
(married an inheritance, ideas above her station, more money than sense).
It silently disparages the neighbour's hearty greeting as she walks past his gate
(secondary modern, Yorkshire drawl, loud tie, cocktail cabinet)
and crosses the busy city street to avoid the Big Issue hawker
(scruffy dog, tattoos, dirty fingernails, grubby collar).
It snaps at the young cashier in the supermarket who offers the wrong change
(skirt like a pelmet. And don't they teach arithmetic these days?).
frowns at a noisy gaggle of foreign students in the Square
(over-indulged, over-dressed, over-the-top over here)
and omits to tip the chatty taxi-driver taking her home
(too pricey, too nosey, too familiar by half).
Alone again, facing another solitary Saturday evening,
she and her familiar second skin settle with a supercilious grin
to deride the hammy antics of "Neighbours" on TV
whilst she picks over a microwaved Menu-master For One
brought back from her weekly shopping spree.

Ali Batt

Beauty Of Life

Oh.. wouldn't I just like to be..
Sole owner of a money tree..
All the things that I could do
Giving, spending, all day through
Oblivious to my surround
My dreamy eyes searched barren ground
Alas, alas 'twas not for me
That damned elusive money tree
But wait.. what's that, something stirred
My eyes espied a wondrous bird
Black as night with yellow bill
Head pertly cocked, began to trill
A heavenly song, melodious sound
He softly hopped on dewy ground
Then silently he flew away
To azure skies .. no hint of grey
I watched him as he soared so high
Even wished I too could fly
I saw new life in plant and tree
How blind I'd been, but now I see
Wealth was not only silver or gold
It patiently waited for me to behold
Here were life's treasures given free
God's boundless love for you and me

Doreen Blakeley

A Day At The Seaside

It's fun beside the seaside,
to run and jump into the waves,
tickle your toes within its waters,
and to explore the seashores caves.

Dig holes with spades and buckets,
build great castles with the sand,
collecting shells and seaweed,
while mum gets all sun-tanned.

Sitting cool beneath the parasol,
while eating giant icecreams,
as the seagulls swoop above you,
crying out their screeching screams.

Stripy deck chairs sit out boldly,
while beach balls bounce about,
dad's been buried deep beneath the sand,
and my! how the children shout.

Many a day while at the seaside,
is spent sitting by the sea,
while summers sun is shining,
there's no better place to be.

Jacqui Bailey

The Gunslinger

Saloon doors swing on creaking hinges
Tumbleweed plucked from the arid desert
Rolls its crazy path down deserted streets
The man in black stands his ground
Mean staring eyes beneath a faded stetson
Leather waistcoat of dirt laden pockets
Weather worn jeans with dust filled creases
Jangling spurs hang on boots scuffed and muddy
Silver buckled belt shining like a beacon
Six gun shooters poised in jewelled holsters
Cowering townsfolk watch from grimy windows
Gloved hands perform their quicksilver draw
Triggers pulled in unison spewing death
Deadly bullets strike their twitching target
Bullying braggart kneels clutching his chest
Crumpled figure slumping in the dirt
Useless weapons grasped half drawn
The stranger wears a killers smile
Smoking guns gripped in steady hands
He turns on his heels in the clutching wind
Blending into the shadows, unseen

Paul Birkitt

The Point Of No Return

The jealous soul, impoverish goals,
Concepts blighted, the weak united,
The meagre myth, the socialist, the rift.
Contempt, the rage, a chance renaigh,
The tightrope of hope, a deliverance speech,
The humbles dreams, the walls to breech.
Shackled to hypocrisy the compatriotism, democracy,
What price the strangest vice, advice!
Solitude for they so prude, elude the limelight,
Dominate the hand of fate, time slips by too soon too late,
Poignantly omitting adversity, avoiding much calamity, the parity.
Sanctioned for piece of mind? Define mistakes collaborate,
Nothing complicated, the masquerade satiety,
Out of life cheated, yet never defeated.

Paddy Berry

Handbag And No Romance

Saturday. Going to a pub. Maybe on to a club
Meeting with pals and gals.
Beer. Lager. Shady dance. Handbags and no romance
Prancing around the leather
Lodger. Low. A lad insane. Let's begin the game
Who's gonna pay, to play?

Drink. Smoke. Trash and violence. Does this make sense:
Commit a sin to win?
Follow the rules. Who's going down? Jukebox in a pub in town
Play their song.
Bottles. Filters. Pints and gum. These are the tunes they hum.
Stuff Pulp and Oasis.

Run fast. Quick. Flee the ground. Stop there. Don't make a sound
Copper spots you and it's done. Banged up. Finished. Twenty-one
First aid. Live aid. Feed and heal. Bread and spread. Latest meal
Birthday? After crime. Happy returns? Lonely time
Visitors? No. Long overdue. Old man now?
22

Diamond. Club. Heart and spade. Thought you had it made?
Don't chance it next time . . .
No! Gamble! Play it! What a rush! Next time: royal flush.
Why not raise the stakes?
Beer? Lager? Shady dance? Stick with handbags and no romance.
Let the town find another.

James Baker

Scents And Sensibility

A summers' evening; light and keen, in velvet fields of emerald green,
Where everything was peaceful as the river ran beside ...
I tripped along through garlic glades - a perfumed fox in purple haze;
That melted in a whisper, and I halted in mid-stride.

I'd chanced upon a rodent scout; who upped his paws and glanced about
But failed to see me sinking within teething of his hide,
And every instinct bristled; 'til he turned his back and whistled;
And I sensed the idyll slipping, as the twinkle left my eyes ...

There were brown rats, and black rats; all sleek-and-run-to-fat rats,
Pouring through the meadow in a broiling vermin tide.
Rumbling and grumbling, the wave of rats came tumbling
And wove a thousand nightmares, as their bodies leapt and vied.

I turned my heel and swiftly made, for the hollow trees of the garlic glade,
Just beats ahead of the manic raid; I leapt across the ride.
To a clutch of roots as ever found. I span my tail and went to ground,
And laid in fear of every sound that passed on either side.

But the songs were of elation - Jubilation in migration ...
That presented opportunities; perhaps I should have tried.
I never took what chance that came; the old, infirm, the badly lame,
I found I'd lost my appetite, and turned my head aside ...

And when at last I looked again, the rats had gone; the world was sane,
And everything was peaceful as the river ran beside ...
A summers' evening, light and keen; in velvet fields of emerald green ...
But it's the last that I'll be seen - for rats I can't abide.

W. Helen Beard

God Help Us

God help us,
In our hour of need.
Make us strong to succeed,
Fill our hearts with love and peace,
Keep us safe wherever we go,
Fill our lives
With sunshine and not a grey sky in sight.
Rid all hate,
Stop all Wars,
Love thy neighbour,
Make peace with all.
Bring a smile to another's face,
Let laughter fill the air.
Spread your love in a world
Which no longer cares.

Melodie Bennett

Another

"Another" like so many others,
it varies little!
Like those before and those to come
Another could change it!
indeed they do!
For why, we will not know,
for Another has past!!

Ian Bingham

My Mom

My mom is eighty two
Knowing I've told you
She wouldn't like it
She goes to market every day
And has even been known to bike it

She told a gent
I'm seventy four
Who went knocking on her door
"Can I take you out my dear"
"Yes" she said "I'll have a beer"

She's not used to all this attention
New shoes and dress
Cost all of her pension

Her new gentleman friend is Harry
She nearly fainted
When he said "Shall we marry"

She said "No
I'm much too old"
To which Harry replied
"You're hearts stone cold"

"But my age is against me
Although you might not think so
I now need a garlic pill
To help me with my blood flow"

Yvonne Bacon

What I Used To See . . .

I look out of my windows,
and what can I see?

I see the most beautiful,
breathtaking things before me.
Way up high,
floating over me,
the clouds, white and grey.
When I look high,
I see the sun,
a bright yellow beacon,
that lights up the blue sky,
the hills,
the trees,
the fields,
the beauty of life.

I don't see,
those wonderful things anymore.
All I see,
is blackness.
I miss, what I used to see.
I miss you and
I miss me.
All I want,
is to see those things again.

Dave Blackwell

A Day At The Seaside

The donkey plodded up and down
I'm sure his face was wearing a frown
It was such a long way there and back
With children perched, like a weighty sack.

Whoops of glee from the end of the pier
Punctuated by screams of real fear.
The roller coaster's desperate race,
While the roundabout turned at a gentler pace.

Crazy golf in the local park,
A dip in the sea, before it got dark.
Fish and chips in yesterdays paper
Then on to the pub for a few pints later.

Angela Ballester

System Society

Electronic world of thunder.
Flashing pixel gaze their under.
Mesmerised by static force.
Pulling them helplessly towards.
An increasing epileptic power source.

Android systems circle round.
The Satellite ships that drift and frown.
Magnetic forces grimace proudly.
Clinging hold so bold and dandy

Data input food of thought
Hyperactive mentally taught
Society changing activating
Little minds persuading
Beaming laser penetrating
Parental guidance deteriorating

Children of the system age
Spurned to be all the rage
Boot 'em up and shot 'em down
Switch 'em on and move 'em round

Senseless glances beaming out
Screaming at their frightful bout
Robotic tuned clones so swell
Powered by a single cell

J.P. Bell

The Little Dears

They make you laugh
They make you cry
They can do strange things
Not knowing why

The things they say
Can embarrass you
In front of friends
Both old and new

They bring you worry
They cause you pain
But some of us go through it
Again and again

And as they grow older
They'll flee the nest
But the start you've given
Is the very best

Yes it's kiddies
I'm talking about
And yes they make you
Scream and shout

But you'll never be
Without them near
Bless their hearts
The little dears

Dawn Bedforth

My Sunflower

As I planted "My sunflower" from seed
I wondered would it grow or be covered by some unwanted weed
Day after day I would look to see
If there was any kind of life or joy for me
Then suddenly one morning to my surprise
"My sunflower" began to rise
As the weeks went by "My sunflower" grew and grew
And now it's so tall I can see the flower peeping through
And at last I can see "My sunflower" in bloom
Yellow and gold and looks like the moon
But now the nights are getting cold "My sunflower" begins to bow
Protecting it's seeds from the rain or the snow
And as I look into the sky
I can see "My sunflower" cry
And now I know it's time to say goodbye
The seeds I gathered one by one
And now "My sunflower" has gone
"My sunflower" has gone!

James Francis Banner

Lucy

All through the night she howls and bays
Taunted through the day by adult and child alike
Coat all mud and matted, on cold concrete she lays
Ears flat, eyes dull. She makes a pitiful sight

Oh! warm blooded creature my love goes out to you
As you pace to and fro in your nine by five prison
No toy or piece of wood for you to chew
No matter what I say your master won't listen

Your bed is a covered wooden box with open door
Sometimes I can only see your muzzle
As it sadly lays upon your paw
Why he treats you so, remains a puzzle

Your canine pal didn't survive the hell
Nor loneliness and lack of human warmth
Now your young have gone as well
All is left is to pad back and forth

The icy wind blows the rain pelts down
The snow so thick, like a blanket embalms you
And by the vicious Jack Frost you are found
By winter frozen stiff, by summer covered in dew

Lucy, Lucy please don't stare
For there is naught I can do
My guilt for you I cannot bear
Even from the authorities there is nothing to gain for you.

Jay Baker

Untitled

Sweet spring, dark winter.
Slides on into oblivion
Never seen never mind
Kissed or never kissed
Loved forever in unison.

Life without caring is nothing
Meaningless and empty, trite
Life should be for living
For needing to be needed for giving.
Today, tomorrow, this night.

Don't waste, my time, your time
This time, for all time.
Hold it, hold on, use it
Mind it , bind it, don't lose it.
Stop the rot, draw the line

Christine Bamber

Magical Moments

Two lovers kiss
Under a moonlit sky,
All they hear is each others sighs
Whispering and murmuring low,
Both feeling a sensual glow.

They could go on
Forever like this,
Holding on for one last kiss.

And as they go
Their separate ways,
There's a promise
Of more pleasant days.

J. Barr

54

The Little Pixie

There was a little pixie,
Beside our potting shed,
She looked so sad and lonely,
All dressed in pink and red,
I picked her up quite gently,
As she was very frail,
Her tiny hands were frozen,
Her face was very pale,
I found some pretty flowers,
And made a little coat,
Then next, I made a bonnet,
With pretty little bows,
Thin shoes made out of tinsel,
To keep the coldness out,
That tiny little pixie,
Would last the winter out,
She found a cosy corner,
Till summer came along,
Then left a little note there,
To let us know she'd gone.

B. Barlow

Thoughts Of Grandma

When I was young, I ran to you,
I told you tales of woe
You'd stoop to kiss my worried brow
Then straight away I'd know,
I had the best of allies
My true and trusted friend
Oh ever steadfast Grandma
My love to you I send.

I pass the gate where you would stand
Though no one else can see
With wrinkled face and care worn hand
You smile and wave to me
Fond memories of you standing there
Are locked within my heart
I'll never let them fade away
We're never far apart.

Rhona Bayliss

Change & Challenge

The stepping stones did glisten in the light of the moon
The water flowing gently played a magic tune
Holding hands so tightly staying side by side
Balanced for a moment then we did slip and slide
Reflecting on our challenge in wild grass we lay
Our laughter seemed to echo, to end a perfect day
At dawn we were awakened by a chorus so unique
Golden rays of sunshine nature seemed to speak
Colours of such splendour the rainbow seemed so near
The mist upon the mountains did slowly disappear
Such beauty did captivate my soul
To stay within my heart when I have grown old
It will not last forever I am sad to say
If the kings of concrete have their own way
The young ones try and try in vain
Living in the trees they endure the pain
Of seeing their landscapes torn apart
Once gone, gone forever they depart
Future generation in concrete jungles will dwell
On a sad note I end this poem, it is my way to tell
Such landscapes are our heritage
Of them to write a thousand page
This England, not now, now never
Will live within my heart forever

Shirley Beckett

The Fae

As twilight mist enshrouds the trees a silent voice still sings,
It sings of truth, beauty and joy and tells of Faerie rings,
If you go to trees by night and listen with your heart,
You'll hear the calling of the souls who've acted out their part.

From the corner of your eye, you will see the changlings dance.
A rhythmic twirl of widdershins jig, a mesmerising trance,
The music of the silent truth will whittle at your dreams,
Until you lose your sense of time, time isn't what it seems.

When the sunlight warms the earth and rises o'er the hill,
If you are lucky you may hear the Faeries dancing still,
They will fade into the trees and vanish without trace,
But you will hear that voice again as you pass by that place.

Do not forget the things you saw and knew then as a child,
Out there amongst the trees and rocks, imagination is wild,
If you ignore it long enough, it will leave this world of waking,
And as it goes it'll steal from you all the things that you have taken.

D.A. Blackham

My Daughter

You were such a beautiful child
(I still am, I still am)
Why oh why did you grow so wild
I wanted to keep you safe and warm
In a world where you would come to no harm
I loved you so much in those happy days
But you turned away to other ways
I grieved for you over the years
I saw you suffer and heard your tears
I had to protect myself, I had to withdraw
I had to think of what life had been before

You were such a beautiful child
(I still am, I still am)
You come to me now our eyes smile
Our arms link, we talk awhile
We tread lightly on each others ground
Not wanting to lose what we have found

You are such a beautiful child
(I love you, I love you)
Time heals all wounds so they say
Time is on our side, we'll find a way
To share our life, our joys and our sorrows
Love will grow stronger, tomorrow
(I know it will, I know it will)

Ruth Baker

A Gnomes Home

15 Rockhurst Drive
That's where I live and thrive
You see, I'm a gnome
And that's my home
There's lots to see
Especially for me
The birds and bees and various trees
Snails and slugs and even bugs
The seeds people sow
the bulbs that grow
And other things like butterfly wings
Wind and rain causes no pain
I imagine I'm alive
At Rockhurst Drive
Which I guard all day
Without any pay
All I ask is that I live
At one and five
For the pleasure I give.

Edward John Baker

Daddy's Girl

I was his little princess, his joy and delight,
I would eagerly await his return every night,
There were things to be done, the rabbits to feed,
Our Alsation to walk, a few miles was his need.

As dad came round the corner, to meet him I'd run
Be swept up high in the air, it really was fun.
Up on his shoulders back home I would ride,
This was MY dad, I'd be bursting with pride.

One night my dad went early to bed,
Mum said he had a bad pain in his head.
I did his jobs as well as I could,
Made sure the rabbits were given their food.

At eleven o'clock mum begged me to wake,
Said "Go ring the doctor for heaven's sake".
I ran to the box, repeated what I'd been told,
He came straight away, I was ever so cold.

Next morning a neighbour shook me roughly awake
Said "Your dad's dead, come on we've a journey to make,
Don't you dare start to cry or your neck I will break
You've got to be good for your mother's sake".

I could not understand, I was only eleven,
Why was MY father taken to heaven.
The pain, so intense, made worse, you see
By the callous, cruel woman who awakened me.

Berenice Mary Baxter

Red The Colour (The Colour Red)

Red wine warmed by the sun.
Red rug my love and I did love upon.
Red sunset melted into cool long languorous night.
Above us myriads of stars,
Looked down from never ending sky.
Red dawn, precursor to the waiting day,
Compelled us now to softly steal away.

Christine Beebee

Looking

Here there is a flower, with its petals gone,
A taste of our tomorrow, an omen of life to come.
Its roots are our foundation, where all our strength springs from,
And stalk our walk through life, short, yet tall for some.
Unopened bud reminds us of days of innocence,
Shrouded from the outside world where nothing else makes sense.
And when the flower comes to bloom in all its splendid glory,
Let loose upon uncertain life, this is our story.
Its brilliance and splendour for all the world to see,
Are apparent as they're gazed upon, outside and free.
As weeks go by, it ages fast, its days become our years,
Until in time life starts to drain, a mirror of what we fear.
Colour fading, strength depleting, fragile and unsteady,
At this point in time we know that we should all be ready.
The final days ungraceful as we suffer in our own existence,
Look at the flower, now devoid of all resistance.
Death looms for all mankind, in truth we cannot hide,
Unlike the flower which grows again, we're swept on a final tide.
And when in spring a tiny shoot breaks out from 'neath the soil,
A journey of our own begins, not in body but in soul.

J. R. Bainbridge

Her Upstairs

Well! It's never quite right for her upstairs; she's constantly got a moan
If she can't catch anyone passing she'll go to the telephone
And there's something wrong, and it's all our fault, so what are we going to do?
The fire won't burn or the tap won't turn, and 'Why have we blocked the loo?'
She'll drive us to drink will her upstairs; she knows we drink anyway
How she thinks she knows is anyone's guess, but she's certain we're sloshed all day!
If we put our aerial on the roof she's threatened to make a fuss;
An indoor one's been enough for her, so it should be enough for us.
We can't have gas because that's not safe, it's sure to invade her pipe,
We shall all explode with a horrible bang - and a whole lot of other tripe.
She doesn't go out, she stays in at home, and nobody comes to call,
She moons about looking pale and thin and driving us up the wall.
Well it's not our fault that she's friendless, it's nothing to do with us,
We're not our sister's keeper, we haven't got time to fuss;
We don't feel rotten about her, we've all got our own lives to live,
We're busily building up lives of our own, there isn't much over to give.
I suppose we could visit her sometimes and 'neighbour' just once in a while-
A bit of a chat and a natter and that, a nod and a bit of a smile;
I suppose we could be a bit friendly and show her that somebody cares...
Could that be all that she's needing - a bit of love taken upstairs?

Brenda Barber

War - The Deadly Game

Cruel and wicked war came not again near me.
My family and I are happy, as we are.
We may not love our neighbours yet murder them we shall not.
Break not my family, shatter not our community,
For the act of war shall always now be beneath me.

I know now the horrors of war, and no
Disguise of honour will lead my sons to your door.
Again men will be shot, gassed, blinded and blown to pieces.
So, again civilians and soldiers will be victims to your game.
I am more learned now, and shall not go to war even with my foe.

War is remorseless slaughter, a bloody ghastly mess,
With devastating consequences yet honouring the dead:
Muffled drum beats, solemn hymns and overwhelming sorrow
Of commemorating Acts for those you were told died in glory!
The fruits of war oh so bitter, with few left living to confess.

War - you lying cheat, you fake, you phoney.
Never will there be a war to end all wars,
And no better world will emerge for us aged heroes.
You've never left a country as you found it
And yet you still encourage the acts of such tragedy.

But wars will one day surely end, when we have all learnt -
A land without conflict is a land without wars,
And a land free of war is a land fit for heroes.

Zhanara Begum (Age 15)

Grandad

Will the sadness ever go away
I know the ache in my heart's here to stay
When I close my eyes you're all I can see
Why did you have to go and leave me
It all seems like a dream
I don't understand what it all means
I keep expecting to see your face
But you've gone to a far off place
I try to smile - I really tried
But it's hard when something inside has died
I feel you with me everywhere I go
And I know you loved me so
But it doesn't stop my tears from falling or my mourning
No-one can take our special memories away
They are all I think about day by day
There is one thing I know is true
And that's words can't describe how much I miss and love you.

Tracy Bradley

This Royal Throne Of Kings

This Royal Throne of Kings, that has known Queens,
Has overheard and witnessed many varied scenes.
In nearly twelve hundred years of Monarchs it has known,
Seven Queens have been; one equal Consort, shared the throne.

Royal status, often envied, constant obligation brings,
Official duties, miles apart, now are possible with wings
Yoke; that bondage can imply, and servitude that stings -
Applies to loyal Monarchs who give service without strings.
Loyalty is from the hearts - of subjects, Queens and Kings.

Throne of Kingdom and of Empire: Commonwealth is now the name.
Housed in Parliament, in London, Freedom's symbol is it's fame.
Rarely on this throne if ever, Monarch earned such warm acclaim,
Only when the Monarch's present does the Royal standard fly.
Now - on ship, plane, car or jeep - proclaims the Queen is nigh
Elizabeth the second keeps our Royal standards high.

Of affairs that are political our Monarch has no part;
For the Commonwealth as body, the throne surely is the heart.

Kings, and Queens too, in times past, have been dethroned and slain
In twelve-fifteen the barons did the Monarchs power restrain;
Not just a temporary measure, but a freedom to sustain,
Gone forever, here, the power that, abused, the throne can stain
So completely that, through "Winds of Change" our Sovereign we retain.

Constance M. Burrows

The Fox

What was that so late at night
How dare he give me such a fright,
It was a fox a whizzing by,
I'm going to follow him and spy!

He jumped a gate and now he's in,
He's making headway for the bin,
I saw him shaking - all a quiver -
Because he found a piece of liver!

He munched and munched on a crust of bread,
He stared at me, and I went dead,
And then he turned and fled away,
To beg or steal just makes his day!

Delma Bowen

Snow Of the World

The tingling in my stomach grew
As I pulled the frosted window to
The silvery flakes fluttered down
The target was the ground
The wind danced and swirled
Really wild around the world
It whizzed and it blew
Did battle as it flew

Maria Burrluck (Age 11)

The Shadowed City

The city hides a thousand dreams-
But there's no bed for me.
I'm a shadow on the pavement,
Without a destiny.

The city hides a thousand hopes-
Wherever can they be?
Lost in the world of make believe,
Where only the blind men see.

The city hides a thousand streets-
Where only dwellers tread.
Without a guide to take you there,
You'll earn no honest bread.

The city hides a thousand tears-
Only the lonely see
Shadows on the pavements,
Who share the days with me.

The city hides a thousand secrets-
That only strangers know-
Only ever told to those,
Who have no place to go.

The city hides a thousand fears-
That stench the night with shame,
Encompassing forgotten souls,
Whose graves will have no name.

Malcolm Wilson Bucknall

Mad March Day

Although the wind was blowing strong,
We thought we'd walk awhile,
And happily we went along
Across each bridge and stile.

Though many were the birds we saw,
And deer and squirrels too,
A greater pleasure was in store-
'Twas like a dream come true.

We came upon them suddenly,
All playing on the ground.
Those wondrous creatures, wild and free,
Were leaping all around.

We counted twenty - maybe more -
All bounding in the air.
In little groups of three or four,
They dashed round everywhere.

They seemingly ignored us
As they gleefully gave chase,
And scampered up towards us
As they ran their rural race.

It really was a life-time thrill
And we forgot our cares,
As silently and very still
We gazed enthralled...at hares.

Anne Brown

The Chimney Pot Across The Road

The chimney pot across the road
Is a very funny shape.
It's leaning over on its side,
Held up by a large glass plate.

A brown spotted pigeon,
Has its nest up there,
So there's bits of twigs and grass and straw
Sticking up everywhere.

One grey stone's all wobbly,
And all the red ones cracked.
Sadly, the cement dried knobbly,
But at least it remains all intact!

Kelly Bond (Age 13)

61

Thoughts While Standing In Tiananmen Square

You lie in plasticised immortality
Beneath the glass in your 'Mau' soleum,
Disturbed, they say, too frequently.

The long, long line of citizenry
Men, women and children, are hastened past
Hushed in solemnity.

They bow their heads, unbelievably
In tribute. They do not know. They think
You, like God delivered them from evil.

The millions, who did not survive your methods
Obviously
Cannot be here
To bring their never-born children
For a New Year treat to Tiananmen Square.

Where today
Fantastic bird-kites soar up into the air,
Cheerfully exorcising the too, too many ghosts
In Tiananmen Square.

Pamela Brooks

Bright Lights

"Can you spare some change"said the boy on the street,
"Just enough for a bite to eat".
They walk right by without a glance,
He never really was given a chance.
The children's homes weren't much fun,
So he decided to go on the run.
The bright lights of the city began to beckon,
A better chance of life or so he reckoned.
All too soon he was on his own.
Without money, food or a home.
So life on the streets became his way,
Begging and scavenging from day to day.
Cardboard city became his home,
Free to stay and free to roam.
Watching his back along the way,
Hoping he'll live for another day.
But then one snowy January night,
He could take no more and gave up the fight.
He had frozen to death in his bed on the floor,
The bright lights of the city were no more.

Tracey Brady

Memories

Every day I see her, 'the lonely one'; she sits and stares into space,
I often wonder why, but never have the time to ask.

Her hair is dirty and unkempt, her face is weathered and wrinkled,
Grey eyes do not see any beauty in the sunny autumn day.
Her hands are knarled and red, little birds flutter around her feet;
She does not move.

Her day is long, as it is day after day, she has no one.
I wonder? What lies deep in her mind?
Memories of days gone by perhaps.
Memories locked inside, she can't see anything else.

Has she known love, a love so rare and true; has she felt the breath
Of her loved one on her face when she was woken from sleepy dreams,
Felt his soft lips on hers, or heard the words 'I love you'.
I wonder?

I would like to think so, for if not, she hasn't lived at all;
Or, maybe she has, and lost it, and maybe that's why she sits alone
With her precious memories.

Eileen Bradley

Lottery Madness

The lottery is a load of madness
And sooner or later it will bring you sadness
Five million to one chance of winning
If you won it would be a new beginning
Mystic Meg is so dull
And the lottery is a load of bull

Dale Winton shouts out loud
Win the lottery and you will be proud
John turns on the machine
And it looks squeaky clean
The machines called Arthur or Guinevere
Then the crowd gives a cheer

The lottery is so sad
The people who buy tickets must be mad
But if I won a load of money
Wouldn't that be funny

I would buy myself a dog
And stuff my face like a hog
The money would not be too bad
Especially for my mum and dad
But the lottery is a load of madness
Sooner or later it will bring you sadness

Laura Bratton (Age 12)

The Tramp

He plodded on blindly,
a man of the road -
it had to be kindly
to give him abode.

His eyes were streaming,
he looked so thin,
His only food
was in a bin.

His coat was scruffy,
his whiskers long,
a pathetic sight,
it seemed so wrong.

Finding shelter must be hard,
as Winter draws so near,
the frosts lay thick upon the ground,
his life so much in fear.

And so the only answer is,
come in from out of the damp,
a home is found for this stray cat,
a little pet named Tramp.

Sheila Boynton

Fragments

Sitting in quite contemplation I look upon the
world with grief, and as an overwhelming sadness
fills the theatre of my consciousness; crying out
for me to free myself from the bonds of moral
twilight; where I have dwelt for years and years,
too afraid to look because I didn't want to see
the pain, the voice of truth struggles out from
within me; and through a dark night of my very soul
I see the fragments I have stored now as a picture
of the whole. Human rights, human wrongs. Genocide,
murder, rape; mayhem of every kind. Paranoia, rage,
hunger; man's inhumanity to man. Drugs, death,
injustices, lost causes, indifference; nothing
works anymore, and as I kick out against the
world I feel nothing. No past, no future, just the
long moment of experience, for I am acclimatised
and too far gone to stop the rot that sweeps
the world. But then, I am not a voice alone.

Martinella Brooks

Rabbit

My rabbit had a habit and showed it to
The hobbit next door
He gave him some potion which
Gave him motion
He ran round on all fours
He cut all his paws
He went to heaven at 11
Now he's back at 47
He sees the hobbit and tells him to hop it hobbit

Andrew Bratt (Age 13)

Newcastle

Smelly and dirty
Car fumes polluting the air
People dashing around like little insects everywhere
Flats big and tall
Old tatty buildings ready to fall
People getting impatient in the traffic
Beeping on their horns
Clickerty clack out on the track
The metro speeds by in a flash
Bridges and chimneys outlined in the sky
My trip to Newcastle will always stay in my mind

Faye Bristow (Age 10)

Reincarnation

I lie here very quietly and I just can't wait to tell
Of all the things I've done recently, I know you'll think I've done well.

I hear you walk into the room, but something seems to be wrong.
Why can't I get up and walk to you? I'm usually sturdy and strong.

I start to shout, but there's a problem there too,
For the noises I'm making make no sense to you!

I feel so frustrated but what can I do?
How can you understand what I'm going through?

You come to my side and look down at me
With eyes so caring, so why can't you see?

I can't lift myself up and I can't even speak
Oh, please won't you tell me what is wrong with me?

I look back to yesterday with the sun in the sky
And I'm laughing with my friends as they all drive by.

Then suddenly the rain comes down with lightening and thunder clap.
Too late I see the glistening bend, the tree, the bang, then black!

I try to tell you what it was like, but I'm afraid I get no joy,
As you whisper "I wonder what you're trying to say, my tiny baby boy".

Elaine Brack

Modern Life

Sometimes the strangeness
strikes me, (of life I mean),
sitting here in a corner of my room
near the source of warmth,
the walls stretch out, elongated,
angled into a diamond shape,
the dim light exaggerates the distortion;
and on the corner of a couch,
my familiar sits, a black well nourished cat,
for I am not lonely, I quite enjoy my life,
it just seems strange, with the space
stretching out, finite, infinite, oblique,
not to have room for one of those out there,
homeless humans not near my source of warmth,
someone to share my finite/infinite space
instead of the infinite cold in the night's icy air.

Monica Bower

Not Knowing

We don't know
We wait
For it to show
Your fear
Draws us near
And I know I'd be proud
At the start
You are my heart
At first the first kiss
But not like this
I'm in wonder
You're unsure
Feeling guilt
If you'd rather
I'd understand
Though less certain
Yet let us hope
We don't face the choice
Not knowing

Madelaine Brennan

The Price Of Progress

A little cottage, to call their own,
Then the children arrive, one by one.
Their village life, was very pleasing,
With lots of fun, and lots of teasing.

They worked very hard, in their little home,
Not for them, was the urge to roam.
Years pass by, and the children marry,
Left on their own, having time to tarry.

With their flowers and garden, they were content,
Then men in smart suits, to their door were sent.
It seems they must leave, where they reside,
They sit and wait, for the shock to subside.

Fred doesn't understand, why he should go,
A man's home was his castle, not so long ago.
To a smart new flat, and that was that,
No flowers, no garden, no one to chat.

When Fred went missing, they searched everywhere,
They found him back home, in his old fireside chair.
When the bulldozers came, he didn't seem to care,
His cottage was gone, now a round-abouts there.

He was not part, of this brand new place,
Of sky-scrapers, tunnels, and the traffic's race,
'Twas not long after, dear old Fred died,
The price of progress, had been paid.

Eileen Briggs

Music Man Almost

The bow lifted, quivered, almost shivered,
With anticipation, months of dedication, delivered,
Here to us unworthy souls, fools, foolish, fools are those,
Who laugh and snigger, they are not bigger, better than he who chose,
To display this passion, in this captive fashion, to anyone who'll listen,
To the beauty of his music, the searching of his song,
Wanting to belong, wanting, wishing, praying with these long,
First, drawn out notes, shrill, only the player knows their power,
The bow dances on the strings, it sings, but causing him to cower,
Is the realisation, hesitation suddenly aware, he is bare,
Vulnerable to the crowd, where only the foolish stare,
At this man, who can play, if he may, he won't stay,
Long, just enough, to show this passion, to say,
Something, to each and every one, but no words are here,
He just plays, plays then strays, but always returns to conquer his fear.

Holly Bradshaw

Characteristics

A babe is born with characteristics
of every sort, and kind.
They are formed almost immediately
in his tiny mind.

Then as he grows up to a man
they develop strong, and true.
It's easy to distinguish them
from every little clue.

There's the strong man, the weak man,
the man whose very mean.
Who wouldn't help his kindred out
when times are very lean.

Some men are sympathetic
they respond to others needs.
Others are so selfish
Their philosophy is greed.

But the kind, and understanding man
reigns far above the rest.
Who can make me feel a Queen,
and with tolerance is blessed.

Mona Brown

The Ophidian Sting

To seek a sensual recess,
A rising ophidian
Casts a swanlike silhouette
In quivering madder.

Piercing vapourous shadows,
To thrust ever deeply
For a nidulant union
In a self-anointed warmth.

A lacuna of pulsation,
Stiffens in response
For a dance of ferment,
In rhythmic undulation.

Fierce draughts are gulped,
Stiffled whispers echo;
An ululation heralds
A supreme convulsion.

The rampant ophidian
Inflicts a sufflated sting,
As a coral mantle suffuses
To envelop glorious languor.

D.W. Brown

Vodka And Knickers

There they were, lying at the top of the litter bin, next to
The bus shelter.
How had they come there?
Were they connected?

A half bottle of vodka, and a pair of black "silk" French knickers,
Thrown together.
Were they "an item",
Left at the same time?

Questions came rushing, my imagination immediately
In overdrive -
Who drank the vodka?
Who wore the knickers?

Scenarios flashed 'cross the mind's screen, with options of love, lust,
Tryst or attack -
What was the story?
We will never know.

Jo Brookes

Untitled

I'm not very mobile, I think you'll agree,
But I have a dear friend who is staying with me.

She stays by my side each day and each night -
In fact she is never out of my sight.

She puts me to bed and she helps me to rise.
She's a real treasure, a blessing in disguise.

Her name's Lena Walker, and as you can see,
She's my walking-stick and she's always with me!!

M. Boynton

Daddy

Holding your hand, so big and broad
You stirred a little, wondered what your thoughts
Time together coming to an end
So much hidden, so much unsaid.

I love you, whispered softly in your ear,
Please not too late for you to hear,
For you no pain I prayed so much,
Gently placed kisses, can you feel my touch.

Your body frail, your breathing slight,
Such courage apparent, refusing to end this fight,
How can I continue without you near,
My life, my love, my father dear.

Barbara Brady

Stone Circle Landscape

Deep dark passages, boulder grey stones,
Beaker people common place, a place called home,
Heavy lintels shimmer in copper tones,
Passage grave landscapes, this place is home.

Long dark passages, bluestones mixed,
Beltane new May day's - the farmers are rich,
Burnt bone in chalk soil, ritual tricks,
Swirling moat waters, bonfires surround,
Beaker people common place, burial ground.

Deep dark passages, boulder grave stones,
Heavy lintels shimmer in copper tones,
Sunlight sharp and streaking, we were not alone,
Beaker people landscapes, landscapes called home.

Keith Boswell

Class III's Trip To The Zoo

At nine-thirty the bus arrived at school to take our class to the zoo,
Each child had a label pinned to its clothes with its name and school printed too,
With great "Gusto" they boarded the bus, excitement revealed on their faces,
Whilst we packed the boot with lunch boxes, straws and soft drinks already in cases

"Don't forget the sick buckets, bags, first aid, tissues and spare pants", someone shouts
"And remember the travel sickness pills for the children prone to sick bouts"
At last we set off on our trip singing, "We're going to the zoo, zoo, zoo",
Back slid the sun-roof because it was hot! - In degrees it was 82!

When we got there the adults were given six children each into their care,
Then we set off to see the animals - "Look Miss there's some monkeys over there!"
Eight thousand people were there that day, mostly children all labelled like ours
In case they got lost and sure enough, one of ours did - in the first half hour!

The loud speaker bellowed his name and school and we searched for him high and low, when
We suddenly spotted him, calmly sitting, in the giant tortoises pen!
Rescue over, we saw lions, tigers, elephants, orangutans too,
Giraffes, gorillas, otters, sea-lions and penguins to say but a few.

The children wanted the toilets so we joined the queue "To spend a penny",
This took ages and for some came too late - our "Spare Pants" sure came in handy!
Then off we went to the picnic field with the packed lunches and cases of drink,
And sat in the shade, quenched our thirst, ate our food - some even had forty winks!

Rested we went to the gift shop to buy presents to remember our day,
then boarded the bus, had the "roll-call", tired, but happy we sang all the way,
The children's sweet voices, singing the choruses, echoed throughout the bus,
"We've been to the zoo, zoo, zoo," was their favourite song "And so sang all of us!"

Kathleen Briers

Without You

Never have I been so alone
Without you
When I think of happier days gone by
I realise I am
Without you
Time will come and time will go
Days - weeks - months and years
Without you
Until the day that my time comes to
Join you
And I shall never again be
Without you

D. Boulton

Night

The moon hung in the indigo sky
A creamy orb
Caught in a tangle of twigs
Its radiant glow lit up the night
Its perfectly rounded form startling
Momentarily hidden
By clouds scudding lazily across it
Silent, like eternal whispers
Each star a silver pinprick
In the velvet cloth of night.

Camilla Buckle

What Is A Dad?

What is a Dad?
He's the one that makes you glad when you are sad.

He earns the money
That pays for the honey which satisfies mummy.

He fixes your bike
The one that you like so you can go out at night.

He services the car
So we can travel far and take ma and pa.

He decorates our room
So depression doesn't loom and helps the population boom.

He gives us security
Which is a necessity to make our life simplicity.

He pays for our treats
Things like chocolates and sweets we love him heaps.

When we are down
He plays the clown and that brings us round.

He brightens our day
In some special way even if there's a price to pay.

He holds us tight
Kisses us good night and puts out the light.

Nina Braines

Down And Out

Cardboard boxes line the streets,
Crumpled bodies no one greets
No chance of a nice warm bed
It's a shop doorway they lay their head
Nowhere to go with nothing to do
Tramping the streets hole in a shoe
Down and out not much of a life
Doom and gloom nothing but strife
Caught in a trap there's no escape
What other road can they take
On the prowl for drugs and drink
All are living on the brink
Hurtling downwards do they fall
No one hears when they call
Winter nights wet and freezing
All the homeless coughing and sneezing
So what's the answer for the down and outs
Can't someone help they're not all louts

Kathy Brown

Tune In

Living only for self
leads ever to sorrow,
So "Do unto others"
is the motto to follow.
We must cease being drawn
into conflict and strife,
find peace from within,
then we'll get values right.
Clear out all the anger
the sleaze and the gloom,
Open up our hearts and
make much more room, for
true beauty that surrounds us - all
the colours, sounds and light.
Come, let us all play our part,
in the orchestra of life.

M.M. Brice

Life

We follow a path each day of our lives
Each step sees tomorrow draw ever near
As the hours unfold do we ever take time
To see the changes that come with each passing year

Where now are the hopes of our youth
The idealism and dreams we held in our hearts
Are we older and wiser or do we look back
Wondering, where did reality start

Each season that passes bring changes
How easy to notice them all around
Yet, day by day, so we differ too
The children we were no more to be found

Though the clarity of our thoughts be less
We learn wisdom and honour, we hope
the world that we once sought to conquer
Is the world that has taught us to cope

The path that we follow may be long
Sometimes, maybe, too long to bear
My hope for the future, was my hope in the past
That we may travel together and care.

Lyn Bradley

Soulmate

And did you know me?
When I gently brushed your lips
To calm the howls of sorrow
In the darkness
Did you see me?
When I danced around about you
To guide your steps
Through yet another door
You may have heard me calling
In icy winds that moaned
On bleak midwinter days
Of your life.
And when the loneliness
Of a thousand lifetimes
Weighed heavy on your soul
I was there
Yes, I was there
Waiting
For you to know
That I am you.

Mary Bradford

The Breach

A gunshot splits the air
Resounding, whip like
Across the back of morning.
Milling rooks erupt in flight
Spilling down from tall thin trees.
Assurance has been tangled with.
Now rabbits quiver in their darkness
Praying, frantic to evade
The hands that shatter peace.

Those nameless hands that claim the day,
That rob the complex of it's store.
Those heartless eyes that aimed out life,
Those blackened eyes that flamed the roar.
What vow knows iron twinned with flesh?
What conscience has this beast?
Skilled in deprivation are,
The hands that shatter peace.

Alistair Bullen

71

Heavenly Land

Cool words girl
Straight from your heart
Good to my soul
Come and feel my kindness
It's straight from eternity

My love goes so high
High as the clear blue sky
Feel the good
It comes from above

Chosen jewels
Brings colourful pleasure
Girl this treasure
Was meant to last forever and ever

This palm tree
Makes me feel so free
This ocean sea
It flows through you and me

Perfect life
Heavenly life
So free of the old strife
Beautiful clothes
Great big treasure troves
It's all yours

Simon Burgess

Morning Glory

Still orange morning,
Day wakens for the dawn,
Dark skies leave the horizon,
And the new day has been born.

In the glow of morning light
We can see the work of Jack Frost,
Come, leave your bed to witness
It's beauty before it is lost.

He has sprayed the trees and hedgerows
With a coat of glistening white,
As if he sought to override
The darkness of the night.

Diamonds strung across corners,
Where spiders' webs are spun,
Soon the warmth of daytime
Will have his work undone.

And sleepy heads who never wake,
Till after the day has begun,
Will never know of the beauty
That was there before the sun.

Margaret Burgess

The Hunt

The riders dressed in red and black up on their horses mounted
Gathered at the village green all ready to be counted
Their spirits high, the weather fair, awaiting word to go
The anxious hounds were barking and weaving to and fro
Upon the air a horn blew clear a sound to set the mood
They went off at a gallop over towards the wood
It was said that an old and wily fox had recently settled there
If they could catch 'old Reynard' what a triumph they would share
Up and over fences they rode with madness in their eyes
All at once the fox appeared at the top of 'yonder rise'
The hounds were all way up in front ahowling as they ran
Old fox already limping played 'catch me if you can'
But with hound and man together he didn't stand a chance
He stumbled and next moment teeth pierced him like a lance
The hunt was nearly over except for cutting off his 'brush'
To prove they'd all enjoyed themselves before back home they'd rush

Joan Brooks

A Love Poem

Wise without Morecambe,
Chips without fish,
Eve with Adam,
Mash without mish.
Rhyme without reason,
Christ without mas,
Year without season,
Lawn without grass.

Life without you.

Hell but no Heaven,
Mind but no soul,
Six but no seven,
Rock but no roll.
Sea but no water,
Wool but no worths,
Bricks but no mortar,
Deaths but no births.

Me but no you.

Neil Brammall

Nightime Meditation

The night sky stretches over the world
Like a large bejeweled hand
Stars hang like pendants from dark blue velvet
Sending silver beams over the land

The moon glides gently across the sky
Casting shadows and light everywhere
Over dark secret woods where animals creep
To the mountains so stark and so bare

A lone hawk hunting his evening meal
Circles silently looking around
All at once spotting his prey
He screeches and swoops to the ground

The shimmering stars are mirrored
On the surface of the lake
The winds breath rustles through the willow
Causing the blossoms to break

They drift away from the waters edge
Like beautiful golden boats
Bobbing under as ripples disturb their path
Then back up again they float

As I sit here in meditation
Contemplating on all that I see
My heart fills with love for the universe
All these gifts that are given us free

Jean Brownbill

Adam Aged Two

During the day,
Adam sleeps
on Anni's side of the bed,
the quilt
wrapped around
like a cocoon
rises and falls;
and birds sing still.
I sniff his hair
and kiss his cheek
his hand dangling
off the bed,
twitches.
I lie next to him
and close my eyes.
Peeping
I check he's real.

T.M. Boardman

Untitled

And now the wind begins to blow
To free the cobwebs from my thoughts
These passages strewn with autumn now
My voyage to remembered haunts
A passing glimpse of sunlit rooms
Of sultry haze and heavy blooms
Now feel the chill of winter's sighs
Think not of seasons as before
Of summer faded from our eyes
Which look in search of spring once more.

Wendy Brett

Steam Dream

The other night I had a dream,
My motor car was driven by steam.
I rattled along a country lane,
Belching smoke like an old-fashioned train.

The boiler lay beneath my seat,
Hissing, puffing and supplying heat.
Steam was rising from my toes,
And made a sauna for my nose.

Now and then I'd stop and get,
A supply of coal in a buck-et.
I stoked the fire up good and hot,
which made me sweat quite a lot.

I entered town in a cloud of smoke,
People thought it quite a joke.
There I was, covered head to foot,
In thick and grimy chimney soot.

But the joke was really on those who scoffed,
In their heads they were quite soft.
For they paid duty and V.A.T.,
While my fuel costs were all tax-free.

David Bull

Christmas Time Again

Christmas time again,
As a child,
My hands held out,
Waiting wild with
Happiness for presents
To be handed out.

The mass of Christ,
The birthday of Christ,
The Yule log, mistletoe,
The holly and ivy,
And winter berries,
As they lay in church.,

There would be
Screams and shouts,
Excitement as
I got the present,
I wanted, a prayer
Was said, and the
Turkey ate, Mum and Dad,
Fell back to sleep

Barbara Brown

Spring's Delights

As the winter fades away,
Gone are the ice and snow and sleet,
The warming sun is shining through
The clouds disperse, the sky is blue.

Grasses springing forth to life,
Covering the ground a carpet of green,
Buds peeping through from earth's recent slumber,
A sight to be seen.

Flowers arise in beauty arrayed,
Each one in their kind proudly showing,
The air sweetly scented, the perfume is stayed,
Their fragrance bestowing.

Spring has now come, the earth is reborn,
The birds winging by are now singing
Their chorus rings out, as high they do soar,
A new day beginning.

Doreen Brown

Egypt

Ancient Egypt
You attract
Many curious cats
Your history is slowly uncovered
Your mystery still intact

Wondrous Egypt
Head of the ruling king
The Great Sphinx at Giza
With a lion's body couchant
Egypt's guardian figure

Mysterious Egypt
What secrets do you hold?
Are the answers right
In front of our eyes?
Many questions left untold

Precious Egypt
Where the sun beats down
Highlighting all your glory
Paintings, the Nile, the Pyramid Tombs
What message is behind your story?

Annette Boxall

Life

Life is full of many different things
Some are animals, birds, fish
Or human beings.

Life can also be such fun
things that make you laugh or cry
Watching everything go by.

Life can be unusual
Flying saucers, aliens aglow
Cheetahs that are fast
Or snails that go slow.

Life can be full of life
Baby, Toddlers, teenagers
Go to school, go to pubs
Full of noise full of life
People getting into strife.

Life is us, all of us
Until we are no longer
Full of anger full of hate
Until we pass them their pearly gates.

Lesley Boyd

It's Christmas

Winter brings the frost and snow,
The holly and the mistletoe,
It's Christmas once again,
Children dreaming of the presents they will get,
It's going to be the best festive season yet.

Christmas is a joyous time,
We celebrate the birth of christ,
The family gathering around the tree,
It is a special time for you and me,
A time to share our love with all we see.

If all the year could be this way,
Showing our love for each other every day,
I think that God in his heaven,
Would smile down on us and say . . .

When I created the human race,
I intended that their lives would always be this way,
Oh what a wonderful birthday,
This has turned out to be,
To see them sharing around their love,
Is the greatest gift that could have been given to me.

Terri Brant

Litter Bug

There is a certain creature
That lives amongst us all
It varies in every feature
And can be small or tall.

Papers, cans and bottles everywhere
Its work is never done
This bug does not seem to care
It spoils the view for fun.

Food left out to rot or decay
A compost heap is the thing
Ready for the garden in May
Gives the veggies a tasty zing!

Rubbish gives off gas under the ground
At Christmas recycle your tree
Shredders can always be found
Save your cards just like me.

Conserve fuel, water, oil and gas
Or the world will be a sad place
Use the sun and wind or alas
Pollution will kill the human race.

Everyone has a part to play
Cans, rags, bottles and metal too
Must be recycled without delay
All can be used for something new.

Anne Brookes

Mum

Oh dark-haired, lady of the night
Who brushed away my childish fears
With soft embrace would ease my plight
And kiss away my fearful tears

How in the morn shed take my hand
And warm them with her comforts touch
This lady of the children's land
I could love her oh so much

I was a child but now a man
Once was blind but now can see
I'd always take my mother's hand
She is forever part of me.

E. Brown

Voice For Gentle People

Where are all the gentle people?
Gone alas, pushed out of sight,
Trodden by the surging masses,
They don't have any rights!

LOUDNESS,
BRASHNESS,
Push and shove,
Force the pace,
It's a race,

It's a disgrace.

Gentle people feel,
Gentle people love,
Gentle people sense things,
Gentle people don't shove.

Gentle people listen,
Gentle people hear,
Gentle people are strong,
Gentle people know fear.

Gentle people are kind,
Gentle people care, just
Open your eyes to gentle people,
You'll find they're everywhere.

Gillian Broom

Timeless

A span timeless, a breath of spring,
Feathered soft, like an eagles wing,
Era of years, changing face,
Smooth, rough, entwined with lace,
Threaded worn, passages of time,
Turbulent, tranquil, together, divine.

Eileen Brown

Do You Know

Do you sometimes sit and wonder
Is there a purpose to your life
Have you fulfilled your destiny
Have you won your stripe

It's all so confusing
How do you find out
What could be the meaning
What's it all about

You see many happy people
Also people who are sad
Nice caring people
People who are bad

Do they know the answer
Have they reached their goal
Will they share their secret
To help fulfill your soul

You feel your life is empty
You know there's something more
But your destiny will find you
No matter where you go

Then at last, you too will know

Margaret Jane Brown

The Tree I Played On

The tree I played on stands tall and high
Branches reaching to the sky,
Birds would gather to sing their song
Happy to sit all day long

Playful days are over now
Climbing carefully up it's bough,
Hiding away never to be seen
In amongst the leaves of green

Many a happy hour was spent
Sitting quietly quite content,
Watching all that went on around
From so high above the ground

The tree I played on is no more
All that's left is just a core,
Where once a towering giant stood
Is just a lonely piece of wood

Sandra Boyde

Snow In The Night

There was snow in the night,
And the pure white scene
Raised a desire to make one's own impression
Upon it . . .
As artists long to do,
In words or paint,
On any fresh sheet, set before them.

What flights of fancy -
What raptures -
Came to mind! . . .
But the random ventures led
To disappointment -
Slush!

A single hope remains:
One morning, soon -
We shall find, yet again -
There has been
Snow in the night!

Peggy Bridges

77

Rwanda Burns

The heart of Africa burns in tribal war
It's peoples in a state of chaos and despair
The agonies, the traumas they endure
To find a haven, they know not where!

They trek the gruelling tracks of hell
Aching limbs carry their burdens and their will
For days and distance no one can foretell
The search for peace and calm, over yonder hill

Children red eyed from constant tears
Many helpless and lost from family ties
Hunger and thirst among their fears
Beg for food in order to survive

The Greed and aggression a lawless attempt
Tribal warfare they can not prevail
The horrors and heartache unable to prevent
A human disaster on a massive scale

The food to live, the world to heed
As despots drink the cream of the land
Our hearts bleed for those in need
We pray that help is close to hand.

Kenneth C. Burditt

The Frog Prince

I should never have kissed the Frog!
But then again I would never have known the Prince,
Never have felt the pain of love.
I should have patted his little head, thought,
'Good little Frog' and not believed a word he said.
He was so beautiful that I fell in love with him hopelessly.
I swear I did not hear his low, Prince-like tones say,
'It cannot be!'
His panache and charm were an act, a sham for all to see,
- 'cept me!
Never kiss the Frog Prince,
For 'tis in the kiss the harm is done!
For in the moment your eyes are gently closed, you are blind.
Then you open them into fantasy,
And it's the Prince you think you see!
But he's the Frog of stone,
- Leave him be!
He's much too busy for the likes of you and me.
Think of all the Prince-like sins his little soul has to atone.
Leave him! Leave him be!
- Leave him well alone!

Doreen Brook

The Moon

Silently the moon appeared from behind the hills
Majestic and cool and calm and aloof
Riding through space on invisible chains
It watched me watching it from my roof

I bathed in the reflected light from a star
Enchanted I watched enthralled by the sight
As in silver it painted the land far below
Changing colours of day to the colours of night

Higher it climbed in the sky and the hours
Brighter it shone as the sun raced away
Now alone and serene in it's splendour
Unchallenged it ruled with the death of the day

Compelled by a force they couldn't resist
The seas followed the moon until stopped by the land
Where baffled and angry they bowed in submission
In frustration they moved and hissed onto the sand

The moon's magic faded slowly losing out to the dawn
Its day over it quietly fell
My spirits sank with it as I watched it go down
I sighed as I stood there and wished it farewell

Richard Brown

Love In Bloom

Flowers help us celebrate Spring
In abundance sweet and bright
Help lift our hearts to the light
Capturing our mood of moments you come
When they burst forth in the rays of the sun

Bluebell for constancy,
For-get-me-not for true love
Pansy I think of you my turtle dove
Tulip means beautiful eyes
Violets fidelity
Add up my love and thoughts of thee

Jonquil I desire return of your affection
See your face in love's reflection
Anemone I won't be forsaken
By you, but that you will taken
By my admiration

To you in all you do
A bouquet of all I feel for you
Expressed in flowers of every hue
For you

D.M. Brown

Photograph

I have at home, a photograph,
Of a bouncing baby boy,
With a tangled mass of curly hair,
His Mother's pride and joy,

He's hanging from her finger tips,
Having just learnt to walk,
As I sit and look at its faded face,
I wish that it could talk,

I'd ask the Mother sitting there,
Of all her dreams that day,
And what things she hoped for him,
I wonder what she'd say?

But sadly now the Mother's gone,
She died a year ago,
And if he lived up to her dreams,
I'm afraid we'll never know,

But I'll keep my faded photograph,
As a reminder of you Mum,
I hope I didn't let you down,
Goodbye, your loving Son.

Ian Bourbonneux

Farming In The 1920's

We have lost a lot of what we had
To the present day of farming
Machines do what man used to do
And taken away the pride and joy of farming

The horseman with his team of horses
Which he fed and groomed and I cared for
They used to plough and drill the fields
And pull the carts at harvest time

You would hear the yodel and the whistle
From plough boys happy in those days
Gangs of men and women hoeing up the weeds
No harmful sprays in those days

The harvest field with its stooks of corn
The farmyard with its many stacks
Each one nicely trimmed and thatched
Which was done by the skill of man

The farmyard with its hen and chicks
Which scratched the soil for insects
The cockerel said cock-a-doodle-do
She laid a nice free range egg for you

Farm labourers were very many
They worked hard with pride and joy
Today the tractor and machine does this work
Has taken from our farms that pride and joy

John Bridgeman

Regrets

Regrets are threaded like jewels
On a necklace of years,
As many regrets as a rainfall,
Of tender sweet tears,
The light is so dim,
The darkness just harbours more fears,
And how many more
On the path that destiny steers.

John Burns

Dan Dan

Dan Dan the funny wee man
Who washed his face in a frying pan
He combed his hair
With the leg over the chair
Dan Dan the funny wee man

Kolieal Brooks (Age 10)

Incompatibility

Are you weary, are you ill, seated by the window
Chin on hand, gaze averted from me?
How can I tell from your forced grin, your disaffection,
Your refusal to answer a direct question?
The radio speaks - The News again! Is it need
Or barrier you have raised to foil communication?
I glare at you across the void, aim darts of fire
At your crab's shell: my febrile fancy is dire;
Smug, inviolate Cancer! Curve of smooth complacent cheek
That bears no portent of disaster, why not burn
In my mad blaze of passion and frustration;
Why no flush at this cauldron of resentment tensed
To scald once and for all your indifference?
Impervious to my pain, how can you be so blind?
You don't mean to be unkind, but your convoluted mind
Issuing evasive word, contentious look, leaves me stricken.
Show something, feel something, damn you!
Shared laughter flown, the loving touch renounced,
The goodnight kiss a mockery;
No longer needed nor swayed by your desires,
Venus, in extremis, folds her hands and silently expires.

Joanna Bowes

Ode To My Love

The pain that I feel inside
Sometimes becomes impossible to hide
I love you more than you'll ever know
My love, please don't ever go
In the past you've gone astray
But we're still together after all we say
If only you'd love me as much as I love you
I've changed my hair, I paint my face
I've shed my weight but it's all in despair
I'm sure I don't deserve all this pain
What did I do to hurt you?
What did I do so wrong?
We even have our own little one
I feel so hurt when he's used as a threat
When he wouldn't hurt a soul
He's just our little pet
Perhaps one day it will all come to light
And who knows
We'll be able to talk and not fight
And then perhaps we will unite
For this I'll wait forever my love

Beverley Bozzoni

Bones Of Glory

An external death
Yet an internal lie
A glove of disaster
That curtains the sky

Rocks of wisdom
Pearls of dreams
A whisper of hope
That tears at the seams

A continuous murmur
Yet a repetitive yell
An angel of innocence
That ends up in hell

A pocket of luck
A handful of snow
A powerful wish
That no-one will know

Bones of glory
That structure the Earth
Gone has the dying
That extinguished all birth

Natalie Cheers (Age 12)

The Pope In Ireland

The Pope he came to Ireland
He came in troubled times,
He begged and pleaded with gunmen,
To turn away from crime.

He preached his message at Drogheda,
Millions came by rail and road.
While across the border in Ulster,
Another terrorist bomb explodes.

He started his visit in Dublin,
To Pheonix Park he came.
A day for the Irish to rejoice,
And forget their country's shame.

It was in the west of Ireland
Near famous Galway Bay,
He preached his final message
On a bright September Day.

The youth are who he turned to
Because the future is in their hands
To change the past of Ireland
And to live in a peaceful land.

May God protect His Holiness,
From the world's many evil men.
And I hope before I die
He'll visit us once again.

Gerard C.V. Burke

Lament

For those who work in factories,
Whose lives are ruled by time,
It's like a breath of heaven, to enjoy
The countryside.

To meander down a country lane,
By fields where cattle graze,
To hear the sound of brook, or stream,
And scent, the new mown hay.

These scenes, to many city folk,
Are just a memory,
As they go on from day, to day,
In total apathy.

Their only piece of open ground,
A playing field, park or green,
Which people tend to foul, and mar,
And use for pets latrines.

Though country folk toil long and hard,
From dawn, to eventide,
They have one legacy of wealth,
They have their countryside.

They have their lovely fields of green,
So beautiful to see,
They have their rivers, woods and streams,
They have their linden lea.

J.J. Clare

What A Job?

I could go join the Police Force, but I really don't suit blue,
I could try archaeology, but wouldn't have a clue
Maybe I'll be a doctor, but I hate the sight of blood,
Or I'll be a plumber, but I'd probably cause a flood.
I could try being a vet, but feathers make me sneeze,
I'd be a ski instructor, but I'd catch a cold and freeze.
I could be an author, but my writings not that neat,
A butcher? I'm a vegan, I can't even look at meat.
I could be a sales assistant, but my need to spend's too strong,
Or maybe a scientist, but my experiments turn out wrong.
Maybe I'll join the R.A.F., but I've got vertigo,
Or I could try being a tailor, but I don't know how to sew.
I could be a psychiatrist, but I easily confuse,
Or even a comedian, but my jokes never amuse.
Hang on a sec, I've got it, I know what job to do,
I'll be a career advisor, like that helpful bloke at school.

Jean Carman

The Road

Have you trod for many years
Down rough and stoney paths
Your stumbling feet are tired, weary
For you have never found the way
Where you could walk with ease
Never dared to take a different path
Or go the way you pleased
Have you been frightened and bewildered
By the roads that twist and bend
Have lacked the confidence and courage
Never dared to find or visualise
Where the journeys end.

Have you followed many false trails
Your footsteps gone astray
Or have taken the wrong directions
And somehow lost your way
But who knows for certain
Which road is the one to take
For each person has a purpose to fulfil
An individual will, the choice
That he or she alone must make.

Pat Brown

Not Missing You

I only miss you sometimes now
Like when I hear your name,
Then I remember how you felt
And then I feel the pain.

Of course I rarely miss you now,
Just every time I see
A pair of gentle sad grey eyes
Not recognising me.

Just when my arms are empty
And there's no-one there to hold,
Then I do begin to miss you,
And the world starts feeling cold.

Sometimes when I'm happy
I see your timid smile,
And I miss your warm strong body,
But only once in a while.

Happy or sad, day or night,
A good day or a bad,
In darkness or in light,
Alone, or in crowds,
Awake or asleep,
Just some of the times I miss you.

Lynda Chambers

Remember Dunblane

This poem is for you - the person who doesn't fit in.
Who keeps himself to himself, and feels the world is against him.
Who has no luck with women, who never hears a kind word,
And has anger in his heart - remember Dunblane.
Look at that photograph, a small child smiling.
You were once that child.
O.K. life hasn't been kind, you never got the breaks,
Not much to look at, little cash - remember Dunblane.
That man who walked to school that day.
He took the most precious thing we have, and for what?
Revenge? A tiny body lying on a blood stained floor.
Did that help him feel avenged?
A child who perhaps one day would have found the cure for cancer.
Poor hard done by you - remember Dunblane.
Those children were the closest thing to angels
This side of heaven. Now they've gone, and we miss them.
Just the silence, and some memories,
And the sound of a small voice, lost on the wind of yesterday.
This poem is for you, if you hurt inside, I'm sorry.
But don't hurt others because of it.
It's not their fault, they're not to blame.
Please my friend - remember Dunblane.

Roger Carpenter

Dementia

I sit in a chair, too big for my frame,
I hear the nurse calling,
But I've forgotten my name.

The minutes, turn into hours,
Which seem like days, I sit,
And stare, in a constant gaze.

I have a family, visit me, they are so very kind,
Their faces, seem familiar,
But their names, don't spring to mind.

One minute, I am aware, then my memory goes,
Oh why am I so much trouble,
God only knows.

I am so confused, in a world of my own,
I am sitting here, when I should be
Going home.

You wash, and bathe me, and comb my hair,
Your tolerance, and devotion,
Your loving care.

My memory's a blur, my mind not so clear,
Excuse if I shout, it's because I can't hear.

I look around, and what do I see,
People sitting, the same as me,
A burden, I never wanted to be,
God has given you, patience and understanding,
To look after me.

June Cameron

Afterwards

Down across the spooky woods imagining . . .
Myriads and myriads of terrors
Waiting in the shadows soon a rustling.
Coming nearer and nearer . . .
A magnificent creature blazing eyes staring
My heart felt like it was melting
Like a pound of butter
Getting nearer and nearing, menacing
Through the rustling trees
With a great big roar!
With an enormous jump!
It leapt at me, I fell into the gully

Michelle Campbell (Age 8½)

My Christmas Wish

My Christmas wish is big
I don't want a red wig
And not a toy wood fort
Or a ball to be caught,
I want a new computer
Nothing like a cycle hooter
My friend has a computer
But I don't want his
That's my Christmas wish.

Jonathon Clayton (Age 10)

G.I.

In the late 30's England was facing
a time filled with hate and mistrust.
The talking was over, the Nation stood ready
into the jaws of war were thrust.

My Mother, a young girl, remembers quite clearly
the sight of that handsome young man.
Her parents responded to help the war effort
to place a G.I. "if you can".

A friendship developed that grew into love
'til a posting took him far away.
They continued to write and always the words
"I'll come back and get you one day".

One letter returned and on it was written
of him they had now lost all trace.
So helpless, hopeless, abandoned, alone,
her memory still holds his face.

My mission today can take nothing away
from the love and support that we've had.
But I'll never give up 'til the day that I die
in the search for my lost G.I. Dad.

Carolyne Calder

Rejoicing

Eyes meeting
Lips smiling
Fingers touching
Caressing
Arms entwining
Tongues seeking
Flesh melting
Writhing
Breath panting
Hearts racing
Earth moving
Climaxing
Passions draining
Bodies relaxing
Contentment reigning

S.F. Carr

Mum

"Dad, she's going."
Her eyes opened as if awakened from a sleep
And her breathing became less deep
Until her last breath was taken.
No struggling.
Her pain was gone.
Pain from a gangrenous leg
Too late for amputation.

I saw an old woman worn out before her years
With painful eyes full of tears.
I saw a young girl dancing in my father's arms
With angels singing hymns and psalms.

I saw myself.

She worked too hard, too long
With little time for pleasure or song
Snatching time here and there
To smoke and drink without a care
And in the end, it did her wrong.

Jeanette Cave

Little Betty

This is the tale of little Betty, who choked whilst eating cold spaghetti
Betty's mum, whose name was Lizzie, got into a right old tizzie
And promptly sent for Mr. Baker, who was the local undertaker
He came with haste and tape to measure, for making coffins was his pleasure
He brought it round the following day, but it wasn't right, I'm sad to say
That's no darned good, Lizz did retort, the blooming things six inches short
But Baker a resourceful man, stood back and made a cunning plan
With saw and drill and two sharp knocks, he made two holes in Betty's box
Bett's feet protruded through the holes, her toes turned up, God Rest Her Soul
Dad said, can't have our Bett with frozen toots, shoved them into his old football boots
The cortege left and as it passed, some giggled and some stood aghast
The graveside reached, the Vicar there but he could only stand and stare
At last he said "God Rest Her Soul" then slipped and fell into the hole
Bett's mum gave out an anguished cry, to save the Vicar she did try
Instead slipped in herself, poor soul, now three of them were in the hole
The man who digs the graves, old Fred "Dust To Dust" he thought they said
So started filling in the dust, two spadesful onto Lizzie's bust
Bett's Dad said "You can't do that there" she's got my pension book with her
He made a grab for Lizzies purse, but missed and spoke a dreadful curse
Which made the Vicar's wife turn green and hurriedly she left the scene
If after dark you pass that way, don't linger, I have heard them say
That Betty and her mum and dad and Vicar also poor old lad
Can be heard to moan and groan, so hurry past and get off home

Margaret Clegg

Sexual Appetite

I watch you from across the room,
out the corner of my eye.
The feelings that you stir in me,
disgorge a longing sigh.
I know I'll have to touch you,
and stroke your silky skin.
To undress and caress you,
the urge just won't give in.
My teeth need to nibble,
My tongue wants to taste.
I have to possess you,
not one part must go to waste.
I know it all seems crazy,
that my need has gone too far.
But then I'm a chocoholic,
and I've got to have that bar.

Dawn Clayton

Melanie

As I go along life's way
I try to live from day to day
I try to live just as I should
And take the bad times with the good

And though I'm sometimes feeling down,
I try my best to smile not frown
For I have friends that share my pain
They make me feel so good again

And I will win out in the end
Because I have these special friends.

Ethel Carroll

The Deadly Necklace

Strung with morning dew-drop beads,
A necklaced web moves in the trees,
Gossamer soft and spun with care,
This awful trap, the Spider's lair.

Enticement is the Spider's art,
And weaves his cartwheeled silken chart,
A compass rose without a scent,
This awesome jewel, a hand can rent.

The unsuspecting insect's weight,
He blunders in, there's no escape,
The more it struggles, the more it's kept,
A flight of freedom, suddenly checked.

The Spider feels vibrations strong,
From the insect's troubled wrong,
And runs unhindered on a thread,
So claims his catch, now stung and dead.

A tiny corpse parcelled in silk,
There's nothing like the Spider's ilk,
Exacting, cruel, without a heart,
His deadly necklace, his deadly art . . .

Susan Clinch

A1

The sun sinks into a cancer sky
Wind blows water bubbles of time
Sperm flies when it's set free
Life falls like ye olde oak tree

Don't wanna spoil, day or night
Never ruin endless plight
Words could not refrain
The feeling of whiteman's game

Seconds become light year
Life death, no life no fear
Same old cliches appear true
Read the mind see right through

How do we begin, never end
Subconscious day dream my friend
No-one to trust or talk to
Communication feeling blue

Stuart Campbell

Emma

How can this child I bore treat me so bad
She's a different person now and I think that it's sad
She used to call me the best mum in the world
But that was when she was my 'little' girl
She'd hug me and kiss me, tell me I was great
What have I done to deserve such a fate
I'm not wanted for company, or on shopping trips
It's not cool to be seen with Mum at the flicks
Even lunch out gives her cause to moan.
"I'd rather have the money and go on my own"
Her little sister cries and says she's so unfair
"Why doesn't she love me like I love her"
I do have my uses on pocket money day
And for washing and ironing and putting away
And cooking but only the things she likes
Her Dad comes in handy for punctures on bikes
My own mother tells me it's only a phase
And that I was once just as terrible to raise
So I've accepted my fate as I remember with tears
My other daughter will be like this in another six years

A. Clarke

After A Visit To Glastonbury Abbey

Men came from Rome, sent by the Pope
To make a home, they had the hope
To build a church which then could cope
With folk at Glastonbury.

The years progressed; an abbey grew.
As generations built, they knew
That faith in God would see them through
To praise at Glastonbury.

The monks serene, all day they toiled;
Their backs were bent, their faces soiled;
They persevered, with wheels well-oiled
To build dear Glastonbury.

The great grey stones were hewn by hand;
Constructed that they would withstand
The ravages throughout the land
At strong brave Glastonbury.

But time and tide, and men the worst
Have sated their unquenching thirst
Upon our heritage, and burst
The walls at Glastonbury.

Yet as we walked the ruins round
And our feet traced o'er hallowed ground
We thank our lucky stars we found
The road to Glastonbury.

Barbara Clarke

The Tree

I saw some workmen plant a tree
Its branches hung dejectedly
Rudely staked upon a footpath new
I watched the sapling as it grew

As early days of spring drew near
I noticed buds and blossom appear
And as they did I must confess
Feeling an inner happiness

But sad to say my little tree
Failed to reach maturity
In great dismay one day I found
Its broken trunk laid on the ground

Snapped in two by vandal hand
It seemed so hard to understand
It is such things as that, I swear
That one finds so hard to bear

Not for profit was the tree slain
How could that be for someone's gain
How sad some bitter mind did choose
That wanton act when all would lose

Now we shall find much to our cost
A touch of beauty has been lost
So useless must such action be
That stoops to rape a little tree

Jack W. Cash

"Goodbye My Love - Farewell"

I thought my life was over the day you said goodbye
I didn't think that I'd survive I thought that I would die.
You took away my self respect my heart you broke in two
You took from me, the love I gave I lived my life for you
I cared for you, I cherished I never thought we'd part
But then you went and left me with a torn and broken heart
Time is a healer so they say and stress you'll feel no more
Now I've regained my dignity I'm stronger than before
My life is calm no anguish there no arguments, no doubt
In fact, I find, I like myself I'm glad, I found you out
No rushing round, I've time for me I please myself all day
There's no more being "home for tea" I go my own sweet way
So really I should thank you dear! For leaving me to cope
I found that life is full of joy and happiness and hope.

Pat Casey

Name

I've claimed the name that soothes my soul -
Ended the game, and finished the role
That for fifty unsuccessful years
Brought nothing, but anguish and relentless fears

Of disapproval in every aspect of life
From a cycling genius, or just being a wife
Who wanted only the best for her children,
Discouragement reigned, coming by the pen

To cause heartache and sorrow, unlovingly sent
Disclaiming the trials and seemed hell bent
On causing the unworthiness of this lost child,
Making living disgusting, and a mind reviled,

So that proving an existence was no mean feat;
Longing for some pleasure instead of defeat;
From all the sickness a human can bear
To a holistic reality in which to share

The love and the caring tied up inside
All covered in pain. It had to hide
Even from the person most trying to mind it
Spending hours and hours in search to find it

'Til at last emerged from the concrete shell
A person of worth who had been through hell.
The growing, the feeling of soaring above
Sandy Chapman, individual and so full of love.

Sandy Chapman

A New Life

A baby is pushed into the world,
Naked and bare, its first breath expelled,
A tap on the bottom it gives its first yell,
Is it a boy or is it a girl,
The mother lays back proud and excited,
The father glows with pride,
Obviously delighted,
The nurse brings tea for the exhausted mum,
She drinks it thirstily,
Scolding her tongue,
The father kisses his wife and child,
The mother so tired she gently smiles,
It's time to tell the relatives and drink to the babies wealth,
Everyone congratulates and drinks to its health.

Nicola Chapman

The Voyageuse

In carefree youth she travelled far,
Collecting joys from different lands;
Strange sensations, awesome sights,
Roasting days and freezing nights.
She savoured food, so rich and spicy
And scaled the mountains, cold and icy.
Warm seas lapped her sun-kissed skin;
Hot sands of deserts stung her face.
Steamy jungles, full of fear
Sensing death was ever near.

Now her world, so safe and small,
Where others tend her every need,
Is full of kindness, hushed and bland
And very, very dull indeed!
But her sightless eyes recall
Vivid scenes from long ago;
Her useless limbs still feel the ache
From long hard treks upon the snow.
In a wondrous world she dwells alone,
Content with memories of youth.
She would like to say,
"I've had my day,
Don't pity me .... but thanks
For caring so ....
        But I must go ...."

Joan Clark

Christmas, The Meaning

Family together in one home
Worries of others rise to the brim
Gathering of the worst and
Good features of family, highlighted

The lunch is fun after the presents
Games and tears
Tired, retiring after all the food
A few drinks to take away the sting
Of conversation

The days ending and the sense of relief
Is coming, as the coats are gathered together
The kids want it to go on
Even when they are ready to drop

They love the day
They don't see the adult failings
Only the pleasure and joy of their family
Children aren't just innocent
But lucky, if only it could last.

Lorraine Elizabeth Chaytor

The Place Of A Thousand Beds

The visitors have all left,
The lights are dimmed,
I have drunk my cocoa and I feel bereft,
Strangely alone in this place of a thousand beds.

I gaze idly at the ceiling,
Follow the patterns thrown there by the light,
It's good that the walls have no feeling.
The scenes they have witnessed would bring them tumbling down.

I hear the wheels of a trolley,
Night sister's voice so reassuring,
She stops by my bed, dispels my folly,
Dispenses night medicines, the boon of sleep.

All is quiet again
And I seem to hear a thousand sighs,
The moans of those in pain,
But not for long, sweet sleep creeps up on me.

Margaret Clabbon

Judgement Day

John Major is no good,
To chop him up would be too good,.
Boil his head is what the rhyme said,
What price we'll pay is what I dread.

What cuts will he make,
How much more can he take,
To trust what he said is our only mistake.
We don't live we survive,
Yes that's right,
We can't settle down to sleep at night.

We have no security left in our life,
I'm still a mother but I'm not a wife.
The poorer get poorer and mothers left alone,
My child's lost his father,
And we cling to our home.

Thanks Mr. Major for crushing our pride,
Come on Mr. Major it's time to stand aside.
Call an election, lets have our say,
Come on Mr. Major it's Judgement Day.

Linda Churchill

The Nightmare

You wake in the night
With a terrible fright
Your mouth feels dry
You want to cry
You remember your fear
And down flows a tear
Your skin is wet
With pearls of sweat
And your chest feels tight
Breathing's a fight
Your shaking all over
From under your covers
Panic is mounting
And it bursts like a fountain
And into the dark you stare
From your nightmare.

Kay Chester

The Gladiator

In the vast arena the lone gladiator stands, amidst the dying and the dead,
Those for whom he had respect, friends he had come to like and love.
The mighty emperor, to content the clamouring crowd, makes the gesture
That gives the other freedom and the right to wander where he will.
But in the warrior's heart there is a sickness and a sadness at the sight of those around him
And contempt for those who have come to see the gory spectacle of death.
Casting his eyes about he picks up a slender spear, strong yet light,
And though drained by combat and many wounds, hurls it high into the air
And watches as it rises in an arc, and at it's zenith drops and speeds towards its mark;
Plunging down it tears through the softness of the Emperor's body
And pins him to the seat on which he sits. All his greatness and grandeur
Are as nothing as he writhes in agony, screaming a hideous scream,
Feeling all the pain felt by those he has himself condemned to die.
By today's event the warrior knows that he has already passed into legend
And that, in the days to come, when men talk of courage, pride and glory,
His name will be upon their lips; Thinking thus and seeking to deny
His captors vengeance and pleasure at long hours of torture
He takes the short sword and sinking to his knees, falls on it.
His life-blood darkly stains the sand as he crosses into oblivion
And beyond, to wherever all men go when life is ended.

Vince Clark

91

Deadline

We teeter on the brink of a great conflagration,
to oppose brute force of conceited aspiration
when speech has mugged all meaning from negotiation
and man has lost his grip on rationalisation.

The justice of a cause seeks universal blessing,
hawks shatter the peace yet fair doves concern expressing
that those who twirl the sword become themselves oppressing
in believing RIGHT is theirs for the sole possessing.

Death leads us by the hand gently to the devil's playground,
as we embrace destruction in this wasting compound
where reality is final, not a film background,
where cries of pain and anguish create deafening sound.

And what will be achieved by this war and privation?
exhausting more Earth treasures to destroy a nation
another blow to nature not regeneration,
no heritage bequeathed to future generation.

The deadline has been set to produce a solution
which may react in turn to reduce World pollution
and safeguard man's survival through its evolution
or blitz the World with fire in crude retribution.

Robin Clayton

The Wee Burn

Seeing my reflection in your depth
stirs an ache in me
for when you sparkled through my life
between stepping stones and bridge.

A time when we shared together
'spricks' in a jam jar
and paper boats tossed by your flow.

Never questioning then
what came before or after
your stretch of company.

Now cupping my hand against your rush,
I hear echoes of your laughter
drowning my questions
in waters too busy for speculation.

Margaret Cameron

Gentle River

Gentle river, gentle river
Bright thy crystal waters flow,
Sliding where the aspens shiver
Gliding where the lilies blow.

Singing over pebbled shallows
Kissing blossoms bending low,
Breaking 'neath the dipping swallows
Burbling where the breezes blow.

Floating on the breast for ever
Down the current I could glide
Grief and pain should reach me never
On thy bright and gentle tide.

Robert Chapman

All I Wanted . . . .

When I was younger I longed to be embraced by you
But I got nothing but a shove to the side
I longed for just a bit of affection
But you just wouldn't swallow your pride
And again rejected the love I gave
Well you were the one who never tried
Now I still long to be embraced by you
But you looked me in the eye and lied

I often wish for a moment just to be with you
But you left not intending to be back
Oh memories, why do I waste my tears
I will not be used as your door mat
To role me out when you think you might
I don't want to be treated like that
I just wanted you to love and want me
As we follow life down this narrow track

I wonder what it would be like if things had been different
Knowing you didn't want me made me sad
When all I wanted was a hug
But you turned away things were so bad
Yet I still loved you all the same
The wanting of your love drove me mad
You held back from me you wouldn't give
But all I wanted was a loving Dad

Sarah Clifton-Brown

A Way Of Life

Give me a man with a heart of gold
Give some light from the dark to brighten my sole
Life is a treadmill
A challenge for man to find his fate
Fight for your own contentment
That is the blight
For these are the words you'll find written tonight
Give me a few of life's pleasures
Give me time to resolve
The problems man finds at reaching his gold
Sentiments of hardship have already reached these shores
It's time to bring back all the times
Lost by doing everyday chores
A human's a human what ever they say
So give yourself the time
On that bad rainy day.

J.D. Cherry

Dear Absent Friend

Gentle words winging their way o'er a vast expanse of blue,
Traversing the countless miles that separate me from you,
Bringing you my warmest good wishes, and a message, which is this -
You're never out of my thoughts, as you're so deeply missed.

For our bond of friendship no mere parting can sever,
As you mean as much, if not more, to me now than ever;
For when I think of you there, in the wide blue yonder
I confess absence truly has made the heart grow fonder.

And even though we, at present, may be so far apart,
Yet certain things remain indelibly etched on my heart -
The warmth of your smile; the kindness in your eyes;
And your face beaming love, like sunlight from the skies.

So, it's wonderful to hear your voice on that long-distance line,
To hear you laugh and joke, to be assured everything's just fine;
And to receive your warm-hearted letters, so thoughtfully penned,
Bringing pleasure at each reading, my dear absent friend.

So, many thanks for so faithfully keeping in touch,
But please never forget, that I miss you so much,
Longing for that day, when, feeling simply delighted,
Upon home soil once more, we are at last reunited.

So, a fond farewell for now, take care, and God bless,
May He prosper your way with unceasing happiness;
But please hurry home soon with the utmost of speed
To a welcome whose warmth is sincerely guaranteed.

Ian Caughey

Orca, The Killer Whale

I cry for the whale who died from grief,
He yearned for a life he could not live,
No partner for him, no oceans vast,
His freedom denied, his kingdom confined,
To a small shallow pool surrounded by fools,
He obeyed commands and learnt his tricks,
Rewarded by his master with pieces of fish,
The children laughed and parents applauded,
This splendid creature in a small shallow pool,
Whose heart was breaking for a life denied,
No ocean for him no wonder he died.

Judith Chaloner

Wayside Inn

How lovely to travel
Fragrant leafy lanes
Deep in the heart of country
Just as daylight wanes.

Discovering a wayside Inn
Aglow with friendly light,
Beckoning hospitality
In surroundings that excite.

The mind, as well as palate
Contemplating wholesome fare,
Wonderfully fresh, and presented
With diligent care.

As reflected in oak furniture,
Glasses, and brass twinkling bright,
Proudly watched over by oak beams
Of old England's strength and might.

Amelia Canning

She's Gone

She's gone,
Do You know why?
I loved her, but she's gone,
Do you know why?
Another life, another man, she's gone
Do you know why?
We had four children and five grandchildren,
But she's gone,
Do you know why?
My life is empty now she's gone but I still love her,
And do you know why?
She just fell in love
That's why.

B. Chawner

Poet By Nature

Within, I'm sure there is a novel.
Each night I soul-search for the plot.
When dawn breaks and still my page lies empty,
A poem exorcises this, the writer's block.

Although my psyche still provides no epic.
No trilogy, no best-seller mine.
My greatest pleasure, past, present and future,
Is the compelling liberation of verse,
Its form, rhythm and often rhyme.

D.L.C.

The Stallion

On glistening hooves that shone black as onyx,
The mighty beast stormed into view.
Its heart pounding with such a rhythm,
As if the mighty ocean swelled within.
Rippling muscle, taujt and lean.
Flashing eyes full of fury.
Grinding to a halt before me.
My heart missing a beat,
Not knowing if the emotion rising within me is fear,
Or fascination.
Shoulders foamy with the sweat of great exertion,
Appearing as if snow on its majestic black cloak.
Nostrils flaring.
I without conscious thought reach out my hand,
The softness combined with the hot breath surprises me.
Turning,
Its pounding hooves carry it from view.

Alison Clifton

The Burning Pit

Her confession came,
a dark raven, of ill omen for my tears,

tears, salt laden and stained with bitterness.

Hail Marys, to the ears of a priest,
for a penance he can absolve,

forgive, if only god I could forget.

For loves vows I try,
but bitter tears stain the consummated cloth,

until death us do part, the voices of innocence.

My confusion came,
a dark omen, from over the river styx,

my face a mask, for the grim reapers last twisted act.

Until death us do part,
for that vow I will leap,

my confession, purgatory to the ears of a priest.

From a life fraught with bitterness,
to the souls in hell, and the burning pit, I leap.

Tears, salt laden and stained with bitterness.

D.C.S. Childs

Love Is

Love is - You and I, lifted into a place, high above everyone else, The days we share, doing even the simplest of things - walk in the park, the street, anywhere together.

Love is - The way, you wrap your arms around me - holding me close, the look that you give me, it tells the world I'm yours.

Love is - The times we love with utter ecstasy, utter devotion and total commitment.

Love is - The ray of sunshine you bring to me and the gentle rain that begins to fall as we reach oblivion.

Love is - The way you hold my hand, stroke my fingers, caress my body, how you gaze at me, sometimes in utter amazement, sometimes in wonder, but always with longing.

Love is - The peak you bring me to,
        The brink you leave me at.

Love is

Valerie Carter

Winter Sky

Mid afternoon,
Winter sky,
The first hint of yellow overhead.

Late afternoon,
Winter sky,
Changing to orange overhead.

Almost teatime,
Winter sky,
Brightest amber overhead.

Dusk approaches,
Winter sky,
Deepest crimson up ahead.

Sunset now,
Winter sky,
Red dips slowly from view ahead.

Evening's here,
Winter sky,
Black sprinkled with silver overhead.

Sarah L. Carroll

Plum Tree

From my kitchen window
I see
One blossom on a twig
Banishing
                Winter's bareness

A joy
Spreads
Along branches
With blushing beauty of
                Spring youth

Festal bridal boughs
Surrender to green maturity
Bees and birds
Are ecstatic with
                Floral sweetness

Fruit gestates
Embryo plums miscarry
A summer gale
Threatens premature destruction

As the crop ripens
From taut green to blood red
Limbs hang wearily
Showing their time is near

Jan Clarke

One Day

Because beyond my hopes there are no feelings,
Every one is waiting to be found,
Each a thought waiting to fade,
So what? Somehow, somewhere we dared,
To try to dare for a little more.
Why the self-same things keep on happening?
Because beyond my hopes,
There are no feelings.

But our paths have chosen different routes,
I hope they've chosen well;
And if our lives again should cross,
Well, only time will tell.

Chris Cannaby

Untitled

It's cold, it's dark, it's raining, people on busses complaining,
Always the worry of yesterday's bills, car, mortgage and household things.
There's people who are homeless living on the streets,
Crying out for compassion, looking for something to eat.
I don't know where they're going, I don't know where they've been,
But I know that each one's special, that's how it looks to me.
I remember one so special, Huggy was her name,
The day she came to Church so high, little did we know,
That she could give to us so many, her kindness and her love,
She always wanted to help anybody but did not love herself.
She struggled through times so hard and drugs they took their hold,
Even when she got attacked, when someone cut her throat, she found it hard,
But kept on going, found the strength, but in it knowing,
That high above the sky so bright Jesus loved her day and night.
Now Huggy was a girl so clever, poetry was her thing,
She used to turn her hand to writing saying where she's been.
She always had her little surprises, you never knew what to expect,
But guaranteed that through it all this girl who sometimes pretty,
Could turn up scruffy, pale and thin and then she had you guessing.
It's now so sad and hurts so much to have seen her coffin,
That lovely girl who gave so much and ended up with nothing.
But though her life so short, so young, she did find time to pray,
To ask forgiveness of her sins and receive eternal blessing.

(In memory of Susan Ann Huddleston Affectionately know as Huggy with much love, Dino)

Dino Christodoulou

Fires Of Hell

This is the tale I have to tell,
Of the vicar's wife who went to hell.
She was engaged at highest level,
Shovelling coal up for the devil.
While up above the vicar prayed,
And prostrate with grief his tears displayed
But little could his wife console,
For the devil had consumed her soul.
He led her with his evil leer,
Into a life of crime and fear.
And taught her all there was to know,
About his captured souls below.
Now my friends you may well wonder,
Why the vicar's wife was sent down under.
It seems she had one little sin,
She could not resist the taste of gin!

Diane Clark

Snow

Flaky snow is falling
Shining in the night
Fluttering in the dark breeze
Disappearing in the night
It's hiding behind the white clouds
So no-one can find it

Laura Cascarina (Age 8)

Strix Aluco

Darkened oasis fringed by
vapoured mercuric light
the sleepless lie listening
to the voices of the night.

This shadowed grove gives sanctuary
to an Owls soundless
flight.
A far off call from a distant woodland
site
is the signal! for the silence
of our oasis
Breaks . . .

And those of us who sleepless still
lie breath caught and
wait upon the serenade of
low and shrill
Owl speak

And he in shallow sleep into
an echo of half heard sound
. . . . . Wakes

Roy C. Calthorpe

Recollections

I would be where winds are calling
Summer from the moorland, flung
In full circle, purple falling
To the vale where apples hung.

Never constant, ever dreaming
Of the grass that greener grows;
Out of mind the sunlight, streaming
Where the heather meets the rose.

Wiser now, unspelled, unfriended,
Yearning quickens to a sigh,
As each dawn, her vigil ended,
Claims the land I left to die.

Maurice Clayton

Creation Patchwork: The Second Day

The vault above us, the abyss below;
An ordered firmament: the second day.
A child's eye view. The primitive need to know
The framework of our lives won't totter and sway.

The arching sky, firm in its distant place,
The solid earth, that shakes not 'neath our feet
Welcoming the toddler's confidence. Protective space!
Explore and marvel and govern. Progress sweet.

We have probed and questioned and shaken the foundations.
In this parentless world, we can pull the sky down on our heads.
The abyss of drugs and defeat issues devouring invitations.
Tossed among the flotsam and jetsam what hope can we spread?

Anchor of the universe, where have you gone?
Will the God we have forsaken reclaim his dying son?

F. Mary Callan

My Valentine Forever

Please be my valentine for just one night,
For you are the best ever, and
Oh! so handsome in my sight,
Just end my search,
And cuddle me real tight,
Then an affectionate kiss,
Will make everything alright.

Lynne Charlton

New Year's Eve

I am here alone, nobody to sing me a song.
December times are cold and long.
A candle shines through a window pane.
No travellers are seen down the country lane.
You are my companion in this pitch black night.
No cheery smiles, just bright yellow light.
But why do you weep, my beautiful friend.
We are together, the old year must end.
Melting wax slides down to the ground.
White tears without the smallest sound.
Your burden is large I can but see.
The drops are full of humanity.
This night is ours so hope and pray.
Tomorrow may bring a brighter day.

Tom Clarke

Winner Takes All?

Life is such that some who play the game
Strive ceaselessly to take the winner's spoils.
They seldom see such beauty as proclaims
Love triumphant over all our tedious toil.
Yet contemplate with awe the tiny star
Of infant hand against its mother's breast.
The misty breath that hangs on icy air
Of wintry mornings,jewelled with sparkling frost.
The dance of teeming rain through headlights gaze.
The joyful peal of laughter ringing clear.
Now burnished sun sets sea and sky ablaze,
But will you see? Or have you ears to hear?
So spare one brief, still moment in each day,
Or find life's greatest riches gone astray.

Vikki Cook

The Bee

The Bee is beautiful full of delight
The Bee is pleasant, most cheerful
The Bee is striped like a Zebra
The Bee is a collector of dusty, yellow pollen
            And provider of sweet delicious honey

The Bee is a happy creature, humming through the day
The Bee is about the size of a one penny piece
The Bee is the colour of yellow, like the sun
The Bee is the colour of black like the night

The Bee can get vicious yet very shy
The Bee can sting if threatened
The Bee can get angry and be bad tempered
The Bee can be afraid and sting and still die

It stings with a needle like dagger
It injects poison - a burning sensation
            So don't touch it leave it alone!

Alexander Cook (Age 10)

Freedom

A carefree bird in a cloudless sky
With unclipped wings and space to fly
A quick sharp beak a beady eye
I wish this were me I'd love to fly

Maybe a fish in the sea I could be
To swim all day would be ecstasy.
Just a miniature fish, not a rainbow trout
Or a fisherman may haul me out
To serve me daintily on a dish,
But an insignificant fish, like me
Could swim all day and remain quite free

Perhaps a snail with my house on my back
To go where I please and leave no track
I'd not even need a case to pack
Fear and danger I'd soon dispel
I'd slide under a leaf and retreat in my shell.

There are times in my life when I long to be free
Of the world and its problems so daunting to me
But wherever I go I have to come back
It's inner confidence I lack.
To bid farewell to my family
Though I've freedom of choice
I shall never feel free.

O.M. Cribb

House-Bound

Grey morning,
Heart-ache.
Tears flowing,
His sake.

Time passing,
Blue sky.
Pain easing,
Eyes dry.

Latch-key turning,
His face.
Ending yearning,
We embrace.

Janet Coulthard

101

Silence

Silence is the refuge
Of the abused.
The last resort
Of the unjustly accused.

Who listens in the silence
Of the lonely night
To the bereaved, the dispossessed,
The sick in mind and heart?

While uncherished elderly
Line the desolate walls of day rooms
In their high backed chairs
The rapacious pockets of managers,
Paid to care by those
Who abdicate duty - are filled.

Listen to the silence
It speaks to those who hear.
Carried on the anguished,
Stifled scream,
Of the child alone, crying in the night.

A conspiracy of silence
Condones atrocities.
Allows exploitation of the vulnerable.
Implies consent.
Refuse to be silenced!

Janet Cullup

This World's Dying

Don't you realise,
This world of ours is crying
Don't you realise,
This world of ours is dying.

Through bitter tears,
The world can see,
I need them so much,
But they don't care about me.

The tears pour down,
But don't sigh or frown,
There has to be a way to help you,
And to help you today.

So everybody gather round,
To help our planet,
Recover from our poison,
And to keep safe and sound.

It needs it.

Nicola Collison

Thoughts Of Bradley Aged 3½

I always know its Sunday, my dad gets up quite late
A cup of tea, and two sharp prods,
And he looks such a state
Eventually he'll surface and on goes one sock
The other one takes ages, his arms just seem to lock
Slowly but surely he'll make it down with us
A long sit on the sofa, then it's such a fuss!
Where's me coat, where's me shoes and where's my blooming hat
It's where you left it over there "ouch" mind that poor old cat

Oh its great now we're out here, it's really not that far
Now it seems I've made it, I'm in my daddy's car
It's dirty and it's smelly, it's falling apart
He'll turn the key and with surprise
It will sometimes even start
That poor old car my dad's got, I hope you never rot
'Cause what you don't know and he don't know
I love you quite a lot

Tony Cranwell

Christmas

Amidst the noise and bustle
Going through the town,
Keeping on the sidewalk
The traffic makes you frown

People dashing here and there
Like a swarm of bees
Going on their merry way
Feeling light and free

The traffic rambles on its way
Throwing out their fumes
Turning left and turning right
Until a red light looms

Wouldn't it be heavenly
If all the traffic stopped
Kept the traffic out of town
And walked until you dropped

Everyone could walk about
The children could walk free
Especially near Christmas time
When there is a lot to see

Pamela Cooper

Will to Live

For the battle of consciousness,
The comatose arrive,
To fight for their life,
With only their wills to survive.

Holding on to their love,
For their family and friends,
They have to fight the reaper,
Who wants their lives to end.

Will-power, character and strength,
There only weapons to fight,
Reaper with doubt and submission,
To end the tunnels light.

It's a struggle in themselves,
And whether win or loose,
They can't give up the fight,
Life is what they must choose.

If they're beaten through exhaustion,
Or their bodies no more can take,
Then if there is an afterlife,
It's there that they will wake.

Hugh B. Cron

Our Little Pup

We've got a little pup, my wife calls her Jennie,
She's funnier than Stan Laurel or even Jack Benny.
She rolls on the carpet, she jumps on the chairs,
The carpet is covered in, you've guessed it, white hairs.
When I get out the broom to sweep it all up
She grabs hold of the stale, that dear little pup.
She's two black ears and a patch over one eye,
She plays all day long till night time is nigh.
She's got a little friend who lives down the late,
She calls to visit Jennie and Boomas is her name.
When they both get together we feel all at sea,
But they soon settle down when we have biscuits and tea.
When I reach for my coat she jumps all about,
She knows when I wear it the old codger's going out.
She crawls on her tummy and tries hard to talk,
I know what she's saying, 'Let's go for a walk.'
So don't buy a pup just for Christmas alone,
They need lots of love and a jolly good home.
When Jennie's asleep she's as quiet as a mouse,
I wished we'd called her Joiner, she does odd jobs round the house.

L. Curphey

Remember Them

I wasn't born when the great war started.
Reading of it now, is not for the faint hearted.
When the second one exploded I was 9 years old.
Now I'm a pensioner but my blood often runs cold.
Memories of the tears and sadness.
Worry, fear, not much gladness,
Sight of the telegram boy bringing bad tidings.
The food rationing, the black out, air raid sirens.
My brother was called up 'yesterday'
Take care of him Lord, we earnestly pray.
So many we know will not come back.
Heartbroken mothers will never recover from that.
Every November we honour our dead.
At the 'Memorial', tears unashamedly shed.
Medals are worn and we are proud.
'We won't forget' the Poppies shout from the crowd.
Fly the flags high, let them be a reminder.
Peace not war must be our binder.

Marion P. Cook

Mr. Wilson

Mr. Wilson died you know,
Though no one really knows what for.
I think he lost his will to live,
You see he never could forgive.
A wife who left him all alone,
With empty heart and empty home.

So they came from miles around,
To see him placed into the ground.
Relatives all, friends aplenty,
All he touched now felt empty.
A gentle man so nice a toff,
These words would make his ex wife scoff.

For she has tried to poison me,
By trying hard to make me see.
Those things I do not wish to know,
Those things that happened long ago.
But then perhaps it's only guilt,
Over the years so steadily built.

By she who left him all alone,
With empty heart and empty home.

Terry Cochran

In The Gallery

Oh!
What joy
To look and see
Colours, changing light,
Faces dark and bright;
A new world revealed
By pictures hung in a gallery.

- By pictures hung in a gallery
Through which we see
The world afresh,
Through artists eyes -
Whose are the best!
Come! Look with me!
At pictures hung in a Gallery.

Susan Cockerton-Airy

104

Despair

I am old and disillusioned, so I went to church today.
With the world in such a shambles I felt the need to pray.
A struggle there to reach the pew, to put the cushion near my feet:
To ease the pain of kneeling, with thoughts of God to greet.

I closed my eyes in reverence, as my palms came close together.
Tried to transfer all my thoughts, as I had reached the ends of tether.
In my humble way, I made a plea for humanity to prevail;
And I asked our Maker there on high, for light beyond the pale.

A century full of suffering, frequent wars that come and go;
To be removed from the thinking - creating friends not foe.
Let our thoughts lie with the children, instill hope and banish fear:
They are entrusted with the future, as the millennium draws near.

I begged the Lord to guard their lives; to protect them with His love;
Shield them from the bullet and bombs falling from above.
Suffer little children . . . . . .has been quoted and been read:
Cosset and kiss them gently - tuck hem warmly into bed.

John Cunningham

Just Wait

Look for it and you won't find it,
Wait, and it will find you,
You won't be able to ignore it,
It'll be a bolt from the blue.

Don't worry you won't mistake it,
Yours will find you one day,
But you must wait, don't chase it,
It will soon find its own way.

It will arrive when you least expect it,
But sometimes it can take a while,
It has power and magic in it,
So it travels in single file.

When at last it does arrive,
Believe and trust in its power,
Then it'll be sure to survive,
Nurture it and watch it flower.

S. Corry

It Breaks My Heart . . . . .

It breaks my heart when kids don't care,
When all they do is stand and stare
And muck around in class all day
With little done and much to say!

It breaks my heart when kids can't write,
When all they do is scrap and fight!
What is a sentence, can they tell?
When they prefer to shout and yell!

It breaks my heart when kids won't learn!
When they're content to sit and turn
And start to punch the child next door
Or drop their text books on the floor!

It breaks my heart 'cos at this rate
They'll really fail to concentrate!
On whom should we direct the blame,
The home, the school, the video game?

It breaks my heart, 'cos life is tough.
They'll learn its lessons soon enough!
So come on kids, give it a shot
It's only this one chance you've got!

Anwen Coffey

Accents

I love the sound of a happy voice and the joy that it can bring
From the softness of the Irish, to the Welsh who seem to sing
The Scottish have a harshness that has their strength of mind
Whilst Yorkshire has a flat cap drawl, a very different kind
The Geordies with a mellow tone of aye, an, nee then pet
To the rounded tones of the BBC and the Oxford cultured set
Merseyside has its Scouse, an accent quite unique
They add a lah to every sentence, every time they speak

The Brummies have a dulcet tone, a rolling high pitched voice
Passed on through Generations, by legacy not choice
Perhaps the greatest accent that has a term real broad
Is of course Lancashire, to the ears, a larynx Lord
Now Bristolians have an accent that has a certain ring
It borders close to Welsh of course, but has no tones that sing

Then there's Cider country, with its straw in mouth appeal
Painting a worded picture, of a Devon so ideal
The accents of the Cornish are rugged like Lands End
With lovely lilting rustic drawls, so hard to comprehend
Now finally to London, where Cockneys speak in rhyme
The sound of accents I am sure, will stand the test of time.

G.R. Cooper

Peace On Earth

With every breath I ever take
With every moment I'm awake
With every day that I caress
You give me more I want for less
When inner peace is hard to find
You touch my heart and soothe my mind
With every single word I say
You shine a light and show the way
When I am lost, I feel alone
And when this world is not a home
You guide me through the hornet's ring
And I emerge without a sting
And every time I say a prayer
You answer me, I know you're there
And so I live and here I pray
Please help me through another day
I have the strength to carry on
I need your help when I go wrong
When I become what I should be
And remember the times you carried me
I'll need your love for all its worth
So I can be at peace on earth

Richard Copeland

Mare

She walks,
unheard,
and the smell of rotting violets
taints her giant step.

Freckled hands,
dimmed by blue candlelight
read
my love-dimmed body
in a room
of shimmering white nightgowns
and potted cauliflowers.

The sound of her feelings
is hushed,
foolproof
to my cardboard ears.

Baking love and bread
has never been sweeter
on a Sunday morning.

Antonella Collaro

Cynicism

It seems to me, there is no doubt
it is the bastards God helps out.
It's plain that all rewards are sadly,
bestowed for treating others badly.

If you're a lying, cheating cad
you'll be well-blessed for being bad,
but be disposed to kindly ways
and you will struggle all your days.

The sun smiles on the righteous kinds;
'Manipulative, hate-filled minds'
is what it ought to say; our Lord
for righteousness gives no reward.

For trampling underfoot the many
there is no punishment, not any.
It's wickedness that's God's intent
for goodness no reward is meant.

It should not be, it makes no sense;
for mild and kind no recompense.
But that's just how it is I find
for caring heart and thoughtful mind.

The Good Book should have in its text
'Rewards in this life and the next
if you do others down, and plot
against them, you will get the lot'.

Deborah Crockett

Battling Boredom

Clutching the remote control
With hands like twisted
Tree roots, she hops
Television channels
Attempting to win
Boredom's daily battle.

Breathtaking scenes of the moors
Fill the screen, winging
Youthful, pain free memories
To mind, transporting
Her from bungalow confinement.

Round one to her.

Boredom counter attacks

Blacking out the screen.
Silence falls:
Last weeks power cut
Notice peeping
From behind the clock.

Today's battle lengthens
Six hours still to go
Before her home help returns.

She sighs.
Eyes closing she calls a truce,
Rests before the next round.

Julia Cutting

The Student

I work damned hard as a student
My brain box is still full of scars
From swotting up this and cramming in that
I'd rather be right up on Mars
Earbashings I take for exams that they make
My mind goes a terrible blank
My adrenaline flows - Oh god how it shows
Must give the old brain box a crank
Still reeling from strain and a deep kind of pain
I go out with the boys for a jar
Don't envy us please
Go down on your knees
And Thank God you're all under par.

E.L. Collins

Now I'm Retired

Now I'm retired, I don't shirk,
Don't know how I found time for work,
Admitted I don't get up at dawn
But I've time for a stretch, or even a yawn.

The experts say, "Get out and mix lass",
So I do, once a week, at aerobics class,
Floor mats and trainers are a must
With a bit of luck, I'll develop a bust.

I make my own jam, pickles and soup
I've even joined a rambling group,
Sandwiches packed, on with me boots
May not look chic, I don't give two hoots.

Out in the fresh air, swinging back pack
Mustn't forget to carry a mac,
Some might think I'm not right in the head
Every two weeks, I bake my own bread.

I've even tried the art of calligraphy
Now look at me, I'm writing poetry,
But I'm enjoying it, life's such a gas
If it comes to the worst, I'll use me bus pass.

Pauline Crowther

A Place With Nature

Come with me to the place with nature,
I'll take you there.
Shelter from the blustering wind,
Just to breathe in fresh air.
The heavy gusts blur my vision,
But I still walk on alone without you.
Share with me the place of nature,
And watch all the season's change.
New buds on naked branches,
Awaiting the call of Spring, in their dormant months,
To bring forth a new wealth of colour and hope.
The season's swirling and turning,
The darkness of winter months into the light of Spring.
Come with me to the place with nature,
I'll take you there.
See the serenity so calm,
Where the Blackbird & Robin are my only friends,
They come up to me so close singing their song.
Solitude of separateness,
Away from all the crowds of people's clutter,
And chaos of traffic.
Escape into tranquillity with nature's freedom.

Louis Crouch

108

A New Poem

I stopped writing poems years ago when the dust
That begot dust settled like snow
The thickening of bird song the rusting of precious metals
Time moving not like a jet more like a sofa
The train had no track somebody with the right equipment
Had whipped it

Ten years ago I was younger such an obvious statement
Ten years ago I would have romanticised such notions
A decade of derailment with visits by appointment only
But one fine day when shadows ran for cover
And ladies baked cakes and cooed through open kitchen windows

You arrived

With a flash of Sheffields finest you slit my arm
And funnelled gold and caramel sunsets and skylarks
And things I had no name for
You placed your feet in my open wound and told me I was healed

I was

I was a black hole rider A devil dancing on the grave
Of apollo I was God disguised as Adam I was the
Snake and the apple and you and I would sit
Burning holes in the canvases of Van Gogh as we threw stars
Into heaven but nothing lasts or so they say
And only yesterday seemed like only yesterday
And today I decided to write a new poem

Michael Clarke

For David

I'll love you for always and forever
You'll always be in my heart and thoughts
We shared so many happy times together
Together our hearts as one

Together we walked hand in hand
We'd sit in the park and dream together
I'd sleep and you'd watch me
You made me believe in your love

Now my heart is empty of your love
I miss hearing your laughter and voice
I'll never forget the happy days
I miss you so much

I'll always treasure your picture
You will never change my feelings for you
The little things we'd say
I miss and love you more and more each day

Maria L. Cowperthwaite

Escape

Distant train whistle
Travellers speeding away
The streets are empty

Elizabeth Cole

Precious

I watched the sun burn down over
the horizon and found the wonder
of you . . . . . . breathtaking.

Amanda Jayne Collins

109

The Every Day Sights Of Shopper, Friend & Family Member

As I fought my way through the crowded shopping mall
Shoppers, mass of bags gripped right like best pals
I could not help notice they walked with eyes straight ahead
Like so correct drones, stepping over and around the make shift beds
To have to confront or notice the contents of the beds their biggest dread
Strewn rag and bone on pavements and in polished doorways
They avoided eye contact with the street people wherever they lay
Thought of as our societies dropouts or non-conformists
Their names used to be on mailing and polling records, now just missing lists
The empty eyes seem to say it all, as they stare from grey weary faces
Some lucky enough to have boots on their feet, though holes and absence of laces
The outstretched grubby hands with pleas for cigarettes or change
The shoppers and suits cross to the other side to be out of range
These extraordinary street people each with their own unique story
Some even fought for us LAND OF HOPE AND GLORY!
Others only children abused and used
No wonder they feel distressed and confused
So I ask you to please consider, the next time you cross the street
What if in the same predicament one of your friends or family you meet
Do you with open arms greet
Or pass by opposite side of the street
Head upwards to the skies
I ask you please remember before you walk on by
Aren't we all someone's friend or family member.

Karen L. Cogher-Adams

Walsall

Walsall is a town ever changing
Its history written down for everyone to read
Been and gone have shops and buildings
As the years keep rolling on and on
In my short lifetime of not quite half a century
I can remember well Walsall's town centre as it was
The George Hotel and even trolley-buses
Preedy's, Pattisons and Henrys too
Being just a few to mention
I can recall four cinemas I think it was
Now we don't have one at all
The market is still there winding its way up the hill
Whereby St Matthews Church stands on top for all to see
Towering above its domain like a sentry posted to keep watch
How much longer can time stand still for this little piece of Walsall
Tall and proud the statue of Sister Dora stands on "The Bridge"
Silently watching faceless people in the ever moving crowd
What would she say and would she approve
Would she prefer the Walsall and its people of her day
Life was so much better in by-gone days it can be heard said
Have the disease and decay of long ago been forgotten
It's a different disease and decay that's carried along with modern times

S.A. Cooper

My Mother, My Sister, My Best Friends

When you were born I was ten years old
To mum and dad you were like precious gold
When you were a toddler you were really quite sweet
It was your turn now and I couldn't compete
As you grew older and reached about five
You were this little girl who I started to despise
In your fourteenth year mum became very ill
The cure wasn't going to come from her taking a pill
A transplant was needed of which she received
Two years later, we were sadly bereaved
The mother of us all and my best friend
Her love and her strength was given to us all
Ten years parted us and a lot more in between
We had nothing in common, together we were never seen
Wedding preparations had begun for your big day, you were just twenty-one
I wanted to help but dad never asked
I started to think our chance had passed
You wanted my approval before you left for the church
The barrier was finally broken for emotions I didn't have to search
Nervous and frightened I entered the front door
The pride I felt, no-one could feel more
Before you left the reception, we hugged very tight
From that moment on, I knew we would be alright
A few years have passed, now dad has gone too
My best friend now has got to be you

Anita Maria Coteman

My Church, My Heaven

My church is my home,
Absent from prayer I roam
Yes I do pray every day
It increases my power all the way

My church is where I will die
My heaven is where I'll be on a high
I'll pray before my last breath
Then Be rewarded in my death

My heaven is full of shining faces,
My church is full of love that races
Knowing my home is my church is right
Knowing there is a heaven is pure delight

Hark I hear the sound of angel voices
Into the bright light full of rejoices
In new pastures the angel leads the way
My heaven I know I will not have to pay

Philip Anthony Corrigan

Mothering Sunday

March, flowers to the church we take
Mothers bake a simnel cake
Children's gifts of flowers bright
Fill Mothers heart with delight
Messages of love are sent
To Mothers far and wide
On Mothering Sunday long ago
Young children in service
Were allowed to homeward go
Picking flowers as they went
For the Mother Church of St. Anne
Small gifts of cake or flowers
For Mum were sent
So today we commemorate
And our Mothers bless
For all the love to us they give
In many ways throughout our days
As long as our Mother lives
So we remember Mothering Sunday
In many ways
As on that one bright Sunday in lent
Fresh Spring flowers were sent

Irene G. Corbett

111

I Want To Paint

I want to paint a tiger's growl
Sore and painful if touched
Black, red, orange, grey for the echo
Stretched and open
I want to paint my sister;s shout
Rainbow colours - sparkling fizzing
Coming out with force
Parting, running, waving about
I want to paint worry, sliding along.
Moving, ticking, sticking to his home
Locked inside, howling, growling
Longing to be free
I want to paint rapids
Blue, yellow with anger pouncing out
Rolling, getting heavy, catapulting the river
Wide, sharp as cut glass
I want to paint buttercups
Creamy white
Bluebells for the sparkle
Soft skin for the touch

Heather Cox

Thoughts Of A Woman

17 years of hardship through labour, love and money
17 years of laughter, sometimes crying, sometimes pain.
I thought we were here forever united as we stand
To share our love through old age - walking hand in hand.
You took control of everything: money, shopping, bills
Never letting me do a thing, I thought (yeah) I understand.
He's such a caring husband but I didn't know your plans.
You said that you were leaving (sorry) and all that ...
You've found another woman and are going to get a flat!
You didn't mean to hurt me or our daughter too
But would be much happier if we weren't two.
I thought I knew him .... But we don't need him.

Fran Coulson

The Daybreak Dawning

They started out for moonlit romance,
With passionate embraces, they danced.
All dancing and embracing over, they
Raised their heads and saw,
That the dawn had broke and the moonlight
Was no more.

P.L. Cody

112

Snapshots

He stands, head bowed,
Blanketed by silence and the November mist.
Red poppies at the eleventh hour.
Remembering . . . . snapshots in time.

He stands, head bowed,
Eyes of innocence look up from his arms.
New life on an Easter morning.
Remembering . . . . his first grandchild.

He stands, head bowed,
Heart filled with pride as she says "I do".
Joined forever at a sunlit altar.
Remembering . . . . his only love.

He stands, head bowed,
Hands tied, waiting for the bullet
As time stood still in a wartime jungle.
Remembering . . . . his longest hour.

He stands, head bowed,
Teachers raging all around him.
Powerful mis-kick and a glass-strewn staffroom.
Remembering . . . . his deepest shame.

He stands, head bowed.
"The Last Post" sounds across the years.
He stands alone in the mists of time,
Remembering . . . . while time rushes on.

Valerie Crookes

My Body Takes Revenge

In the darkness
I reflect.
In the darkness I see all of my life
Laid out in front of me,
Silky, strange, sad and spring green.
In the darkness
I extract small amounts of joy
From great amounts of sadness.
Suddenly, in the darkness,
My spine rips out of my back,
Upwards from the base
And wraps itself tightly around my neck.
In the darkness
My spine tightens it's grip
And I spit blood
As my vertebrae and neck both crack.
In the darkness
My body finally takes revenge,
And kills me.

You Would Not Let Love Die

If I were cold in deaths sleep,
Where I would not here the lark
Or ramble through Summer Corn,
You would not let love die.

If I were old from weary tread
Or sick with fevered brow,
You would not let love die.

And I run free to swallow words,
To touch the empty glass and
Blow the starry meadow into
A Great New dawn where love lives.

Bill Cummings

Roger Curry

113

Ode On Rejection

Do not let your will be conquered by this -
Thorns may fall from the gardener's shears
And pierce bare soles as part of Fate's cruel twists
Ebbing blood and the bitter stinging tears
Begin to drown your will to strive again.
Yet wear no scarves of itching nettles,
Nor let the darkness, nor the hailstorms be
Your companions, nor let your heart feign
To be an empty place where dust settles,
Where cobwebs choke and blind a soul which used to see.

But let rejections burn be soothed by this -
A cooling stream of reason through your brain
Telling you that all is not amiss,
That lesser men have suffered greater pain
And risen up from their despair to hope again.
Observe the beauty of a turquoise sky
And smell the musty fragrance of her hair
As she leans across to fix your tie,
And of these simple joys become aware.
Thus free yourself from melancholy's share.

Deborah Cox

My Lucky Day

If the weather promises to behave
This could be my lucky day
Nothing is going to get in my way
Early mornings water sun
Brings no happiness for someone
Like things of the distant past
Everything been and gone
Life just passes everything by
No-one says hello anymore, just goodbye
Living by excuse, living a lie
All beliefs are all but shattered
There's nothing left for me to matter
You weren't there when I needed you most
Just drift through me, the ghost
The weather was nothing new
It only brought wind and rain
But to me all it brought was pain
I know I shouldn't be this way
One day soon will be my lucky day
If only the weather promises to behave.

Steve Cooke

True Friends

What are true friends?
They are there when world's at the end
When you're sad
They're beside you when you're glad
To reach out a helping hand
Give all they can
Share all feeling
All your dealings
Help each other
To make your life fuller
Know your moods
Help if they could
Give a listening ear
To troubles and the fear
Lift your spirits high
When you felt you were going to die
Give you all the love you need
Always doing a kind deed
Friends are there to share and care
Make things brighter
Lift your heart lighter
A true friend
Stands by you to the end.

Marie Coyles

The Factory

It stands cathedral like high on the hill,
The noon day siren sounds and out they spill.

They pass Joe on the gate and show him a card,
The money is poor and the work is hard.

Unions help little when conflicts erupt,
Their hands are tied by owners corrupt.

Workers stand long in cavernous rooms,
Dangerously stretching over deafening looms.

It's Friday and Jack brings brown envelopes round,
It's never enough, they blame the fall in the pound.

They're different today though, they look too small,
Joan opens hers quickly then stares at the wall.

She's unwillingly joined the ranks of the redundant,
The reason they give is 'Cloth's too abundant'.

'Cheap imports flood in from faraway shores,
The price of cloth drops and this is the cause.'

It's harder for Joan though for she's the breadwinner,
Her husband is ill and grows ever thinner.

So the few that are left soldier on but are bitter,
They've given most of their lives to be treated like litter.

But at the end of the day the table needs bread,
So they stay at the factory for poor money and vote red.

In the hope that one day the country sees sense,
And the hard working man gets his recompense.

Jane Coleman

Emma Jude

I remember her as if it was yesterday
As she sat making little caps
Tasting an egg with great relish
And at eighty eight danced a jig
Her eyes became dim she needed care
Became an inmate of a hospital near
She sat all day yet cheered her friends
The last I saw of her she was confined to bed
At ninety four she was laid to rest
On a cold winter's day in Barrington
A soul at peace

Joan Cook

Thin Sliver Of Time

I recall clearly the feelings of before and after.
The thin sliver of time that shattered my life.
Order and Organisation are a thing of the past,
Since I answered the telephone late Monday night . . .

My stomach somersaults, overbearing sense of nausea possesses my body.
Heart beats irregular, confusion and recognition dominate thoughts.
"What?" Is the only word capable of leaving my dry mouth.
Sit, I have to Sit. Everything appears white. Numbness.

Silent purring informs me the caller has placed the receiver.
Stale smells of alcohol, aftershave, entwined patterns of
The flowered wallpaper are all that my senses register.
"Could it be?" Instinctively it is confirmed.

Now the law must be changed. Male voices must be heard.
Tender touch and smell of newborn flesh, looks of innocence,
Irrevocably lost due to Ones Rash, Undignified decision.
My Child was aborted. It would have been three today.

Mark Crane

Fountains Abbey

A canopy of velvet blue, studded with splashes of cloud that drift as sea mists do -
Shelter for the ravens - sleek black - and witchlike in their cunning look
as they search for rocky ledges - where once fine windows eyed the folding glens.
Pillars of strength - that once served fine arches - and cornices that point to
the Heavenly sky - now laid bare - to the tramp, as well as the King of England's land.
Touch for one still moment - and feel the warmth of all that lived and laboured here -
Can you not hear the patter - patter - of those sandalled feet - and smell the cloth
that adorned each advocated monk - listen for the chime of bell that called each
servant from his meditation and deep austerity - and see how the shadows lengthen
over granite stone that once was knelt in sufferance to the ominous knell of doom.
These cells that held a life -no better than the chains that manacle a beast of danger
entrapped in this vast mausoleum that for me - speaks only of the faith and devotion -
that so many held - and died an everlasting death to show their trust in the one that
knows above all others. Walk if you will down the ivy clad cloak of the crumbling
cloister - and reflect for some seconds on who has walked before - feel the power in
your tread as you resume your idle walk - and lift your face to the dying sun - as
so many have done - in years gone by - and sigh. And can you truly commit your
words that it is the warmth of the sun no other reason - for the peace you feel -
For everyone - and every action - that in the name of love and honour - has been
done. Leave me now - Go! - Let me sit awhile upon this weathered step - to reflect -
and to give my own words the debt I owe - to all those many, many monks -
of long, long time ago.

Valerie Cubitt

My Life, My Spirit

On horse back I ride,
Through the cold night air I glide,
Alongside my honour and pride.
I am not afraid,
For I have my shield to protect me.
To save me from horrors and doom.
From all nastiness and gloom.
I proudly ride on,
Like a knight in shining armour.
Charging into battle.
The sun rises, my fearful worries melt.
At last I've found what I've been looking for,
My delusion, dream stood before me.
I reached out and touched the bright, golden flames,
I caught it,
To bring the spirit of the flame into my soul.
For that is where the spirit lies,
Beyond the golden gates of the fire,
Waiting for me to give it freedom and life . . . .
My life, my spirit.

Rebecca Council

Dreams Are But Memories Of The Future

Would that my dreams had wings to fly,
Would then the night stars light the sky,
To show the path that may help me find,
Dreams I lost and left behind,
When came the night, I stopped dreaming,
For true then shone my winter years,
When my dream eyes did not long ago,
See bright for me a future glow,
A dream foretelling with my earth years done,
Of everlasting years, eternal years to come,
Years that promised never ending light,
Years of joy, where comes no night,
But here, alone in darkness, I now live my life
While my dream eyes search through timeless space,
Drifting on clouds filled with memories, memories of a future,
That can find no place for me, for astride the wind
Speeds now the eve of my winter years,
As new and swifter wings have grown,
Speeding faster than the wings of life faster than my earth years flown,
And I feel that as we are soon to meet friend death,
I may ask one thing of thee, could I in lasting sleep a traveller be,
That I might help my dream eyes find those dreams I
Lost and left behind when came the night I stopped dreaming

J. Cuthbert

Shadow Of Solitude

She comes in shadows on my wall
Her voice a whisper, she speaks my name
Upon the stair I hear her footsteps fall
The spectre of solitude is haunting me again

She comes in shadows in my heart
To wreath me in the chains of sorrow
Twilight fades into a night so dark
That I am blind to thoughts of tomorrow

She comes in shadows in my soul
The gold of summer turns to winter time
Shivering, I stand in the bitter cold
As the lady puts her hand in mine

She comes in shadows so beguiling
Though I believe she means me no harm
When I see her face, so sadly smiling
Still I fear this dark lady's charm

She comes in shadows of the night
And finds me wherever I may be
Then I am lost to the world of light
Wrapped in the arms of that dark lady

Paul Crudgington

Matt The Mad Inventor

My mate our Matt
Does not have a cricket bat.
Scientific mind a mess.
Sure he does his very best.

Mist and fog float through the room.
Bits of wood and witches broom.
"Eureka Dad it works this time,
I made Mom a washing line."

You put the battery over there
Then sit upon this rubber chair.
Connect it up then off we go.
Thunder claps and lightning show!

Peg the washing on the string
Then pull it with this plastic thing.
Not too hard or it will break.
Not that hard for goodness sake!

Lights are out for miles around.
I think we should be on the ground.
Flying high into the sky
What do they mean by tumble dry?

My mate our Matt
Does not have a cricket bat.
Instead he makes things, this and that.
My mate our Matt.

S.J. Cook

Dead End

Some crazy couple in Taiwan - had their parents 'tie the knot'
I can't believe I'm hearing this where does the madness stop
They only went and had them wed in their coffins upon their funeral day
No sooner man and wife than their bodies were carried away
I really see no point in having the poor devils wed
I mean no disrespect but their parents were already dead
Were the couple crazy a screw loose in their head
If I was their shrink I'd have them certified instead
A wedding's the last thing on their poor parent's minds right now
They've got to be the only couple I know who needn't worry about mad cow

Lynn Cook

The Paper Pendulum

The paper pendulum that hides the cloud
The future calling that beckons loud
The paper state an empire born
Will leave its mark in time to come

Storms the like of none before
That rip the roots and raise the score
Of trees that one by one
To the will of man succumb

Economies must grow and prosper
As each new fad we seek to foster
This paper world goes round and round
Communication without a sound

The pace of change grows ever faster
As each technology we seek to master
And developing countries, are told to learn
Be green, be careful the way you burn

Now we face the final problem
Of endless needs, but not resources
So to the earth, we go, cap in hand
But, where there once was soil, now only sand

The wind blows wild without the trees
Mother nature now on her knees
As the trees that are left, still one by one
To the will of man succumb

Chris Davies

Mouse

I dread the cold, dark night when the house cat comes out
I try to hide but she hunts me out
I run away, my life is precious
She pads after me her slow, casual strides never matching my hurried ones
I dart quickly into a bush, waiting and praying for her to go past
She doesn't, she stops and looks wildly around,
Her eyes flashing like green torches in the dark night
A quick scratching in the grass catches her attention
And she pads silently after it, softly like the hunter that she is

Alex Corker (Age 12)

The Ruin

It lays alone, so stark and bare
The old stone ruin in the field down there.
With sightless windows swaying in the breeze,
Surrounded by the old fruit trees.

The untouched stones that once held life,
Belonged to the miller and his wife,
They worked the stone, a daily tread,
That helped to make the staple bread.

Now alone, in sad disrepair,
Once tidy rooms open to the air,
A drunken, swinging, broken pane,
Bangs to and fro in the driving rain.

I stand and watch as images pass
Before my eyes 'cross the trampled grass,
My mind alive with those bygone days,
Of the miller's life and his ancient ways.

Elizabeth A. Cook

My Person

My person exists 'By the Grace of God'
But my actions are mine alone
My conscience is my morality
And will judge upon what I've done

I can be pure of body, mind and spirit
Not every hour of each day my personal limit,
I can deed good. I can deed bad
Whatever lesson will be taught, I'll be glad.
Welcoming pain, I appreciate my health
Accepting poverty, helps me know wealth
Being selfish, enables being selfless
To do a good deed, for another in distress,
If my person helps someone
Then I have achieved
My God helps me fail
My God helps me succeed
My God can be availed
When my person is in need

My will alone is my ruinous course
My God's will has all my perfection, undoubted
Between He and I my God has most force,
My God again to my person, has reported.

M.R. Cross

Simon's Seat, Appletreewick

A trail of
wispy cloud
drifts lingeringly
round the summit rocks
while, just below,
snow which fell at dawn
like sprinkled icing sugar
coats the moor.
On lower slopes
rich ochre of wet winter bracken
spreads a warmth
belying the cool day.
At the foot
thin black lines
of dry-stone wall
form asymmetric swards
of varied green.
A grey and wintry
sky enwraps the whole,
while song of blackbird, finch and tit
hangs merrily on the air.
Beautiful creation
reflecting, echoing, praising
bountiful creator.

Beth

Dogs

Dogs are of every kind
So I'd like you to sit back while I find
The dog you like best to sit and caress
the alsation with its striking marks
Boy I'm scared when he barks
The poodle with its lovely curls
Neat and nice as it sits and curls
The sheepdog a lovable dog
With streaks of black and white
Easily noticeable at night
The boxer with its fowl face
Plods along as if in a race
The labrador smart and tall
Always so handy with a ball
The old English sheepdog fluffy and cuddly
A friendly face he's got not to be forgot
The greyhound slender and slim
He always looks poorly and thin
So here's my story to the end
I hope I've made a friend

P.A. Conroy

Bleached

Colours bleach
Bleak streets
Scream defeat
Deafen with the snore
Don't budge
Rush, hurry, rush, hurry,
Routine debasing scurry.
Grey drudge
Bland fudge
Flatulent slug
Bloated flab
Pasty drab
In lethal drift
Flat
Sapped by apathy
Drugged with lethargy
Drunks lurch
In endless search
Vitality leached
Colour bleached.

M. Davies

Pains Of Remembrance

Just a hint of a movement was all that it took;
Her throat closed in moments as the past opened up.
Attracting attention was a little blue suit -
The back of a golden blonde boy choosing fruit.
His father's worn face told a thousand short stories;
As he reached to pick berries blooms blushed in their glories.
The rain-sprinkled trolleys fought bravely for space;
Only hers stood stock-still: her heart shot through like lace.

She was mesmerised - smiling, she thought he'd come back;
Hurried feet took her over Time's fathomless gap.
Reliving the joys, needing wrongs to be right,
Tricks of the mind made a fool of her sight.
Mistaking his features for ones of her own,
She just didn't see that by now he'd be grown.
But the instant it dawned her whole core paid the cost;
Silver-soft offerings for the child too soon lost.

Slowly, she regained her sense of reality;
Warped wheels in motion brought back some normality.
She could feel prying eyes, yet she queued like the best;
Her tanned, slender legs cried out loud for a rest.
Trundling her bags, catching scents on the breeze,
She found her way home with the simplest of ease.
Another day over, put away with the others;
The pains of remembrance for forgotten once mothers.

Angela E. Crosbie

The Message

If the world were only filled with love
What a peaceful world it would be
Where love would override this hate
For each man and beast to see

Because love is the basis of faith
Where trust can truly be seen
So remember to love one another
To help make this more than a dream

Wars would be a thing of the past
Prejudice wouldn't ever exist
A basis for the brotherhood of man
For hate would never be missed

They say we are here for a purpose
Well Christ came to show us so
His love always came through shining
Through his sorrow and deepest woe

What can be gained by suffering?
Why worry about the colour of his skin
Surely its the person we should love
The quality that comes from within

So take this message as a warning
Should hate carry on destroying so
There'll be nothing left in this wide world
To love, to hate or even grow

Christina Musgrove Cowling

The Odds Are On

I'm not lady luck, I married Mr Chance
I was bowled over, by his romance.
The days when he won, the tips were right
Loosing stepped in, so did the fight.
I thought he enjoyed a flutter
Not a gambling nutter.
Visitors don't come any more
There's not much furniture, past our door.
The bailiffs came, with no remorse
Money borrowed, for the racecourse.
Wages lost, poor excuse.
Addiction, can't break loose.

Carolyn Coyne

Last Thoughts

Dear strings of my heart
Play me a tune before we part
Make time stand still for a little
while
I'll make believe I'm a boy again
Laughing so full of joy again
Dancing with my only love

Dear youth of the past
It was so good while it did last
I'll make believe that we're young again
Reliving loves first spring
Having a wonderful fling again
Oh how the years they did fly
Swiftly by

Dear love of my heart it hurt me so
When you had to go
I'll be with you in a little while
I'll close my eyes and then
I'll be just like a boy again
Dancing with my only love

Last winter so so cold
And you were so old

Thomas Walter Cunningham

How Could . . . . ?

How could you leave me?
How could you go?
If only you knew
How it's hurting me so

We had it all made
We were destined to be
We were people in love
Guess you just didn't see

How can you smile
When you've taken mine away?
I just can't go on
If I'm feeling this way

Come back to me baby
And make our love true
'Cause how could you leave me?
I'm lost without you.

Emma Darby

Pilgrimage To The Home Of Dylan Thomas At Laugharne

Through a shed's grimy window
I catch a glimpse of a poet's open soul
Bereft of life now, alone
A table scattered with papers, books
A dead man's work place
Dust blankets photographs on walls
Small shrouds hiding a testament
Echoes of a life mummified
The shriek of gulls and the sea's cry
Prayers over this abandoned carapace

Stone-walled cemetery in the fading light
Headstones marble white
Battle for supremacy with the coming night
A wooden cross marks his grave
A simple sentinel for a lost cause

What am I doing here, come from the valleys?
This man is a stranger, dead before I lived
What right have I to trespass in his garden?
Yes, we come to visit the dead,
Say our prayers and linger, callers uninvited
The dead have no choice but to suffer us, silently.

I have come to this place, a pilgrimage to a shrine
In hope of stealing something - inspiration?
I will carry home only a photograph untaken.

Kevin Cooper

The Loss Of Our Mother

We only have one mother
To teach us right from wrong
You taught us how to love
And to understand
We know you will never leave our hearts
And always be by our side
A guiding light from above

Janette Cousins

Untitled

Oh does the heart pounder
Upon its being
Does it wonder
Where upon seeing
The loneliness engraved
On the silent wings
Of the gentle soul
Its destiny unknowing

Francine Delabracherie

123

Village Undeserted

The church, school and pub
The village triplet of traps
Religion, learning, the boozy hub
Snares are set, unseen perhaps

Rain the first of holy water
Falls from the blessed hand
Upon the infant son and daughter
The showery sacrament waves a wand

A few to church will come
To repent and pray (sooner or later)
Yet afterwards on going home
Will still feel thus a traitor

School the memory lingers
First the chalk and slate
Blotting paper, inky fingers
The vain attempt to educate

The chestnuts chandelier
Leafy sycamore in its prime
A tavern nestles near
The church bells chime

Here the weary traveller
Will rest, slake his thirst
Here the rampant reveller
Demon drink accursed

G. Collinson

The Golden Days Of Greece

Achilles hero of the Trojan War
He laid proud Hector in the dust
Godlike to the very core
But was slain by an arrows thrust

Bathed in the waters of the Styx
His immortality to gain
But one heel which was unsubmerged
Robbed him of his life and fame

Still the glorious days of Greece
And of its heroes will be told
With lions still to guard the gate
To Mycenaes treasures of solid gold

Lord Byron loved this country so
The ultimate of gifts he gave
For when the fever laid him low
He relinquished his life
For an early grave

And so the golden days of
Greece are gone
Along with Aphrodites arms
But now Greece captures
Tourists hearts
With its golden sun
And scenic charms

Dorothy Dawson

Changes

It's funny really, in a way
How things happen, day by day,
Though things don't seem to change that much,
Suddenly you're out of touch,
People you would see so often,
You'll never see again at all
And the small children you saw playing,
Have now grown up to be so tall,
Those little children you saw then,
Have all got children of their own,
Though you never really notice it,
Time creeps up on you bit by bit,
And all the friends you thought would stay forever,
Have moved away to return never,
It's funny really in a way,
How life changes day by day.

Gary Dimmock

Finding Happiness

While in pursuit of the things you like
You have no care for day or night
No care for rest just work no play
Until the time someone blocks your way

Maybe we find it at the end of time
Maybe we find it's yours not mine
Maybe it's a symbol of hope to say
That it's the wish you made the other day

As life unfolds and time goes by
We've seen the lows we've seen the highs
But have you found that special one
That makes your life complete and done

Yet you may think you've got it all
But suddenly you hear that call
And loneliness is back again
So gushing back comes all the pain

Vikki Doris (Age 13)

Stroke Victims

Porridge and Toast
That's what Mum enjoys the most
But the long night waits ahead
It's the part that I most dread
"A B C D" - moaning deep
Uneven breath, but asleep.

Nerves on edge
Patience raw
Must keep calm
Try once more

Head on pillow
Sleep, please come
"Oh Dear"! "Oh dear!"
Sighs restless Mum.

Abandon bed, kettle on
Muffin bounds across the floor
"1 2 3 4" counts my Mum
Wristwatch says half past four.

Cup of tea
Two 'Rich Teas'
One for me
How long will it be?
Before Porridge and Toast
That's what Mum enjoys the most.

Anne Decalmer

What The Sister Said To Me

When I was a little lass I always had a yen
To be like the nurses on Emergency Ward Ten,
I'd act like Florence Nightingale aglow with tender care
And hoped I'd meet a Doctor like the famous Kildare
So at seventeen I enrolled a student nurse to be
And as I donned my uniform here's what Sister said to me
Always take care little nurse
And you must put your patients first
You'll work like a slave
But think of all the precious lives you're going to save
You'll do the work of seven
But your reward will be in heaven
And when you reach those pearly gates your face tired and old
You'll meet the man of fate your future to behold
What makes you think he will say you've gained admission here
I've been a nurse you'll proudly say for many and many a year
The heavenly gates will open wide as Peter touches a bell
Come in my love and choose your harp you've had your share of hell

Harriette Dawson

The Birds "Still" Sing in Dunblane

Pain, Shame
Dunblane
An act so profane
To mention totally, totally insane

Fateful day, devil came
After events, after aims
Community saw, society came
Organisation! to blame

Meek, mild, six year old child
Themselves only on trial
Save them, sadly
Their names logged on file

Clergy is reading, those little mites
Graveside, families cry
Cut deep, their souls in pain
Young to old, the scars remain

Eye-witnesses tell you
Holding back disgust, shrouded shame
Hurt, hear them exclaim!
The birds "still" sing in Dunblane

G.A. De-Natale

Dark Nights

Home from work
Have my tea
Watch TV

Home from work
Write a letter
That feels better

Home from work
See a friend
On the mend

Home from work
Take a look
Read a book

Home from work
Have my tea
Watch TV - maybe!

June Davies

Old Woman's Tale

Sparkling eyes, turned watery red
two sunken hollows, in my ageing head.
Surrounded by hair now white and fine
that once, so ebony black did shine.
Weathered cheeks, where no longer roses glow
the words that once flowed fast, now come slow.
Lips that cannot always find the cup
many kisses sweet did so lovingly sup.
Ancient, straining ears cannot hear the bell
yet could so many little secrets softly tell.
Frail hands so shaky and callous worn
helped many a neighbour's child be born.
Feet that happily, danced the night away
from these wretched legs, now often stray.
Weary heart, fighting so hard to beat
once, pounded to burst at my lover's feet.
Listen well, let my tale be told
I too was young and not always old.

Marina Davey

126

The Ruins Of Lindisfarne Priory

You push open an old wooden gate,
Old grave stones stand proudly,
The crisp, green grass under our feet,
St. Aiden gives a warm welcoming,
As he points to the ruined priory.

An arched doorway cries,
At this awful state of misery,
I look round the doorway,
And see, a giant rainbow arch,
It is calling God to help.

I peer round an extremely wide pillar,
It looks out to a grass courtyard,
Even further along, on a hill,
Cows and sheep graze,
Not only looking at the ruins, but the blue-green sea.

I swiftly move to the well,
Deep, deep, down
The water seems to shiver,
Because of the cold wind blowing,
The well was never going to end.

High, high up,
A passageway stands,
Higher than anyone could ever reach,
Only small like a window,
This priory was like a heart that had been broken.

Evette Jayne Davies (Age 10)

Night Frights

What are those noises in the night
Whilst under my sheets I hide?
Are they ghosts, monsters or demons
Which turn me rigid with fright?

Each tiny noise fills me with terror
And shivers quake my body.
I pray that I'll be left alone
And not be an ogre's dinner.

I don't know where they come from
Those spectres of the night,
There's nothing to fear in my bedroom
Until I turn out the light.

Sally Davies

The Kiss

Golden shoulders, languishing forward,
Froth of love dreamily caressing,
A slender neck thrown back,
In sheer joy and captivating the moment,
Forever. So beautiful, so untouched,
Just love, long awaited,
The longing satisfied,
Knowing that this would come,
One day,
Tempting, the kiss that lingered,
Like it would never end, never cease,
The kiss went on being,
Forever.

Angie M. Davies

The Morning After *(With apologies to Clement C. Moore)*

Twas the night before Christmas when all through the house,
Not a creature was stirring, not even a mouse,

Except for a feller who wore a red hat,
Who had a white beard, and was ruddy and fat,

I watched open-eyed as I sat on the stair,
As he cuddled my Mum, as he ruffled her hair,

Then he sang a rude carol, and poached a few kippers,
And took off his wellies and put on Dad's slippers,

He opened some presents and tried on three ties,
Then attempted, but failed, to eat seven mince pies!

And he drank my Dad's whiskey, the saucy old tyke,
And rode 'round the hall on a shiny new bike!

Twas the morning of Christmas, joy spread through the house,
Save for Daddy, who sadly, was grey as a mouse,

So I said to him "Daddy, where were you last night?
You should have been here, for you missed a great sight!"

Peter Davies

New Year Resolutions

From many friends all quite sincere
Comes the wish A HAPPY NEW YEAR
Said of course with a cheerful tone
For seeds of hope have now been sown
Printed on a card or better
Like older times in a letter
But before it can make its start
You really have to play your part
Now's the time for resolutions
They do have some good solutions
Change is what living is about
So take the plunge or you'll miss out
Take your pick and remain in charge
The rewards indeed could be large
Start it steady but keep it up
That's how champions win the cup
You could become a millionaire
For fortune goes to them that dare
Well anyway the best of luck
All you need is an ounce of pluck

Harry Derx

Treeson

You stood there quite majestically
Proud and so erect
Waving to the whistling wind
Clouds above bereft
Shadows you bestowed as gifts
To nature far below
Birds made use of trunk and bough
Shelter from the foe . . .
As leaves dislodged in winter
Earth welcomed fruitful guest
Your work there so magnificent
Environment a quest
Through each and every season
Not a moment ever bleak
Until the time your sap ran dry
When they felled you in one sweep . . .
Took many years to grow in strength
Then in no time at all
No more environment complete
Man voted for your fall . . . . .

Margarette L. Damsell

Sailors Lament

The foaming deep will bless the sleep
Of those who lay below,
From years gone by, who answered the cry
And for sailors they did go.

Their loved ones pleaded for them not to go
Yet they bid them farewell from the shore,
Placing them in God's merciful hands
Knowing they would return no more.

Now through the darkness of the night
While cold winds moan and into bones doth bite,
They watch the lighthouses flashing light
Guiding sailors home.

Seagulls screech their mournful cry
Above the waves they daily fly,
So sailors round the world will be
Aware of the dangers of the sea.

God bless them all, both young and old
Out on the seas in the freezing cold,
Please send them all back safely to shore
To the loving arms of their families once more.

Victor Day

Brussel Soup

Never eat brussel soup
(I assure you it's not the right thing to do)
I tried to do it once in my life,
And I was sick!!
That could happen to you!!

Graeme Darbyshire (Age 9)

The Grandfather Clock

The Grandfather Clock, lovingly polished when remembered,
is only missed now the gap in the hall is still walked around, and I catch
myself, waiting, for the hour to sound by a now mute chime.

Regret; for not appreciating his depth of colour, for not being in awe of his history,
for not taking the time to polish and deepen his shine, for not staring for hours at his
face, with its minute details, each line with a story to tell.
For not remembering him before his colour began to fade, bleached by the sun.

Elaine Dalton

Untitled

To start a poem, is an inclination to roam,
To dream a dream, far away from home.
Picturing colours, that play a part,
A mind of creation, that exemplifies art.
A world that can revolve, with words, and imagination,
To explore, all the realms of fashion.
This applies in every sense, to whatever is decreed,
The beauty of the soul, we need, not greed.
To focus on everything, that governs our thoughts, how we think and feel,
Whether it is fantasy, or what is real.
Either way, constantly probing, the mysteries we face,
A parcel, that makes up, the human race.
Whether it is colour or creed,
We all need, to fulfil, the same need,
After all, we all have mouths to feed.
With reality, things could be realised,
To confront the problems that materialise.
Single thought, sometimes can pave the way,
Despite, what others, with proffered help might say.
Deep thought, can leave a pattern to follow,
Like other ideas, prove negative and hollow.
So, you might be able, to strike out anew,
As, you have obtained, a different point of view.
This will give you an inner strength,
And bolster, your confidence to great length.

Bruce Dann

Good Health

Good health is such a blessing;
Which we must learn to appreciate,
But alas, we only realise its importance,
When it begins to deteriorate.

Most of us sail through life,
Acting rather dense,
When all we need to maintain good health,
Is to use our common sense.

Such as losing that extra weight,
Which plays havoc with the heart,
Or cutting out those cigarettes,
Which tear our lungs apart.

And taking a walk each day to improve the circulation,
While enjoying the fresh air,
And perhaps,
Having a good conversation.

Mary Daly

Severn Bore

On a cold grey day we stood, nerves aquiver
Awaiting a phenomenon peculiar to this river,
When a full moon, and a high tide, the way will pave,
For a long travelling tidal wave,
An awesome sight when in full flood,
With a following wind to make it good.

Fairly soon our waiting was rewarded,
And everyone excitedly applauded,
As our ears detected an increasing roar,
Heralding the imminent arrival of the bore,

Full six feet high, travelling ten miles per hour,
Moving upstream, getting gradually lower,
A full fathom depth of water following behind,
Which we could see when it "Reverted back to kind",

Coming upstream against the flow,
Across the river all in a row,
You can see that its water, and of it there's lots,
Moving upstream at a high rate of knots,
The complexity of this phenomenon I cannot comprehend,
The spectacular sight of the wave without end.

Marilyn A. Davis

What If . . .?

Let's suppose the aliens found a planet floating around,
and when they went to look at it everything stayed aground.
They had the knowledge and the means, so made a thing called man,
they made a woman just for him to make life as they can.
They watched the people multiply and make their own domain,
they sent them new ideas just to see how they'd sustain.
The people soon learned how to live, but reproduced too much,
the aliens took care of that with natural disasters and such.
The aliens got bored with that and introduced some stress,
the people seemed relieved there was a reason for their mess.
It soon took over all their lives, if they wanted it or not,
This was when the aliens introduced alcohol and pot.
Some people used it wisely to take the stress away,
Others they abused it and made stress part of the day.
These people struggled on with it and thought "well this is it",
the others thought "to hell with that I've got to get out of this pit."
Striving to get better they all gave their lives their best.
Because it suddenly occurred to them "what if this life's a test?"

Lorraine Daniels

One Day In The Past

Failing eyesight, wrinkled skin, hair of grey,
But memory is good of a bygone day,
Memory is strong to recall, young lad, a dog,
Two friends always, a bond so strong.

Short trousers above bare knee, bare feet strong,
Race through heather, rough and brown,
Heather bells swish and ring, no problem to him,
Faithful dog by his side, what is time.

Stretched out upon soft green berry moss,
Skylark soaring high, full of song,
Another noise comes to his ear, just a grouse,
The curlews cry, is that a corncrake I hear.

Clear blue sky, soft white clouds,
Almost a breeze to ruffle the grass,
Discover a nest swarming with ants,
Study them closely, carrying their eggs.

Squawking peewits swoop and dive,
Drumming wing feathers, sound alive,
Far in the distance, is that a crow,
Could it be a gull, out over the flow.

The naval anchorage full of ships,
Swing at anchor, await new trips,
Peace and quiet surround the hill,
Could this be wartime, and be so still.

Doug Delday

The Loss Of A Loved One

So many things spark off the memory,
and for you and me and countless others,
small things remind us constantly -
we, the lonely windows, husbands, mothers
of a life once known, now gone for ever.
We live in the present, but long for the past,
and though we smile, we cannot sever
the longing for that someone which will last
as long as we live and have a memory,
and can think back to a happy carefree day.
Our loved one's eyes are closed, they cannot see
or do they, as we weep and pray?
There is no escape, we have to survive,
we, the ones that are left behind,
lucky, or unlucky to still be alive
remembering what 'might have been' in one's heart and mind.

Tina Deacon

132

Sweet

On a sun-soaked rock I bask at leisure,
Sweet words rain down like morning dew
To refresh me with forgotten pleasure
That all of me is dear to you.

Honeyed words which leave no doubt
Of how your tender heart now tends;
You'd rather be with me than without;
You need me, so we'll never end.

Your fragrant breath, a floral breeze,
Which whispers nothings in my brain,
Says something's wrong, and there I freeze,
To hear the tune of your refrain.

Sweet words, like syrup, make me sick,
Dripping from your sugar-mouth placid.
Naive, I received the smooth word-slick
Like a newborn child baptised in acid.

Claw-torn flesh slides thick and hot
Through my skull, as everything within me falls,
Leaving a hollow gourd; skeletal pot
Of nothing, 'cos you took it all.

Rachel Davenport-Williams

Help Me Please

You know, I sometimes wonder,
Why my life is all asunder.
I find myself alone, in a darkened room,
Surely this is not my lot, someone will come soon.
I try to fathom out, why fortune let me down,
Dear old friends, I used to know, no longer around.
This life I lead, to me, holds no appeal,
No point in going on, I've just lost the zeal.
My life, once full of love, enough to keep me strong,
Now I'm told, it seems, this is where I belong.
I have difficulty remembering, from whence I came,
This is not surprising, with every day the same.
People come to see me, with them I've no recall,
They stay, for a few minutes, return, no not at all.
So why am I allowed, to continue in this vane,
I tell them I'm happy, content, but it's only feign
Death will kill the pain and make me whole once more,
And when I return, I will do it differently
Of that you can be sure.

G.W. Davies
(Carer)

And The Sick Shall be Cured

She grabs up a slip
And lets her huge jaw gather
On a thought provoked by dreams
Half heard and understood.

Shielding her perfect knowledge
From the rest - touched by God
She has advantages - she chooses
Dribble as her system.

She cannot vote - or is it sit
In the Upper House? - yet here her money
Is as good as anyone's:
All are equal in the eyes of chance.

A democracy of coloured balls
Chips away at social walls;
While History lessons concentrate
On the numbers one to forty-eight.

Alan Dorling

Remember

Now you are old and grey my love
rocking in your chair,
take a trip down memory lane
and I will meet you there.

Dancing eyes, soft warm skin,
think of me, you're young again.

Come with me a courting,
drift and reminisce,
laugh and love together,
remember that first kiss?

Darling what a kiss that was
you set my heart a whirl,
it had to be from that day on
that I would be your girl

I didn't want to leave you
or die, when oh so young,
but soon you will be at my side,
back where you belong.

Now you are old and grey my love
no one seems to care
come, take a trip down memory lane,
for I'll be waiting there.

Valerie Di Franco

Fly Past

It seemed that twilight, rose and purple lit
Made candelabra of descriptive branches,
Shades of transient and penitential people,
Crickets private Gloria dizzying the haze,
The haze where better days
Pursued, like spirits lost, old shadowed ways.

Then, in formation, constancy occurred,
Where sea birds, through a passage way, a pause,
Like aspirations, swept forwards buoyed by God.

Throats protracted like beacons, silver white, in cloak,
Of massing ether smoke,
Shot, salmon pink,across and silence spoke.

No arguments, detriment, disturbed
Alignment as rhythmical as music,
Symphonic winged those swans, high pitched
                    In flight.

Ruth Daviat

Absent Friends

It's many years since I was a Ted
"You're not going out like that" mother said

But go out I did without a row
With all my mates, "Where are they now"?

There was Bill and John, Dave and Ted
Where are they now? Are they all dead?

Saturday morning, all go for a bath
Saturday night, up the pub for a laugh

Sunday was pictures, in the Old Kent Road
Some films were new, most films were old

Each night all meet at the local park
Chatting up girls, just for a lark

My lovely mates, Where have they gone?
What happened to Fred? What happened to Ron?

I suppose like me, they are old and grey
Living in places, that are far, far away

But as I write this, I say to myself
Well I'm still alive and in good health

So to all my friends, wherever you are
Look to the sky, you will see a bright star

That star is me, looking down on you
My absent friends, the old and the new

George Dickens

To Spring

Farewell Winter welcome Spring
And all the beauty that you bring
Lighter evenings brighter days
Joyful signs in many ways
Fresh green grass begins to grow
Dainty flowers their heads do show
Buds and bulbs to please the eye
Songs of birds up in the sky
Just look around and you will see
That all best things in life are free

Dorothy Everett

Christmas Candle

Not some cold, distant star,
To guide those journeying from afar,
But the warm, welcoming glow,
Of a candle in many a window,
Lighting the way,
On the eve of Christmas Day.

The wayfarer, seeing the candle-light,
Would know that there'd be a welcome within,
From the chill of the night.
Should two wayfarers from afar,
Happen to come by;
Be on their way to Bethlehem;
Their newborn would have better
Than a manger, on which to lie.

Denis Dolan

135

Lazy Days

In the genteel elegance of Oxford
The picturesque Cherwell
Meanders slowly past tended gardens
Where respected dons dwell

In this city of waterways, hidden
In the trailing willows
Below the graceful iron bridge to
Unite where the Thames flows

An idyllic scene one lazy afternoon
Filled with summer sounds
The air heavy with summer's fragrance
Evident to all around

A solitary punt nudges along the
Grassy bank carelessly
But hush! the occupant is sleeping
It seems quite soundly

The youthful face is shielded from the sun
Covered by a boater
With head on cushion, he lies extended
In flannels and blazer

One arm relaxed hangs over the side
Trailing in the water
While all the time his life blood drains away
Leaving behind a crimson trail

T. Daley

The Garden

There is a little garden
Which I do call my own
Where all the shrubs I harden
And all the seeds are sown

I work there in the Spring
And in the summer too
And to all my friends I bring
To show them what I do

In the corner there's an apple tree
Which if I give a little shake
Drops its apples down to me
So an apple tart I'll make

There's roses climbing round my door
And ivy up the wall
Heather, daisies and lots more
Oh ho I love it all

The luscious green of the lawn
The colour of the flower bed
And with the wakening of the dawn
The place where my feet tread

What would I do without you
I ask myself each day
You're the only thing to me that's true
My life would be oh so grey

Catherine Elliott

The Spark

In the busy street a woman fell;
No-one spoke.
In the way, she lay concussed and shocked;
No-one paused.
At last a young boy stopped and raised her up;
No-one helped.
"Shall I call an ambulance?" he asked;
No-one looked.
"Thank you, no. I think I'll be alright".
No-one heard
Except a young girl passing close to them;
"Want some help?"
"Cheers", he said. They stood the woman up.
"Can you walk?"
"Yes", the woman said. "We'll take you home".
"You're very kind".
Each took an arm. They slowly walked away.
No-one saw.

Pauletta J. Edwards

Kathy's Kitchen

I sing hour after hour
Morning, noon and night.
I can rehearse in here
practice my meek, quirky little Jewish ma routine.
I find easier, nicer inside
my formica, stainless steel sleek, chamber.

Whilst I am at my work, baking, stewing, advising.
My voodoo eye can still probe and prowl
I am still as sharp as a canteen of bottom draw cutlery.
I see it all.
I felt the hooks of marriage and motherhood cut and cut.

Everything here is kosher.
There is a place for everything in the larder
honey, blood, sugar, knives, cookies, arsenic.

My coffee pot is always hot.
Hungry mouths, zealous wives, vulgar inlaws
arrive to blemish my kitchen.
Clutter my afternoons with their affairs
every one of them expecting me, Kathy
to wash their dirty linen.

Once they have gone I sing too loud
so as I can drown destruction, decay, infidelity
I yawl brazen, so I can't hear my broken heart thump.

Nicola Daly

Remembrance Day

How sad it is
That all this time
Has passed, and still,
In every clime,
Men bearing arms,
Tribe against tribe,
Race against race,
Creed against creed.

What troubles those
Who sell the means
To maim and kill
The babes
Who once were cradled
In their mothers' arms.

Bea Ewart

To A Cherished One-Keri Downes

We who are left oft wonder why
Someone we love it seems must die.
We may no longer feel their touch
But they are with us just as much
Because our memories are so clear
We cherish them and hold them dear.
Whilst time may heal the wound in part,
We know deep down within our heart
That nothing can take those away
Who're in our thinking every day.

D. P. Downes

137

Perfection?

The vivid orange, dramatic red, a myriad of colours flit through the sky.
Something to do with trapped dust and solar flares say the scientists.
Trying to explain the lights,
The sinister lights in the sky.

Next propaganda and lies, lies stuffed down our mouths, our throats. Lies!
Churned out constantly by the media.
The lights are nothing to worry about, nor the tremors that wrack the weary world.
I feel we are being watched.

The voices in my head, are they real?
Or just the last cries of an anguished mind?
Nobody is in control, anarchy rules.
Our very own fear of the unknown is ripping the world apart.

The world is gone, disappeared.
A nasty blot on the Universe, erased.
All hopes, dreams everything just gone.
The voices tell me we didn't deserve to live.
I now live in a perfect Universe.

No newspapers screaming out the news,
No hate, no fear, no joy, no love.
Why must I live in eternal torment?

I float through space, totally at mercy.
Why do these creatures wish to control my body and my mind? Why me?

If only they had given us more time,
All we needed was time . . . . . .

Marie-Claire Dibble

To Spring

Here we are at the start of Spring
Now is that not a lovely thing?
The grass beginning to grow,
And the birds beginning to sing
Spring bulbs are starting to flower,
Heavy rain turning to showers.
Days grow brighter and longer,
Seeds that we planted grow stronger,
Spring is such a lovely time
Even helped to create this rhyme!

Bert Enston

Please

After the battle
I bleed and plead
Please can I have some water
Please, please,
If I don't I will die,
Please, please, please.

Richard Essex (Age 9)

138

The Blasted Motor-Car

When I was small, still in my pram, my mother often talked
To other folk she'd chance to meet whilst going for a walk.
But now one seldom sees such mums, they don't go walking far,
They put their babes in kiddies' seats inside their motor-car.

And some years on, with friends to school, we'd walk there rain or fine,
We'd lots of fun, and have to rush to get there just in time.
But now no groups of kids are seen, they all go there with ma
En route to work she'll drop them off quite safely from her car.

And after tea when I was young, I'd walk alone to Cubs
And all the rest of the family would stroll to friends or clubs.
Not so today, they stay at home, to watch their TV star
And if they *have* to venture out it's in their lovely car.

On Saturdays with all at home, we'd do the shopping first,
Then if its fine we'd take some food and drink to quench our thirst
Sometimes to Epsom common or the downs (not quite so far),
But now its supermarket and the coast . . . by motor car.

Each Sunday now, the roads come live, a cacophony of sound
Of radios and shouting, with families jostling round
All wielding cloths and buckets, no spot allowed to mar
That pride of their possession, their sparkling motor-car.

My neighbours are unknown to me, it's such an awful shame
For once upon a time I knew each person by their name.
I never meet a soul these days, it gives me quite a jar
To know my isolation's cause . . . that blasted motor car.

Norman Dallen

Car Boot Sale

Car boot sales are very strange things
Where else could you buy used life belt rings
Broken toys and dolls with no heads
A glassless greenhouse, a roofless shed
Pens with no ink, cups with no handles
Disgusting pot dolphins, wickless green candles
Totally useless unwanted tools
Games for six players without the rules
TV's with no picture, radios with no sound
Shapeless Hula Hoops that used to be round
Thirty pence for this, ten pence for that
A very bald looking brown Welcome mat
Gloves without fingers, plants without leaves
Knives without blades, coats without sleeves
Yet people flock there and spend lots of cash
On things that later in the garage they stash
Of course you can bet on this without fail
These things will be out at the next car boot sale

Paul Duddley

Four Seasons

Scudding clouds and snowy mounds
White sheets across the downs
Winter's grip is all around
Mother nature's tender hands
Will change the scenery of this winterland,
And so it came to pass,
Snows receding down to the grass
Crocuses and blue-bells everywhere
Spring has come on the land and in the air
Sounds of birds whistling
Ah! sweet music to the ear.
And as the days get longer
Time to relax and ponder
The wheat's all in, animals in their prime
Makes summer all worthwhile
Days begin to shorten
As leaves begin to fall
Horse chestnuts lying everywhere
Waiting to be conkers that's all
And so the overcast skies return once more
Snowflakes fall gently over land and moors
Four seasons come and go as they always will
So if you don't mind I'll finish this poem
I'm only allowed twenty four lines you know

Gordon Dangerfield

Sister

Sister you're a special friend
We have so much to share.
The memories of our childhood,
Someone to show you care.

The love I always have for you
The feelings are so true
To have a younger sister,
As wonderful as you.

I love you little sister,
You mean so much to me.
It hurts if you are poorly,
The feelings can't be seen.

So let me tell you something,
I should have said before,
I love you little sister
And every day much more.

L. Evans

Alone In The Dark

Alone in the dark
Scary lanes that make you shiver
Trees look like they're whispering
Twigs that remind me of grabbing hands
Owls hunting for mice
Spooky noises make you shiver
The wind starts to whistle
Sticks break when I step on them
Thunder crashed
Lightning sets a tree alight
I run out of sight
Through the park
Past the canal
Home at last

Samantha Dwyer (Age 9)

140

Thoughts From A Cave

Dry and acrid was the taste of the cave
As he licked and he smelt and hated;
He remembered the truth of the bitter outside
And he sank back angry.
Dead were his thoughts to the realms of truth,
Of the despair, hate and suffering.
They detested each other and fought with the world
To create yet even more money;
But he sank into the gloom and damp of the cave
And wept for their utter misery
Wretched is the word to describe their hearts
As they fight and quarrel and mope
Around the tired globe. But none can redeem
The state of repair that man has provoked;
And he sat in the mud of the floor of the cave
He hung his head and cried; as he thought of
The people above whom he'd known, and now
Alas had all died.
"Why me?" he shouted and heard it repeat with
Yet no retort to his cry.
For he knew that he was not the one
To right all the wrongs of the world, but
Only he had survived
The destruction of the real world.

Jane Darke

Battle Of El-Alamein

A procession of queues, sixty miles long,
Queuing for rations and water.
Queuing in queues, north to south,
Queuing for prayer, before the slaughter.
Queuing in depth, queues shaking with fear,
Desperately anxious, the mine field is clear.
'No-Mans-Land', five miles across.
Queues move en-bloc, beneath a full moon,
Queues never ending, progress to the slaughter.
Queues onto death, queues uninterrupted,
To form greater queues, this side of heaven.
God alone doth decide, who queues into heaven.
Queues left behind, form queues, non-believers,
Ghosts of the future, queues of the past.
Beneath shifting sands, queue the hidden reminder,
One million 'tin-cans', classified mines,
Meticulously arranged, add to the slaughter.
One million warriors, forming queues,
These men of courage, queue undaunted,
Into battle, once give the cue.

C.R. Drury

A Lover's Dream

Dreams are born when sleep descends
As daylight melts to dusk
We pray with all our hopes and fears
To God in whom we trust

We dream of love and happiness
With all our hearts desire
We search through all life's mysteries
With passion and with fire

In dreams we find contentment
Success in all we do
Imagine it were possible
That it would all come true

Our dreams do sometimes come to pass
Some small things dear to heart
In dreams but not reality
Lovers stay and never part

Hearts are never broken
In all our wildest dreams
And love goes on forever
Like a never ending stream

Each dream we have comes from the heart
No one can take its place
Other hopes have tried in vain
To a lovers dream replace

James Dow

Golfing Daze

I walked out to the first tee
In clubhouse, eyes were upon me
Far ahead the marker flag
Par three, my legs began to sag

Hit the ball with style and flair
It flew off, I know not where
Could it be on wooded bank
Stream, gully or undergrowth rank

Ball is lost and no mistake
Fresh one from my bag I take
With third shot, managed to land on green
Ten minutes on, worse putting ever seen

Shot seven holed at last
Other players go on past
Second tee, marker out of sight
Green is between trees, to the right

Up the fairway, take a drive
At last I seem to come alive
Will I make next green in three
Cross water hazard that I see

With nine iron and lots of hope
Straight in water, what a dope!
Around course, I soldier on
All my nerve and five balls gone

Harold Roy Ellis

The Good Old Days

I'd love to turn the clock back to days gone long ago
We hadn't got much money because the wages were so low
But we never went hungry or even felt the cold
A coal fire burning and a stew to fill the fold
Didn't have a telly, we had lots of games to play
Wooden hoop, a skipping rope or spinning top all helped to pass the day
We used to use mums old clothes to dress up for a show
Then charge each one a farthing and watch their faces glow
we had a long walk to school and back again
And tried not to be naughty or else we'd get the cane
No computers or calculators ruled our day
We used our brains, it was much better that way
We all could do shopping from an early start
Because we'd learnt our tables off by heart
We always had a lot of fun, and if we were very good
We might be bought a lollipop, a very special food
Yes give me back the good old days, although we were a little poor
They were so very happy, but alas won't come back no more

P. D. Dugdale

Annie

Pregnant? Pregnant? A mother to be?
Good Lord no! No, no, no, not me,
You've made a mistake can't you see?
There's no new life, here inside of me.

Let's wait a while, do a new test,
I'm only a little late, so I think it best,
You're sure then, I'm expecting a baby?
You're sure then, it couldn't be maybe?

Through utter despair, fear and distress,
I see clearly now, how I got in this mess,
But I don't want a baby, there's no father to be,
I'd have no job, no money, no life, no more me.

What now then, have I an option?
Can I go through with abortion? adoption?
Do I go on and become someones mother?
Or do I close the door on the life of another?

The birth of my daughter I'm sure was meant,
Her smile, her touch, her kiss heaven sent,
I love her more than I love any other,
Of course I do, for I am her mother.

Jane Melanie Durkin

The Price

There's a price to pay for being alive,
In spite of the pleasure that we all derive.
There's pain, sleepless nights and a long weary fight,
When troubles and trials creep up overnight.

There's a price to pay for taking one's pleasure,
Not thinking of others, hell bent on all leisure.
When the good times have past and the barrel has run dry,
One regrets one's past actions and tries hard not to cry.

There's a price to pay for that innocence lost,
Never stopping to consider what would be the cost.
Life looked at no longer through rose coloured glasses,
With eyes opened wide life's bliss simply passes.

There's a price to pay for that long love affair,
That real close allegiance makes one more aware,
Of the day when the partnership ends for all time,
Then one wishes for days that were once so sublime.

Audrey Donoghue

People Street

People street, I have walked your way,
Down Northumberland Street,
This street that keeps changing of joyous
Occasions and different ways.
You leave yourself open for many
To entertain the meaning of life,
From acrobatic to a juggler,
To a musician, to some mysterious
Person or some other, to a Christian
Spreading the word of truth,
To a Budhist who practices his
Belief in Buddah.
I am sure there are many others.

People street, I have walked your way,
Meeting these people they have so much to say,
Preaching the word of a politician's life,
Speaking up for animal rights.
Gay rights, homeless rights, people's rights.

Facism, racism, all are out to win the fight.

These people are the people,
Living the Northumberland way
Of life!

Peter Dotchin

Tiger

One beast of beauty, one heart of strength
One soul of courage, one body of length
One coat of disguise from a catch at bay
One leap of attack in the midst of the day.

The art of survival from day to day,
To raise up it's young in the hope that they may,
Continue to live as free as should be,
Not encaged like a slave, give them the key.

Over many lands they silently roam,
Sleeping in the shade when the sun is full blown,
Prowling when cooler, with grace and ease,
Running and pouncing through the great plains like a breeze.

With eyes that glare with a touch of light,
And a great mind that ticks over by day and night,
An air of supremacy and of elegance,
A great animal to see if you ever get the chance.

Denise Alison Dye

A Stroll On The Beach

I love to stroll along the beach
With wind in my hair, sand at my feet
Listen to the waves lashing the shore
Gaze at the seagulls as they circle once more
Observe jet planes way up high
Leaving a vapour trail across the sky

Away in the distance boats roll and sway
Cutting the waves as they go on their way
Fishing or pleasure, motor or sail
They all play a part and they never fail
To blot the horizon or straggle the shore
Some drift out of sight to be seen no more

People about me walking their dogs
Children build sandcastles, some play leap-frog
As donkeys pass by there are cries of delight
The children they carry so gently in flight
Radiate happiness for all to see
Bringing back many memories to me

Of times I spent on New Brighton shore
With bucket, spade and sandwiches galore
A bottle of lemonade to help quench the thirst
Towel and comb, a few pennies in my purse
Day return tickets for ferry and tram
After many hours of fun it was home to our mam
A meal and a bath, night prayers were said
Before being safely tucked away in bed.

Mary Dunne

Forsaken Love

I watch you lying there asleep and contented,
Whilst I'm awake, alone and tormented,
To smell your sweat, so sweet and muskish,
I lay and cry and sweat with anguish,
I listen to your groans and sighs,
At last you're asleep I hear no more lies,
But what goes on behind those eyes,
I long to touch your body of perfection,
But dare I try for fear of rejection,
I want to taste your lips of wine,
But their flavour is no longer mine,
All these things I'd love to do
For the only one I love is you,
If you only felt the same for me
Each day when you awaken,
Then my love for you would not be forsaken

John Ewing

Snow

Snow is falling
Soft and white
Even frozen in the night
Ice like glass
Twinkling bright
I can feel it all the time
I can see all the snow
Fluttering down

Kayleigh Evans (Age 8)

New Show

Why does the grass always grow so green?
Tender young blades so fresh and clean.
Summers sun to burn and scorch
Beating down like a fierce blow torch.

Autumn time and cooler nights
Refreshing dew the grass delights.
From brown to green the blades all turn
No summer sun to wither and burn.

The winter frost the growth to stop
A pearl of ice on each blade to drop.
From green to white in one fell swoop
All growing things their heads to droop.

Overnight the spring appears
Leaves of green like tiny spears.
Life awakes from dormant sleep
To look around the world to peep.

All fresh and new the fields of green
New flowers of spring new dress so clean.
Lush green growth from deep below
Natures wonder a whole new show.

L. J. Draper

Do It Myself or D.I.Y.

Time now to smarten up the room
Create brightness out of gloom
Roll up the carpet, place out of way
Shove furniture into window bay
Stand on steps and wash the ceiling
Scrape the walls, old paper's peeling
Fill the cracks with lots of plaster
Wish I could work so much faster
Go to the shops to buy wallpaper
Deciding which is such a caper
So many patterns which shall I choose
All kinds of colours, shades and hues
Matching paint also to buy
That colour there I think I'll try
Paint the windows, and paint the door
Oop's! Another splash lands on the floor
Fetch the brush and mix the paste
Must take care now, don't want waste
Lay paper on the pasting table
To hang it right, I hope I'm able
Why then do I stand and frown
I think I've hung it upside down
Tell me please, then why 'Oh' why
Do I do all this D.I.Y.

Gwendoline A. Ellis

Christmas

'Twas such a Christmas, very long time ago,
When there fell such a lot of wonderful snow
And carols were sung freely, with smiles and mirth,
Gentlemen in breeches stood, wide at the girth.
They said "Merry Christmas, We Wish You All The Best",
They said it with joy, and oh such a zest.
But if it snows now, we're not at all glad
We shudder and shout and look rather sad
"The car will get stuck dear, what will we do?"
"We've got things to buy - we must get it through"
The car park is so full of snow, what a bore
All the shopping's to do - oh what's it all for?
We are stressed out and weary, run off our feet
At the end of the day we're feeling quite beat.
So all in all I suppose it's our game
The winners, the losers, they all play the same
But spare just a thought in the maddening rush
Take a little time out, listen to the hush
For if you pause and let it, the magic <u>will</u> show
And your thoughts will be happy, your heart it will glow
The spirit of Christmas will be there for you too
But <u>you</u> have got to let it come shining on through!

Jacqueline Duffy

146

Enjoy Your Festive Season

Enjoy your festive season, for Christmas time has come,
It only comes just once a year, enjoy it everyone.
Childrens eyes how they glow, when they see the Christmas snow,
Coloured lights, like fairy land, twinkle all around,
Carol singers at the door, what a joyful sound,
Christmas holly mistletoe, adding to that Christmas glow decorations hung on high,
The shouts of merry Christmas, as peope hurry by,
Christmas trees, bring pure delight, covered over with coloured lights,
Peeping out of windows bright, in the darknes of the night.

Santa Claus he visits every store in town sitting on his magic throne in his bright red gown
How the children love him as they form a queue,
Seeing the wonders of old toy town is quite the best thing they can do
But do they know the reason of why we celebrate
Listen to my little tale tell it to your mate
We celebrate the birthday of a very special boy
Who fills our hearts and fills our minds with God's eternal joy

That tiny babe so meek so mild the son of God the holy child
So raise your glasses inthe air and drink a toast of Christmas cheer
A happy birthday little one who gave his life for everyone
And as the Christmas bells ring out and as the carollers sing
Just take a little time out to glorify your king
Thank him for the food you eat and all your Christmas fare
And if you know a lonely soul invite them in to share
For Christmas is a lonely time when someone lives alone
So show your Christmas spirit and invite them to your home

Eleanor Dunn

Private John Fudge 1897-1992 Somerset Soldier

He was so brave my beloved Dad
He went to war, he was just a lad
His mother's tears, followed him that day
He left his home, he could not stay
Duty King and Country calling
Across the sea to Flanders fields
Over a stream that Somerset fought
Dead and dying counted for nought
A yard of land they gained that day
Oh what a terrible price to pay
Dad was wounded all day he lay
In mud and blood until a comrade came
Home he was sent back to the farm
With shattered legs and wounded arm
He didn't grumble or complain
Said he would do it all again
His dreams were haunted evermore
With memories of that dreadful war

Vera Dyer

147

Spring

Winters rages fading having put gardens asunder
Natures reawakening from her annual slumber
Gone are the cruel winds that cut like a knife
As woodlands and hedgerows slowly come to life
They seem to send a message of silent reassurance
A splendid reward for winters endurance.

Mother nature bursting with energy after her resting
The air seems alive the birds busy nesting
Under leaves in the woodlands there is a rustling
A hive of activity hustling and bustling
Preparing for new life is all around
Both in the air and on the ground.

As we walk on an unfolding carpet of green
Glimpses of crocus here and there to be seen
Primroses in bud waiting their turn
To show off their colours amongst tufts of fern
Then spring moves on at a breathtaking pace
Buds of flower and leaves opening as if in a race.

To my mind there is not a more pleasant sight
Than a glorious spring morning at first sunlight
The dew like scattered diamonds glistening
For the first cukoo all of nature seems to be listening
Narcisuss and daffodils mildly competing
Nodding their heads in a silent greeting.

Miriam Duddridge

Winter

Winter is bleak,
Snow is at it's peak.
I lift my eyes and the snowflakes dance,
They tickle my lashes and I wipe them away like tears.

I tug at the nuzzle of sweater at my neck,
I roast with the chestnuts by the flame.

I share a sherry and a cosy mince pie 'with a friend'
I glow with the fire. I raise the glass to my lips.
I find 'Winter' so intoxicating.

Joan Emmens

The Drummer Boy

He stands a witness to this torturous war,
the memories stay, forever more.
The sight of a man, torn down by another,
soldier for soldier, brother for brother.
He kneels at a mound, with a cross in his hand,
bowing his head to the brave of the land.
His eyes close shut, as he feels the pain,
remember . . . remember . . . remember . . .
Wraths of smoke fill the weeping air,
the drummer boy stands so pure and fair.
He stands like an oak, as others fall,
unaware, of each frightened call.
Tension rises, and the drum beat quickens,
the enemy advances, the mist, it thickens.
When all of a sudden, the drum makes no beat,
the boy lies slain at a warrior's feet.
Silence spreads throughout the field,
smoke becomes the only shield.
The war is over, no more battles to fight,
no bloodshed, no pain, no hatred or spite.
The boy stands up, and stares at his grave,
he'd died for his country, home of the brave.
The time has come, and he looks to the sun,
he reaches for heaven, his duty is done.

Magda Dyson

Another Clear Sky

Have you ever walked into a dark cloud?
So dense with sadness and pain
You feel the sun that once lightened your life
Will never come through again
And as hard as you try to disperse the gloom
Searching for one ray of light
You can never find a gap to see through
Not even a star in the night
With no motivation and self-esteem at a low
And your confidence shed like a skin
It seems harder and further the longer you go
As the cloud holds you stead within
Take a deep breath stand as tall as you can
And reach to where you cannot see
For there you will find the light you once saw
Shining for all you will be
No matter how hard and wearing times are
We have to march head held high
Because our pride is the strength that is always there
To keep these dark clouds from our sky.

Kenneth Robert Edwards

The Tramp

Tattered medals on his chest,
Dangle from a woollen vest,
The tramp that day had travelled miles,
Yet still acknowledged people's smiles.

London streets were hard and hot,
The gold of tales there, he found not,
As on the streets he begged,
A cup of tea, a slice of bread.

The soup was free and smelt so fine,
It came each night at the same time,
Wearily he joined the queue.
Among the other unfortunate few.

The night was cold, where could he sleep?
In winter's depth, when snow was deep?
In shop door he made his bed,
And dreamed of being warm and fed.

Charity offered Christmas cheer,
In warehouse home, no need to fear,
Comfort, warmth and food,
But January brings time to brood.

How had he come to this position?
He had no answer to that question,
Only knew his days would end,
On the road, without a friend.

Jean Everest

Nature Renewed

The outstretched arms of leafless trees
Reach up towards the sky
"Witness my unsightliness"
Their sighing voices cry.

And yet to me they are
A thing of beauty still to see
For when I see them next in spring
How lovely they will be!

Then buds and shoots will come again
When winter's frosts have gone
And nature will renew itself
And all life carry on

Small creature now will wake again
(Their hibernation finished)
And flowers and plants will thrive and grow
Their beauties undiminished

And as you follow pathways
Lined with summer scented flowers
Then bring a book to read with you
Or while away the hours

Or stand quite still and look around
At all that you perceive
I guarantee that once you do
You never want to leave!

Marie Egan

You Clear The Path

You clear the path and lighten the way
To help me through each and every day

Your love is undying
Your words are always true
Oh Heavenly Father, how I love you

Sometimes I may stray off this narrow path
But you and your tender love always brings me back

Life seems dark at times
It gets hard to go on
So you shine your light, that leads me on

I know you're always there for me
And that you'll always care for me
So today my Father I'd just like to say
Thank you for guiding me on my way

Ellie

Red Rum

Racing stories can be told of the past and years to come
But listen to this story about Billy and Red Rum.

It's only human nature to love an equine beast
But to ride a horse like this one, feelings never cease.

I tried to tell the racing world - they did not seem to care
The truth, the work, the team - we had it all - seems so unfair.

We hit the road at daybreak, returned so late at night
Travelled back on motorways, guided by a light.

His food was warm, his bed set fair - he's glad to be back home.
I read his mind and knew his thoughts - a legend here was born.

His pride and class, his ability, was much to his proclaim
Three times he won round Aintree - the place of his domain.

New stars are born when old ones die - this one once stood brave
His triumphs and his victories shall be written on his grave.

Now this immortal hero will lay at Aintree's post
For all the world to see and read the times he passed it most.

On people's minds, in people's hearts, aware of all the fame
Three statues stand - some big, some small - but none of them the same.

As time's gone by and feelings changed, I asked the Lord above
To tell and prove to everyone how much this horse we loved.

Billy Ellison

Going Back

I want to go back to that little cottage small
With roses and ivy climbing up the wall
I wish to turn back some chapters in my book of life today
Longingly to happiness and yesterday
To the green fields where I once did play
And the little wooden church, where as a child I used to pray
Years have passed and now I am old and grey
But I will always remember yesterday
Times have changed and life goes fast
My memories will always belong to the past

Marion Edwards

151

A Part . . .

His words twisted in her mind like a knife,
A knife whose blade was sharpened with spite.
Her confidence sliced with each twist of the blade,
As a mockery of her life he'd made.

The scene in her mind, replayed in full,
She felt the strings of her heart pull.
She'd been warned by others of what he was like,
But to her, he'd been a welcome ray of light.

They'd been together longer than most,
Even though their happiness, now, a mere ghost.
She'd long convinced herself they were a part,
Of a perfect picture. A work of art.

But like many a picture, the colours fade,
As the years roll by, until a decade.
Cobwebs gather around the frame,
But who, and what was to blame?

Over the years, dirt had gathered behind the glass,
Had formed a barrier between present and past.
Now that barrier had become a force,
Which had pushed their marriage to divorce.

Now she faced a future without,
His presence there to question and doubt.
What would she do? How would she cope?
She didn't quite know, but was full of hope.

Elaine Evans

Ianto's Revenge

The Chapel was packed that Sunday night
With all pews jammed . . . solid tight
When the Reverend Pomfrey Cadwalader Jones
From the pulpit preached in a voice that moans
And pointing a finger at Ianto he said.
Damnation on you - you were caught in bed
With one rom the village a name we all know
She's known near and far as Prudence the Pro
But Ianto in temper stood up and faced all
You're wrong Parson Pomfrey it weren't her at all
His voice loud and clear - cut the air like a knife
I wasn't with Prudence . . . it was your WIFE!

Trevor Edwards

152

Only Love

How dark the sky, no sun to warm our world
What have we done to God to make him,
Try to make His voice heard
He gives us love the greatest gift to be given to man
Yet we turn away to seek happiness elsewhere, if we can.
The simple things of life are best
Yet we pass them by, for who knows, just try the rest
Who do you love above all else
Is it yourself or some other
Do you treat each man like a brother?
Is your life so full of greed
That you are not aware of another's need?
Do you honour your father and mother
Or send them off to be cared for by another?
When you cast your eye on someone with plenty
Does your life seem to be empty
Even though all you need is at hand
Do you worry because it is not quite what you planned
Where are we going, what do we care
With our world declining, pollution fills the air
Only God will give the answers
To protect us, from our greed
He will meet us to help us every day
And we can hear him if we pray

Pat Ellwood

Laboured Exchange

What bitter irony is this.
Which creates the nexus of new generations in yellow and grey.
To be shown hope in puerile plastic,
Whilst bawdy murals scream their silent proclamations,
Heralding the attempted new dawn.
Emanations of hope grasped by freezing fingers,
To throw themselves into the breach, to dart their futile furtive glances,
Towards other lean scavengers. Their comrades without arms, toothless in survival,
With grim hands locked onto freshly painted tickets.
Fixated by the watchful stance of suited custodians,
Silently they stand in grim abandon(ment).

Groaning loudly in an atrophous shuffle, they stagger,
Slowly around in mournful musings. Screaming in semi silence
And weeping with the pain of lost humanity. Lost forever.

Some eager eyes scan for sustenance, looking for life, hope, movement a job.
Anything to animate not analyse. Moving easier with the iron rations of promise,
He signs his release with a lessening meagre joy.

Used and extinct they head back to their grounds,
Weak unassured and knowingly abandoned. Left out to graze and die.
The "civilised" have no reason to ask why.

Simon Evans

Christmas Visions

The shops are aglow brimming with Christmas fare
Inside the magical grotto Santa sits in his chair
With a coat of warm red with a white fur trim
All the little children, lined up to ask of him
All their desires, to arrive on Christmas day
Fat bulging stockings with lovely things for play
Christmas eve, in every household in the land
On the radio a rousing brass band
Playing Christmas carols as the work gets under way
So the dinner on the table will be festive fun and gay
A hive of activity, stuffed turkey, Christmas puddings full of spice
A sip of Christmas sherry a warm glow inside so nice
The hearth is warm and cosy as the fire burns its log
Stretched out and oblivious to all lays the family dog
The children are excited and can't wait for Santa to come
But mum and dad in the kitchen will be glad when all is done
The snow outside is falling getting thick and deep
Faces at the window curtains pulled back for a peep
As the evening draws on inside the church so still
Suddenly the choir boys voice rings out so sharp and crisp and shrill
Candles flicker with their yellow golden light
A sense of wonderment this Christmas holy night

Rosalyn English

Serious Problem

The roads keep being built at all cost
How will money value what's been lost
The trees are falling down globally
And every country is ridden with disease
Some homeless people need your food to eat
The rain itself can keep them off the streets
Our prison institutions are all full
But a sex offender lives just outside Hull
The problem with pollution carries on
Coz your aerosoles are nothing in the storm
The problem as you see completely washes over me

Euphorian Escape

Winter's Eve

Tiny silver stars in a carbon-paper sky,
Deep meringue paletted earth,
Penetrating air seeking pockets of warmth
And a stillness, an infant soft stillness
Drawing together enchantment
Vibrating with beauty.

Ann Ermel

War At Sea

Calm but ready for the unexpected,
All is fine to the naked eye,
But underneath those still waters,
A shoal of anxious fishes lie.

The sea-weed's loading the shells up,
The sword-fish are held sharp and strong,
The seals are planning an escape plan,
For the wait for the storm can't be long.

The sun is beaten by blackness,
The wind is caught by the gale,
The elements are moving too fast,
The powers of the sea mustn't fail.

Sea-fish charged on their sea-horses,
Shells were thrown from the sand,
The waves fought back a desperate claw,
The sea eats away at the land.

But the storm is forced to surrender,
As the sun begins to come out,
Gulls call their howls of victory,
The ocean army all shout:

"The storm has been defeated,
The armies of the sea did their best,
We're going back to the depths now,
For a peaceful and well-deserved rest."

Jenny Foster (Age 14)

The Answer

So, you ask me why I love you
Well, I'll try to make it clear
It's the laughter that you bring me
Every day of every year.

It's the love that never falters
And the strength that never fails.
Like a rock that never alters
Though beset by storms and gales.

It's the gentle, thoughtful caring
For the others that you meet.
It's the firm and upright bearing
And the absence of conceit.

It's the hatred of deception
And respect for truth and right.
It's the quiet determination
When you need to stand and fight.

In the days of pain and turmoil
You are there to hold my hand.
With your wisdom and perception
All my fears you understand.

Yet you ask me why I love you
When your love has been so true
And the years filled with goodness
Just by living them with you.

Doris Fewster

Stormy Eyes

A whisper in the wind, that floats through the air
A soft breeze that sweeps away your stare
The soft clouds above, from within discontent
Your eyes match the sky and a million tears are sent

The storm stirs the river
The sudden harsh wind causes a shiver
No words are spoken
Yet another heart broken

The wind that sweeps a tear
A sudden loss of fear
A blink of an eye
Leaves only one last goodbye

Rebecca Alisha France

Children

We've heard it said that children,
Are a blessing in disguise,
The look of loyalty and trust,
You see it in their eyes,
They've got no room for secrecy,
Diplomacy, or tact,
They talk about the strangest things,
All matter of a fact,
They never feel, they have to spare,
Your feelings, or your pride,
Their lives are like an open book,
There's nothing there to hide,
They say exactly what they think,
Not always, very kind,
Yet we accept quite easily,
And never really mind,
The magic years will soon be gone,
Let's cherish what they say,
For soon they'll join the adult world,
And so, grow up one day....

June Fricker

Why?

Why do you make me suffer like this?
You've broken my heart in two.
You just don't realise how very much,
I really do love you.

Why don't you feel the same as me?
Why don't you really care?
I've got the answer to these questions;
Life just isn't fair.

I feel the tears roll down my cheeks.
I said I'd never cry,
Now look what you've done to me,
I just want to die.

Just when I thought I had some luck,
I thought you liked me too.
I find out that the door is closed,
And I just can't get through.

Rachel Ferguson

Tramp

Dirty, unwashed, smelly, unloved
Abused by life, cheated and shoved
Lost and alone though oft in a group
Living on handouts, so tired of soup
Dishevelled, untidy, a tramp in all ways
Trying to fill all your tedious days
Shouting and frothing, swearing and spitting
None want you near to where they are sitting
Unsociable, grouchy, mad and confused
A wealt on the system, our charity bruised
Desperate, forlorn, bitter, aggressive
Arrested development with behaviour regressive
A pitiful indictment of our caring society
With our smug indifference and our well practiced piety
You're so far beyond our ability to aid
We simply assume it's a choice you have made
We would like not to see you, to feel all that guilt
To picture your face when we're warm under quilt
You are grubby, uncouthe, unruly and coarse
And all we can offer is a twinge of remorse.

Anthony Fuff

156

The Clan

Once upon a time three mums, three dads -
(A nice even mixture of lasses and lads . . . .)
Set out one morning while skies were still grey
To find new snows and pistes - come what may.
There were also three husbands with their lady wives -
In love and so happy - enjoying their lives.
Eight charming daughters - lovely ones, all,
And four stalwart sons who'd grown handsome and tall.
Four pretty sisters - a lively quartet -
And a couple of brothers - great pals, you can bet.
Four aunts and four uncles were there to be found,
With two nephews and six nieces somewhere around.
And then were the cousins - the last count was eight -
Could there be more? . . . we'll just have to wait!
Relations by birth, relatives by wedlock -
Bringing in the in-laws, creating a deadlock . . .
Then two mothers-in-law - (if one isn't enough!!)
A couple of fathers-in-law - quite heady stuff
Four grandmas, four grandads, playing major parts
To eight super grandchildren -bless their hearts.

Surely that now completes this long detailed list -
'Cos to tell you the truth, I'm "totally piste" . . . .
For that sure was some party - seventy four there, but, when
You get down to basics, we were still only ten!!

Dorothy Fieldsend

Reflections

Reflections of days long gone by
time lost forever, tears fill my eye.
Reflections of that childhood toy
fond times, when there's been joy.
Reflections of that special first kiss
and loved one's you so dearly miss.
Reflections of memories so precious and glad
and painful days when life's been sad.
Reflections of what might of been
gone forever, and never again seen.
Reflections of that magical place
like the divine beauty of a serene face.
Reflections of deeds that you regret
etched on your soul, you can't forget.
Reflections of how foolish men be
out in the cold in life's lonely sea.
Reflections that will make you cry
leave you confused, and asking why?
Reflections of all that has past
always with you right to the last.

Nicholas Fletcher

Heads You Lose

I gazed as an innocent
Not blinded by deceit
At an ocean
So beautiful
So heartstoppingly breathtaking
And tried to explain
To the man beside me
About living like the ocean
Without
Constraints
Oppressive pasts
Less than glorious presents
And unimagined futures
Just there
Constant ebb and flow
Time immortal
Of no consequence
To me
Now
Heads you lose

Lynn M. Frazer

Unpaid Slave

I have a little family
A husband and two girls
The things they get me doing
Often sends me in a whirl

They have me fetching this and that
"Where the hell's my tea"
They never stop to think
About poor old me.

One day they pushed me
I thought I would snap
Fetch this, fetch that
I got in quite a flap

Then I said enough's enough
Come on kids behave
"Who do you think you're talking to"
I'm not your blasted slave

I think they need a skivvy
Or maybe even a maid,
But I'm not doing it anymore
Unless I get well paid

C. Frisby

Dunblane Disaster - Why?

Yesterday we were happy kids
Without a care in the world
Today we've been torn apart
Oh why? Please tell us why?
How did we allow this man
To kill and mame at will
Now we've lost our friends
Oh why? Please tell us why?

Why did young children have to die
At such a tender age
Now guns are easy to obtain
Oh why? Please tell us why?
Though our laws are out of date
With what has happened here
No more laughter no more joy
Oh why? Please tell us why?

Why should our parents suffer
The death and carnage here
Brother, sister gone forever
Oh why? Please tell us why?
And young lives have to share
The loss the hurt the pain
Now their pals will be no more
Oh why? Please tell us why?

Danny Foster

Village Awakening

Overnight the village held green to blossom in the dawn
Soon, a myriad twitterings will drift over ears of corn
Crystal light seeds the way, for all to dance in its bloom
Reborn, a shimmering landscape, from the bed of nature's loom
Chimneys and thatch above the mist that swaddles field and bog
Frolicsome squirrels playing hide-and-seek in a hollow log
The farrier checks his bedside clock just as the cock is crowing
Room lights through bull's eye panes in cottage windows showing
Spectral looms the church, gazed on by stone figures in prayer
A gravel stride along the way, a groom bridles the mare
The cattle's breath, cotton white, churns with the mist of morn
Billhooks sharpened in readiness to lay the hedgerows of thorn
Majestic, the mute swans mirrored, upon a pond of polished glass
Gossamer wings spread soaring, into a sky of burnished brass
High above the rooftops, a rook raises its crackling caw
Such stirrings throughout the village, a part of country lore.

Kenneth C. Francis

Release!

I want to release the inner me,
I want to release the me no one knows,
I want to release the person I used to be,
I want to release the innocent person I once was,
I want to release the hurt inside me,
But I don't know how!

I want to release my talent,
I want to release my love,
I want to release my feelings,
I want to release my pain,
I want to release all my trapped sorrow,
But I don't know how!

I want to release all the wrongs,
I want to release all the love held deep within,
I want to release the love of all animals that I've held for so long,
I want to release the thinner inner me,
I want to release all that's within me,
But I don't know how!

Please can someone show me how,
How to get rid of the pain,
How to loose the clown I've held so near for so long,
How to loose these metal 'chain linked' bars around my heart.

I've hidden myself so far inside I don't know how to release me.
Very few have had a glimpse of 'me'.

Michelle Faccenda

Late Swallows' Flights At Wressle

Swallows are performing their last
Flights of summer; and will soon meet
For discussions between phone-masts
Prior to their southward retreat.

Weather-moods are changing here,
Caught as this month is, between two
Seasons. Cooling winds inspire fear
In their hearts. More bid adieu

Each day. Birds of lively feather
Revelled in their freedom, soaring
As they will, again, in nether
Climes, when gales here are roaring.

Gillian Fisher

Count Your Blessings

As we awake each morning
The birth of each new day
We should count our blessings
And to God we should say
We thank you, for your creations
How beautiful they are
The sun, the moon, the sky above
The twinkling stars afar
So bold the trees, so sweet the flowers
The giant seas that flow
The crops that feed a multitude
On this our earth below
So when at night we sleepily
Lie down to end the day
Just think of God, and all He gave
For His work, we can never repay

Nora Fisher

Endangered Animals

For a life full of awareness it isn't much fun
Nor seeing your head on the end of a gun
Dashing through bushes with family behind
What's wrong with the huntsman, have they no mind
Beauty within nature is not what they see
But a nice opportunity to make a nice fee
To kill a nice tiger would make a nice gown
Maybe you'll be smiling, but they'll have a frown
But can't you see just to leave them be
And let them be free like you and me

They're nearly all gone and to be seen no more
But wait just a minute it's against the law
The animals don't think their life is bad
So why take it away and make them mad
Something must be done and done straight away
Or there'll be nothing left in the distant day
Just think of it now, to see no animals, no wildlife
But to see tusks fall to the ground, from a sharp bladed knife
But why give these animals a life full of fear
Can't you see Mr. Huntsmen all it sheds is a tear.

Catherine Fletcher

Allusion to Life
*(Dedicated to Ewan McGregor
who passed away on February 1st 1997)*

All summer long
I did clasp fast
To the branch of an elm.
The winds blow strong -
He is at the helm.

Novice bud in spring,
Soon to explode
Bright, leafy green.
Sun, rain and wind me coat
Fluttering bird on wing -
Holding to His theme.

Summer meets autumn,
Colours of vibrant hue.
Blustering winds blow,
And I must let go -
Gently floating to bottom,
Settling on the river below.

Winter chill appears -
My life expended, I surrender in His arms.

Elvee Fenning

Footprints

He lifted his son
Offering
Proud

No word
Just eyes
In still span
Held

In the welling

There in the footprint
Yet unwashed by time
He saw himself
The child
Held
I the memory
Holding

Eclipse of shadows
Glinted the edge
Of fused worlds

Gurgles drew fresh eyes
Printing the newborn earth.

Alasdair Fairbairn

Now Your Car Has Gone

I feel so lonely now your car has gone,
Left contemplating zig-zag tyre marks imprinted on my heart,
Love letters written in oilspot on tarmac.

I stroked your shiny nearside wing,
Stroked the warm firmness of your skin,
Parked still. Awaiting your return I watched,
Passing by every day as every day passed by.

Imprint of your back, faint on vinyl seat,
My imagining hand slipped round its contours,
Caressing orgasmic dials of temperature, oil pressure, speed!

I clocked up the numbers of your absent miles,
Tried to peer through your toughened-glass mind
Into the soft-seated centre of your consciousness.

Now your car has gone. You have driven your gadding miles
To some citadel on a pink dioxide cloud,
Piped organ music playing cassetted wedding marches,
To cosset another girl.

I dab up your oilspot with pink tissue
And weep into it under my pillow at night.
Wheel-marks have crushed our tenderness.

Now your car has gone I cannot drive it.
There is no room for you in mine.
When you tire of your giddy direction and break up,
Break down in your own garage. Don't pull into mine!

Evelyn Friend

A Feline Friend

Mystery surrounds you
Majestic in your beauty
How many changes
In this world do you see

Were you once in Egypt
Lazing by the Nile
Or at a warlock's side
Predicting our lifestyle

Perhaps this is your first life
In this century
And as you journey through the ages
Will you remember me

Jean Fyall

Waiting

Time and people pass me by
When alone with thoughts
Of you and I,
Thoughts of a romance just begun,
When two hearts would beat as one.
Two lovers locked into the bliss,
Of each others tender kiss,
Yet alone am I.
As I walk with my face.
Turned to the sky
Soon, very soon I know you'll come
And the agony, the agony of waiting wil be gone
You will smile and say - hello
Oh God I love you so!
And then to avoid other eyes
We will walk with our faces
Turned to the skies.

M. Fitzgerald

161

Early Hooking

It sure makes me mad, I feel so annoyed
To see school children smoking, when they should avoid
The smoking habit, at that early stage
You'd think they'd know better in this day and age

Young ones who light up, how my heart wishes
That they'll stay only, with hot chips and kisses
Instead of inhaling from filter tips
Or drawing on a king size between their lips

One can lead to ten, and ten into many
Much wiser are those, who do not smoke any
Thus leaving their lungs, healthy and clean
Without all the staining from that drug nicotine

What medics have said, what they have been told
It's a shame that some of them may never grow old
When they start smoking at that early stage
You'd think they'd know better in this day and age

Albert Edwin Fox

Villanelle

The willows weep into the stream
Each day as I go walking by
My mind's disordered in a dream

Where thoughts are rarely what they seem
And with each dawn will surely fly.
The willows weep into the stream

Rippling the waters all a-gleam.
I stop and look, and wonder why
My mind's disordered in a dream -

But I recall moments supreme
When we went walking, you and I.
The willows weep into the stream

And so do I - a sorry scheme
Since Nature cruelly cut the tie
My mind's disordered in a dream.

Now that I walk alone I seem
Only to see hopes fade and die.
The willows weep into the stream -
My mind's disordered in a dream.

Eric Ferguson

Christmas Wrapping

I make coloured words
to wrap around tiredness -
the windows of life seem short
winter's blackness pulls me down.

I wrap coloured gifts
embracing in paper my love -
my family of gifts is perfect
I gather them like a brood of eggs.

. . . the house is bleak now
the fire inside burns low
I am sustaining though losses
like candles in the night . . .

I wrap now the emptiness of loss,
I wrap it in my words,
the bleakness I walk in surrounds me,
please, love, let go, let spring come.

Nicole Fordham

162

13th March 1966

Why did it have to be a day that will long be remembered
With sorrow and with pain?
All because of the horror that came to Dunblane.

13 is an unlucky number - now we all know why
Terror and murder came to Dunblane
But we question "Why".

Why did this happen, to children so small,
And to the Teacher who led them to the Hall.
They didn't know what madness was due
We couldn't protect them
There was nothing we could do.

This sadness inside is for the families left,
How can they go on living and feel so bereft.
They each must have found a strength to face each new day,
I wish I could help them in some small way.

I think of them often - my thoughts are drawn to them.
They are so brave and accept their grief.
Their pain will ease - But When?

Barbara Froggatt

Mona Lisa

She held a sensitive secret;
By night she embraced the glittering stars
By day, remote in your emporium,
A museum of antiquities.
A prize born noble for mankind
With a smile to beguile the enchanted dreamer.
And there in your sweet repose
The painter who inspired to compose
An Icon to a poets solitude
And a lover, to you, the creator.
Even Gods could not forsake her,
Death has bequeathed your beauty.
Captured with seasons in colours of life
A creation enthroned on a threatre of light,
Celestial is your countenance.
Crowned in your source of glory
An enigma, unique, for eternity.
Elusive, profound, refined and unfading
Enduring the fame of immortality.

Nubia Liana Farquharson

Storm Warning!

Storm clouds congregated - clinging together
Formulating a field of force beyond Man's cognisance:
Tongues of flame licked the carefree sky -
Twisting, tangling, choking sense and reason
Spitting fire and forking fields:
Battalions of thunder clouds
Cannoned through the sepulchral night -
Ricocheting, rounding, resounding in Earth's bunkers:
Night's black hands stretched fingers of Fate
Into every crevice - the sky bled black
Earth's bowels and bosom suffocated in putrefying odours.

Suddenly a silver spear of light penetrated the black blood -
Spreading, searching, surmounting, caressing clouds, kissing cosmos
Collecting cool moonbeams stringing silver stars together
In an ecstasy of Evolution:
Diamond-hilted silver stalagtites resolutely mirrored rainbows
Whilst Sun's sensuous rays called, beckoned,
From behind receding banks of buried black cloud
Rose like saffron silk - smiling on tender Earth.
The lemon souffle ball rotated changing into deeper shades of gold
Gold to gold on gold until the velvet orange orb spanned space -
The sun has risen once more . . . . .

Paula Lee Fox

Autumn Gold

I walked a path of autumn gold
Laid strewn a field of scattered poppies
Do not hinder, do not touch
But glance and remember
Walk on - leave lay where I rest

'Twas for thy future
We fought and perished
So forgetful are ye
The band marched
The trumpets blared

As dusk drew in
The poppies reminded us
One last time
Remember
'Twas for thy future
We fought and perished
'Twas for thine own future

Kirstin Ferry

Retirement

A man's idea of heaven
Is a place to dwell
A book a bed a drink
And maybe a wishing well

But these things don't come easy
There's a rough road on the way
A slip up here a slip up there
And there's hell to play

Life's lessons can be very harsh
Mistakes can cost you dear
But once you put things right
The way ahead is clear

Remember faith is vital
Always play the game
Be fair be firm be honest
What more is there to say

Ted Forty

164

Mother's Special Day

Oh! to be a mother in this day and age
A chapter book story written on every page
Mother's Day is special all throughout the land
Rejoice for that unique lady bring out the brass band
She deserves the pampering the love and affection
Given to her today and always
Each rhyme note or verse played today is sincerely conveyed

Your dear fine mother the grandest lady in all the land
She was always chosen for you given every command
Her love for her children is boundlessly great
You stop and treasure her give time to contemplate
One only has one mother no one can take her place
Like the Lord and gentry she walks in grace
Look after her now and always she's such a golden lady fair
With endless comittment looks after your every need with full care

Denise Frost

In A Day's

I walked at speed
dreaming of the girl I'd meet
the girl who'd teach the art of love
the girl who I would love
the girl who'd love me

I walked slower
dreaming of the children we'd have.
The blonde haired girl
the freckled ginger boy
with the girl who'd love me

I walked slower
dreaming of growing peacefully old
sitting in a chair with a radio
Children visiting once a week
growing steadily old
with the girl who'd love me

I walked slower
dreaming of my death
would I out live her and die alone?
or would she out live me and die alone?
or would we leave and love together
or would I forever be
with the girl who'd love me?

Paul Fletcher

Inclement

The wind seizes and drags
Carport roof
Turns the corner
Scattering shattered plastic
On conifers
Cats crouch beneath, shocked tails aloft
Eyes like moons show fear
Paws tucked under, safe.

Rushed on by the wind
Bag on my arm, tugged forward
Pushes me along each road and alley.

A funnel of pressure
A dance uncontrolled
A tune without colour,
Or shade.

A litter lifter
Dispersing scrap paper
Whirling dead leaves from live
Scattering seeds.
Merciless, biting,
Unrelenting.

Janet Farley

The Chase

"Tally Ho" - 'Tis the cry
Wagging tails of hounds that bay
That cunning fox - oh so sly
Heads the chase throughout the day

Red coated horsemen mounting up
Thirsts are quenched from stirrup cup
Faces that are now aflush
All ready for the coming rush

Those hounds are all excited now
Followed by the thundering hooves
Leaping over fallen bough
Pounding of the earth that moves

Crafty fox that twists and turns
Moist noses seek to find the scent
But their brush tailed quarry spurns
They don't know which way he went

O'er fields of green and river bank
This madding crowd of horse and hound
Heels that dig intothe flank
So spurred on by trumpet sound

The cunning fox they chase this day
Is too clever - gets away
Nay well it was oh so much fun
A day enjoyed by everyone

John Fletcher

Sibling Love

You let blood seep
from your flesh to punish me
you said
Cold steel
Gun grey
You hurt yourself to hurt me
in return, you explained
You wrap your heart
in barbed wire because
of my actions
Gun grey
Cold steel
Your eyes are filled with anguish
Your tongue forked
Sriking out at me
Cold steel
Gun grey
Your dark blood has
snaked a path down
your wrist to prove
a point that wasn't needed
Gun grey
Cold steel

Cheryl Frith-Clarkson

Untitled

Thank goodness it's Friday time to mellow out
Time to relax not scream and shout
So many demands, so much to do.
All the work's been landed on you.

Everything's wanted right now this minute,
You don't even get a say in it,
Typing, wages, invoicing to be done
When will I get all this work done

When you've a minute make a cup of tea,
Cor blimey boss is there only me!

After this work is done the weekend can begin,
Now who's turn is it to get the drinks in.

Lisa Jayne Furbey

Fever

Saturday night on goes the telly,
There we sit with knotted bellies!
Someone gets lucky, alas not you.
We're off again to line up in the queue!
Another week another pound,
Oh why can't people keep their feet on the ground!
So many of us hooked it's a shame to say,
It could be you we're told so again we play!
How many people would part with their cash,
Without the incentive to win a big stash!
How about giving that pound of ours,
To keep our NHS solid and sound!
Rewards would then come from knowing at least,
We'd helped some poor sole, maybe in our street!
Sadly I admit I'm one of the flock,
Buying a ticket, if I win could mean a new frock!
I never dreamed I'd get caught in the trap!
Gambling fever, we all need a good slap!
The opera and arts are given fat cheques,
Why not the unfortunate, can't they also be blessed!
The lottery is of course a good idea,
If it went to the needy, and not to our peers!
So lets see a change, and make it soon,
More for the sick please, they don't ask for the moon!

Jackie Gaish

Alone

The winds of time caress my cheek, the touch of it is bare,
whilst all around me, I can hear it's music in the air.
But I am not a part of this, as I stand outside and wait,
for loving arms to enfold and kiss my hurt away.

For although my heart is broken. I remember all the times of gentle breeze
and sweet embrace and your lips that brushed my eyes.
But that is in the past now, and I must go alone.
Forever seeking that I have lost and forever on my own.

But sadness is only a fleeting thing, of memories dead and gone,
and you will always be part of me, as your touch still lingers on.
And so I tread a different path and solitary I must be,
for that is the role I have chosen, from birth to eternity.

So do not weep my dear ones, for this is how it was decreed.
Forever to be thankful of the love I truly gave,
and I will love you always, yes, even to my grave.

Jill Fox

167

Wars

We decorate to commemorate
A war in all its glory that's the saddest story
An eye for an eye a life for a life
Death and destruction is a soldiers life
Shooting and bombing plus wars of the words
Have you ever heard anything so absurd
Wars are for winning
Wars are for losing
Wars are the end
Wars are they worth it why do we pretend

Boy

There is much more beyond the garden wall,
Beyond the fenced in field, the boundary lane,
So much more beyond the village wood,
The rolling hills, the grey town hall . . . .
And though these city streets the eye detains,
And feet now stand where others wandering stood,
Remember this, that all ways lead to where it all began,
The dreams, the hopes, the boy within the man.

K. Ford

Cuddles In Cadlelight

Home is where the heart is,
So they often say.
Part of mine is with you,
The room near, so far away.
In heaven, you are above
Watching the world down below.
Knowing who is grieving,
How we miss you so.
Reflecting on the past,
Loving memories that linger.
We walked this lane now full of spring,
Threw pebbles in the sea.
Cuddles in candlelight,
Words of love we whispered.
It seems like yesterday,
You will always be remembered.
Forgive me is my plea.

Zoë Fail

Gift

This is a very special gift
That you can never see
The reason it's so special
Is because it's from me
Whenever you're feeling blue
You only have to hold this gift
And know I'm thinking of you
You can never take a look inside
Please leave closed
Just hold this special gift close to your heart
'Cos it's filled with all my love inside

Bonnie Frier

168

The Paradise Trail

Sundown sets the seal of passing day
And paints the sky artistic pastel shades
While lengthening shadows stretch across the land
And darkening trees hide deep in woodland glades
O'er western hills the black backed clouds arrive
While strings of light adorn the street below
To gleam like fireflies moving through the night
Each within its arc of halo's glow
The evening star its lone appointment makes
Before the dew its teardrops starts to weep
And white-bright planets sail their nightly course
Across terrestrial oceans wide and deep
Meanwhile from eastern rims where dawns shall break
A pockmarked silver disc is seen to rise
The beacon lamp that lights the travellers path
And leads lovers on the trail to paradise

John B. Freestone

The Old Woman

The old woman tends her little plot
She seems so proud of what she's got.
While other people stand and stare
She carries on without a care.
She stops occasionally for a while
And looks around with a smile.

She picks some flowers and some veg
Then disappears behind a hedge.
She's done this now for many years
To hide the pain and the tears.
She carries on all alone
Now her beloved husband's gone.

That garden was their pride and joy
Where their spare time they would employ,
Growing plants and sowing seeds
To supply their family's needs.
She still continues on her own
Even though her family's grown.

She carries on despite her ills
And having to take numerous pills.
The aches and pains that winter bring
Are gently eased by the coming spring.
As the growing season has begun
Her health is restored by the warming sun.

G. Gallo

Spoilt Summers

Disaster has struck us
In the Haven today
Wildlife is dying
On Haven bays.

Oil is streaming
Through the sea
The birds now
Will never be free.

I stand on the pier
Looking out to sea
Now there are no
More summers for me.

Children disappointed
No more clean summers
All because of those
Big oil tankers.

Siân Goodman (Age 13)

You're Special

You're special, have I ever told you that?
Funny how I knew you'd shake your head,
Just shrug it off, and carry on.
For that's your way, you don't want praise,
Or fuss; no medals, no certificates of merit.
No making out you're any better
Than all your sisters on this earth.

You've things to do? Of course you have!
So put them first again, instead of you.
For I guess it satisfies you deep inside,
Attending patiently to all their needs;
Their little whims, desires, their endless appetites.
Go on then, smooth their path out yet again
The way that only you can do so well.

But when you've done all that, it's time,
Yes time for you to sit and listen
Very carefully to what I have to say.
No really, please, just humour me,
And leave those tiresome chores for someone else.
Come close, and let me pamper you for once.
You're special have I ever told you that?

Alan Glasby

My Daughter

One bright Autumn day
My world fell apart,
My daughter was born
And took over my heart.
My nice ordered house
Was no longer to be.
But nappies and teddies
Were all one could see.
The crying and tantrums
Had me tearing my hair
Then one dimpled smile
And I hadn't a care.
The months hurried by
And food hit the walls,
The washer blew up,
And she started to crawl.
What happened to walks
To reading a novel
To leasurely lunches,
A house, not a hovel.
But, one year is now over
Her birthday is due
And I'd not change a thing
Because Katie, I love you!

Susan Green

The Question

Wherein the eye doth beauty lie,
On land or sea or in the sky,
Is it in a maiden fair
With rosy cheeks and golden hair
Or in a butterfly brightly coloured and so rare.
Seeking nectar from the flowers there
The flowers in a woodland dell
The mosses on a wishing well.
Or in a stream on a summers day,
A lake or loch or water way
Maybe it's the birds, converging in a mottled throng,
Competing for the title of bird of song
The animals too all have their place,
The badger and the fox.
The otter fishing furtively among the weed and rocks,
So much beauty you'll all agree,
Ever more and more to see.
Life is good if you look around,
There's beauty there it does abound,
Cast your eyes from earth to skies,
Then you'll know where beauty lies.

Charles Graham

170

Love Lies Bleeding

Old Simon was a spider of the large and hairy kind,
The sort that nervous ladies try to keep out of their mind.

His legs were long and dangly, boggly eyes bulged out in pairs,
And whenever he paraded out he drew some withering stares.

The lady spiders shunned him, they cared nothing for his charms,
And would not let him clasp their spidery goodies in his arms.

Simon had to face it, for romance he had no flair,
If no spider chum would have him, he would have to look elsewhere.

He was desperate for a partner, any size, or shape, or hue,
Any class, race, or religion, in fact, <u>anyone</u> would do!

Next day, whilst in the garden, espied a gorgeous girl,
Her name was Millicent Muffet, and she set his heart a-twirl.

He could recognise a winner, this was no passing whim,
And he watched her stack the compost with a lusty, lecherous grin.

He galloped up to meet her as on the ground she sat,
But with a rear end like a hippo, she squashed poor Simon flat!

With his dying breath he begged her would she grant his last request?
In a state of apprehension, she said she'd try her best.

So Simon lies in state now upon polish smooth and oily,
And features on her sideboard as a most unusual doily!

Miriam Glover

Night

The smoke of darkness chokes the day
Creeping through keyholes seeping 'neath doors,
Whilst glowering gloom filters the glass
Unstoppable, except by its maker.

Automatically, appears the pilot light
Faintly bright, this faithful vanguard of the night sky.
Heaven's escorts gleam eternal, masterly kindled,
Unstoppable, but divinely controlled.

Night plus his accomplice Time, looters of the day,
Steal generously to grant sweet rest.
The blessings of sleep, healer and restorer,
Unstoppable, is this celestial gift.

Margaret Greenhalgh

The Ruin

Heavily wooded trees dark dreary mist, ancient ruin mediaeval church cenuries old, heavy stones scattered over the woodland floor, the wild wind opening up the tree branches the ruin a misty picture of crumbling apart.

Broken church doors lying in decay rusted metal an empty gateway, the golden key gone the bell tower silent standing alone rising through the mist fungus growth a ceremony of burial.

The church roof fire damaged the weather cock hanging upside-down its place taken over by the owl staring eyes searching out the land, broken slates in-bedded in the wooden pews, rain flooded floor only living plants allowed to grow.

Blind screamingbats no bodies of hymn singers, or the bowing of heads, only climbing plants no growing stones, Angels anger alter with no cross born again christians only animals and plants, stain glass window no light shining through, a tangle of splintered glass its honour and glory gone.

Clergymans ceremonial garments once a parish force swallow up by the sacred ground, dwarf gavestone sunken in rich soil names chip away by time, ghostly sounds dreams of fading years, closed eyes, the mediaeval church God's heaven now at peace just left to die.

Garrett John

Bang, Bang, Bang

Bang, bang, bang
Shouts the gun of a German man.
The bullet flies through the skies.
So black, dull and grey.
It hits my skin,
I'm not sure where.
My mind goes blank,
My face goes white.
The warm, red blood pours out.
The horrid sounds of war,
Slowly, slowly, slowly
Are no nore
The smell of rain, death and pain leave me too.
The only thing left now is the slow, dying beat
Of my heart.
Surely I won't live.
I want to die
So others can survive.
I'll die for my country.
I died for my country.
War, war, war,
Please,
Be no more.

Louise Gibbons (Age 13)

Enigma

I was born in pain
A stranger me,
To parents, who,
Behind their eyes were crying.

I live in pain,
A stranger now,
To people, who,
Behind their truths are lying.

I will die in pain,
A stranger then,
To children, who,
Behind their lives, are dying.

James Greene

172

It's Not My Fault If I've Got Fleas!

They treat me as if I'm an alien
"Don't touch him, he's got them," they shout
I circle their legs 'til I'm dizzy
They cringe and then throw me out.

They say, "Take your fleas round to Margaret's."
Or, "Get lost and go hunt for some mice!"
How dare they when they're just as dirty
It's not my fault if I have some lice.

I do what I can to avoid them
I wash twice a day, even more,
I choke all the time on my hair balls
I lick 'till my tongue becomes sore.

They think they're the ones with the problem
"He's a filthy old moggy," they say.
I don't get the cuddles I used to
They don't get the string out to play.

But I am the one with the itches
I have to go through the pain,
Then in all my anguish and suffering
They throw me outside in the rain.

But the worst thing of all are the lotions
The collars, the sprays and the cream.
They put me through hours of torture
If only all this was a dream.

Debbie Glover (Age 14)

The Princess's Veil

The veil cascades white tulle,
Flows down the aisle, billows
And sails on flagstones.
In our throats bubbles of joy
Burst into waves of cheers.

Glass beads caught in the netting
Tremble like tears,

A spell disintegrates the fragile web
Fraying the gossamer weaves,
Leaving the princess shipwrecked,
Castaway on their land.

And our enchanted dreams
Dissolved in the maelestrom.

Michelle Gunner

M.U.F.C.

Manchester United are the best,
They beat all the rest,
Beckham, Giggs and Cantona too,
Trying their best to get us through,
Man United is like a dream,
And this is my favourite football team.

Emma Jayne Gosling (Age 12)

Hopeful Love

Please my dear I hope you'll phone
Or come around when I'm alone
To hold me tight, kiss me all night
And tell me how much you love me

Tonight it's cold, I'm so alone
Thinking of only you
Wanting you here, so very near
To keep me nice and warm

What can I say to let you know
How I feel today
I've tried to stay away from you
But it's hard for me to do

My mind is clear, it's my heart I fear
Will let me down again
I'll have to try to get by
And not think of you.

Pamela Ann Grant

Holy Analogy And Just A Thought - Three In One

Controversial as it may be
is the eternal triangle
of the Father, the Son
and the Holy Ghost.
Created in his image
could this be me
in my Parent, Child
and Adult?
Fundamental assumption
of what I could be,
the complete person
in all its supremacy,
the reflection of God.
In me.

Maybe.

Irenka Goldsmith

Family Life

There's nothing more special than family life,
The love of a mother, a daughter, a wife,
They're held by a strong, an unbreakable bond,
It lasts all through this life and also beyond.

Family life will always be there,
We learn as a child how much we can share,
We always feel happy, we're always secure.
The love of a family will always endure.

All families are different, they vary in size
But each is so special as seen through our eyes,
They're there in the bad times as well as the good,
Supporting as only a family could.

Perhaps if we studied our family life,
It would help to lessen the trouble and strife,
Your family loves you, it doesn't ask why,
You have love from your birth till the day that you die.

So three cheers for families and all that they mean,
The best institution that there's ever been,
Family life is a gift from above,
Enjoy it! Life's greatest example of love.

Sheila M. Gannon

The River

I walk down to the river
That flows to the sea
See you walking behind me
What can you see
See soldiers a dying
See blood running free
In a second we'll be there
So keep following me

So why are we fighting
Why is it so
In some foreign country
We don't even know
Come the morrow of slaughter
Come the morrow of blood
When death fills the air
And a sea of red mud

An uneasy silence
When each count the dead
But the river flows on
In a bright shade of red

So why are we fighting
Why is it so
In some foreign country
We don't even know

Ian Gallagher

Mutavi

I have trod the sacred places,
Where time's velvet river runs,
Stooped to drink from holy waters
Burned by heat of endless suns,
Humbled, stood before my Maker,
Felt my heartbeat in his palm,
Fled through cackling realms of chaos,
Just to reach a place of calm,
Been below the depths of lonely,
Felt the touch of evil hands,
Followed empty paths to nowhere,
Been a stranger in my land,
Crept through flaming halls of madness,
Known the white-eyed lunge of fear,
Cried alone a million night-times,
Just to reach myself, and Here;
Mind-flow cleared of choking jetsam,
Able now to really care,
After seven years of struggle
    All I needed - He is there.

Lucie Guilbert

But Why

There is never enough time to do the things we wish.
But why?
The years shrink to memories,
They just seem to fly by.
One moment we are young and so full of life,
The next it's old age,
With all the pain and strife.
As life's young dreamers we behave as though -
We will live forever.
As half of a young love-struck couple,
We expect to live out our lives together.
But in what seems like no time at all,
One of us is gone.
And the survivor, alone
Is forced to soldier on.
Then all too soon our own end it nears,
But why,
Why are we so short, so short of years?

Steven Gamble

Tribute To a Friend

We are all sat down in silence,
Waiting to begin,
It's half past six, time to start
The first Sunday Evening Hymn.

It's a favourite tune of mine,
And to our feet we rise,
I sing it very loudly
To everyones surprise.

A loud noise from the back,
Someone clatters through the door,
Could have been more quiet,
Late again! As times before.

Once more into the silence,
We bow our heads in prayer,
Proudly, next to me he sits
Upon the empty padded chair.

Then he starts a' scratching,
All around his quarter hind,
As the service carries on
No-one seems to mind.

Oh dear, what is he doing?
He's cleaning out his ear,
Please don't you start your purring,
You old church cat, so dear.

Pamala Girdlestone

The Aegre

Making annual pilgrimage,
Where peaceful waters flow;
A product of an early age,
Of times so long ago.

Where salt meets fresh with supreme force,
Their waters to collide;
A lunar's power to endorse,
A gravitational guide.

From Humber's shore to Torksey Lock,
A tidal wave of wonder;
Cleansing banks of debris stock,
With sound like distant thunder.

Landscape changes may be seen,
On leisured stroll of bank, down stream;
But, Aegre's might survives all tests,
Come equinox she knows no rest.

Flow on, sweet waters of the Trent,
For evermore without relent;
Let Aegre's force remain sublime,
Refined tradition of our time.

Stephen R. Garner

Sunrise And Sunset

My thoughts are with you
When the sun does rise
The beauty we find in the skies
Reflects our love, so strong and bright
Showing to all our wonderful delight
In each other, yes it's true. . .when the sun does rise
My thoughts are with you

My thoughts are with you
When the sun doth set
A colourful finale. . .and yet
Reflective of hidden delights
When in your arms I stay at night
Majestic and powerful, just like you
When the sun doth set
My thoughts are with you

Ginny

In Fields

Cradled in fields, by chattering stream,
He sits enrapt by time.
All worries and cares evaporate,
As memories unwind.
Young child, again, runs the summer breeze;
Climbs high the old gnarled oak.
Pure ecstacies, long forgotten, since this man from childhood awoke.

Long gone that adventurous schoolboy:-
Versed well by work and life;
Reined-in by responsibilities,
To children, home and wife.
Betrayed by battered ability;
Forced early to retire.
Mind too bemused and muddled by frustration's smouldering fire.

He bids the comforting stile good-bye.
Turns easier feet to home.
Hears, again, the high-soaring skylark,
Feels sun, still soft and warm.
The scent-laden wind keeps enchanting.
Distanced, now, earthly cares.
And the young boy keeps on running to prove he'll always be there.

L.J. Giggins

Elliot George

There are things in our life that make us smile,
Happenings, events that we love for a while.
There are things that hurt and make us cry,
Leaving us feeling we do not know why!
Sometimes there appears no rhyme or reason,
Just the years passing from season to season.

At first there was joy and hope,
And then the whole concept of trying to cope,
With the loss of our baby son.
Our hearts he had already won.

Just a life inside,
Our hearts were opened wide.
All our hopes, all our dreams,
Disintegrated it would seem.
Our seed of love was sown,
But we were never destined to see you grown.
Sleep with the angels baby boy,
Knowing you such a short time our only joy.

Norma Grundy

Never To Be Forgotten
Thirteenth March 1996
Angels Of Dunblane

We all stood still, we all were shocked
We took one step back, just to take stock
We cannot start to think, or possibly comprehend
The fear in those angels, as their lives were brought to an end
The horror all started on a normal school day
Now all that the people of the world can do, is pray
For:-
**Melissa, Emma, Victoria, Charlotte, Kevin, Rosse, Emily
Sophie, John, Joanne, David, Mhairi, Brett, Abigail,
Hannah and Megan**
These little children were sent to heaven
Along with their teacher, **a hero called Gwenne**
She died protecting her charges, we'll always remember when
So just to remind you, again once more
We can't stop their hurts or heal their sores
All we can do is share their pain
The devastated people of Dunblane
They say that memories are golden
Well maybe that is true
We never wanted memories
We only wanted you

Trevor Gill

Dream Flowers

I dreamed
Upon a flower
And all of heaven
Exploded into colour
The sea revolved
The sun stood still

Graffitti
On the wall
At the corner of my street
Danced
With barefoot children
High-stepping broken glass
Toward the swings

Such colour
Never seen before
Streaked my sleep-screened lids
It did not stay
Memory put it in a frame

These flowers I give to you.

Audrey Greaves

The Poppy

The poppy with petals of bright blood red
A symbol of all the soldiers dead.
On fields of flanders they flourish and grow
And soft low winds their seed doth sow.

The poppy with seeds of deadly shade
A symbol of all the deeds to be paid.
On fields in Asia they flourish and grow
And small brown bodies the harvest do mow.

The seeds of the poppy ground to dust
A symbol of all the pain and lust.
On streets in darkness they flourish and grow
The poeple who sell the harvest they sow.

The poppy with petals of bright blood red
A symbol of all the narcotics we dread.
Dead hospital patients flourish and grow
And soft low winds their ashes doth sow.

H.W. Griffiths

178

Summer Days

Where hollyhocks and sweet peas bloom,
Pansies, lavender and broom.
The scent of roses fill the air,
The old man snoozes in his chair,
And bees buzz lazily around
The snow white daises on the ground.

Where jasmin and the cornflowers grow,
And bright red poppies gently blow
In the soft and gentle breeze.
Life is pleasant, quite at ease.
The washing mother has just done
Is fluttering gaily in the sun.

On lovely summer days like this
Our country garden's perfect bliss.
The lines of cabbages grow tall
And peaches nestle 'gainst the wall.
The marrows ripen, start to swell
And everything is doing well.

Soon the summer days will fade,
We'll eat the jam that granny made
On crusty bread by dancing flame,
But somehow it's not quite the same
As having tea upon the lawn
Under the sun so bright and warm.

Barbara Gingell

The Cormorant

Alone he stands -
Crucifix on the rock.
Wings outspread to dry.

Silently watching, waiting,
This greasy, black
Reptilian bird.

Vulture of the seas
He flaps lazily
Across the waves

Then up, up
Into the swirling wind
Preparing for the kill.

Plummeting, he punctures
The mirrored surface
Like an arrow

Transforming in a splash
From bird to fish.
Wings pressed close.

Then down, down
Into the wet darkness.
Killing to survive.

Gullet crammed
Heavily he rises
Then home, home . . . .

Louise George

A Promiscuous Miss

They said, "She was the biggest *slate,* "or words to that effect,
A *female dog,* a filthy hog, a *jade,* not delicate,
They quoth, "She were a *wobbly* gal," they durst not meet her eye,
This woman who doth walk the streets, resembling *pastry pie.*

But glint her jewels like *morning frost,*
'Gainst passions that run hot,
Her painted fingers should they point . . .
At you! Would you swear not?

Gemma Edwards Gill

The Magical Isle

A man and his friend turned round a bend and a wondrous sight met their eyes
They stood amazed, confused and dazed, the splendour was such a surprise
The grass was blue covered in dew, with flowers of silver and gold
And a musical sound came out of the ground with a magical tale to be told
Sparkling rain with a lovely refrain was sprinkling the beautiful flowers
And a colourful light from rainbows so bright, brought warmth and magical powers
The sun beamed down on a colourful town, with streets of yellow and green
And trees of pink made the visitors think, stranger sights they never had seen
They passed through a wood with toffee for mud, then a palace of gems met their view
They stood at the gate awaiting their fate, wondering what next they should do
A queen was sat with a red spotted cat, whose eyes flashed purple and green
While her sparkling gown outshone the town, dripping pearls of aquamarine
She ran to a hill which led to a mill, where the water had turned into wine
And peaches and plums awaited the chums as she told them to sit down and dine
She sprinkled some stuff with a flash and a puff that whisked the two men far away
They fell through the air but hadn't a care and didn't know quite what to say
Breaking their fall they crashed on a wall and wondered where they had been
And neither was sure if their wonderful tour was really a colourful dream
They took a deep sigh and again tried to fly but firmly rooted they stood
So the man and his friend just couldn't pretend, this time they were back for good

Juliet M. Green

Without You

To shout aloud yet not to hear,
To be apart but not to fear,
You bring the joy and take the pain,
As if the sunshine on the rain,
I see so much and need no sight,
Your love to me my guiding light,
To be my dream but not be here,
Your heart to place inside my tear.

J. Gillen

Rank Oxidazation

Tangled, yet ordered,
their lifeless forms respire.
Dead, but alive,
Their rusty redundancy recycled.
Ugly, but beautiful,
Revitalised riddles.
Menacingly tame,
Pathetically majestic.
They're humanly inanimate,
Futuristic relics.

Chris Gillet

Kiss And Tell

In this town of despair,
A rainy cloud hangs overhead,
Bringing out the tormented soul in
The animals cry,
While people lay in their dustbins
Of suburban hell,
Maybe the devil played kiss and tell,
And has given us our own cell,
Within the prison walls of our own soul.

Cheryl Gelder

Deafening The Silence

The peace and quiet is nature's day,
A summer time for making hay.
Or hazy dreaming in a flask of tea,
And river swings from the tallest tree.
A warmth of face and a glow of heart,
Lapwings and swallows it's time to depart.

For the vibrant hum of all the creatures,
Has lost the wood to concrete features.
A wildlife movement for the roads,
Fill in the ponds and drive out the toads.
Where badger setts became service stations,
Killing nature through motorway creations.
These monster paths are for ferrying man,
To those allotments of Eden now privately ran.

David K. Green

A Wedding Prayer

May your lives be long,
Heartaches few,
The best of luck,
In all you do,
May worries be absent,
From your door,
And memories so pleasant,
Be ever more,
May sunshine and roses,
Live in your heart,
And bonds of love,
Grow from the start,
May each day begin,
Like the first day of spring,
Each waking moment,
May your heart sing,
May your lives be blessed,
With happy days,
A guiding light,
With you always,
May love and peace,
Come your way,
This is my prayer,
On your wedding day.

Tina Griffiths

Nature At Work

I'm looking out of the window of time
Watching the wonders, working outside

The sky is blue, the trees are green
Swaying about on the breeze

Some of the roses, are still in bloom
Most of them are no more

As I watch through the glass
A butterfly comes on by

It's snowy white wings, waving to and fro
How graceful, and serene

How wonderful to see, nature at work
Watching each element, taking it's turn

The sun, the rain, and the wind
Working together, in harmony

E. M. Gee

The Haunting

He haunts me
Yes, he haunts me
This adonis
I see his visage now
The strong jaw-line that will not compromise
Such stature
Yet such doubt
I cannot follow
Yet I cannot wait forever
This dilema grieves me
Oh creaky back, away with you
I know the current price
I also know that more adventure follows.

Amanda Green

Lost Love

Ideas we planned were not a few,
disappeared like the morning dew.
The joys we shared when at play,
are lost to the dryness of decay.

Birds sing and fly to their nest,
my heart yearns for a loving rest.
I long to sing our song at last,
instead of living in shadows past.

I lie awake in a misty night,
thinking of freedom from my soul's fight.
I close my eyes to hope and pray,
that love will live with us and stay.

Marshal Green

28th November

Plump, pink-pouting pigeons with grey backs and clerical collars.
Blobs of partridge and pheasant, and untidy gatherings of rooks.
A dark line of plough, newly thrown over amidst the frozen earth.
A 60 watt sun lighting the fields through a frost-evaporating veil.
Bird scarers sailing like yachts through green and white old chenille fields.
Pale plough perfectly striped like subtle deck chairs, beige and silver.
Grey, dazzling tarmac; pale lemon as the sun slides on the wet surface.
Baby blue sky with a smoky rim hugging the bare branched hedgerows.
Small spherical birds pecking at the seeds and water by the washing line.
A crashed car in the High Street, a testament to the black ice we cannot see.
Winter is here!

Michelle Gibson

The Dream

Last night I lay sleeping,
Dreaming, dreaming, dreaming.
The moon rose high, stars shone bright,
Air was filled with sheer delight.
Beautiful voices singing,
All the bells were ringing
Which came from the 'Heavenly Heights'
Suddenly a door opened and a voice called from within,
Learn of me my blessed one, before you enter in.
I looked up and saw a kind and gentle face
With such a loving smile,
The scene then changed within a little while.
Down to earth with a bump I came
Waken to reality, like so many times before,
To find the alarm bells ringing
Later the postman knocking on my door
Good morning madam, there's sunshine on the way
I think it's going to be a heavenly day.

Madeline Green

A Fern

Unfolding as a fern on a warm wet day
Bringing forth new fronds from wet clay,
Besides many roadsides, on the hills afar
As winter browns take on a new green star,
It looks like a little star as it unfolds
Then rises out on a stalk long and bold,
It nods in the gentle breeze when it is grown
Acknowledging its whereabouts, it likes its home,
All is provided in the hedgerows and the glades
Nature nourishes with its food that it makes,
So strong and so sturdy when fully grown
So green and so healthy, so strong and so sure,
There the fern will stay for many a day
Gladdening many a heart that pass that way,
Like a carpet of green now it is seen
Awakening from its sleep of a winter dream,
So as you pass the green fern on the roadside today
Spend a moment in thought, who made it this way,
All to gladden our thoughts new life springs through
Everywhere and always God made this for you.

Lillian R. Gelder

183

Making Space

Crippled vision . . . you almost killed me, -
sucking on inadequacy.
Whispering that all I see -
prevents me being free.

Stunted reason . . . You almost fooled me, -
limiting my boundaries.
But spying my own epitaph -
finally cancelled out my pleas.

Futile mission . . . You almost enlisted me, -
to force me along your own path.
Confusing my reason, my inner path -
to act upon my own wrath.

Hunting this treason to every corner of psyche,
twisted me around to be, -
every dying persons confident.
But a foreigner to me.

Stephen Edward Glover

Dreams

What are these things that play in my sleepy mind?
That leave my outer self behind,
That create a collision of my thoughts
And imagery of all sorts.

A contrast between fantasy and reality,
Visions that only I can see,
Making things happen to me and you,
Creating yet another déjà vu.

The choice of what type is not up to me,
Romance, horror, real life, or mystery,
I wish I could choose, it's just not fair
When I end up with horror, and another nightmare.

They try to distract me when I'm awake
And assume my thoughts are their's to take,
These things that lead my mind astray
Call themselves dreams, people say.

Louise Ghosh

To A Canterbury Lamb
(One of many put down when a triple-decker transporter over-turned on the A2)

Soft head on hard shoulder,
how far away your close to
Canterbury field?
How near the path the expectant
pilgrims trod?
Came you with a promise of the
resurrection that is Spring,
Blow-dried by the March wind
and rinsed by April showers?
Across the meadow did you
hear the Easter bells,
An organ playing and choirs singing
'Worthy Is Thy Name'?
Note how gentle were the hands that
held you in the summer sunlight
streaming through the stained
and ancient glass?
Soft head on hard shoulder,
and good and hardened men did
weep, and sighed the more
for the ones that journeyed on.

Peter Greaves

Pictures

Pictures show on a postcard
Nothing like years ago
When things were clean and crisp
When trees grew tall
And rivers flowed

In a time without traffic
People walked they would sing
A time without dirty rivers
Life would roam
A fish could swim

But now a dirty claw
Drags pollution near and far
Nobody laughs nobody sings
Fishes die for they can't swim
Pictures show their decay
We all must learn one day

Ray Hart

I Love You

I love you with all of my heart
My whole body has taken part
For these messages my mind receives
My heart untangles the net my mind weaves
My love for you is eternal
Which explains why to my life you are the kernal
Forgotten days, months, years
My undying love for you has caused no tears
I love you, I've often said
This is as true as blood is red
The purest of expressions
Is how I give to you my impressions
You are my one and only boyfriend
Don't break my heart as it will not mend
Disclose your love to me
Those humble words, as sweet as can be
It makes no sense when were apart
From start to finish, finish to start
To you I have to say
I've always loved you in everyway
For every minute of every day.

Judith Gray

Today

Where, oh where are my ivory towers
Where has the bright rainbow gone
Lost in the dim of life's lonely hours
Ago when life was just a song

Where are girls that lifted my thoughts
Are they around, somewhere hidden
Lost, with others, they now will consort
Never more to come for my bidding

And where are the dreams that were mine
Achievement, ambition still await
Long lost in the deep abyss of time
Time is now, moreover too late

Yesterday allowed to depart and fade
Tomorrow we shall never see
Together a supreme masquerade
Today is totally all there'll be

Yet life is further, a dream, a song
Full of golden treasure
Time's span will never be too long
Live it, share it's pleasure

Clive Goodare

The Four Seasons

Sunshine and showers
Primroses and pretty flowers
Rainbows with their colours bright
Isn't it a lovely sight
Nice bright sun and sky so blue
Gardens are made just for you.

Summer days are a delight
Up above the sun is bright
Magic moments of the day
Mystically just fade away
Everlasting hours of fun
Relax enjoy the nice hot sun

Apples falling from the trees
Up above the gentle breeze
Tints of brown and also gold
Underneath the trees is cold
Make a date, go to the park
Nights will soon be getting dark

Wet and windy, very cold
Indoors is best I am told
North wind blows perhaps some snow
Temperatues are very low
Everyone should wrap up warm
Ready for the coming storm

A.P. Godfrey

Estate Agents Blues

What is this nightmare called "The chain"
Everyone a loser with no-one to gain
More permutations than a game of chess
All players united in deep distress

The recession has only fuelled this curse
The only thing moving, the funeral hearse
'For Sale' signs spoil the idyllic views
'Sold subject to contract' makes headline news

Estate agents bored just twiddling their thumbs
They fight over crosswords til 5 o'clock comes
If 'Joe Public' enters their empty domain
It's "Do you need any help" again and again

Who's to blame for this pityful mess
Thatcher & Reagan's an educated guess
A grocer's daughter and a B-movie actor, please
No wonder two nations are down on their knees

M.A. Gallagher

Xmas Dinner

"I'll kill that chicken", our Bert said he gripped it by the neck and head,
The bird let out a mighty squawk Bert dropped it like a red hot fork.
"I'll do it", Jack said in disgust "I'll kill that chicken if I must".
He screwed the neck round even more the bird squawked louder than before.

Jack's face turned white as a sheet he looked unsteady on his feet,
Both muttered then "We cannot stay, see you all another day".
Shouting "See you later Ma" the chicken pair ran to their car.
Thinking I must do something quick I layed it's head across a brick.

Saying to young brother Ned "Fetch the chopper from the shed".
He swung it hard and cut right in the head hung down from a piece of skin
Chicken jumped up on its feet ran in circles round the street
It's little heart soon ceased to beat then it was a lump of meat.

Some work in the slaughter house, now I can't even kill a mouse.
We don't keep chickens any more buy oven-ready at the store.
Fifty years that chicken's dead but still it lives! Here in my head.

Ronald Guest

Our Pattern Maker

With God as our pattern, with God as our guide,
His love will support us, along lifetimes ride.
Life is a mere journey with which we will cope,
With God alongside us, with Faith and with Hope.

Remember to tell him our problems and woes,
And respect his decisions for what comes and goes.
Remember to thank him for all blessings past,
He loves us his children, with a love that will last
At the end of our journey, who's there by your side.

The Good God who carried us, along paths hard and wide.
He will greet us with kindness and help us reach home,
To Blissfull tranquility, no more to roam.

Rita Goodwin

Bowen Peak

We breathed in pure New Zealand air
You and I on that mountain top.
Below, defined, beyond compare
God's hand which said forget me not.

Bryan S. Hart

To A Solitary Dandelion On The Hammersmith Flyover

Whence came you, lone dandelion?
Small, solitary, bright,
Wafted perchance, by some capricious breeze,
To lodge your tiny seed
Within some minute cavity.
Your roots precarious hold
In a chance particle of earth.

Bravely, you hold high your head,
Your yellow yellow head,
Green slender stem and leaves
Buffeted by exhaust blast.
Alone, amidst the roar
Of London's noisome traffic.

Today, you seemed to wilt,
O'er come by petrol fumes;
Yet, if your day is done
Your past played out,
You have not lived in vain.
You have, if for a fleeting space,
Bestowed a moments brightness
To a jaded motorists eye;
A benison of grace.

Leslie Grant

My Silent Scene

As I sit here waiting,
Paint brush in my hand,
Whilst I'm contemplating
The beauty of the land
All around me changes

Clouds that dance up in the sky
Ducks on the river passing by
A blade of grass, a wild bluebell
Rabbits playing without a care
Have not noticed I'm even there

How I love this silent scene
Shh, they will never know I've been,
But you and I know that's not true,
Because I brought them home to you,
Undisturbed, unaware, in my painting
For all to share.

Sharon Hill

Feelings

I used to be so loving,
and cared about all things.
So gentle was my nature,
to beast and living things.
But now I am older the love
I had has gone,
For my feelings have all changed
now, the fear is so strong.
So empty is my heart and lonely
as can be.
I wish I could be loved again,
and be free as I could ever be.

C.J. Glover

Rainstorm

I see it racing on the windows,
I hear it pounding in the street,
I feel it trickling down my spine,
Forming puddles wide, dark and deep.

Pitter patter, swish and swosh,
Giving our world a refreshing wash.

The bugs all start their marching back,
To nests all cosy and warm,
The birds will all take flight,
To find shelter from the thundering storm.

Pitter patter, swish and swosh,
Giving our world a refreshing wash.

Now the rain begins to calm,
The cobwebs seem to glisten,
The sun prepares to show its face,
I see the birds, I stop, I listen.

Pitter patter, swish and swosh,
Giving the world a refreshing wash.

Owen Hall (Age 12)

Water Shortage

The running water talks to me,
Does it talk to you?
Or does it only talk perhaps
To just a very few!
Water heating in the kettle
Daily sings to me,
I wonder if it sings to you
Waiting for your tea.
Filling up the bath tub
Almost to the top,
Do you hear the water pleading
STOP! STOP! STOP!?
Do you use the garden hose,
And the sprinkler too?
With only fleeting thoughts for those
Who need it more than you.
Perhaps you do not bother
What the water has to say,
But all of us should do so
For we need it every day.
Water chiefs make statements,
The press and others too,
But saving water in a drought
Is done by me, and you.

Joan Hancock

Anger

Anger is doing R.E.,
Or falling off the smallest tree,
Anger is going round a roundabout,
And when my mum balls and shouts.
Anger is mum telling me to tidy my wardrobe,
Along with taking everything out.
Anger is my brother and sister telling me what to do,
And my mum telling my sister to go to bed
And saying you go too.
Anger is when Nichola whines,
When my poems do not rhyme,
Anger is when Carrie sings,
And when the bell goes ding ding ding.
Anger is my cousin Gemma,
Who causes us a big dilemma,
I am feeling hot and bothered,
I don't feel like being smothered.

Nichola Harper (Age 10)

Cheat

I knew that he'd been cheating I'd had my doubts for days
The moodiness had left him he'd changed in many ways
He smiled at night when he came home and showered twice a day
He'd even beg to take our son out to the park to play
He'd disappear for hours on end then turn up pleased as punch
And sit and watch the telly and refuse to eat his lunch
A neighbour said she'd seen him she knew just where he went
And so I finally had the proof of how his time was spent
I waited for two minutes after he had left the house
Then followed him on tiptoe as quietly as a mouse
I watched him go into the pub but I stood right outside
I peeped in through the window and could scarce believe my eyes
He promised me he'd never cheat was more than life was worth
He'd pledged it on the very day of our two year old's birth
I watched him and I trembled as he brought her to his lips
And lit the first of twenty from a box of filter tips

Yvonne Hampson

Dream Dragons

The dragon is a mythical beast,
With leathery wings,
Eyes deep as mines,
Some say he's from the early times.

His rippling muscles, clean and lean,
He flies the sky like an aero-machine.
Causes havoc wherever he goes,
With spines on his back and claws on his toes.

He served the witch
And wizard too
But they had not one single clue,
Of the power and beauty within his soul.

But lovers of this beast,
Fight to survive, no losers to live.
To keep his memory we have to give,
Mind and body to make believe.

Let thought, emotion out in words.
The break of day, the song of birds.
Keep feelings down so deep within,
Inside your soul.

Wash out pain and bitter means,
And let yourself fall deep within,
The world of dragons,
A world of dreams.

Lee Samantha Hainey

A Glimpse Of Paradise

I like to walk among the fields
Just like so many do
I find it so rewarding
And it does my soul renew
I am not often lonely
For all Nature is my friend
I just enjoy the countryside
And would it all defend
We do not have to go afar
To some exotic place
To find the Peace and Quiet we need
Our stresses to erase
Just sit in some small garden
Take it easy for a spell
Relax and count our blessings
Try on kindly thoughts to dwell
Give ear to all the bird songs
And the humming of the bees
Just marvel at the butterflies
That flit among the trees
If we can do this now and then
And look up to the skies
We could no doubt feel free
And catch a glimpse of paradise

H.S. Hawkins

Living With Leukaemia

It all started when my back began to ache.
The doctors didn't believe me, and thought I was a fake.
They gave me some pills to ease the pain.
It went but then came back again,
Then I met a man called Dr. West (who probably saved my life)
With a very painful bone marrow test.
They sent me to Newcastle to the R.V.I.,
Where I was reassured that I wasn't gonna die.
I thought I was a vampire as they gave me some blood.
Whose ever it was it did me a load of good.
And if I could ever thank them I gladly would.
They took me to theatre and put a Hickman line in my neck
When I came out of anaesthetic boy did that not wreck!
I've been on drips for hours on end
I don't mind what goes in, as long as it mends
Then there was radiotherapy at Carlisle
I didn't really want it but tried my best to smile
I met a man called Professor Proctor
Who I have to say is a very good doctor
The end of my treatment is now in sight and the future is looking bright.
When I do eventually get to the end
There is one thing I have to say to both family and friends.
Thanks very much for all your support you've given me right 'till the end.

Gillian Heron

Grandchildren

There are three little Yorkshire girls,
Full of fun and bouncing curls,
They are the sunshine, and to me,
The new generation in my family tree.

One's named Katie, she's a beaut,
Then there's Kellie, oh so cute,
The third one's Lisa, very pretty,
They'll all go home soon, that's the pity.

But still we've had them all for tea,
So we won't grumble, Grandad and me,
We must be thankful for mercies small,
We might not have had them here at all.

Therefore in gratitude we'll say,
They are welcome here, just any day,
It is THEIR love, sets them apart,
And helps to keep US, young at heart.

Mavis Hemingway

Dreams

In the warmth of a shadow
I think of all brand new
Of a new born puppy
The thought of all that's true
A rainbow bowing
Across a shining sky of blue
And a tiny little smile
From the photograph of you

In the mildness of a breeze
On a warm summers day
I think of mellow ballads
Playing quietly, far away
And the thought of you beside me
Upon the dreams on which I lay
I want this to last forever
And this alone to God I pray.

Jojo Henry

My Christmas Wish

We're going to have a party,
They'll be lots of things to do,
Christmas cake and crackers,
Lots of fun for me and you.

The smell of roast turkey,
In each and every room,
Everything will be ready,
Very very soon.

Santa will be coming,
With presents in his sack,
It's great to see the children,
Smile, play games and laugh.

Christmas cards and trimmings,
Make us all feel good,
But Christmas time's for sharing,
The precious gift of love.

So try to think of others,
Not as fortunate as you,
Be happy and enjoy yourself,
But wish them all, well too.

Here's to a Happy Christmas, a Happy New Year too,
A wish that all your hopes and dreams
For the coming year, come true.

Sharon Hill

Safety Net

You were my safety net
I fell swiftly but surely
I was catapulted
Like a ricochet bullet
On the rebound, yes
But I was surely bound
To fall for all your charms
Or even lack of them

It seems at times you were a willing net
I fell swiftly, you caught me with ease
Such calculated ease
I was at times captivated
Propelled by some unseen force
Unseen, yes but not unknown
By previous encounters of majesty

Pauline Hatch

Snow

Have you seen the snow
Fall from the big white sky?
In the frozen night air
A blanket of snow is falling
From the clouds
And people are turning it
Into snowmen.
Like shining iceburgs,
Shiny as ever could be seen
Snow tastes like ice-cream.
Glittery snow is falling
From the sky.

Dominic Hamilton (Age 7)

192

My Wife

She's always there no matter what,
caring and loving as if I were a tot.

When I was ill she was more like a nurse,
comforting and worrying to keep away that hearse.

When I got better I returned as I was,
demanding and moaning, well just because.

But now I've found out she is seriously ill,
so serious in fact, that she's made out a will.

I'm in a turmoil and lost for words
she's always done everything even fed the wild birds.

Well it was up to me, my turn now,
I would wash and feed her and wipe her brow.

I said many a prayer over the next few days
and promising God, that if she lived I would change my ways.

Then to our surprise she got really well,
as if a magician had broken a spell.

It's hard to believe but very true,
She's her old self now, as good as new.

I've been given a chance to start a new life
to look after and care for my very dear wife.

Dennis Hinchey

Night Time

"Sleep little one"
Said mum and switched off the light
and went away.
It was scary.
I waited and waited.
I crept out of bed and on to the floor,
I heard people talking.
A sudden jump crept up on me,
and gave me a fright.
I ran into bed and pulled up the covers.
Soon I'm thinking, then I'm asleep.

Celia Hall (Age 7)

Snow

Snow is frozen
Frozen as a freezer.
Snow is as white as a sheet,
It sparkles when
The sun comes up.
Snow is crunchy and crisp.
Snow is so icy,
It is so cold.

Daniel Hare (Age 7)

The Seaside

Go to the seaside it's nice and cool
The sea is calm
The fishes swim slowly by
Paddle in the nice cool waves
Or you can swim if you are brave

Bring your buckets and spades
Build lots of sand castles with flags on top
Children playing games
Blazing hot sunshine melting ice-creams
Dripping ice lollies over sandy toes

Looking for pebbles and seashells
Climbing in rock pools
Playing with the seaweed
Picking up stones looking for crabs
Crabs moving quickly sideways

Sand in your sandwiches
Picnics sitting on a mat
Sitting in the shade of an umbrella
As sailing boats pass gently by
Cotton ball clouds, bright blue sky,
Suncream, sunglasses and a floppy hat
This is what makes my day at the seaside!

Rebecca Halstead (Age 8)

This Wonderful World

Imagine a world without birds
How dreary this life would be
Picture a scene without trees
With no leaf or blossom to see

Think of a barren like garden
With no pretty flowers on view
Think of a world without greenery
Where no grass and wild flowers grew

How sad if no butterflies fluttered
No bees to produce golden honey
No sun to shine, no sky of blue
Not one single day would be sunny

How dreary our world would be
If creation was moulded this way
With no nature's blessings around us
To brighten our lives through the day

Pam Hackney

On A Cold Winters Day

Looking out on a cold winters day,
Made all my thoughts just float away.
The fields were covered with snow and frost.
In this wonderful white world I was lost.
The snow was glistening,
I was shivering,
Before me was a beautiful sight,
All that snow for a snowball fight.
Icicles hung from window ledges
Robins hopped about in the ice covered hedges.
Snow was on the ground and pretty high.
"Snow, snow, snow," I heard children cry.
Snowflakes fall and softly hit the ground,
So delicately, not the slightest sound.
I have seen this sight many times before,
And every time I see it, it means so much more.

Marie Hawke (Age 12)

Just A Little Dandelion

I was standing at the bus stop
In the pouring rain
When I saw a little dandelion
Growing from a drain

Little yellow flower head
Half closed against the rain
Waiting for the sun to shine
To open up again

Forgotten was that dreary wait
My heavy shopping bag
My aching arms and tired feet
My spirits on the flag

For just that fleeting moment
My spirits rose again
To see that little dandelion
Growing from a drain

Phyllis Hall

The Inner Strength

Inner strength prevails
It must
Outer strength it fails
Not just

The inner strength combines
Destiny's balance
Weaver of unfaltered lines
Truth portrayed not chance

Truth from heart deep in the soul
These words are meant not just for thee
The meaning goes beyond the role
My thoughts are here for all to see

My thoughts will go beyond this page
As truthful words reveal my plight
Our destiny's succumb to rage
Strength now shown by outer fight

As webs deceit untangled just
Roles meanings heard throughout the land
Lies unveiled and shown as must
Balance restored, truth etched in sand

Keith Hall

War And Remembrance

How many of us get married and then divorced
It happens to the best of us of course
When does it all start to go wrong
Why does the music leave the song
I suppose if the answers to this we knew
The number of divorces would be few
But as it happens we don't know
So into a life of hell most of us go
Though not all end up in court
Others have no choice but to abort
Think carefully before taking those vows
Chances are they will lead to many rows
Marriage isn't all it's cracked up to be
Go through with it and you'll see
Here's a bit of useful advice
Don't marry someone you entice
Live with them first in sin
See if your relationship can win
If you manage to win this first round
Then maybe in matrimony you can be happily bound

V. Hamley

The Fate Of The 'Sir Galahad'

There she lies, at the bottom of the sea.
Aboard her, men of gallantry.
It came so fast, when all were in bed.
The dreadful fate, of the 'Sir Galahad'.

The enemy bombarded the 'Galahad's' deck,
And left the ship a burning wreck,
As young men, blazing, screamed in agony
Others, risked their lives to set them free.

Now that peace prevails way o'er that land.
Let us not forget our brave young lads.
Some returned, but left a heavenly band
Dead. On the decks of the 'Sir Galahad'.

Jennifer Hayward

The Thames At Eventide

Tall stands the clock o'er shadowing the bridge,
As dusky ships 'neath arches glide,
Splitting the emerald sheen as ridge to ridge,
The rippling river is cast aside,
And bustling traffic heeds not the quiet,
Which waters bring at eventide.
Could I but for one instant hold,
The picture which I now behold,
Then memory would in time release,
An instant of eternal peace.

G.A. Herd-Lewis

A Mother's Struggle

Recall a frame of tender care,
that stooped to meet my kiss.
Reminded of the life she led,
the people she tried to help.

The nights she'd toil,
coming face to face with fire;
Helplessly she'd bow her head.
Endless struggles, with hardly any rest.

She grows older, knowing there's no choice;
struggling's all she's done her life.
Looking at me she tries to smile.
Only I know what struggles hide behind that tender face.

Nilmini Hattotuwagama (Age 14)

196

Olly The Octopus

My name is Olly the octopus
And I live under the sea
I can't stay long to sing a song
Before the humans come and catch me
My life is full of swim away
Sometimes I think what is the day
I'm scared of just a simple noise
Then I meet up with those nasty boys
They beat me up upon the street
Soon I can't stand on my eight feet
I go away in great great pain
And humans come and chase me again
I go and visit my best friends
To tell my unluckiness never ends
They comfort me for hours until
They say they feel a scary chill
I have a feeling it will be bad
I turn around and get real sad
I see humans about to fire their spears
So I shout my loudest and hurt their ears
I get away with my tentacles scraped
They find me again this time I escaped

Barney Hall (Age 10)

Chemistry

That magical night I was captivated by innocent conversation,
Oblivious to the impending see-saw of despair and elation.
Each hour I fought temptation by keeping a safe distance,
While unknowingly taking down the barriers of resistance.
In true monogamous fashion, I struggled to keep away,
Supplies of will-power dwindling with each passing day.
A few days to avoid you did not seem too long,
Then the magnetic pull, increased to extra-strong.
Eventually I was overwhelmed by all your winning charms,
Seduced by a crazy longing to be held in your bronzed arms.
I felt very nervous, perhaps you feel the same.
For me it was love, not some lighthearted game,
You stirred emotions within, that filled me with fear,
I wanted you to leave, while I wanted you near.
Our mutual needs for affection surged to the fore,
I asked you to go away, I dare not ask for more.

It was a devastating experience to find "The love of my life",
Then remember you were someone's husband and I was someone's wife.
Soon you were gone leaving only memories and fears,
A few hours of love, ended with a life time of tears.

Judi Hill

197

Experience

Accept your life, for what it is
Nothing is permanent
The rough, the smooth, the sad, the glad
Dispense with your lament

Life will hit you hard at times
Companions may be cruel
Never seek revenge my friend
This is a fatal tool

Select acquaintances old and wise
Who can teach you all the ropes
Experience cannot be surpassed
Fulfiling your dreams, your hopes

Do not fear, your own voice
Your liberty is guaranteed
Each is entitled to his choice
Some may, or may not heed

Let your mind be haunted
Haunted with respect
This is your key to peace of mind
You are poised, sincere, direct

Thank God for your life
With all its imperfections
We are all brothers and sisters
Branching in different directions

Margaret Hazard

New Year's Eve

Once again we gather with friends,
and wait for the midnight hour.
New resolutions are firmly made,
as bells ring in the tower.
Out with the old year, welcome the new,
on this last night of December.
Then holding hands, sing 'Auld Lang Seine',
and nostalgically remember.

Reflecting back on previous months,
did the joys exceed the tears.
Did summer dispel the winter gloom,
the pain-filled days of fear.
How much success have we enjoyed,
of plans made long before.
And did we really make progress,
for peace in the world for all.

Now comes the first of January
the start of this brand new year.
We have such good intentions,
just now they are very clear.
As time goes on and weeks slip by,
and mundane life returns.
Will we remember 'New Year's Eve',
and from the past year learn?

Renée Halford

Third World Blues

Skinny ribs, no clothes no homes.
Across the desert all day they roam.
A babe in arms, others dead, left behind
Life to them is so unkind.
Water so scarce, food little or none
Desert scorched all day by the blazing sun.
Death and disease wherever they go.
Their hearts so heavy their pace so slow
Why I ask must they suffer like this
When God made the earth it wasn't his wish
He provides enough for all nations to feed.
So why does this happen? It's western man's greed!

Joyce Harding

T.V. Set

In the corner sits the television set
Why do I not know how it works yet
It entertains me nightly both comic and tragic
Yet for all I know its workings could be magic

On it I've soared through space and time
With the volume down its like watching mime
Yet when it comes to when it breaks down
All I can do is sit with a frown

I've mastered the washing machine
And learned how to clean
All things domestic I've mastered you see
But the workings if the TV set is a mystery to me

I can ponder the world and watch sport until I die
And watch documentaries and learn how birds fly
See distant oceans and countries afar
Places I couldn't get to sat in my car

So there in the corner sits my TV set
I haven't got around to turning on yet
And I think 'Will I sit here and slowly vegetate
No, I'll go to the pub and get drunk with my mate'

Martin Harty

Only Memories

Watching the first leaves that fall from a tree,
Letting us know spring and summer has come and gone,
And Autumn will bring the wet winds and the chill to the air,
A reminder of snows to come, bright blue skies are fading away,
When dark mornings are coming our way again, it's a sure sign
Winter is back with a forceful fear.
Sitting by the fire, with a hot rum toddy,
Stew and dumplings, and stories from long gone,
Only to be revived for eager young ears, all excited hugging by the fire,
The room filled with warm air settling down covering us, a blanket of love.
Oh, only memories, as I turn over to sleep, grasping hold of yesterdays papers,
Resting my head on the rags below on the floor,
And the cardboard box to sleep within.
I will dream the dreams that only for the few, the lucky ones,
But alas it's no longer for me, but a reminder from the past,
Dreams that haunted me, reminding me,
Of treasure that I once grasped and once held dear to me.

Angela Hamill

The Worlds Unique Village

Once upon a time and far, far away,
A village developed, named Clovelly.
Built into the cleft of a cliff
Where two centuries ago, author, Charles Kingsley lived.
'The Water Babies' being his claim to fame
With other stories too numerous to name.

Down steep cobbled street you can wander at leisure,
Visit his home now an archive of treasure.
Post Office, craft shops, two chapels and more
With quaintly built cottages, roses gracing the door.
Donkeys stand waiting so patient and still,
In times gone by they pulled coal up this hill.

Boasting a harbour curved round by the shore
Extreme weather sheltered, spy trawlers galore.
Set high on a plateau overlooking the sea
A Celtic cross stands, with a view of Lundy.
Steeped in history from 1100 A.D.
This picturesque hamlet holds tranquillity.

So if you're ever down North Devon way
The World's Unique Village make your first stay.

Barbara Hellewell

The Old School

They sit around their table
Hand picked for the cameras
To keep the conversation true
Do they really know? Have they felt
Life outside the green belt?
Experts of course they are
But on every street?
Once perhaps to canvass
To touch the real world
Their boots don't look worn
On T.V. they reassure
Of course their hearts are pure
How dare we question such conviction?
Do they make mistakes and falter
Or ever question their addiction
To "their" world?

Gordon Heathcote

Thank You

I have made mistakes
These have caused some tears
I hope I have not failed you
I am wiser through the years
I have written these words to thank you
For being here for me
Especially over the last few years
They have been so hard you see
I have lived my life the wrong way round
Topsy-turvy you know me
Sometimes I wish things were different
We live like that don't we?
Thank you for being here with me
You are my true best friends
You never judge or criticise
With you I don't pretend
I may not say it often
My thoughts are very clear
I love you more than words can say
You're held in my heart so dear
I hope one day I'll make you proud
As I am proud of you
I love you both so much indeed
I am so pleased to have you two.

Anne Hickson

Untitled

It was like a massive hall
Tables and chairs here and there a stage in front
As we walked awkwardly into the room
A stranger showed us where to be seated
As we sat and converged a boat drifted past and stopped
We walked onto it as if in a dream
It drifted away in a red and yellow cloud.

Jo Harvey

Yesterday's Dream

Alone in the world
No-one hears her cries
No-one is there to wipe away her tears
From a sadness she has built up over the years
Memories of a lost love
The moment she was cast aside
Never to be a bride
Hurt pride, she locked herself away
And her beauty left her on that day
She lost that twinkle in her eye
Beneath which now only pain lies
That distant look of far away
Her thoughts trapped in yesterday
No more a smile there'll be
She lives her life on a memory

Sandra Heath

Fascinating Illuminations

Looking out of my window what is it that I see?
Fascinating illuminations that often capture me
The sun begins to rise mixtures of golden red
Stretch out far and wide above my weary head
The April morning blossom is scattered all around
Grass shimmers and glistens from the dew drops on the ground
The aroma in the air smells so fresh and sweet
And birds of many kinds merrily begin to tweet
New buds now appearing upon the branches of trees
Soon to be a travel stop for butterflies and bees
Cobwebs and their patterns gleam with a frosted glow
And now the airs much cooler for there isn't any snow
So looking out of my window, what is it that I see?
Fascinating illuminations that never fail to capture me

M.A. Hirons

Spring

Today is the first day of spring,
Gone the long cold winter chill.
It's proclaimed by birds as they sing,
A new season of warmth, the trill.

Gone the long cold winter chill,
Buds on the trees break out.
A new season of warmth, the trill,
Emerging flowering bulbs sprout.

Buds on the trees break out,
Farmers the turf ploughing, symbolic.
Emerging flowering bulbs sprout,
Playful lambs gambol and frolic.

Farmers the turf ploughing, symbolic,
Winter misplacing its polar mantle.
Playful lambs gambol and frolic,
The arctic grip lost its strangle.

Winter misplacing its polar mantle
Its proclaimed by birds as they sing.
The arctic grip lost its strangle,
Today is is the first day of spring

Harrold Herdman

A Secret Told

My mind recalls a distant past
That happened so long ago
And I now write this for you
Hoping one day you will know.

Looks can be very deceiving
And a past could be no more than a lie
But when I think about this time and again
It's not for me to ask you why.

If it's really truth you spoke
I really feel deep for you
There is nothing I can do or say
To help in any way.

Your innocence was shattered
Your love now hidden aside
What a shame this ever happened
To someone who seemed so kind.

Even after such a short time
Of knowing and caring for you
I hope you'll find some help
In whatever life you choose.

Gill Hewett

Friendship

Your gifts come as no surprise. I know you well
You gladden my heart and weave a glorious spell
I forget the years of persecution, of bleak oppression
When I fell into the pit of deep depression

You and your daughter shower me with respect
Your love you show. You push aside my pain
I turn and watch my anguish go
Well into the night I hear your words of peace
And feel their healing powers
You gladden my heart
Through many lonely hours

I've known the grey insides of mental institutions
Been supplied with bitter pills to mask the pain
Yet you through friendship turn my mind to pleasure
Bring rainbows, flowers nodding in the rain
A glass of wine a friendly word or two
Undoes the wrongs committed in the past
And I believe though all the world's corrupted
That I have found a friendship that will last

Janet Heslop

202

Blind Alleys

Parallel with ours, another world is with us
Though we exist on this, our present plane,
Striving for whatever brings us pleasure -
Power, glory, everlasting gain?

Dreams of youth are often lost in conflict
Ideals fade in fending off despair,
Seeking answers to our endless questions -
Is there hope or anyone to care?

Distracted by the needs of this existence
Survival is an ever-present thought,
Sometimes beguiled by avaricious yearnings -
Are bitter-sweet, and never what we sought

Look beyond, and find the truth that beckons
Shake off the shackles which confuse the mind,
False goals that seem to promise freedom -
But, more deeply, are we then confined.

The Universe is wide and ever-reaching
Uncomprehending, ego fails to see,
As clouds of doubt and fear obscure them -
The Truth beyond the Mystery.

Brenda Hilton

Poetry

I took to poetry
A while ago
Before I could read
Before I could write
And even before I could talk

And now I've got thirteen 'A' levels,
'O' levels, GCSE's
And an Honours degree,
I CAN'T REMEMBER THE WORDS.

H.P. Hayward

Our Garden

With natural attributes unblessed
A shady patch of heavy clay,
Our garden lies in dormant rest
As Winter slips away.
But then when Spring and Summer reign,
These faults soon fade, and once again
Our garden is transformed with care
Into our own Oasis, where
We can among the flowers dream
Each flower true to colour scheme,
A cool and shady place.

Kate Hannis

Misunderstanding

Play with words
        with care, my dear!
Once spoken, they disappear.
Where? - In thin air?
No, like sharpened weapons
or healing hands
they find the target.
What was the aim?

So often I failed to hear the caring
        in your tone
Because of fear in my own.

So often I thought you meant
        with what you said . . .
And I missed the meaning.

Why didn't I ask before?

The words we chose had no feeling
        on their own.
Why didn't I listen before?

I then suppose we stopped receiving,
        became alone
And could not stand anymore.

You silly thing (I love you so)
You silly thing (I wish you'd go)

Why didn't I trust before?

Seija Henry

Facets Of Love

True love reminds me of a rose,
Which buds, then blooms and grows.
Thorns, protecting it from harm,
Afford refuge, as a lover's arm.

Love between a child and mother,
Is unique, a bond, both discover.
Strong as diamond, lasts forever;
Death its brilliance can't sever.

Friendship, lasting through life,
Surviving joys, challenges, strife,
As open as space, knows no bound;
Such precious love rarely found.

Kindness afforded to a needy man,
Reminiscent of The Good Samaritan,
Placing another before own interest,
Surpasses human love's highest test.

Love is vulnerable to hurt, distress;
Without it can be no true happiness.
A life alone with none other shared,
To Solitary Confinement is compared.

Perfect love was revealed by Jesus,
Who gave up His life to redeem us.
This sinless man showed God's love,
Opening a pathway to Heaven Above.

Janet Hewitt

You Are The Love Of My Life

My heart is on fire with deep love and desire
To hold you in my arms forever.
My emotions so palpable like never before
Because you are my true love whom I adore
The touch of your hand is like magic
And the loss of your love would be tragic
For you are the love of my life
So divine you are you entered my life like a shooting star.
Desirable, delectable, how precious you are
And my worship of you will always ensue
For you are the love of my life.
Together forever I hope we will be
For loving you is so, heavenly.

Patricia Anne Handel

Ghosts 'n Ghouls

Are there ghosts in this world, in which we exist?
If there are, they are visions, easily missed,
They're supposed to 'live' on the same plane as we,
But with different 'vibrations' so we cannot see,
At the end of the day, it is still my boast,
There is no such thing, as a Genuine Ghost.

The 'Ouija' board is a favoured way,
To call the spirits by night and day,
But it only works when you're drunk or drugged,
Or unless by someone, the rooms been bugged,
So listen to me, hear me howl,
There is no such thing as a Spectral Ghoul!

Poltergeists haunt, and throw things around,
To prove to the world that Spirits abound,
They can wreck and spoil an entire room,
Filling the sceptics with fear and gloom.
Hear my opinion, I say it looks,
Like there is no such thing as Real Life Spooks.

Clairvoyants and Mediums, prove only to most,
There's no such thing as a 'God damned' ghost,
The gullible listen and believe what's said,
My contention is - when you're dead, you're dead.
So listen to me, I want you to hear,
There is no such thing as a Gifted Seer!

Harry Hemingway

Bad Patch *(Remembered)*

I press the bell tug the cord and bang the walls
But no one comes. They never do.
Out through the bars beyond the courtyard
I can see into the pink room, the table and chairs room
Where pretty young nurses sit reading Cookson
While wrinkled old men stand thumbling, mumbling
Dribbling the remainder of their tiny insignificant
Lives down crusted chins and buttered shirts
Caressing stubble while forming opinions on today
Tomorrow and yesteryear; pink stone and paintbrush
For company, a muffled radio and a ten a penny picture to call home.
Out in the corridor a notice reads:
IN THE EVENT OF FIRE ALL STAFF TO GATHER IN 'E' WING.
The rest of us to gather in 'D' wing, if we can remember our alphabet
                                                    Not me
I don't give a damn about fires or wars or earthquakes or anything else.
                                                    Damn them
Damn everything, everyone.

Sam Harlow

Flowers

A cocktail of colours fit for any eye
Bright as any rainbow that arches in the sky
Fragrances and perfumes exquisite and fine
The flowers of the world are mysterious and divine
From giant sunflowers that stand tall in vibrant yellow
To red roses that girls love to receive from their fellow
Tulips in rows like guards on duty
Orchids in all colours showing their beauty
Freesias are always a mum's favourite gift
They give a hard day just a little lift
Lily-of-the-valley a brides special flower
Crocus emerge from the ground in a spring shower
Pansies in bright colours with darkened faces
Candy Tuff pops up in all different places
Carnations and Gypsophellia for the birth of a child
With flowing ribbons of pink or blue soft and mild,
Sweet-peas send a strong aroma into the air
Chrysanthemum blooms are arranged with care
Yes, flowers brighten up any miserable day
They often mean more than words can say
A gift from God heaven sent they must be
A wondrous glory for every eye to see

Lorinda Hammond-Marshall

The Poets

There are "Thinkers", that are writers of "Stature"
There are those with no literary name
Yet humbly make deep impression
When they rise in freedom's name
Heroes and heroine this isle of England has
Singers and dancers too, orators "just a few"
Poets we learnt at school
Yet only Shakespeare's words <u>still</u> rule
Poetry of words, a motion picture make
Leaving to posterity all in its wake.

Jessie Florence Harper

Lady Of The Loo

Somewhere a little old lady is sitting
Daily she sits, just doing her knitting
Beneath her feet, a carpeted floor
With bowls of flowers within every door.
This haven she treats with scented spray
A labour of love she does every day
Do visit her at a comfort stop
As she tends her loo?
It's the very best pot.

Dolly Harmer

206

Industrial Accident

Blowing down Grey Street towards the river
A couple hears the cheers from Pudding Chare.

Night club kids grab a kebab and chips before
Plunging into the crowd to play the game once more.

Last throw Christmas shoppers clutching Fenwick's bags
Dragging fraught children and dragging on taught fags.

The buses pulling out of Eldon Square
And the girls pulling in the Robin Adair.

Coloured lights flash in plastic trees
And signs say what's on sale and what's free.

A few miles down the river,
Working the last half shift to pay for Christmas,
A young lad opens the nitrogen valve
And begins to fill a pipe with a dodgy weld.

Paul Hanson

A Letter To My Father

I talk with you in my mind,
Words I never said.
Sparrows on your table,
The thoughts inside my head.

Of walking in the woods,
Memories of Summer days.
Skein of geese flying,
Of all your funny ways.

Boats on rivers, my captain,
You will always be.
Starlings on your grass,
The truth you made me see.

My father, my hero,
My force against the dark.
Foxes in my garden,
On me, you made your mark.

Prepare a place my father,
As your roses seek the sun.
The robins in your garden,
Welcome me, when I come.

Susan Hoskins

Bills And Ills

There is always a fear of dread
After awakening in the morning making the bed
That the post will arrive with the bills
Enough to give anyone the chills
Envelopes often brown or white
Can bet that you are usually right
Be it, gas, water, electric or phone
Makes us all in need of a groan
That prices increase without much warning
Check the bank balance, no time for yawning
Not much respite for us these days
Constantly caught in many different ways
Postal deliveries can bring joy at times
With friends on holiday in different climbs
But the fear and dread is still there
To what the postman's delivery might bear
More money to pay for that expense
Leaves us all feeling rather tense
Never mine leave it for another day
Perhaps we might win the lottery on Saturday

A. Higgins

No Electric

What a night, without no light
The electric has broken down again,
So out comes the candle while we wait in vain,
No T.V. or radio no wonder we are glum
That's all we can do just twiddle our thumbs,
Dad gets up and gets a drink
Mum looks and gives a wink,
"We'll have a bottle of Scotch", says dad
But mum says "Tea I would rather have had",
While they dither and fiddle about
It's, a laugh the candle goes out,
There we all sit in the dark
It really is a lark,
We can't see to do a thing
All we can do is sing,
Dad gets cross, mum looks lost,
Then on comes the light and we can see
Thank goodness we can now watch TV

Joy Hall

The Baker

At four o'clock he's out of his bed,
To bake his pies and cakes and bread,
There's cobs and rolls and loaves and baps,
And lots of other little snacks.
And while he's cooking frying and baking,
Those little furry eyes are waiting.
Their tiny feet scamper over the floor,
Those pesky mice are out once more,
They nibble the cakes and icing toppings,
And leave behind those little droppings.
They gorge themselves with lots of goodies,
And fill their little bulging tummies.
Scurrying among the plates and bowls,
They squeeze themselves back through their little holes.
The baker sees the flour and crumbs,
And little currents nibbled out of his buns.
He's tried his cat and little traps,
To try and catch those hungry brats.
But all the time he's watched and baited,
Those little furry eyes just waited.
Because they know next day at four,
He'll be up to bake his bread once more.

Graham Hancox

208

I Do Not Wear Rose Tinted Spectacles When I Write

Happily they sit in church on the pews.
Pious morality a colour worse than death.
(It can cause such harm)

Others are like sitting ducks for the
Religious propaganda.
Or should that be "morality"?
The thick plastic that hides the iron arm of control . . .

Is what the patriarchal church tries to inflict on us all.
It damages the eyesight until all they can see is black.
(Although it must be confessed that the preacher
gave them all blindfolds).
They didn't want to see reality - only condemn it.

Clare Harwood

Wildlife Sanctuary

You animals find this place as wild as the tides
Of the sea; the landscape you roam in as fresh as the dew
In the morning of Eden; the lake where you drink in its sides
Reflects from their feet to their crowns the hills made for you

By Nature's hand alone. The only flaw
In your wilderness, putt-putting sounds of the motor-boats
That send you rushing to cover of trees from the shore,
Your paradise dreams disturbed until each one floats

Out of sight. Dear creatures, that one jarring note is the mark
Of your world, for nothing around you is what it seems -
You thought you lived in a forest, you live in a park -
From largest to smallest, even the lake that gleams

Was planned by Man. Can't you see the half-submerged trees
That were caught in the water? Lifeless now, but teak
Is slow to rot. Men felt on a whim they would freeze
This landscape with lake for you. Their benevolent streak

May not last. Without honour the safety of sanctuary fails
(So found the innocent kin of usurping kings
When dragged to death from the very altar rails).
You elephant, antelope, warthog, wild free things,

Your zoo is too big for you to see the bars.
You are saved from outside by thin fences of kind intention,
From a world that's senselessly savage, a world that jars
With Nature: the juggernaut world of Man's invention.

S.R. Hawk'sbee

Well Of Tears

Many thousands of years man has been on this earth
Through stone age, ice age, virgin birth
But still we have wars and people are dying
'Till all that's left is a mother crying

We cheat and rob, and kill and lie
And before too long our planet will die
But do we worry, shall we care
When all that's left is a world that's bare

All our future children should learn from our mistakes
Let them see where we went wrong, we must for all their sakes
Because if they don't heed the warning of these past thousand years
All that will be let is a well of tears

S.A. Harrington

So Another Year Goes By

So another year goes by
Do you some times wonder of the star in the sky
What ever; For love is his forte
I bring you greetings this day
To show you from my scribe why and for what reason
That my wish and joy, goes to you this festive season
Because we do and must celebrate the great light
Of the special child sent to man that night.

Jacob Harris

Sanctuary

Away from the noisy city.
Away from the crowded street.
To somewhere serene and peaceful.
To a place where the air smells sweet.
A peaceful spot where I may hear
The song of a bird on high,
And feel the warmth of a golden sun,
As it shines in a cloudless sky.
Where no buildings blot the landscape,
Or exhaust fumes foul the air,
Where only animals roam the fields
As they graze on the green grass there.
Here I could find contentment,
Free from worry, fear or care.
A valley steeped in silence,
A sanctuary rich and rare.

Graham Hamilton

Caedmon

Caedmon in the tongue-tied wastelands
Of a barren place,
On the far-stretched reaches
Of a race's reckoning,
Harrowed by the smell of night,
Through the chase packed quarry,
Huddled in fear to his religion.

Waiting in the wilderness
With mind reached out,
Pleading for conception, empty-mouthed.
Then it came
In a dream,
And his chains snapped like tinder,
In the forests surrounding.

C. Hill

Suburbia

If all the front gardens were tidy and neat
How pleasant 'twould be as we walked down the street.
Tall daffodils thrusting their spikes through the ground,
Then midsummer roses ablowing around.
Snow winter-white heather, new hope for the Spring,
Pink, frail almond blossom where blue tit-mice cling.
Mauve lilac and lavender, rosemary blue
And herbaceous borders of dazzling hue.
Geraniums marching in orderly style
With alyssum scenting their feet all the while.
No rushing in cars, but a short walk instead
To view Mrs. Potter's delphinium bed.
If all the front gardens were planted with roses
What colours for eyes and what perfumes for noses!
If all the rose bushes were carefully tended
And if all the flowers were perfectly blended
Each one with another, a bountiful pleasure,
To walk down the street would bring joy without measure.

Thelma Harborne

Spud

I have a dog, his name is 'Spud'
I take him training, he's not so good
He does try hard when he's in the mood
But most of the time, his mind's on food!
He wanders about just sniffing the ground
Or causes me stress by jumping around!
I try to make him concentrate
Then sit him down and tell him to 'wait'
But again he's not interested, he just wants to play
What chance do I have to make him obey?
He looks up at me with his big brown eyes
As if to say "mummy, let's say our goodbyes
I want to go home now, I've tried my best
I'm wanting my dinner and needing a rest"
I agree - we'll call it a day
Can't cope any longer, it'll make me go grey!
I guess I slightly exaggerate
He's not so bad - just not so great!
But I don't care if he's not very good
'Cos he's still my baby - my little Spud!

Marie Hinsley

Whirls

Serene, a grey winged statue peers,
Alone upon mossed turf.
Whispering winds blow far, around its form,
As green grass blades, bow beneath high winds,
Here we'll turn to gaze, to watch the spirits of mid air.
Oh sweeping winds blow fast, when the winds blow free,
Haunting winds blow far, now you and I,
Shall feel the spirits, roaming free,
High spirits of mid air, we'll watch the leaves,
Now carried high, upon the bracken way to fly.
A vast Autumn fall of golden hue,
Whirling mellow leaves that turn,
With dancing leaves that fall,
Oh when cascading, we'll watch thee fly.

Christine Hare

Cold Air

Through out the cold air
Do we take a walk, do we dare
Do we hesitate before proceeding
Do we appreciate going out before needing to do so
When were out, will it rain or will it snow
Can we see the sun one more time
Can we possible make it shine
Cold air is not what we always expected
I think to myself that a lot of old people feel neglected
Cold air I can feel rushing through my hands and feet
Old people I know they'd rather be home in the heat
I would like to help them, but intend to go my own way
At least I know the cold air is not here to stay
My circulation is highly affected by the cold
The doctors agree, I should be highly protected so I'm told
Through out the winter I feel the cold air
But do we risk ourselves out there

Simon Hart

Red

Red is for the robin red breast
We love to see at Christmas.
The blood oozing out of a cut.
The blazing red fire that keeps us warm in winter.
The juicy red apple we like to eat.
A fire engine speeding down the street.
The brake light on the car.
The tomato ketchup that makes a mess.
The romantic red roses for the girl of my choice.

David Johnson (Age 10)

Idea

Oh ancient rocks!
You who have held
The seeds of conscious mind
The womb of thought!
Travelling down the ages
Through mortal time.
Sent from the timeless to eternity,
The journey and journey's end.
To bring things to a point,
To bring things to florescence,
Consummation in all things
Since the immensity of all things
Lies in the Idea.
Beyond sight,
But in souls' desire,
Yearning beyond the stars,
And the far away blue heavens.
For the "One who dwells in the High and Lofty Place".

Henrietta Hick

A Night Out

The lights were dim, in the place we met
He sat by me in the discotheque
Said "Hello" and lit my cigarette
I saw his face in the glow of the light
Smiling and handsome, for me just right
The place was packed, it was Saturday night
The dinner was lovely, I was full of joy
To be out and about with an attentive boy
I was flattered by his devoted care
No mention of the difference in age
To offer going "dutch" I didn't dare
On the way home, in his little old car
Broke down twice, didn't get far
Got it to a garage, then started to walk
A beautiful night, we didn't talk
No need to, there was nothing to tell
We knew each other so very well
Happy to be together regardless of time
I was so proud to be out with someone so fine.
Hope to repeat it someday soon
Maybe next time there will be a harvest moon
Home at last it's been such fun
My night out with my only son

Evelyn Handforth

Sunken Village

On Sunday mornings - and perhaps others, too,
The bells swing silently,
Moved by the current of passing fishes.

In the surrounding churchyard
Damp ghosts gossip, whispering
Of their morbid drownings,
The unfairness of double death.

Eels slide along the street,
Entering the shops, the empty
Bakers and greengrocers and barbers
With nothing for the weekend.

They say, - whoever they may be -
That once a year,
At Hunter's moon,
The village surfaces,
Heaving itself above the jealous water
Which gushes foaming from the church conning tower.

Then the ghosts shudder and sigh,
Moan and grumble,
They should have been lifted,
Transplanted,
By their uncaring descendants.

In Pompeii the living perished, too

Ann Harrison

The Winter's Wold

Here January's rimy scene unfolds,
Shows winter's wold subdued.
Now blows the biting east wind keen,
Across a landscape white.
The robin's song unheard above the whine,
Lost amidst the frozen, tortured, gorse.
No comforts sent herein to ease,
Whilst natures whims confound.
Tired grasses yearn for summer's breeze,
Gripped tight in frost bound earth.
Days now dawn then quick recede,
Memories fanciful of spring's long past,
Picture nature's garnished shrines
With flowing swards of daffodil,
Her monument profound.
The wold our everlasting friend,
In winter's cold embrace sleeps on.

Ray Hand

214

Celandines

Farewell the winter hour, often dark and bleak'
Golden celandines fain court the sun's timidity
To flaunt their burnished stars against winters grief,
And all excited glow above the heart-shaped leaf.
Beauteous as innocence before it is forever lost
To tears of unbelieved reality indelibly embossed.
Out-stretched petals, slivered gold, adorn the sun-bathed grass,
Blossoms all a'lingering before the precious hour should pass . . .
The precious hour will fleet away, brightened petals strain unfurled,
Soon to fade and fall as dust among the wreckage of the world.
The joyous child, in eager haste, now stoops, with eager face,
To clasp the linear stems, then up-turn glance, and hurry on a'pace,
A'feared of all the dipperling shade trespassing the bower,
Shadowed o'er by scudding clouds, forerunning to the coming shower.

Frank Henson

Remedy

Unbelievable, the best time of my life; the only time I ever got things right;
Sitting there with you all night, being there with you, for you; rarest of pleasures.

All those fires, those months of vast, intense and yet invisible fires
That sealed your presence deep behind my eyes;
All those speechless moments, listening to you speak,
Keeping me from all that was to come and make me weak.

I'm hungry for you; I'm flayed alive and lost,
I'm torn for you, a jagged, ripped reminder of all that seemed to happen there between us,
Hoping I could be the one to bring you home.

The quest for lack of lonliness besieged me there,
I wished for you, I wished your happiness would
Soon arrive, including me would be a miracle, but that aside,
I wished for it to come at you, gushing through
The channels, carrying positive and permanent release to calm your questioning.

Could I help you on your way in all of this?
Just tell me what you need, want, wish for, and let me bring you back again, out of sadness;
Heavy skies with cold regrets do clear,
And if I stand in the light I'll get out of your eyes,
And if I stand in the shadows I'll get out of your doorway,
But only when I know that you are happy now.

Past hurts, past hauntings and deceits, the giving in, not recognising past defeats,
Delays, distractions, I have been there too; now let me be a remedy for you.

I wish I'd known, I wish I'd known
That I could be the one to bring you home.

Wendy Hanstock

215

The Lover

Never have I met
Someone so real
And I can't help
This way I feel

I think of a world without you
It makes me feel sad and blue
Never have I thought
Loving you could be so true

I know not what you need
I know not what you want
But I do know what I feel
And I think you know this could be real

Every time you go away
Feels like emptiness inside
A lot of tears I have cried
But you are always on my mind

Your life should be filled with happiness
With love and sweet caress
Not much of this you possess
Which is why I would like it to progress

A man of such beauty
Who could ask for more
Which is why I want you to know
It's you I adore!

Michelle Hewer

Mary Virgin Mother

Whatever our sin
Whatever our sorrow
Mary is with us
Today and tomorrow

A light in the darkness
A hope in despair
She'll save us from danger
We know that she cares

Hope rests with Her
The Saviour of all
Pray to Her daily
Answer Her call

When down and depressed
Worried and scared
Call upon Mary
Give Her your prayers

Help when it's needed
Love when it's sought
Through Her saving grace
To Heaven we're brought

Glenda Jones

Lost Generation

They were so young as they marched to war
And saw death and horror they never saw
Before some came back to tell of that horror hell
People shout no more war
Then another war starts same as before
Another generation called to fight and serve
Why don't people be good on the good earth
War is wrong God in the bible said
If we go on killing no-one will be left to bury the dead
So turn to God and serve
Be good on the good earth

George Hall

Love

Limpid eyes, ears pricked
And throbbing purring greeting!
A cat I love, that isn't mine
Gives back that love at every meeting.
Has she a name?
I've never heard it spoken.
Not 'cupboard love' she never gets a token.
What is it then, a mumbled word of love?
An ear that's scratched? A fondling of her side
As she rolls from side to side
On the pavement in the dust?
Even in the rain, the pavements cold and wet
She never fails to express herself
Her damp coat turned to jet.
She'll emerge from under a car,
From under a hedge, from around a wall -
I could never pass her by - never at all.
She'll follow me, tail held up high,
Then skip in front and my oh my!
I nearly step on her!
So what strange bond exists between us two?
This cat that lives with someone else
Yet loves me true.

Joan Hall

The Quietness Of Rowell

Such a lovely place to have a home,
With a special peace, I've never known
Surrounded by nature, far and wide
And a beautiful garden, which is their pride.
There's plenty to do in the length of a day
You suddenly could get called away,
To guide the cows to the top of the lane,
And watch they don't come back again.
All part of life in this wonderful place
And the sweet smell of nature,
Blowing in your face.
Back to the garden where there maybe,
A special place, where you sit for a while
And think of things you have to face.
But wherever you stand in the garden,
It takes your breath away,
There's life growing all around you,
In a wonderful array.
A long way from the busy roads,
And down some winding lanes,
To the quietness of "Rowell"
I will come back again.

Judith A. Healey

My Godmother

My godmother is special
In oh so many ways
Her beauty is astounding
Her voice is full of praise

I've never heard her raise her voice
Or shout in any way
That's why I chose Aunt Glenys
To be my mum today

God he helped me choose her
For this special day
He knows she is so special
In a special kind of way

Gemma Jones (Age 11)

A Magical Trip

the pearly sprays of moonlight sparkle against the wall
Surrounded by depths of water and mist we fall
Pushing the force deeper and deeper into each other
Tearing, biting, screaming, fighting but we don't suffer
Our separate lives unfold to become one
Fading into the rain, moulding our bodies into the sun

We are Gods praying to the night
We are vampires dreading the thought of light
We are the dead, lost and now we've returned
We are the living with no feelings of concern

Now that the twisting blinding drops of rain subside
All that is left is for us to hold each other tight and cry
Remember the unicorn burrowing its horn into the rainbow
The perfect body of the goddess making love to us in the snow
Remember when we became the mystical king and queen
Dancing in the sparkling fountain wearing gold sequins
Our separate wondering thoughts being shared
Realising that we could love each other and care

Thank you for sharing this trip with me
Thank you for leaving and setting me free

Maxine Hall

Annabel The Goat

She came to me in all her splendor her coat the sleekest brown
She stood so demure as I looked her up and down
It was then I fell in love with her much to my dismay
Her beautiful face not more than an inch away
I gave her free reign on the front field
The well stocked front garden she took to in her stride
It only took two days for her to show her mettle
Her warm and cosy shed I soon had to fettle
I found out that my neighbour was also a great friend
Or so thought Annabel as her sheep she chased around
Her milk was non-existent the reason for her stay
She looked into my eyes and quickly ran away
A friend was what she needed so our neighbour said
So a rare breed Golden Guernsey we shelled out money for
Annabel took one look and head down made her charge
Not in here she made a stand could we put the other goat
A new shed we had to buy to house the Golden Guernsey
At last I had the milk that was so badly needed
Adding up the cost made me understand
Why people bought their milk from the man who came around.

Elizabeth Bell Hewitt

Visiting Dad

At Christmas I cut holly,
Coiled it into a wreath,
You stood by me in the garden,
But I did not see you at the grave.

At Easter I picked a host
Of golden daffodils, a posy of primroses.
You walked up the lane with me,
But I could not find you in the cemetery.

Summer, sweet pea with scissors snipped,
Such colour, what fragrance.
You wandered by the flower beds,
But the graveyard was empty when I went.

Michaelmas daisies, dahlias bunched
In my hands. You watched smiling.
By the headstone, having filled the vase,
I waited, but you did not come.

I hear your footsteps cross the yard.
The sheep crowd round you in the field.
You turn to look from the tractor seat,
Or lean on the gate and adjust your cap.

Through the seasons I have gone to find
You so easily at home on the farm.
But when I visit the churchyard
    You are never there.

Kate Harkness

My Father's Coat

It is old and it is beautiful
It's colour lovely brown
It was worn by my dear father
In the country and the town
My father loved to wear it
In bygone days of yore
And now he's gone I love to wear
The coat my father wore
It was part of a legacy
He left me in his will
And 16 years further on
This coat I am wearing still
I have worn it at many functions
Pulled apples in tall trees
With it's fashion and wearing potential
I can wear it where I please
And like my father I have worn it
In bygone days of yore
I will always be very proud to wear
The coat my father wore
This coat holds precious memories
Of a loving father kind and true
Sweet precious childhood memories
And happy manhood memories too

Jack Howie

Reflections

Cast thoughts of concern and doubt away
Then think about some halcyon day.
Reflect upon your inner thought,
Where only true peace of mind can be sought.
Close out thoughts of doubt and fear,
Your way may then become more clear.
Speak words kind sincere and true,
Such as you would wish to listen to.
Relax, maybe meditate,
You'll find it never is too late,
To find that peace you contemplate

Brian Hughes

Christopher

Christopher was a little boy,
That lived in a world of his own,
He had no mummy or daddy,
Nor did he have a true home.

His mummy and his daddy died,
In a car crash, when he was two,
All he has left is a photo of them,
And a bible saying "Love will renew".

No one seems to want him,
No-one seems to care,
No-one to give him a cuddle,
Or show him love is still there.

He is 7 years old now and is growing fast,
All he wants is a true home and lots of love that will last,
The orphanage is the only place he has ever known,
To him, this place is security and his only home.

He doesn't ask for much in life,
Just to be guided on his way,
By a loving family, who will help him along,
And show him the difference between right and wrong.

He didn't ask to be alone,
But with a true family and a real home,
They can give him the love he has never yet seen,
Until that day comes, he can only dream.

Barbara Holme

Anger

Anger is when my brother is nasty to me,
When I fall out with Katie,
Anger is when people leave me out.
If my mum starts to shout.
Anger is when I don't know what to write,
When I can't get to sleep at night,
Anger is when it's not fair,
When my socks are not in a pair,
Anger is when I'm feeling blue,
What does anger mean to you?

Sarah Hill (Age 9)

Holy Fire

Baptism bound in holy pews,
Of this ancient religion,
Above, soaring arches, flared,
Proclaim our new devotion.
Twisted pillars of granite oak,
Solid against the storm,
And crypt darkness, waiting, needing,
Listening for your footsteps.

Hazel Hopes

Living A Lie

Pretending we're together
When we're really apart.
Pretending we're in love
When we've lost all heart.

Three years of saying,
But not meaning, "I love you"
Three years of replying
And Lying, "I love you too".

We say it's for the children,
The reason we live this lie
Fooling no one, they know
We've said good-bye.

We only deceive ourselves
Friends and family can see
The only story tellers now;
Are you and me.

Marie-Louise Hull

Rabin

Lived his life,
Brought to death,
Everyone hung,
On his every breath.

Campaigned for all,
The guns to cease,
Wanted quiet, but more,
Wanted peace,

Shot down trying to finish,
What he had begun,
In cold blood,
From an assasins gun.

A world united,
His ultimate plan,
Wrecked by a bullet,
From a countryman.

Timothy Hughes

Scary Hairy

In between the bits of pipework that run underneath the sink
In the corner where the wall and old bath panel try to link
There are gaps and cracks and even a considerable hole
Which is partly hidden by the stuff we use to clean the bowl
While to us these dirty crevices may look an awful sight
There are others who will seek them out because they are just right
And it happens that the one in our bathroom was duly spied
By a visitor who subsequently made her home inside
There's a dusty patch of webbing in the corner by the floor
And every day its owner seems to grow a little more
It hides away until you're sitting prone upon the loo
Then when it knows you can't escape, it wanders into view
While you palpitate with knickers down around about your feet
Cold sweat will make you tremble as you swiftly leave the seat
With bated breath you hurriedly commence your exit path
Only then to see another monster lurking in the bath
With the hoover motor roaring you return in to the room
And with gleeful smile observe as they are sucked up to their doom
But the silence of the cupboard lets them crawl back from the pipe
To creep up to your bedroom and give you another fright
Now the two you thought were vanquished have produced a family
And the evidence is there in every room for you to see
Having found that scaring humans is a fascinating game
They ensure that generations of their offspring do the same.

Andrew Hodson

The Fox

He hurries and he scurries, my goodness how he's scared.
He'd like to take a little look, but wonders if he dares.

Last night he didn't have a care, the world seemed safe and sound,
But now today is different . . . . it's the chasing by those hounds.

His mother taught him how to run, and frolic, hunt and play.
She never warned him that he'd be hunted himself one day.

He hears a sound of "Tally Ho", and knows they must be near.
He'll have to make a run soon and overcome his fear.

The dogs are getting closer now - they're ready for a kill.
Whatever has got into man, that this gives him a thrill?

The fox has made a run for it, across the field he starts . . . .
The hounds are quick to follow him, wherever he may dart.

Poor little fox just has to hide, he's running short of breath.
He looks for somewhere safe to hide. He's not ready yet for death.

The pack of dogs have found him - his life was very short.
His tail removed, men and dogs go home. Can we really call this sport?

Laura Hobbs

Marriage

The wonderful thing about marriage (I think),
Is washing the pots every day.
Making the beds and cooking the food,
You don't get a great time to play.

Cleaning the bathroom and dusting the stairs,
Washing those dirty old clothes.
Cleaning the windows and polishing the brass,
Rubbing that brass till it glows.

Peeling the potatoes and doing the greens,
Making a pudding each day.
Fetching the coal in and cleaning the grate,
As I said there is no time to play.

Hoovering the carpets and polishing the floor,
The times gone before you can blink.
There's hundreds of jobs and the money's not good,
Still, that's the wonder of marriage (I think).

A.B. Hughes

My Yorkshire Terrier

A perky little fellow,
With a coat of steel blue and tan,
A mind as quick as lightening
And a best friend to man.

A friendly greeting is always assured,
Morning, noon and night,
His big brown eyes are staring
As I come into sight.

He goes to fetch my slippers
As he looks at my friendly face,
Part of his daily greeting
As he goes off at such a pace.

When strangers call at the house,
He's there to look them over,
Brave as a lion, despite his size,
He's certainly no pushover.

A lot of love and a daily walk,
It is his bit of pleasure,
And in return,
Has given me, a love I will always treasure.

Although I know when we have to part,
There will be lots of tears,
But many happy memories,
He brought me through the years.

Hazel Hough

The Home Coming

I walked from the twisted wreck
That exploded round my head
I walked for miles in the dark
Endless fields through a park

Then suddenly I was home
Mum was crying she dropped the phone
Dad was shaking pouring whiskey
Did he really walk right through me

They talked as if I wasn't there
About a crash - no survivors
She cried my name again and again
A silent scream was all I made

The time stood still as I materialised then
For one last moment I waved goodbye
Before my journey to Heavens Gate
My home coming had been made . . .

Frank Howarth-Hynes

A Cardboard Box

No one cares, he's on his own
A cardboard box that's become his home
Sleeping rough in door-ways, under bridges of decay
Ragged clothes and hungry to face another day

Weatherbeaten face, older than his years
Hostile world around him, eyes reflect his fears
Circumstances beyond him, add to his depression
Another forgotten statistic, caused by the recession.

Rita Humphrey

Celebrate

Celebrate because it's over
Celebrate because we won
Celebrate because we're at peace
Europe is as one

Be happy because I went hungry
Be happy because food was scarce
Be happy because I lost my home
For the innocent life was unfair

Be scared about the air raids
Be scared about the bombs
Be scared that one day you might die
When Hitler's parcels fall from the sky

Be heartbroken about your loved ones
Lost on a far distant shore
Be heartbroken they never came back
You won't see them anymore

Be praying for the prisoners
Be praying for the dead
Be praying for the Germans, Brits and Jews
As they lie on the death beds

So celebrate because it's over
Celebrate because we won
But be sorry it ever started
Because it never should have begun.

Tracy Hulley (Age 15)

Lachrimae

A face of parts
And sorrow and tears

Softly in my dreams appears
abstract, romantic but feared.

Shades of light, so cruelly thrown
dapple
its mournful crown.

Grey are its sea-salted tears
rolling down the vivid years

Driven by such guilty horrors

Soon my face disappears
in its place, this sorrowful face leers.

A face of parts
and sorrow and tears

from within such anguish
inevitably appears.

Peter Illing

Outcasts

You ask me why? The eyes beneath the unkempt hair
Grew weary, his voice was rough, as if you really care
Clutching the empty bottle, he drained the evil smelling dregs
And hurled it at the wall, I saw his trembling legs
Give way, as falling on the ragged bed
He fumbled in his pocket, and looking at me, said
"I am one of hundreds meths, drugs, the lot
Misfit, outcast, layabout, a drunken, broken sot
Your modern world, society, turns from me in distaste
Do gooders shake their heads and whisper
Oh, dear what a waste."
He laughed, his pallid features creased in silent mirth
I felt that I was looking at the loneliest man on earth.
The box like room was stifling, the filth beyond endurance
I turned to go, but was held by the searching perseverance
As shaking hands empties pockets, I waited, at a loss
The hands withdrew and silently held out the Victoria Cross

Irene Hustwait

224

Senior Schooldays

With dignified tempo and August design
We reign in the fifth Form and Sixth Form sublime;
We view from a lofty disdain each new kid
And make sure they do whatever we bid!

For Seniors and Prefects and Captains are we
Whose Word is the Law in all Dignity;
We have our own Study and Places at table,
While those lesser fry have to go where they're able!

The Staff consult us, the Headmaster too.
We don't put our hand up to go to the loo!
We come and we go, more or less as we please
And do all our study in comfort and ease!

And when school is done, we don't rush with the crowd,
We're far too official, we're much, much too proud;
We stay on to plan and suggest with the view
Of making the School much better for you!

Then, Duty behind us, we go to our homes
And get down to study with masses of Tomes
For 'O' Levels; 'A' Levels or G.C.S.E
As befits the High Office of Authority!

Reg Hunter

Another

The air was heavy with the suggestion of sex
As a draught blew around her picture
Displayed for all to see in a reticent corner of his mind.
Another's lips pressed closer to his.
The reasonable man is not excitable
He has normal powers of self-control.
Books on religion, philosophy, morality stood upright
Taunted by primitives emblazoned on scarlet walls,
Beneath exotic skin gleamed under scented oil
As stealthy snow fell layer upon buried layer
Unseen through the half-uncurtained window.
Drenched silk shuddered upon contact as it was removed,
Stiff-collared shirts lay in ruins
Thrust carelessly beside her unopened letters.
Conquered by the overwhelming opulence of hot flesh.
Disreputable darkness mixed with wanton whiteness in the secret dusk.
While deep underground the phone rang consistently
With fervour
From the undisclosed regions of his heart.

Katherine Hubbard

225

The Prisoner

She had a parlour
It possessed her
Private, perfect and polished
"A tomb of rich lavender wax"

Sacred, sparkling glass cabinet
Trophies of bone china tea cups
Wasted weekly - used rarely
"Waiting for a funeral"

Footstep free carpet
Carefully placed cushions
On wrinkle free sofa

Posh parlour grate
And Wedgewood ornaments
Dusted daily
"Gazed at often"

Shining brass companion set
"Never glinting in the warmth of a fire"

She stares in horror
Old bed placed in the midst of her perfection
Commode near by
"Her prison now complete"

S. Hulley

The Moon

The moon between the clouds at night,
Is the most wonderful sight.
Surrounding stars in a certain way,
Romantic things two people say.

Unbelievable the effect it has,
Like the sound of distant jazz.
Harmony and expressions mixed,
The stare is held indefinitely fixed.

Flowers and chocolates can't compare,
With the moons reflection in the nights warm air.
Fading deep into dark space.
Changing making a new and different place.

The sun arrives although it seems,
That the moon holds peoples favourite dreams.
Similar but not the same,
Like the start of a whole new game.

M. Hobbs

Do Birds Fly In The Fog?

Do birds fly in the fog?
Eyes straining to find their way,
Little brains frantic with worry,
Senses and judgment overtaxed?

Do birds fly in the fog?
Moving forward blindly,
Heedless of what dangers lie ahead,
Of unseen forces sweeping across their path?

Or do birds take shelter in the fog?
With fate postponed eluding fear,
Laughing at fools who struggle against
The awful, fleeting power of the unknown.

Jennifer Lyn Howard

The Silent Waltz

An air is there when the music fades
That draws these two together,
Though they remain unaware
Of the ties that will bind them
When the cloak of mystery falls
And crashes around their feet.
The swirling of robes
And the murmurs of speech
Are silenced as they near.
His hand outstretched, she looks in his eyes;
She sees them both in a ring of pure gold.
He looks deeper into her gaze
And knows he's captured her heart.
Closer they will be for now and forever
As they dance their own steps
To a distant beat of the silent waltz.

Jenny Hughes

Dead Blossom

Why should ever innocence die?
White blossom has fallen
on concrete.

And a man, who once was a child,
to whom the laughter of summers by-gone
is unwanted memory now.

For to the stained snow,
the pure sky will show,
as a mirror,
the cruel wounds of time.

Barbara Hughes

Imperial Flight

She moved her wings in wavering cascading motions
As the sea yet again tore the landscape,
She was hundreds of feet above the crashing waves
But she saw it all with her eagle eye.
She saw the landscape slowly disappearing
Her nesting places being torn from the earth,
She would swoop down to the sea with agonised angry cries
But the sea was far too busy to hear her screams,
She swept down in defiance to fight the power
That was taking away her home.
But she knew if she touched the power
Her flight would be gone,
She was alone in flight watching the sea tear up the ground
She was helpless . . . . like her nestlings.
So cruelly snatched at and pulled away to drown
She screamed her wrath and anger as tears fell from her eyes,
Her children were no more, never to taste the skies.
She cursed the sea and dashed the land
And vowed never to give up the fight,
For imperial was she the queen of the sky
And the power had taken her children to die.
She vowed to return in the darkness of night
And continue her vengeance in imperial flight.

G.B. Horne

First Aid

Whilst sat at home, one summers day
My son and daughter were at play
In the garden, I thought Safety First
But what was that, a noise outburst
A crash, a scream, I jumped from my chair
My heart in a panic, my mind in a scare
Ran into the garden, there lay my son
I looked for movement, there was none
What could I do for my son who was in need
I had that chance to learn, that chance has gone.
Who is this coming, a member of St. John
Over the fence he did climb,
Speed of the essence, the race against time,
He brought my son round in just a short while
As I looked on, I saw my son smile
Tomorrow I must go, to learn a new trade
To become a master in the art of FIRST AID.

R. Holmes

Grandma's Unplanned Trip

The birthday lemonade was poured, when Grandma trod on Rob's skateboard,
Grandma had come to celebrate, she never planned a solo skate.
She whizzed across the white tiled floor, and then out through the open door,
Into the street she sped with ease, remembering to bend her knees,
She cruised down hill, around two bends, she hadn't time to wave to friends.
She passed the shops, she passed the church,
She gave a wobble and a lurch,
She saw the vicar stand and stare, and hoped he'd offer up a prayer
Police car sirens wailed and whined, but Grandma left them far behind
The railway crossing up ahead, Gran hopes the lights will stay at red
The lights are green, her path is clear,
She's heading now for Carter's weir.
The water's deep, her speed is fast,
This nightmare trip must end at last
And as she makes her final dash,
Gran knows there'll be a mighty splash.

Elizabeth Hughes

Christmas Through The Eyes Of A Child

Oh what joy I feel on this Christmas Eve Night,
I look all around me and see a wonderful sight.

Streamers on the ceiling,
Cards on the wall,
Presents on the sideboard,
For me, Mom, Dad and all.

The Christmas Tree Glistens,
With all its tinsel and lights
And right at the top sits a fairy
So heavenly white.

Outside the window
The snow starts to fall
Soon covering the fence
The driveways, the lawn.

I'm off to bed now
To sleep and to dream
Of the lovely things
That tonight I have seen.

R.S. Hughes

Hope

Hope is a door that never closes,
A room wherein one's soul reposes,
Hope is all things to all people,
The cross we see at the top of the steeple,
A shining light when dreams are low,
With joy becomes a golden glow,
Suffusing all the inner eye sees,
Rippling out over land and seas.

Hope is a gift we are given when born,
Never to leave us from morn to morn,
Always to dwell in the depths of our being,
Despair and despondence ever expelling,
As Phoenix it rises from long-dead ashes,
Spiralling upwards - our dreams it surpasses,
Lifting the spirit with love excelling,
Life's sin and sorrow ever dispelling.

Hope is a light that never grows dim,
Illumines our body without and within,
Present in the darkness of Stygian gloom,
Blazing forth when faith comes home;
To live in thoughts humbly expectant,
Of earthly sorrows simply transient,
A spark creating another sense,
A living flame no flood will quench.

Elizabeth Hope

The Disregarded Battlefield

Grim caretaker of bygone hours of pain,
Of quietness where once brave deeds were wrought,
Where raging conflicts to and fro were fought,
Where men for freedom and for right were slain;
Impassive watcher of the bleak terrain,
A wilderness enfolding sufferings bought
By conscripts with but one demanding thought -
This fearsome hell must never be again;
Where hardened warriors came at length to die,
With tired minds and memories afar,
Imploring nations never more to vie
In bloody feuds that hope and truth debar:
But still humanity must weep and sigh,
For still the Martian gate remains ajar.

W.H. Hodkinson

Criterion

Judgements are chameleons of time
A paradox to a death from a birth
Ever changing 'twixt vile and sublime
Weaving destiny for Man and Earth

One agreement whether elder or child
Could be suffering for other's unseen
The key to right shifting and beguiled
In bondage of law or ignorance mean

What measure or gauge principled matter?
Is avarice the stone of criterion?
Should seas of compassion reign over latter?
What fulcrum levers judgements on?

Why eons of hunger and drought in nations
Billions decaying to skeletal dust
Creatures succumbing to oil and radiations
Extinct and consumed by judgmental cost?

Carry on blinkered shall be ill-fated
Heading to darkness and poisoned air
Earth unsustained and stripped naked
Humanity without: crying despair

If love is the scale to read the balance
How can nation's cruel advances barter?
Watching after, caring all-sides parlance
Must be judgement's new criterion charter

Linda Hoult

Lawn Maintenance

Why to lament, old time unspent,
With views that grow much longer?
When grass still green, will go unseen,
In creasing what you ponder.

Old lawns unkempt, from time well spent,
Ooze fresh grass fumes and flowers;
When mowers and fun, and jobs well done,
Leave space for happy hours.

Enjoy the grass, enjoy the flowers,
Think not of uncut scandal.
The grass grows right, when out of sight,
It's nothing you can't handle.

Chris Hollingsworth

If Only

If only I had not eaten that cake
Or the apple pie I decided to make

Nibbled tasty crisps, ate some sweets
Plus other known forbidden treats

Always on a sensible diet next week
Alas again lack, the control I seek

If only I'd been firm with my urges
I'd be the slim person that never emerges

Yearning for those slim model looks
That I envy from reading fashion books

If only I'd stuck to the promised plan
But now I've gone and made a strawberry flan

Never mind do more running, burn up the fat
I really could be much bigger than that

Always make the most of the way you are
Be grateful for good health, better by far

Indulge in moderation then no need to ban
Won't then have to say again and again

If only . . .

Maureen Howell

The Grandchrildren

The grandchildren call,
The tall and the small,
Their works of art adorn my walls,
Not for me the Rembrandt's and Van Gough's,
Just one eyed pussycats,
And funny shaped dogs.

"Nan-nan" they shout
"What's for our teas?"
I think please God can't I have any peace,
But when they have gone giving
Me a hug and a squeeze,
I think did I really want
That bit of peace?

Vera Hunt

232

Solitude

Sat alone, all wet and cold,
watching the snow falling;
No one to love, no one to hold,
hungry! thirsty! I am calling.

People ignoring my gentle cry,
as they hurry to their home;
My life is ruined, I want to die,
another night I am left to roam.

Why can't they see I am alone,
needing food, warmth and love;
Tomorrow will be another clone;
I wish I was a beautiful dove.

Then I would be able to fly,
sail away from all this hate;
On the hot sandy beaches I would lie,
and find myself another mate.

Never again will I give my heart,
to another man so easily;
'Cause the pain I felt when we broke apart,
devastated me completely.

Now I have absolutely nothing,
no home, no pride, no life,
I'm alone with just my memories,
in my isolated life.

B. Jacobs

The Garden

I wonder, Dearest, if you see
How beautiful the garden grows;
When spring adorns the apple tree
And June bedecks the Damask
Rose.

This precious plot I daily tend;
A loving task we used to share,
And it's so easy to pretend,
In leafy shadows you're still there.

Now those busy hands are still,
Hands that made these borders
bright,
Summer's promise to fulfil
With fragrant blooms for my
delight.

When spring time crowns the apple
tree
And June bedecks the Damask
Rose,
I wonder, Dear, do you still see,
How beautiful the garden grows.

Stella Hodgkiss

Seasons

Buds 'n' blooms are all around,
Breaking through the frosty ground,
Growing bigger day by day,
For it's Spring time, natures way,
Reaching up towards the sun,
Now that Summer has begun,
Opening up their pretty heads,
Standing tall in their flower beds,
All too soon, Autumn has come,
Greener and greener the garden's become,
Petals are falling, leaves dropping down,
Insects going in deep underground,
Winter's here, soon snow will be falling,
Out in the garden, children snowballing,
Not a sign of a plant or flower there,
As they're waiting for the Spring of next Year.

F.P. Hone

Vancouver Island

Hiawatha's spirit lingers where his feet have never wandered
On this island's sheltered sea-shore, far from distant Gitche Gumee.
This horizon, full of splendour, quite defies a fair description
So majestic are those mountains, snow-capped mountains of the coast range,
Glistening in the winter sunshine, glowing pink at evening sunset.
That, and other secret glimpses peeping through the distant valleys
Paint an ever-changing picture, changing moods, forever varied,
Making this a perfect setting whence to contemplate the future.
No environment could ever quite surpass in unspoilt beauty
This remarkable creation, still untouched by bricks and mortar,
Still preserved for nature's purpose.

Here the pioneers had laboured, clearing land for cultivation,
Cutting down prolific woodland in their zealous indiscretion.
Worthy though their good intentions, came the need for some reflection
To examine consequences of a reckless exploitation
Of some selfish enterprises which ignored the rights of others.
These minorities created such unrest in those whose foresight
Visualised the widespread chaos which results from such intrusions,
Such abuse of nature's garden that the government enacted
Common sense decrees protecting these defenceless trees from people,
Irresponsible invaders of this realm of rich resources . . . . .
Introducing CONSERVATION

John Hobson

Green September

A green eyed boy of gentle ways
Took my hand in autumn days.
With smile as warm as summer haze
He held my heart in September.

Alone each night with such tender dream
September flowed like a peaceful stream.
Out love grew on like an evergreen
Through the lovely nights of September.

Yet still the thoughts of my yesterdays
Lingered on in these autumn days.
My green eyed boy of gentle ways
Was losing my love in September.

In a lonely square under starry skies
We kissed and said our last goodbyes.
And with tears that shone in his green eyes.
Our love passed by, like September.

Sandra Humble

Winter

The sky above is sad and grey
It's now December, no longer May
The leaves have withered on trees so bold
My fingers and toes tingle with cold

The woodland creatures are fast asleep
In nests and burrows warm and deep
They rest and dream and wait for Spring
And all the beauty that season brings

In the park the lake is frozen
And ducks and geese appear to be skating
Winter's magic is everywhere
Whoever could think it cold and bare.

Carol Howard

Evening Sunshine

Late evening sunshine, splitting the heavy clouds,
sending a piercing shaft of brightness
down. Even those ominous, dark clouds
suddenly have a silver halo - no less -
and - see, how the garden colours glow!
Listless flowers raise their heads, and nod in gratitude,
whilst silent birds find voice, and start to sing again.
There is an expectant air; suddenly a gayer mood.
A solitary butterfly appears, and alights
for a moment, opening and shutting dazzling wings -
preening - before joining another, and flying off
together, two such small, delightful, coloured things.
You have the feeling, all and everything rejoices
with the coming of this one small show of light
and warmth. It highlights the vicious gnats
that, appearing from nowhere, fight
and dance, in airy abandonment.
The tireless bees take heart, and
set to work, on last pollen-laden
flights - a willing, eager, little band
of workers. Their cheerful drone makes
a perfect end to a summer's day
that began by being sullen, dull,
and set in such a melancholy grey.

Joyce Hockley

Corners Of My Mind

I've searched a thousand thoughts or more
To see if I could find the secrets of the Universe
As deep down in my mind I know I hold the secrets
To the mystery of life
The sweet soft sound of water flowing softly through the vale
The sound of softly falling rain
The whispering wind at night
The night and day the sun and moon
That gives the world its light

All in all part
Are part of the mysteries
I've searched the whole world over but nowhere could I find
A place that would hold everything
Like the corners of my mind

Sylvia Hopcroft

Beginnings

Begin,
      birth;   a seed changed by time,
               flowers into a perfect
               innocent being,
               breath

Begin,
      story;   fantasy words reflected gems
               in the eyes of a happy child,
               peace

Begin,
      game;   a whisper hidden behind
               hands of a silent room,
               listen

Begin,
      life;   after the innocent age
               descends, ascends,
               mountains

Begin,
      death;   new life perhaps somewhere, elsewhere,
               anywhere I don't know but
               I have begun,
               journey.

Jenny Hodsoll

Survival

Can we survive
      on fields of green,
And never walk where
      others have been?

Can we survive
      in this age of greed?
Too many people, animals
      and mouths to feed!

Can we survive
      in this modern world
Of too many machines
      and computers untold?

Can we survive
      and be on our toes
To keep alive?
      God only knows.

Shelagh Conrad Joynes

The Enchanted Garden

O' loves sweet spirit fleeing
O'er yonder shimmering pools
Whilst two lovers cry
Stay with my soul
O' beauteous spirit beyond the velvet sky
As twinkling stars cast silvery shadow
Amidst yonder swaying reeds
Gently floating amidst yonder boughs
Whilst onward life's stream flows
It's sweet arraignment onward
Stretching far beyond life's vale

Fred Houghton

The Panther

Silent as the night,
On a cold winters eve.
Shining, yellow suns,
Glare from the dark, murderous form.

Leaping, bounding,
Full of life.
Black Satan moves,
Through the undisturbed trees.

A yawning roar,
Echoes long and deep.
Scraping paws,
Silently carve the defenceless offering.

No redress,
For the wretched creature.
Its life is extinguished,
Revenging some past sin.

The dark ungodly shadow,
Departs the deathly scene.
Then stops and turns,
Acknowledging his own dreadful fate.

Janet Hood

Easter

The snowdrops grace my garden,
Assuring me anew
Of life that is eternal
And love forever true.

Of victory after striving
And through the darkness light.
Of strength in seeming frailty
And beauty infinite.

And - beyond all understanding,
Peace now and pardon free:
Since Jesus rose from death, and Lives,
For us, for them - and me.

Past depth and breadth of measure,
More than words can ever say,
Are the glory and the comfort
And the joy of Easter Day.

Gwendoline James

Village Life

Wanting to take my shoes off
I reach the last part of the exhibition
And the picture of a woman standing
Against a stone wall in a grey village street

She wears a rough woollen scarf against the cold
Looks into the distance
Her eyes holding mine - I am that distance

Eyes imponderable, enduring
And I hear her say
I have witnessed peace and war
Where are my kinfolk, my children?

On either side of her, there are men
Sitting in rows, staring into the lens
Drinking, arms round each other's shoulders

- And children (not hers) playing in stubble fields.

Barbara Hughes

In Remembrance To Our Grandad

Sadly I glanced at your old armchair,
Wishing you were sitting there,
We knew you were the very best,
For often we put you to the test.

Our tears you used to wipe away,
On each, and every day,
As the years went rolling by,
We often used to hear you sigh.

To us you were a friend,
Right to the very end,
I wish I could of held your hand,
The night you went to the Promised Land.

You said, we must not weep, or mourn,
But without you, life is so forlorn,
Life must go on, so you say,
For we will meet another day.

Dear God our loss is your gain,
We know now, he has no pain,
Please gently lay him down to rest,
For to us, he was the best.

F.H. Hounsell

Mid Life Crisis

I woke up one morning all perky and bright
Then suddenly felt that all was not right
I ponder a while then quick as a flash
Think yes, tonight is my big birthday bash
You know of course which one I mean
The dreaded five o' and I'm not very keen

Now yesterday's gone, I was feeling just fine
But then of course I was forty-nine
I don't think I'll bother to get out of bed
I've so many notions going round in my head
Will I be able to cope now it's here
That is the thing that I most fear
Shall I get up, and start a new job
Or mope around here, like a big fat slob
You tell me, as you've had your five o'
I suppose you will say yes have a go.

Vera Hobbs

True Friends

Friendship lasts forever within the heart of a child.
Perceived through a pureness and with little demand.
In time one discovers,
Most people use and abuse.
Loyalty and trust become friendships cold rules.

With both the above, believed when true and
Each one defined through an action or two,
It comes as no revelation and no great surprise
That very few friendships are destined to last.

Through sharing belief and sharing each other,
Both lives become richer and stronger together.
A mutual appreciation, heart felt and pure,
Builds a close friendship, doubtless and sure.

Loyalty and trust then become something you do,
Given in friendship and not through a rule.
Once united together you are completely aware,
That nothing can divide you because
You are what you are -
- And that's friends forever.

W.C. Holt

The Angel

Mother I saw an angel today
She would not go away
She asked me if I would like to go to heaven
But, I did not know what to say
She said, I could leave this world behind
To a place of beauty, where I would find
Happiness and joy, where no tears are shed
I could not answer her, only bow my head
She took hold of my hand
She was as cold as ice
Her face was beautiful, she was very nice
I said my mother would cry for me, if I go with you
She replied, That's alright, she can come too
My mothersmiled, she looked as happy as could be
As I held out my hand, for her to come to me
We held hands with the angel, she said close your eyes
When you wake up, you will be in paradise
At the gate's of heaven, we did stand
My mother and I still holding hands
The gate's opened, we went through
To a place called heaven
Where peace and happiness we found
There we will stay, forever bound

Margaret Howard

The Transformation

He sat and stared at his life,
Which hung on the wall like a painting,
Its colours fading with age,
Its clarity marred by the dust of time.

Trapped in the eternal Now,
He fought off another dead-end dream,
And destroyed a new concept
Before it threatened to give birth to reality.

He could not find the new life,
Hidden deep within the shadows of the night;
He lit the last candle,
But still had time to win the fight.

Hope had never left his side,
Keeping him warm in a cold universe,
Which to him was the room
In which his thoughts had lived and died.

He knew it was time to leave
And move on to another place,
Before the hand of fear
Took the key and locked the door.

He walked out of the four walls
That had been his home and prison;
Nothing left but that light within,
Which had set him free to be himself.

Anthony Hunt

Natalie

I remember, I remember the day that you were born
Your little fingers holding mine that warm September morn
'A little girl' the nurse told me perfect in every way
The daughter I had waited for had come this special day
You were such a clever girl excelled in all you tried
I could say you weren't special but you would know I lied
For twelve short years I had you until that fateful night
When I had a frightening phone call and God turned out the light
A car had knocked you over nothing would be the same
You never opened your big blue eyes when I repeatedly called your name
You died on New Year's Eve and left this empty space
Natalie how I loved you and still picture your little face
You'll always be remembered for the special gifts you had
But when you were taken it left me oh so sad!
So until we meet again just wanted you to know
I love you - and miss you why did you have to go?

M.E. Jones

Memories In Patchwork

The patchwork quilt she made with love
And patience o'er the years,
Its deep rich colours tell a tale
Of hopes, and dreams and fears.

In lamplight glow, she'd sit and sew,
And wile away the hours,
With each neat stitch, a memory
She stored 'mongst patchwork flowers.

The smooth white satin filigree
Was once her wedding gown,
The centre piece she worked around,
The jewel in her crown.

The patches blue, and green and pink
And shades of deepest red,
Grew through the years,
And proudly laid, upon her feather bed.

As time passed on her eyes grew dim,
Her fingers, once so nimble,
Were old and frail, too weak to hold
Her needle and her thimble.

The patchwork quilt grandmother made,
Holds happiness and strife,
A treasured heirloom passed to me,
The patchwork of her life.

Maureen Bevan Jones

Words

Words are FOODS
Smell them
Taste them
Chew them
Swallow them
Digest them

Words are KNOWLEDGE
Read them
Learn them
Remember them
Know them
And use them

Words are MUSIC
Feel them
Listen to them
Play your beats to them
And let yourself
Dance to them

Words are WEAPONS
Arm yourself with them
Try to form them
Reshape them
Defend yourself with them
And win your battles of life with them

Semba Jallow-Rutherford

Alone In The Dark

Lightning flashed as the trees came to life
The wind whistled like a werewolf
Animals scream like bats flying past
Twigs crack like the trees are coming to get me
I see loads of dark figures
All around me hooting and howling.
The lightning looks like sharp teeth coming to eat me.
My heart pounds, as the darkness closes.

Mark Jones (Age 10)

Lying In Wait

Lying awake - what is that noise?
Pubs let loose - boys will be boys.
Boozing after time till half-past-two,
A man's gotta do what a man's gotta do.

Smashing telephone boxes in,
They're high on drugs. They like the din.
Working three jobs and claiming dole;
Neighbours dare not tell a soul.

Rubbish strews across the lawn.
Needles dumped, condoms and porn.
Drunken parents. Foul-mouthed kids.
Wheelie bins without their lids.

Gardens with borders of doggy-do,
Using the porch as an instant loo.
Cars with no tax, no wheels, no doors.
Kids young as five shouting 'Up Yours!'

Stereos blaring at all hours of night;
Pensioners huddling and shaking with fright.
Existing inside a council estate
Is like being on death row . . . . with a very long wait!

Megan S. Jameson

Journey Of Life

Enter from the free wide world
To the flat secretive island
Walk round the rings of time
Like a maze
Above the witches fingers, bold eyes gaze down
On a forest of tall strange, silent trees
The air full of the sound of humming bees
The monstrous giants with furious claws
Desperately clutching on to life
Hopeless
Clasping on determinedly
Dying
Gone

Sally Jones (Age 15)

Time

If there were no yesterday's
I would have nothing to regret
No memories to remember
No bad times to forget
The struggles of today
Is what I have to face
But time ticks on and ages me
With little or no grace
We all need our tomorrow's
To help us on life's way
Try to wake with a smile
It's another new day.

Amanda James

"Spirit Guide"

Mystical figure appears
Carrying a diamond headed spear
Mercury eyes ease hidden fear
Closing elderly hand over a few pebbles
Upon opening tightly grip
Pebbles were no more
Profound words followed
(many turn to dust, those with wisdom shall not)
Person of vision felt to be Methuselah
Light of life remains clear
Ending of struggles near

Alan Jones

Morning Muse

The pygmy butterflies flitting in and out of the jungle of giant weeds
The sky a stark scarlet claret in the morn
Corn growing long golden and strong in the fields beyond
The myriad birds pecking at bread laid out on the ground
Their heads busily bobbing up and down
I thrill as I hear the train whistle shrill
Taking commuters to work others to play
Speeding smoothly along the track
Past curious grazing animals in the field
Then out of my daydream and in for a cup of tea
And the reality of the news on T.V.

David Julian

Corridors

This maze of corridors that life takes us through,
Doors leading to sadness or sights that are new,
Once doors are opened we cannot return,
We take new pathways but seldom we learn.
The sadness we find is not always our making,
Doors we should pass, chances we're taking,
Hallways we've stood in, which way should we turn,
Doors we have missed and forever will yearn.
Our lives are all signposted but we don't always heed,
Paths sometimes taken for guilt or for greed,
Running past windows filled with warm light,
Ending in alleyways filled with black night.
Stepping off tracks that seem long and a bore,
Wandering through openings, still wanting more,
The roads are so long, where will it all end,
Come take my hand and travel with me, my friend.

Karan Jackson

Home

There is a house that stands,
Tall, out on the hill.
With flowers cascading,
Down the wall.
The gardens front, mid and rear,
All from an artist's pallet.

The house is not any other house,
But my house.
With the welcoming porch,
And the fresh cut flowers in the window.
The sounds of happiness run through,
The welcoming rooms.

I feel the house takes hold of my troubles,
And carries them as they were its own.
The responsibility of life is blown away
As the following river of pleasure,
Drowns dark fears and replenishes it with light.

Comforting sounds stray from the kitchen.
As delicious aromas fill the air
The chinking of cups and clanging of pans,
Herald the hub-bub of evening,
And I am glad I am home!

Julia Houldsworth (Age 14)

The Sun

There is something that
Makes me hot and get
All red and brown
And when I run it
Always slows me
Down but when
I work so hard
I always get hot
And sweaty but
When I play on
The fields I always
Get hot and sweaty
But when I get under shelter
I am cold

Liam Keefe (Age 8)

November

It's dawn, a cold November sky,
The mist creeps o'er the grass and high
A seagull flaps his lonely way to where and why.
Winter waits suspended while the earth is still asleep
Reluctant trees bend in the breeze
Their leaves they strive to keep.

Let the Autumn come though
Accept the cooling blow
Life is like the seasons
A moving ebb and flow.

Skies of grey soon change to blue
Dark clouds melt away
Take heart and know the earth survives
With Spring another day

Constance L. Jackson

My Children

When God graced me with my first child I couldn't believe my eyes
It was as though an angel had emerged through the perfect cloudless skies
With eyes the colour of chocolate and hair like strands of gold
The most beautiful face I've ever seen a real Irish beauty I'm told

The first few years were fun something different to do every day
But you have to make the most of it as before you know it they're up and away
To give your love to a child is so very rewarding it seems
As nothing stops it getting stronger not even their very loud screams

Then God granted me with another so we waited with anticipation and joy
And then nine months later out came our gorgeous little boy
A real little terror and rogue but a heart made of strawberries and cream
With a face as before, angelic with a temperament calm and serene

These words can not describe even by swearing on an oath
Just how much you two mean to me and just how much I love you both

Alison James

Old Warrior

Marching along so proud with your medals so bright,
Your eyes do deep in sorrow.
Thinking of comrades you had to leave behind,
In the fields of mud and sorrow.

What tales you tell of long ago.
Of battles that were won and lost.
Remembering friends and comrades,
Who lost their lives so long ago,
Never to be forgotten.

The horrors you had to endure.
The smell of fear and death around,
You've never forgotten.

Mud, damp in those trenches so deep,
With rats and fleas encrusted.
Cold which reached your bones.
Even now the thought makes you shudder.

Fields where friends are left behind
Now covered with poppies so bright and red.
Rest the friends and comrades, never to be forgotten.

Margaret Jackson

245

Why Was It So?

A child of man, that we all know,
Thoughts as pure as driven snow;
Innocent and free from care,
Playing with others, likewise, there.

Not yet aware, that soon there'd be
A messenger of infamy;
Bringing death with every stride
Towards a place, where none could hide.

Too late, they saw his evil face
Gazing with a cold embrace;
No time, to stop the spitting flame,
Cutting short, their childish game.

Across our world, deprived and lost,
Rivers of tears turned and tossed;
Increasing, as they spiralled more
Then came to rest, at heaven's door.

For a thousand years, we'll mourn their loss,
As in our hearts, upon a cross
There is embossed, in grief and pain,
A town in Scotland - called Dunblane.

Bill Jamieson

Tramp

Star speckled sky his ceiling,
Grass underfoot his rug,
His meagre diet, to him appealing,
Fresh air his only drug.

Boots of leather and cardboard,
Long since past their prime,
Replacements he just can't afford,
Lack of wealth his only crime.

His heart he avails never,
His feelings are his alone,
Solitude his only endeavour,
Compassion he has never known,

A God fearing man to be sure,
Neither wicked nor even dismayed,
He reasons that the bible is pure,
And Commandments to be obeyed.

His mind works in mysterious ways,
Rejecting all thoughts of a home,
Intent on spending his days,
In the nomadic world of his own.

Brian John King

Dannielle: Sleep Little Princess, Heaven Awaits

D early loved and missed by all
A beautiful princess going to the ball
N eatly dressed in her white satin gown
N ever shall your face fall upon a frown
I nto the ball you came with a swing
E veryone saw you shine like a diamond ring
L eaving the ball, you dropped one shoe
L ovely sweet Dannielle, we'll always remember you
E ven now you are asleep

You are in God's arms
for Him to keep
Sleep tight, take care, Dannielle,
Wherever you are
xxx

Lisa Jessop

Delos - The Sacred Isle

We taste the warmth of centuries
Reflected from the scattered stones
Of Delos, daughter of the sea,
And feel the breath
Of golden gods and goddesses
Whose temples and forgotten shrines
Lie hot and broken
In the bright Aegean sun.
A pillar here and there
Denotes the place where once
The priests and acolytes of old
Extolled their praises to the gods,
Where festive maidens danced
And sang sweet harmonies to those
Whom we and passing time
Have long consigned to myth.
A marble statue stands forlorn
Between tall, fluted columns
With the open sky beyond,
As if still pondering
Upon some lofty, long-remembered hope
That time might work in other ways
And resurrect the sacred isle
Of Delos in its golden days!

Gordon Alexander James

Someone

Someone who can look
Deep into my eyes
And understand
Why the whole world
Empties itself out
Onto my shoulders

Someone who brushes away
My tears
And does not wonder
Why they still glisten
Like crystals
In the sun

Someone who smiles
When I smile
Even though his fears
Suppress
Every chance of happiness

Someone who is
Someone
But yet
No-one
My soul mate

Ayesha Kanji

Shipwreck

The darkness torments me, I feel frightened and threatened surrounded by sea
There is nobody around to offer comfort to me
But yet there is a turbulence - I do not think that sharks play
If my legs only tread water, will it keep them at bay?
The cold seeps deeper, the minutes stretch into hours
Will I survive? It will take all my powers
But I can and I will, I was not created to be a shark's kill
Is that a ship's engine I hear, feeling a thrill
Then I panic in case they are not very near
The truth is, I have no strength to cheer
The water envelopes me from the sway
Will I possibly see the dawning of day?
The moon is bright, the stars stand out
Mustering my energy I try to shout
With no hope left feeling benumbed and bereft
Even desolation cannot make me weep
Paralysis means it's the long long sleep . . .

Julia James

Death Sentence By Poisoning

I mention two cousins distinguished by colour,
One viewed with approval the other with horror.
From false information the public receive
Via a media who'd have us believe
Grey squirrels attacking his cousin 'tis said
And must be controlled where there are no reds.

Who foresters killed 'till the late 1940's
Gamekeepers also since 1903
When a club was set up 'Highland Squirrel' by name
In its first thirty years 85,000 slain.
'Twas said the red squirrel could never revive
In the lower two thirds of U.K. to survive.

Greys habitat oak woodland where they thrive
On acorns unlike their red cousins, 'tis said.
The damage they do is exaggerated
Far exceeded by costly research to
Damage they do to mans' interests.
Apart from a few valued beech, possibly
In timber trades April to July.

When squirrels strip bark from the beech. There's no need
For killing grey squirrels anywhere else.
Whose debut on TV delighted us all
Even the government acknowledged that they
Don't believe the red squirrel is mugged by the grey.
While allowing 'control' in such cheap, cruel way.

Alwyn Jolley

Touch Of Glass

A glass paperweight is heavy
And smooth in my hand.
It is warmed by my touch.
Glass comes in many colours;
Green glass reminds me of the sea,
Waves crashing like frothy cream
Over seaweed covered rocks.
Glass rescued from the sea
Turns opaque and secretive
With no sharp edges.
Broken glass is like cubes of ice
But does not melt in my mouth.
Stained glass makes kaleidoscope
Patterns on a sunlit floor.
Beads are made of glass,
Circling my wrist like drops of blood.
Glass is all around us;
Delicate and fragile as life.

Sue Johnson

Untitled

My life is nearly over
The shutters are going down
It's getting really dark in here
In the shadows of my mind
My soul is drifting upwards
To the bright light in the sky
My heartbeat is getting fainter
And a hand reaches out to me from high
I am going to the place of peace
I'm going to rest my woes
In that loving place above
I go to the God of love

Tracy Jennings

Coming Home

The beautiful green view rolling by
Is very pleasing to the eye,
The fields made like patchwork quilts, hold the cattle
As I listen to the rattle, rattle.

The trees, some short, some tall, swaying in the breeze
All this I see through a purple haze,
In the distance rolling near are the hills, the best
Scene yet, for I am returning to Somerset.

I sit and watch this beautiful terrain,
As I am returning on a train,
As I near the station with racing heart,
I say again we will never part,

Never again to leave the soft green earth,
Soon to be beneath my feet,
Or fight a war for my home land, or die upon some
Lonely stretch of sand.

I smile with mirth, I have come home
To my place of birth,
And as I walk away towards my home,
I know I will never more be alone.

For waiting there is a girl with two children,
Who I will never leave again,
I have fought my war, with body shattered
I now return to all that matters.

The Soldiers' return

R.I. Jones

Rememberance

Birthday good wishes, perfect bliss
An opportunity I must not miss
To show appreciation of strength given away
To people more needy, every day

With your world experience of good and bad
Achieved in your travels as a Lancashire lad
We learn that life's school is hard
Proving true past thoughts written by poetic bard

So we live on as the Lord decrees
Interspersing rejoicing on birthdays like these
Saying sincerely Best wishes to you
In contributing happiness in what you do

John W. Johnson

Totally Bombproof Schoolmaster

My daughter was frightened of ponies, but she wanted to ride out with me.
Our advent said "Totally Bombproof". The second reply proved to be.
His coat was all patchy and dirty - he didn't seem much of a find
But though he was shabby and scruffy, his eyes were bright, gentle and kind.

He was hard to take care of in Summer. He foundered if he ate a blade
Of the lush grass, so he spent long hours in the shelter we built in the shade.
Now trusted and loved by our daughter, who rode him whenever she could,
They had lessons and hacked out together and, if he could please her, he would.

A very small pony, eleven two hands, he sadly had soon been outgrown.
Luckily, then, our young son took him on, the first interest in riding he'd shown.
Ritchie, who's cottage stood next to the field, fed him apples at his garden wall,
He kindly took over at holiday time, mucking out, laminitis and all.

Now over twenty, Snoop bravely continued to take my son riding with me
But, sadly, next summer his apple-friend died and the pony had aged, we could see.
Soon the children were weeping for Snoopy. I ached to take their grief away.
"Ritchie's feeding him apples in Heaven", was all I could think of to say.

Judith A. Jenkinson

Newlyweds

Gone were her wedding finery.

After a hectic day we were at last
Alone in the bridal room.

Both our hearts beat fast.
We wanted the night to reap its ecstacy.

She stood there removing her stays and knickers.
All that remained was a lace low-cut nightdress.

My fond gift was a pendant of forget me nots.
It hung from a gold chain.

She put it over her head and unbuttoned her night attire.
Then exposing more and more of her beautiful cleavage.
I leaned over and kissed her rosebud nipples.

Soon we were eclipsed by the firm
Contact of our intertwined bodies.

The gift she gave me was enduring love.
WHO could ask for more.

J.F. Jenkins

Dreams

Did you walk across the fields
And through the wooded shade,
Did you see beneath your feet
The little elfin glades,
Did you see the fairy cobwebs
Glistening with dew,
Each morning fresh and new.
Did you see the lovers dreams
Trapped there in the silver streams,
Or are your eyes closed to the fragile things
Your ears deaf when the wild bird sings,
Your heart as cold as the dark coal seams.
Are your dreams lost in the elfin glade
Where shafts of sunlight break the shade,
The evening stirs the Rowan trees,
The fern fronds curl in the nights cool breeze,
You trapped the wild bird in the elfin glade
Where the violets grew in the gentle shade,
But no love do the cage bars bring
And the lonely birds heart has ceased to sing,
Are the dreams still there in the elfin glade
When the door is opened to the cage.

Janet James

What Is Love?

What is love,
Love is sharing,
Caring,
Giving,
And loving.

Love is strong,
And long lasting,
Love is never wrong,
And all embracing.

Love is weeping,
Laughing, sighing,
And for keeping.

Love is glowing,
Like an ember,
Love is to remember,
When like the ash,
It grows cold.

Pat Kings

My Girl (The Teenager)

Clumsy, hurrican like
Body pumping like a radiator
Clothes laid about like stale puppies!
A million teenage thoughts
Sink into the wallpaper
But fresh babe a newly born you are . . .
with your deep sea eyes
And your go on mum please, just this time, I'll pay you back . . .
Explosions in your hair, with your diet of gel, hair spray
And gallons of the finest electricity to pump up your head . . .
Our time has gone girl, yours is fresh and tugging at your skin . . .
Go on join in eat it all up get as fat as a mountain . . .
Life tastes lovely eat it all, leave the brakes off don't stop . . .
Wear your life like your finest outfit!
Let no one stain it, tear it, or borrow it
It's yours and yours alone!

Garry Jennings

I Had It Done, My Way!!

Imposing buildings, corridors I curse
Little rooms with bed and nurse
A doctor there - what could be worse
Telling me what they're going to do
What they're going to put me through
I think to myself, there are other ways
But no-one listens to what I say
I feel as though I don;'t exist
And I;m only a number on the list
they don't give you time to stop and think
While washing their hands at the hospital sink
"Come lie on the bed, this won't hurt a bit"
Why do they lie - they must think I'm thick
I'm getting annoyed now - and will not comply
Their eyebrows are raised - it's obvious why
The doctor with temper begins to give in
You would think I'd committed a great mortal sin
"I want it done my way! Is that so bad
Not pushed and prodded and made to feel sad
they did do it my way, after a fight
I knew I was naughty, but wasn't that my right.

Shirley Jones

River Boat Games

Before geometry
And algebraic manipulation were my heaven,
I played elaborate river boat games,
When I was only seven.

Along the golf course edge,
Another Tarzan in the trees
Swayed high above the elephants,
And tumbled in the breeze.

Northward bound,
The Flying Scot was mine,
Child's hand upon the regulator
When I was only nine.

The clocks run down
An old man's dream,
The pirate ships, a cardboard toy,
Wild elephants, a mongrel dog,
But the railway train's REAL STEAM

Brian E. Jordan

Autumn

Autumn is the time of year when,
Birds migrate.
Hedgehogs hibernate,
The Autumn artist has visited
The forest.
He has splashed the colour of
His Winter pallet among
The trees.
To signal that it is time to
Sleep.

Jack Kenwright (Age 10)

I Believe In Yesterday

Do you ever wonder - just what the hell went wrong?
Murders, rapes and mugging - the sick become the strong.
Drink and drugs and violence - replace the contented soul.
Why can't we love each other - and once again be whole
Do you ever wonder - just what the hell went wrong?
Today became tomorrow and yesterday was gone!
Yesterday: not perfect - still far better than today.
For in the name of progress - much was lost along the way.
Gone, are all the values - which gave meaning to our life,
Enlightened self-interest - it just fuels the growing strife.
Loving, sharing, caring - they're fast going out of style.
Many hearts have grown so cold - only profit brings a smile.
While the devil and his cronies, spreads lies across the land.
The lonely become lonelier - the weak become the damned.
More, more, more, more, more, more, more - that's all he seems to say!
Do what you're told, and do it quick - or you won't get your pay.
Don't care about pollution - don't care about the old.
The only things to care about - are those that can be sold.
Will we ever learn our lesson - not to listen to the snake.
To listen to our hearts instead - stop repeating the mistake.
His fruits are always bitter - for they lose us Paradise!
But yet we keep on eating them - and disregard the price!
And in return for all we've lost - what can we say's been gained?
E - lec - tron - ic gadgets. Oh! Paradise regained.☺

J.M. Knight

Christmas Tree

Now trim the christmas tree please do
baubles and tinsel in ev'ry hue.
The fairy overlooking all
lights too glisten though very small.
Novelty choc'lates then to hide
amongst the needles hanging with pride.
Bows and ribbons also delight
'neath the branches presents in sight.
Warming the heart a wondrous scene
a cosy log fire glows how serene.
This peaceful season of goodwill
carols to sing a joyous thrill.

Margaret Jackson

Formatt

Don't hide me in your distant past,
Or promise things that will not last.
Don't worship me like a holy shrine,
Or say that you will not be mine.
Don't shine a light on all I do,
Or be someone that is not you.
Don't tell it to the talking tree,
If you've asked me and I don't agree.
Don't bang the drum and shout out loud.
Unless of me you're very proud.
Then I'll carry you like a beautiful scar,
And who told me this?
THE TALKING STAR.

Andrew Johnston

Will Anyone Come?

The day is so terribly long,
Just sat here waiting to die,
It seems that life is wrong,
And that soon I must say goodbye.

I watch the clock, counting the seconds,
The chance to talk to a friendly face,
Please someone visit me, I beckon,
In this morgue of a retirement place.

I miss all my daily routines,
When I worked and especially shopped,
Now my purpose in life seems to mean,
Eating and sleeping, everything else has stopped.

Lemanie Kelly

Untitled

In all the worlds of Venus I have known
A feline grace is here and there disposed
To vaunt itself and let the others stare
And then retire alone and be reposed.

I had once a lover like a cat,
Slow moving, elegant and wild and wise.
He gave me warmth and his vibrating laugh
And all the world had nothing but his eyes.

Alison Jacobs

Death

Death comes first,
Grief comes after,
Sadness and sobbing fills the days that follow.
Eyes fill with salt tears and trickle down grey faces.
Everything you do, you remember,
Everywhere you go, you remember.
Death.

Death is so greedy - it takes and takes,
Leaving the living with holes in their hearts,
Stranded and lonely they feel, for a long time
Passing the days with only thoughts of their loss.

April Louise Kent

Searching For Myself

Who's path do I walk?
On whose feet do I tread?
Chasing a source,
Who's presence I dread.
Who's light do I shade?
Who's air do I breath?
Who's heart do I break, as I wilfully leave?
Into unknown I invade whose space?
Who's dreams and ambitions are these that I chase?
What do I crave, or hope to achieve?
Who do I worship?
For who do I grieve?
For who am I longing?
For who do I search?
And suffer this pain.
For what am I striving?
Then what will I gain?
I know not the answers,
I'm seeking to see,
For who am I searching?
ME ME ME me!

Leisha Johnson

Remembering

At the beginning of the Springtime
when everything starts out new,
as buds appear and lambs are born
I remember you.

In the brightness of the Summertime
with skies of perfect blue,
when the warmth of the sun touches me
I remember you.

As the beauty of the Autumn
shows its golden colours true,
and I walk through the crisp fallen leaves
I remember you.

In the cold snow of the Winter
when the frost shines in the dew,
I feel a special warmth inside as
I remember you.

Christine King

It's Just All Natural

Where the sun shines
The moon doesn't
Where the glittering sparkling Star sparkles
The cloud doesn't
Oh! NATURAL things last forever

Oh!what could we do if -
The tiny star did not
Sparkle.

And the glowing moon
Did not glow so grandly
With its charming glow!

Oh! I could just feel the warm sun
Upon my back
Shining brightly from the sky
If it did not shine so brightly
There would not be any light in the
Bright blue sky

Samia Kouser (Age 12)

The Wind

The wind, the wind, oh what a terrible thing,
It blows by day and blows by night,
Its shivering touch freezes the air,
Icicles hang on trees all bare.

The wind is like a ghost that howls in the night
It sends great shivers down your spine.
With the hurling and swirling of dustbins and litter
This wind is turning very bitter.

Stray dogs and cats do cry,
Trying to find shelter in the night,
A rat a tat tatting on the window pane
Old Jack Frost visits again.

For his frosty bite freezes your heart,
His weary moan echoes all around,
Beware Jack Frost will bring you sorrow,
Oh go away wind and come back tomorrow!

Lindsay Ann Jackson

Rail Link Blues

When you buy a house just look around
What could be built in the fields that surround
Could it be a road or railway line
A superstore, not what you had in mind

A country view, birds in song
Didn't last for us, the Channel Tunnel came along
Widen the road, International Station
9,000 cars parking, a new era for the nation.

But not for us, worst affected
House prices tumble, homes rejected
Car fumes in the bedroom when the traffic is slow
What it will do to our health, no one wants to know

It won't be long, before work starts
My view will go as the diggers embark
Dust will follow fumes into my home
Many will suffer, I won't be alone.

When you buy a home, there will be no guarantee
In ten years, you could be feeling like me.

J. Kempton

Jack Frost

Wintry day, Frosty day
Oh what tricks Jack Frost can play,
Whilst we laid in bed all cosy and warm
He's covered the landscape with a glittering charm

Jack Frost is an artist
His patterns I see
As I look at the window
How many designs can there be

I see snowflakes and icicles
Circles and squares
Threads of pure silver
Like my granny's hair

Better dress quickly
Put on something warm
Stroll in the crisp air
So peaceful and calm

Margaret Kent

The Twelve Hours

One o'clock, two o'clock, three o'clock four
Someone came knocking at my door
Five o'clock, six o'clock, seven o'clock eight
I asked them to go back to the gate
Nine o'clock, ten o'clock, eleven o'clock twelve
Santa Claus came with his elves

Stacey Mather (Age 11)

Unborn

Farewell my precious so small and so weak
A life pure and simple is what you tried to seek
If this could of happened what joy you would bring
But you must go now darling, with the angels you'll sing
The angels that greet you will take you into their home
They will love and they'll hold you, you won't be alone
Although I'm not with you my love's not denied
So wait patiently sweatheart till I can walk by your side
Your face and your smile is what I long to see
I love you my baby you are still part of me

Vicki Lambourne

Strange Feelings

What is this thing possessing me, that when I look I do not see
And cannot talk when I try to speak, or if I walk, my legs go all weak
My hands start shaking, then I start to sneeze, have I an allergy or some terrible disease
Maybe a fever or something far worse, should I call in the doctor, or visit the nurse
This feeling that makes my throat go dry, and I need a drink so badly I could cry
My stomach is turning and my face is bright red,
Could something I've eaten be affecting my head

I slump to the floor as I sit on an imaginary chair,
Fraught with confusion gave the illusion of one being there
Something I can't touch, something I can't see, whatever it is it's got a massive hold on me
Always searching my tormented soul, never achieving any worthwhile goal
Strange sensations filling my brain, am I having a breakdown or going insane
Negative feedback doing its evil deed, holding me back while others succeed
Going along with its powerful force, prevents me from taking a more positive course

No need to be sad and so full of doubt,
I'm beginning to understand what this feeling is about
It's becoming clearer could I be right, is this feeling love at first sight
Thinking of her at night, my heart just aches, and stays that way until the morning breaks.
Being lovesick is the term they use, could this be the reason for my mental abuse
Her hair, her eyes, and skin so pure, just give me a glance I know you have the cure
Never had thoughts for children, marriage or a wife,
But that all changed the day she came into my life.
I visit the same place every single day, just hoping to see her look my way.
She beckons to me, she wants us to meet, my torment is over my world is complete.

Brian Lorkin

Who Am I?

Just who am I?
You keep on telling me
Who I am
But how do you know?
Were you blessed with insight
A god damned foresight
To preach your rights
To turn out life lights
You're not part of my dreams
The places I'll go
Just like I always told you so
You're not part of my destiny
So go on and leave the rest of me
Just let me be.

Emma Leigh

Wanting

Hand me happiness and I will take it
Hand me truth and I will discard it
For the truth is not always your desire
For desire is want
Want is not need
Need is essential to keep life in your grasp
What you need is not always your dream
It is not wrong to have a dream
It is not wrong to want
So take with both hands and never let go
For what is a body without a soul?

Carmen King

258

The Impossible Romance

Mystical darkness,
The Age of Innocence.
Dawn and Dusk divide us.
I gaze across the universe
To see her dancing shadows.
I reach with my beams to warm her,
To reach into her core.
But the clouds frown;
Would I truly burn her with my touch?

He is the source of life I can never be,
The centre of the Shades of Blue.
His colours dazzle.
In the four corners of the world
Gravity would not be the cause
Of my falling stars.
But here the Night is my master,
I am but the cliche of the earth dwellers;
Romance personified!

Two worlds,
One destiny,
Eternity, together, apart.

Milena Kullack

The Gambler

I gambled, persistent like the winter rain,
wishing lady luck would turn.
Blackjack, Poker, I played the lot,
to re-cap my losses, alas in vain.

A slippery slope I'm sliding down,
visiting every betting shop in town.
In life I've found my little nook,
just a shame I'm out of luck.

The bet is on, I can't resist,
Flies on the wall, even snails,
my money's out, well, what's left.
I'll lose, I'll lose, I must desist.

They took our house to clear the debts,
my wife made it clear, no more bets.
So, here we are, out on the street,
how on earth do we make ends meet.

They left me they did, my wife and kid,
I've blown it now, life is no fun.
Let it be a lesson for the future my son,
Let's hope you never get to gamblers anon.

John Kitson

Reflection

At some time of the day
We look at ourselves
One day while looking
Is that grey hairs?

Time passes by another surprise
That's right!
Crabs legs at either side of our eyes.

A few years on, red veins around your nose.
How we all end up looking no-one knows.

Hair on your head going quite thin
Next thing you know you have hairs on your chin

Reaching old age but still feeling vain
We'll never look like sixteen again

Trim your chin, perm your hair,
Day cream, night cream, if you really care.

It doesn't really matter how we look
After all the batter could be tatty,
"It's what's inside the book".

Mary Kitchen

My Northumbria

Come to Wild Northumbria where the rivers flow free,
Through woods and valley bottoms, in their journey to the sea,
Passing lonely hamlets and busy market town,
A sight to gladden every heart and lift the deepest frown.

Listen in the quiet of hidden valley in the hills,
To the skylark sing his heart out in silver notes and trills.
To imagine in the stillness, the distant tramp of sandled feet
Marching in formation up and down a Roman Street.

Sheep and cattle grazing, peacefully turn as one,
To watch the pony-trekkers on holiday in the sun.
No fear of Reiver Bandits or Vikings from the sea
Coming from out of nowhere, causing them to flee.

Ghosts of long-dead miners are the only ones you see.
As reclaimed heaps are tamed now, planted with shrub and tree.
They seem to be imprisoned in the grey and dusty scree.
But motes of sunshine dance along, you blink and they're set free.

All the landscape's peaceful, battle hymns sung no more,
Just the laughing singing river as it rushes for the shore,
The clouds of heaven fly freely in the wild Northumbrian sky.
Silence settles once again, now the tourists have passed by.

Nancy Knight

The World

When will it end, how did it start,
How did I get my beating heart,
Is it flat or is it round,
How on earth was this world found,
Why is there morning and why is there night,
Why is there darkness and why is there light,
There is laughter there is fun,
There is sadness too, for some,
Why do people like to kill,
Why are people sometimes ill,
Why do children often cry,
Is it 'cos we have to die,
We enjoy life as best as we can,
From having parties, to a caravan,
All these questions and many more too,
Who has the answers, I don't...do you?

Stephanie Lord (Age 12)

My Endless Love

I think of you every minute of the day
I think of you with every word I say
When I see your face, it makes my day
Your beauty, no-one else can portray

My love for you will never die
Though some would say I tell a lie
My love for you will last forever
I know that it will never sever

I'm sorry if I have hurt you before
I now know I love you more and more
My love for you will last all eternity
It will not rub off like a novelty

I love you with all my heart
You could say I've loved you from the start
I believe it was love at first sight
Since then I've know, you're my guiding light

I wish you would love me as I love you
It's a dream I hope will soon come true
You may think this poem has come out of the blue
But for you there is nothing I would not do

Andrew Kane

Untitled

He's short and fat, of uncertain age
He makes us laugh, oh yes not half
When he is on the stage
His pants are large, his jacket torn and tattered
He has a hat, they call it that
Which has been badly battered
His shoes for size are out of place
Perhaps he had them from his dad
Tied up with bits of broken lace
His face is painted red and white
This I suppose to match his nose
But what a lovely sight
Oh the pleasure it doth bring
To see him fall and that's not all
He even tries to sing
Now and then he seems to make a
Very stupid blunder
But that we know it's just not so
And so perhaps we wonder
Who is this man we have just been seeing
To some you're a clown, no please don't frown
To some a human being

Augustus King

Grandad Joe

In the Autumn of my memory years
My thoughts take wings to fly away,
Leaving joy and happy memories without fears,
Of my Grandad Joe, for whom my love will stay

He worked in the mine, from being a boy
Until he was seventy years of age'
Crouched on his knees, for most of his shift
Until he came up again in the pit cage.

A charming man, was my Grandad Joe
So full of love and fun and knowledge.
As a child I roamed the lanes with him
Picking wild flowers, and watercress from the stream.

On Sunday morning, no work below ground,
He would dress in his best, a rare sight.
His homburg hat, smart suit, flower in his lapel,
His watch and chain and walking stick just right.

He loved me dearly as a child, he made me strong,
And as I older grew, he was always there to share.
The many heartaches I had to endure and bear
Until he left us in his ninety-sixth year.
   "God Bless" Grandad Joe

Doris Kitching

An Old Man's Sorrow

The old man in the bus shelter,
Has no home to go too,
He sits slumped with the world's cares on his plate.
What with the rain and everything,
His rheumatics are killing him,
And the ache in his heart doesn't help.
The lines on his face echo the years,
Good or bad it's hard to tell.
His hat tilted slightly to one side on his head,
Has a tattered old feather,
It too has seen better days.
His coat is buttoned tight,
In a brave effort to keep out the cold.
It was a present donated by an acquaintance
The old man has served his country
And loved his wife to distraction,
Till she died.
And now sits on the damp hard seat,
Forgotten, ignored and alone.

Carolyn Kirk

The Old Mirror

Oh Mirror! What times can you reflect?
What from your memory can you resurrect?
In the antique shop window there you stand,
How far back can you cast your mind?
Were there crinoline dresses and men in tights?
I bet you've seen some unusual sights.
Gangsters and their molls dressing to kill?
In the black and white movies they gave us a thrill.

Oh mirror! Would your image show young soldiers off to war?
And the tears of loved ones when they returned no more.
Have you seen people with secrets looking forlorn?
Some of them wishing they'd never been born.
Do you retain my likeness while I spectate?
What feelings like pictures could you emulate.
Have you seen laughter and gaiety, horror and shame?
What images are trapped inside your frame?

Oh mirror! What sights you must have seen
Through the years that now have been
Young women dressing for their very first dance
While the men are pruned to charm perchance?
Have you seen joy and happiness, lovers caress
Have you copied these lives with great duress.
If we could see beyond the glass seal
A life time of stories you could reveal.

M. Kennedy

A Dream

I feel so weary so I'll take myself off to bed
The pillow feels so downy soft as I lay down my head,
Now come with me to a land of dreams
One that's filled with excitement and love
There will be no nightmares containing screams,
Let's travel from this land of damp and cold
And as we travel continental countrysides unfold,
How we got across the sea, I'll never know
But the air's now filled with a warmer glow,
How thrilling it is to see how different people live
The world belongs to everyone, and each have differing talents to give,
We all fit into natures store
And if the world worked as God intended, there would be no poor,
Some countries have a surfeit and should gladly give
To help the people of less fortunate nations live,
And what's been seen tonight as my dream speeds on
Makes me hope, when I awaken, I remember each one,
My hearts filled with love for all the worlds poor
And I'd like to try and help even the score,
Oh! good, I've not forgotten, as I open my eyes
My dreams flash with clarity before my eyes.

Carole Diane Kettle

263

My Admirer

"I wish I was gifted like you" she said
"You can make any words rhyme"
"You play the piano and sing in a choir
And your dancing is always in time,
I wish I could bake a nice cake" she said
"And your scones ooh, they taste so divine
Your kitchen smells good, when you make yorkshire pud
And the men think you're still in your prime,
I wish my complexion was wrinkless" she said
"And my hair was as sleeky as lime
To walk down the street with court shoes on your feet,
Must surely feel simply sublime
I wish I was gifted like you" she said
"Oh mother, you make my heart climb
You're lovely you know, though I'm sixty four
And today you have reached eighty nine!"

Lynne Kirby

Save Your Gown

Prayers and storms and waterlily.
They found three in the lea.
Christen me, marry me
And then you can have me.
Pikestaff and pigskin,
Hemlock and wine.
Grow your venus-hair, my dear,
Another time.
Corncrake and jackdaw saw
The killing of the Saints
And when the sun returns again
The moon will have her mate.
The Harvest Queen has never seen the cross,
The ivy and the cuckoo will never know my loss.
Brandied apples and avarice, save your gown.
The sky is a furnace that burns above the town.
'A ring, a ring of roses and we all fall down.'
Meet me at the knoll with the death bell.
Let's dance back the rivers of hell.
Meet me at the Wedding Tree at dawn on Willow Lane
If you want to do the same.
Witching hour, Virgin's Bower, in the Chapel grounds,
I thought I heard you sing as I held fire in my hands.
A ring, a ring of roses and we all fall down.

Chris Kemp

Reasons

Pity was not the feeling I had when I returned
It was more a pang of remorse because I had taken so long
Childhood memories of the place were mixed
Large, friendly, in a time warp

My visit was for a different reason
A new found friendship and it's cultivation
A "sense" of deja vu was not apparent
Although I knew the old haunts well

Sadness possessed me when old ties were sought
Some had changed, many remained unaltered
The decision to go back was out of my hands
Regret was not what I felt

To retrace one's step is to lay the ghost
Painful thoughts surface only to be repressed
I reviewed the place with new eyes
Experience of the years an aid

"Large friendly, in a time warp" still rang true
The reunion of old thoughts with new emotions
Was cleansing, refreshing and vital
For our recent association to survive.

Margaret Kirkham

Brothers Of The Underground

Brothers of the underground sleep the life-long sleep
Crawl along the gutters like larvae in the dark
Wriggling towards the light.

Commuters throw a dime and it tinkles on the tiles
And glints like an inspirational flash
Under the drab florescence.

Each day they maul the plastic bin liners for the haute cuisine
Or gulp the moonshine from their plastic cups
Thrown down by travellers.

And each eye that passes looks but does not see
Because each life is filled with triviality
And the brothers of the underground watch you and me -
Desensitised . . .

Barbara King

Help I'm Burning

It happened when she was six years old
A little dark haired girl I've been told
She went to warm her little feet
Thought she would give them a proper treat
So to the fireside she up and went
This she did without her mum's consent
Then the flames to her nightdress flew
Higher and higher and bigger they grew
I'm burning I'm burning was her cry
She truly thought she was going to die
Then her mother came on the scene
You see she had heard her sister scream
A blanket then was wrapped around
That little body so charred and brown
To the hospital she then was rushed
Her mother's heart was really crushed
The doctor said "She might live for one hour"
So to God they prayed for some of his power
To save this little girl from dying
And to tell the doctors to keep on trying
It seems that all these prayers were heard
Because I am still here to print these words

Lois Kerron

Dunblane . . . 13.3.96

Say nothing just now
Please don't talk of love
Don't mention forgiveness
Or heaven above

Insanity preferred
Of that there's no doubt
The mind locked away
From the evil without

I'll hurt alone
I'll weep without sleep
Remembering promises
I never will keep

Too angry to listen
Too sad to decide
Whether you're near
Or there by my side

Talk to me later
In maybe a week
But at this moment dear Lord
Please don't speak

K.J. Langley

My Dad

Oh Dad! Why did you have to go
We all loved you so
You had your three score years and ten
But how much I've missed you since then

I'm being selfish, I know you were in pain
But we will never see your like again
You were the kindest man I've ever known
Caring and wise, you looked after your own

You worked hard all your life
On the land that you loved
You taught us how to work the land
And how to tend the beasts in hand

No-one will ever know what you went through
I knew because I was close to you
I hope there is an after life
If there's a heaven, with my brothers' you'll be there

Through good times and bad, in summer and fall
You gave us the greatest gift of all
Your enduring love!

Janet Knevitt

266

Me & 'H'

Lately I've been HONEST, HURTFUL and some say HEROIC,
How long will I last?
Living with 'H' has changed all of our lives,
Will I be with you next Christmas Eve at Mass?

Is 'H' for HELL or is it for HEAVEN . . .
'Have I done something terrible' will be your first thought.
To be sentenced with HIV is to be cursed with the gift of seeing the beauty of
LIFE . . .and to make my parents cry.

I cherish every moment, speeding on the existence I inhale,
Indulge in existential gratification and the superficiality of the day . . . Drink
my favourite drink, Milk,
Smell my loving Dogs' bad breath again and again,
Feel the discomfort of damp socks through my split Nike.

I still find the courage to Love and time to watch Godard films while it rains outside.

It's funny, you may think disgusting but I do regret one thing.
I regret not indulging in more of the same that brought me this disease.
For a cliche is a cliche because it is true,
I better the cliche by having had two lovers instead of one.

Believe me I have been ANGRY, ENVIOUS, DESTRUCTIVE,
but months have passed as I stand here a fine figure of a Man . . .HANDSOME,
ENERGETIC, IRRESPONSIBLE,WISE.
I will still explore this 'H'eart shaped place for all eternity,
. . . or until I die.

Michael Lamb

Poverty

Upon reflection I recall, standing lonely
Asking for milk on my rice
There was no milk
Only rice
A field of dreams too evasive for me
To grasp
Only rice and poverty dwells here
Blue tinged toes, naked toes
There was no socks
No milk
Only rice
Why was my needs not tended to?
Always lonely . . . cold
With blue tinged naked toes
Asking for milk on my sparse
Portion of rice

To Heaven

Along came a man, threw up in the sky
A dead man in the grave.
So sad, so sad, it melted.
And now no moon up in the sky.
So sad we cry.

Stephanie Lane (Age 6)

S.E. Lea-Morris

World In Backwards Perspective

Flowers in my heart,
books in my head,
I read my floral sketches
whilst lying in my bed.
I see an open book case,
I look upon the floor -
my streaming world of scribble
is heading to the door.
Words that open locks,
cans without the key,
all this mixed confusion
is a metaphor of me.
The sky turns suddenly pink,
I'm filled with unaware
my life is slowly wandering
but all I do is stare.
An open ended answer
looks me in the face,
so all I do is imitate
while staring into space.

Kirsten Lyon

Space

In space it's dark
It's go lots of stars
rockets go u and fly
Like a bird in the sky
Will I ever get to fly?
Fly up high - up high in space.

It's just where the fireworks go
BANG! BANG! BANG!
All the lovely colours crackle
Shooting stars go BANG! at night.
The blinding sun is bright
Jupiter, Mars, Saturn are planets tonight
Always
Machines bang! whoosh! crash.
Along the midnight - sky in space.

Rachael Lundy

Autumn

The wind came out the west, and hurried on,
Trembling the aspens by the river side,
And birds sing plaintive now that summer's gone,
As certain as the river's onward glide
Through unreturning leagues, to meet the sea.

The swallows twitter round the moss grown eaves,
And trees are barren loves in every lea,
Filled all the air is now with dying leaves,
Falling as woven dreams upon the earth.
For Autumn's come in russet, brown and gold,
And lost forever is the summer's mirth,
No more shall tales of silver Spring be told,
Under a bright young moon of loving May.

The light is fading on the purple hills,
A thrush is piping out the dying day,
Twilight the mystic strews the dust that fills
With purple dusk, the valleys near and far.
Forlorn the earth seems in the fading light,
Naught through the wide world shines, save one sad star,
And gladly, gladly, sinks the land from sight.

W.H. Lunn

Thoughts In January

The January sky so dark and grey, as though wearing a frown,
Windy days with snow filled air and muddy shades of brown.
People with faces, tense and stern, no smiles of greeting now,
Wrapped up warm against the cold and lines across the brow.
Not many like these cold grey days when winter is abound.
But listen and imagine new life stirring under ground.

The snowdrop so fragile and gentle will soon begin to show
To appear as a promise amidst the cold cold snow.
The first welcome tips of daffodils, crocus and the like,
Bright green patches of grass emerging near the dyke.
Enjoy the calm renewal of life you know that time will bring
The glorious reunion of winter merging into spring.

Dorothy Laverack

Molly

I opened the sitting-room door quietly
So as not to disturb her rest,
She was, as I thought she would be,
Not really looking her best.

Her hair needed brushing or combing,
To cut it, I really must try,
I marvelled at time slipping by me,
How quickly the years had flown by.

Just three years ago she came to us
With her belongings - including the chair,
Every day she used it to rest in,
To sit in it - no-one would dare.

Oh how all the family love her,
She shares all our ups and our downs,
She loves to be with my husband,
With my son she is always the clown.

I know that she won't be long with us
For I see she is ageing so fast,
She really has blessed all our family,
She'll be loved right up to the last.

I suddenly heard a car draw up,
She stirs at the sound she knows well,
She gets up, albeit so slowly,
And walks, barking, to the sound of the bell.

June Linscott

Alive And Kicking

The suction hissed
They pushed and pushed
A raised, clenched fist
My waters whooshed.

"A boy", they cried
The tears fell
We sobbed and sighed
Hearing his yell.

He screamed and screamed
Legs kicked the air
Of this we'd dreamed
A son so fair.

Wide open eyes
Head full of hair
Small gasps and sighs
Hung in the air.

Tom's little bro'
How proud he'd be!
God's gift bestowed
So plain to see.

Dreams have come true
Hearts ache no more
Songs burst anew
Souls now restored.

Ceri Lusk

269

Breath Of Love

Sometimes you stand so near
I can almost feel you breathe
A whisper of breath that brushes over my heart
Like a gentle fanning breeze
It cools the blaze that burns my soul
To a smouldering cindering ember
In the ashes lies the love
That was so touching, and so tender.

Just as the soft hush of breath
Can extinguish the burning flame
As a snuffed out candle's light
My love, to tame
The breath can easily stir
The dying charred remains
As bellows blowing through the dust
To resurrect the fiery flame.

Signs of revival from the ashes show
Licks of fire that leap and glow
My heart aspires to such comparison as this
Sweet breath of love
Smothered my love's sweet kiss.

Carole Ann Luke

Sisters

Hear me my sisters
My blood runs through your veins
My heart feels your pain
Let the invisible cord
That binds us
Draw us in close
Even though the path we chose
Says no right of way
Let each parcel of pain
That lies deep inside
With so many labels
To set free first
We can never decide
Let this be a step to freedom
A new age
A feeling of being
Born again

P.M. Lightfoot

Starlighters

Curtains slowly parting, crescendo starting.
With great anticipation, an audience awaits.
As darkness descends, stars soon to appear,
To bring forth joy, laughter, maybe a tear,
Their delight, a parade of crinoline ladies;
A face of smiles, behold the star.
With each crescendo, - An encore of echoes.
Finery, colour and costumes, finale.
Nay, - there is no end, stars are forever,
Stars that shine and shimmer in a velvet sky;
To light your darkness till light of dawn.
Guiding stars for mariner's travellers - to home.
Across lands and seas, life a jigsaw of pieces,
Where we try to fit and smooth the creases,
Guided by the greatest show of stars.
Remember at the end of a hectic day,
The starlighters are on their way,
To lighten and brighten those hurting affrays
So part your curtains, choose your star.

Des Lamb

Me

My Mum's not my Mum
And my Dad's not my Dad.
But they're the only ones that I've ever had.
The caring the loving
The feelings of love,
The playings, the teachings
The bad and the good,
Are all locked inside me
I hold onto them tight
They're mine they were given to use as I might.
My family are borrowed;
And the feelings I have
Are warm and affection, tenderness and love.
Borrowed they may be
But to me they are mine.
We're there for each other for most of the time.
All this I do have
Yet the feelings I hide
Are that of a great hurt, down deep inside.
Yet one thing I know of this to be sure
All the love I do hold, I'll never be poor.
So my Mum's not my Mum,
And my Dad's not my Dad,
Yet to no great surprise of this I am glad.

Linda Law

Wish

A pot at the end
    of what a rainbow
A frog that turns
    into what a charming prince
A fairy maybe
    at the bottom of our garden
All dreams
    all hopes
A war that kills
    in far distant worlds
Children that starve
    in front of there eyes
Choices they cannot dream
    hope is all that's left
This is now
This is reality

Jan Lister

Loneliness

I feel weak but nobody cares
I'm ragged and old going up the stairs
Of an old building that I lie in
Full of tears I'm always crying
Drunkards and dropouts are all around
Nothing but rubbish and scraps on the ground
I pray each night my eyes will see
A new beginning in the morning for me
I beg and plead to feed my hunger
But nobody hears me while I'm down under
Can somebody help me
Can somebody care
All I need is an answer to my prayer

S. Lloyd

271

Christmas Eve 1996

Where is everyone?
All those mad Christmas shoppers
Dashing to and fro like clockwork
Spending plastic cash, being merry, always on the go

You won't find those types here - no chance!
Not here at the Gellie Loch - the middle of nowhere
With the sun beating down on my bare fleshed neck
It almost feels like a frosty summer's eve
But it's only four in the afternoon

It casts my ghostly shadow as I hike the trail
Everything gets painted a glorious golden hue
From the magnificent rays it sends out
A sight money couldn't buy

Swans, like live balls of cotton wool
Glide elegantly upon the Lochs mirror surface
Which breaks the monotony of their reflection
Ever so gently and with great ease

So I find a spot and plank my weary legs
And watch the swans drift off into a shadow
My sight acknowledges the golden object in the sky
As it peeks through broken clouds
It's slowly evading my optical view
On this day - Christmas Eve 1996

Scott Lowe

Weight Watching

I'm trying to lose a bit of weight
So I don't put much food on my plate
I don't eat fat from any meat
I nibble a carrot instead of a sweet
I eat Ryvita instead of bread
And I don't eat a thing before going to bed
Then I wake up in the middle of the night
My tummy is rumbling so I put on the light
I head for the kitchen and get the bread
I cut off a slice and with butter I spread
To lose a few pounds I'm doing my best
But how can I help it when my stomach protests

Rosetta Lee

The Shoot

The mist curled quiet fingers through the leafless trees one dawn in late September,
A day that began for me an early start, a special day, I looked around the glade.
So quiet still, above the trees the cloud, dark shadows made a curious pattern,
Slowly pass - and then a beam of light
To touch with gentle fingers and chase away the night.

Too soon the sound of voices, the tramp of many feet
Among the bracken dry and brown - my heart began to beat
So fast, I stood transfixed, and listened to the sound
Of tiny woodland creatures - so nervous on the ground
Above, the birds gave out their song, the rooks with raucous cries.
Joined company with the wheeling wings that swept about the skies.

Men's voices now, harsher still as each took up his stance.
The dogs and beaters, busy now with purpose did advance.
Then suddenly, the flash of wings, bright patterns in the sun
And Hell became reality with the firing of the guns.
The dogs retrieved and once again, the men resumed their kill,
And as I watched, above my head, a feather floated down,
In timeless beauty, tipped with gold, it touched the ground - was still!

Olive Lumb

Lottery Fever

Saturday night, it's 8 o'clock,
Sitting erect, adrenaline amok,
Pen is poised, the button is pressed,
Please let it be my turn I try to impress.
This time next week I'll be off to Mauritius,
Drinking champagne, surrounded by riches,
On a sun soaked beach if dreams can grant wishes.
Contemplating the rest of my life,
If only the first out could be number 5.

The balls are all rolling, which one will be first,
Bottom lip bitten, I'm ready to burst,
Every Saturday is the same situation,
As I hold my breath with the rest of the nation.

The first one out is number 3,
Well there goes the jackpot, it's definitely not me,
Still chance of five more, that would be great,
Not this week anyway, no chance with 8.
The finger points it could be you,
Certainly not with number 2.

Back to reality, dreams are on hold,
No luck this week, I have not struck gold,
But one day I know it's going to be me,
Who one day will win the National Lottery.

Linda Lane

273

Farewell Friend

We sat there in the twilight
The time was past for tears,
We listened for the heart-beat
Reviewed the passing years.
Remembered things of childhood,
Children now full-grown,
Loves and lives and friendships,
The people we had known;
The hardships and successes
Which punctuate our lives,
The goals which seemed beyond us
To which each one still strives;
Remembered days of sunshine,
Skies of red and gold.
The pale green leaves of spring-time,
The frosts so white and cold.

Soon Spring-time will be with us,
This winter will be o'er,
The birds high in the tree-tops
Will build their nests once more.
For now, we sit at twilight,
The time for tears has passed.
She sleeps a deep, untroubled sleep
And welcomes peace at last.

Sandra Low

Stop The Wheels

Union chairman, brilliant tactician
Serves his brothers with attention
The conniving works manager, conjures up a plan
To get rid of this clever union man

He is dismissed for being too cute
Bringing the company into disrepute
Major meeting then is called
The men not liking this at all

They decide to strike on Saturday each week
The chairman's future was still looking bleak
Then lo and behold from out of the blue
He was reinstated, looked too good to be true
The manager was told to clear out his desk
Possibly on the dole with someone else

They did not feel they had won a great fight
It was more about ones civil rights
The greatest lesson to us all
United we stand, divided we fall.

James Loughran

The Seashore

Soft white clouds out of reach
Ocean splashing on the beach
Rays of sun on my face
This is such a peaceful place

Sitting on a sea washed stone
One could never feel alone
Seagulls flying with such grace
This is such a peaceful place

Tiny rock pools still and warm
Baby crabs will do no harm
Stones and seashells have a race
This is such a peaceful place

Now the sun is getting low
Soon the moon will start to glow
The clouds are trimmed with silver lace
This is such a peaceful place

Patricia Lambourne

Brothers And Sisters

How I detest the engrossing daily woe,
Of evil indignation choking my soul.
With tempest tantrums and temper led torment,
Who is the figure whom I dread with fear?

This monstrous mutant is both a villain and a cad,
It is my sister, the result of my mother's mistake.
Arguments ripen at the arrival of her presence,
Angry snippets force my mind into total confusion.

Emotions erupt in a sea of outrage,
The tone in her voice like a beast in its cage.
My sister and I reflect family deformity,
Two contrasts in a world of conformity.

Viscous vexation infests my philosophy,
Encore injury in the mind of each opponent.
Harmful hatred is so terribly unkind,
Yet further failure in the progress of mankind.

I'm crumbling quickly, both day and night,
I've reached the limit of her menacing bite.
Like wilting petals from a Rose in Autumn,
I've fallen in a hole of absolute abnegation.

Passionate dismay is dramatically involved,
Is this really how humans have evolved?

Jonathon Livingstone

Natural Gold

Every week the lottery produces millionaires
So many people hoping to win, or just get shares
This lust, and greedy attitude is blotting nature out
Money can't buy everything of that there is no doubt
Look around the countryside and see what people miss
Have you ever walked in showers and felt a raindrops kiss
Or in the summertime relaxed in hazy wooded glades
Nowhere could you ever buy such natural dreamy shades
Paddling in a running stream invigorates your feet
There isn't a chiropodist could offer such a treat
Sledging down a snowy slope with cheeks all aglow
There isn't any makeup to put on such a show
The music from the birds in song the cricket and the owl
The butterflies the squirrels and a dogs occasional growl
The dandelions the daisies the bluebells what a list
Buttercups are surely gold the millionaire missed

F.S. Lowe

Yesterday

It seems like only yesterday
We played in fields of green,
Our mothers hardly worried
When we could not be seen.

Pony tails and dirnell skirts
Lime green socks we wore,
Blue suede shoes and drainpipes,
Dancing till our feet were sore.

We managed to enjoy ourselves
Rock-n-roll, our passion.
We hardly had a bean to spend
But we really were in fashion.

Soon we were getting married,
Dressed head to toe in white,
We had to grow up pretty quick
When money was so tight.

We took our families to the seaside
We went by train or bus,
One suitcase carried all we'd need,
No passports and no fuss.

Now our children and grandchildren
Fly all around the world
They think they have an exciting life
But I wouldn't change mine for theirs.

Eunice Lee

Cathy Said . . . .

Not altogether my story.
I cannot tell of my own.

I played it, speaking with notes,
With the rush of ivory, ebony keys
And hands almost as frozen as my heart.
I remembered all, in spite of myself.
Yet still, I could not weep.

I still feel nothing for life,
So I must guess at what could have been,
By reading other people's stories.
And when I examine the mess in my head,
And ask, "Who the hell am I?"
I recall that Cathy said,
"I am Heathcliff".

Somebody else's story.
I cannot write my own.

Bryn Leshiye

The Entity Within

Emptiness full of darkness.
Fear. Unknown. Evil.
Lonely, yet not alone.
Enclosed, encapsulated by nothingness,
motion, but vision remains still.
Darkness that can be seen.
Calm, yet sensing something is there,
or will be coming soon,
a presence, not a being.
Something invisible, but can be felt somewhere
within the chamber of nothingness that surrounds me.
Silence. Sadness. Selfish.
Released, thrown into the unknown realm of reality
or fantasy, that cannot be controlled,
yet is controlled by the presence that is both
near and far, strong and weak.

Hannah Lee

Train

Rumble trundle view-line flying
tickets bought by craft and lying
many the victim in danger of dying.

Huffing, puffing, rail lines humming
passengers worry! themselves they are bugging
why sing this song? they've done no wrong.

Priests of all factors; soliciting their makers,
doctors, plumbers, candle-stick makers,
Poets and tinkers, and many great thinkers.

Workers and idlers, now remembering their mothers;
with rich men and poor men and many do-gooders,
with no blame at all, 'twas the fault of their brothers.

Managers of orphans, out on the make;
while the kids had the leavings they ate the cake,
then prayed to God in heaven above,
that they would not get, too early a move.

Rumble, trundle, smoke pores from the funnel,
with nothing to stop it, the train heads for the tunnel.

No turns or twists or sideways move,
this train runs onward as though in a groove.
the passengers it carries have done themselves well;
now they're on their last journey
for the next stop is hell.

Norman Lowe

Emptiness

How long the day, how slow the hour
Now you're no longer here.
How steep the path, how hard the climb,
When all is dark and drear.
I look for you, in every dream,
Where once you were in truth;
When life brought only happiness,
And love was in its youth.

But now there's only emptiness,
For love won't live anew;
And dreamless sleep is all I crave,
For dreams do not hold you.
The hidden sighs, the silent tears,
Grieve for your cold goodbye
Which left me to walk on alone,
But did not tell me why.

Beryl Laithwaite

Guinness

Tall, dark and beautiful
Gracefully sinking
Descending, cascading
With a silk smoothness
Like mink, sleek, full-bodied
Clinging then sliding
Leaving no trace, save for
Insecurity.
An aftertaste bitter
As jealousy, yet
Refreshing as the dew
Whetting, encouraging
No polite request
But expectant pulsing
Gaining momentum
Good looking, good natured
She is my bête noire.

David Laud

The Beginning Of The Rest Of My Life

Introduced in a nightclub by a mutual friend,
I knew we'd be together right until the end,
We'd got nothing in common, they say opposites attract,
I would never believe it, now I know that it's a fact,
After two and a half years together I finally proposed,
I knew that our families would not be opposed,
We started making plans for our special day,
When we'd be together on the 11th of May,
Nearly five years had passed when the big day came,
I knew from the very first moment things would never be the same,
Now that we'd got married all that was missing was a child,
There was many a happy time spent in bed, sometimes passionate, sometimes wild,
It didn't take long to get pregnant, it was sooner than we thought,
So we started to make a list of the things that will have to be bought,
When we went for a scan we were in for a great surprise,
For as the midwife switched on the machine we couldn't believe our eyes,
We had planned on having two children but never expected twins,
Everyone's saying it's going to be hard, this is when our life begins,
From buying one of everything it is now double,
They say one's bad enough, but two's asking for trouble,
But I can't wait for March when my wife gives birth,
Because I know our babies will be the best things on earth.

Mark Lancaster

Time

Time to sit, gaze and wonder,
Marvel at what we see up yonder.
Time to think of what's up there,
Do we know? and do we care!!!

Time has let us reach the skies,
Time to reason was it wise?
Probing into the unknown,
Into darkness all forlorn.

Time to think of us on earth,
Give us credit where it's worth.
First help us humans here below,
Then to the cosmos you may go.

Time to give us better days,
Improve our lot in many ways.
Give us all a decent share,
Of what's going, that is fair.

Time to learn to the sincere,
Time to walk without fear.
Time to live and be at ease,
No more violence only peace.

Albert Edward Lloyd

Untitled

You lay beside me now,
Still and sleeping.
I sit for hours,
By the light of the moon,
Just watching.
You are so beautiful.
You who taught me,
That a lifetime,
Is a time of life,
Of living.
You who with a single smile,
Can calm my deepest fears.
You are so precious to me.
Whatever I'm thinking,
You know.
Whatever I'm feeling,
You understand.
Your kiss transcends all sensation,
It is boundless,
And so is my love for you.

Stuart Lello

Picture Frame

The frame hung on the wall
Pretty picture did display
Children playing gaily
Upon a winter's day
Snow had fallen softly
Hats and muffles donned
Shiny ice upon the water
All frozen to the pond
All the people chatting
Balls of snow strewn all around
You could hear all the laughter
Though the picture made no sound
The little boy seemed lost
All tracks were covered in snow
The laughing girl in red
She knew which way to go,
In the corner stood a tree
Its boughs all heavy with snow
In the sweet shop doorway
Children huddled in a row
All had come to life
Once Autumn turned to fall
In this exciting little picture
In the frame, hung on the wall.

Mary T. Lowe

Child And The Cherry Tree

After stark, dark winter
White before green.
Everywhere blossoms show up
Extravagant as brides in their lace.
Vanish almost as quickly
In a puff of wind -
Spring's snow a soggy brown on earth.
Don't cry, little Laura. Dream on!
Pioneering leaves fold open,
Transparent in the sunshine,
Toughen to power stations, energising
Fruit to form and swell.
Our garden tree's too big to net,
But bird and worm can't eat it all
And if we care to pluck some at first blush
Then they will ripen in this bowl.
And on a summer day we'll lunch
On yellow cream and tangy fruit.

Christine Leonard

Glen

I'm wondering, through glades of green,
Remembering, things which once had been
Even now, I still hear those voices
Telling me, you had but one of two choices
I knew in my heart, that they were right,
I just couldn't give up without a fight
I also knew deep down the thing, that I should really do
But found it so hard to part myself from you
So many happy years we had been together,
I wanted so much for it to last forever
Inseparable, I would hear people say
As they watched us run, walk and play,
Then I looked in to your tired, old eyes
And the doubt, no more, could I disguise
The pain of your suffering the heartache, the sorrow
I knew then, one of those choices had to come tomorrow
It dawned bright, on your last day as side by side, we both did lay
You lay in my arms, as we said our goodbyes
You were so brave, it was I who cried
One last look, you gave to me you seemed to be saying
Don't cry, it was the right choice you made for me.

Tricia Laye

279

Childhood Memories

Hurt faded with time, subconsciously hidden, but still there
Those bad things - the sickness, poverty and fear.
They still lurk in the archives of the mind
Intermingled with sirens and droning planes -
Hard to decipher after all these years - lucid are the good things,
Laughter when the chicken's carcass ended on the floor,
And the sweet taste of raspberry cordial at that festive time of year.
Unforgettable the old stocking full of nuts and simple toys,
And still ringing in my ears the sounds of Christmas -
Carols on frosty air and the salvation band loud and clear
Comforting as Grandma's tender song.
Grandmother so gentle yet strong - the heart of our family
Quietly guiding, calming, taking all our troubles upon her aching shoulders.

It was cold then, when undercover of darkness Jack Frost left his mark
Turning simple window panes into magical works of art.
It was so cold then, and wrapped in hood and woollen mitts
Worked by mother's tired hands,
I ran the shore just as I did in summer
But then - in winter's iron grip the snow lay white and smooth
Stark against a dark and menacing sea and a sky as black as ink.
Even then - a child so young - I loved the isolation and the howling easterly wind
A wind that cut deep into the flesh, but could blow away all sadness
And the longing that gnawed away inside me - the longing to sit on father's knee
And listen as he read to me. Did he ever read to me?

Jean Ann Larner

Hiding The Shame

With the rising of the sun
Pushing back the blindness from my eyes,
Those things I once chose not to see
In a brilliant light become clear to me.

I cannot hide behind eyes of shame
That gift of man's: Acid rain,
Nor turn my back on Mother Earth
When roads cut through her fertile worth.

Forests burn! Oceans so black
I cannot see a clear way back.
So with man's great hand he may destroy
This land of green and oceans of joy.

Paul Shaman Loft

A Dream

We were walking by the river
The moon was shining bright
Your love kept me warm
On that cold dark night

You told me that you loved me
You told me that you cared
You told me all your secrets
And the promises we shared

You walked me to my door
We kissed by the light
I know it was only a dream
But it felt so right

Samantha Kay Lamming

Streets Of London

The streets of London
Have held some exciting moments
King and Queen coronations, weddings of royalty

All the horses of many proud men
Come out in their hundreds on these special days
Dressed in regalia it makes us so proud!
For the streets of London hold many memories
The crowds they come in millions just to see the sights.

The streets of London also
Hold horrendous memories!
The bombs of terrorists
Marches going wrong!
People dying in bloodshed for a cause
That happened hundreds of miles away

So we take our London and hold it
In esteem for it is the greatest city
We have ever seen
To Brits it's our Empire
The home of our Queen
Long live London
And our special Queen

Esme M. Lander

Echoes Of The Night

As I sit and listen to the echoes of the night
I hear a train a rumbling along its onward flight
Can it be a sleeper or a City Link maybe
With some weary traveller or commuters far and wide
Reflecting on the meetings or taking down some notes
Dreaming of a nice warm bed or a restless sleepless night
Onward ever onward never turning back
As it goes its distance along the busy track
Life is like a train as it ever trundles on
Facing new tomorrows with the freshness of the dawn
We must be just like that train ever going on
Filled with hope so we can cope with all life's trials
That come along to try us every day
May we gaze ever upward to the heavens above
And thank the Lord with all our hearts for His ever gracious love.

Audrey M. Lawrenson

My Baby Has Gone

My baby has gone
The Mother sighs
She looks at the picture
And wipes her eyes

She turns the page
It brings another tear
It brings back a memory
She holds so dear

My little girl has gone
She tries to close the book
It has to be this way
Perhaps I'll have another look

My lovely lady all grown up
This photo tells another story
Mother and child outside a church
The wedding dress and all its glory

My baby has gone
Well that's as maybe
She is married now
But she is still my baby

Keith McDonald

A Sad Farewell

Goodbye my friends it's time to part
To continue on life's way
Although it almost breaks my heart
I must return another day
But whilst I'm gone do not forget
The times we shared together
Do not be filled with much regret
And take care our links don't sever

Remember every one of you
You're special beyond compare
And may I say a big thank you
For always being there
There when help was needed
And did never once complain
Your advice I always heeded
No compassion did you feign

I only hope you all do feel
As fondly as I do
Of memories all so real
Which will always stay with you
May all your thoughts be pleasing
Not of the tears or pain
Think not of me as leaving
But until we meet again

Nicola Martin

A Letter To Dad

I had a friend who had to go
And why you did I just don't know
I only wish that you could see
How much you really meant to me

I had the chance to say goodbye
As I held you in my arms I cried
We only had a little while
And then you were gone, you'd died, no more smile

I know it sounds daft but it makes me feel better
To write these words to you in a letter
I cannot post it and it makes me sad
But I'll always love you my dear Dad
I'll never forget you how could I?
So with these words I'll say
                    Goodbye

Valerie Ann Littler

Life's Roses

Why is it that those nearest and dearest are taken from us?
When least expected.
They vanish as quick as the wind and the rain disappear.

Our love for those close to us
Blossoms as though it is a Blossoming Apple Tree
Only the blossom disappears, as does most loved ones.
The blossoming tree may only blossom for a year
And then loses it's leaves.
Our blossom can grow throughout a lifetime
Yet the leaves are lost suddenly.

Love develops like a Rose,
It begins as a seed and buds as it grows,
The Rose and life grow and grow
The larger each becomes.
Unfortunately all have to die in the end.
A Rose wilts and fades into the ground
Humans grow old and wither up
Eventually they too fade into the ground.

All is lost when a loved one dies or goes
As with a Rose there is a gap.
The Rose and a human leave
A space for new life to begin.
As one dies or wilts away
Another appears or begins to grow.

Samantha Malster

An Early Morning Call

Heron drifting through the sky
Seeing all with its beady eye
Suddenly spotting down below
A pond of fish he could swallow,
Gently he dropped from the dawn
Landing on the lush green lawn
Slowly he crept to the waterside
Then with his beak he made a dive
Pulling out a fish that was still alive,
But as he looked up what did he see
A man shouting and waving a stick at he,
Today he feels he's met his match
So quickly he drops his catch
And lifting his wings he flies away
But beware he'll be back another day.

Martin Mitchell

Determined Action?

Futures Unknown -
Captured by Hourglass
Pasts already gone -
Determinants of Present
Active participation
shifts the sand
Passive marionette
falls through the neck
Engulfed in sand
Or building sand castles?
The Future determined
Until the tide turns

Steve Messenger

Destiny

The stony eyed destiny
With its eyes so cold and small
Presenting and penetrating
A scene beyond the wall

A place that once removed
Could turn your life around
To confirm yet disillusion
A future to be found

The secret is hidden from view
Though time knows the way
It's underneath the mountains
And where the moon does stay

The answers are beyond me
The questions are too vague
In depth of my serenity
Destiny like a plague

Uncovering the unexpected
Revealing all the treasures
To open up the box
And smiling at the pleasures

I kneel amongst the flowers
Unearthed beyond the mind
And close my eyes to feel content
A dream where truth flies by

Sonja Maughan

Ageing

From babyhood to boyhood,
From youth to grown up man,
Time makes its steady progress,
Says, 'Catch me if you can'.

A man thinks youth is very young,
A youth will scorn a boy,
A boy thinks babies useless things,
A baby's mother's joy.

And when a man is middle aged,
He thinks himself just fine,
But 'junior' thinks him very old,
Dad says he's in his prime.

Grand-Dad has reached that certain age,
Of three score years and ten,
For him each day's a bonus,
'Til he hears that great 'Amen'.

Great Grand-Dad's over ninety,
And he thinks they're all so young,
It's good to hear Great Grand-Dad say
That there's still much to be done.

So ageing is a lovely thing,
We learn much on our way,
The joys and sadness all combine
To make our special day.

Joyce Mahoney

"22"

Corrupt and broke
I choked the pheasants throat
With daydreams and a smile
I kept my sanity for a while
Albeit drunkenly
Like an inebriated tree
With liquid limbs
Spending time on fancy whims

Mark James McWalter

Memories

The memories of long ago
We were so gay, but very slow
We took such pride in all our clothes
Right from our heads down to our toes
We mended this we mended that
We even made flowers to put on our hats
The men went to war to fight for us
And never did they make a fuss
If it wasn't for them we wouldn't be here
Thanks to them to fight without fear

Patience Millard

Out Of Place

She looked sadly 'out of place',
Standing near the bar,
With a look of tears upon her face,
That are never all that far.

The tears did fall from those
Fair eyes; as she was all alone,
Her friend had left her to her woes,
Not wanting to hear her moan.

She had made mistakes, now left
With regrets of days long past,
Which cause her to feel bereft,
They hit her with a chilling blast.

A man caused her undoing,
Abused her, by saying he was in love, but
Where is he now? That man with skill in wooing?
It is not known, which is a door left unshut.

She would not want to see that face,
Which haunts her day and night,
The past that makes her 'out of place'.
Yes, she would have him forgotten, quite.

Natasha McDonald

No More Lonely Nights

It's the golden crescent
Against a matt black sky
Shining so bright
That catches my eye

It's the cold nip
I can feel
That gives me today
My winter chill

In your arms
My life's reborn
Now my heart's
Not tattered and torn

In your arms
I lie each night
Knowing that
It's all right

When I wake
Each morning I feel
Love and Happiness
I know are real

Emma McLeod

To Spring - A Confusion Of Thought

Beloved herald - dare I claim you?
Dare I name you yet the solace of my lonely heart?
Incessant dreamer - must I doubt you?
Know about you, yet keep silent in a world apart?
Unknown intruder -
Usurper of the heart's solicitude,
Love's creator -
Late offspring of the soul's ingratitude,
Elusive phantom - strangely haunting,
Cruelly taunting, yet the prologue to my heart's rebirth,
I must receive her, thought tormented,
My resented fate inevitable to the earth.

Intangible mist that hides the future from my eyes,
Veiled predictor, grasping fate between your hands,
Be kind. Do not destroy the faith I placed in you.
Be wise - or I may never see the distant view.

Muriel McNeill

Waiting With Hope

In a far distant land a baby was born
In a manger He lay at the first light of dawn
To the world He brought the message of Love
From the One we call "Father" who guides from above

He told of a "Father" who is not just above
But is here every moment and surrounds us with Love
Now Jesus walked this same path of life
To teach of a "Father" who is with us in strife

His life wasn't easy the end was all pain
I'm sure if "God" asked he would come back again
When the path you are treading is painful and steep
Try to be as a child and so gently creep

When your heart is broken and you're in despair
Why not go to the "Highest" who loves and cares
And "He'll" move all the rocks and take away pain
Then into your life "He'll" bring sunshine again

If I try very hard and give of my best
Till that moment in life when I'm called home to rest
Then I can show the "Great Teacher" who suffered great pain
My life was not wasted it wasn't in vain

Lilian Milsom

Coming Home

As I sit at home trying to ignore it
He's there watching, in his replica kit
Ninety minutes of hell, 'till he's back home again
But will he even make it onto the train
You may think it is because I'm fed up
But really I wanted to go to this round of the cup
"Oh no dear no place for you, not now anyway
Too much fighting" what a stupid thing to say
So instead I sit here and worry all alone
And hope and pray that I don't hear the phone
I know if it rings it will be bad news
Opposing teams don't mix, not with booze
It's not even the fans that fight half the time
They're too busy singing that stupid little rhyme
But those who use it as an excuse to war
They shouldn't be allowed near, not any more
A year that's seen football come home to so many
Should be followed by one that makes it safe for any.

Tamsin Macdonald

Fifty

When I woke up this morning, I didn't feel any older
Although the crick in my neck's now a pain in my shoulder
My face is still pleasant, though I have the odd line
The body is more bulky, but the teeth are still mine.

I can't understand it, I still feel twenty one
But the truth's on the cards, where have the years gone
I'm no longer a girl, but a woman mature
The mirror confirms it, but my mind is unsure.

Of my three score and ten years, only twenty remain
Oh if only I could live my life over again
I'd perhaps be a film star with my name up in lights
Or a dancer, or model exploring the sights.

As I open my cards now and read out 'YOU'RE FIFTY'
I shouldn't feel sad, I'm really quite nifty
It's only a number, it doesn't mean that I'm old
My life started at Forty, or so I've been told.

But time doesn't stand still, and the tide will not wait
Youth cannot be captured with a trap and some bait
It can't be revised, re-kindled or saved
Maturity follows wisdom on the path that we've paved.

Pamela Margetts

Composition!

The merry-go-round of youth
Leaves squandered minds
Unrecognised potential
Immature reasoning

Two thirds of your grey matter are
In animated suspension
Awaiting Genesis

What! Is the key
To release these imprisoned cerebrum
A keyhole of knowledge cannot suffice
Enrich these prodigy cells!
Offer them diversity
Create a stimulus

When the brains orchestra plays,
A cataclysm of notes
Compose it

Angie Mac

It's Good To Have Wings

Flying is the bird,
No sound to be heard,

Flying through the trees,
There's a slight breeze.

The air is still and there's a
Bit of a chill, but to fly it's a thrill!

When I steal the other birds' food,
They always think I'm a slight bit rude!

Because I have long legs,
I can see over the other birds' heads.

For me,
Living in a nest
Is best.

No petrol do I need,
Though I can go at a high speed.

Joseph McMahon (Age 8)

In Appreciation

How proud, how grateful, am I for this gift,
Through youth, 'that pain', I could not realise
How wonderful this bounty, such a lift,
Seems, fortune cloaks herself in much disguise,
That we may miss her, never hear her tread,
Too quiet her footfall on unheeding ears,
Yet, not too late, as many teardrops shed
That, I'd 'abandon' her in future years . . . .

This life long gift I cherish now, as one unto
Her bosom, mother nestling child, and too,
Unfinished was her beauty 'loaned'
Like roses growing 'midst the nettles wild . . . .
. . . The rose hath thorns, and too the nettle stings
One for its beauty, the other to 'impose',
Self preservation, ammunition brings
Anticipating 'pain', her 'dart' she throws . . . .

Take not away, my folly, nor my strife, nor hurt,
That led me to this path of mine,
Just leave to me the 'nectar' of my life
So I may die, in reveries sublime . . . .
For what is 'life' without this daily bread?
The sustenance on which I can survive,
If not for 'words', I am not born and bred
I'd starve and hunger, and not feel, 'alive' . . . .

K.A. Millington

Alzheimers

Something closed the shutters of her mind.
Her eyes stare blankly into space.
I wonder is there silent screaming there,
Just beyond the lax expression on her face.
I still recall her repartee' and laughter,
The giggles round the teapot we would share,
I can't for life of me conceive
She now lies dormant in a ward somewhere.
Dear God if tears were all it needed
To lift the torment and set free
A soul, imprisoned by its circumstance,
They'd spill to overflow the sea.

Margaret M. Marklew

Sisters Of Serendipity
(For Shane)

I can now understand
how women become groupies:
listening to your lament
soul-strung from the heart -
the next beat in anticipation
emotional overflow on your strings,
each cord a word of wisdom.

Majella McCloskey

Clairvoyant Night

Tonight I experienced something quite common,
I went to City Hall to see a clairvoyant,
He sat there and spoke of spirits, life and death,
And kept the the audience amused by his depth.

I was quite impressed by the way that he spoke,
As if he knew precisely what we thought,
He mentioned names and how people died,
Then asked if we knew them, which was a surprise.

My friends thought that he wasn't for real,
And took it for granted he must be a fake.
I listened curiously, to determine my point of view,
But couldn't decide whether it was really true.

Some names that he mentioned did make some sense,
To people who were waiting for news of their descents
At the end of the night, we laughed at the show,
And finally agreed: How could he know.

He came to Hull just for the night to fill his pockets,
Paid by all the soft type,
They believed in him, like some people do,
But to me and my mates, it was all
HULLABALOO.

Margaret Milner

My Prayer For You Annie

I pray you will always
Be healthy and strong
That no-one will ever
Do you any wrong

I pray the sun will always shine
And you will always keep that smile
But most of all I pray you find

The things that money
Just can't buy
And if God will let it be
I would like to be around
To see you on your Wedding Day
What a proud Grandmother I would be

Denise McIntyre

Is It You

Did I hear you call my name
Has my search come to an end
Tell me you were never lost dear
Then my heart can finally mend

Have you returned to me
Or is it just another dream
Have we been reunited
Or are things not what they seem

Let me slumber once again
Where I can hold you in my arms
Feel your breath upon my face
And succumb to all your charms

Do not rouse me from my heaven
Leave me here where I do lie
For if this is not my love returned
Then I shall search until I die

Janet Merola

Forest Walks

The forest pathways touched with bronze
Littered with balls of burnished wood
And their forsaken casings.
Ponies grazing 'midst the thinning trees
The ground silvery beneath their feet.
Their misted breath a token
Of the chill to come.
A golden haze heralding the arrival of the sun,
A welcome glow defying the onset of winter.
Drooping Elders rich with ripened fruit
Adorning the hedgerows
While spotted Toadstools straight from picture books
Allow glimpses of colour through a damp bracken.
In the distance a Peacock calls
As he forages through the undergrowth.
And in a clearing rabbits play,
Enjoying the last remnants of warmth
Before enduring the trials ahead
When winter will have all within her grasp.
But for the moment, is there anything more tranquil,
More giving of its solitude
Than the forest of an English Autumn.

Isobel Mitchell

Remembering

I remember the town where I was born
It was quaint and so called small,
I remember the pavements old and worn
And the buildings seemed so tall,
I remember my house at the top of the hill
The door was painted green,
The windows and the window sill
It now seems like a dream.
I remember coming home from school
Over the iron bridge,
Up a small street, across the road
And up the long narrow ridge.
My dog was there to meet me
So faithful and so true
I would only have to whistle
He knew that was the cue.
It's all so different now
The development came you see.
They took the heart out of my town
And with it, half of me.

Sheila Merriman

Is It Time

It's nearly time I can see
Your wobbly stumbling legs show
There's not long to go
My duty to fulfil
I won't let you down, no way
You begged me today
To take you one more time
Could be your very last
Down your beloved valley
You only just made it
We only just made it home

The sadness I feel and see
In your eyes
You know as well as I
The valley is in spring flow
Rejuvenation everywhere
Except in you and me
You are nearly empty
But I am full

Kenneth McDonald

Father's Cactus

No flowers now, just yellowed lobes which droop
Anaemic through neglect by trembling hands,
Long unremarked by aged eyes, which dupe
The watcher with pretence of sight, while stands
But memory of so-familiar room
To guide the frail steps to basic chores.
He cannot see the cactus, blind of bloom,
For only habit guides him - every door
And chair and shelf and step fixed in the mind.
The plant remains, and in its withered stance,
Surviving, void of choice, in leathery rind,
It mimics its old owner, lives by chance.
Yet once it shot forth fiery spears each spring
To truly earn the 'Easter Cactus' name:
Once, he was young and vigorous of limb
With strength now vanished as the cactus' flame.
And when he dies, as soon must blind eyes close
On burdened, lonely days, will cactus die,
Too long his sole companion? - No. It glows
In radiant triumph at his liberty.
Its spiky trumpets burst from shrivelled stems,
The graceful crimson curves confounding thin
Atrophied digits, while its petalled hems
Dance on the sour sand, new hope to sing.

Ruth Marsden

Subtle Silence

Weeping willows will cry no more,
Laughing hyenas turned to dust,
Waving tides forbid the shore,
Springs of time left to rust.

The sun on the horizon will never appear,
Snowflakes at Christmas cannot fall,
Stars in the darkness glisten so clear,
Why did God put an end to it all.

No rabbits nor frogs to bound and hop,
No doves to glide so elegant to ground,
No trees in the forest left to chop,
Not a movement to be seen, to be heard,
Not a sound.

The earth has stood still
Without any warning,
Human race bitten by natures fang,
Has the time come, for a new dawning,
Or could this be the next big bang.

K.G. Mason

African Violet
(Dedicated to a Political Prisoner)

Vulnerable,
Yet strong
In the Faith of humanity:

The cry of the yellow within.

I blossom, I die
Condemned for the right
To live:

The cry of the yellow within.

Confined to this cell
The body of many,
The mind of insanity:

The cry of the yellow? Creator of rights?

Nothingness
Speaks out
To Nothingness

Alison McNeil

291

The Early Years

I am skating on a bubble
Twisting and twirling
Posing and pirouetting
Faster and faster
Faster and faster
Chasing the colours that ripple in and out
That flaunt and float just out of reach

I must acquire some new skates
Some new expensive skates
That will leave behind
Those other skaters
Who push and jostle as they pass me by
"Keep off! The blues and pinks are mine.
For you the browns and greys."
My conscious thoughts are dulled
As concentration on the contours of the dance envelopes me

There are other skaters
Far away from here
Skating slowly calling faintly
But there's no time to question why
Just time for dancing on the skates
And catching at the colours
As the colours change

Norah Mitchell

Dead River

Beneath lifting spans float
Ghosts of boats, blackened corpse
Lost in warps of death's dire wraps,
Token scraps of life that was
Heavily come, so lightly gone.

Wharf's skeletal shadows strut,
Pecking guts of phantom ships like storks
Hauling mawks of memories.

Hollow echoes scream along
Pier's cold throng of puddled
Stones where muddled souls grubbed
In bloodied empire's trade;

Gristle born for grist down
Mill's dank drowning holds, and
Dint scored bold for treasure moved -
A measure of their worth.

Geoffrey Maine

Forgotten?

Shrouded in obscurity
Hardened by adversity
Into a past I flee
Where treasured are my memories
With closed eyes I hear a sound
Laughter which my heart has found
And through the magic of this our place
I gaze again upon your face
Where I breath within Phantom Embrace
Pandoras box lies open
Nothing left inside to see
For I have thrown away the key
While waiting on the final fee
I step down from society
In emptiness there are no needs
Locked away my pain can't breed

John Christopher MacDonald

The Bluebell

When autumn is over
And winter is gone,
I rise in the spring,
To shout at the sun.

In a coat of silver,
And a coat of blue,
I sing my rude chorus,
As I bathe in the dew.

In woods of deep slumber,
I tip-toe on,
Hushed by a mist,
I dance naughtily on.

In pots of plenty,
And vases so fine,
In children's stories too,
I am so divine.

But as the year passes by,
Into summers full dress,
Old age comes a creeping,
And steals my blue vest.

For now I am naked,
And my song is all spent,
So I hide under ground,
Until I repent!!!

Paul MacMillan

Jurassic Park

It all started 65 million years ago,
Today scientists thought they could do it,
Unfortunately for us they did.

Only a handful of people knew,
They should have told more people,
That way it wouldn't be so deadly.

I agree with Ian Malcolm,
You cannot keep them locked up,
They will break free.

As usual Malcolm was right,
They did break free,
And we've got to stop them.

Some of them are killers,
And they're coming for us,
If we're not careful we'll lose.

If they're not killers they're still deadly,
They will crush us, eat us and beat us,
In other words they're all dangerous.

Even our best experts are no match,
Because they will always be stronger,
We have no choice but to run.

I said they couldn't do it,
But unfortunately they did,
They created DINOSAURS!

Chris Masters (Age 12)

Snow

Snow is cold and frosty,
It's bumpy, crunchy and soft.
When the sun comes out
It sparkles,
Glitters and twinkles as well.
When you look at the snow
It looks flaky and bumpy
Snow is lovely to see
Sometimes
The snow looks like ice-cream.
Like I said
Snow is lovely to see.

Toni McNiece (Age 7)

The Outing

Have you ever been to Selsey Bill?
To buy the crabs they have to sell,
The sheds and boiler standing there,
With the old bath full - no room to spare,
People standing in a queue,
Not having a lot to do,
The talk of fish is in the air,
How to cook them - some quite rare,
At last! the crabs all pink and hot,
Are taken out of the boiling pot,
Wrapped in newspaper - that's your lot!

Jean Miller

Deflowered

You planted a little seedling
And waited for her to grow
In nature's time she sprung forth
Pure as the driven snow.

Her tiny form grew stronger
As each day passed she grew,
Then the bud began to open
Revealing her loveliness to you.

And as she bloomed, but not yet full,
You pushed your way inside,
Although bruised and torn she struggled on,
But the heart inside her died.

She was no rose, she had no thorns
Protection she had none,
When in full bloom, her head hung low
The damage had been done.

Though years pass by you watch her still
You have no guilt nor shame
She'll have no peace 'till you are gone
But forever the memories will remain.

Yvonne McCartney

Pavement Panorama

Zimmer framed pensioners
Race shopping trolleys
Misogynistic males
Brandishing brollies
Trike riding tots
Burn up the track
Miss you out going
Get you coming back
Buggy pushing Mums
With attendant brood
Meeting more Mums
Much fat chewed
Walkmanclad skateboarder
Scattering the throng
Oblivious to invective
Ears full of song
Loose bowelled doggies
Squatting here and there
Make going 'walkies'
Another cross to bear
Pavements are dangerous
Don't even have a code
Never ever cycle there
It's safer on the road.

Leslie Marshall

Love

In our darkness, the wonder of where it ends
where it begins
though invisible, its names are many
have we yet to taste its sweet scent
petals in the wind are we
given down to us as children
left to understand its meaning as the autumn come
do we all wish for the angels touch
whispering tenderly, in arcs it moves
creating the tears, the hopes
more devastating than any war
the making or the breaking
giving and taking
books of old describe its eternal beauty
for those of fortunate creed
touch me angel
let me feel this thing called love

Andrew McCartney

A Changing World

When I am older I will bear a knife,
Secluded within my apparel,
Without the public eye but within reach of a trembling hand,
As a token of a changing world.
When I am wiser I will seclude myself
Within my terraced castle, gun at the ready,
Without the reach of a deranged society, safe from its demands,
As a token of a changing world.
When I am richer I will flee to the mountains
And create a fortress,
Entreat the eagles to feast within my tower,
Stout refuge against a humanity which denies the meaning of its name,
As a token of a changing world.
And when the world is changed,
I too shall be overrun.
I will flee my fortress
And rain death and terror on a world not designed for me.
And I will change this land.

Beware, I watch your every move.
Beware, I do not approve.
With sword of iron and banner unfurled,
I claim my prize: Your changing world.

J.G. McCutcheon

Out Of The Womb

Shiver queen
Singing in monotone
The sky beneath you is failing
But you still have the scent in your hair.
Cold blooded mother
Burning your babies into shape
You've moulded their voices into gilded wings
And peeled from your vision, they can fly again.

I've learnt from your nauseous state
To wear my scars with nervous pride
And do without skin
If I have to prove that I'm white
On the inside

Monochrome day
Cloying round my neck
Choking me into fist-clenched submission
And viscous denial slip-sliding
Through my consciousness
And leaking from my pores.
I know you smell it on me.

Jessica Matthews

Treasure

Something to have
something to keep,
something to look at
laugh at, and weep.

Sharing emotion, or
a fragile object,
something to look at
which you have always kept.

It came into being
to your eye, to your heart,
is it something with which
you will never ever part?

Because it is special
a child or
a diamond.

Treasure it always.

Hayley Claire McCann

The Sunday Event

On a bright sunny summers day
Assorted cars gather in coloured array
In our village field or on the green
Quite the largest crowd we've ever seen
Beware of the mud and tricky parking
The odd stray dog always barking
They come with canopies, stalls and trailers
To display their goods and regalias
That obscure book one's longed to buy
Or rapidly outdating hi-tech hi-fi
These bargains could be heaven sent
Just to fever the event
But life has a paradoxical contradictory side
Thieves, villains their stolen loot can hide
Then on mistrust one should not dwell
For most are honest, that wish to sell
So have a go, take part in this scheme
To satisfy the antique collectors dream
A simple idea to give so much pleasure
For one person trash to another treasure.

Gerald E. Miller

In Yonder Tree

There sits a bird in yonder tree,
And he sings merrily down to me,
Good cheer, good cheer.
Such a joyful song he sings.
That to my heart he brings
Good cheer, good cheer.

From morning light till evensong,
He sings the whole day long
A choir of angels in his voice
Beseeching me, REJOICE! REJOICE!
When little bird you fly away
To far off lands across the sea,
I hope you will return some day
To sit and sing in Yonder tree.

A.J. Macdonald

The Boatman

Hold my hand, the boatman said,
Nothing to fear, nothing to dread,
All aboard, on a journey we go,
You're safe with me, as I gently row,
Sometimes the journey for some, takes a while,
For others it's short and enjoyed with a smile,
The boatman knows those who are afraid,
So he holds their hand until the fear abates,
The boatman is busy, always full,
Plenty of passengers, never a lull,
Tirelessly he rows, from shore to shore,
Never empty, always room for one more,
It matters not to him, if it's night or day,
It's a job he does without reward or pay,
Climb on board, he says, as he holds out his hand.
No need to be fearful, we shall soon safely land,
You're not on your own for very long my dear,
Loved ones are waiting, they are so very near,
See in the distance not so far away,
A bright light shining, listen to what I say
There's love and there's laughter and beauty all around,
Soon to be surrounded and on very firm ground
So don't be afraid, please dry your tears
The boatman won't harm you, he takes away your fears

D.A. McGowan

Travellers Woe

Come close now,
And forgive me, my innocent child,
For leaning heavy upon your tiny tolerant shoulders,
Many age old troubles,
We have struggled, together,
Unwilling to comply, to conform.

Forgive each spilt tear,
Upsets dampening our usual spirit,
As God blesses you,
Especially your encouraging smiles,
And acknowledges contentment,
When once again, we travel on,
Though our family roots remain forever buried.

Come now child,
In good time, these regrets will be yours,
As your will stands others tests of strength,
Their attempts to change your mind, to change styles of life.
But forgive society, (apparently civilised)
Never to understand,
For their ignorance discriminates
Against freedom in god's land.

Lisamaria Miller

Sign Of The Times

You can keep your fresh air and your sun shine,
Just give me my couch and my telly,
When anyone asks me to change my ways,
My answer is "not on your nelly."

Give me my couch and my telly,
I'm sure I will come to no harm,
If I feel the need of fresh air,
I just watch Emmerdale farm.

You can talk to me about exercise
Of every kind and sort
Give me my couch and my telly
I'm not a lover of sport.

There's one thing that telly has done
Which has affected the whole of the nation
It has to be said, it has killed stone dead
The art of conversation.

J. Mallison

The Snow

They're white
They're crispy
And what
Do you think
They are?
They're all
Crispy and
All different
Shapes what
Are they?
They melt
They run
All gone.
You can make
All different
Things. The
Next day,
The next
Night, all
The things
Are melted away
Snow flakes.

Kirsty Marrow (Age 8)

First Love

I often lie awake at night
While others are asleep
No one hears my sorrow
No one hears me weep
You are someone very special
Someone set apart
You left me with special memories
Engraved within my heart
I treasure the love you gave me
And the days we were able to share
I just hope you find happiness
With someone who will care
My happiness was with you
Now my days are glum
Now you've gone and left me
All I have is my mum
She does her best to console m
But she will never know
How deep my love for you is
I will never let you go

Carly Morgan (Age 13)

Pepsi

When Pepsi died we broke our hearts
for all our lives she was a part
we knew that she was always around
although sometimes she made no sound.

Now she's gone we miss her purr
but have to smile when we find her fur
she would wind herself around our legs
for food and drink she always begs.

For seventeen years she shared our lives
always there by our sides
waiting patiently to welcome us home
after a day of being alone.

We would laugh when she played a game
she always came when we called her name
now the house seems so cold and bare
knowing that she is no longer there.

Ann May

The Children Of Dunblane

A class of children on one innocent day
Were playing so nicely as the sun dimmed away
A man from the bushes who wanted to play.
Jumped up on the children as he gunned them away.

A one minute silence went around the world
The hearts of the parents travel through people's souls
Flowers were layed in shapes of hearts
The school was shut down for the spirits to depart.

The world that lay in silent peace was lost within the wind so deep
The figure of this silent shape whispered through the wind of change
The sweet children of Dunblane
Sang this song again and again.

We hope that for this Christmas Day you remember the children from Dunblane
To pray for them this Christmas Eve while sitting by the christmas tree
We pray that when you're all in heaven
That you remember the good times that your family had together.

Cassie McEneaney (Age 11)

Betrayal

I gave you all I had to give,
You crushed my dreams, my will to live.
How could you leave those letters for me to find?
Didn't you know they'd destroy me, devour my mind?
The song you wrote for her tore me apart,
Each word is a dagger in my heart.
When you told her "If you want me, I'm yours,"
You can never imagine the pain you caused,
How could you say that in front of my face?
Then walk off and leave me, back to her place?
All the nights I spent at home alone,
Were you with her? Should I have known?
I cannot believe that liar was you,
Was it fun, did it amuse you,
To see me cry, to hear my screams,
To see me losing all my dreams?
What you did to me, you just don't care,
But still when you need me, I'll be there,
When your life is empty and your world seems black,
You can count on me, I won't turn my back.

Wendy Marshall

Love

What is Love?
Let us define, in the verses of this rhyme.
Love is a natural bond that should be there all the time,
It is a warmth, an affinity, almost a feeling of Oneness,
For those that experience it, a reassuring completeness,
Some do not need love, and prefer to be alone,
But for others without love, only emptiness deep down.

If barriers exist of personality or other
It is hard for love to be felt for another.

Love combined with attraction becomes a new sensation,
Perhaps only temporary, it is called infatuation.

Love as a source of strength, can be offered as a life line,
To those that suffer an emotional , or personally difficult time.

True spiritual love is neutral, yet warm,
An affinity, a bond that cannot be torn.
The love from god is complete in every way,
And can be felt by all those who believe when they pray.

Love is the natural bond between man and womankind,
Yet often in this world it seems hard to find.
But if no barriers existed of breed, culture or race,
Misunderstandings and differences Love would replace.

Robert Mason

Untitled

A 'room for the night' in a local inn, was all that Joseph asked
So that Mary, his wife could rest a while, to ease her aching back
But there was no 'room in the inn' that night, for Mary and Joseph to stay
Though there was a lowly manger, with lots of clean warm hay
And so, they did find shelter - nothing palatial or grand
Yet here the saviour of the world was born, I'm sure just as God had planned
For had he been in a palace, with all he wanted on hand
He could never have reached out to the needy, when later he fulfilled God's command
Had he not known a humble home, with parents who loved and cared
He would not have been so very aware, that the love he knew had to be shared
And so from his birth, and right up to his death, his life had been carefully planned
Geared to learning the lesson of life, preparing to understand
And all of God's planning to bring us His Son, was to show us the right way to live
So He gave us a precious part of himself, the most wonderful gift he could give
Christmas has a tremendous message, within it solutions and healing
A story of love in its splendour, the power of God revealing
The manger - the baby - the miracle birth, the life that was truly divine
The cross, the death - and the rising again, were because of God's love for mankind
So never take for granted, the precious Christmas story
Hold it always in your heart and to God be all the glory.

Fran Merrett

My Holiday

We went to the seaside my sister and me
We went with our mum to Burnham-on-Sea
We went over the sand dunes down to the seashore
And watched the boats sail out until we could see them no more.
We played in the sand and got sand in our shoes
Then a little pink crab bit one of my toes.
We made a big sandcastle and paddled in the sea
Then we were all very tired,
So we went home for tea.

Sasha Lianne Morse (Age 9)

Space

Mum and dad we are going to space!
Look at that rocket, we're going on that,
Whoosh! Off we go bang, bang my head goes
Mum look at me upside down! Get down you silly girl,
Mum, dad, look out of the window there is Jupiter,
Orange, pink, what nice colours,
Mum, me and dad are all excited,
Where are we going to? Mars? Oh no! The bright red one,
Dad, how come it's always Mars?
"Because I like the colour of the bright red planet"
"Oh no" we're getting closer, closer and closer,
Mum I'm going to sleep! Me too!
"I can't stand on Mars!" said mum.

Katie Marsh (Age 10)

Little Jewels

Little jewels sent from heaven above,
There's no hatred in your heart, you are made from love,
Some of you are white, while others are coffee brown,
The Lord knew what he was doing, when he sent you tiny angels down,
He is asking mankind not to throw his gift away,
That innocence be taught tolerance and kindness every day,
In the playground, tiny tots hands clasped so tight,
Black and white, catholic and protestant all unite,
God is smiling in His heaven, as He views this scene,
He heaves a sigh, He knows what could have been,
Some of you will encounter racism and fear,
Your creator asks you to turn to Him in prayer,
You are the future of this human race,
So unite now, and put his plan in place,
Sometimes some of these little jewels are called back home,
We wonder why, maybe the Lord wants them for his own,
Every time a jewel is lost, I'm sure it joins the stars,
And looks down upon this earth, with all its scars,
So treasure these little jewels from far flung lands,
We are nothing without them, the future is in their hands.

Val Matthews

Snow

Snow on the grass
And icy on the path
And snow on the houses
That falls down.
Snow as white as a ghost
As soft as a feather
And as glittery as you see.

Stacey Metcalfe (Age 7)

The Test Of Time

A tall strong handsome man with so much love to give,
A small sweet pretty girl who he longs to be with,
They gazed into each others eyes and the lady drifted away,
She floated on a sea of love and said in heaven I'll see my love one day.

The handsome man went on a wave of life missing her so dear,
Wishing he was with her, hoping she was near,
They loved each other more than life, more than anyone will know,
He kept her picture by his side until it was his time to go.

One cold January day as he was lying in his bed,
A beautiful angel came through the door and kissed him on the head,
As he rose he looked at her, smiled and took her hand.
The feeling of them both was joy
And together they walked into the heavenly land.

Donna Barbara Meins

The Beatings He Gave Me!

I got to the door it was 10pm
I was 10 minutes late.

My hand shook with fear,
Fear of what or who was behind the door,
I quietly nudged it shut.

There he was,
Sat in his arm chair,
Face as red as blood.

I turned to run,
But was too late,
He was hitting me,
Hitting me so hard!

I sat there motionless,
Crying from the pain,
The pain he'd left within.

I sat alone in this room,
The pain inside hurts so much,
I must be silent not a sound,
He cannot hear the hurt inside.

The house is silent
He had gone,
Gone to get drunk,
Then to return
And hurt me once again.

Tracey McHugh (Age 15)

Gwladys

She sits alone in silence
With her magnifying glass
Struggling to read the paper
Hoping to make times pass

Her home is full of memories
Of happier days gone by
Her life she gave to others
I've often wondered why

She passed by her chance to marry
And sacrificed her life
To nurse her dear old father
And his sick and ailing wife

All her life she nursed the elderly
Worth her weight in gold
Yet who is there to care for her
Now she herself is old

She doesn't want a nurse maid
She struggles on her own
She'd rather be independent
Than be put into a home

There's years and years between us
In fact there's 53
Yet that doesn't seem to matter
She's a dear, dear friend to me!

Lorraine Meredith

Loving Hands

I love to look at your strong firm hands, that have helped me through the years
They held mine in times of happiness and strengthened me when there were tears
They wrote me loving letters when we were far apart,
Those letters now tied with ribbons, with memories kept close to my heart
They consoled me when in labour, and helped to ease the strain
Then holding our new baby, they took away the pain
I watch them while you're driving as they guide the wheel with care
I know in my heart they will get us safely there.
In the years we have been together I have learnt to love those hands
It's good to know I am loved by someone who understands
Even though the years are rolling by and your hands become lined with age,
In my book of memories, they are entered on every page.

Margaret Meadows

Two For You

Two for you is my poem to view
So here are my thoughts written down for you
Two is a number when you add one to one
Two is for tea and served with a scone

Two's company but three makes a crowd
Two hands on a clock which goes round and round
Two sides to a story when telling a tale
Two sides to a coin, a head and a tail

Two humps on a camel two wheels on a bike
Two wings on a bird or a plane in flight
Two hands, a left and a right
And two wrongs don't make a right

Two eyes to see this wonderful land
Two ears to listen to this poem in hand
Two feet made for walking to travel around
And two fifty p's do make up a pound

It's good to speak for a short time
When two friends chat on the telephone line
Two makes a couple that joins each life
And when they get married they become man and wife

Make your own version read and compare
And see how many two's you'll think of in pairs

E. M. Mallett

War

Men go to war and women cry
Their tears flow as their men folk die.
Since time began and life was seed
Men go to war and women bleed,
They bleed from hearts that will not heal
From wounds that only women feel.
Women raise their sons to men
So the cycle begins again
The sons go forth and sow the seed
They go to war and women bleed.

Florence Matthias

Transience

Seek the wind in the trees
and it is gone.
A snowflake, one,
very soon none,
the torch that shone
so rarely on.
Where is reason?
Each life's season?
As fleeting as a breeze.

Ken Merry

Your Poem

The love poem I wrote for you
Is now so widely known.
Young girls throughout the world
Claim it as their own.
Hold the words against their breasts,
Close their eyes and pray
For the poet who took pity
On those lost along the way.

I remember when you loved me
The world was at my feet.
We ran along the river banks
We danced along the street
I wrote your poem by candlelight
As you lay by my side.
I read it to you softly
You held me and you cried.

That now seems so long ago
My happiness is gone.
Your love for me has died a death
Your poem lives on and on.
When your memory haunts me
And wakes me in the night
I try to read your poem again
But I never read it right.

Ron McWilliams

Ghost Train

I went to Blackpool fair
When I got there I did stare,
It was dark like a bats brain
There was a sign "The Ghost Train"

I got in a car which was a skull
It went through the door it was dull,
Big eyes glowing in the dark
I heard a sound it was like a bark.

I looked up and saw a skeleton hanging
Through the next room noises banging,
The train was going on and on,
Then I came out and saw the sun.

Daniel Melling (Age 10)

Leaving

I didn't mean to leave you there, without even a goodbye
But please understand how hard it was, you know I'd never lie
I realise I have hurt you by doing what I have,
But please find it in your heart to try and to forgive.

I've tried to tell you many times how much he means to me,
But you wouldn't stop and listen, you didn't want to see.
You've made me choose between you, all you tried to do was prove
That he really wasn't good enough, you said it wasn't love.

But you've got to understand that I just need to be free
To be with him and love him for he means the world to me.
We know we belong together, we knew right from the start
And I know that he will cherish me, I feel it in my heart.

Don't think I''ve found this easy, it's not the way I'd choose to go
But you have to realise your disapproval made it so.
Don't think that I don't love you, and I'm sorry for what I've done
But it really was the only way, oh please do forgive me mum.

Dianne Mamwell

Rainbow

The clouds above are threatening to shroud the wistful sun
And drape it in a shady mist before the day is done.
A cascading flood of water withheld in high restrain, can
No longer hover o'er the earth and burst in a torrent of rain.

We see the watery heavens as a semi-pellucid sphere, then
Perceive a break between the clouds and lightness then appear.
At last, all darkness now dispelled though the sun is still opaque;
There, triumphant in the sky - 'a vision of God's own make'.

A riot of pastel colours and fashioned in an arc;
It's the sun's rays on the raindrops and there has made its mark.
With violet, indigo and blue; orange, red and green, and
Gently merging at each end, are yellows and golden sheen.

And, right across the heavens this beauteous beam of glory,
Sets a question in our minds - could there be an authentic story?
What of the very first rainbow? Well, God showed his majestic power,
When, as a token of regard, He made a covenant with Noah.

For when Noah came out of his ark, God set a bow of light -
Across the sky, just after the rain and made all earth seem bright.
This, a traditional story found in books of early times,
Can be changed or accepted or along some other lines.

Whether it is true or not - there's no one can deny. . .
That joy and perfect beauty of a RAINBOW in the sky.

Patricia McGowan

Memories

Memories are something we'll always keep
some memories come back and
haunt us in our sleep.
Memories can be very special, those
are the ones we treasure in our hearts
and souls they'll stay with us forever.
Some memories make us glad, some upset us
and make us feel quite sad,
memories no-one can take away as they
stay with us night and day.
Some memories can make us beam with pride
some can be so bad, the past we want to hide.
People and things can come and go as this
I already know.
But memories of the past and yesterday
with me I know will always stay.

Patricia Mackenzie

Friendship

I looked into your eyes,
And myself came back to me,
Clearly as in twin mirrors,
With such startling clarity.
The essence of your soul came too,
And bonds were formed that hold
The world forever, with you close,
In real friendship's ring of gold.
Some call it love. For me, I know,
That all such names compare,
And friendship, love and oneness,
With togetherness, are there,
And always will be while life lasts.
Our eyes still meet and share
A wonderful companionship.
I know . . . . and it is rare.

Pettr Manson-Herrod

Reflections

When I look in the mirror, the face that I see
Is not the face of the girl I used to be
With eyes ashine and face aglow, those tender years so long ago
Hair thick and brown, skin blemish free,
An attractive face that used to be.
Those teenage years when the world was mine
Exciting years full of dreams sublime
The age of maturity when the future looks good
The face that looks back as a mature face should
Look again in the mirror, a picture I see, of a bride on her wedding day
Could that be me? Those war years when we must part
Just a few special days, and the fear in my heart
Now the face of a wife and mother, older now, but with each other.
Our joys and sorrows, our future together and all our tomorrows
Now hair not brown but white, wrinkles and dentures, eyes not so bright
Spectacles needed to read and write, anti wrinkle cream to use at night
Limbs less supple as they used to be, fingers clumsy and slow,
Can't hear as well as I used to and my memory is fading I know
My seventy four years, seem but a day, I still get out while I'm able
A senior citizen with a "sell by date label",
So mirror, mirror, on the wall, help me to like what I see
With all my faults and weaknesses
I am what I am - Just me

K. McQueen

Bird Song

Please God don't let them cage me in and take away my freedom,
You gave me wings to fly the sky,
Not sit and wait for death to come.
Can you not open their eyes to see,
That I belong up in the trees
Or resting in rocks and skimming the sea
Not pining away in front of T.V.
With little toys that are all the rage
Cluttering up my tiny cage.
I do not know the taste of fruit,
The colour of leaves, or bark under foot.
To feel the wind under my wings,
I am so sad I cannot sing,
So please make them see they are being cruel,
To cage me up like some precious jewel.
Just let me go to find a mate,
To build a nest and propagate.
That's all I ask, is to be free,
To come and go just as I please.

F. Middleton

306

Dance Of The Fireflies

Still is the night, light is the breeze, faint is the sound of the rustling leaves.
Moonlight from heaven downwards doth pour
Casting shadows that dance on the damp forest floor,
Where the mould on the leaves is a wondrous sight,
Glowing in darkness with a soft phosphorous light,
While up in the air attracting the eyes, a swarm of glowing fireflies,
Whose lights seem to dance on the nights soft breeze
'Gainst heavenly stars that can be seen through the trees.

Spiralling upwards the flickering lights, dance to the rhythm, the rhythm of the night.
Their music is the sound of the rustling leaves
And creak of the branches as they sway in the breeze.
And the chorus is the owl that hoots up above
As the fireflies dance their courtship of love.
Whilst nightly creatures in the forest below,
Look up in wonder as they dance to and fro.

Onwards upwards into the trees the dance continues on the nights soft breeze.
Like fairy lights they shine in the night, their dance of love is a glorious sight.
The rhythm heightens in their dance above.
And for a moment in time, there is consummate love.

Cool is the dawn, gone is the breeze, no more the sound of the rustling leaves,
As the sun arises and spreads forth its light
And the light from the fireflies doth fade from sight,
Such a wondrous vision is lost to the eyes,
'Tis the courtship dance of the fireflies.

Joseph Michaels

Going Home

I am out at sea and far from home
If I was a seagull I'd swoop over the foam
I see the liver birds in my minds eye
Faster and faster I would fly

I've been away for such a long time
I wonder if Liverpool is still mine
I hope she opens up her arms
And holds me tight with all her charms

I hear her voice
I smell her air
It won't be long before I'm there

So carry me home you mighty ship
Because this will be my very last trip
I see the Mersey in my minds eye
I'm coming home to you to die

Anne Murray

Alone

A breeze of feathers
Tickled the Column's nasal.

One, two, now twenty
As the archer let go with a twang. . .

Energy died as nature conquered,
The city fell silent.

Paranoia: are you after me?
A cuckoo spots an empty nest.

Food, sodium chloride regenerates
But weight out-does speed.

Own to live: Own to die
Birth and death; nature thrives.

Matthew Murphy

Spring

The blackbird dark, with beak of yellow, sings his song, this feathered fellow,
When evening comes with crimson hue, purple tinged and darkest blue,
He sings his song, to mark his space, a silver sound like fragile lace,
His song is perfect in the air, reverberating everywhere,
On rooftops there, with chimneys tall, where curling smoke blows over all,
Smoke that twists and turns on high, sending trails into the sky,
The blackbird sings as if to say, that Spring at last is on the way,
The hedgehog in his den awakens and dressed in spiky armour takes
His walk across the lawn to see, how the gardens changed since he,
On that day when Winter's blast sent him to his sleep at last,
A sleep that lasted Winter long, until he heard the blackbirds song,
That awakened him from his repose, he searches with his black tipped nose
For food to fill his empty frame, a tasty morsel he will claim,
He scurries, scuttles through the plants and all this time the blackbird chants
His song from high as if to say, that Spring at last is on its way,
A warming sun begins to stir and sprinkles colour everywhere
As dormant plants begin to grow and wondrous flowers their colours show,
Primrose dainty, crocus bright, reaching out to warm sunlight
Spring sun-light that dapples trees, enhancing growth of new green leaves,
Leaves that grow again each year, until the Autumn shades appear,
Then tumble down and swirling round, an amber carpet on the ground,
Then Winter takes its dreadful hold, dull grey skies and bitter cold,
But now the Winter days are done and feathered fellow sings his song,
He calls from high as if to say, that Spring at last is on its way.

Janet Morton

A Letter To Freda

This letter that I'm writing I hope it reaches you first post
I know you are somewhere in heaven with the Holy Ghost
Sorry I can't get to find out your postcode
Nor the district, box number, lane, street or road
So I'll just address it, care of Jesus Christ
He will see you get it post haste within a thrice
Yes somehow I know you will receive the words of this letter
I'll wait for you to talk to me when the line is better
Of course as I write it you can follow every line, every word
Read it out aloud, it doesn't matter if you're overheard
Because I want the whole world and beyond to know
My prayers are for you sweetheart, and I love you so
For I miss you more than words can ever say
My thoughts, my deeds, are with you every moment of the day
I think and remember your lovely cherished smile
The fondest of memories live on with me all the while
I can feel you so near me dear, I want to touch
Oh please God let me, that's not asking much
Let me hear your soft voice telling me what to do
It's so lonesome and heartbreaking here without you

Leslie Moate

"Life Goes On. . ."

As I stand here by your graveside, the pain's too much to bear,
For I know when I awake tomorrow, you will not be there.

I can't believe He's taken you, they say He takes the best,
He decided that your time had come, and laid you down to rest.

I have no will to live now, why doesn't He take me too?
For a life of pain and misery, is all I have without you.

It wasn't meant to be like this, this wasn't what we planned,
Never will I touch you again, or even hold your hand.

You promised me we'd be forever, you promised you'd never leave,
How could you be so selfish? How could you let me grieve?

I tried to wake you from your sleep, you never even stirred,
I didn't get to say goodbye, you left without a word.

There's so much I didn't tell you, so much you need to know,
He didn't even give me the chance, before He let you go.

So I just wanted to tell you, that your life was not in vain,
My will to live is stronger now, as part of you lives again.

Although you will not be here, your spirit will live you see
For my will is for the life I have,
Which grows inside of me.

Tracy Murrell

The Lovable Rogue

There is often a time, and often a place,
When I think of you fondly, remembering your face,
It could be daytime, or maybe at night,
Whatever the time, it's a wonderful sight,
Sometimes it's whiskery, others it's smooth,
But it's always kissable, if you approve,
With you I relax, in you I confide,
I wish that more often, you were at my side,
Life is interesting, enjoyable and serene,
Completely relaxing, whenever I've seen,
Your character deceptive, rugged and rough,
Though beneath the facade, its tender and tough,
I am happy to know you are there now and then,
And delight in the thought of seeing you again.

Valerie Morgan

The Childrens' Dance

We'll dance in the dawn and through the blue day;
We'll dance like the stars in the wild, whirling spray
Away on curled waves as they surge up the bay.

We'll dance in the morning when the sun rises high
To the whisper of leaves as the wind rustles by
And the larks pour their song on the earth from the sky.

Then down the cool gardens through noon's blazing hours,
Where fountains fall splashing in cold diamond-showers
And freshen the faces of sweet-scented flowers.

We are the children who dance like the light
Dressed as the moon is in silvery white,
Frocks fashioned from stars on a fine summer night.

We'll skip through dew till the thin mists rise
And the glow-worm lamps burn green, and the skies
Deepen, rose gold, as the daylight dies.

We'll fade like pale flowers, and turn into dreams
Caught in the gleam of the moon's magic beams
As they shatter on glass of deep pools and dark streams.

When gales come and winter, sad earth wrapped in grey,
In a numb frozen silence we stay hidden away;
But we'll dance through the spring on the first shining day.

Diana Momber

Liverpool Garden Festival 1984

Come to our garden festival
Which was opened by our Queen
Set in the heart of Liverpool
We hope you like our scene
We are having lots of visitors
From many country's too
Hoping there's a lot to see
And many things to do
We have had our share of troubles
This Liverpool of ours
And hope things are looking up
With our festival of flowers
Thanking all the planners
And the workers too
But most of all we want
To see our dream
Come true
      And it did!

E. Moneypenny

Untitled

You turned me on
Like a light
I felt like Oxford Street at Christmas.

You blew me out
Like a candle
At the end of the day.

Brenda Molyneux

310

The Awakening

I have just awoken from a dream like sleep
I am looking at the ocean so blue and so deep
I feel such calm peaceful and free
For the first time ever I am me.

I now have time to see beauty in flowers
Time unfolds before me, I have hours and hours
I don't feel tired stressed or pain
Just relaxed in this white light, there is no rain.

I look in your eyes, what do I see?
Your sorrow and grief, please don't cry for me
Can't you feel me? I am right by your side
Drying your tears and being your guide.

I'm not gone, I'm here in your need
I'm the sigh at the end of the poem you read
I'm the light in the dark, I'm a kiss on a breeze
I'm moonlight on a lake, I'm the thaw in a freeze

When your time draws near, I will hold your hand
I will carry you in my arms to this treasured land
We will spend eternity together
We will be happy and free for ever and ever

So when my love you feel you have to weep
Remember the memories I gave you to keep
I am not dead, I am right here
Holding you tight, and quelling your fear.

Angela Monk

The Merchant Banker

The message is clear
There's no one here
Stars are passing one by one
I plunge deeper - still they come
As I stare into infinity
Pinpoint planets pass by me
Ever falling, never landing
I feel myself resist, then drawn in.
"Look away" - I hear me cry
Still more stars go sailing by
You're hooked on the PC Screen Blanker
My friends think I'm a Merchant Banker.

Andrew Mountain

311

Best Things In Life

Give me the best things in life
All that is free
I want trouble, nor strife
Just tranquillity

Give me fortune, a pot of gold
To buy things I've never had
Have fun, before I'm old
To be happy, not sad

I need sunlight, not rain
To shine down on me
I don't want misery or pain
Just harmony

I can't be weak, make me strong
To help me to defend
I want to stay young
Until the very end

Let me feel happiness, not gloom
I don't want to cry
Let me smell flowers in bloom
And see birds fly in the sky

Give me faith and hope, not charity
I need love, not hate
I want a lifetime guarantee
Everything on a plate

Diane Murphy

In Love? Or In Lust?

Want to hold him want to kiss him
Want to stay
In his warm embrace forever
In love? Or in lust?

Standing in a room
Doing his own thing
And my eyes fall upon his face
I find myself drifting into trance
Just gazing at his face
He looks up and I quickly look away
But he knows I've been watching
In love? Or in lust?

When alone together he makes me laugh
Such a good feeling inside I have
He holds me and I never want him to leave
In love? Or in lust?

I will not deny that I have had
Passionate thoughts about him
Or that I gaze only upon his face
But this is only natural
In love? Or in lust?

Andrea Murdock

Untitled

I have the strangest hobby, I'm sure that you'll agree
For I like watching adverts, which appear on our TV
If on channel one or two, I realise my mistake
And quickly, with remote control, switch to commercial break,
The never ending story of the lady in Gold Blend,
And that little Andrex puppy, I could easily befriend,
Then there's Northern Upholstery, with furniture and stuff
Although it's on ten times a night, I'll never see enough
Direct Line Insurance, I really do adore,
I sit there in amazement, as the phone saws through the floor
I like the Oxo woman, she always makes her point,
But I've got to keep on watching, in case she burns the joint.
I think I'll start a brand new craze, could be at the hub
And become the Founder member of the advert watchers club.

R. D. Moses

Trust Me

"Trust me," she said
And you did.
You allowed her
To take you
Running through the blades of grass
Shredding your feet to ribbons.
You allowed her
To take the stars out of the sky
And hurl them into your eyes.
You allowed her
To feed you exotic fruits
Poisoning you to the brink of death.
You allowed her
To meet you in your darkest nightmare
And play with your fears till dawn.
You allowed her
To burst through into your daydreams
And casting flames, scorch your every thought.
You allowed her
To dance through your head
Implanting herself in a fertile corner.
You allowed her
To pilfer your soul
And as you watched her
Hurl it up into the dark night,
She left you
Longing for more.

Ann Moffat

Chocolate Spread

Chocolate spread,
Chocolate spread,
I love it with fresh bread.

I spread it with a knife,
And make it really sticky
But I'm really picky.

Chocolate spread,
Chocolate spread,
I love it with fresh bread.

I get it on my face,
What a disgrace.

Chocolate spread,
Chocolate spread,
I love it with fresh bread.

Rachel Norman (Age 11)

Disparity

This town, this fetid slum
Devoid of love
Governed by despots
Where conflict reigns supreme
Where realism is non-existent
Servile to the moralists unwritten laws
Prevalent where morons dwell
Continually contemplating plunder desperate to exist
Their language is heathen
Know it at your peril
The downward spiral beckons
Who dares to oppose, incurs suspicion
Segregation follows
The final link is broken
The door is firmly latched on the other side
There is no going back.

C.A. Moggach

The Big 40 Enigma

Oh dear, is this it, have I lost my get up and go,
I see a different person in the mirror, I can't believe
It's so.
I need someone to tell me, I still have a teenage
Physique,
Although deep down I realise some reactions are
Getting weak.
I imagine everyone is looking, I'm sure they can see the signs,
The greying hair, the slowing down, and the inevitable
Face lines.
No longer do I spring out of bed, I need to take extra care,
It's only to be expected, I'm not twenty-one I need to be aware.
So when I come to terms with all of this, it doesn't seem
So bad,
I begin to notice those with walking sticks and zimmer frames,
Then I almost feel glad.
At least I can get about reasonably well, although age is
Beginning to show,
I don't want to join those ranks quite yet, there's still a way to go.
I'd started to get depressed, and then I met a friend who is
Seventy five,
He's worked hard and now he's writing poetry, he says it's great
To be alive.
Age is no criteria, he says he's going for the "ton",
So what is life about, I feel ashamed, I'll forget age from now on.

Reg Morris

My Dream Is Long

I dreamt in fear so long a dream
I walked the shore, but when I turned
The sand had gone, I waded on
And so believed the night would end.
Then I was in a field of green
And they were there, looking my way
But did not play, they seemed at rest
So I was too, until they cried,
The field of green turned crimson red
          And they were dead

I turned away and struggled on
And those in coats of white stood strong
I shouted loud, though silently
No one had heard, they would not see,
The victims now were different souls
With tortured minds, they bled, they moaned,
I tried to reach, but could not touch,
The weakened limbs, the crying eyes,
Again I turned and hoped to wake
          But did I sleep

Luciane Murfitt

Changing Seasons

Skies lighter, new life unfolding
Buds burst in colourful hue
Daffodils dance in abundance
Springtime and all is new.

Hot days and long light evenings
Jasmin's perfume filling the air
Butterflies hover in large numbers
Summer is here.

Russet leaves falling gently
Trees once again looking bare
Seasons have changed all too quickly
Autumn I fear.

Swirling mists arriving with the dawn
Beating rainy days
Grey and forlorn
Thick frost on the grass
Wild life disappears
Winter is here.

Doris Moss

314

Summer In The Countryside

The emerald green grass,
Overgrown by poppies,
Sways in the cool summer breeze.
The smell of grass cuttings,
And honeysuckle,
Casts a spell over my nose,
When I breathe deeply.

The butterflies flutter past,
Landing on the blackberry bush,
Bearing its unripe berry.
A dog lies in shelter of the sun,
His uncoordinated breathing,
Sending the fallen pollen,
Back into the now still air.

The children play on the swings,
And mother sunbathes,
Whilst I listen to the soft,
Sweet chirruping,
From the nearby chaffinch,
And her newly born.

Ava Néputé (Age 14)

The Farm

I walk by the side of the hedgerow
Happy in my tread
Berries and flowers abound
Birds fly overhead

The sheep lie huddled together
Chewing, content as can be
The horse runs around in a field
'Tis a beautiful sight to see

The cows move slowly to greet me
Belinda, Patsy and Joy
I feel about seven years old
As happy as child and toy

The goats, the geese and farm cat Sam
All add to my wonderful day
Oh - to visit the farm all the days of my life
Aside Jackdaw, Rook and Jay

Anita Mularz

The Sussex Bandstand!

I have waited patiently for this week in July
When the R.E's would come down our way.
To sit and listen for a couple of hours
And dream of that tall dark handsome soldier!
Although he is not so young, his hair has a touch of grey
And the shy smile lights up his dark brown eyes.
His solo spot has set my heart a thumping
And all too soon the concerts ended!
Now I eagerly await the next day.
Here I am, sat down, so keen, there's at least another hour
Until they appear on the scene!
But I contentedly sit and wait, the wind is chilly
And the sun has gone, it makes no difference to me!
Just as long as I can sit and daydream 'til my bandsman plays!
I'm too old to catch his eye, to him I'm probably just one
Of many out front, bespectacled, a sea of grey
With my crossword book, I've not even noticed
It's upside down and I haven't even given it a look!
Now it's over for another year, will my handsome soldier be back?
Or retired and trumpet put away?

Well! I will still have him!! On my C.D. to play!!

Barbara Morris

Life

Life videos in sharp focus now.
Live immortal scenes - 'know-how'.

See vivid, clear camera shots,
Define, zoom in -'on-hold' life knots.

Newborn hearts blossom nowadays
Canvas flowers froth all pathways.

Artistic dances step childhood acts
Timeless beauty outlives time pacts.

World languages converge earth rivers,
Wise-pen words, whilst sword-hand quivers.

Equality-freedom seeds sow
Justice, happiness, love must grow.

Human mortals shadow clock-toys-
Fate winds blow - 'fast-slow' turns girls, boys.

Who can control lifes watch winder?
Or glimpse God's fleeting view finder?

Special times-memory freeze-frames,
Moonbeam mirages encircle names.

Kaleidoscope scenes haze road steams,
Heat raises up elusive dreams.

Born-truth revealed through child eyes;
Tears dry, heart-held times make men wise.

Hilary Ann Morris

Remembering

Tears are escaping from my eyes
Through the mirror of my mind
Reflecting forth so many memories
I believed were sealed and signed

Like the finding of my treasure chest
And apprehensive to turn the key
To unfold scenes of long ago
Afraid of what I might see

Releasing the lock of my inner self
Into the dark recess lurking below
Will I be able to handle it
The truth must be revealed to know

On venturing the secrets of my heart
A healing calmed me when I delved
Into hidden feelings put on hold
It seems for eternity had been shelved

Reminiscing among the forgotten past
Has enveloped me in happiness again
Not only is my whole being at rest
Erased is all sorrow and pain

Soft echoes are now calling to me
Flowing swiftly along on a breeze
Whispering away grey evil shadows
Time now for acceptance of peace

Tricia Mary

Rude Awakening

As daylight breaks it begins
Rustling, hustling - is it the wind?
No, there's a frantic scampering, a sudden squeal
Am I asleep - is this for real?

My senses reeling, what's that I hear?
Was that a footstep creeping near?
A clump,a shuffle, something soft
Is there someone in the loft?

I'm awake now, well only just
What is it that's making such a fuss?
A squawk, a thump, a raucous hoot
Oh, 'tis only a Starling in hobnailed boot!

Stella Norris

Alphabet Of Love

A touch of a hand
Brush of a cheek
Caress of a loved one
Delightful memories to keep
Each moment a treasure
For each one to hold
Given one who is lonely a gem to enfold
Hearts are so fragile and easy to break
It needs pure love for one to partake
Just give love a chance be honest and true
Keeping love in the heart to last your life through
Love can be shown in so many ways
Most growing deeper day after day
Never keep secrets from one that you love
Opening your heart can solve many things
Putting two heads together is better than one
Quote your misgiving and things will come right
Regrets are forgotten and driven from sight
Sigh of contentment and happiness begins
To love and be loved
Unites two hearts into one
Value this gift given to you
When love guides your heart
X amount of joy you possess
Your wildest dreams will be answered
Zealous love to impress.

Mary V. Ciarella Murray

Nests

A mossy twig here
Intertwined
Built piece by laboured piece;
An arbour of peace
Safe from the predator
The storm and the cold.
All creation needs a nest;
A form in the ground,
A decorative bower; a sheltering rock -
A Home Nest where love can bloom and grow.
And in the Palm of His Hand,
God holds the Nest of the World
To His bleeding Heart,
Overshadowed by the Glory of His Cross,
Where all nests find their starshine,
And tears give way to rainbows
Radiant in the joy of Resurrection's Dawn.

Marie Adèle Newby

317

Life Or Death

Why is there sadness?
Loneliness builds up in a troubled soul
A fire burns in hell for every tear shed
And is God real?

The earth goodness shattered and slayed
By the piercing knife of evil
The red soldiers fiery and glowing
Overcome the clear, heavenly guardians

For every death, a battle is lost
And somewhere in hell a celebration is held
Painful living in a bad dream
Trying to overcome the chaos and madness

Words of sin and pain
Vibrate among society
The fury builds up a bomb
Just waiting to explode it's bad feeling

The journey to the bright light
Is so rigid and hard
Like a vertical mountain
Impossible to climb without aid

A time when the Earth
Is swallowed up by money, disease, war and hatred
Are the devils' games
His ambitions and his winnings

Natalie Moore

Autumn Walks

Morning sun lies low on the horizon, the sky is a lilacy-blue,
The air is cool and still, the ground is covered with dew.
Brambles grow on the hedgerows, hips and haws abound,
Peace and quiet around me, birds adding soft, sweet sounds.
Away from the hustle and bustle, away from the traffic's noise,
I walk alone through the fields, savouring Nature's joys.

Golden evening sun,casting shadows so tall,
Dusk is slowly creeping, over fence and wall,
Creatures are settling slowly, soon to be quiet and still
Night is not very far away, just beyond the hill.
Peace will soon fall again over the sleeping Earth
Until the sun arises to give the new day birth.

Christine Naylor

318

I Have Got

I have a lunch box
I have a badge
I have a packet all in one
I have a baby (not really)
I have a van and a car
And a lamp with the children all about

I have a TV that everybody likes
I know people that most people like
I go to a school everybody likes
I've got a video I like
I've got an art book that Jessica likes

I've got a fire that keeps me warm
I've got a pen that I write with
I've got a flower pot that I made
I've got the matchbox to light a fire
I've got the old lady that swallowed the fly

We've got a mirror that we look through
We've got glasses that make us see
I've got some dice that I play with
I've got slippers to put on my feet
I've got a sore lip

I've got a teddy
I've got a bedroom that I sleep in
I've got some parents to look after me

Nathalie Needham (Age 5)

Shadows On The Heart

When age had robbed him of mobility,
And daydreams trembled to senility,
The changing seasons became all his days,
As by his window, constantly, he gazed;
Kaleidoscope of summer's verdant green,
Merged to autumn, into winter's scene;
No trumpets heralded approaching death,
As, vap'rous on the air, his frosted breath
Hung in frailty, and sight dimmed,
To last obscurity; sweet robin, weep,
And wait no more, patiently, for
Crumbs, about his door; though bitter
Wind may moan, in winter deep,
Forever he lies wrapped in endless sleep,
And soft as snowflakes, on your
Breast so red, sighs dark December's grief,
For he is dead, and sorrow's icy chill
Enfolds my heart, ne'er to be warmed again,
        Or love impart.

Dorothy Neil

319

The Moment

Time was, when I was there.
I lived and strived
Towards the future, to another time.
I had desires that I yearned to fill.
Always hoping, searching, until
A moment came to cherish, sublime.

Memories hold time long passed,
Sometimes clear, but oft-times dimmed.
One is told that time stands still,
Yet, how does one know when to grasp,
That finite moment 'ere it has passed.
But one came to me, pure, unsought.

My mind dwelt not on material things.
As the end of day was drawing nigh
My gaze turned upwards to the sky.
There the sunset filled the scene,
Such was the sight, words can't describe.
That's the moment etched in my mind,
Pure, immutable, undefined.

Norman Nicholson

Haze

I lay back in the grass
and traced the scars of planes etched into
the sea above

The air was pure, fresh;
grasshoppers and butterflies
my only other company

A pure fleeting vision yes,
occurring only when I closed my eyes
and breathed . . .

I roll to one side and my hand closes
on another, warm and
fragrant like wild flowers

Almost worth missing the uncertainty
of life ahead,
to be buried here now
safe
and contented.

Ben Nurdin

December Days Of A Little Child

Hurry home to crackling fire,
Hot soup bubbling in the pan on the hook
Grandad asleep holding a book
The cat looks up stretches and yawns
The dog opens one eye then just licks his paws.
The brasses ashine with the bright flame from the fire.
Grandad wakes up puts tea in the pot,
Gives me some soup it's lovely and hot.
Some bread freshly baked by Mother that day,
I'll have some more soup then go out to play.
I'll just play for a while with my friend from next door,
Then indoors I'll go to sit by the fire.
Grandad will tell me some tales of yore,
Mum will appear soon to bed we will go.
Goodnight, God bless, a kiss until tomorrow,
Mum tucks me up warm, kisses my head.
My dog, my cat, come to the foot of the bed,
Goodnight darlings, God bless you both.
I'm tired now so to sleep.
God bless you all, my day is complete.

Lena Newton

Peace, Be Still!

The night was dark, the sky was grim
The sea was rough as the tide rolled in,
And there I stood on the beach alone
Wondering why I was so far from home.
The sand was soft beneath my bare feet
Was there someone I was meant to meet?
The waves rolled in still higher and higher
As the church bell tolled the midnight hour;
The sea was coming much closer to me
I turned around and started to flee.
Why at this hour was I on that beach
What or Who was I trying to reach?
I fled along the cold, damp sand
Wasn't there anyone to give me a hand?
I was brought to a stop by some high cliffs
And fear made me feel so cold and stiff;
I could not move, there was nowhere to go
And the waves still came, quickly, not slow.
I tried to climb though full of fear
My mind was stunned I could not think clear,
I screamed "Help! Please someone help!"
Then a voice so calm as that of yore
Said "Peace, Be Still!" and the waves stopped
As they had done ... those centuries before.

Madge Nyman

Snow

Snow is bubbly,
As bubbly as a a bubble bath.
It's freezing and smooth.
Snow is like ice-cream
Soft as a feather.
It is crunchy and bumpy,
As cold as a freezer
And white as a sheet.
It sparkles and twinkles
And it is glittery.
Snow is white.
It's like a skating rink.
It is very slippery.
It tastes like water.
It's like a blizzard
And like a storm.
It looks like a cloud.
Snow comes down from the sky
As soft as silk.

Jodie Oakes (Age 8)

Sky Ships

The frolicsome wind is upon us today
And likely to stay with us, so they say.
Bothering the trees and all in its path
Upskittling everything - such a laugh!

Scudding clouds and lots of small fry
Across the skyline hurrying by.
All shapes and sizes pushed along
With a whining, clattering, joyous windsong.

Where are you off to, great ships in the sky?
Is someone steering you, and if so, why?
Have you a train to catch yon side of the world
As puffing along the skyline you're hurled?

And if you reach where on earth you're going
Are you finished all your to'ing and fro'ing?
Or will you come back to dance up on high
And call us to share your pie in the sky?

Phyllis Norman

The Word

The dreaded word we don't want to hear,
Is the thing that most of us really fear.
It attacks the old when least expected,
When it's a child we feel rejected.

It strikes the sick when we think it's safe,
The weaker the body it's the road we pave.
It comes with diseases and can cut life short,
It can even happen with fitness in sport.

We know it has to come to us all,
For some it is harder to take the call.
Some say it's good to see the way to the gate,
Not to be afraid of it must really feel great.

It can come to a son or a daughter so dear,
That bad empty feeling it makes us all fear.
We all know we are living to do it,
And misses no one, that includes the fit.

When it's a mother our hearts just break,
Our dearest person it's so hard to take.
The one we turn to when things get bad,
After we've spoken we are not so sad.

We know our mother is our best friend,
And it's hard to bear at the very end.
But we all know what she would say,
Some one has to go first to pave the way.

Grace Nellies

A Little Innocent

Your days are numbered little daffodil,
Yet it isn't the spring wind or frost that wicks
Your delicate yellow frame.

Surrounded by glass,
Your life ebbs into water.
You need your sun to live,
We take you to remind us of a sun that we have forgotten.
Your fragile colour brightens this dull terrace house.
For that, and that alone,
You must die.

Paul Noble

This World

I hate this world of greed and lust.
A place where you cannot learn to trust.
To watch your back at all times
And keep your eyes open wide.
A blink too quickly and you're a victim
To a world of latent sickening.
Noses in the air, ridden with self pride
Attitudes of people that will never subside.
Trying to break barriers which are artificially there
Put by people holding so - called prestige
If only they would notice those in need.

I hate this world of lies and deceit.
That gives you false hopes and never peace.
Always conflict and despair
Fill my dreams with nightmarish flare.
Commiserations to us that dare
To speak aloud and say what's fair.
To bite one's lip and admit defeat
When you are not heard, but seen and befit
What others, presume is right
But you are weakened and cannot fight.

I hate this world of greed and lust.
A place where you can never learn to trust.

Saima Nazreen

Silver Shoes

She dreams,
Of twirling bodies and silver shoes
Of lacy skirts and body stockings,
She smells the chalk
Stepped into the floor
And the spicy smell of warm bodies.
She feels the beat of the music,
In her mind
For wheels cannot feel, her legs are useless
Beyond repair,
Like her car.
She sighs and weeps her tears,
For spangley lights and silvery shoes,
And the rhythm of the dance.

Barbara Nash

On My Way Home

Tonight I saw my place
On Earth
Beneath the soft delight of the stars.
I looked -
Into emptiness and everything-ness
And saw myself - AWAKE!
The miracle and the beauty shrouded
In an infinite veil.
The soul - its focus.
Perception - pinnacle of the senses.
A silk expansion of what? And why?
And what of WHAT's and WHY's?
Am I the centre of the universe?
NO! You are what you were before
　　　Your turn
　　　　　On the
　　　　　　BIG WHEEL.
Repenting my sins I bowed down in glory.

Michael Newell

Armageddon

The explosion is silent, the pain is sudden,
the bombardment of life, it's Armageddon.
To think yesterday, here stood the city,
now all that's left is an air of pity.

The world is empty, the world is dead,
the rules of God have now been read.
The foolish humans chose to ignore,
their greedy behaviour led them to war.

I'm up here now with the rest,
seeing heaven at its best,
seeing the innocent in a trance,
we pray to God for another chance.

He says to us "what have you done?
The world I created has now all gone!
You think I'll re-create all the land,
at the click of my fingers or the clap of my hand?

You controlled the world like you were me,
I just watched and hoped you'd see,
hope gradually slipping away,
now we've reached the final day.

I'm sorry I can't do what you ask,
I won't complete this final task,
it's not because I cannot do it,
you had your chance and went and blew it!"

Andrew Whaley and Paul Nixon

Moods

Over your face the shadows fall;
As sunlight dies on a silent pool
And you think sad thoughts,
And I wonder what you dream.

But the waters come to life again;
As do your thoughts;
And sunlight and shadows flash into being;
And you are alive again.

M.A. Newport

My Valentine

My valentine has been my love
For fifty years and more.
Must be that the Lord above
Intended us to score.
Among our many blessings
Are children one-two-three,
Who helped to form the branches
On our growing family tree.
Now life is getting shorter
But love will never alter
For my valentine and me.
We now have great grandchildren
Sixteen to date
There may be more
It isn't too late.

W. Ordidge

Where Is My Springtime

I stare into the misty morning
The naked trees stand tall
They have lost their coats of green
In the winter's fall

Sometimes I feel like trees in winter
Open and exposed
Longing for springtime
When I can be reclothed

Oh where is my springtime
My flowering daffodil
My new grass in the morning
Upon which the rain does spill

Come fill my heart with joy
Let me look into your eyes
And down by the river
Come sit here by my side

Find me my love
And I pray that I find you
Bring my heart out of this darkness
And let your love shine through

Let us leave the tides of heartache
Far far back in time
And the brightness of the future
Be yours and mine.

M.J. O'Rourke

Unsung Heroes

Dedicated to their calling
bound by the hippocratic oath,
stitching cuts and wounds appalling,
or treating an unsightly growth.
Knowing they are always needed
whatever time, by day or night,
patients asking to be heeded,
soothing our nerves when sick with fright.
Through sleepless night and hectic day
to always smile tho' feeling rough,
expected to know just what to say
sometimes wishing it was enough.
Wondering if we ever stop
to think they might be feeling low
often working until they drop,
rarely thanked for what they know.
Bedside manner and healing hand
to make the patient feel at ease,
hoping they will understand
good or bad news, we're hard to please.
No other work can be compared
so little outlet for emotion,
carry the thought we know they cared
and be grateful for their devotion.

Ann Odger

In The Night Sky

Spikey sparkling polished star in the sky above us,
Little yellow wishing star climbing, higher and higher,
Dazzling twinkling little star.
Flying overhead,
Little tiny fire ball
In the night sky.

Flying golden dashing
Star through the galaxy.
Like a little light.
It flies past Jupiter, Saturn and Mars,
Like a little fading blur,
In the night sky.

Kirstie Osborne (Age 8)

Sun

A mischievous cloud blocks out the rays,
As it dances and threatens its worst;
You know in your heart that it's not there forever,
But still feels a cross you must bare.

The lightening explosion erupts in your ears,
And you know you're going to thunder;
The infernal noise, stops and it starts,
While you shout to be heard asunder.

A torrent of water appears fore your eyes,
The noise slowly becoming quieter;
The torrent eventually eases to droplets,
As the storm at last passes over.

The beams start to sparkle from between the clouds,
As the light finds its path slowly clearing;
A twinkle, a shimmer, what more can we ask,
A smile, we again find we're sharing.

Then shining upon us with a smile so fierce,
We're warmed through to the core;
The anger we felt for the tempers once shown,
Disappear along with the storm.

His tempers flutter along with the wind,
As his tears trickle down with the rain;
Though my son, to me, is always my sun,
For his smile and warm heart I have gained.

Lorraine Oakes

My Wish

If I could have a wish to choose for just one day
I would change into my costume
And with the Dolphins I would play

We'd laugh and sing and have great fun
Swimming from shore to shore,
We'd talk, dance and communicate in a way
That humans don't.

When the day is over and I must go home for my tea,
I'll shed a little tear as I'll be sad to leave,
But when I'm feeling lonely and all alone
I'll always remember my sea friends in their home.

Terrie Oakshott (Age 9)

Nice One Dean

Today's the day, I knew would come,
When mum finds out what I have done,
It was three weeks, or maybe more,
And here we are, at Nan's front door.
With hugs and kisses,you can't ignore.
Nan ushers us in, and closes the door.

'Nan where's Grandad, I've something to tell him.'
'Dean, he's in the garden, fixing the netting.'
'Hello Grandad, gee, have the fish all escaped'
Says mischievous Dean, with a smile on his face.
'Ah my boy, you've come round at last
'Better help me, fix this netting an fast.'

'Grandad I'm sorry, please let me explain,
You know that cat, next door is a pain,
I tried, I tried to chase him away,
But the bird he was after flew away.
I ran after him, all over the garden,
Till I fell over, oh I beg you pardon.'

'And Grandad, that's how your netting broke
It's that cat's fault, and that's no joke.
Don't worry Grandad, all is not lost yet.
That cat, will soon be off to the vet.
It's sure, he'll be sorry he tangled with me.
When he tries to eat that toy fish for tea.'

W.J. O'Toole

Winter

Winter is so cold and cheerless
Coming frosty, bold and fearless
Like a panther ready to pounce
Upon an unsuspecting prey.
Winter skies a miserable grey
With icy winds that chill the soul
Creeping into every home
Sending shivers, not wanting to leave the world alone.
Striking sometimes with a vengeance
In winter finery - a bleak and snowy coat,
Covering the land by day and night
Until warming rays of sunshine break the spell
And winter is no more.

M. Owramenko

Told To Have Faith

I am told to have faith to believe in your Lord,
by those that have faith in you. I am told not
to question but just to believe, and believe,
all that you say is true.

I am told understanding will come in good time
if I have faith in the bible your book, but I'm
still of a mind, of my Mother's advice, don't
leap until you have looked.

Why oh Lord, did you not write one word, in your
bible, I can not understand, but I envy those,
who believe in your word that was written by
other hands.

In order to believe I must first understand, to
have faith I first must have trust,
to put my life in anyone's hands,
believing in them is a must

I want to believe in a God out there,
but like others I've not seen the light,
but I'll try to do good and learn what I can,
tomorrow might give me new sight.

Keith Onslow

Sister's Love

There is no love like a sister's love
The growing of ones minds
The little things you say and do
The kindness that I find
To see your face to see you
Smile means all the world to me
For big sister I've looked up to you
Since I was only three.
But now I have grown older
I'm glad you're by my side
Because big Sister there is no other
Like you, I'm glad to find,
And when our days are over
And we are up above,
I hope you're still my sister,
Because you're the one I love.

Lindsey Oare

The Lord's Day

The great Creator in His gracious way
Gave six whole days for us to work and play.
He gave the seventh to rest and sanctify,
The day to praise the Lord, just you and I.

Just stop and think your purpose on this earth,
How you depend on God from day of birth;
God's kingdom doth reside within thy soul,
Join in His heavenly house, obey His call.

The Sabbath Day that God did sanctify
He asks us all to keep it clean and dry;
Why can't we live and keep it as we ought?
Instead of turning to a day of sport.

Judge not the sinners on their way to pray
If in the crowd you crucify His day,
But if in doubt, just read the Holy Book,
You'll find the answer there, just have a look.

Richard Orritt

The Thing

There is a Thing with a mission,
In its mind, body and soul.
It has a mode of action,
Now it only needs . . . . . a victim.

A fox strolls in the Forest of Dreams,
Unknowing that on this peaceful, perfect day,
He is hunted.
The Forest will be peaceful no longer.

The cold-blooded master checks its plan,
Then, swiftly, sharply, it strikes.
Like comets the hunter and the hunted collide,
The hunted had no hope.

The fox prays for mercy,
As the Forest's vivid colours begin to fade.
Sadly, the fox dies a slow, painful death.
Now, only his last thought remains:

"What is this brutal Beast?"

The Hunter rests, smiling, content,
A thought flashes into its mind:
"This game is too easy,
It seems that Humans can never fail."

But the man is wrong.
For, in the Forest of Dreams, there is always
        HOPE

Bhavnaben Patel (Age 15)

Friends Forever

You are a star that shines so bright
Up in the shy that holy night.
You shine so strong you make me cry.
For you left me oh so soon you died
To mourn and weep for your soul
Your memory I am proud to own
But on that cold night, not so long ago
When they took away your heart and soul
They took my heart along with yours
So we can be together
Heart and soul as one
You are my friend forever

Sue Owen

Snow

Snow floating in the sky
Night time birds
Over the white trees.
Snow that is white
As icing sugar.
A man says goodnight.
A boy falls asleep.
No-one is awake.

Lee Pettit (Age 8)

My Next Door Neighbour

My next door neighbour had a childhood disorder,
He didn't eat worms from the ornamental border
Or rub something fluffy on the space 'neath his nose
Which is perverse when you think, but normal I s'pose.

My next door neighbour had a penchant for steel,
Sharp angles, cold surfaces, unpleasant to feel.
He didn't clutch teddies to his small heaving chest
But irons, carburettors or house bricks were best.

My next door neighbour had a thing for tin foil.
He lined all his clothes and remained totally loyal
To the habit until when he started to date
And he found undressing was at too slow a rate.

My next door neighbour became a minimalist,
Now he's in hospital on the critical list.
He's covered with sores from chairs with cold arms
And stony faced women with goals but no qualms.

Sally O'Reilly

Face To Face

Stark pain etched on my face is plain to see
a weariness that eats away each night
hangs like an omen mirrored within sight,
your peace never extended toward me.

I see your pale face, glowing in slow dark,
built upon a perfect circular shape
descended not from some far distant ape,
by man created measuring life's spark.

Alarm must raise by pre-determined act
your hands encompass space throughout a day
to own three is unusual today
which may from fate seek sleepers to distract.

Bland face has no emotion to express
two hundred years or more of settled form,
but wasteful night-long vigils I perform
a senseless dose of self-inflicted stress.

Read from you information none can mock
source facts supplied can never be but true
a forecast when the nightmare's end is due
because you simply are my faithful clock.

Richard O'Yorke

Remembrance

Two minutes isn't much to give
To those who fought and died
And not forgetting loved ones
Who till this day have cried.

To Flanders field where poppies grow
Our thoughts return to long ago
And in Remembrance they still live
Two minutes isn't much to give.

A lonely field so far away
A jungle in the heat of the day
A raging sea so cold and deep
Are memories we all should keep.

This debt is ours to those who died
Repaid each year with loving pride
They fought our fight so we could live
Two minutes isn't much to give.

So don't forget those long days past
And live in hope that peace will last
They gave their lives so we could live
Two minutes isn't much to give.

Frank Osborne

Everlasting Blossom Of Fruitfulness

Are we a fragrance - a beautiful show
An abundance of blossom that does endless grow
Do the rains come and the showers fall
Whilst our blossom stands proud to be seen by all

Are we a beautiful show for all to see
With our fragrant petals saying "look at me"
Do we protect ourselves from the rain's harsh fall
And shield ourselves from the sun's hot scorch

If a man walked by and a hungered be
Could he reach down his hand and pick fruit from you and me
Or would our blossom stand proud showy - in the way
Beware lest he curse us this very day

Some trees grow but blossom with no usefulness
A sweet smelling fragrance - no fruitfulness
They're a beauty to behold nice to the eye
But what value have they to the needful passer by

Some trees like a peach their blossom supreme
A showy affair like a beautiful dream
It seems to take ages but gets there in the end
A succulent fruit the hungry to tend

But what of the vine - which through Christ we're a part
So little the blossom the fruit is the heart
The sun does scorch, the rain beats in its day
The pruning knife cuts deeply away all of its uselessness
So men can see the fruitfulness of Jesus to meet their need

Sheerah Ruth Peachey

To Ken . . .

I need a man, whose eyes can say,
"I love you" every single day.
I need a man whose lips are warm,
Who'll hold me close and safe from harm.
I need a man to touch my cheek,
One look from him, to make me weak.
I need a man, whose arms are strong,
To hold me close, all the night long.
I need a man to buy me flowers,
To comfort me, in my lonely hours.
I need a man who dreams, my dreams,
Who helps me, and supports my schemes,
I need a man who used to be,
The one and only man for me.
Where is that man? Where is he now?
I'd like him to return, somehow!

Joan Oyston

Night-time Fright

It tickles my feet
I jump up with fright
Whatever is this monster
That's come in the night

It makes me shiver
As it crawls up my PJ's
Making my legs cold and clammy
It's got to where my teddy bear lays

I start to cry
Because I'm wet and cold
Mum please come and help
My bottle has a hole

Stacey Purath (Age 10)

The Cross Of Love

A small leaded window pane, where the light comes shining through
It's shining bright on the cross of love, our brother just for you
We look at the cross so often and imagine you standing by
Then as you gently smile at us, tears just fill our eyes

We read your name in gold letters time and time again
The letters stay so clear and bright when in the pouring rain
We read your name out loud and hope that you may hear
Then look at the glowing cross of love feeling you are near

We many times forget and say, we'll just go and see our bri
And as we call and say a prayer we feel you standing by
For we were your six sisters and you our only brother
How you left us oh so quick was cruel for our dad and mother

You always said in your fifty one years, if I go let it be quick
We knew you were ill for some time but only you knew how sick
We tried in vain to save you but you had come to your end
We wonder now do you know the many hearts there is to mend

Now as we tend to your grave and do the best we can.
People may visit you and say, I remember that man
Will they look at the leaded window pane, light shining through
We wonder do they see you there, near the cross of love as we do.

Shirley Ann Quinn

My Cousin

My cousin tickles me
My cousin makes me laugh
My cousin plays with me
And he acts daft

My cousin and me play football
My cousin is my best mate
He is a fan of Huddersfield Town
And they are great

Joel S. Pollard (Age 8)

War Heroes

Shot men are falling to the ground,
The noises are extremely loud.
This is getting extremely gory,
"Dulce et decorum est pro patria mori."
Boots in mud, mines in the grass,
Death has got no upper class.

Gas bombs explode around brave men,
As they fell, ten by ten.
"Come on lads!
Here we go!
To spoil the Nazi show!"

John Pool (Age 9)

Flowers In The Thistle

For little flowers, the world is cruel
On Wednesday morning you skipped to school
Clothed and fed, full of beans
Heads full of thoughts and childish dreams
Your lives ahead, you'd lived so little
Oh life is cruel my flowers in the thistle

You met your little classmates
Happy at play, without a care
Although you were the new initiates
Your innocent love you were happy to share
But fate and life can be so fickle
To budding flowers in the thistle

People ask how could it be
How could anyone fail to see
The beauty in your angelic faces
And trade such views for empty spaces

Your faces are etched in my mind
As stone with a chisel
But the colours are gone
No more flowers in the thistle.

Robert Powell

Loves Dream

Where loves young dreams go to and fro
On the river of life where do they go
Tossing upon the crest of a wave
Who'll end up being loves slave
When the one you love is beyond your reach
To another your feelings you have to teach
To share with one your life and love
And make your vows to one above
Through life's road you will wind
And hopefully true love you'll find
So take my hand and off we'll go
Through life's journey forever more
And though at death we must part
I will love you forever with all my heart
And hopefully if we meet again
It will be a Paradise lost to a Paradise regained

C.A. Pope

At The Helm

I know a place
A land-locked prow
Where I can be helmsman
To the planet Earth
Feel the roll and turn
Beneath my feet
Watch for sunrise
Over Eastern hills.

I know a place
Where a living mast
Unfurls green sails
In chaotic breezes
I can take the wheel
From immortal hands
That hold our course
Into tomorrow.

Tricia Pearson

Oregon Song

I've followed you for mile after mile
Yet you never seem to stop
I'm still wondering where you're going
And beneath which mountain top?

From strength to strength I watched you grow
Whilst Alpine shelves protect you from snow
White frothy ribbons adorn every boulder
As your cooling waters cover their shoulder

All around you, mountains so high
That all I can see is the blue of the sky
Those rugged peaks that help you to flow
Together, you make a spectacular show.

All the trees that grow along your banks
For centuries now, they give you thanks
Just now and again, I hear you roar
You're letting me know, I can see you some more

Through canyons you've been, what else have you seen?
Maybe playtime and laughter where children have been
With love and romance along your side
Your beauty will not make anyone hide.

I'll think of you when I'm far away
Remember me too, if just for a day
You've given my mind, the peace that I need
My own special river, I wish you God speed.

Doreen J. Pickering

After Winter

After winter, cold and bleak,
The first light touch upon the cheek
Of warm and balmy air of spring,
Now, as every year, will bring,
Not the welcome of release,
But the first faint stirrings of unease.
For the winter's cold hard grasp
Does not conflict with life's stern task,
But the unaccustomed lightening
That's in the air of early spring
Belies the truth with smiling skies,
Does not, like winter, harmonise.

Doreen Priestley

A Prayer

Beat gentle heart
And kindness flow
Time is here for me to go.
Lord in Thy Heaven far away
I yearn for peace but not to stay.
Here - "In Heaven is called" our earth
My soul awaits your re-birth.
Loving Saviour that I may be
As a winged dove
On my way to Thee.

Olive Panzer

Progress

So let it free the surge of blackened tar
Pouring over core and patchy battered stones
With boiling treacle reaching crevices afar
Dripping into the earth, searing pockets, like poking bones

Filling the pipe covering trenches, unsavoury sight
With a lesser form of harmony you would expect
Thick greasy black unlustrous in its flight
Until the surface dark, complete, remains unflecked

Smokey rollers baton down rough hewn black
While steam and smell insult the very prim
Then finer layers are smelted on the track
The treacly ooze now fills from rim to rim

Now cranking, squeaking rowdyism fills the air
Iron bolts and jolting crank shafts shake
The once trim fields where wildest flowers did stare
Where peace and dreams belonged beside the lake

Phyllis Page

Heaven

There was a man from Devon,
Who every night at seven,
Went to the pier,
For a pint of beer,
And thought he was in heaven.

Mark Pilkington (Age 11)

Fog

The fog is an owl,
Swooping down towards us,
Stretching out its talons,
Ready to catch its defenceless prey.

The deadly hunter,
Will cover your village,
With a grey swirling blanket,
That will haunt the Earth forever.

Jonathan Pollard (Age 10)

A Patient

Our hospitals are on a par with world war trenches far.
Yes a good fight fought, but also the slow dying death fraught.

Do you realise bed three is dying, while bed two and four are sighing.
For comforts they'll get as homeward they trek, but bed three has nothing, he's dying.

If only he could go with no bustle and moans, in a neat little room of his own,
But no he accepts his food, sits in his chair, all skin and bone,
Don't they know he's dying.

Wait now, wait now it won't be long, in bed number three is a sweet young thing
With bright blue eyes and dimpled hands, ah me!

Remus Poll

335

Heating System Blues

'Twas installed when I was young.
Like a dream it boiled in the corner.
The heating system blues came after.
'Twas over ten years ago it went wrong.
To prove it'll never work, never stay.

Oh when you were repaired in surprise.
The blues returned it switched on 3 am.
Freezing us at tea time till fixed.
Just for once be the thing that behaves.
Touch wood blues will stay away awhile.

It still bubbles and cackles in the corner.
Spring leeks to remind you it's there.
How could we forget when it froze last year.
Radiators have a party of their own,
So bubble and cackle in the corner.

I shouldn't speak too soon it's so vain,
You play the heating system blues so well.
Even the cat stared once at the row.
One day I'll know how to handle the demon
That bubbles and cackles creaks into action.

E.J. Potts

Too Late

Gone; gone for ever. No warning,
Suddenly you have deserted me.
To no avail a desperate cry.

Too late! Too late for good
But long delayed intentions.
Too late to make up for neglect.

Unthinkable not to behold again
The smiling face that
Brought me joy, delight.

No more to hear your voice
So comforting and calm
Soothing my troubled mind.

How can I bear the future
Dark, alone knowing there is
No return? You're gone for ever.

Oh, had I once again
The chance to chart
The course of our lives.

Too late! These cruel word
Need not be spoken
Never.

Ruth Peel

Fulfilment

When I no longer see the beauty in a rose,
or fall in love with girls of seventeen,
then bury me and, without thought, dispose
of what I have become, not what I've been.

When I no longer hear hope's call upon the wind,
nor gather strength for what tomorrow brings,
prepare my beir, and do not dare rescind
the triumphs of my yesterday's brave youthful flings.

I do not bow to night, for I recall the glory of those days
when I was strong and loved and courted o'er.
I still have sight of me when I was young in all youth's ways,
and none can steal from me what's gone before.

Thomas A. Pendlebury

What's In A Name?

I don't think it likely that Somerset Maugham
Has ever attempted to infaugham
His readers that the Duke of Gloucester
Was once no more than a wicked impoucester,
Nor yet that at one time the Earl of Leicester
Performed as Good Queen Bess's jeicester,
During one of her visits to the Vale of Belvoir,
By playing the part of Bottom the Welvoir;
But I think it more likely that someone named Beauchamp
Would always be ready and willing to teauchamp
That if they catch sight of a name spelt Chalmondeley
There is no need at all to just stare at it dalmondeley,
Nor on seeing a name that's written as Vaughan
Does one need to feel just a little faulaughan;
While someone who's known by the name of MacLeod
Must surely feel extremely preod
That a famous compatriot, one Douglas Home
Was once our Prime Minister, though he might fome
At the strange way the Somerset people say Frome.
But of one thing I'm certain - if I were Lord Beaulieu
I'd ensure all my letters concluded "Yours Treaulieu"

G.E. Perrett

Mam's Poem - Christmas 1996

We thought about some whisky
And we thought about some gin
We thought about a crystal vase
   To put some flowers in

We thought about some chocolates
   And perfume crossed our mind
We thought about some slippers
   But we didn't know what kind

We thought about some vouchers
   For a gift of your own choice
   But we didn't think it right
She likes surprises does our Joyce

We thought about so many things
   But this is what you got
And you'll like it and you'll use it
   If you want to do or not!

L. Parker

My Sister

She's very fussy,
And a bit too bossy.

She thinks she's fast,
But always ends up last.

She thinks nothing's funny,
But when she laughs her nose goes runny.

She thinks she's the best,
But really is a pest.

She's got long black hair,
Which looks like a grizzly bear.

Even though she's like a blister,
She's enough to be my SISTER

Soleman Patel (Age 11)

The Steamtrain And The Guinness Can
(Ode To Andrew)

Beauty is in the eye of the beholder so they say
We all have different views of "What is art?"
"The Haywain" or "Sunflowers" is a standard persons taste
But to some three piles of bricks a foot apart

The beauty of the written word is plain to understand
And music has the power to move the masses
A concrete bust or sculpture can affect in different ways
As can windows made with different coloured glasses

There could be beauty in a photograph or even in a building
There is beauty in some objects made of metal
But I only know one person who could love a Guinness can
The one and only Andrew "Caveman" Kettle

I couldn't understand the simple point he tried to make
He spent ages in an effort to explain
That the can from which he poured was an object of high art
I thought the contents had affected Andrew's brain

His argument continued as he strained to win the day
But came the time we knew he was insane
His well considered view was that the beauty of the can
Could be compared to a classic old steam train

Now Andrew works at H.J. Heinz but is sure to get the sack
His supervisor will not know what he means
When he explains that he did nothing in a seven hour shift
But see the beauty in a tin of Heinz's beanz!

Stephen Parker

Endless Night

I hate this room
With all its gloom,
And this great bed
Which held the dead.
The furniture so very dark
That in the dust, you leave a mark.
The feather eiderdown and pillow
Which feels like drowning in marshmallow.
I just pretend to be asleep
And curl myself into a heap.
I snuggle close up to the wall
And hope I'll slip through to the hall.
But this I know will be my prison
From nine pm till half past seven.
Till the sweet sound of the clock
Means, the door, she will unlock.

Jacquelyn Prosser

Flying Sheep

Flying sheep,
Are what children call the clouds.
Clouds that look so near,
Yet are really far away.
Slowly, almost lazily drifting,
Letting the wind choose their destination.
Changing size and shape,
Like dawn changes into dusk.
Slowly moving across the sky,
Until they disappear beyond the horizon.
As one cloud goes, another comes,
An eternal flying sheep cycle.

Rachel Potter (Age 15)

Come Forward Old Friends
The World Is A Stage

There is an image of summer.
A warm and forgiving image,
when the table in the corner window of the cafe
played host to the paper and pen.

Many dreams were forged at that table;
Many fears died along with the cigarette-butts' fiery smiles.

Unwritten and undevised entities wait behind the bleaches for a curtain-call,
hoping for a part in a Broadway hit; dreading a miss that is
destined to be forgotten until the creator meets his Author.

Unfortunately some were lost.
Some by miscarriage alone, who never saw the ink;
never given a tabloid prize or given the challenge to stink.

Those who fought played a futile game,
for it was chance that had the decisive say.
Chance that inspiration would jump into the creators eyes;
then take nothing, create a something,
dress it in persona and give it a past.

A mother, a father and brother is added and a loved one
who's dead for a reason unanswered; until the end when the web is untangled;
The performers disband and the portrayed become shadows;

Then the table is given another visit and the entities collect for Act one,
once again, hoping for their curtain call,
hoping for a speaking part and a stage to perform.

David Edward Plant

There Is A Bird Called Lemon Curd

There is a bird called Lemon Curd
Its wings are made of honey
Its beak is just a blob of jam
You'd think it rather funny.
And on its head there's chocolate spread
Its tail is peanut butter
Two legs of chunky marmalade
And feathers all a-flutter.
And you should see it try to fly -
A sticky mess up in the sky
But when it lands it's worse than that
For then it's just a gooey splat!

Helen Price

Marriage

Marriage means a lot of things
Brand new clothes and wedding rings,
Lots of presents from your friends
Kettles, clocks it never ends.
These are nice but not essentials
Take no notice of credentials
If you're after married bliss
Make sure you remember this,
Lots of loving, giving, caring,
Most important is the sharing
Work together is the aim
You will win the wedding game.

Jill Phillips

My Dream

I dreamed I saw the man of my dreams
With short blonde shiny hair
His kiss was soft and listless
His eyes were blue
His hands were warm and gentle
I dreamed he was walking in a sunset
Walking on the sandy beach
The waves were calm and quiet
It made me think
My love for you
Was meant to be
He was looking at me
I was looking at him
Together we watched the calm sea swim
I dreamed I heard the seagulls cry
Cry because of happiness
I saw them cuddling loving each other
Like a family
I dreamed I saw the man of my dreams
Fun and laughter is what we had and what I need
My dream I saw was like me
Like me in paradise.

Dipa Patel

Waiting

A ghostly figure stands alone,
an Abbey just beyond.
He can't escape this lonely place,
for here, he once belonged.

"Twas here he met his lover,
they lay beneath a tree.
'Twas here that he proposed to her,
as he knelt down on one knee.

But the war had called him,
before that they could wed.
Their faces, oh, so sodden,
from the tears that they had shed.

She waited till she heard the news,
that he had lost his life.
As for his beloved?
She became somebody's wife.

He had waited all these years,
would he never learn?
For now she had another,
and, would not return.

Jean Marie Palmer

Outer Space

Planets hot, planets cold,
Sun crackles shooting stars
Rockets bang, feel excited,
Space ships, sending rockets.

Jupiter all different colours,
Orangy pink, hazy purple.
Sun bright, dark sky,
Rockets whoosh, blended colours.

Comets floating in the sky,
Space ships blown up.
I feel lonely I am sad,
When is this over I am frightened.

When I come back down
I am with my mum and dad.
I do not feel frightened any more
Now the journey's over I would just like to say goodbye
And be home in warmth and comfort.

Jennifer Phillips (Age 10)

Island

Lighting fires in the minds of children,
awakening dormant primitive thoughts.
Shackled by so called civilisation,
oppressive regimes run by aggressive monsters.
Freedom gained only in grotesque death,
swinging at the end of a rope.
Pain numbed by alcohol and drug abuse,
always bubbling beneath the surface.
If only they'd listened to you,
they know the truth now, too late.

Look after your loved ones, young and old,
institutionalised aged before their time.
Cruelty waiting to strike at your estranged child,
better dead than life with a tortured soul.
Rest in peace Mark,I hope you can,
let down by a society which should have protected.
Your dark island will never rise again,
gone forever into ignominious disgrace.
If only I'd known, could I have helped,
a shoulder to cry on, a friend in deed.

David Thomas Price

The Seasons

The snow lies crisp upon the ground
From the birds no joyous sound
Biting winds and swirling flakes
Frozen ponds and frozen lakes

How I long for the spring
When the birds all sing
When flowers awake to natures call
Spring I like best of all

After long dark nights of winter
What pleasure the spring flowers bring
When daffodils are in bloom
We know for sure it's spring

Seasons come and seasons go
Bringing sunshine or bringing snow
From long dark nights to lighter days
What a joy to feel the sun's warm rays

Maud Pickering

A Lonely Grave

Upon Islay he lay
On that saddened May Day.
Prince Christopher George
Unsung but adored.

On this Island he found
Peace all around.
May he find it again
In the land of 'no pain'.
Such heavenly bliss
Where the Angels may kiss
Unite him with those
From who's birth-right he rose

In splendour the Royals render,
More tears on the grave.
Where you lay,
School children mourn and say
'Flowers for a teacher not a Prince'. I like this!

Alma Paget

The Free Peace Sweet

"Another day."
Just one more day to get through.
Keep the child at bay,
So I can find some space to look to.

A thousand ideas, an imagination swimming in circles.
Swirling to overcome,
A ghost ridden smoke of hurdles.

"Just another day," drowning in an air of silent tears.
I'm starting to decay,
Being swallowed by my own betraying fears.

Flying alone, an inner peace releases my dead heart.
A kindred shadow,
Takes my hand, guiding me back to the start.

"It's just another day," broken and empty the two lost dolls.
Searching out the way.
The beginning of a parallel of souls.

Belonging nowhere, alive, in the space between dream and life.
A vacant stare,
Will you save me from playing with the knife?

Belong in the inside, can I really find my freedom there?
A dangerous ride,
Together we can make it, if we truly care.

"Its just another day, another day of living."

Donna Payne

Reflections

I look through my window and what do I see?
A mass of colour for all, and its free,
Blues and yellows, lavender, red, white and gold,
What more can one ask for the eye to behold
        Outside my window

Nature is wonderful, I hope you see what I mean
'Cos amongst all these colours, are all shades of green
Each blending together, to form a bright scene
        Outside my window

Relax in your garden, in the park, by the lake,
See the beauty around you, as refreshment you take,
Then, when duty calls, and inside you go,
Thank God for the Blessings each one can know
        Outside your window

W.M. Pearce

342

The Train To Heaven

This is the journey of life, calling at all stations to Heaven. For those who know the Father who resides there, they are certain to be on the right train. The passing landscape ranges from a bland nothingness to a rich beauty that touches the soul. As the train of life surges forward, forward, forward past scenery that is ever changing and yet the same. As I gaze from the train and feast my eyes upon a scene of fleeting serenity, I recall some of the stations I have passed on the great journey. Some can be vividly recalled, such was their greyness and desolation, sometimes shrouded in the pall of a night closing in. I would long for the train to continue along its path, but alas it would sometimes long remain. Some stations have come so pleasingly into view, I joyfully recall. Daintily adorned with cascading blossoms, immersed in the bosom of the warm golden sunshine. I would long for the train to delay its progression, but alas it would sometimes pull quickly away. Many miles back I passed through a tunnel, I could see only a dark void. But in faith I knew that the tunnel had an end, although my eyes could not see it. And now I am amongst vivid colours, alive and vibrant. I see flowers, hundreds of them, and I savour the passing fragrance, that wafts through the open window as the train passes slowly by. But I am acquainted with the certainty that my journey's end will one day come. And someone might say to the Lord on their arrival day, that they were taught that on the great train journey of life they shall never see His face, and they may never hear His voice, but He will always be close by. These words they may deeply ponder, and the Lord will tenderly reply that it was He who was driving the train.

David Pestridge

Boris The Spider

I'm Boris the spider, I'm big black and hairy
I wonder why everyone thinks I'm so scary
Nobody likes me they all scream and run,
Whenever I go out to look for some fun.
Fully grown people will jump on a chair
If ever I try to go out anywhere.
I've things to get done, just like you, every day,
So why won't you let me just go on my way,
Couldn't you try just being my friend,
Instead of planning my grisly end.
I'm really quite lonely and live by myself,
In my nice cosy web at the back of the shelf,
I'd love it if someone would just call for tea,
But as soon as I move, you all scream and flee.
There must be someone, somewhere in this land,
Who could have me to play, or just sit on their hand.
I'm sorry I fill you all so full of fear,
As I sit on my shelf and shed my silent tears.
So next time you feel me tickling your arm
Please stay and play, as I mean you no harm.

Lyn Prosser

Playtime

Come out and play, come out and play, I'm calling to you today
please come out and play, I know lots of good games,
we won't play two the same, I promise! I know you soon get bored
but, you need relaxation, you need to let go and have fun,
you need to jump, shout and run. Come out and play,
relax, take a seat, watch you're in for a treat,
I will be sweet and nice, I won't tease or cheat, well not more than twice!
Oh! please come out and play, come laugh and be gay, times too short to worry,
life is fun, you won't be sorry. Come, let me see you smile,
as we play, I'll be good, as we play, you'll feel good. Come out and play
now...today; I've been knocking at your door, answer soon forget the chores!
If you play, I'll help you with the chores...later!
Oh! but, listen, my feet are itching to play like a kitten!
Are you going to answer the door? Yes, I hear footsteps in the kitchen;
the latch is lifted, the door is open, I see your smiling, mischievous face,
you are coming out to play! I take your hand, you take mine,
Oh! we're going to have a happy time. Hold tight away we go,
we mustn't run too slow...you know, our time is precious, not to be wasted,
freedom is ours for a short while, freedom to laugh, play, with a happy cry.
Oh! I'm so glad to be alive, playing with you, holding your hand,
playing with you as the sun sets in the land.
We are having fun aren't we? Thank you...thank you, for coming out to play with me!

Carol Pigford

The Old   Vs: The New Covenant

A stone quarry outside old Jerusalem,
A howling mob with stones in their hands.
A woman, trembling, and weeping, kneels on quarry sand,
"She must be stoned to death, according to our Mosaic Law."
Accusing her of crass adultery, with sundry men galore.
Calmly seated near this woman - a man, doodling on the floor,
He challenges the mob, "The sinless one to throw the first stone".
Shame faced, one by one, they quietly slink away, to the woman's relief.
The seated man asks, "Where are your accusers that gave you such grief?"
"There are none my Lord", He absolves her and adds, "Go and sin no more".
She falls prostrate at His feet. SHE LIVES, FOR EVER MORE!

N. Palmer Chamarette

Reflections

The reflection in the mirror is so unkind
Nothing like the person I saw in my mind
To recapture the youth that once stood there
I can only look and forlornly stare
I turn away from the mirror unkind
I'll look at the image inside my mind

Robert Purvis

Yeti

There is a man that walks the Earth.
8ft tall but not much worth.
He's covered in hair nearly all over.
But seems to have appeared from nowhere.

Juliet Pyke

Immediate Thought

I watched the programme, I read the book,
I studied statistics, I understood.
I looked and wept, I listened and sobbed
In a few minutes I understood.

His pain and misery, heartache and loss,
His worries, responsibilities and undesirable thoughts,
His emotions in turmoil, the isolated circumstance,
His suffering so great I understood.

No matter what it is or how it happened,
No matter where I am or who I'm with,
I have friends, family, support and security,
I have a life full of love, trust and honesty.

I now wonder if I really understood,
It's easy to say and good to hear,
BUT
To be alone, to be frightened,
To be addicted or homeless,
I now know it takes more than a programme.

Sarah Payne

Do You Care?

How many give a thought or care
That Christ was born on Christmas Day?
How many know how that sweet babe
Did pay the price our sins to bear?
Who showed mankind Christ is The Way
To bridge that gap 'tween God and man.

This festive season always brings
Tinsel, baubles and worthless things.
Too much to eat, too much to drink
At parties just because it's fun.
The drunken driver at the wheel
Gives not a thought for God's own Son.

Take time, reflect and pause a while;
Why do we always celebrate?
Rejoice, give thanks within your heart
That Christ who loves us came to earth
That we might rise from death to life
Forever with Him in Paradise.

Nina E.M. Parsons

Spring

Bluebells bloom in the woodland glen
The stream slowly trickles by
Birds are singing in the trees above
Beneath the blue blue sky
Spring is the start of life anew
When lambs are born mid the morning dew
The darkness of winter has passed away
Spring begins with a bright new day
But memories of you stand still forever
Spring will come again when we're together

J.M. Pollard

Me

Middle aged, short and fat
Never knew the names of Take That
Even my hair's turning grey
Hate computers, they're shocking
Mourn the passing of stockings
And I never seem to get enough pay.

I wish I was back in the sixties
Tune in, turn on, and drop out
When the Beatles were gear
And no-one was queer
And little Lulu she couldn't half shout.

Now the world's gone mad, everything's wrong
Like the words of a country and western song.

My dog died the other day
The day after my Pa passed away
My pony's gone lame, and I just can't start the car
The cattle are ailing
And the fence needs renailing
And I sure do miss dear old Ma.

I wish I was back in the sixties
Tune in, turn on, and drop out
When the Beatles were gear
And no-one was queer
And your Dad could still give you a clout.

Steve Payne

Taj Mahal

Ethereal, that heaviness, white floating
Above darknesses of pain, mass uprising
Closing love with beauty, upraised by doting
Despot, prises viewers' eyes, so surprising.
His frenzied grief brought frenzied light creation
Detached from truth the marvel can be pretty
Beautiful; sun or moon-stroked stone formation
Formed in formaldehyde. Oh! what a pity.
Cold marble, whispered dome, built twenty years
Or more by thousands damned impressed endeavour.
Whose grief, whose toil employed, whose endless tears,
Whose thrall of passion should enthral forever?
My love no wealth no regal heights can claim
Yet reprints may outlast his marbled frame.

Robert Peel

The Angler

The river was dark and flowing fine,
He sat on the bank alone;
And his treasure was a rod and line,
The river was his domain.

Shelter above was the silent sky,
All the world was in his eyes;
He pondered as the ripples pass by,
A silver salmon his prize.

For the river has a thousand eyes,
He alone has only two;
He studies nature that makes him wise,
He may catch a fish or two.

Happy man with pleasant thoughts to bide,
On the river side alone;
Full of glee with basket by his side
And the river bank his home.

A moonbeam shows the float on his line,
Starting to dip and to rise;
Gets his reward for patience this time,
A silver salmon his prize.

Yes, the river has a thousand eyes,
To angler a cherished home;
And now with silver salmon his prize,
So how can he be alone?

Dennis Parkes

I See A Fool, And Then I Don't

He's just a fool
A clown in fact
He just larks around
And puts on an act

He won't have a brain
Just an empty head
By the look of him
And by what he has said

But as life goes on
And when you're in need
It is that same clown
That will do the good deed

So don't judge a book
By the look of its cover
It's the goodness inside
That stands one from another

Bert Quennell

A Souls Food A Spirits Flight

Music is an artist painting pictures in your mind
Music is the special love who's there when you unwind

It unites the world in joy and hope
It makes a blue heart soar
It depicts our moods and feelings
Our thoughts our dreams and more

It doesn't matter if you're musical
Or if you can't sing in tune
Celebrate an everlasting youth
Join in, and rock, rap, or croon

Michelle Poole

To My Wife
(Our Roles Reversed?)

A curious thought was on my mind.
Should we some morning wake and find
that in the night we changed would be;
that I'd be you, and you'd be me.

You'd smoke your cigs from morn 'til night.
The ashes on your clothes a sight.
You know how anxious I would be,
if I were you, and you were me.

You to the football, pubs, would go.
While I'd attend a flower show.
How different our tastes would be,
if I were you, and you were me.

I'd tell you when to change your clothes,
and brush your hair, and blow your nose.
A funny place this world would be,
if I were you, and you were me.

If I were you, and you were I,
would you do things to make me cry?
Or would you kind and loving be,
if I were you, and you were me?

We'd view the world from different slants,
if I wore frocks and you wore pants.
But really, love, would it not better be;
that you be you, and I be me?

Keith Ian Platt

The Clock On The Wall

Happiness is
When the clock hits top gear
Or when a man says
He just cannot hear

Sadness is when
The clock finds reverse
Or when things don't get better
They only get worse

Yet if I could invent
A clock that is kind
That points out the good
And you don't need to wind

Then life would be shorter
And soon pass us by
Yet could we still smile
When the time comes to die

And if clocks could have hearts
Instead of those springs
Life could be full
Of wonderful things

But heartless they are
When the finger won't slow
And you look at the clock
Then say . . . . . time go to

Stella Parker

Winter Is Here

Jack Frost had his fun last night and painted all the rooftops white.
A rime of frost lay on the grass and tender plants stood dark and drear,
now, I know that winter's here.
The earth rests in it's winter sleep,
but soon spring bulbs will peep up through the cold hard earth
and nature comes again to birth.
Soon spring will be with us again,
March winds and April rain.
Each season following swiftly on,
Each with a beauty of its own.

Jean Phipps

Daisies

Sweet simplicity, fresh and bright,
You lift your face when you see the light,
You may be small with a heart of gold,
Stark and white but never bold.

When winter's gloom has passed away,
You re-appear on a summer's day,
You are easy to find, not very rare,
We walk in the meadows and you will be there.

The children's favourite, loved by all,
And by their elders, when they recall
Playing happily, on a summer's day,
Making chains, passing the hours away.

Through the years that come and go,
The daisy survives as if to show,
Grandness and complexity are not always the best
Keep your originality to compete with the rest.

Valerie J. Purdy

Alone?

Imagined idealogy, the writers friend?
Of a world full of comfort
Heartaches easy to mend
Write not of life's sorrows, woes
Lakes of fallen tears
Loneliness, destitution, abandonment
For in that quagmire of self pity
You may start to sink, deeply
And find cries for help, unanswered
When those about you fail to listen
Or maybe leave, simply unheard
Search for life's brightness, and then
You may find your sun
Seek out the song of nature
And you will hear the chorus of souls
Take comfort in the warmth of love
Wrapped arms around, you will feel
Reach out to help some other
Their support will be your guide
For only those happy in their isolation
Will ever find themselves truly alone.

Jane Porter

Snow

White as white can be,
Snow all over the ground.
It twinkles in my eye,
Sparkles in my hair
Like a white sheet
On the ground,
Soft and crunchy white.
The snow
Soft as silk laying on the ground.
Snow on your shoes
As you come inside.
Flaky and feathery
And it's so cold.
Wrap up warm
It comes smooth as silk
From the sky
Winter's here,
Wrap up warm.

Natasha Reed (Age 7)

Life

Whether it's hot; whether it's cold,
whether it's raining,
every season is for drinking,
every season is for drinking.

Whether it's expensive, whether it's cheap,
whether a lot or less,
every season is for drinking,
every season is for drinking.

She spends every time with me,
through every difficulty she is with me,
every season is for drinking,
every season is for drinking.

She taught me to live,
sad or happy she will stay with me,
every season is for drinking,
every season is for drinking.

I'm not worried about eating,
I will drink, and offer others,
every season is for drinking,
every season is for drinking.

M. Padhiar

Snow In May

It was the month of May
Thought we were seeing things today
For snow was falling from the sky
We saw the snowflakes going by

It's supposed to be spring
The birds have started to sing
The flowers have started to grow.
Getting covered in snow

Hills are a majestic sight
Have been covered through the night
With their caps all shining white
A glorious sight in broad daylight

Constance Price

Sea Song

Shushing, swirling sounds of sea,
Curl and crashing crescents from clouds of foam,
Form frolicking figurines which dance,
Dashing, daring the land that lumbers lowly,
And wandering waves wends its way,
Across oscillating oceans,
To die in darkness depths.

Tracey Parkes

Dew

Have you ever noticed the beauty of the dew,
On a cold and misty morning, just as the sun breaks through?
The wonder of the patterns made by spiders into whirls,
Are as wondrous but more fragile than any precious pearls!

Think of the dew as tear-drops, caught within those lovely webs.
Turned from sadness into gladness, as they lie within their beds.
Look for them in hedges and in grasses short and tall.
You'll not be disappointed, I know you'll love them all!

Gladys Payne

I'd Like To Live Inside A Book

I'd like to live inside a book
Where there is no need to look
At important things in another world
I'll just stay here all warm and curled
Like a baby in a mother's womb
Safe inside my fragile room

The ignorance that creates my bliss
Spawned from an innocence I long have missed
Is heaven in my tired eye
That has been blackened by the dye
Of war and famine in another place
I'll just stay here in my own space
With the knowledge that tomorrow brings
Another set of trivial things

But when I do have to leave
And crawl out from my daydreams sleeve
At least I wont have to face
Prejudice against my race
Or bombs and guns, my family killed
Or knowing my stomach will never be filled,

Still
I'd like to live inside a book.

Shaun Parry

My Winter And Spring

Decades of a fallacy, the living of a lie.
History the betrayer, you or I?
Striving with every tear, with every fall.
Your covenant from the loins, you cannot recall.
I testify night and day, as you prematurely wither away.
The elements torment me but my roots are firm,
For I know that cometh the winter you shall be no more.
But I shall, I hope, in the spring be forever more.
The tranquil breezes will caress the soul,
Whilst you shall be gazing up in awe.
Weeping 'I could have been up there singing hymns of praise'.
But your grasp was too weak, the wind blew, you trembled.
As yet my season of autumn.
Dark skies as the darkest of destinies.
But rays are beaming through the canopy.
They have entered my heart, my soul.
Abide in there forever, forsake not me I pray.
I am holding on - waiting and hoping,
For my winter and spring.

Shaida Parveen

351

Verses At Sunset

When the world and I stood side by side
When the day was young
And my life was younger
Where the wind was my friend
At the opening act of the play
Where I gazed to my time
And remembered it's ending
For I prepared for my death at my birth

Through the scenes of the world
I've wondered and waited
Through the ways of the earth
I've stumbled and faulted
As my life takes its road
Far beyond this dead land
Just as man took his hand
As destroyer of man

So its now only time
That stands in my way
And I know that the world
Is turning and learning
But when shall we see
The earth shield her eyes
Away from the sadness that litters these times

Alan Pollard

The Midnight Passage

The walls rumbled,
The people tumbled.
Adults' fears,
And children's' tears,
Gathered by the midnight passage.

Everybody killed,
The atmosphere stilled.
The people dashed,
As the train crashed.

The people dead,
Nobody tread.
And from this day,
People lay,
And hear,
It happens every year.

Carly Reilly (Age 11)

600 Babies

I've got 600 babies or did I just miscount
It's like a school assembly when we all go out
I really don't mind it's such good fun for me
But you should hear my husband when he comes home for tea
Where's this lot come from I often hear him say
I'm sure there wasn't this many when I looked the other day

I've got 600 pairs of hands or is it only one
I have to keep on going there's so much to be done
I've all those dirty pots to wash and change another nappy
I'm never on my knees I'm deliriously happy
I like to stay up all night and soothe a crying child
And next day at the crack of dawn I watch them running wild

I've got 600 Blessings that's how it seems to me
I love to hear their laughter and delightful squeals of glee
To see their glowing faces watch the little things they do
Each day is quite amazing there's always something new
It really doesn't matter that life's sometimes inside out
I've got 600 reasons why I love to just miscount

Helen Phimister

Sea Wind Strumming

Hark to the surf on the distant shore
And the breeze that's rising and shrill -
My thoughts go winging away now
To a ship that's sailing still,
As it docks near and the decks clear
For a cargo trading
Till the night clouds start to gather
And the day is fading

Watching the high tide come rushing past
Sets my spirit now all aflame -
For I must sail and I will sail -
Across the trackless main,
To life that's free on the endless sea
Where the ships went whaling,
Through the storms' clash and the waves' crash -
Then for haven sailing.

Oh to be free from this land-locked lee!
Then to wander far and wide,
And to view earth's teeming oceans
Where leviathans still abide -
And hear the echo of voices rise
To a shanty-chorus singing,
Till o'er sea swell clangs the last knell
Of the watch-bell ringing.

Don Ferrers Panting

Arran

An island of treasure, and that is a truth
For the sights and the sounds are all there
Each curve of the road is a scene of delight
Wether sunshine or mist in the air

The mountains rise high, decked in so many hues
And the burns flow with ease in the glen
The primrose shows yellow against the green bud
And the blue-bell sways in the wind

Seals bask in the sun, and play in the sea
And the birds wheel and call to each other
The stones on the shore have a story to tell
Of which we will never discover

So hasten ye back to this Island of joy
And look for yourselves at this gem
So peaceful, so pretty and calm to the mind
You'll return again and again.

E.B. Powell

The Man Who Is To Blame

Kicked out, discarded by Man
Not knowing that death could be their fate
The animals in the compound hopefully wait.
What is the life of an animal
To him who feels no shame?
He knows it can't fight back at him
The Man who is to blame.

The fox, the otter and badger
All hide from the Man with his dogs
That tear them to shreds for fun.
Domestic pets tortured and maimed
To amuse the Man that has no shame
The Man who is to blame

Yet when the Man dies
It's assumed that to Heaven he'll go
But the Lord sees all that happens here below
Will He welcome the Man
Who caused so much suffering and pain
Will the animals be there to meet their tormentor again?
Surely then he'll feel some shame
The Man who is to blame.

Hilda Potter

Life Goes On

I'm trying to make, something of my life
Don't have to be, somebody's wife.
The good sometimes, outweighs the bad
Memories I have, of what I once had.

When I sit, and wonder why
I realise I was, just living a lie.
When I think about, being a wife
Being used, to get him along in life.

Used to help him, along the way
He'd no intention, whatsoever to stay.
To take all those years, off my life
All pretend, being for him his wife.

9th of June, and 9th of September
Dates in my mind, I'll always remember.
Two reasons for me, to carry on
The birth of my Daughter, and my Son.

Carrol Lesley Robinson

Clouds

As I look up to the sky
The wonders that I see
It's full of lovely clouds on high
They look so soft to me

I sit and study them one by one
They're like pictures you see
An old man's face
A skirt of lace
And a honey pot for a bee

As I sit here watching
They're gently rolling by
All shapes and sizes
And pictures to my eye

It all changes very quickly
Just when I blink my eyes
Not a cloud left to see
Only the blue skies

Pat Robinson

354

The Millenium

What is the Millenium?
A time to look back
And a time to look forward
Looking back we applaud the good things done
But are dismayed at the hurt suffered by some

People will be celebrating
Do they know what?
Or have they forgot?
Whilst they are enjoying life
Others have little or nothing
No hope, no treasure, no job and no leisure

So while they enjoy fun and laughter
Will they remember -
And then some time after
Resolve to do something
To eradicate the imbalance
That is what we should be hoping for
And a fullness of life for all restored

Let the nations rejoice -
Sing with heart and voice
With uplifted spirit
Affecting everyone
And pray God's will be done

Edna F. Pine

Untitled

The voice within my head
It bears a name,
It says I will make you jealous,
Cause you pain.

I'll replace your devotions,
And destroy your emotions,
Till all that remains
Is vengeance filled veins.

Your blood will run hot,
And your heart miss a beat,
As you put down the gun
And fall from your feet.

Now, all that is left
As he lies dead on the floor,
Is a cold, empty corpse
As the blood starts to pour.

But I will be there,
I'll take you with me,
To the deep depths of hell,
Where jealousy lives free.

Hannah Ratcliffe

What Have They Done To Me?

My confidence has gone,
There's nothing left.
I don't even know how to dress.
Do I look good, no, I feel such a sham.
I'd buy a new outfit but I don't feel I can
Wear it with pride and walk down the street
Feel good from my head and down to my feet.
I feel so drab - yet everything's new.
Oh what, just what, am I going to do?
I must look good - I must feel right,
But everything I try I feel such a fright.
I tried to think - Well don't you look good.
But I don't inside although I should.
I tried so hard to get it right.
But all I feel is - It's just not right!

Gaye Read

Labyrinth

Life is full of twists and turns, which all of us befall.
Born into a labyrinth, full of corridors and walls.
For each of us it's different, we make our separate moves,
like pieces on a chessboard, some win and others lose.
I've hit my share of obstacles and once I lost my way,
I strolled along in sunlight, when it suddenly turned grey.
Trapped inside a fierce storm, tempestuous and bleak,
I fought against its icy blows, but I was far too weak.
Then even when the storm had passed, the wind and rain would come,
banishing the sunlight, 'till once more my strength was gone.
It took some time, then finally, the sun began to break,
I travelled down a warmer route, the storm left in my wake.
I made it through the labyrinth and in blinding rays of gold,
there stood within the centre, a treasure to behold.
I walk a different labyrinth now and know not what I'll find,
but in my heart I'm certain that the clouds are far behind.
I'll take each road as it comes, until my life is through,
and stand against adversity, but not as one, as two.

Joanne S. Reeder

Second Life

Though mine eyes no longer see,
And amber - like blood ceases to flow
Your thoughts and dreams come clear to me,
Although in life they did now show.

My soul relives another life,
A life the living can't understand,
I must go on without my wife
My spirit at your side will stand

Step softly on the ground above me,
When you visit my resting place.
Think? Your thoughts, I now can see,
Yet in life there was no trace.

Stay strong, live long, we're never apart,
I'll light the dark that lies ahead,
You'll always be close to my heart
Even though my body's dead.

As you stand, so deep in thought
You yourself may deeply sigh,
Life 'gainst death so fiercely fought,
To really live, one has to die.

Remraf

Untitled

Hungrily,
He sucked at
The large nipple.
She felt the
Itch of excitement
It stirred up within her
For a moment -
Then it ended
Just as quickly,
Once again leaving her
      Cold.
(Would it _ever_ happen again?)
The sucking continued.
He had not even noticed
The slight change in her -
It was a good thing
She thought
Quietly to herself
He would learn
Soon enough
The needs of a woman.
But not from her

It would never
Be her.

Natasha Reeskens
(The Wet Nurse)

Ernestine Truelove Doesn't Like Washing

Ernestine Truelove doesn't like washing,
she likes splishing! and splashing!
she likes splashing! and sploshing!
But Ernestine Truelove doesn't like washing.

She likes the rain and loves splashing around
in the puddles that fill up the holes in the ground.
She likes to go swimming with her best friend Milly,
but washing, to Ernestine Truelove, was silly.
"What is the point!" the girl would complain,
"tomorrow I'll just get dirty again!"

But mum made her bathe every night, without fail,
and every night Ernestine Truelove would wail,
"The water's too hot! and this soap makes me stink!
and if I have to get bathed one more time I shall shrink!"

"Shrink? don't talk nonsense," her mother said giggling,
"Now I'm trying to wash your ears stop wriggling."
But as usual Ernestine struggled and thrashed,
till everyone else in the bathroom she'd splashed,
Dad, at the basin shaving his chin,
and mum, trying to wash her, both soaked to their skin.

Then at last, bath time over and spotlessly clean,
in bed with her teddy, climbed a tired Ernestine.
"But why mum," she asked, tucked up and yawning,
"do I have to get washed again in the morning?"

Walt Richards

Alley Cat

Behold the alley cat!
King of all cats.
He sneaks in the streets,
Who miaows in the middle of the night?
Is it the alley cat?
He scavenges in bins.
Looking for a bite to eat.
He dishes old fishes for his mates.
Then home he goes!
Who knows where he sleeps?
Who knows where he goes?
Nobody knows!

Andre Reynolds (Age 11)

A Rash Attack

I've got measles all spotty and red,
Doctor says I must stay in bed.
I heard the birds singing in the trees.
My curtains blowing, with the breeze.
The sun keeps trying to get through
The lovely sky of azure blue.
Soon my measles,will all be gone.
Then I can get my school work done
My friend Sally, she looks a sight
She caught my spots, last Friday night.

Rachael Yvette Rodgers (Age 13)

What Are We Doing To Our Children!

God sits upstairs in His heaven, and shakes His weary head
As He looks down on this Earth that He gave us in good stead,
He thinks back over the many years, back to the beginning of Time,
When earth was just an empty space before Man was in his prime.
He had this dream of making Man and a Woman for his mate
And put them on this Earth, this was to be their fate,
He taught them how to love each other with tender loving care,
He said to them "No matter what happens you must be good and fair,
"Nurture this planet with all your might and sow your seeds of love.
And I will watch over in my Heaven, and help you from above".
Because they did as He had asked they were rewarded with a child,
The most precious gift anyone can have - a baby meek and mild.
And so our Earth went on in time, and we just grew and grew,
But we've forgotten what God taught when there was just a few,
Some of our children are not loved, some are left to grow wild
Others are abused, and our children are defiled.
Children are committing crime, they seem not even to know
What's right or wrong - good and fair, sadly this is so,
They're victims of war and robbed of their childhood,
They don't know anymore the difference between bad and good.
All our children are innocent and they just cry out for love,
Because one day we'll have to answer to Him, upstairs, above
"What are we doing to our children?" This is what He'll say
"Stop and Think and Love one another, it's too high a price to pay."

Vivienne Yvonne Richardson

Laura

She falls asleep upon my knee
I pick her up so carefully
Her curls fall down from her face
She snuggles up to my embrace
I lay her down on to her bed
And kiss her gently on her head
She heaves a sigh and frowns a while
Looking at her makes me smile
She is my sun by day and my stars at night
She fills my life with a light so bright
She is snow in winter and birds in spring
I love her dearly more than anything
I will protect you forever so never forget
Having you my Laura I will never regret.

C. Ridpath

Secrets Of The Night

Whispering secrets in the still of night
so faint so soft hardly heard at all.
But yet oh yet must surely be
the echoes of a humble call.
Sleepy shadows resting now
so wisp so low so not to be seen
but how oh how do they close their eyes
a midnight calm that has ever been.
Twinkling stars through the dark vast sky
so clear so bright may show the way
but why oh why the only light
reflections of a new born day.
Mysterious moon disappearing from sight
so full so round play a magical game
but not oh not descending now
dancing in time a flickering flame.
Delicious dew of the early dawn
so pure so fresh a welcoming sign
and soon oh soon the world awakes
sharing the secret yes all is fine.

June Roberts

The Love Of A Soulmate

One night a man did waken to hear his young wife cry,
He listened for a moment, and then he asked her why
She said that she was sorry but she couldn't help but cry,
Because she loved him so much, and what if he should die?
The man he was much older and he knew that it might be,
So he answered very wisely, for what must be, must be.
What if my life should cease to be, and then what would become of me?
And what of love that I have known, would it be gone and you alone?
Though my body you'd no longer hold, in spirit you would me behold,
And if you wish to see my face, then see our children, watch their grace,
For every smile they show to you, and every word they speak of me
Within their eyes and laughter, there my presence you will see.
And watch the tide upon the shore and I'll be there with you once more,
The wind that blows within the tree will whisper love to you from me.
Then as you walk in the summer sun, and think of me with happiness,
The breeze that gives its kiss to you, will be my tender warm caress.
For love as strong as we have known, in death does not abate,
For in our lives we have lived as one. You are my true soulmate.
His young wife smiled a thoughtful smile, and held him close just for a while
For now she knew they would never part, as long as he was in her heart.

Sandra Robinson

The Invite

My friends invited me but I didn't want to go
I dressed with feeling but Oh! so slow.
At last I was ready, a knock at the door
My friends beckon, I'd better go I don't want to seem a bore
The drive was exciting the pace seemed fast
It wasn't long before we reached the gaff dazzling lights!
Happy people, why did I worry about it after all
Tonight I feel like the belle of the ball.
The butterflies in my tummy have all but gone
I feel much more confident to carry on,
I walk through the doors I see through the haze
People merry at a gaze
Music vibrant, drink divine
Close couples in cosy corners secretly talking hands entwine
The bandit machine takes its time
Gobbles the coins at an alarming rate
Never mind its only a race
To see who gets the pot of gold
Maybe you, maybe me,
You never know it could make my evening complete,
Considering I didn't want to come I am having lots of fun!
But all too soon it comes to an end!
I'll never forget the invite from my friends.

M. Robinson

The World That I Used To Know

Where is the world that I used to know?
Where love and friendship and flowers grow.
Where people could walk without being mugged.
Where pavements weren't littered with souls who were drugged,
Into oblivion so they couldn't see
What goes on around them, to you and to me.
Sexual freedom which brings so much scorn.
Unwanted children, by children are born.
Children who ought to be learning at school,
Not being taught by somebody's fool.
Being a woman before being a child
Is rather perverse to be putting it mild.
What memories will they have to relate to their kids?
A life of regrets of the things that they did.
Not much of a heritage, perhaps no father's name,
Then the child that they bore grows up just the same.
Why must it be so just to complicate life?
For that's why we live in a world full of strife.
So just let us think before it's too late
You never get anywhere by just tempting fate.
I could sit here and weep, but while my tears glisten
I am afraid that no-one will listen
But it was just a thought we should all try to face
To make this world a much better place.

Margaret M. Ramsden

Lockwood

Lockwood was once a holiday spot,
Huddersfield the place to shop.

Huddersfields' water came from the river Holme,
the allotments were the first to give fresh veg at home.

Bentley & Shaw made their beer,
now the rugby union will make us cheer.

Mountjoy school put you in good stead,
the Baptist church gave the good book to be read.

Lockwood was once a holiday spot,
now Mecca has made it a hot shot.

Janet E. Rodrigues

The Other Side Of War

People queue up for hours waiting for any food that's going
ration books held tight in hands,
hoping for plenty but not knowing,
an air raid siren goes off, warning the enemy's on the way,
people run in fear of their lives,
they'll queue another day.

Writing a letter to their loved ones in trenches far away
with love and compassion in their hearts, praying they'll be home one day.
Then the dreaded telegram comes, the one you always feared
time suddenly stands still, all hope is lost, the feeling very weird.

Someone's son, husband, father, brother, just another body
is it really worth all the pain for a letter that said sorry.
They give their lives so readily for a better, freer land
so that people have the freedom of speech and can walk along the sand.

So much blood is spilt, so much tragedy to follow
because people can't communicate, it has to end in sorrow.
Boys and men lie thinking of their families so far away
when they've put things right and won the war then they'll be on their way.

With death and destruction everywhere war eventually comes to an end
the guns at last lay silent, they've decided to surrender.
Will anyone learn from these lessons so that it's not all been in vain?
Let's work together for a better land and please God peace remain.

Janice Reeves

Cotswolds
(Bledington, 19.2.97)

The squally rains held us in,
Full February leaking.
We nestled against limestone,
Downy as any stone can be:
Porous with wind-whipped centuries
And snug with long-accumulated
Tawny Gloucestershire sun.

While the rain beat out a path
Towards the steep-pitched hills
All day, we were huddled, exposed,
Absorbed by the great and gravid
Undulating woolsack of the wolds.

Spencer Redfield

Rags Bottles And Bones

I know a man his name is Bart
He rides about on a horse and cart
Around the country homes
Asking for our rags, bottles and bones
Where he goes to no-one knows
Or where he gets his trinkets and clothes
Yet he's always out and about
And you can always hear him shout
As he walks over the cobbles and stones
Calling out any rags, bottles or bones
So if you see this grand old chap
Don't forget to give him your scrap.

John Ramsden

As The Years Go By

How could it have happened
Where did it all go?

All the friends, the partying
I used to love it so

All the letters and the phone calls
Things they used to say

Hurry get your glad rags on
We'll have some fun today

So off we'd go and sure enough
We'd dance the night away

We giggled and we flirted
And we really had a ball

Now suddenly it's disappeared
There's nothing left at all

Vicky Ray

Is It The Way?

Is it the way he smiles,
that would make you walk a thousand miles,
bare foot over desert sands,
just to hold him in your hands.

Maybe it's the way he holds out his arms,
which so quickly and easily soothes and calms,
that fiery temper so quick to ignite,
the burning passion throughout the night.

What about the look in his eyes,
which reminds you of the bluest skies,
or the way you hold him, oh, so tight,
that can get you through the darkest night.

Rachel Rowland

Oh Mighty Ash Tree

Oh mighty Ash Tree majestic there,
Towering over all you survey,
A cold Eastwind is music to you,
As your bare boughs dance and sway.

Oh mighty Ash are you wiser than I?
As you slumber through the winter deep,
Your life juices stored safe in your roots,
Whilst mine freeze trembling no warmth to keep.

Oh mighty Ash are you more benevolent than I?
When in stifling heat you cast your shade,
Whilst I lay dreaming in your care,
Your rustling leaves sweet symphony made.

Oh mighty Ash are you stronger than I?
Your strong limbs a stairway to heaven,
And mine so puny when compared,
And aching limp from a long life striven.

Oh mighty Ash are you more stable than I?
We both sway trembling in a ferocious Northwind/
A lesson to both some are mightier than we,
And if not humble, then we have sinned.

J.R. Richardson

Fighting Luekemia

This is a poem for a girl I know,
Who must have been very frightened,
But didn't let it show,
Her initial diagnosis didn't look bright,
But we knew at the end of the tunnel there would be light,
We all clearly remember that awful day,
As we stood around the bed that she lay,
Months have gone by, where does time go?
Where she found the strength I will never know,
We all had, and shared, a hidden fear,
But be sure of this, let me make it clear,
None of us ever gave up the fight,
And Gillian's recovery is now in sight,
So now I wish to raise my glass,
To you Gillian, you're above first class,
You're head and shoulders above the rest,
In fact Gill you're simply the best.

Wendy Richardson

Words

If we said what we feel,
Instead of hiding thoughts so real,
Would we hurt the ones we love?
Leave alone those thoughts,
Don't bring them up above.

We must care what people feel,
Don't hurt with words those thoughts revealed,
Forgive what people say to forget the pain,
Words are strong,
They can stain.

Try hard to say kind words,
A lot of thought before you speak,
Make not a friend or loved one weep.
Kindness in what you say,
Can go so far from day to day,
Can mean so much to someone dear,
And, if kind, will bring you near.

Joan Roberts

The Salmon Leaps Of Teifi

Fast falls the waters of Teifi
To tumble and flow,
Over green moss stones
And salmon's brief show,
Into the calmer collected pools
Of blue cerulean glow,
And shady nooks
Of the waiting streams below.

Finding for a while
The quiescent moments away,
And early evening's catch
Of soft whisperings of spray,
That lie within the silver light
Of the river's deeper play,
Yet far beyond
The dark falls of rushing day.

Norman Royal

U.F.O.

When my dad was a watchman, working at night,
He took me and my brother to a Bransholme building sight.
Me and our kid used to play in the rubble,
We had a good laugh and we got into trouble.
We played a game called U.F.O.,
We used to shout it out and grab a breeze block and throw.

One time we played it when I was sat in the sands
Then our kid came round the corner with a breeze block in his hands
I looked up in terror and shouted "Oh No!"
But he held the block above his head
And he screamed out "U.F.O.!"
Then he went and threw it, it hit me right on my head,
So he ran away as fast as he could while my hair was turning red.

My dad came around the corner with a look of disbelief,
He sat me in his car and wiped up the blood, with his trusty handkerchief.
And then he said "right I've had enough, to that site you'll never go".
So we never had another game of that bloody U.F.O.!

Peter Reilly

Whatever The Weather

Weather, weather, weather,
What will you do?
Rain, Snow, Blow or Shine.

Whatever the season,
Whatever the Month,
Weather is still there,
Whatever!

Will you blow the clothes dry,
Or water the gardens,
Cover in carpets of white,
Or light up the world.

Whatever weather will be,
We cannot predict,
The Weather men try,
Sometimes their right.

Whether today or tomorrow,
The weather will be,
Whatever it wants to be.

A.L. Reeve

The Cruelty Of Life

See, the people sitting there.
All that they can do is stare!
No-one, at all seems to care,
That they face life in despair.
They have no homes, no hope, no life,
All they face, is poverty, misery and strife,
Their children cry,
Their babies die,
There is no sunshine in their sky
To health and happiness,
They have said goodbye,
Now all they can do is wait to die.

E. Reid

The Second Hand Shop

"Come in" said the old man
"Look around. Touch and feel."
I entered and saw around me
Relics, unwanted gifts,
Parts of peoples' lives
Used, abused, unwanted.

Dust had settled on old wardrobes,
Clothes smelt musty and sweaty
Tangled with shoes that had walked a million miles.
In the corner lay piles of mattresses
On which lives had been created,
Given and taken away.

I walked across the cracked linoleum floor
Seeing the decay of existence
Spread around me in organised heaps.
The slow death of materialistic objects
Once loved, all forgotten,
Awaiting rebirth.

I sat down on a broken lopsided chair,
A second hand life on display for all to see.
"Come in" said the old man,
"Make yourself at home."
I did
And never left.

Sue Rhodes

Condemnation

I can't believe your futile mind.
How could your thoughts be so small?
Why are your actions all so blind?
I can't believe you exist at all.

I could understand if you were insane.
How could you know what you were doing?
But you're not insane, so you take all the blame.
I could understand if I too sought to ruin.

To us it's a crime, to you an obsession.
One which you tend to with the greatest of care.
But your lack of regard for human emotion
Means all that awaits you is condemnation.

Marianne Redfern

Babe
(Dedicated to my wife Chell)

Oh come to me darling
Oh please come to me,
Kiss me, caress me,
Make sweet love to me,
Squeeze me tightly.
Hold me harder my dear
Bring your face nearer,
Nearer to me,
Oh babe kiss me sweetly
Tell me you love me.
I love you madly
Words could never say.
So babe love me forever
Never never go away.

Len Rye

365

Paradise Lost And Regained

My poetry has flowed like an endless stream from my mind,
For many weeks my teeming brain has written words refined.

But suddenly the train of thought ran into the buffer,
Words scattered to the wind leaving me alone to suffer.

I tried and tried and tried again to write a modest verse,
But the words eluded me and became a constant curse.

After a long week of endless toil, hopeless and forlorn,
I fled to the forest on a fine, sunny winter's morn.

The beauty of the surroundings blew all my cares away,
A little thought became a word and called its friends to play.

Alec Reynolds

One Minute Of An Hour

The sea sepia blue,
Where the horizon
Joins the sky with azure glue.

One wave, one cloud for two,
One drop of spray
And not a raindrop all day.

One ray of sunlight
Seen in a prism, a rainbow
Encased in the eye's prison,

One grain of sand for you.
In a rock pool
A universe to view.

I'm a millionaire in my imagination,
Seeing you in an eiderdown
Of brine, asleep on the shore;

The survivor of previous wrecks,
I'm cast adrift once more.
Our footprints wash towards the meridian,
Our memories stretch beyond oblivion,
The fossils of dinosaurs.

Stephen Roe

Dunblane

Little children faces glowing
Hurry in to take a seat.
Kindly, caring, smiling teacher
Bending down each morn to greet.
Then their parents, very trusting.
Believing that each precious child
Would be safe and well protected
From the perils of life outside.
Came the day a bad man found them.
Running happily around the gym.
Full of evil cruel intention
Great disaster he would bring.
A short time later on the floor
Bodies lay from right to left.
Teachers knelt among the children
Feeling sickened and bereft.
Around the world the bad news travelled
Causing shock and disbelief
People in so many countries
Sharing in the pain and grief
Now written in our history
There forever to remain
The horrifying story of
The primary school Dunblane.

Jean Rule

Today's Christmas

As Christmas approaches we head for the towns
where lights and tinsel add glitz and glamour,
our ears are deluged with different sounds
as over the tannoy carols clamour
and through the still air bells ring out,
as people converge from near and far
and adults chatter and children shout
and rush around with wallets ajar.
Not far from the high street where merriment marches
the streets are unlit and cold and grey,
hunched in a box underneath the arches
or shivering alone in an open doorway,
crying out for attention behind shuttered doors
are the people whose family are far away
and those who have no means or cause
to celebrate this Christian day.

Wendy Ray

Only A Son

I look at your picture once again, it helps
To ease a little of the pain.
To think, when we all started out not really
Knowing what it was all about. We were all
Excited and so thrilled, but not now I've seen
My mates killed.

Someone once said,time heals all, would they
Say that? Seeing us crawl, some on bellies
They have no legs, even going over a lot of
The dead, today I tried to save a mate, he
Slipped from my grasp to a muddy grave.

I try to imagine roast beef and wine, but all
We get is mud and slime.
Closing my eyes, I picture you both, hearing your
Plea two years ago. 'Don't go my son' I hear you say.
'You are but sixteen and a day'.

You were right and I was wrong, joining up to end
Up in the Somme.
Hot tears spill on your picture, I am not a hero,
Only a son, who is really missing yer.

As I hold my stomach together I pray I am able
To finish this letter
As I write this, in great pain, I only hope losing
Our lives was not in vain.

Rachel Robertson

10 Minute Talk

"Die, die, die," cried the 9 year old, as he
Emptied an aerosol can over just
One ant. His mother smiled indulgently.
At my call, she turned round, her shaking hand
Holding a freshly-lighted cigarette.
A curly-headed little girl ran out
Of the house, asking a smiled question.
"I will come and show you what to do next,
As soon as possible," Mummy answered,
"When I have finished talking." The boy asked
Interested questions, politely.
The elder girl stood some distance away,
Smiling shyly. Her mother looked at me,
Also smiling. The sun was warm. As I
Ran for the last bus I felt I could do
Anything.

Paul A. Reeves

Sweet Dreams

I surrender to the darkness, the drug that is the night,
Only to awake once more, filled with heated fright.
My journey has no direction, or impetus to start,
Endless, useless hours, weigh heavy on my heart.

I do not hurt or hinder, or seek great wealth and fame,
I only wish, not to cringe, at mention of my name.
Ashamed of who I am, disbelief at what could be,
Self doubt and apathy please take off, and set this Spirit . . . .
. . . . FREE . . .

TO BE, TO HAVE, TO WANT, TO NEED . . . ALL SO 'SELFISHLY!'.

A.J. Regan

Winter Darkness

Paper chains of love unreal,
with violets of complexity
and through a tunnel of
mis-shapen haze,
a distinctness of the day.

Untamed and definite
is the night,
with countless dismal dreams
and hopes that turn but to ghosts,
cold, cold, as the winter's sun.

Margaret Reed

God And the Universe

Avaunt thou puny satan
Surprise no future gain
To will god's vast creation
Along a leafy lane

When the world has thrice turned over
When the planets thrice again
When the sun is growing clover
Maybe we shall meet again.

S. Rosenthal

Childhood Memories Of Marsden Rock

The hallmark of my childhood is what it means to me
The rock that stood majestically her cold feet in the sea
With time and tides eternally this grand old rock kept pace
With summer suns and winter snows beating on her face

Softly nestled in her green hair many species of sea birds
Others flying, crying, wheeling, watched with wonder without words
But what was hidden in her bosom as huge waves lashed her sides
A treasury of little caves revealed with the ebbing tides

Thus came our chance as children, to explore those wondrous caves
Golden sand spilling between our toes with tiny rippling waves
Jelly fish, crabs and seaweed all amongst the rocks
Boys scratching off the limpets, little girlies lifting their frocks

As we joyfully gathered sea shells and smooth pebbles by her shore
We children in the thirties never asked for anything more
Most photographs and pictures display this old rock standing alone
New ones show her now battered and scarred, truly and sorely worn

But I shall always see you with crowds enjoying the summer sun
Adults and children, dogs and all, having so much fun
Throughout my life from childhood you have played a vital part
You are my ROCK of AGES but really you're GOD's WORK OF ART.

Joy D. Richardson

A Special Child
(Dedicated to Ella)

New-born baby like a rosebud,
Fingers tightly curled in sleep,
Diagnosed as having problems,
Anxious parents wait and weep,
They will guide her through life's pathways,
As she grows from day to day,
They'll be there to love and hold her,
Should she fall along the way.

She will never know the heartache,
Behind her parents loving smiles,
Never understand their sadness,
As they walk her through life's miles,
Looking down at all the babies,
Sleeping now across the hall,
This little baby with Downs Syndrome,
Is theirs, the loveliest of them all.

Marian Rokyckyj

She Is

Her strength overwhelms,
Her beauty astounds,
I am afraid of her
But to look away would
Show my weakness,
My insignificance,
My lack of understanding.
And yet when enveloped
In her embraces,
Her gentle caresses,
I feel a part of her,
I am in awe of her.
Destructive, Powerful,
Beautiful, Gentle . . . .
She is the sea.

D.A. Randle

A Cottingham Grave At Christmas

After sprinting hard up the frosty path, I halt,
Panting at the rusty gates,
Now almost pearly in the greying winter light.

I step inside, passing
A freshly turned pile of clayey soil.
I turn between the stones, over the
Frosted mounds, searching out the grave.
The plots seem strangely unfamiliar, festooned
At this time with wreath and bouquet.

Ah, there it is; the once white marble, greying,
The once black inscription, greying
But still so beautifully understated:
'Philip Larkin, Writer, 1922-1985'.

So, here he lies, this Christmas, and forever,
Hull's greatest and one of Britain's best
With a poppied wooden cross and single primrose,
Girdled by housewives, seafarers and gypsies,
Here, in Plot 81.
I stand in awkward, sweating reverence.

Behind me, I hear the clank of spade and shovel
As the digger, donkey jacket, bobble hat and steaming
Twilight breath, loads his wooden cart.

So, cooling, I turn and trot for home.

John Riley

Unrequited Love

Alone and uncertain of what I must do
Just sitting and waiting - my mind's in a stew
Am I awaiting your visit as a reason to fight
Over some empty promise to call me last night
My ego is damaged - my suspicions arisen
Solitary confinement in my own mental prison
So, what's the way out?
Dig a tunnel to sense
Or see how far there is to climb
To finally breach your fence?

Jane Roberts

Poetry Reading, With Wine, '97

With fortitude, launched, our poet began
    well-supped with best fruits of the vine.
    Ready, I think, to go on, (steady man),
    there's Latin the very next line.
Em see em ex see vee wun wun, therefore
    this year, if I've fudged the date 'right.
    Scan's up the creek, I'll just lie on the floor,
    I may be a little bit tight.
Promised the royal poetical fringe
    one's non-alcoholic, one must.
    Dead loss when one's head is muzzed from one's binge;
    I'll vent this verse reading non-plussed.
I agree with things you haven't yet said.
    By a muse quite often I'm seized.
    Rip'd denim jeans brought me offers to wed.
    The vicar seems hopefully pleased.
Tright-rusted friends; they're in focus then fade.
    Out front, with worn foibles laid bare,
    no doubt, you're afraid odd renderings were made.
    Forgive me, 'tis divine to err.
I raptured in time, with fervent declaim,
    that Rubysh-at oh-mike-I-am.
    Incapable now,but I'm glad you came;
    I'm off home, as quiet as a lamb.

Michael Roy

The Gentle Ways Of Nature

Way up high in the mountains
Is what surely must be paradise
Luscious grasses enriched by rains
A magnificent scene greets the sunrise
Few yards away lies a beautiful lake
Peaceful, gentle, barely awake
Especially at dawn a fabulous scene
As such as I have never seen
Thousands of lotus flowers start to unfold
Bright vivid colours - so very bold
A carpet of pink, in glorious display
Soothing, easing one's cares away
Each one delicate and beautiful
Perfectly placed in the waters cool
But the noonday sun will soon beat down
Mother nature is wearing her crown
The flowers will close, their day is done
Tomorrow yet again, more flowers will come
And so on forever, the wonder of it all
As mother nature takes great care of it all

Joyce Roberts

A Victim's Song

'I'm not, I'm NOT,'
Knot. Knotted,
In and out, up and down,
In and out,
Round and round,
Screaming pain
Internalised,
Living life
For others' eyes.

The sky is blue,
The pit is black,
The rope is all
That stops the fall,
Yet scars and burns,
While yet it turns,
And turns
And twists
Her bursting heart.

Rona Rowe

Today

Here is today,
As yet untouched - unspoilt
Ready to unfold hour by hour
As petals on a fragile flower
For you to chose what you will do
With all this precious time.

Don't spoil today,
But use as best you can
Each of the gifts that you possess
And fill it with your happiness
Let not your chances slip away
They may not come again.

Enjoy today,
It comes but only once
Don't sigh and moan and wish it past
But do your best to make it last
Enhanced with love and hope and joy
Accept - and be content.

Remember today,
And all good things therein
For soon it will be on its way
And then be known as yesterday
Another fleeting memory
Receding into time.

Ann Rickhuss

Forthcomming Attraction

Coming soon, Jesus of Nazareth
With full supporting cast,
Descending from the heavens,
Ever swiftly ever fast.

Trumpets will be blasting,
Through the skies to wide applause,
The return of the messiah,
Here to finally fulfil his cause.

Are you ready for this spectacle,
Of such power in the skies,
Are you ready to go with Him,
When there's no time for goodbyes.

Do you think you will be ready,
To climb the golden stairs,
Or will you still be doubting,
And left behind with your affairs.

The angels will be singing,
What a joy will fill the air,
When Jesus makes his entrance,
And his spirit everywhere.

The Lord's grace is so sufficient,
He has set a place for you,
At his table in the kingdom,
But then the choice is up to you . . .

Ian T. Redmond

Street People

Plastic bags, prams of rags, cardboard cartons, string,
Cigarette butts, polystyrene cups, sad, dirt darkened skin
Unkempt beards and matted hair
Hungry, homeless, humourless with despair,
Are the Street People
Abandoned vehicles, derelict buildings, doorways, passages, stairs,
Ducking delving, gutter searching, a life entirely theirs,
For finding food and keeping warm, is all they strive to do,
Each endless day and one night home, for old and young ones too.
The Street People,
Rejected, neglected, victims of chance are they,
Society has let them down, relentlessly they pray
In alcoholic dreams they see, tomorrow they will be strong,
Visions of hope, stability, to the streets they will no longer belong.
The Street People.

Catherine Robinson

372

Winter Window

Clustering snow crystals obscure the birch bark
As they float on their slow descent
Through still air which recently battered at our windows as it was driven by
Siberian blasts to gain admittance.

Cold white velvet covers frosted green and
Petrified leaves are fixed in metallic postures.
Twigs play percussive rhythms to the spasmodic tune the wind begins singing.

Where are the birds?
We might glimpse them sitting dully, as if conjured into
Place or chattering abrasively suddenly to one another, in sparse groups.
Few are apparent around the garden where many were feeding a summer ago.

A pigeon goes swiftly to roost within the branches of the black firs which fade in
The greying twilight.
Almost mid-winter now and deeper and darker the starless nights which steal up on
Us silently.

The only comfort is companionship which like warmth from the fires we kindle in
Winter hearths livens grey days and softens what otherwise is cold and harsh.

Chris Rowley Langford

To A Blackbird

Sing again Blackbird
With all your heart
Sing for the springtime
Let winter depart

Sing for the rebirth
Of all living things
And for the beauty
A new season brings

Sing for pink blossoms
The beauty of Trees
Warm sunny days
The murmur of bees

White scudding clouds
And azure blue skies
Days in the garden
Bright butterflies

Sing again Blackbird
For when we hear you
Joy is reborn
And hope springs anew

Margaret Radley

My Perfect World

In my perfect world there would be no wars,
No violence or crime,
The nations all would live peace -
Oh, what a world sublime!
There would be no battered children,
No animals in distress,
And the leaders of all countries
No more their countrymen oppress.
Refugees need no more search the world
Travelling hopelessly to find
Food and safety for their families
From the terrors left behind;
The thousands living on the streets,
Cardboard boxes for their home
Would all have friends and shelter
And no longer need to roam.

Of course this is just a dream world
And we must face reality,
But we need to hold on to our dreams,
As I'm sure you will agree;
I dream that sometime in the future,
Not in my life span I know,
My perfect world may come to pass
When peace and tolerance flow.

Freda Rogers

The Idol

A vista of eternal-ethereal grasslands; in Dream, as life so Dreams!
My thirsting soul is quenched by a surfeit of land's richness.
In verdure, alien pollenations upon a nocturne of sweeping savannah.

Incarnadine aura vitalise this ether of lower atmosphere, my goal stands within
the beyond, slicing through the limitless horizon; an incision enacted by surgeons of
the Chaos, out of which is weaned Order!
It's presence enacting apocalypse, obliterates the curtains. reveals the Cosmic Drama.
Within these infinities serene, wheels the cradling empyrean, wherein birth is given
to lustrous Stars, in the cold nakedness of heaven's fractured Textures!

The Edifice is exact in its poetic form, the matter is Pure,
yet cognition eludes - as the beautific and Terrible form extends
into a higher dimension.
that which we can perceive is an Eidolon of Symphonic prowess,
in presence of this mass, the Terrain is buckled,
within Shadow and Compass; in form, the Grace is Supernal! It rests
upon the very air in sensuous supination. No less a Monument,
no lesser Temple "beneath the Lotus-hued light of great nebulae",
than would sate the hearts of questing Pilgrims from the Gates
of worlds beyond, (within quintessence of light!)

Mark Rogers

The Missing Christmas Tree

Where's the tree
Two little boys
Went down our street
To the Christmas tree shop
And the man came
Around from the counter
He went "chop, chop, chop"
How will we get it
Through our door
It must be six foot or more
Christmas tree, Christmas tree
Where are the lights to be
Bright baubles and bows
I just want you to know
How special you'll
Always be.

Jeannette Reynolds

Gypsy Lord

We met one warm and starless night,
And stayed together 'til morning light,
He promised me, through Romany law,
His life, and love,for evermore,
I thought I'd love and need no other,
Then my dark-eyed gypsy lover.

He tempted me with endless lies,
With dusky skin and flashing eyes,
Lured and loved me, left and shamed me,
Cast me aside, but chose to blame me,
When I was gone he took another,
My dark-eyed gypsy lover.

S.J. Rostron

Cursed Are The Curious

What wretched God this life donates
Forged on earth from love and lust
To be denied anything, fulfilment

Holding, needing, seeing, dreaming

Like the needling of a thousand pins
Each kiss lodged fast upon my heart
This twinkling in anothers eye
Ignites each spark in butterflies
Swoon each and every aphrodite
Yea, never may they part

Wanting, needing, touching, having

Like burning heat it scalds within
Each pain filled fix my pleasures touch
This lusting in another's flesh
Fans each flame in more excess
Shame other loins of would be pain
Never may we part
Yea, never may they part

Craving, craving, craving, craving

What tortured bliss each day dictates
Not youth defined this life and love
To be fulfiled in anything, denied

Kit Richards

The Green Man

Perfect May morning
I set out for Slad,
A way of white parsley,
The verges Spring clad.

I stopped at a layby
Wood end of a track
And wandered across
Toward the "Wool Pack".

Outside the entrance
I spied the Green Man,
Cream dressed for Summer
Half pint in his hand.

Old pewter his pot
Old silver his hair
Viewing the valley
Alone he stood there.

Few words did I hear
Lee side of the porch,
"You show promise boy,
Carry the torch".

Gold flashed the sky -
Emerald the Sun,
The Green Man had gone
And my visit was done.

John Rumming

A Flowering Grave

The bright light shines the redness glistens,
A high pitch noise vibrates the wall,
Two entwined with crystal tears
A room of love for a small bud of life.
The strands of silk grow,
Unfolding head raised the first step,
A mamma, a papa, a scribble in red,
The symbols the signs orals a mine!
Winds turn a tide roars, more boarders a form,
Two stems strained a young flower or thistle.
Roots merge fresh buds, an array of colours that call.
Cracks of time the petals shrivel fall, they crawl.
Peace the air is still a mist of fog with mystic
White shades of frost no longer pink floss.
As black shadows stare,
Two stand, acid drops fall to the soft wet soil,
That embrace a wooden lair.

M. Raynes

Spring Flowers

Oh wonderful sunlight
Amidst the morning haze
Showing greatness of creation
Descending your silver stripes
Beating down in random ways
Upon flowers of Spring
"How delicate you seem"
Your colours afire.
Transforming shapes into elusive array
As you bud into bloom
Bringing forth happiness
From petals and stamens; So agile
Feeding beauty to gardens around
Exotic fragrance enriched
By early morning dew
So frail . . . so meek
Sunlight so bright
Relinquishes heavens power
As aroma slowly fades
Far into eternity
Petals and leaves wilt
"Why do you die?"
Remains a mystery to this day
Never to be forgotten.

Victoria M. Revell

Untitled

I see your face before me,
In thought, in dreams in prayer.
No matter where I look,
Before me you are there.
Your touch is warm and tender,
Your kiss is soft and sweet.
The first time that I saw you,
You swept me off my feet.
My thoughts of you are precious,
More precious to me than gold.
For you my love grows stronger,
As another day unfolds.

In dreams you're there beside me,
In thoughts I see your face.
And in my heart I know,
No-one can take your place.
In prayer I pray to God
One day you will be mine.
Then we can share our love
Forever and all time.
Oh how I wish that I could show,
Just how much I love you so.
Then my darling you would see,
Just how you mean the world to me.

Sylvia Ranby

Reflection

At eventide, when gently glows the lilting light
Upon these trivial thoughts transformed by it to such
Romantic depth; when shadows play and tease the night
So tauntingly to roll them in its velvet clutch
Making of them mere nothing as their source departs;

At this time does Reflection come. With wings outstretched
And fleeting feet she skims the silky sea of gleams
So softly as to slide in leaving mem'ries etched
All unawares, to surface in the pool of dreams
And fantasies she swims in through our sleeping hearts.

Julie A. Rayner

Love Of Her

My love for her grows stronger,
With the dawning of each day,
As I lovingly caress her,
And loving words do say.

As I hold her in my arms and kiss her,
Her tender lips meet mine,
With her bosom pressed close to me,
The feeling is divine.

All these loving actions
Excite me all the time,
And make me feel quite content,
To know at last she's mine.

But alas I'm only dreaming,
As I have done for years,
And awakening to reality,
Fill my eyes with tears,

Jack Robinson

Help

Times are hard and this we know
Days go by but still we grow.
Laughter, glee are all amiss
Where is all the joyful bliss?

Sadness, woe and heartache too
Loneliness is nothing new
So much we hurt, so much we cry
Sometimes we wish that we could die.

A helping hand, a listening ear
Someone to wipe away the tears
It's all we ask, it's all we need
Just someone to plant a caring seed.

We need the strength to get us through
To stop us feeling down and blue.
A guiding soul to make us see
How happy we should really be.

G. Rush

Treasures

When I was young, I was inclined to clasp
With eager hands; life's treasures. Now repose
Is mine; the perfect peace of one who knows
That God's good gifts are well within our grasp.

Firstly, the evening stars effulgent light,
That jewel gracing heaven's pearly throat,
The crescent moon, a slender silver boat,
Sailing on distant, dusky seas of night.

With breath withdrawn I have beheld above,
The tints of twilight, lovelier by far
Than gems, and look in vain for joys that are
As bright as truth is, or as strong as love.

Throughout life, as the darker days pass by,
The grey is gilded by the kindness shown
By strangers, and the sweetness of my own
Child's kiss upon my lips, that ends my sigh.

For joy intangible within the breast
I thank God, and for glimpses that he gave
To mortals of that life beyond the grave,
Where dwell eternal beauty, peace and rest.

P. Ransley

Husband

Precious love is hard to find
You mean so very much to me
A man, so gentle, warm and kind
True love I thought could never be
You turned the key and opened my heart
To so much passion I never knew
Our love will keep never to part
The love and laughter because of you
You reach the depth of my very soul
Together we share such intense pleasure
Love like ours is a passionate whole
Memories of love I will always treasure
Your loving smile makes my day
Rising with the waves of life
A look that says - we've come a long way
I am so proud to be your wife.

Pauline Richmond

I Tried

I tried to teach you how to love
and how to have some fun
I tried to teach you how to work
until the job was done
I tried to give you values
and show you how to live
I tried to teach you when it was
the time for you to give
I tried to teach you never to say
'I've had enough'
I tried to help you through
when times were really rough
I've always tried to be there
as your mum and your friend
And I'll be there
until the very end

Jacquie Smith

It's A Crying Shame

An elephant walked out of the jungle
His body all of a quiver,
He was feeling very thirsty
So he stuck his trunk in the river.
A crocodile swimming nearby,
Saw this thing splashing about,
Swimming quietly under water,
It grabbed the elephants trunk.
The tug-of-war that then started
Went on, at a furious pace,
When, - there was a loud crack!
They both staggered back!
The trunk snapped, from the elephants face . .
'Jumbo' - now minus his nose-piece
Cried, through tears that were big and runny,
Said, to the 'Croc' - who was smiling,
"I thuppoth you thing thath funny .?

A.G. Revill

378

The Basement

I've dreaded the dark black basement all of my life
The spiders all black and hairy
Along with the green dragon flies
I've seen the black basement but never been in
But scary as all I went in one day
To find that the green dragon flies
And the black spiders
Were only old boxes to life
But every now and then a black hairy thing
I see from under the door

Elizabeth Reed (Age 10)

African Memory

Where the Libyan desert meets the sea,
By the cool green marsh and the dune,
I saw the pink flamingoes fly
In the light of the crescent moon.

With their broomstick necks they headed south
For the dusty plains of Sudan,
To the rosy lakes of Nakura
And the shade of the marsh-tree's fan.

And my heart flew with this caravan
To the land that lives in my dreams,
To the forests red with Nandi flame
Where Kiliminjaro gleams

Marjory Reynolds

A Town In The Rain

The paving stones are wet and dirty grey,
Mean little gardens at their inner edge
Where gallant flowers struggle to survive.
The buses pass and spray the filthy rain;
It does not reach to where the flowers wait.
Poor tortured trees grow spaced along the way,
Their limbs lopped off to form unnatural shapes.
Large blocks of flats rear up and hide the sky,
Net curtained windows, cataractic eyes
Obscure the tenants in their concrete jails.
Far, far beneath this human ant hill is
Rich soil where once a fertile meadow grew
And cattle crazed and farmers made their hay;
And there were hedges where the wild birds sang.
I long to be at home again and walk
Where only grass is underneath my feet.

Penny Radclyffe

The Human Race

This world could have been a better place,
If there was no such thing as the human race,
For man destroys, all that he sees,
The soil, hedgerows, birds, insects,bees,
He is not only content with that,
For he will often kill, both dog and cat,
Even turning on his fellow man,
Will try to kill him, if he can,
So here we have 'The Human Race,'
We should be ashamed, to show our face,
For centuries, on and on it goes,
When we think it is over, the answer is no,
The more we breed, there's more decay,
We see it happening every day,
Do we help to make it stop?
No! We are Human.
  We are the ROT,

Pam Richardson

Falling

I'm losing my grip,
I'm falling down this hole,
I've tried so hard to fight,
And to retain my soul.

But as time passes,
The hole deepens,
My head spins,
And my heart weakens.

I had a grip on the edge,
But somehow it slipped,
I plunged into darkness,
And my heart skipped.

I've not yet hit the bottom,
But it'll be with a bang,
I'll try and get out of this rut,
But I don't know if I can.

Kelly Smith

For Sale Or Return

Love, its fresh, its new. A
Gentle caring love so true, folk
Declare 'it's from heaven above.' But
On whom may I bestow this love.

Hi there hi hi. Any bidders any offers
Or are ladies only interested in my coffers
A frozen love that needs unthawed, I need
To share, to comfort. So ladies where is cupids' dart!

So, love and care on offer for a lady to share,
A love so strong it will perfume the air, a
Strong wild love, free as a bird, must this
My plead continue on - unheard.

So ladies out there. Love on offer. Love for sale
With tender loving care, a male who needs
To share. So beloved ladies please
Do respond to this lonely lonely male.

Duncan Robson

Paradise

Paradise - what have we done to it,
We have made it into a rubbish tip
By polluting land, sea, and air.
And nobody seems to care,
We have caused extinction of hundreds of animals
And it's all done by us the people.

Thinking about the state of the world can be depressing
But can we do something!
No - we will have to wait
Until it can be bought back into a paradise state.
By the one who came to earth before
Who gave His life and so much more,
He is God's son Jesus Christ
This world He will turn back into paradise.
In the meantime God expects us to live His way
Look after the world and His laws obey.

When Jesus does return He will give us eternal life
To live in a happy, peaceful, beautiful world called paradise
But first we must go to God and our sins confess
And ask Him for His forgiveness,
We must also believe in the one who died for us
Our one and only Saviour - Jesus.

Linda Roberts

My Boy

A babies first step
That winning smile
It says it all
A tottering one foot in front of the other
Like a drunken footballer trying to kick the ball
The triumph, the cheer as you urge them on
One more wobbly step - but the legs are gone
Legs look like jelly feet on wrong way.
Haven't you done well - we'll call it a day
Struggling to get up and have another go - can your
Nerves take it! I really don't know.
It's hard to watch
Your bursting with pride,
Tears in your eyes - your not bothered to hide
He's done it! Four steps to your arms
You hug him and kiss him - then he falls
To his bum
Oh it is great to be a mum.

Sue Rawnsley

The School Concert

Arrive 7.30 and drop off your child. The concert starts promptly at 8. (God help the
parents who mislaid their tickets, and suffer the wrath of Miss Blott on the gate.

Great, a night out! Loads of laughs? Entertainment? Easier said than done! (The
thought of those little school grey plastic chairs, shaped solely to numb one's bum!)

Oh well, she's excited, rehearsed it for weeks. Perhaps just this once I should try . . .
to get it together. Be there 7.30. Encourage her, don't make her cry.

It's just that the odds seem all stacked against me, to exit the house on time. And I
can't find her clean socks,or pink plastic hair band . . . "No you can't . . . put it back .
. . that is mine . . ."

And why don't I have enough fingers, to master the art of a pretty French plait?
Why didn't I mend that hole in her jumper? Stain Devil the oil from her back?

At last we're all in, and the doors quickly close, as we grope for our seats in the
dark. The hall is quite stiflingly hot and I'm sweating, and Luke needs a pee . . .!
Should have gone when we parked'.

The man on my left suffers bad halitosis. The one right in front's 8 foot tall. The
children are coughing, I can't hear the words, and I haven't seen Hannah at all.

Ten minutes before the curtain is raised, for the interval, marking half time, I have
to take Luke for his pee, he can't hold it. (Why is it that kids always whine?)

I've been so incredibly patient so far, but when will my daughter appear?
Oh there she is, in the back row of the chorus. Her finger in somebody's ear.

We're on the last song now. It's time to go home. I'll wake up my husband again.
Up come the lights, quick, grab for the coats. Pretend we must rush for a train.

"Yes Hannah, we loved it, and all saw you wave." (from the back, her 2 minutes of fame.)
"Just get in the car. It's late and Dad's hungry." (Next week, Luke is doing the same!)

J. Richardson

Time

What is this thing, man calls time.
What is its reason, what is its rhyme.
This thing called time that rules all
Creates builds up, then brings about fall.

We are but droplets in Times great sea
It will not wait, for you or me.
We are but a passing phase.
Whose memory Time, will finally erase.

Living mankind's memory, finally fades.
Written words lingering, like dark shades.
People of the future, deep in wonder
As upon, the written word they ponder.

Terry Ratcliffe

Snow

Snowflakes fall
Like a blanket of
Freezing snow.
White as a sheet,
Crunchy snow,
Soft as a feather
'Till all the snow melts.

Thomas Smith (Age 8)

Eye Surgery

In the hour before the hour
Of the remaindering knife
I found myself in a lost bower,
Trace of a hope once in another's life

Remaining in the scents of lemon-mint
Rosemary, bay. The old clumps sprawl,
Hiding his flagstone: no hint
Of the path that eye saw to an order in all.

Well, my derelict eye shall soon submit
To the surgeon's way, retrieving an order
Overcome. Men might yet forestall,
Turn back the raindrop that would fall

In its ordered course, to pass from sight
Beneath the surface of a weed-fringed pool.
I could not take the sickle in my hand
Here, where I see that already thought was blind.

Now a breeze in this garden goes on its way
Through wiry invisible stems of hawkbit.
Flowers swirl like fireflies in the light of day
Over those frail palisades, wire of an unseen border.

Paul Reeve

June's Candles

The dark room shines.
Tiny buds of light open and blossom in the
Small black space.
"That's better, now we can find joy
In our apprehension."
The blinds are closed to the Sun,
He is not visible.
They are only visible in their own dim lights.
"We are our own God."
Their ego burns brighter every day.

Soon laughter turns to sorrow as they begin to
Realise they are slowly bleeding away from
Sight.
Their imprudence has confronted them with
Their own unexpected mortality.
They become hollow and sink into the night.

Daniel J. Rapley

Pet Food

What do you get Jude
When you eat pet food?
Hamster burgers,
Poodle pies,
Gold fish fingers,
Corn cat ash,
Hot dogs,
Pig pies,
That's what you get Jude
When you eat Pet Food,
Sounds good to me,
I think I'll go and have my tea!

Nicky Smith (Age 11)

383

What Every Girl Should Know When Seeking A Post

First scan the papers and look for a post
Then write and convince them you're the 'girl with the most'
A letter arrives, an interview is set
An important decision to make - a permanent I must get

The hour approaches, I rehearse my prose
I apply personal freshness and then check my hose
I knock at the door and enter therein
I try not to notice the number of chins!

I smile at him sweetly and answer his questions
(Was that the wind blowing, or his indigestion!)
I say what I can do - and what I do better!
And "Oh yes, if necessary I can type a letter"

Now as you know folks I'm not one to brag
But in this job I'd be wasted and find it a drag
I resist his invitation of a lift in his veh-ic-ular
Especially when he says he wants to take down my particulars!

You then join the dole queue as you need the '**bread**'
But don't let your guard down, be positive instead,
And when your turn comes and they holler out "**NEXT**"
Do keep your mouth shut about your personal effects!

Ann Slee

Finding Peace

Finding peace is where we look,
In a paper in a book,
With some knitting or a pen,
Someone's letter read again,
In the garden with the plants,
With the birds their song enchants,
Going for a quiet walk,
Forget the work forget the talk,
Be at peace your walk employ,
Tranquil steps your feet enjoy,
Peaceful time we all must find,
Noise and gossip leave behind,
Empty words that have no fire,
A silent prayer has more desire,
Calming thoughts are what we need,
If in this life we shall succeed,
God's peace can put our minds at rest,
With His help we do our best.

Margaret Scrivens

Dreams

My dreams are as a dove in flight,
That hope for peace and love.
My fears haunt me through the night,
And I pray to the Lord above.
The heart beats like the drums of war,
My eyes see grief and tears.
The voice speaks of terror afar,
Yet no-one ever hears.
My ears hear the cry of pain,
From men, women and children.
Will their suffering be in vain,
Or will peace return again.
Why can man no longer care,
What happens to our land,
All the suffering that is there,
Can no-one understand?
So let my dreams come true, dear Lord,
All nations live in peace,
May all world leaders give their word,
To let strife and suffering cease.

J.E. Simpkins

As The Crow Flies

Broken windows empty eyes
Staring out at grey pennine skies
Blackened buildings empty rooms
No more resound to the clacking looms
The weaving trade has left this town
Cheap labour's brought the weavers down
The masters to increase their hoard
Broke down the looms shipped them abroad

Black as the night the carrion crow
What can he see what does he know
Is he drawn by the scent of death
The rattle of that final breath

Over the hills the footwear dies
Different masters same old lies
Cheap imports have killed the trade
Textiles footwear foreign made
Cold empty fingers pierce the murk
Weavers clickers out of work
From handloom to the factory floor
Cold destiny the poor stay poor

To warmer climes now does he fly
But who can hear his warning cry
Muffled by the clacking loom
No one heeds his croak of doom

Will Scribble

Three O'Clock

The spirit's at its lowest ebb
At this hour of the morning:
The darkness deep, the world asleep,
When dread walks without warning.

Awake alone in heedless arms
Feel isolation's scalpel.
Chimera slips into the void
Swathed in dementia's mantle.

The rhythm of the other's breath
Would seem to shroud a sighing:
The rattle of a fetid gasp,
Lost echo of the dying.

The fitful quiver of the heart
Will not be stilled by prayer;
The mind contracts before the dark
And wrings the logic there.

The corners hold our primal fears
With no light for revealing
The innocence, or ridicule
The shadows are concealing.

No sleep arrives, no respite yet
From ceaseless cogitating:
The terrors stay, the ghosts insist,
'Come dawn, we shall be waiting.'

Madelene Simpson

Look After Love

If you take love for granted there might come a day,
When too late you'll discover, life got in the way.
You became so involved in everyday worry,
Too busy to notice, you were in such a hurry.
The signs were ignored, and as if out of the blue
Things came to a head, you hadn't a clue.
But if you look back, I'm sure you will find
You've been going through life as if you were blind.
You neglected to listen and became unaware
Of the other one's needs, forgot how to care.
So just stop for a moment and try to recall
That wonderful feeling, that first made you fall
In love with that somebody special, and then,
Be sure not to let life take over again.

Patricia Scott

Recipe For Love

God took a good helping of kindness, together
with gentleness and warmth from the sunshine above,
he added heaps of affection, patience, understanding,
and an abundance of love.

Then he put in sensitivity and sincerity, as well as
a large measure of strength,
he mixed in tolerance and compassion, all of these
gifts heaven sent.

He then topped it with a huge sprinkling of tenderness,
laughter, joy and happiness.
Then stood back to admire his work with pleasure
a masterpiece no less.

He knew his new creation was special
and deserving of a name like no other,
and so because of the goodness within it,
decided to call it
    MOTHER

Maria Smith

Wind Is Like An Animal

It ripped through the night air,
Fierce, angry and violent,
Like a wild animal, maybe a bear,
As he moves through the woods with intent,
His growling can be heard as he nears his prey,
Like the wind as it howls through night and day,
He was hungry,
The wind was angry.

It's time to sleep, he's had his fill,
He tries to find a place to lay,
A comfy spot near a shaded hill,
Is where he'll spend a restful day,
Just like the calm after the storm,
When the wind stops on a winter's morn.
The bear was in peace,
The wind was at ease.

The bear wakes from a nice long rest,
He is happy, content and ready to play,
He runs through the trees, which way's the best,
Oh who cares, it doesn't matter, I'll go this way,
He plays like the wind when it's just a breeze,
Tossing and playing with flowers and trees,
The bear is playing,
The wind is swaying.

R.A. Self

Deadlier Than The Toadstool

The streets lay
still and deserted.
Gone was the everyday
bustle and laughter.
A dog barked hoarsely
shattering the silence.

An explosion and a
blinding flash,
with a core that was
white hot.

the intense heat
burnt everyone or anything
to a brittle piece of charcoal.
The gamma rays destroy the
body tissues and you become
a shadow on the wall.

But above all the pall
of white smoke, rose as
a huge mushroom, like a
funeral pyre, a headstone
over the dead.
Even more deadlier than
the Toadstool!

Rosalind Smith

386

The Dark

We all live in the daytime,
While the sun comes blazing down,
But we all know that as the day moves on,
Darkness comes along.

He sends his troops to kill the blue sky,
And sits back to watch the sun die,
Then he becomes the moon,
Letting down a shimmering light,
As his troops become the stars,
And lay far out beyond Mars.

Now that he rules the sky,
He thinks of all the things that die,
The mice, caught by the swooping owl,
While the fox goes on his nightly prowl.

A comet goes zooming by,
Which means that he will die,
The light is coming along,
And now the sun is strong.

A fierce battle commences,
And the darkness has to retreat,
But he means to come back the next day,
To make the sun pay.

Tim Self (Age 12)

Nature At Work

I hiked amongst the hill-top trees
Where rare birds find their habitat
And resting on my bended knees
I watch them feed their young, and sat
In silence amidst nature's show
Spellbound I could not rise to go.

The squirrels scurried here and there
Ran swiftly through the wind-blown grass
Avoiding not the small mounds where
Ants stood aside to let them pass,
About their business for the day
The ants marched off another way.

A rabbit jumped behind a stone
In search of food I do not doubt
He may have thought himself alone
Apart from insects all about
Not to mention the butterflies
Kaleidoscope across the skies.

The Sun shines with a godlike smile
Upon the lives of creatures all
Who are prepared to climb the stile
Without the fear that they may fall
And grants them when their labours cease
The comfort of a lasting peace.

Alexander Smith

Winter

The wind around the tree tops moans,
It's howls like banshee's cries.
The clouds race one another,
Through the dark and stormy skies.
Window panes are lashed with rain,
Unyielding to it's might.
The willow sways, but does not break
As twilight turns to night.
The wrath of winter rages on,
Oblivious to man's cries.
The warm spring morn will take its time,
Till winter finally dies.

Linda Storer-Smith

A Helpless Child

She's just like a child still needing her mum,
But in many ways she's all alone.
With everyone to stare,
She doesn't understand,
Oh why is she this way.
People different staring at her,
They laugh and walk away,
It could be one of there's maybe.

Corrine Sandford-Smith (Age 12)

387

My Box

In my box I keep my life and all the good things
That happened in the past
And all the great things that will happen
I will keep in my special box

My special box is made of pine and leather over it
And silk over that and gold over the silk
And all my stickers
And when it's mad it makes it snow
And when it's happy it makes it sunny
Me and my special box

I will go in at midnight and open the gold handle
When I do it makes me feel really happy and peaceful
When I go inside the box
I will go to a land of fantasy and fly on my box

I go on rides on the box and when I get off
I'll be dizzy
We will get ice cream and have lots of fun
Every night
Me and my special box

Mark Smith (Age 9)

Seasons

When one awakes and sees the trees
With leaves just turning brown
Rustling wind high in the boughs
And acorns falling down

You realise that once again
Winter is almost nigh
Brief cold days and colder nights
Did not the summer fly

All too soon the summer days
Pass by and bring instead
The need to tend to fires
And a warmer in your bed

But never fear the time goes by
And 'ere too long you'll see
That spring is here and birds do sing
How happy I will be.

Brian Sandford

The Airport Lounge

Like a child's first day at school
My heart is racing, my hands are cool
I glance at the clock upon the wall
Is your flight the next they'll call?
I want to turn and run away
Perhaps I shouldn't have come today

You remember me young, but today I feel old
My heart is racing, my hands so cold
You went away without a word
You broke my heart, I haven't heard
Why now should you bring back the pain
That I thought I'd not feel again?

And like a child's first day at school
My heart is racing, my hands are cool

But then I guess that you've changed too
Perhaps you're feeling as I do
And like a child's first day at school
Your heart is racing, your hands feel cool

Joan Shillabeer

388

Thank You

Just a little 'Thank You' by word or note or air
Creates a happy aura, it proves you really care
It may be for a present whether small or great
Or perhaps a kindly action to a relative or mate

The value of the present is neither here not there
What really matters is to show you really care
The parcel wrapped and posted we think of them opening it out
Hoping they like the contents we've chosen with thought

Maybe they'll call this evening, we wait for the phone to ring
Or maybe the postman will call with a letter tomorrow morn
Days pass without a word, we begin to feel cross
We sought to give pleasure, was it not to their taste

'Tis such a simple word 'Thank You' yet it conveys such a lot
Thought, appreciation and common courtesy without it we're not worth a jot

M.E.M. Schlette

Our World

Our world is full of wonderful things like
Plants, birds, trees, rainforests, rivers, oceans and plenty
More. All you have to do is open up your eyes.
Look at the birds the rivers and the seas.
Try a bit of food or drink.
Try some water that's all you have to do.
It's not so hard.
Just open up your eyes
Look at the sky and I am sure
You won't want to close them again.

Amanda Shaw (Age 10)

Brighton

From my room I see the crashing, frothy sea,
I can see the funfair lights
I can smell the fresh salty air which burns my cheeks
The laughter of happy children rings in my ears.

Once the sky darkens, the funfair is still open.
The sweet smell of candy floss and toffee apples still linger
The funfair lights look brighter than ever.

The sea grows restless, it crashes violently on the pier
But still the funfair goes on
Seagulls squawk in joyful glee
People walk along the beach whether it is dark or daylight
Then when the clock strikes twelve it all falls quiet.

Charlotte Slattery (Age 10)

My 13th Christmas

I have been here in this world for 13 years,
And every second of the day is worth it,
But now I'm getting older, things are different,
I have to think for myself, do everything,
It feels as though the whole world is upon me,
I'm so happy, but yet so sad,
I don't know what to think,
But Christmas makes me think,
Think so hard that I cry,
It's not just any Christmas,
It's so special.
It's nothing like it used to be,
It used to be a proper Christmas,
But now I'm at Grammar School,
No Christmas plays, no Christmas parties and no Christmas work,
It doesn't feel the same.
It's hard to come to terms with the feelings I have.
I feel as though I have missed out on so much,
I feel so confused, grateful and happy.
I want to make use of what I've got.
It's so hard being a teenager, especially at this stage,
I have to think about my whole life, make decisions,
This world is such a beautiful place, I want to explore,
But people stop me, I've got to stay in one place, all the time.

Ruth Shepherd (Age 13)

On The Beach

Rows of coloured beach huts line the promenade,
Each individually decorated with a different facade.
Driftwood and seaweed left by the ebbing tide,
Pretty coloured seashells washed up alongside.
Bedecked with towels and windbreaks, using every space,
Suncreams and potions smeared on every face.
The salty smell is everywhere, so different from town air,
It gives a sticky feeling to skin and clothes and hair.
Water held in rock pools make playgrounds for small crabs,
Assuming they're not found first by fish-net wielding lads!
Children armed with buckets and spades dig furiously in the sand
Build a castle, grand, with a moat separating the land.
Mums and Dads soak up the sun and watch them hard at play,
Prepare a picnic lunch for all, on a tartan blanket laid.
The ice-cream van approaches selling lollies and ninety-nines,
People queue and wait to buy in long untidy lines.
With food devoured and paddling done, it's time to make for home,
Plenty of sun for everyone, unlimited ozone.
A last long look at all the sights, the beaches, coves and bays,
The memory will linger on it seems, when finding sand for days!

Susan Small

Night Games

Dreams will not the pitch-black night relieve,
A cold pervading darkness deep and dense,
Severs sleepless minds from normal sense;
No eye can hopeful change perceive,
No prospect of approaching dawn retrieve.
Time makes the crowding darkness more intense,
The less that's seen the more the mind invents,
Creating images which sense could not conceive.

But just as sanity begins to drift away,
Dawn draws back the shroud of dark despair,
A skylark's singing fills the silent air,
And through thin curtains first-light pale and grey,
Brings reassurance with each welcome ray.
Gradually the eye becomes aware,
Of bedroom clutter scattered here and there,
At first in outline only, but then on full display.

Getting up I shrug off all remaining gloom,
A crowing cock proclaims the break of day,
Long strands of morning mist drift far away,
And brilliant sunshine floods throughout the room.

From when I leave the cottage until the eventide,
With everything but morbid thoughts my mind is occupied,
But when the day is over and I watch the sun descend,
I wonder as the darkness falls if it will ever end.

A.K.S. Shaw

This Is War

Women and children run for cover,
Hoping and praying for their lover.
The smell of gun powder fills the air,
The sound of screaming everywhere.
Many wounded many dead,
Its starting to drive me out of my head.
Claret fills the gutters and pavements,
All of this to make some statements
Nothing is sacred anymore,
All my memories are now so sore.
Now there is no peace or love,
I await the day I see that dove.
Maybe one day there will be some kind of law,
But for now all I can say is this is war.

Hannah Sheen

One Second

One second later
I can have sex
But not watch it
For another two years.

One second later
I can drive a car
But not down a pint
In my local.

One second later
I am an adult
As time obviously makes
A great difference.

Gary Shipsey

Wheels For Life

Twelve years old, does anyone care.
I'm firmly stuck in my wheelchair.
If only I could, get out of this hell
and just for one day, I could feel well.

Ordinary children just go outside
my legs won't work, I stay in and hide.
I did try to get out one sad day,
I fell on my face, took my pride away.

I go to the disco and watch others dance.
I get excited but there isn't a chance.
Just can't do the things that you can do,
how I'd love to wear pretty clothes too.

The doctor says, "Now I've no idea
how long you're going to live my dear.
You could go on for years you know
or maybe it'll be next week you go."

So I carry on and smile a lot
people say, "You're happy," but I'm not.
A death sentence I'm under every day
not fair, I can't even go out and play.

Sometimes I cry, heaven knows why,
I just get sad and stare at the sky.
People look at me and think, "What a shame."
Please God take me, I'm not to blame.

K.J. Simpson

A Message From A Loved One

Don't weep for me by my gravestone,
because I am not there.
Please don't shed your tears for me,
and don't cry in despair.

Your heart is full of sadness,
I feel your grief and pain,
but I am all around you,
in the gentle falling rain.

You feel that space around you,
that empty void of time.
If only I could tell you,
I feel wonderful, I'm fine.

I take your hand, I dry your eyes,
if only you could see,
my life is free of pain,
of toil and drudgery.

I whisper words of comfort,
I kiss your tear stained cheeks,
if only you could hear me,
before you fall asleep.

My loved one, please don't worry,
have faith in God above,
one day we'll be together,
in our Spirit home of love.

Margaret Sadler

Bonfire Night

The silence of the night skies
Were suddenly awakened with screeches and cries
With shooting stars so pretty and bright
And terrific bangs to give you a fright
With bonfires soaring and flames leaping
Faces burning and eyes weeping
Smoke bellowing and sparks shooting high
Up and up into the night sky
All these things we remember
It's Guy Fawkes night on the 5th November.

Jean Smith

To Jessica
(With love from Grandma (april 1994)

The first time that I saw you on that September day
And touched your tiny little hand, you stole my heart away
Your Mum and Dad so very proud and happy as could be
That a new and tiny branch was added to the family tree

As weeks and months went quickly by I watched you smile and grow
And now you have a little tooth that's just begun to show
To hear you laugh and chuckle is such a sheer delight
You have your way of getting things. Yes! even in the night

And as you start to grow up, learning more and more
And begin to toddle on your legs instead of kicking on the floor
You'll find lots of things to interest you all wonderful and new
Making you a special person with a distinct point of view

In a world of busy people always rushing here and there
I only hope you grow up prepared to take your share
Of giving love and help to those worse off than you
And whatever else may happen to yourself always be true

And when my eyes are not as good as once they used to be
And my face is full of wrinkles from lifes ups and downs you see
I hope you will remember to come and visit me
As I did you on that September day in 1993

Elaine Shaw

Nonchalance

I have to try very hard not to mean too much,
Even though I yearn for your touch,
It takes time to teach not to feel too deep,
When life in general keeps me from sleep.
I've got you now, that's all that counts,
The past is dead, the future long from now,
I waste my time in idle verse,
Lamenting happiness making me not better but worse.

Would that I could, that I knew how,
This eternal bleakness of my soul to dispel,
To use the light your presence brings,
To turn the winter of sorrow into spring.
But I cannot, no matter how I try,
As they say "Once bitten, twice shy"
And being once struck by lost loves pain,
Paint everything black again and again.

Simon Skelling

A Lancashire Tale

The Lancashire fog lay everywhere, the streets were full of gloom,
A pretty young lass stood all alone in a firelit room,
She moved nervously to the door and gazed down the dreary street,
There was no welcoming figure there was no welcoming feet.

Sam was very late tonight the shift had finished long ago,
Surely if something had been wrong someone would have let her know.
Her mother had been widowed young, with three small babes to keep,
She pulled her shawl around her tight, tonight there'd be no sleep.

She thought of Sams warm smile and his strong arms around her tight,
She thought of life without Sam, it brought tears she had to fight.
Soon dawn would be breaking her hope was fading fast,
When suddenly she heard footsteps "Oh Sam you're here at last".

The men marched down the cobbled street their faces black and grim,
The worn out looks had said it all "Sorry lass Sam's still in",.
She leaned against the door post not knowing what to do,
Although she'd seen it all before, you don't think it will come to you.

How long she stood she didn't know she couldn't really say,
With stiffness in her body she sadly turned away,
Then all at once on cobbled stones familiar footsteps heard,
She turned around and there was Sam, but neither said a word.

For many a lass would grieve this day and many a child would cry,
But they had been reprieved this day and it wasn't for them to ask why.

Pat Saxon

Living In The Hang Of Gallows

I cannot change what should have been,
I cannot change the shadows,
I cannot change what I have seen,
Living in the hang of gallows.

I cannot change the yearnings,
I cannot change the sallows,
I cannot change love's burnings
Living in the hang of gallows.

I cannot change life's webbing cant,
I cannot change the deeps and shallows,
I cannot change the devil's chant,
Living in the hang of gallows.

Nor can I change what will be,
Nor change the things to come,
Nor know of any certainty,
Until on those gallows hung.

Steve Sheppard

Home And Retirement

Home is a place we all love best.
A place to relax in, and sit, and rest.
We do our chores, and every day,
We go out and about, come what may.

The time doesn't matter at all these days,
It is ours to spend, in all kinds of ways.
We meet up with friends, and have a nice walk,
And a laugh and moan and a lovely talk.

We can have a short sleep, and a lovely read,
And of course a nice cuppa and a little feed.
Retirement can be a time of leisure.
A time to look back on memories we treasure.

Margery Scowcroft

The Night Of The Still

Enchanted mountain highland child
How minor witchcraft fires her mind
Weaves blissful spell when dreams are wild
Melody haunting words unwind.

Drinking soft moonlight lay home beach
Bewitched by whisky lapping shore
Stranger comes riding briefed to preach
Old legend brewed in glass blown store.

Maturing years slink through veiled glen
Rainbow of movement breaks thin chain
Illicit shadows rowing men
From river Ness dry casks regain.

One dozen portrait necks embrace
Examine gently torchlit glass
With daring magic finger trace
Honesty content of each class

Awaken those fools who write law
Seeking vast taxes can't collect
But wrench its heart by tooth and jaw
Squeezing club jokers they select.

Obvious ploy to slip the breach
Travelling passport all alone
Departure lounge too far to reach
Stepping towards man's duty clone.

Robin Smith

Memories

Today I'm feeling lonely
But then that's nothing new
I live each day, surrounded by
A mist that once was you
I never thought I'd lose you
But deep inside I knew
My rosy world of colour
Would one day echo blue
If I could only say goodbye
And lock you in my past
Then find a key that's strong enough
To make my memories fast
Then I could live my life for me
Looking forward, not behind
But peace and happiness I feel
Live in the past, in my mind
So when my life gets me down
There's nothing else to do
But find the path that leads me back
To yesterday and you

Shirley Ann Slater

Christmas Thoughts

Sing a song of Christmas, of Mistletoe and wine.
Of sumptuous food and chocolate on which we all will dine.
Presents underneath the tree just there for one and all,
And children hoping secretly that Santa Clause will call.
People wrapped up warmly singing carols in the snow,
Roasting chestnuts in the fire which gives a warming glow.
Then off to church at midnight and there our praises sing
To little Baby Jesus, our newborn Infant King.
But what we must remember in what we do and say
Without this blessed Miracle, there'd be no Christmas Day.

Janet Short-Windsor

Childhood Days

When I was very very small our yard was my domain
I'd always play outside in it, unless it turned to rain.
It used to be the very place to see all there was to see
A spiders web, just like lace, a dizzy bumble bee
The spider used to peer at me from a tunnel in the wall
I'd stand and watch it catch a fly, be glad I wasn't quite so small.
I'd wander up the garden path to see what I could see
I'd often stop and have a laugh, pretend there was someone with me
The sun shone bright and life was good, I was happy as could be
I'd dig and pull some flower heads off till mum called "It's time for tea"
In I'd run and sit right down, I really couldn't wait
Mum would say "Just look at you, you're really quite a state"
Dirty hands on my clean cloth get down get to the sink
After tea you're in the bath "Oh Good" is what I'd think
Dad came home with his snap tin to meet him I'd be so pleased
To see if he had left any in "Oh joy some bread and cheese"
Just look at that child my Mum would say "She must have hollow legs
She's eaten all her meals today and still she even begs".
Pots washed up and I would laugh they'd look at me and know
My clothes came off and round and round the table I would go
"Mother control that child" my Dad would say "She is quite wild" and in the bath I'd go
Newspapers on the clothes horse to protect me from the draught
Water spilling on the hearth, while Mother laughed and laughed
Off to bed, tucked in tight, "God Bless love, nighty night"

Mary Shearer

My Grandchildren

I have five grandchildren, three girls and two boys
Their ages ranging from three years to twelve
The girls are very special to me
The boys are my treasures oh yes you see
They all have their own identity
And I love them beyond compare
I remember the times upon my knee
Their first steps and their smiles at me
I love each one for their own special ways
Because they all give me their love
Which is priceless today
I'm here for them always
My home is for them
Be it laughter or sadness they come to tell
Yes I am their Grandma, so proud be it too
My five dear dear grandchildren
Are loved through and through

Rita Smart *(nee Brooks)*

The Argument

You're evil,
I hate you,
Then why don't you go?
You Bastard,
I loathe you,
I love you,
I know.

Alexander Sharp

The Pain Of Life

The sun comes up, the sea remains black,
Clear water tries to squeeze out,
Weeping in sorrow.
The paralysed giant lies still,
Sentencing the sea to death.

A young seal breaks free from the oil's hold,
Motionless on a rock he lies - horror fills his eyes,
He collapses, joining the sea of oil and pain.

Oil creeps forward armed with the weapon of death,
Taking the life of a puffin,
Then a fish,
A seagull.

Skomer lurking on the horizon,
Oil lurching forward.
In an instant it is upon Skomer,
Slowly torturing,
Sticky wings,
Poisoned water,
Burnt skin,
The oil sleeps on a bed of death.

Julian Sayarer

Why Do The Birds Fly South?

How come the birds fly south?
How do they know the way?
They gather together on top of my house,
On a chilly October's day.
With a flutter a twitter and one big flap,
They rise up out of reach,
Then fly for a thousand miles or so,
And land on some tropical beach.
There they stop,
All winter long,
Relaxed in the sunshine,
Singing their song.
They'd be happy over there,
Or so you'd think,
With loads to eat,
Plenty to drink.
But one thing really puzzles me,
It's driving me insane,
Is why the hell they ever bother,
To fly back home again?

Snappa

Here I Am

Here I am tall and green,
Leaves falling in the stream.

Children playing around my bark.
Keeping my roots in the dark.

Rabbits making dens below
Sparrows come to and fro.

Spring, Summer, Autumn goes
I wonder how much I've grown.

Abigail Savage (Age 9)

People Like Us

Second class citizens they're thought to be,
Or the mind of a child,
In an adult's body,
But they are still human,
With minds of their own,
Their thoughts and feelings,
Yet to be known.

People cross over the street,
Or stop and stare,
They whisper and point,
Without a care,
Unkind names and comments are made,
Are people ignorant or just afraid.

If you just say hello,
Show that you care,
Or talk to them,
Acknowledge they're there,
You'll realise they're people,
Just like you and me,
With the right to make choices,
And the right to be free.

Susan J. Smith

Emotion

Come with me, help me to
Evaluate this feeling we call emotion.
You give, you take this intangible force
We call emotion.

A written word, a song of a bird,
A musician's masterpiece
They each play their part
Within this feeling we call emotion.

A single voice, a thousand voices,
One painting, may be many
Give and receive once more
This feeling we call emotion.

The welcoming sound of a new-born babe,
A merciful release for some solitary soul,
Give and take once again
This feeling we call emotion.

Your coming was of no avail,
It is within ones self
To give or receive
This feeling we call emotion.

Isobel Scarlett

Exhumation

Beneath broad Beeches under their cooling shade
A shallow grave in the woods they found,
While probing and searching with rods all around
There a gruesome site their eyes did gaze.
The body emaciated, slowly decaying,
Eye sockets sunken, skin yellow and shrunken,
Hair matted, balding and grey,
This body once was young and gay;
The stench so foul of rotten flesh,
Maggots writhe in its guts enmeshed,
Finger tips and toe bones exposed
How long has it been buried, no one knows.
Worms and Moles have had their fill,
While under ground the soil they till
Generating some new life to live again,
Is this re-incarnation or pretence!
Whatever the answer, it's a horrifying experience.

G.S.H. Seymour

Starsky

He's buried under the apple tree
His body at peace his spirit free
No more pain to mar his grace
No more stress shown in his face.

A beautiful cat, a friend most true
But oh the pain without you
A family grief we all must share
Isn't it fortunate we all really care
I know the house is silent now
But your presence is strong and how.

Always here to comfort the night
You tried I know, a useless fight
The body was weak but until the end
Your eyes said I'm still your friend.

The hurt is bad without you here
But I'm sure you'll understand the loss that's so dear.
You left us so quickly no time to reflect
You went out with grace just what we'd expect.
Quick silver's your life any less is no good.
So rest in the ground as a hero should.

Goodnight and God Bless you'll always be free
But I will not because STARSKY was me.

Catherine H. Smith

Shamrock Lady

She strides through the World with a jaunty gait
And a twinkle in her eye,
Emerged from the green land across the strait
Bidding forty shades goodbye.

Speaks softly her brogue with a gentle voice
Her laughter delights the air,
Yet politeness is always her first choice
Whilst firm, she is always fair.

Her figure is trim and her hair is down
Twin butterscotch are those eyes,
She never distorts her face with a frown
For her wide smile never dies.

There is honesty about herself
Which cannot remain unseen,
It is not glitter and it is not wealth,
But a patient heart serene,

William Smith

Kevan John

From the twinkle in your father's eye and your mother's come on smile
Nine months later you arrived my son and heir our only child
As a baby you were well behaved and at night you slept right through
We would breakfast on boiled eggs and soldiers and a cup of tea or two
All done and dusted and clean clothes our shopping we'd begin
We bought in bread and spuds and milk as well as baby dinners in a tin
Then back home to feed you lunch and change your nappy again
We would play rough games that made you sick but what is one more stain
First years soon go, time flies past hey presto you have started school
I could tell you would do very well you were nobody's fool
Primary years soon pass and here you are in uniform for the comprehensive
Time rushes on five years soon gone you've had your education that's intensive
Now you're prepared for what this world will now start to throw at you
Enjoy yourself while you can, time will pass like you're still as a statue
As a young man you've turned out alright though you put us to the test
We are proud to call you son you now stand one of the best
As the grim reaper gets ever nearer from life's chains to set me free
With you and your life I can go on for in you there is me.

Alan Sharrock

Dark Skies

Dark skies gave darker shadows on the footpath as we walked,
I saw the rain and felt it hit as we began to talk.
But there seemed so little more to say and no more that we could do,
We'd tried it all and lost our way - broken dreams for me and you.
I'd hoped that we could work it out but sadly I was wrong,
Those days are past for you and me though our love had once seemed strong.
I hope that in the future there'll be a rainbow after rain,
Our lives have drifted far apart but perhaps we'll love again.

Paul Sanders

Maths And Myths
(A Muse In Fifty-two Words)

In the beginning there was the word and the word was <u>CREATION</u>.
Cosmic Radiation, Energy And Time In Organised Nuclei.
In time all things developed, diversified or died.
Animal, plant and all manner of life,
Co-ordinating in natural compatibility.
<u>THE LAW</u>! In the beginning of the end there was <u>MAN</u>!
<u>THE END</u>!

R. Peter Smith

Black And White

Nightfall floods the town,
A town of deserted cafes,
Naked mannequins and red lights.
By day, crammed with story telling pensioners,
With black and white memories,
Of when everything to see
Was sand dunes and farmland;
Taking advice from wise voices,
From the drains.
The hobbling war veterans,
With a pint of Tetley's, talking politics,
And of the dark distant past,
Eroded by the claws of the solid brown tide.
Where are our sons?

Broken bottles bombard the bastard boys.
Back then they used to take snuff,
But now, it's the hard stuff.
The stormy night belches
A streak of light from under jet black stallions.
The spitfires crash.
Death and destruction radiate
From a raging, demonic sun
On the dark water.
And the photographs burn.

Mark Shuttleworth

The Mirror

Oh mirror that once
Told only the truth,
Now you show that
I have lost all my youth.

Must you be right
So much of the time
And do you need
To show, every line.

Once I could face you
without any fears
But not any more
After all those years.

I don't want to clean you
You see too much now
Could you not change things
Yet, I . . . . . don't see how!

C.J. Scott

My Temple

A friend asked me - where is your place
of worship - my reply from my heart I have
temples everywhere - the sky above and earth
below - my love of nature looking back at me -
always reminding me of his loving hands of care
my temple is always there - at night I have the
stars higher than any building I can see - my
place of worship is everywhere - the moon when
showing and looking down on me - my place of worship
is everywhere - I believe he loves all his earth - my
places of worship and temples are everywhere.

Rowland Patrick Scannell

Young Tommy

At Adolph's instigation, and George's invitation,
He dressed himself in khaki and he went
To a world of booze and darts,
Where they practiced martial arts.
He was introduced to sin and youth mis-spent.

Then they sent him to a land replete with flies and sand.
A culture shock which shook him to the core.
He had come to fight the Huns
Who unleashed their mighty guns.
So young Tommy cried 'till he could cry no more.

They don't breed one who kills, in the Dark Satanic Mills
So he thought this war malarkey rather odd.
Should he shoot his fellow man?
Or join the one who ran?
Or fall upon his knees and pray to God?

So he prayed to God almighty that he'd soon be back in Blighty.
But the war was vicious, bloody, hard and long
Yet the chinless wonder spoke
As the band played "Hearts of Oak"
And they sent him back to England with his gong!

John Scholes

Mauritius - My Home Island

The wind blows gently in the casuarina trees
I sat, nonchalant, admiring the vast Indian Ocean
Deep valleys, grassy mountains.
Green fields, rushing fountains
Golden beaches, rocky coast.
These are the things I miss most.

Morning: First I watch the clouds
Forming shapes before my eyes
Sometimes horses, sometimes crowds
Of silver shadows in the skies.

Night: The stars, they dance and play
Until the dawn breaks for the day
They form patterns of delight
As they shine with radiance bright.

The wind blows gently in the casuarina trees
I sat, nonchalant, admiring the vast Indian Ocean

René Seren-Dat

• *The casuarina is a tree with jointed branches and scale-like leaves.
The branches have a somewhat feathery look, like the cassowary bird.*

Merry May

A lovely month is merry May
When all around is bright and gay,
With blossom hanging from the trees
And songbirds singing as they please,
And cuckoos singing night and day
And all is bright in merry May.

Young maidens blossom as the trees
Showing off their pretty knees,
Young swain stop to stand and stare
Admiring maidens everywhere,
Cupid fires his bow their way
And all is well in merry May.

The linnets song is sweet and clear
Lending music to an ear,
Daisies bloom on stems so slender
Buttercups glow in golden splendour,
Mayflowers in the fields so gay
All this and more makes merry May.

Children dance with steps so light
Round the maypole in colours bright
Skipping, laughing, round and about
Weaving patterns in and out,
Rowan and Alder make ribbons so gay
A gift for your favours in bright merry May.

Edith M. Smith

Untitled

Autumn leaves are falling,
Falling to the ground,
They flutter down from way up high,
Without a single sound
They now have lost their colour
They had the summer through
They hid the birds nests from our eyes
But made a lovely view

It seems it is a pity
They have to go this way
When they have been so beautiful
Why ever can't they stay
We now wait for the springtime
When new buds will be found
But we still have the evergreen
That stay the whole year round

Julie Smith

Day Break

When the banks were high
and rivers flowed by,
you got out of sight and
appeared,
again.

The sun shone, bright,
as the day was alight.
The dream came true,
and our love said, I love you.

Joseph Sagnia

Bedlam

My nerves are frayed, I know no peace,
My life is just in uproar,
What made it so? I'll tell you more,
Just listen now to me.

Children squabbling, dogs are barking,
Budgie squawking, breakfast burning,
Husband singing, radio blaring,
BEDLAM reigns in my house.

Rain on my umbrella beating,
Thunder cracking, bus brakes squeaking,
People pushing, always rushing,
BEDLAM reigns in my street.

Copier purring, printer whirring,
Tea trolley clanking, doors keep banging,
Workmen drilling, telephone ringing,
BEDLAM REIGNS where I work.

Some say heaven is a restful place,
Full of joy and sweet contentment,
Just my luck if I reach there,
To find it's purely BEDLAM.

Pauline Smith

To Undo

How have I dwelt
In the pit of deceit
Bowed, scraped and grovelled
Near Satan's feet?
How have I travelled
With weights that grow
And tendril-like, throttle
All sweetness I know?
How have I listened
And taken each arrow.
That pointed my heart
Towards fear and sorrow?
How I have peace,
And arrive home anew.
To beat out a pathway
From here to undo.

Amy Seed

Ornamental Fantasy

Just after dark when all is still and the birds have gone to bed,
Peep from your bedroom window, but do not move your head.
For there upon the patio you'll see the strangest sight,
Mr. and Mrs. Hedgehog upon a 'Harley' bike.
And as the stars begin to shine and the moon his face doth show,
They pack their little side-car and wonder where to go.
Should they go to Bognor, Brighton or Penzance,
Glasgow via Gretna, or maybe across to France?
And while they sit and ponder, discussing this and that,
The moon he makes his journey across the world and back.
Then suddenly it's morning and the magic starts to fade,
Their destination's pending, with no decisions made,
And the 'Harley Davidson' hedgehogs once more remain at home,
Parked still upon the patio, as silent as a stone.

E.J. Sherwood

Bedtime

"Right that's enough, you snuggle down."
I bend to kiss goodnight.
He panics, "Just one more, last time."
But I'm turning out the light.

I talk to him in whispers,
An eternity it seems,
And watch him as he fidgets,
Then drifts quietly to his dreams.

His breathing rhythm changes,
To long and slow and deep,
And at last I know I've done it -
He's finally asleep.

Floorboards show me no compassion,
Every tiptoed step is heard.
The door creaks loud - I'm sure he'll wake,
He hasn't even stirred!

I close the door behind me,
And the tension slips away.
In bed myself within an hour,
It's been a weary day.

Andrea Smith

The Scarecrow

I thought you almost spoke to me
When I passed the other day
Then I recognised your cheery grin
As your arms began to sway.

The wind raised your tatty titfer
As if in apology
I have known you for so long now
You seem like a friend to me.

You idly watch the world go by
As your master toils around you
While your funny little carrot nose
Seems to twitch in the morning dew.

At night your lonely silhouette
Brings a quickening to my step
But in the glare of the noon day sun
I wish I could stop for a chat.

You are out in all sorts of weather
Come hail and rain or snow
With a cheery smile for everyone
My friend, the lonely scarecrow.

Doreen Sutch

Blue Innocence

That man made path you have taken
better company than Man you now keep.
On broken wings you have risen, this dying world forsaken;
few will know and even fewer weep.

Shadows come and go, the sun rises;
the world keeps turning and the manrats race.
You were nought; the irrelevant and defenceless Man despises,
what he has judged and sentenced to oblivion with words alone he will replace.

You knew no words, asked no favours, could not fight or sanctuary find.
The shadows came and stayed, the sun set on a fading wing.
No epitaph, no splendid past remembered by a better world, for Man is going blind;
Recall and smile a rye smile for me in days when darkness is king.

The world is dying; when Man is no more I may be free;
I am a Man, the guilt is mine, yet my despair and regrets are true;
so if we meet and you see a friend, reach out and call to me.
For, Blue Innocence, I reach out and call to you.

Dave Shea

The Dream
(A Mixture Of Thoughts)

She saw the trees a quivering
The trunks so still and tight,
She saw the earth a moving
On this dark and mysterious night.

The air was full with thunder
As the lightning struck the earth,
She felt so stark and naked,
It came to her from birth.

This mystery feeling inside of her
That longed to get out,
Then she felt with wonder,
What was it all about?

For the lightning it came
Across and from up above,
And thought again
Is this what is called love.

Then she awoke from the dream, it was so real,
Was it a dream? as the night ended so still.

But it was there amidst the quiet sound,
Of what she heard, and whispered,
As she sat, in her nightgown.

But why did she quiver in wonder?
As the dark clouds and thunder rolled away,
In this mysterious quietness that had come to her, this day.

Leslie Smith

Blustery Day

I Say! It's a blustery day,
The winds in the trees a-whistling away.
Stealing the leaves off their branches once more,
What a colourful cascade as they fall to the floor.
Red, yellow, orange, brown,
Make a beautiful blanket to cover the ground.
But, in an instant, that blanket is blown away!
What a dazzling display, on this blustery day.

Dave "Snappa" Snape

My Cat

Once I had a cat called Susie
Who was really very choosy
She went for a walk
And liked to stalk
She never came back
And we were very sad
An old lady phoned up and said
Your cat has had a little mishap
I found her in the road
I nearly overflowed with sadness.

Joanne Sydenham (Age 8)

406

Moonlight

A brilliant gem in the midnight sky
The moon beams down on passers by
All creatures that stalk within the night
And all who steal home 'ere morning light
All these the moon beams put to flight.

Within the shadow of the church tower.
The barn owl seeks refuge within his bower
Moonlight reveals headstones haphazardly strewn
Of rustics only to the village known.
They had their loves and joys perhaps unseen
And now at peace they lie, as in a dream.

Alone and pensive this scene I beheld
For many years in this village I dwelled
And as the owl lets out its mournful cry
For long lost youth my heart did sigh.

The reaper, the plough hand are all here at rest
Of childhood follies can we no longer jest
The moon with silvery shroud
Enhances toil, the weary and the proud
I turn; she still beams down her rays
And in melancholy mood, I think of happier sun drenched days.

Dorothy Sheard

Journey To Christmas

Cold the way, hints of snow,
With a pale Advent sun,
Braving the clouds,
Touching the furthest hillside,
With gentle light,
So quietly.

The trees, without their green,
Yet, glowing red berries,
Or golden leaves,
Like candles in the woodland,
Gave soft light,
In welcome.

Then the town, busy shops,
Lighted windows, streets, trees,
Pheasants hanging,
Luxury with courtesy, love that came silently,
For the coming,
Of Christmas.

Kathleen Scatchard

Me And You

You say hello,
I hear goodbye.
I start to laugh,
You start to cry.

I say I'm sorry,
You hear me patronise.
You say you're happy,
I see pain in your eyes.

You say you like it,
I say I don't.
I say let's go there,
You say you won't,

I am scared,
You are bold.
You offer your hand,
I shiver from the cold.

You were weak,
I was strong.
I was right,
You were wrong.

Rachel Start

I Think Of You

I close my eyes, and I see your face,
I can smell the freshness of your hair,
And though, oceans divide us, and keep us apart.
        I think of you.

I touch your face and kiss your eyes,
Lingering longer, upon your lips.
I long to hold you, in the night, and,
        I think of you.

Jungle surrounds me, in a foreign land,
Everyone's hostile, so I reach for your hand,
My own private thoughts, from the prison of my mind,
        I think of you.

Am I dreaming, is this real, I need you so much,
I'm frightened, I miss you,
Oh! just to feel your touch,
        I think of you.

Why am I here, does anyone know,
I didn't volunteer, but still had to go,
And though Death is all around me, and calls to me once more.
        I think of you.

Though time is our enemy, we must try to be strong,
I miss you, I love you, surely that can't be wrong,
So, until we meet again, on some distant shore, called home,
        I will think of you.

David Simpson

Love Will Reign

How savage are the wings of hate,
That smites upon love's young face,
Tearing the very soul apart,
To throw away love's sweet heart.

As deadly as a poisoned cup,
This hate so fierce when stirred up,
Much more stronger than death's sharp sting,
Love's foe fights with bitter wing.

Death steals in quietly at the end,
And love's friend peace, he does send,
Hate will destroy and nothing gain,
For at the end love will reign.

E.A. Sherriff

Reflect

Our life on earth is short
How should we use this time
With love, with kindness
And thoughtfulness for others

Are we worthy of our space
Or are the hours taken up
With spite, jealousy, disregard
Uncaring of other people's lives

Stop, think, take care of
What you do and what you say
For this is what you leave behind
Forever and a day

Joan Stephens

Best Friend My Mum

I turn to you when I feel down
I know you will always be around,
To help me to listen to give me advice
The words that you say always seem wise.
You make me feel happy when I feel sad
You are the greatest friend I ever had.
When I'm upset you are always there
I'm really amazed how much you care.
You pick me up when I feel so low
You have your own problems but they never show.
A shoulder to cry on is always there
A love like ours I suppose is rare.
When I am mad you get the abuse
Because your love I know I'll not lose.
I admire and respect you I like all that you do
I hope I show love to my children like you.
You are my hero my best friend you are my mum.
You are all of these things all rolled into one
I would not change one thing about you
I'll need you forever mum I love you.

Dawn Scanlon

Tomorrow

Mustn't eat red meat
Only eat white.
Plenty of vegetables
That'll be alright.
I've had all my calories - well what's a few more?
The plans for my diet have gone out of the door.

Wonder what's for pudding
A big chocolate eclair.
Start the diet tomorrow - well I don't care.
"Tomorrow no breakfast" that's what I said,
Perhaps just an egg on a bit of fried bread.

I smelled the bacon, just off the grill
Maybe a rasher - tomato sausage as well,
Toast and marmalade, is that butter in the pot?
Before I realised, I'd eaten the lot!
Stamina, willpower - I've got plenty
Tomorrow I'll start (for years about twenty!)
Keep trying to get a little bit thinner.
So, I'll manage that diet . . .
And then EAT MY DINNER!

Margaret Schofield

Road Rage

It's what it is known as, this so called "Road Rage"
That resembles an animal locked in a cage
His temper is fraying, his patients are thin
Hith his foot to the floor, he thinks he will win

Dodging and weaving he believes he's so cool
But down in reality he looks such a fool
Cursing us all with fingers and fright
He pays no attention and through a red light

Flashing his headlights, honking his horn
Looks similar to a baby that's just been born
Stuck in the traffic, he tries changing lane
Toeing and froeing he thinks he will gain

In summing up these people we see they have no sense
No courtesy, no manners and a brain that's rather dense
So do us all a favour and stay off public roads
Take a trip to the local pond and join the other toads

Dean Smith

Just Dreams

It's hard to explain the way that I feel
And the reason for wishing my dreams could be real
I dream of my childhood, my mum, and my dad
My brothers and sisters and the friends that I had
I dream of the yesterdays, sunny and calm
Of midsummer picnics, when we came to no harm
When the world seemed a safe place for children to play
And love tucked you in at the end of the day
I dream of the warmth, and the absence of greed
Of the help we received in the times of our need
I know that these dreams are part of my past
And the saying we use, is "good things never last"
We're creating a future that's violent and tough
Why can't we say that enough is enough
Go back to the days of kindness and trust
Don't crave for possessions, don't make them a must
Let us stop being selfish and gain back our pride
Make a world fit to live in, and work side by side
I know these are dreams and I know they're not real
But I've tried to explain the way that I feel

June Simkin

410

My Favourite Room

In front of the fireside in my old rocking chair
To and fro I lazily sway,
Above the mantle the grandfather clock stands
Tic toc tic toc as around goes the hands.

My budgie chirps away in his neat little cage
Cleaning his feathers till it's time to eat,
I seem to have been in my rocker for such an age
When the door bell rings maybe a visitor to greet.

Alas it is a false alarm
So back in my room I go,
The walk to the door didn't do me any harm
And it's nice to get back to the fireside glow.

My old battered wireless stands on the shelf.
Blaring some good music out,
Just now and then I find myself
Tapping my foot and forgetting my gout.

The worn woollen mat which I made out of rags
Is placed in the middle of the room,
This is solely for my dog who is called wags
To stretch out and his fur to groom.

I love this room so comfortable and warm
I feel so happy here,
I never venture far and roam
For I love this room so dear.

Vera Skelton

Space

Space is dark, space is big
The sun crackles very loud
In the olden days they thought
The earth was flat
They thought they would fall off the earth
If they went too far
If I went outer space I'd be very happy
I'd like to see shooting stars
Lots of bright colours
All mixed up and blended nicely together
I don't believe in U.F.O.'s
Or aliens in outer space
I do believe in planets and people
Floating in the air

David Sullivan (Age 10)

The Cry Is Sudden

The cry is sudden!
Yet not a cry at all.
A moan . . .
A groan . . .
No, none of these!
From deep inside the wail which startles
Is as primitive as labour.
A grasping and clawing at the future
By contracting out the past.
Where then is the creation?
Left only is the remembrance of
Past pain;
And the certain knowledge of
Future ache.

Lynnzie Stirling

The Freemen Of England

Let me lead you by the hand.
And take you through the meadows green
Of England's pleasant countryside,
And we'll survey the distant scene.

Of times long past, of many men,
Who broadcast seed and tilled the land,
Who sweated in their daily toil,
Both weak of mind and strong of hand.

Their wives worked hard from dawn to dusk,
To feed the men and gleen the field,
And many at an early age,
Exhausted bodies they did yeild.

They gave their love to families,
Their children never saw long years,
They struggled with the elements,
And through frustration shed their tears.

When Cromwell called men from the field,
They took up arms against the king,
In this great cause they shed their blood,
But no one did their praises sing.

So when you walk through meadows green,
And see the freemen plough the soil,
Remember then the distant scene,
Of simple men, blood, sweat and toil.

J.E. Sharpe

Winter Poem

Whoo Whoo Whoo
Whistling wind blowing through the trees
Icy icicles falling of the roof
Foggy fields and frozen feet
Chilly children cold and weak
Hedgehogs hiding in the fields
Frozen robins in the trees
Woolly scarves and woolly pants
Children playing the streets

Louise Speakman (Age 9)

Your Word

Thank you Lord, for your word,
Thank you Lord for things you've said,
Thank you Lord for the bread,
Thank you Lord for the wine,
Thank you Lord for being mine
Father friend special brother,
Help us Lord
To love each other.

Barbara Ann Spicer

412

Angry All The Time

Somehow always ready to roar,
Always wanting to bite.
Somehow always ready to shout.

Don't know my problem,
It makes me feel good all over.
Don't even know their problem.

Feeling of their fright,
The domination over their weak minds.
Feeling of the colour red.

Never thought why my anger is so,
Memories come from childhood.
Never thought if I could live without it.

Seeing the sweat trickling down,
Making me feel on top of this world.
Seeing my power, and hatred in their eyes.

Needing to be loved,
Anger takes away my needs.
Needing my heart to be touched.

I'm angry all the time,
Enemy of peace and faith.
I'm angry all the time . . .

. . . Anger is my love,
My mother, my father and my brother.
Anger is my life.

Jatinder Sondh (Age 14)

The Financial Adviser

Sleek new car pulls up outside,
Sharp cut suit and hair to match.
A pin striped knock upon your door,
Accompanies a smooth exchange.

Tell me all I'm here to help,
I know what's best for you and all.
I'm next to God in the order of life,
Trust in me and you'll be saved.

With worried eyes he questions you,
Tuts and sighs with a practiced art.
He plays upon your worst most fears,
Of death and all it means.

No need to risk your family,
And leave them to the wolves.
The world is mine to promise you,
But in return I'll take your soul.

The price is high too bloody high,
He's got you backed against the wall.
Sell your soul and trust in him,
Or face his wrath and trust yourself.

Michael Staples

Snow

A shimmering blanket of brilliant white
It comes in the morning and also at night
We don't pray for it's coming
Nor cheer when it goes snow.
The farmers that hate it packed tight by the door
They curse as they search for lost sheep on the moor
They'd as soon be without it they'd rather not know snow.
The children with snow fights and races on sledges
Sliding down hillsides and crashing through hedges
Their world is a playground wherever they go snow.
You can't love it or hate it or store it away
Long for its coming or to just go away
Though it's cold to the touch it leaves you aglow
We'd all be much sadder if we didn't know snow.

William E. Spence

Eden Cottage

Somewhere there's a grassy pathway
Wandering deep through leafy glade,
Where the chaffinches sing sweetly
In the sunlight-dappled shade.

On the verge there is a clearing
Where a timbered cottage stands,
Encircled by a well-kept garden
Overlooking pasture-lands.

Plumes of wood-smoke rise up slowly
From the chimney, - and close by
A shallow rippling brook meanders
Mirroring an azure sky.

Nearby, voles and timid wood-mice
Live their hurried secret lives,
And bees, with pollen heavy-laden,
Lumber, drowsy, to their hives.

This then, is the home I'm seeking
In the country of my dreams.
Somewhere, surely, it is waiting . . .
Or if it's not, - then so it seems!

Marjorie Swindley

Haig Pit Whitehaven 1916-1986

Headgear gaunt on a cliff top high,
Winter gales lash the foam flecked Solway,
Ghosts and memories of days gone by,
Haunt the old abandoned pit.

HAIG - proud Cumbria's last deep mine,
With seams that ran far out to sea.
Decades of miners stood in line,
To ride the cages to the depths below.

Heartbreak years of tears and pain,
Falls of roof and gas explosions,
Loved ones claimed by deadly methane,
At William, Wellington and Haig.

There's abundant coal still out there.
It's lying many fathoms deep,
But it is staying there, old colliers swear,
Where Opencast can't reach it.

The rusting pulleys wind no more,
Standing tall in silent tribute.
To generations gone before,
Who fought so hard for Cumberland coal.

And now the site has been reclaimed,
With grassy green replacing grey,
But Enterprise though much acclaimed,
Can't eradicate the Past.

Charles Storey

Without

Dark room, set alight by burning candles,
Dark room, full of fears and disappointments,
Broken hearts,
Shattered dreams.

Day break, set alight by morning sun,
Day break, where dreams are reality,
Blurry eyes,
Sunken hearts.

Sunset, thoughts of the past,
Sunset, hope for the future?
Blank minds,
Blank life.

Claire Sutton

When The Cat's Away!

Does the house come alive when we're not there?
Do the chairs from the bedroom clatter downstairs?
Do the ornaments gather for a cosy chat,
Sitting in a ring on the fireside mat?
Do the plants move about and have a moan?
"I'm on the window-sill all alone."
Do the pictures slip from the walls to join in,
Greeting each other with a welcoming grin?
Does the cutlery jump from the sideboard drawer,
Parading about on the kitchen floor?
Does the vacuum cleaner waltz around
Dance with the mop and play the clown?
Do the dusters shake, rattle and roll,
Chasing the polish around the hall?
When the handle's turning on the door,
There's a human foot on the hallway floor,
Does a whisper silently die away,
"The owners back again to stay."
Do they settle back to wait awhile,
Till the travel brochures appear in a pile?
Knowing now it won't be long
"They're looking at holidays in Hong Kong!"

Jesmond Swift

Obsession
(Dedicated to a special friend)

I gaze into your gorgeous eyes
So loving, blue and bright,
Just as warming in my heart
As the stars I see each night.
Your gentle touch upon my skin
Sends shivers down my spine,
I often wonder how it would feel
To know that you were mine.
The thought of moving from your side
Leaves me in depression,
How could an everyday teenage crush
Lead to such obsession?
I need you near me all the time
To keep my spirits high,
I want you there at work, at play
And even when I die.
But even though we play around
There's something I must know,
Is it all a friendly game
Or do you really love me so?

Tanya Stephens

Love, Peace And Unity

Looking through my window so high,
I see many things then have to sigh,
But oh, how quiet things seem to me,
That's just how I like it to be.

Up so high from the maddening crowds,
Being among the snow white clouds,
That's how peaceful the world should be,
No fussing or fighting,can't you see.

"Love thy neighbour", so the bible says,
Let's all sing, rejoice and give praise,
For we all have only one life to live,
And we all have so much love to give.

Let's join our hands and let the world unite,
Make peace with your enemy before tonight,
Let's live in harmony, let peace be forever,
Let's live in love, peace and unity together.

A. Stawicki

Good Old Yorkshire Memories

We'd listen to wireless on a night,
Not many pennies, things were tight,
On mantlepiece ticked the old wooden clock,
I'm dressed up for dinner in my best silk frock,
Sunday roasts were great,especially pork leg,
With dripping jelly on Monday on home made bread,
Once a week it was Derbac soap night.
No nits in our family, hair shining bright,
Washday was Dolly Tub, blue bag and mangle.
The sheets used to get into such a tangle,
Ironing boards out and a packet of starch too,
Why didn't blue bag make clothes blue?
Our clothes smelt of mothballs, in our wardrobes they'd be,
To keep away moths, which we never did see,
At weekends we'd have liquorice root and gobstoppers too,
Dad grafted all week but he got his treats too,
He'd smoke a few fags and drink some beer,
Have a red glowing face full of good cheer,
Some people lived in prefabs with corrugated lids,
Some had no electric, no pennies no quids,
We were taught respect and respect we got back,
In this day and age, of this there's a lack,
In those times things were hard but people were sincere,
Fond Yorkshire memories, gone now I fear.

Elaine Spalding

A Headland Point

With gorse and heather and grasses grown,
Above the sky! endless space unknown,
Whilst far below, the vast sea rolls by,
With shimmering glistenings and a gentle sigh,
A ghostly cry of a seabird's yearn,
A restless breeze for the tide to turn,
Far below your weathered heights,
Sail boats swing to the headland sights,
The horizon speared with a sunlit ray,
From a peeping sun, and clouds of grey,
Distant ships from far off shores,
Butterflies glide, and the seagull soars,
Whitehorses top the rolling waves,
Upon craggy rocks, then foam and shaves,
Thistle of purple, yellow of gorse,
The cricket chirps, without remorse,
With various flower of wild account,
Upon this summit of a headland mount.

Michael Stewart

Untitled

Why do we have to be this way
Man against man every day.
Anger, malice, lust and greed
Children dying and in need.
People passing on the other side
Heads in the sand they try to hide
Lots of people want to take
Most of them are on the make
If only more would start to give
To help the others who want to live
Perhaps we'd never have to see
Babies dying on T.V.
Perhaps we'd never see the pain
Of people crying out for grain.
If only we could all unite
Brown or yellow, black or white.
A treasured gift then life would be
Safe in the hands of you and me.

Norma Tannahill

416

Winter In My Garden

Looking out of my window what a glorious sight to behold
The moon shining down on the snow covered ground
Which glistens like diamonds and gold
Not a footmark to spoil this wonderful sight
On this cold and snowy winter night.
Only a day ago green shoots were peering from the ground,
Now they are covered in a snow white blanket
And sleeping safe and sound.
When the snow has melted away
The shoots will grow again, soon to flower in the Spring
Amidst the sun and rain.
All the birds will be singing again,
Robin and Blackbird and Thrush,
No longer needing so much feeding as in the winter rush.
I shall miss the visiting Woodpeckers
Who fed on the peanut holder.
They will not be around again until the days grow colder.
This winter I saw a hedgehog rustling among the leaves.
I put out some food but it disappeared under the apple trees.
If we all look after out birds and hedgehogs
Throughout the cold winter days,
It will give us memories to treasure
As we go our different ways.

Margaret Dawn Stratford

Lady Of The Night

As I lay still, in silence alone in my bed
A whirl-wind of thoughts flow through my head
I gaze out of the window, it's there that I see
She's there once again staring at me

I see her light a beautiful sight
Serene, like a dream, at spectacular height
Her sigh is the wind of aged old dreams
She carries the history of life, so it seems

Without her the night would not be the same
The stars are her pictures, the sky is her frame
She cries the rain of a thousand years
Then gently and softly absorbs all my fears

Her torch of silver burning so high
Within the clouds, in darkened sky
A shining heavenly, wondrous sight
This shimmering lady of the night

Old, wise and such beauty, blessed with grace
Yet no bodily being, no humanly face
She is sister of nature, a melodical tune
This beautiful lady of night, is the moon.

Carol Steeden

Just .. ME!

This is me;	-	not as I was born to be.
This is me;	-	born to be free!
Look at me;	-	what do you see?
Look at me;	-	in my misery.

This is me;	-	to all, a mystery.
This is me;	-	longing for ecstasy.
Look at me;	-	you will not find . . .
Look at me;	-	what are the secrets of my mind?

This is me;	-	deep in thought.
This is me;	-	for peace, I've fought.
Look at me;	-	without a sound.
Look at me;	-	waiting to be found!

This is me;	-	a creative soul.
This is me;	-	aiming for my goal.
Look at me;	-	with past life so cruel.
Look at me;	-	everyone's fool!

This is me;	-	striving to be . . .
This is me;	-	as I can see.
LOOK AT ME;	-	PLEASE, - LOVINGLY!
This is me;	-	hoping soon to be . . .
This is me;	-	almost, - as I long to be:

	-	A spirit free;
	-	eternally;
	-	just; - 'ME'!

Rosemary A.V. Sygrave

He Who Drinks Alone!

Don't mistake the glint in his eyes,
For the sparkle of a man alive.
It could just as easily be a tear,
As he recalls the bygone times.
The hands that had provided,
For a family long since gone.
Now embarrass,
As they find the glass so hard to cling on.
Don't take exception to his silly lopsided grin,
For this just masks the pain, that aches from deep within.
A lifetime of experience deeply etched upon his face,
Bears testament, that he once ran, in our human race.
And as he rises, stumbles, dreading the thought of going home,
Spare him a nod, a smile, it's so lonely being alone.

Graham Spencer

The Train At Platform One

I'm called, 'Winston Churchill', irascible ever.
Cascading through tunnels. Exploding through heather.
Approaching the station , my form growing larger,
Into Dundee . . . like a ghost on a charger.

Wailing or hissing at re-tarded Schemes
Transporting people with turbo-speed dreams.
People perceiving their window-wide viewpoint
Reflected in shadows and mists at their dew-point.

Dreams of perfection, with trains just on time.
People believing in Life! How sublime.
With baggage secure and everything handy
Mobile cahoots put on ice with the *shandy*.

'Click', go my doors. Amber lights flashing.
Out jumps the man with the duffel bag, dashing.
In flow the Guides. (So good to be cheery.)
'Cheryl come on now- you're making me weary.'

"Will the lady named 'Wilkins' come back to Enquiries?
Your raincoat is there with your personal diaries".

There stands My Brother . . he's bound for the coast
With a glint in his windscreen that is no empty boast.
He waits for the whistle, but strains at the leash
Muscle-bound . . . pants . . . like a dog for the beach.

It's time for departure. Your journey's begun.
So wave your 'Goodbye's', as we leave . . . Platform One.

Brian S. Sweatmore

Eastern Contrast

Great deeds were done in Knossos, fine men took flight,
To grasp the horns of raging, charging bulls
And painters took to brush, with much delight,
Their actions, to record upon the walls.
Kings, princes, courtesans had time to strut
Within the rooms, to bathe, to dress, to eat.
Before their gods, perchance advance the foot;
Obeisance slight, felt justified as mete,
And mete perhaps, but Ephesus saw Paul.
No sword, no gold, the Word alone, withal,
That strips mankind of all pretence at God,
And holds us equal, 'bove and neath the sod.

Leslie Stephenson

Married

Married for four years
Alone the past three
Sat home on the sofa and watching TV
Gone are the roses
Gone are the nights upstairs in the bedroom
The passage of rite

His presence still lingers
His shoes by the door
His coat button mended
Her fingers still sore
He asks for his dinner
She listens with ears that hear not a sound
But the passing of years

At parties the kissing of strangers' goodbyes
Affects not the heart by the weeping of eyes
She peers through pink curtains
And watches for light
Sweet dreams of a future asleep in the night

She knows in a second the passing of pain
Umbrellas the routine that's life's daily rain
And sometime in yesterday life left to stay
Bags packed and departed
Just married away

Julie Stuart

Christmas

In the distance I can hear the bells
Ring out across the snow
Telling of a Christmas
Of oh so long ago

Of when all the trees were shimmering
In their lovely snowy gowns
And there is peace and joyfulness
Everywhere around

Of the time when there was one big star
Shining in the sky
Looking down on a stable
On a lonely hill top high

And in that lowly stable
Layed a baby dear
Who had come to save the world
And drive away all fear.

And every year at Christmas
When bells ring out so clear
I look up at the moonlight
And think of that baby dear

And in the magic of it all
I feel my heart soar free
And in the silence of this winter world
Peace settles over me

Mary Symons

Tantrum

Clashing, smashing upon the shore,
The waves are angry, ready to roar,
Hurtling down with an almighty "crash!"
Reaching for the rocks, grasping, grasping,
Then dragged off backwards, gasping, gasping . . .
Slimy seaweed getting tossed around,
Driftwood bobbing up and down . . .

The sea grows calm, the sky's washed clear,
A million glittering crystals appear,
A soft breeze blows, the palm trees sway,
The sea's tantrum has ended,
It's a beautiful day.

Joanna Stiles

The Old Brown Clock

At home, the clock stood ticking time upon the mantlepiece,
A roaring fire in grate beneath gave warmth, welcome, great relief
To those who entered from chill winter blast
Of a grim world, when will war be past?

It ticked the minutes, hours away,
As each day it sat, did Mother pray
Her dear son would come back soon
From fighting on the Somme at noon.
But hour by hour the clock struck clear
And ne'er did William come so near.

Once a week she wound it up, gave it a dust with cherished touch,
For this old clock, gift from her father
Had stories true but like no other,
It had seen her sisters married,
Grandson born, while brother tarried
With his lass, but now he's gone
But still the clock ticks, relentless on.

But years have passed, the clock is silent
No cherished hand will wind
Time itself flows silent on
Only memories are left behind.

Elizabeth M. Sudder

Again

Again,
The sun is nice and warm on my skin,
The beach I lie on is warm and soft beneath me,
The partial shade of the tree gives gentle respite when needed,
The mixed scent of Jasmine and lavender drifts,
The glass I raise to my lips is cool,
The drink is reflective of life itself,
I've not tasted better,
Cannot the world be like this always?
At least this sense of serenity and calm,
This sense, this feeling that flows and soothes,
Then, a sound, a noise, intrudes,
Reluctantly, I open my eyes,
And my senses tell me of . . . .
The warm bath,
The room I am in,
The winter outside the window,
Time to dry,
And clothe,
And go to work,
Again.

Ellanor Spinks

Saturday Night

Our attempt, pathetic and cold
To please each other, or our
Selves if we are honest was
A disaster if truth be told
Chitty chat was sweet
Really direct and cool
Laughter fell as did tears
When you declined to meet
Under my terms again,
Although I hid it well
From your mocking gaze
Pity and irritation the same
As the Saturday night before
I told you my secrets
You revealed yours
You advised me,
"Ambassador of Liverpool", I mocked
"Is that what I should do?"
"Yes", you replied "Give me a ring",
"Okay" I sighed as the door I locked
Behind you after saying goodbye.
Bloody patronising fool I mumbled
As you walked to the station
No doubt feeling as relieved at our parting as I.

Lisa Swaine

November

November is the time of year
When fireworks are screeching bright
And you remember long lost years
When Guy Fawkes made this night.

When the fireworks go bang
Some little children scream and cry
As they watch bright colours
Bursting in the sky.

When the display is over
We go on the rides for a fright
Then drink some pop, hop into the car
That's the end of fireworks night.

Lianne Sydenham (Age 11)

Silent Magic

Be still - Let your spirit be quiet,
Watch clouds build castles in the air,
Breathe softly - remember -
And be glad.

Be still - All things are possible,
Listen to your heart - to the sea in a shell,
To the murmur of waterfalls
And be thankful.

Be still - I am with you
Forever, through time and space,
Whisper my name
And I will come to you.

Be still - My love is yours,
Be gentle - hurt me not
I'll be there always
Should you call.

Mary C. Thomas

Open Your Eyes . . . . . .

Rushing about, tearing your hair
Grumbling and muttering "it's really not fair" -
The wealthy enjoy a luxurious life
Whilst the rest struggle on with worry and strife . . .

But where is the happiness with 'all on a plate'?
The joy in achievement is well worth the wait . . .
The rich may have assets like silver and gold,
With villas and vistas of wealth untold

Just look around you, open your eyes,
Feast on the joy of sapphire blue skies
The birds and the animals are ours for free -
Along with the beauty of yonder tree

Happiness comes from a heart full of love
For nature's wealth - a gift from above
Don't envy the man with material things -
You're free as the bird - just hear how he sings!

Di Spottiswood

The Storm

the night had started clear
Not a cloud was in the sky
But by the strike of midnight
Not a piece of earth was dry

The rain and hail had lashed
Everything in its path
Down the chimney it blew
And landed on the hearth

It crashed on the roof tops
And through the open doors
It banged on the windows
And saturated the moors

The thunder and the lightening came
And just as quick was gone
But the short time it lasted
The winds had been so strong

But when the sun came up
We opened up the shutters
The only signs of the storm
Were the overflowing gutters

Susan Stevens

Saint Andrew's Son

It's the seagulls song that draws me on
Forever calling me
His raucous cry, with piercing eye
Compels me to be free
To sail again, and taste the salt
That runs within my veins
To sail again neath heavens vault
Where Lord Neptune reigns
I feel it now, like lover's arms
I'm drawn towards my fate
To reap again from silver farms
Would be like heaven's gate
But now it's gone, the seagull's song
I walk the rotting piers
With memories eyes, I see the throng
Of bustling filleteers
With row on row of fishing ships
Of nets and barrow boys
Their ghostly voices in my head
Tell tales of ancient hoys
But now they're gone, a life times lost
My friends the race is run
You'll know me now, as you did then
I was St. Andrew's son.

John R. Surgey

On The List

Recycle all your paper,
Bottles, rags and tin
Don't discard the dinner
Keep for the compost bin

Look at product labels
Be careful what you eat
Wipe the tops of tables
Make meals without much meat

Cut down on cholesterol
Ban butter; spread the marge
Take vitamins and dextrose
Keep fit and don't get large

Drink only mineral water
Pure juice and herbal tea
Coffee contains caffeine
Unless, of course, it's de-

Be nice to your neighbour
Learn psychology
Leave all household labour
To the new technology

Rise above all problems
The world will still exist
And come the year 2000
There will be another list

Judy Stiff

I'm Deaf, You See

I'm deaf, you see,
I know my place,
A misfit in a public space,
I'm deaf, you see,
But from their faces,
A contagious disease to blight all races.
I'm deaf, you see,
I've got no brain,
Fit to be teased again and again.
I'm deaf, you see,
It makes me blind,
No need to hide insults from my mind.
I'm deaf, you see,
I'll take the blame,
For dragging down the families name.
I'm deaf, you see,
But it's still me,
Why not any sympathy?
I'm deaf, you see.

Phillip Stybar

Are We Really Better Off?

Life really isn't very fair
Most people it seems just do not care
If others can survive or not
Some have nothing, others a lot.

It's a shame we cannot seem to share
Or prove to others that we care
When you see how some have to survive
You'd think they would be better off dead than alive.

Yet would they though, I somehow doubt
They probably think we are the ones without
When I see the way they live
They don't just take, they also give.

They don't rape, steal and kill
Or take drugs until they are ill.
And though their plight often makes me mad
They probably think it's WE that are sad.

Steve Sydenham

424

Journey Starts (And the Magic Continues ...)

Leap the fence that doesn't exist,
How else to get inside?
That tallest field of chequer board squares,
The perfect maze to hide,

Play hopscotch on a dragon's back,
Ride o'er Pegasus' wings,
Race with the minotaur there and back,
Beware the harpies sting.

Wish upon that lilting star,
That drifts on ocean skin,
Gaze as far out as you can,
Just as you gaze within.

Such singing lessons as you might wish,
True, getting your head wet,
As you join with the willow fish,
Sweet melodic duet.

How high on high do you see?
Above the never ending Necksore tree,
Look down and around to ground to boot,
As a compass points it's arrow root.

Continue on your mystic quest,
Sights, smells and sounds adore,
Delight in all you witness,
On your way through Dragonmoor.

George E. Spinks

Space

I might be going outer space
I am excited,
I wonder if it will be an adventure?
Looking at all the planets and stars,
Jupiter, Mars, Venus and Pluto,
Wondering if there is any life out there,
I hope there will be all colours pink
Orange red or yellow - all colours,
Or it could be just dull?
I hope I find something there
Then I will be special
And not stay up there forever!

Rachel Tomlinson (Age 10)

The Moon

I look at the moon so still and fair,
You'd think that someone lived up there,
Though habitation, none it seems
Still it lingers in my dreams

Mary Strickland

The Winter Flu's

The winter is the time of year
Full of happiness and of cheer
We celebrate christmas and bring in the New Year
Probably drink a little too much beer.

There's lots of ups and a few downs
Especially when the flu's around
If the flu catches hold, it's not just a cold
Especially for the young and the old.

We wrap up warm, stay inside
Hiding from the flu outside
We do our best, wear our vest
Hoping to keep the flu of the chest.

But it's all in vain
We start to feel the aches and pains
Soon the flu takes it's grip
It's like doing up the tightest of zips.

We take some pills and Lemsip
Hoping that it will bring back our 'pip'
But really there's not a lot we can do
Just lay in bed feeling blue . . . .

Suffering the effects of the winter flu's.

Mark Summers

Quiet Patience

Ears pricked up - Green eyes alert
Tail curled around her - like a skirt,
Sitting upright at the door -
I wonder what she's waiting for?
Her huge eyes stare through opaque glass
Watching something - unseen - pass,
Her tail-end gives a little twitch
Her head tilts forward - just a pitch.
She has no wish to leave the house
Or stalk some non-existent mouse;
An engine sound is heard outside -
And suddenly she comes alive,
She stands up straight - her tail aloft
The purr within her throat is soft.
Her mistress enters through the door
Laden down with food galore!
Her eyes look up with mute appeal -
The time has come for her next meal!
She glides ahead - straight to her dish!
Will it be meat this time - or fish!

Patricia Surman

Spring

Oh for the joys of Spring
The first crocus or daffodil
Peeping through the snow
Lambs frolicking in the field
The mad March hare
Oh for the joys of Spring

Oh for the joys of Spring
A rippling stream
The melting snow
The grass so green
Oh for the joys of Spring

Oh for the joys of Spring
The trees bursting into life
The young deer playing
In the fields the rabbits are courting
Oh for the joys of spring

M.J. Tiley

Our Mel

You came to us when you were three
A friend for life we thought you'd be
We never thought you'd break our heart
When fate played that final part

We talked and laughed day by day
You always had a lot to say
So full of love and thought were you
A caring child that was true

Something you'd say would make us smile
We didn't know we'd have you, for such a short while
So full of life and vibrant too
Now you're gone what will we do

Our memories of you are so sweet
You always wanting something to eat
Giving me hugs, sitting on my knee
I know you thought the world of me

You'd come in and out as if you lived here
That's why to us you were so dear
Just like a child of my own
That's why now I'm so alone

Your future planned happy and bright
Such hopes and dreams you had in sight
Who could have known that fateful day
They would all be washed away

You were in the centre of my heart
When the road played the final part
We didn't have time to say goodbye
That's why we sit and cry and cry
For you were only ten years old
And worth to me your weight in gold

Joan Spratt

Cloudburst

Caught, like fugitives in the glare of spotlights.

Our creeping skin varnished and blistered simultaneously by rain,
Faces a bar-code of sopping hair, teeth a chatter framing laughter;
Our pink tongues curled like serpents 'round the scent of wet April.
The pavement is a ripple beginning at your feet. What we would sacrifice
In this fraction of brevity for the perfect sanctuary of a steaming kettle.

Paul Summers

Eyes Of Time

The eyes of time are left behind
The future of today is tomorrow
A dollar earned is a dollar spent
Don't beg nor steal or borrow
The innocence of a child is the wisdom of man
Through a child we can learn and do
A child won't lie for not understanding why
The pain of telling the truth
And as the story goes to the end of the road
Only we can pull a child through
In the back of our minds we can show them why
What we lie about is only the truth
So do no wrong for wrong is bad
We are here and we don't know why
As long as we're clean and free from sin
No tears will cloud our eyes of time

Paul Trotter

I Will Always Praise The Lord

Everything I love is in God's world
Blue skies, green trees, the sun's golden ray
Music and laughter, in company of friends
The happiness that comes from Him each day
Everywhere I look I see God's work
His creation of all things great and small
Mountains and seas, the stars that shine
Changing seasons, the rains that fall

Everywhere I go I am led by God
He is never out of my reach
He is there to comfort and sustain
And his wonderful love to teach
Everything I do will be for the love of God
He will lead me along the way
He will love me forever I know
And I will love Him, come what may

Olive M. Stewart

Poppy Field War

They grab a helmet,
Gun and shield.
They go to fight,
Then to die in a poppy field.

Woke with sounding,
Of the lark.
Fight again,
Until the dark.

Off they go,
And leave their wives.
Then to be killed
With guns and knives.

Leave their wives with
Doubting fears,
Leave the kids,
With dripping tears.

Remember all those,
Who are dead.
And wear your poppy,
Shining red.

Cait Tabbinor (Age 10)

The Noisy Traffic

I hate the noisy traffic
It is like the roar of a dragon or the crash of thunder.
The red cars shooting by are like fireballs in the sky.
I hate the big red buses,
They are are like monsters towering over me.
The sound of the engine is deafening,
Like he is ready to pounce and eat me.
I hate the long lorries,
They are like boa constrictors ready to wrap around you.
If you looked down at the world,
You would think that they were army ants crawling all over their prey.
I hate the noisy traffic.

Sam Toole (Age 9)

Kids!!!

What is it about our children,
That drives us completely mad?
What turns them from lovable angels,
Into horrors, both evil and bad?

Why won't they do their homework?
Or give a hand with washing the pots?
What happened to our darling offspring?
They used to be lovable tots.

They've turned in less than a fortnight,
In to slobs who love punk, rave and rock.
My god! Our kid's a teenager,
And it's come as one hell of a shock!!

So why, when they pass G.C.S.E.s
Do we shout it out so loud?
And when they get rid of their 'L' plates,
Who are the ones feeling proud?

They're still our darling angels,
If we look inside for the good.
They're really not all that bad,
It's just that they're misunderstood.

They are trying to find their own place,
Before they are suddenly hurled.
Into the nightmare of chaos,
That is OUR OWN GROWN UP WORLD!!

Angela Taylor

A Friend Of Mine

Dear lady, dear friend,
A poem just for you.
A very special verse
For a person who . . .

"Knew a friend of mine"

You knew my friend,
Maybe better than me
Because you wanted to
And I couldn't see . . .

"This friend of mine"

But when she left
I found out then
That this person
Knew how and when . . .

"To be a friend of mine"

My mother was this friend,
The one you can't replace.
Dear lady I wish you well
And though you can't take her place . .

"You are a friend of mine"

Geoffrey Thacker

An Air Of Indifference

A newsflash is broadcast on our screens
Pictures of fighting, gunshots and screams.
A war is declared in some far distant land
Their allies are called on to give them a hand.

Are we disturbed by this latest news
Of conflict between the Muslims and Jews
Or Catholics, Protestants, or Christians alike
Or feuding between the black and the white?

Is it headlines so often, we no longer care
About bloodshed and suffering and total despair.
We see people homeless, all shedding their tears
Shall we mind if this war continues for years?

Do we merely ignore it, get on with our lives
Not cry for the children and husbands and wives
Whose faces we've seen all contorted with pain?
They've so much to lose and nothing to gain.

As we turn off our sets, settle down for the night
Do we think of the victims, their terrible plight
Lose sleep over ways that this war could be solved
Or forget - and be thankful that we're not involved?

Karen Tyas

His Plan

God created men and women
to help make up a planet,
he had the task of finding lots
of species to put on it.
He started with a fearless mammal,
man, giraffe, pet dog and camel
then went on to plants and trees
followed by our birds and bees.
He insisted we have sea and sand,
rock and valley, mountain land,
rivers, fields, huts and hills,
houses, cars and telephone bills.
So many things he made to please . . .
. . . . so why did he invent disease?

Rachel Taylor

Remember Me

Remember me remember me
When times are hard to bear
Remember me remember me
Just think and I'll be there.

Don't think of me as missing
I would not be so unkind
Just close your eyes awhile
I'll be there in your mind.

You cannot be alone for long
When once you've loved so true
Just listen to a bird a song
The things we shared together.

And if you're sad and feeling blue
And the years have seemed to flee
Think of a love that was so true
Remember me remember me.

Harry Toomey

He Really Was My Dad You Know . . .

He really was my dad you know,
The Lord took him too quick.
Here one day, gone the next,
I really can't explain, you know,
Just how I feel today.
All I know is . . .
That I'll just never forget.

He really was my dad you know,
Never having said goodbye,
I feel so upset inside.
My heart aches and I'd like to cry,
But, what's the point in that.
It wouldn't bring him back.
And I just know, that I'll just NEVER FORGET . . .

He really was my dad you know
Always shouting to people "Hello"
And now he lies, oh so quiet,
But what I have to remember is,
That one day I'll be with him
And until this day comes,
I just know that I'll NEVER FORGET . . .

Susan Tiffany

In Torment

Imagine another life
How do I live with this strife
Frustration and exasperation
Seen everywhere desperation

Imagination soars high
I am in between I sigh
It could be so true
What else can I do

Instead of a sinner
Everyone become a winner
Love and forgiveness
Less chance of permissiveness

Where has world peace gone
As mankind fights on and on
If only an ideal world
Would soon to be unfurled

V.A. Tunstall

Life On The Farmyard

For the farmer its been a grotty day,
The cows splash through the puddles, and mud.
Splashing their fresh cut hay.
They make their way into the milking shed.
The farmer's hoping for a high milk yield.
So on his capital he can build.
The chickens nestle down amongst clean straw and hay
Many large brown eggs they will lay
The ducks paddle to a nearby pond
Hoping for some stale bread, to be thrown in
Because of bread, their very fond.
Two tabby cats appear hunting for rats and mice
To catch one or two would be very nice.
The dozen geese look for fresh grass,
Before settling down under an old large ash.
The turkeys in large pens are kept
Separate from ducks and hens
The large cock bird begins to crow
As the sun begins to lose its glow.
The farmer settles down with slippers and pipe
Looking quite contented
Knowing his cereals have been gathered in nice and ripe.

D.G. Thompson

Sunrise Over The City

There's a beautiful sunrise over the city,
Of this we should be aware,
It's shining and beaming and glowing,
Would you notice if it wasn't there.

What a beautiful sunrise over the city,
And it's shining into this heart,
It feels like, I'm bathing in beauty,
Could a day have a better start.

Watch the birth of the sunshine on the horizon,
Let it filter into your mind,
Chasing the dreams from the darkness,
So bright and so warm and so kind.

Yet so many people don't see this,
In there hurrying bustling storm,
The sun rises higher and higher,
They are missing the glory of dawn.

There's a beautiful sunrise over the city,
And it wants you to know that it's there,
It's shining and beaming and glowing,
How sad if you don't care.

John Tearne

Fate

Where can we find peace of mind
How can fate be so cruel, yet sometimes very kind
I met my soul-mate just by chance
It was fate not only circumstance,
Looking back the memories are so worthwhile
Many events can make me smile
The joys, the tears, the dreams, the fears
Are all tied up with fate
But circumstances have occurred
Now life is very sad the dreams of future
Happenings have gone cruel fate has made things bad.
When the light of your life has just gone out
There is nothing left of joy
You rally against God and all
Not knowing which way to turn
Or where you are going,
You pray to God to take you
From torment into peace
But that's no help to others
Whose love and needs would cease
Oh peace of mind don't evade me be there as my destiny
Stay with me forever and ever to fulfil life graciously.

Barbara Tunstall

432

Imagery

The Sorcerer opened his global hands,
and the light that was trapped stampeded the land,
his eyes were as cloudy as a thunder storm
and when the crying had stopped an ocean was born
the water rushed in and swallowed the ground
and pastures fresh on dead fields were found.
He threw a rock across the waters against the incoming tide,
and a pale moon rose across a dying sky.
the sun came down to bare its soul
and rainbows sprang from hidden crock of gold.

Somewhere on a cliff top on a jagged rock,
the sorcerer looks out and is taking stock,
a crystal ball is pulled from a pocket concealed,
he screams "show me a world that's no longer real,
I've given you back your world your reality
give me now my imagery".

Some say eh walked through a mirror t his ancestral past,
that would explain the trail of broken glass,
some say from the cliff top his life he took,
but I saw the flash in the dark and the flight of the rock,
and all that I tell you is no lie
I saw it all in the tear from a conjurer's eye.

Pog

It's Saturday Mom

I woke up one morning and jumped out of bed,
"Stacey it's seven thirty" my mother had said
I dashed in the bathroom, I thought I've so much to do.
I had a wash and brushed my teeth, after using the loo.
I went down the stairs,as quick as could be,
I sat down for my breakfast, and my cup of tea,
By the time I had finished it was quarter past eight.
My mother said "Stacey you're going to be late".
I quickly got dressed ready for school.
I said to my mother, "I'm not late as a rule".
My mother said "Hurry up everyone else, will be gone".
I said "I've just realised something" it's Saturday mom!

Stacey Timmins

The Good Old Days?

Do you remember the days of the old tin bath -
oh come on now, please don't laugh.
It's Friday night and the copper's on
and you stand in line to get your bathing done.

The water is ladled from the old copper tub
and if you are lucky you may just get enough.
You're thankful if you're the first in the queue
because that water will be for quite a few!

You grab a towel and rush to the fire,
the flames leap up the chimney higher and higher.
The smell of home made bread wafts across the room
and you feel safe and warm in this loving cocoon.

The kettle sits a humming on the black leaded grate
and the cat lays curled in a purr-fect sleep state.
But if you were truthful things were not always this good,
there were things you would change, if only you could.
Like the old brick privy that stood in a row,
and the flipping inconvenience if you simply had to 'go'.
The luxury tissue wasn't there to be unfurled -
you usually ended up with the "News of the World".

The lime washed walls were flaking with damp
even though they'd lit the tilly lamp.
And often you'd find the "News of the World" on the floor
'cos it had fallen from the nail on the back of the door!

Penny Thacker

Shivering Shadows

Your sweet sustenance
reshapes my tight wooden sides.
You whisper sweet things to me,
caressing every part, inside and out.
You deliver to the spider a necklace too precious to be placed
upon my motionless body.
The tempest enlivens my hardened soul,
making my creaking limbs sing with anticipation.
You enshroud my rotten body in pearls,
and ask nothing in return.

Johanna Tovey

The Dream

I awoke last night to a wondrous dream,
Of such happiness the world has never seen,
No more wars to shed man's blood,
For peace reigned again and it was good.

To walk in safety down the street,
The hungry nations with food to eat,
The crippled man arose and walked to the door,
He was quite unable to do this before.

The lady with cancer lay in her bed,
Threw off her blankets, "I am better now" she said.
A mum with children walked out of her door,
"I've never been able to leave it unlocked before".

The homeless had houses in every land,
In countries green, or the desert sand,
What was the answer to all I see?
Only one answer could there be.

For the good God had come to earth again,
He walked the lands and cast out pain.
From continent to continent and shore to shore,
The world was at peace as never before.

Hubert B. Taylor

Three Wishes

Soft, gentle, I saw the snow fall
Loud and clear I heard the robin call
A christmas tree so green and tall
The bough of holly hanging in the hall
Snugly lies a baby in his manger stall
Three wishes of peace joy and love to all
These simple words so easy to recall
Are forgotten, because of man's need to destroy all

N. Tate

A Friend

He came into my life and I found peace
He smiled at me with his eyes and I saw peace
He put his hand in mine and I felt peace
And all I need in life is peace

Catherine J. Till

Evening Tide

The sea gently touches the sand
Making rivulets with her hands
Grasping fingers tighten like bands
Straining to claim her precious land
Her arms embrace the rocks and sand
Engulfing the shore with both hands
The evening tide will not stay long
Just long enough to sing her song

Janet Tomlinson

A Workaday Day

Wake in the morning, stretching and yawning,
Wanting to go back to sleep;
But the day has begun
The alarm clock has rung,
Duty calls one to work for one's keep.

Under the shower, could linger for hours
But time does not permit.
Rummage around
Till clean clothes are found
As the clock quickens its tick.

Eat Weetabix quick give loved ones a kiss,
Sprint up the road fast to the station.
It's pouring with rain
As I jump on the train,
Relieved there were no cancellations.

The day passes by my oh my, how time flies!
It's time to be heading for home.
But I'll be back tomorrow
And there'll be no sorrow.
I love it, so why should I moan?

Wake in the morning stretching and yawning,
Wanting to go back to sleep . . .

Dorothy Tucker

Killing For Kindness

A mind awry
An evil eye,
A thought to kill
A child at will.

Killing for kindness
To lessen the pain,
Torture for obsession
To link your chain.

Your soul will be sold
At the gates of hell,
The infernal underworld
Shall cast upon you a spell.

Where you will be immortal
But chained to the ground,
Excruciating pain
A deafening sound.

Paul S. Taylor

The Hand Of The Lord

The hand of the Lord reached down from the sky.
Touched the woman and said don't cry.
Your daughters with me now in heaven above,
Where their is no hatred but only love.
By day she rides on a white horse with wings,
By night she sleeps with the angel that sings.
At this moment your hearts filled with pain,
But believe me some day you will see her again.
So look in the bright sky and think of love,
There is a heaven above.

Antony G. Taylor

Good Old Days

Memories, of days gone by
Of summer times, when nights were short,
And days were long
And the sun did shine on and on.
Doors and windows open wide
To let the summer breeze inside
Babies safe out in their pram
Watching children having fun.
Off for walks, down the lane
Catching tadpoles, from running streams,
And watching farmers work in their fields.
Many a daisy chain was made
With buttercups picked,
To take home to mam.
Sunday came, dressed in our best
Off to church with all the rest.
Family lunch, was a treat.
Roast beef, and Yorkshire pud,
Sometimes we would walk up mountains high.
Now I know, they were just hillsides,
Or catch a bus to the seaside.
For we had no car, for the ride.
I sit and wonder, how things have changed, still for me.
They were, the good old days.

Dorothy Trilk

A Day And A Nightmare Ride

I rose at seven wishing for some heaven after a restless night
Got out of my bed in a dream with my eyes nearly shut tight
Held them open with fingers and gazed at the clock in despair
Felt so tired and ached all over after riding that long nightmare
Gripped the counterpane as morning came, held onto the bed
Felt so tired ached all over still a thundering there in my head
But came back from beyond to greet, a tired and merciful dawn
Thanked my stars it had been a dream, my body and spirit torn
Washed my face and gave a grimace at the ravages I saw there
Got out my comb to tidy my dome, straighten my crumpled hair
Put on my hat still feeling flat, drank of some morning tea
Went out of doors nearly on all fours, a weary and tired old me
How I got through the day really can't say, that time's just a blur
Here sitting in my chair recovering there, like the cat I fairly purr
With ecstacy comfort and bliss as my whole self recovers from ague
Feet on a stool I fairly drool with the comfort now from my laze
Soon to bed for a good nights rest, hoping no nightmare again
As I close my eyes in blissful sleep, having emptied out my brain
To succumb to sweet limbo

Philip Temperton

Night Walker

Can I control myself for I'm like the scales
Let me bathe in the Midnight Blue
This aching void that was nearly complete
Consoles with the Midnight Blue

For this child in his arms finding safety and solace
Has come to such harm by that pernicious promise
Met destruction and fire from the words of the liar
Yes I've let go my covers again

Once how sweet those covers were . . hung like those dreams half forgotten
And I the fool on that pedestal now alone and detached from the bottom

So I must love myself with a freedom of mind
That I'll find in the Midnight Blue
And fill up these gaps with the good that I've seen
Starting over more learned and new

And the pain and the ache that I know still remain
Excels with pre-morning fresh dew
Not covered in grey for I know that I must
Learn from it to work it all through

Lesley Thornton

The Question About Babies

Where do babies come from?
Do they fly through the air without a care?
In the beak of a stork with a nappy and shawl?
Oh where do babies come from?

Do they come from the shop with a bottle of pop ?
Or appear with a plop in a ready made cot?
Oh! where do babies come from?

Do they come out of your head one starry night?
When you're fast asleep and the light is out?
Oh where do babies come from?

It's funny but lately my mummy looks chubby,
Do you think a baby could hide in a tummy?
I didn't think babies could play hide and seek!
Oh yes! I bet that's where babies come from.

I asked my Dad if he could explain.
Was I right about babies and did I do the same?
"Yes!" he said, "It's like a watery room
Where you can swim and feel happy,
It's called the Womb".

C.M. Trimm

Northern People

The people from the north are like their countryside
It goes on for ever and ever, it just cannot hide
The rugged hills and jagged lines
They are working people with active minds
With their identical houses and streets
They are really friendly to whoever they meet
Down to earth with arms on the wall
They say good morning to one and all
With their well worn lined faces
They just don't put on any graces
Some people would say they are nosey
They often have coal fires to make their house cosy
With their back yards backing on to an alley
Where everyone's got time to dilly dally
Where corner shops still give credit
They deserve a hug they deserve a merit
Without the salt of the earth where would you be
They are real people just like you and me

Cath Thomas

Flash Of Light

In a flash of light the Lord spoke to me,
He made this great world for all to see.
The tiny birds, flowers and the trees,
Still silent waters, and rumbling seas.
He made the woman he made the man,
The grunting pigs, the silent lamb.
He made this world and worlds beyond,
The fragrant rose the babbling pond.
God made this world for me and you,
He taught us all the good things to do.
At night and day we must all pray,
This is what the Lord did say.
Without anticipation,
There will be no reincarnation.
In a flash of light the Lord spoke to me,
He made this great world for all to see.

Carol Tibbles

Gemini

Safe and warm in my slumber
A veil of darkness all around
Up above a heart beats
Bump, bump is the only sound
As I'm moving around
I am feeling, gently breathing
Something in the dark
Who kicked my leg
And kissed my head
I'm squashed so tight
I long to stretch outright
The darkness has gone and the light is on
No more pushing and shoving
I can open my arms and point my toes
I bet if I tried I could touch my nose
With rush and a push I'm out in the light
It wasn't a fright but a great delight
For my brother and I were born tonight

Heather Townsley

439

Dawn

The man who was free was unafraid;
The light was red behind the tree;
Grey-haired clouds above smiled undismayed,
With streaks of gold that could not be stolen.
And not being touched they passed away.

And the man who was still was unafraid,
As the moment rested,
Stayed behind.

He prepared his breakfast and ate it,
Eventually.

And then painted in pastel the memory
Of the red light that sparkled
Into a glow
Behind the tree -
The conifer tree that stood up straight,
In the rock-garden,
At the back,
Like the man who was still,
Yet unafraid.

Grey clouds above smiles undismayed
At the secret of ETERNITY.

John Thorn

Hope Eternal

There was his Love, out walking,
by the waters side,
bare feet lapped,
by a gently flowing tide.

Her golden hair, as gossamer,
on the soft breeze did fly,
pale were her cheeks,
no smile touched her eye.

He called out her name,
but she did not look or stay,
could it be the breeze
carried his voice away?

He reached out to touch her,
but no substance met his hand,
nor was there a footprint
where she'd walked upon the sand.

T'was then, bitter reality
pierced that troubled mind,
and the tears of sorrow fell,
to flow forever with the tide.

Florence M. Vass

The Blue Expanse

The sun reflects of the blue expanse,
waves break on rocks in a watery dance.
Different species swim side by side,
arcane places for creatures to hide.
Braid seaweed sway to and fro,
plankton drift and go with the flow.
The role nature intended are played out by prey,
some survive to live another day.
Sunken galleon from an age long gone,
the sound of the whale as it sings its song.
Dolphins glide the surface like a skimming stone,
oil, harpoon, nets soon we will be alone.
The sea can be cruel but also a joy,
only man so careless has the ability to destroy.

Dorrien Thomas

440

Beauty Fair

Swift the flow of fortune's fate
So beauty, that fair mien doth make
Alluring to the wayward eye
In its mortal outward guise.
With Aphrodite's charm endowed
And Cupid constant at her side
Fades, but inner beauty doth abide
Not marred by Foible's fickle pride.

Emotive beauty is twofold.
Happiness with infectious charm;
Sombre sadness and broken dreams,
Delicate hurt with Time to heal.
Sweet sorrow has its role to play
And bring the balance to full square.
Without sadness as a measure
With what can happiness compare?

How is awareness heightened found
Celestial imageries profound;
What human hand or thought could deign
Such bounteous beauty's boundless reign!
Viewed from heaven's window high
Great endeavours in endless time;
But thank for mercy's constant care
To blissful inner peace repair.

K.C. Thomas

Holding Back The Years

Age could never catch ME out,
Of this, in youth, there is no doubt.
But then along comes Father Time,
Hour-glass in hand, calling your name,
And telling you that you're the man
Now approaching mortal span.

Take care! you can't do what you used to!
Eat your gruel, now you can't chew
The juicy steaks you once enjoyed,
And watch that spice and curried food,
You really must do what you're told,
Your stomach now is growing old.

Don't be lifting all that stuff,
You'll do your back in sure enough,
So never try to cut the lawn,
And get to bed before the dawn,
This aint no way to carry on
When you're a senior citizen.

So do you gently acquiesce?
To save the trouble and the stress.
Or do you fight the march of time?
And say that you're not next in line
As many forebears tried to do,
And join the ranks of Victor Meldrew.

John Thompson

Home For Me Is . . . . .

Wherever I can lay my weary head
Can by some kind soul be fed
A home, a place to dwell, I have not
A subway with a blanket is my lot.
Sometimes a cardboard box comes in handy
To shelter from the cold of winter
To have "four walls" so many complain about
In being between them instead of getting out,
To have as such to complain of would be fine by me
But I'm always "out", never in, I have no choice, you see.
Spare a thought, if not a penny
Family, home, I have not any.
Home is for me . . . . well, wherever I can lay my head.

John A. Turner

The Dream

The sun is shining in the sky,
The birds are flying way up high,
Wind rustles gently through the trees
As I dream of you, my sweet Louise.

Fair of face and sweet of tongue,
But oh, you are so young.
Your long brown hair, lies in a plait
Coming halfway down your back.

As I sit beside the gentle stream
Still of you Louise, I dream,
Childhood days, full of fun,
How I loved to see you run.

Sadly dreams don't last for ever,
Not in our stars, we'd be together.
When I close my eyes, I see your face
And no-one else, will take your place.

Mary Winifred Taylor

Dawn Watch

In silence of the early morn,
I sit and watch the coming dawn
As day unfolds, what will there be
Waiting there for you and me?
The morning star that showed her light
Gives way to a far brighter sight:
The star that gave her birth, the sun
Becomes a far more brilliant one.
Its glow is spreading far and fast,
An orange tint upon the frost:
And way across the fields of snow
The light of distant houses glow.
The world begins to stir and wake.
And people to their journeys take.
The trees stand tall, their branches wide,
But now no longer birds can hide
And find the shelter of their leaves,
Blown and scattered by the breeze.
The sky is growing lighter now
And night unto the day doth bow
The rosy sunrise starts to fade
A new start to the day is made.

P.J. Thorpe

I Bonded A man

Hear the chords of rhythmic music playing to the ear
Who can hear the words I chant, lament about?
Does the heart not rend into pieces when seen before the seer?
A band on edict is playing songs of doubt.
Ructions in the audience stir up a mighty roar
Resounding lyrics strip away the peace of living fact
A band on edict marches on again to take the floor
Single-handedly it seems I carry on the act.
The darkness of the concert hall dispells all lights
The place is filled, yet I alone am here
Convinced I was of certain truths not rights
And still a band on edict plays to feed my fears.
Here the chords of rhythmic music sound like painful cries
All the tunes of lonely hearts recorded decades before
Still a band on edict never stops its sighs
Never ending solitary "On the show must go!"
From where did it come a band on edict?
By what authority?
When shall it cease it's lonesome playing?
When comes security!

Tatty

Just Me

Why do people stare at me?
Why do people glare at me?
Why do people look down at me?
Then they seem to frown at me
I feel so alone in this chair of my own
It's not my fault my bones have not grown
I might as well be in a world of my own

I seem to be as small as a rat
But everyone else is a jungle cat
They're agile, they can jump, skip, play and all that
These things I can't do I'm no match
They are not happy with what they've got,
But compared to me they've got such a lot

There's no point of going to town,
They just look at me as though I'm a clown
Why don't people just accept the way I am
It's not by choice I am who I am

I don't need shoes or socks for my feet,
I wear them to make myself look neat
But I do need a wheelchair unlike you,
Why not hold my hand and see me through

Yes I am disabled I may not look the same as you
But I am part of this community
Just like you!

Charlene Vincent (Age 13)

History And Biology

I would speak of another time
but that would be to remember
not to render up what was,
like bidding for Kennedy's rocking chair:
"an artefact of a president
and a time and an affliction".
The interleaved space I would touch
is not there then,
but here now
in the many layers of meaning -
though that draws on the past.
The life that was in the past
has gone, but supports the present
like mould growing in a decaying timber
which hyphae finely penetrate
and slowly, minutely feed on
by enzymatic exudate and reabsorption.

Adrian Tellwright

Winter

Darkness descends like a bird of prey
Carefully shrouding the light of day
Moving so softly you scarce can tell
Except for the toll of a far off bell
Whispering shadows flickering lights
'Tis the beginning of long winter nights
The old oak stands with its boughs all bare
Looks for the sun that's no longer there
Clasped in winter's cold gnarled hands.
Endures its embrace and understands
For in a short while a new life begins
As a brave little snowdrop tirelessly wins
And stands so defiant as if to say
Though your branches creak and sway
Take heart for spring is on its way

Betty Hatfield Thomas

Remora

To look at you un-nurtured, un-nourished
Pathetic in your sight
Your body cut in two
The dead part dying
The other restrained
If only the dead would cut loose
And let the other live
Instead,
You stay - ungrown, unloved
Beautiful in your sight
Yet nothing inside
Glowing bright to the world yet nothing.

You hang there trying to lose
The part of you which doesn't grow
But it lingers
Pathetically by your side
To hinder you
Unless,
You break the stem
Break it in two
And save yourself
Your beauty will become yours not his.

Tracey Thomas

Waiting For Wings

Once I was young,
beguiled, entranced.
Eager for life,
pursued, romanced.
Lively and bright,
such savoir-faire!
Healthy and strong,
with glossy hair.

Look at me now;
youth passed, mirth spent.
Caught in a web
of discontent.
Trapped in creased skin
and clogged up veins.
Vanishing hair.
Departing brains . . .

Hopelessly lost
in binding snares.
Desperate to know
if someone cares.
Waiting for wings
of sovereign power.
Ready for Gods
appointed hour.

Jean Vines

Deep Within Me

Rejected, alone, I leave you to live your own life,
Before there was hope,
Hope that one day you would be mine,
The two of us; a pair.
You said no, without reason,
My intentions were good,
You'll never know.

Now my affection is out,
You know how I feel.
I pass you in the street,
I feel you laughing inside.
Cruel, careless, cold,
I gave you my life,
You gave me death.

Mark Tredwell

In Search Of Day

In silent thought I walk alone,
Step by step into the dark unknown,
Praying for dawn's early light,
To escape the shadows of the night.

Softly, slowly, with weary tread,
As if by unseen hands I'm led,
Deep into the dark cold void,
Where light and warmth have been
destroyed.

My mind is in turmoil, it knows no peace,
Waiting for this hell to cease,
Arms outstretched to find my way,
Eyes open wide in search of day.

With breathing quick and pounding heart,
I pray for the darkness to depart,
To release me from this self made hell,
And my torturous dream to dispel.

In desperation I start to shout,
"Lift this darkness, and let me out,
Send me from this cold dark tomb,
Back to the safety of my room."

My prayer is answered, there's a glint of light,
Breaking through the jet black night,
A sharp deep breath of cool pure air,
And I awake from my mad nightmare.

Michael Tipper

Gone

He'd left no coming back
Off on his motor bike with his pack
Left her alone to cry,
No-one to wipe away the tears in her eye
A child clung to her skirt,
Another one playing outside in the dirt
He said it was too much
"Oh his cruel words how they hung in the blue air"
But now he'd gone she was left in despair
They were poor then
But now without her precious Glen.
Life had to go on,
And not be wasted
The smoke trail was still hot
Like a chicken that had been basted.

Rachel Todd

The Car Race

The lights change
As the race becomes insane
The wheels spin
As the race begins
Faster faster faster
To make sure I'm in front of the master

Corner one
As I show the others how it's done
Corner two
It's easily done by a few
Corner three
As I say whoopee
Corner four
I want more

Lap one
That's how it's done
Lap two
As the crowds say phew
The fuel is low
So into the pit stop I go
Eight seconds past
And boy that is fast

Off I go
And I must not be slow
The chequered flag is in sight
So the master begins to fight
Two cars collide
That's the end of their ride
I'm the winner
So home for my dinner

David Vale

The Little Robin

The robin hops jauntily
Onto a sprig of ivy
Chirping so loudly among
The snow filled trees

The robin's red breast
The only colour around
Dancing frantically to and fro
Among the soft white snow

We hang the nut bags on the line
The robin's hanging there upside down
Just like a circus clown
During the winter months

We always know when Christmas comes
The only time he is around
The nicest bird we seem to find
Always around at Christmas time

Margaret Vale

Street Life

A little old lady walks the street,
Head hung low, no shoes on her feet.
Dirt on her clothes and dirt in her hair,
'Why is life so unfair'.

She begs for money and begs for food,
But the response is cruel and always rude,
Without a friend and a loving home,
She wanders the roads all alone.

At night you can hear her softly weeping,
While everyone else is warm and sleeping,
Dreaming of the life she once had,
Before it went so terribly bad.

I know this lady and so do you,
She's the one who seeks help from you,
When she sits on the corner of the street,
And begs for money and food to eat.

So, next time you see her, don't walk by,
With a stare, a tut, and a sigh.
Give her a smile and help her too,
'Cos you never know, it could have been you!

Kayti Tooth

Living Life

Take one breath of happiness,
That envelopes our soul
Clouds of contentment are illusions to behold.
We stand on terra firma
Bringing reality to mind
Lest we lose ourselves in dreaming.

Cross out the angers of the day
Leave stress and woe behind
Let go despondency, fly away
Take pleasure with sight and mind.

These never ending feelings
For oneself and others too
Drift over us in spasms
As to colour and shade our view

Dorothy Ann Twigger

The Wonder Of Winter

Embrace not the grey of the winter despair
Let not your heart, feel the cold chilling air
Be warmed by the beauty, that none can deny
The white frosty morning, the blue of the sky

Icicles like crystals, reflect the blue of that sky
Frost falls from a branch, as a bird flutters by
Coldness does bite, but with a freshness so clean
And a haze in the air from one's breath can be seen

The snowflakes that fall, so silent to the ground
Each flake, a caress, and not one, makes a sound
Silently falling, white kisses adrift on a breeze
Resting on rooftops, amid the branches of trees

The kiss is so gentle, it marks not its place
As nature with grandeur lays down its white lace
Serenity and peace reign, below sky's of grey
Soon to be shattered, as in the snow children play

What more can one ask, for peace in your heart
A peace for all ages, in which all play their part
The old, they remember the child they once were
The parents out playing, and to the cold give no care

But winter we should remember is nature's time of rest
And the bitter cold weather, is to rid plants of pest
Thus spring and the summer glory before us is laid
And winter, my friends is the price we have paid

Albert Volp

Home

The cold woke me up from my cardbcard bed,
you see I live under the arches by the railway shed.
It's not much of a place but I can call it home,
if only the rats and bugs would leave me alone.
Off down to the Sally for tea and toast,
then I've got to listen about the holy ghost.
They try to change us but it falls on deaf ears,
I'm off now to the pub for a couple of beers.
Two turn to three and three turns to four,
I will probably end up laid on the floor.
Half past eleven it's time for my bed,
just down the road by the railway shed.
My cardboard box looks wet and cold,
still it's a place where I might just grow old.

P.D. Thomson

Let Scotland Take My Pain

Away to a wild and passionate land,
For fate has dealt me a cruel, cruel hand.
To purple heather and melting snow,
To bare rock face where the lichen grow.

To a crumbled, ragged shore,
Where only eagles soar.
To the darkest lochs that hide the years
And bear the kilted soldier's tears.

Under skies of bleakest grey;
I'll touch the spot where a kinsman lay.
I'll caress the cold and blackened stone,
And hear,the haunting voices moan.

I'll let the wind steal salted water from my cheeks
Draining the pain as it speaks.
I'll hear the calmest water roar
And feel the power of nature's law

I'll visit lonely graves and haunted moor
And feel the lives of those that went before.
Upon applecross I will stand;
And embrace this glorious forgotten land.

Upon a lonely beach as the day is stolen by the night
I'll surrender my sword to the emotional fight
And murdering the silence with a battle cry
I'll feel the pain begin to die.

Emma Vigus

Slinx

There's a little green monster called slinx
When he finds some gold
He blinks!
When he sees some chocolate
He'll pinch!
When he's going to rob
He thinks!
And when he comes home
He stinks!
That's all about Slinx!

Warren Unsworth (Age 8)

Chess

Pawn moves forward,
Rook moves back,
Queen moves forth to take and attack.

King retreats
Bishops defend,
Soon the game will surely end.

King is cornered
Knights too late
And then I shout, "Checkmate!"

Sam Whitfield (Age 11)

The Flower

Compare our love to a tiny seed,
It is born.
Will it turn into a weed?
Or flower in the early morn?

This flower has now matured,
The pain I had has now been cured,
And as I look to see its beauty,
I see you and all your purity,
But will the flower last long?
Could our love turn out so wrong?

You've seen it too I am sure,
The warmth, the glow, it's so pure,
That's the work of mother nature,
Like our love we must nurture,
Let us not allow it to die,
Let us not say goodbye.

Is our love really like the flower?
Has it had its final hour?
Is it withered, dead and done?
Or is there another seed peeping through into the sun?

L.D. Vasiljevs

Gone

There was a young girl small and sprightly
Trod the world so very lightly
But age came quickly cloaked and masked
And took away the young girl fast

The person left was just a shell
Of days gone by but who could tell
The gilded lily crushed and blown
Gone forever from hearth and home

Dreams were shattered and hopes were lost
As driftwood in the sea is tossed
No more to know much less to care
As thoughts upon the heartstrings tear

A woman now to face the world
As life before her is unfurled
Days are gone the young girl lost
But only one can count the cost

Patricia A. Thomas

And Larks Sing Overhead

At last the guns are silent
and larks sing overhead;
here upon the battlefield
they seek and count the dead.
Fine men, in their youthful prime
cut down like ripening corn;
once, happy laughing lads,
now broken, shattered, torn.
Ten score and more in khaki,
three hundred in field grey,
they came to fight each other, but
it matters not this summer's day,
for here together now they lie
as brothers in eternal sleep;
mourned by loved ones far away
who plant red poppies as they weep.

David T. Wicking

449

Home Is Where The Child Waits

Home is
Where you stop and wait like a child
Home is
Where you sit, confused by all the contradictions,
Interrogations, professionally lost and forced to
Accept it without fear
Home is
The whole world for the poorest man,
A house for the rich man,
They both just don't know it.

Home is for me everywhere I don't belong
In the world
Except
My house in the heart and soul
Which is terrifying and beautiful.
Every place is an exile in comparison.

Z. Von Roretz

Reflections Of An Old Man

I am bound to a wheel-chair, there is something the matter with me!
You see, my legs are missing! yet my mind is as sane as can be.
I am lame and old, I know. Yet don't look at me so sad!
For I've travelled to many lands as young, for that I am glad!
I've climbed high mountains and swam fast flowing streams,
I still do it today, but only in my passing dreams!
Yesterday I could read and write, I too had ambitions opened wide,
Till the world dictated my life, sent me to strange lands, part of me died!
I went to war, I fought with great men with clothes, cold and wet,
To dig holes and hold our positions strong, what a waste of sweat!
There by my side, running blood discharging sounds of death,
And wheezing throats fighting in vain for breath!
Today I am told, 'You lucky one!' though recounted different harms,
Yet returned home with missing legs and distorted arms!
Today it's still 'Good and Evil' that squeeze each other flat against the wall,
And one has the power to take and takes it and keeps it all!
Such scenes of devastations, that appear to mock the wiseman's rules,
The peace and order, the beauty of knowledge we all learned in schools!
If society is to be for 'all kind of man' we must reveal the rot under the skin,
It is time we sit and think, and share out the horror that lives within!
Now I have many grand-children crawling around where is supposed to be my feet,
Yet their teasing games help my spirit to stand the heat!
Social life is difficult, morning till night, just looking at my face;
Yet every new day I find I am still alright, I must be winning the mortality race!

Leigh Von Stauffenberg

Last Entry

As I look across this land
A stripe on my arm and a gun in my hand
I see the buildings that have been raised to the ground
And the days carry on without any sound
I'm free from the law but imprisoned by this mask
Just a solitary soldier who's been left with no task
As I shuffle through the rancid flame
I search for someone to share this blame
I write this diary and I prey it be read
Because there's nobody here everyone's dead
I walk and search with little hope
I'm all alone and with this I can't cope
So if this diary is ever read
Don't look for me for I too will be dead

P.J. Venemore

Words

If words can paint a picture
I hope you'll picture mine
I see a field of fresh green grass
And many flowers fine
There's daisies white and buttercup,
Give off a golden hue,
Purple vetch, poppy's red
And cornflowers of blue.
Surrounded by a hedge of may, a blackbird on a bough
And in the corner of the field I see a brindle cow
A pathway leads o'er distant hills
A cottage stands alone.
Sweet smelling cover by the way.
A song thrush to greet me each new day
If words could paint a picture
A blind man then could see
The beauty of the country side
That's home sweet home to me.

Margaret Vinall-Burnett

Blackpool Football Club

There was a team from the pier
Who never scored for a year.
Blackpool is their name
Football is the game
And now they're all on the beer.

Stuart Waterworth (Age 11)

Red

Red is a colour that people fear
It is a colour of hate when people die
Telephone boxes and lists of other things like
A Doncaster Rovers kit
The red of the cross of health and heart
That red moment in life
But those socks that mum got you
For Christmas are terrible!

Alasdair Weeks (Age 9)

The First Little Pig

Sucked in by the saw wood sales man
You erect a make shift hut
And call it home to independence.
Determined to keep the wolf out
By hook or by crook,
By the hair of your chinny chin-chin.

The familiar pink skin
Of loved ones vanish.
Upturning and dismantling the past
As fast as nails fly through deal.
Brick houses are for pensioners!

You live in this despite our warning
Rub noses with coarse-haired hogs
Unaware of who goes there
The door is paper thin, condom thin;
No protection against the huff and puff.
While you blast loud music,
Asleep in your deaf heaven.

Noelle Vial

Why
Slimming

The pages stared me in the face
Join Slimming World it said
I thought about it but in the end
Reached for the bics instead

Then suddenly it struck me
Why not give it a go
It wouldn't hurt to lose some weight
I would give it a go

The pounds they came off slowly
But stayed off all the same
It really is so friendly
You're known by your first name

Two stone lighter here I am
Happy as can be
I knew that day the advert
Was meant to change me.

Gillian Washbrook

Happy Birthday Son!

When some parents say I've sacrificed for you!
Don't believe them David it's just not true,
Just take a look at me and your Dad, having you wasn't really so bad!!
Giving up work was a bit of a gas the lump in my front gave me a pass
Never to queue or to stand around, like a ship in full sail that had run aground!!
Remember the grommets and fingers in tins,
The drawers that you fell off and cricket bat things,
Tarzan swings and sofa's too, ropes over the Beck and trips to the zoo!!
On Scarborough front you smiled and you laughed
And run over old folks who got in your path!!
In Spain you were sweet a delight and a joy,
You dug deep for England with a new plastic toy!!
So the giving was small that we've had to make,
The sacrifices nil on the path that you take
The love that we give, we get back every day,
It grows and gets stronger wherever you stray,
When you went to the States our hearts went there too,
The boys also missed you but then always do,
The closeness you have with your brothers is rare
And you're never afraid to show that you care
So the laughter and love shine bright through the tears
The pain and the pleasure of your first 21 years!!!!

Judith Irene West

Romeo And Juliet

Romeo and Juliet
Fell in love when they first met,
From families they both regret
Montague and Capulet.

Romeo a desperate man
Finding any way he can,
To figure out why the ban
On this love that they began.

Romeo cried and cried
To find his Juliet had died,
And though their families tried to hide
It was because of the love they both denied.

Romeo tried his best
To give this love a little rest,
Neither family was impressed
To find a dagger in Juliet's chest.

Judith Williams (Age 15)

Modern Life

Whatever would the old ones say
If only they were here today,
To see us dashing here and there
Never having time to spare,
No-one stops to have a chat
Must keep going - can't do that -
No longer do we care to see
The greenest grass, the tallest tree,
The little birds within the bush,
Horses, Cows or Meadows lush.
For modern life is one big scramble
Run everywhere - no time to amble.
Computers rule our very lives,
It's mobile 'phones now - no more wires.
We drive to work and drive to school,
And shopping on wheels is the rule.
Machines do all our work at home -
Just press a knob - no need to moan!
But somehow life has lost its meaning -
No more is happiness a-gleaming.
So just before it's all too late -
Stop! Take Stock and Appreciate!
Take time to look around and say -
Thanks for the beauty of each day!

M.A. Winn

First Impressions

If an alien did land, handed some invitation,
What would he make of us and our 'wondrous' nation?

On the surface we seem to be, as flawless as a crystal
Lots of people ignoring, the machete and the pistol;

We leave it to others, to sort out our troubles,
Offer a helping hand, and some warming cuddles.

We blot our problems from our conscious minds,
I think that's ignorance, that's what it defines.

We're a G7 country, a name that I do hate,
For we still have terrorists, and scourges of the state;

Sometimes I envy the developing nations,
Without responsibilities and political delegations;

If the alien reported back it would hand us fame,
For all the wrong reasons, it would blacken our name.

Daniel Whitfield (Age 14)

A Child Of War

I heard a child laugh,
In a land where there were no children.
Just empty shells with vacant eyes that stare
Into a distant place,
Where broken spirits go.

I heard a child laugh,
Where the ghosts of ancestors were moaning.
Where toys were weapons of destruction,
And games were death,
And innocence a mockery.

I heard a child laugh,
Where hearts were cold and the Book of Life
Had fed the last forgotten fire.
And souls were damned,
And skeletons the furniture.

I heard a child laugh,
And the sound stirred in the hearts of all mankind.
But we awoke, and saw the carrion,
And twisted crosses,
And peace doves - dead upon the ground.

The laughter of a child, it seemed
Was but a sad and long forgotten dream.

Ronnie Whitaker

If I Were Not Me

If I were not me, I would rather be,
A cat, oh it would be lovely to sit
By the fire on a big fur mat,
Or lying in a box like a curled up fox,
Search the house for a bed,
Where I would lie my sleepy head,
Eat my food when I was in the mood,
I would not be a tabby they're too shabby,
Or maybe a siamese but they get fleas!
Run and catch leaves blowing in the breeze,
Pounce and chase my ball
Running up and down the hall,
Stalk out at night without getting a fright,
In the day I would run away to next doors pond,
Of going there I'm fond,
And bring back a fish on a dish
For my tea, oh yes! a cat,
A cat would suit me purrfectly!

Rebecca Wilson (Age 9)

Deaths Cold Winter

The stench of vulgarity burns through his eyes
One man's trust becomes another man's lies
Time will be drawn from the apocalyptic sigh
Generations of man were born to die

Hell on earth as the button is pressed
Time to die is decided it is now stressed
The youth of today will be tomorrow's gains
Ripped torn and beaten they cry out in pain

Nuclear winter deadens the sky
Lost cold survivors will surely die
Radiation sickness burns through their veins
No hope of cure to kill the pain

World leaders awake from deep underground
Entering daylight, not hearing a sound
Deformed mutants once human beings
Move through the ashes all not seeing

The treasure of life so often taken for granted
Is now taken away with our bodies planted
Until the sun will rise to brighten our day
Human races resilience will find a way

It will rise from the ashes and begin a new
Procreation must start from first the few
Until one day we can live as one
When world powers unite and the weapons are gone

Andy Wisniewski

The Madman

Within the shuttered room
The madman screams
He a tortured soul
His mind a twisted maze of agony
No lustre in his eyes
No light shines here
Only dark deep shadows of despair

What demons did the mind unleash
What torments haunt the brain
And is insanity hell
By just another name
And from deep within the shuttered room
The madman screams again

David Whittaker

For My Husband

Your lips touch mine I tremble
My body seems to ache,
For that rich embrace you give me,
Every time that I awake
You tell me that you love me,
Every passing day,
We'll both grow old together,
Which makes me want to say,
That I love you too my darling,
I know that I am sure,
That our love will last forever
Until there is time no more.

Vivianne Watson

Dunblane

They were mummy's wee darling
And dad's little pet, their world was so new
Their hair was still wet
They held hands together and skipped up the lane
On that bright spring morning that ended in pain

And he who once was a child such as these
Left home that same morning, his hate to appease
Society shunned him, his anger was blind
He'd show them no mercy, he'd pay them in kind

What being could do this, to break life's rule
To appear like a ghost in the middle of school
To sacrifice children, to end all their hope
Leave loved ones the grief a lifetime to cope

There's news that affect us our whole life long
John Kennedy's death, the first atom bomb
Dunblane ranks among them and in its own way
Reflects sad indictment on our world today

But without seeking mercy and still crying why
Can society in general hold its head high
Do we create monsters, give them a name
When the thread finally breaks
Can we handle the pain
But my heart is so full I've lost words to say
For the horror that came on that bright spring day

James Andrew Wilson

Emotions

The greatest emotion, here on earth
To see a wife, who has just given birth
Emotions run high and tears flow
Soft and white, like driven snow
A beautiful girl, or a handsome boy
Everyone, is filled with joy
Tiny fingers, tiny toes
Bright blue eyes and tiny nose
So innocent, in every way
Nine months of waiting, for this day
All the pacing, to and fro
Is over now, you can take things slow
You're waiting now, for the doctor to say
That they're both fine, they're going home today
Grandparents and family, all come round
Celebrations, then abound
To the parents and baby, raise your cup
Look forward now, to he, or she, growing up.

Peter Edward Waines Briggs

Old Faithful

He did not ask a lot from life
He was faithful to the end
A comfort when I felt alone
A true and noble friend

He did not moan about the world
Or of the people in it
Life to him was full of fun
Each day, each hour, each minute

Now he is gone, the house is quiet
What would I give to see
That funny face, that happy look
The joy when he greeted me

Who is this I speak of?
Would you say the description fits
A brother, father, son or friend?
No - just a little dog called Fritz

Bill Williamson

456

Getting Old

The time it rushes past you
Hours are short every day
There are jobs you really ought to do
And things you have to say

By the time you really think them out
Those things you should have said
The light has gone before you know
It's time to go to bed

I'll leave that 'til tomorrow
And give a little smile
But leave and leave what do you get
A massive great big pile!

If we know then, what we know now
Things would not be half so bad
We'll do the things in half the time
When we were just young lads

Things are so much bigger now
And go so very fast
No longer see the horse and plough
And items never last

We must move on, old times must die
Forget the past we're told
No tears must fill our memories eye
Just because we're getting old

Thomas Wise

The World As We Know It!

Throw your arms around the world
Let it know you care
Be happy and contented
With all around you there
Look at all the badness
Look at all the good
Look at all the sadness
You would change it if you could
What can you really do
That would put it right
Only God alone
Can make them stop the fight
He can try with all His power
He can try with all His strength
No matter what the outcome
He will make you swim the length
So why not leave Him to it
Let Him try His best
The truth as we know it
The world is just a test!

Teresa Weller

From Mocks to Employment

My Mock exams, I will defeat,
English and Maths, I know I'll beat.
My Mock exams, they are really tough,
But I think I've done quite well enough.
B's and C's will be no sweat,
Art and German, they're no threat.
Now I'm nearly finished that's a lot off my mind.
I've been helped by my parents they've been so kind.
I will try in the long run to help and reward them,
If I get my GCSEs, a good job I will get for them.
Programmer or Repairer, Computers the job for me,
When I'm earning my fortune,they'll be dancing with glee.

Christopher Wilkinson

Time

My rhymes, if not exactly frivolous are meant to be taken lightly
Although they are sincerely meant - they are mostly given brightly

What I really want to say now - I may not be able to express
Time - although measured quite precisely - is nothing more or less

Than what each individual gives and takes each moment of each day
Not really spectacularly, but in each and every way

A smile, a wave, a bright hello
Small things, small actions bring a glow

The simple little pleasures
Are worth more than treasures

Fleeting moments that are so precious - wasted years that have flown by
But isn't every moment precious? - ones that make you sad, make you laugh or cry?

Time is of the essence - what is the essence of time?
Time is what you make it - is what's said in this rhyme

A tiny hand in your hand - making you feel big and strong
And yet humbling in its own way - if you know where you belong

A tiny star up in the sky - so very far away
That we look upon tonight - was there - but yesterday

Not yesterday - last night - but many "moons" ago
And yet we see it now - we see it glow!

How strange is time - seconds, minutes - hours, light years fly by
Don't waste time worrying about it - but live it - 'til you die!

Janice Marie Wilson

A Gift From God

Thank you Lord for the flowers and trees,
For the gift of the birds and bees,
For the darkness and the light,
The sun and moon shining bright,
With the stars in heaven above,
These wonderful gifts you gave with love,
Along life's pathway as we stray,
We think of you Lord every day.
Hoping dear Lord you hear our prayer,
That some day your home we share.
When you call us Lord to meet,
In your safe keeping we will sleep,
From your heavenly home above,
Most of all you gave us love.

J. Willson

The Sign

I watch the branches of a tree
as they blow in the wind
I think of the future
as I gaze serenely up at the stars
I think of my life as I single out
an individual branch with precise vision
as it dances in the breeze
thrusting upwards
it's twigs projecting like fingers
toward the sky
and as I look up once more
in the direction of my branch
a shooting star rages through the night

Ross Wilson

458

Seasons

Golden daffodils are glowing, absorbing the sun,
Welcoming springtime, nature's tasks have begun.
Animals awaken from their lengthy rest,
Bird's returning and yearning to feather their nests.
Warm is the air, aiding long daylight hours,
Lush emerald lawns complement sweet, scented flowers.
Swift, static cloud gathers, sending storm chilling sights,
Drenching, quenching, mother earth's droughted delights.
Swirling debris collected, from autumn's first fall,
Dressed in tones of amber and crimson, to greet winter's long call.
Trees shiver bare as their final leaves tumble,
Kissed with frost to add sparkle, crinkle and crumble.
Bold blue skies surrender, unto grim shades of grey.
Dominant darkness, steals the light's precious ray.
White crystal falls,soft, silent and clean.
Covering, smothering, all to be seen.

Patricia Watkins

To The Children Of Dunblane

Dunblane, the place that shook the world
As news of murder was unfurled
Innocent children in their school
Were killed or maimed by an insane fool
Although it happened some time ago
The mum's and dad's still want to know
How this man got guns and knives
And then set out to ruin their lives
The hurt of that day will always remain
We must make sure it can't happen again
Let us take a lesson from these girls and boys
Who never again will play with their toys.
We must make sure they did not die in vain
If we can do this it may deaden the pain
And help all the parents who were left behind
And we hope go some way to their peace of mind

Idris Williams

Essex

The countryside in Essex
Is there for all to see,
Churches windmills and stately homes,
And even a brewery,
Beautiful towns and villages,
And entertainment everywhere,
Stop awhile and consider,
Of taking a holiday there.

J.E. Willis

Snowdrops

What a really wondrous sight,
Snowdrops growing so very white.
With their heads held so high,
Faintly you can hear them sigh.
On the ground of grass so green,
Tiny flowers, always seen.

Chris Waltham

Goodbye

I fall apart each time I hear your name
Now you've gone, it's not the same
For the first time, I gave someone my heart
You told me you cared, and we would never be apart

I held you in my hand, like a bunch of flowers
Love and happiness throughout the hours
Folk who live near you, said you had to go away
Someone who played foolish games, and couldn't stay

I never thought our love would end
Thought it was, from heaven sent
I can't judge right, by looking at wrong
Now life's path is bleak and long

Water will never wash away my tears
As I've gone through these lonely years
Like a bird, you left the nest and flew
All I have, is sweet dreams of you

The petals of the flowers they have wilt
As life spirals on a downward tilt
I go through the storm, my head held high
Knowing you never said goodbye

P.G.S. Walker

Amidst The Mayhem

Bloated flies
Drink the blood of carrion
Whilst crops of corpses quickly grow
Lying dead a whole battalion
What they fought for
No-one knows

Images
Of men saluting
Men of courage, nerves of steel
To valiant battle they went running
Though searing pain
Was all they'd feel

On and on
They struggled blindly
Trying to fight their unseen foe
But groups of soldiers mortars finding
Amidst the mayhem
Red sky glows

A.R.M. Wassell

I Wish I Was

I wish I was a robin,
Perched upon a bough,
But there again I'd hunger now
Finding prey among the snow.

I wish I was a hedgehog,
All prickly in a ball,
But maybe then I'd find it cold
Just sleeping in a hole.

I wish I was a snowdrop,
So delicate and white.
But there again the snow would fall,
And I'd be out of sight.

Maybe I should be a tree,
Standing firm and bold,
A wind may break my branches,
Then no blossom I could hold.

Barbara F. Ward

Motherhood

Being a mother is wonderful
Being a mother is great
What else can I say as I look
All around me and think "what a state"?

There's more grass in the kitchen than outside
The living rooms scattered with toys
But what would I do without them
My baby girl and two lovely boys?

Steven's first, he's six and at school
Learning quickly to read and write
Nathan's next, three and full of mischief
He stands on his dinosaur to turn on the light!

Rebecca's eight months, and so beautiful
She's just about learned how to crawl
Growing up with two big brothers
She already seems wise to it all!

I look in the mirror sometimes
And can't believe I'm the mother of three
But I say thanks to God every day
That he showered these blessings on me.

Carole Walker

Time And Space

People may wonder
Of the vastness of space
And if it's only humans
That are here within this place

Yet as we are reaching
Other planets further out
One day a signal from one of them
Hopefully may come out

One day within the future
This may sometime come true
Then will the scientists
Tell of all onto you

If this should so happen
I hope to us they'd converse
Then no one can say
That we are alone in this universe.

Ian B. Wilkinson

A Dedication To My Daughter-In-Law

No angel is more beautiful, than June with her enchanting smile.
Her eyes out-shine the brightest stars and constellations in the firmament.
She's endowed with many virtues, charisma, charm and grace.
This gem so rare, is rare indeed, among the human race.
Her heart is warm and tender - a priceless pearl within her shell -
She always looks so happy, when sad, she masks it well.
She's a paragon of virtue, a joy indeed to see,
She brings so much happiness to kin and friends, and me.
She turns winters into summers, autumns into springs,
I don't know how she does it but, she really does such things!
Her gentle voice, her warmth, her tenderness,
Will brighten e'en your darkest day,
She'll make your troubles vanish, and drive your blues away,
So count your blessings one and all, if you by chance, should meet her,
For though you travel e'er so far, no girl, will you find sweeter.
She may not be perfection, may have some human flaw,
But all who know her, love her dearly; none more than I:
Because she is, my wonderful Daughter-in-Law.

Henry Ward

Just Out Of Sight

Be not dismayed in your sorrow,
Though sad you may be at this time.
The darkness will gradually vanish
And for you the sun will again shine.

Your loved one, her life has not ended,
She has only just slipped out of sight;
For she will be with you in mourning,
Till your thoughts can be turned to the Light.

She will also reflect on your sadness,
For you too have slipped from her sight -
As she gazes on you from the spirit,
She's aware of your mental fight.

Gain strength from the love she now sends you,
The love that will heal all your pain.
Just think of the joy of re-union,
When you are all together again.

I recently heard of your sorrow,
I don't know you, so you may think it odd -
But I feel that your daughter has touched me,
To tell you to keep faith in GOD.

Alan Webb

Untitled

A bird in the sky
Souring the heights
Can you hear its cry?
Unencountered
Do you know what it's like?
The clouds of rain
Come down causing pain
Floods of sea
Flow like tears
Salt water of the fish
That swim on land
Over fields
A wall of water
Swallowing the world
Washing away pollution
Fences of lands
That no-one owns
Rocks are hurled
Onto a nomans solution

P. Winterbourne

Till Death Do Us Part

To love and to cherish until death do us part.
The strong wedding promise that has broken her heart.
She looks at her bruises, they'll be easy to hide,
Glad nothing is broken - but her spirit and pride.

She stares through the window of their lovely old house,
The confident young bride now timid as a mouse.
She thinks of her husband as charming as can be.
She recalls other times being happy and free.

She listens to the songs of the free flying birds,
Her emotions are tied in tight knots by his words.
She just wants to leave him - but he'd never let go,
Her life seems so pointless - just a marriage for show.

To love and to cherish until death do us part
The postmortem report named the brides broken heart.

Lynsey Whitmore

Reflections Of Christmas Past

High on the hill, I stood alone,
On a cold and frosty Christmas morn,
I gazed in awe at the village below
A wondrous sight, all covered in snow.

Not a sound could be heard, but the sigh of the trees
As they bowed their heads to the gentle breeze
Snow flakes dancing in the air,
Like little fairies, prancing there
Bewitched, bemused, and still alone
For this was just, the break of dawn.

Children, they will soon arise
Joy and laughter in their eyes,
For this is the time of loving and giving
But most of all, love, it makes life worth living.

So I give to you, this gift of love,
Sent with a blessing from above,
For nothing in life can ever compare
With the wealth of nature
Waiting out there.

Margaret Wilson

Does He Take Sugar?

"Does he take sugar in his tea?"
"Hello! Why not ask me?
I might have a disability;
but to answer for myself I still have the ability!"
Just because I'm in a wheelchair,
It's not that people don't care,
that much I know;
But it's a problem wherever I go.
"Just 'cos I'm not stood up like you,
does not mean there is very little for myself that I can do"
Many people think we're sick
and most probably a little bit thick.
"Well, how many 'O' levels have you got?
As many as me, I'll bet not!
I also have a University Honours Degree!
A brainy sod that's me!"
To my mum, people will say, "Is this your son?
Tell me, how's he getting on?"
Mum's reply is, "Why don't you ask him?
He's certainly not dim!"

Michael W. Williams

The Night The Moon Stood Still
(A.D.73. Memories of the Captain of the Guard)

Though forty years have passed away
The scene is clear as if 'twere yesterday
Behind the Cross, beyond the hill,
That night the moon stood still.

The moon rose first, an angry red,
Then stopped, transfixed, behind His head.
The wind sighed low, the night grew cold,
When I returned, it glowed pale gold,
Behind the Cross, beyond the hill,
That night the moon stood still.

Two women, maybe three, were huddled there,
A stifled sob, a whispered prayer,
Borne on the night wind to the listening ear.
The guard eased his stance and scraped his spear,
And the dark rocks, grew darker still,
Below the Cross upon the hill.

I have watched many as they died,
Slain by the sword, or stoned, or crucified.
I felt somehow that the Man from Galilee
Forgot His agony just to pity me,
And something strange was wrought upon that hill
The night the moon stood still.

William G. Waller

The Cure

For years and years they searched and searched, but no cure could be found, that ray of hope that had flicked bright, soon dropped to the ground, but they could not give up, they would fight until the end to find the cure that will save his only real best friend.

But time was running out and they had to put their friendship to the test, to find the one thing they wanted the most, the cure, the gift of life, the only thing that would never let their friendship die.

But the cure was only a dream, a hope for the future, something his friend could never have, but it did not end there, for in a way he got a cure that took all the pain away, it showed him a way to fight, to keep going on, to never give up hope when things were going wrong.

His friend showed him all of this for their friendship gave him something, no cure could have it gave him hope, it gave him strength for the cure was inside their hearts in everything they did, for they knew by just being friends they had and always will have, the cure; a friendship that could never end.

Michelle Weatherstone

Red Peril

You're a cocky little fellow
As noble as can be
Guarding your precious territory
From high up in your tree

Warding off intruders
With your song so sharp and clear
Attacking with tenacity
Those who venture near

Yet how can one so beautiful
With your breast of crimson fire
Fight against your brother
With consequences dire

When your feathers are ruffled
Your encounters may end in death
It's sad to think such a beautiful bird
Will never again draw breath

But when all is said and done
I'm still so glad you're here
For your captivating singing
Always fills my heart with cheer

I wonder if you realise
You're held in high regard
And you bring many people joy
Just visiting their back yard

Robert Warren

Clock Duel

Clock ticking on town wall spying talk
holds constant quiet to listen
unspoken words drawn from terror stalk
each sentence where harsh verbs glisten.

Rhetorical questions brain may like
no answers fired come gunning
what danger lies in each quarter strike
stands erect to face time running.

Fraught arguments fly from front to back
whilst handling support by seconds
when honesty my excuses lack
dual truth towards me beckons.

Count sixty points in one target zone
spread evil apace for sorting
'tween equal space speaks red devil clone
a factor not for distorting.

Word weapons rise to spill anger foul
by mistake invokes vile voodoo
in defence appeal to healing soul
but revile myself, a cuckoo.

Frederic Wakefield

A Royal Invitation

The little mans trousers were a deep deep green and his coat was a brilliant red.
His bright eyes twinkled as he looked at me as he stood at the end of my bed.
In his hand he held a letter tied with a ribbon of blue.
The Fairy Queen has sent a note I have to give to you.
She would like you to come to her party to be held in bluebell wood.
It's a royal invitation so I really think you should
On the day of the party the Fairies were waiting for me
Some dressed in pink and others in blue they were there to serve me tea.
There were acorn cups of lemonade and cakes of sugar and spice.
As if in a dream I ate fluffy ice cream and everything else that was nice.
Soon old Mr. Owl sitting high in his tree blinked his eyes and said
You have all had a wonderful party but now it is time for your bed.

A.F.J. Wakeford

Toil

Why doth we all toil?
And some burn midnight oil.
Work lays heavy on the brow,
Beginning to look like a farmer's sow!

If I were not to work,
A few weeks only could I shirk.
Bailiffs and others would then call,
My house and chattels gone by fall!

As sure as night followeth day,
We strive for our meagre pay,
Bosses and masters careth not,
Would they have us 'go to rot'?

If one chose only to steal,
The constable our collar, he would feel!!
Dammit I've just made up my mind,
Gather goods and chattels, antipodes I'll find.

Would it be the better, or worse?
Did that gypsy say in my curse?
Perhaps I'll tarry here a while,
Sup some beer, put on a smile.

Then the thoughts would fade away,
Try work again for measly pay.
I'll ask yon vicar, what he thinks,
Probably say 'your idea stinks'.

R.A. White

Our Best Friends

Dogs make you laugh
Dogs make you mad
They chew the best shoes
You've ever had

You take them for walks
Into the park
Early mornings
And when it gets dark

You throw them the stick
They bring it back
You throw it again
Then that is that

You make your way home
You let your self in
The dog beats you
To your kitchen

While making your meal
You give him his meat
And then settle down
With him at your feet

Christine Williams

Through Fishley Bridge

Cold, clear, diamond-cut, iced water.
Harsh, naked trees, bowing low, held by icy clutches.
Paralleled walkways, bridged to keep their distance.
Suspended above, a fine white winter mist.
Sun, as a golden chandelier, mirrored on iced orange iridescence.
Hark! sounds of woodpeckers, greenfinches, robins, how beautiful.
Nature providing rich red berries, consumed with relish.
Dense foliage, summer stubble cropped short standing proud in a raiment of hoar frost.
Deep frozen, fossilised footsteps beneath our feet.
The only remaining proof of passing children, excited pets,
Lovers deep in romance or fishermen to numbered stations.
We are as invisible, leaving no trail, no sign of life.
Crisp and cold, iced time stands still.

Pauline Helen Webb

Untitled

We rode into the desert
The light rushing low over the ground
To a bloodspot, in the west
Towards Pakistan.

And the night opened up
Above us like a fabergé egg.

And the stars rained down
Through my eyes gathering,
Like disintegrating silver snow
Somewhere inside me

And I thought,
I have never seen so many stars
Heading towards the city
I fell asleep.

Sitting straight up
In the sharp thin air
Exhausted.
And feeling like
I'd been crying.

Claire Whitefield

Sweet Fourteen

They said our love would never last
Because we were too young.
They said that it would finish
Just like it had begun.

But years have passed with ups and downs
We've weathered thro' some tears.
With little ones to swell our joys
Our hopes, as well as fears.

The time has past, the kids all gone,
And once more we're on our own.
Not quite as many kisses,
But deeper love has grown.

For patners this is what we are
With all the things more shared.
No other couple in the world
Could have been better paired.

We will as ever always be
The same as from the start.
Altho' in years we have grown old
Young love stays in our heart.

Dorothy Witt

My Old Bow Wow

I've met some men along the way
Who were happy enough in their own sweet way
With their Borzois and Sheepdogs and Sheepdog-fleas
And trembling Whippets that shake at the knees
With their Chow Chows and thoroughbreds that pee in the flowerbeds
And sit in the window for hours
And their runny-nosed Bulldogs that look like frogs
And yap yap yapping Chihuahuas
With their bow-legged Dobermanns and slobbering wolf-hounds
And whimpering needle toothed Griffs
And their nonchalant Bloodhounds with sorrowful eyes
And hyper-sensitive sniffs.
With their tartan coated dancing Pugs
And vastly superior Afghan rugs
And Pointers and Pincers and English collies
And darling Jillies and lady Mollies
Oh no!
You can keep your poodles and chinese noodles
And sly eyed German Alsatians
There's more choice wow-wow in my old bow wow
Than a hundred and one Dalmatians

Nick Watkins

The Police And The Public

To gain respect in all that you do,
First and foremost, you must be honest and true!
Your uniform stands for all that is good,
And when you are wrong you know that you should,
Stand tall and be counted. Then, in the eyes of
The public, you're not weak! you are strong.
You're an excellent copper, and where you belong.
We all make mistakes, it shouldn't cost you your job.
You're an excellent copper, not a thug or a yob!

So many people have been hurt through the years!
I have watched smiling faces turn from laughter to tears!
For the sake of a policemen, who has to be right,
To turn an investigation in to a life long fight.
Not to mention the cost nor to who goes the bill!
Some pushed so far, that, they just might even kill!

It's a crazy old world, so let's slow it down.
Let's work together and turn it round.
You don't always have to be right!
It's OK to sometimes be wrong,
And if you happen to be a copper
You're not weak you are strong.
And you will make an excellent policeman.

Douglas Wellington

O.A.P.'s

Hand in hand grey heads nodding across the sands towards the sea
Clutching shoes but old feet lagging, no names no cares just 'he' and 'she'
Years before they'd walked for miles along this beach towards the rocks
His auburn hair so thick and flowing matched his sweetheart's tousled locks

Now, their movements much more laboured, toes just scarcely test the water
He grips her arm above the elbow, she turns and totters starts to falter
All too cold the effort beats them, I hear her warning 'Watch the tide'!
He loops his arm around her shoulders her faded eyes meet his with pride.
Their love still there for all to see, I watch them as their hands entwine
Old hearts still beat for one another, reminds one there is 'Love Divine'

Shona White

Untitled

Our bed is a raft
In the sea of our life
Where together we float
Sated, elated, delicious delights
Tingling excitement
Erotica nights
Engrossed in the sanctuary of loves after glow
Lost in each other
Found in each other

One

Timeless
Limitless
Infinite
Love

Gillian Wallace

Cold May

The blossom has tucked itself
Into the hedge,
The whole corps de ballet
Heavy, sad and pink,
As out of place in this
North-Easter
As a flock of ballerinas
Choreographed on an
East Anglian cliff.
Bedecked, bereft,
The show is going on.
But where's the cast?
The Sun,
The praise of scent in
Audience applause?
The light
The drawing warmth
To lift them up?
Reviews will show
Winter has won,
On points.

Olwen Way

To Poetry

Poetry is for anyone who has a thought to share,
Holds dear a memory, truth or passion, and wills their soul to bare.
No need for special powers of reason or imagination:
The only effort called for is the strain that brings elation.
The inspiration for poetry is found in every niche of Nature,
In familiar sights and sounds which to the sense give pleasure -
The wind rippling ripe summer corn, the bounding of a hare or stoat,
The loud cadences of a warbler's song from such a tiny throat,
Or in cerebral concepts which deep in the mind recline,
And which through the miracle of thought exalting words divine.
Poetry is a frugal craft whose material needs are plain:
No pricey pigment, brush or canvas, or musical instrument to gain.
Poetry, too is economic with words, because for every chosen line
Two more, like unwanted potsherds, one must necessarily decline.
The origins of poetry are lost in the mists of time,
Long before the advent of metered verse and rhyme:
Even Cro-Magnon man, who fashioned tools so fine,
Might have made his hammer blows with words and tones align:
While Homer, father of world poetry and famed for the Iliad,
Has been a model for aspiring laureates, both modernist and trad.
So pick up your pens you budding bards, those precious words select:
All thoughts of measuring up to Wordsworth do not entirely reject.
You will find some words in verse sublime which written in prose seem trite,
And one day gain the laurels for the treasured lines you write.

David Walker

469

Winter's Song

Clocks go back, dark days are here
Mornings are lighter, some small cheer
Trees no longer dressed, branches sad and bare
Gardens void of colour, gardeners no longer care

Mist and rain heavy, high on the hills
Rivers and streams at last the rain fills
Leaves to kick or soggy with dew
Wet on the path, they stick to your shoe

All is not lost, log fires are glowing
Lights on early, Christmas carols now flowing
Families together, presents for all
It won't be so long now, spring soon will call

The white winter world we discover one morning
Everything silent, the soft snow still falling
Out to have fun, children gather their sledges
Sliding down hills, ending up in the hedges

Clocks leap forward, longer days are now here
Gloves and hats put away for another year
Goodbye to winter at last spring is showing
Snowdrops, daffodils and the March wind is blowing

C.J. Welling

A Reflection Of You And Me

Look in the mirror and what do you see,
A reflection of you and me.

Look in the water and what do you see,
A reflection of you and me.

Look in the crystal and what do you see,
A reflection of you and me.

Walk by the roadside you'll see,
A shadow of you and me.

Look in the mirror,
Look in the water,
Look in the crystal,
Walk by the roadside,
And you will see a reflection of you and me.

Margret Wilson

Thanks For Being My Friend

I met your family first time,
And wished I'd known before.
We got to know each other,
The time when I was low.
I was blind to my direction,
My mind I had to mend.
In you I found some comfort,
Thanks for being my friend.

I can share your moments,
And watch your family grow.
Take some love, give some back,
While time goes to and fro.
Through all my weary travels,
And where in life I end,
I'll not regret, the day we met,
Thanks for being my friend.

John Ernest Wileman

Stand And Stare

When the sun goes down,
That's the time you've got,
Enjoy the day and say, so what,
Find time to stand and stare,
To see what things are really there.
When young it's just one big rush,
When older, don't let them push.
The days have gone, they do not stay.
You've made your hay, on that you lay.
Just look at the wondrous things you've missed,
While lingering on the stage of abyss.
Look at a flower or up at the sky,
I'm sure you can if you really try.
Take plenty of time to look around,
All this you've missed when underground.
In your short span of life, be good,
Then you will inspire a descent bud,
That in their time, will enable them,
To take their turn to stand and stare.

Geraldine Ward

Wishful Thinking

"Do you think they'll choose me?"
Said the fir tree to the oak,
"No I certainly don't think so,"
Giving him a poke.
"You're small and frail and ugly,
Not the kind they're looking for,
Someone tall and graceful like myself,
I'm sure would suit them more."

The little fir hung his head
Quite sure the oak was right.
But who should come with stealthy steps,
In the middle of the night,
The father of a family
Too poor to buy a tree.
"This one's fine," he muttered,
As he quickly pulled him free.

On Christmas morn all decked in gold,
He thought about his past.
His branches spread, his head held high,
He gave a happy, breathless sigh,
"I'm a Christmas tree at last!"

Sandra Watson

Cats At Night

I was walking along,
One ink black night,
When suddenly I came across
A frightful sight.
I saw two cats
Rolling about, on top of a wall.
They were fighting,
And I told them they would fall.
Their paws scratched
And their tails twitched,
As they fell over the other side
Of the wall into a ditch.

I laughed and I laughed,
And out of the darkness,
They once more appeared,
Both of them looking very weird.
They shook themselves
And they washed themselves,
Then they turned to me as if to say,
"You were right, but go away!"
I smiled, then turned to go on my way,
Leaving them to fight again or play.

Tracy Whiting

A Gift From Heaven

We do not know if you're a girl or boy
It won't be long now before you are born
This is the closest mum and babe can be
What colour hair
and what colour eyes
will you have to see?
I hope you will always be very happy
It's re-assuring when you
kick probe and push my tummy.
Is it a foot, arm, or leg I can feel
or a prod kick or stretch with the back of your heel?
Why have you not arrived yet?
Contented where you are I bet.
I want to see and cuddle you
and do all the things a Mum can do.
When I'm busy you stay still and quiet
no doubt asleep, I pray you're alright.
Often worried, but down inside I know
it's when you are still you sleep and grow.

Linda Whitelaw

The Old Church

The cool, dark silence held no fears for me,
Echoes of Eternity dwelt within this place, cocooned by granite walls:
Those stone guardians of the Love which cannot be spoken.

An all pervading calm brought peace to those who would listen
To the sound of centuries past; A sound like a thousand whispers,
Murmurings of life and death, of happiness and sorrow:
All pregnant with Love, such Love.

Pale dead flowers lay on the marble altar,
Sunshine playing games with their shadows,
Imbuing their presence with light and life.
Stained glass windows watched from above,
Their rainbow colours reflecting like Love Incarnate.
Dusts motes danced in sparkling patterns As if drunk on the Holy Air:
"Look at us", they seemed to say, "be like us".

The beauty of neglect hung heavy
Defying the remorseless hand of time,
Mocking the passing years with deserved disdain.

And where, O Man, were you?
You are this church, it came from you:
An umbilical chord with the Infinite,
For you are part of each other.
Perhaps one day you will return
In awe and silence and wonder.

Michael Ward

The Rainbow

We sat in the car
In the field of Christmas trees,
And watched the rainbow through the glass.
We watched as the bright colours slowly faded,
Leaving half a rainbow.
Some half-forgotten rhyme
Formed at the back of my mind.
'Richard of York gained battles in vain'
I chanted to my grand-daughter,
And there's supposed to be a pot of gold at the end.
The problem was,
Where was the end of half a rainbow?

We sat in the car
Watching till the fading colours finally died.
Our attention caught the lightening
As it flashed across the sky.
Electricity at its most dangerous,
Closely followed by the inevitable rumbling of thunder.
A perfect setting for a horror film.

We sat in the car
Contemplating fish and chips.
Scrapped the idea.
Watched the raindrops chase each other down the wind screen.

We've been here far too long.

Betty Walton

The Rooks

OUT
OUT
OUT
Black voices rasping
Ragged cloaks shred and tear
Rooks fall and rise
Patches of night on a strengthening wind

FLY
FLY
FLY
Wind taken shouts
Nodding heads and a crackle of sticks
Jubilant and safe
In the wriggling arms of a strengthening wind

J. Watkinson

The Trekkie Widow

If your man,
Is a trekkie fan,
And you just can't,
Be like him.
Don't put up a fuss,
Let him watch if he must,
For the Enterprise
Soon will be docking.
Back down to earth he soon will come,
Then you'll have all his attention.
But I forgot
Only one more week,
And you'll be back in detention.

Betty Ward

The Penny Tray

I wish to tell you if I may about a shop with a good display
Of sweets and chocolates that look so gay,
But the kids barge in and you'll hear them say:
"Mrs. Simpson, can we have something from the Penny Tray?"

The boxes of chocs and the sweets on display are of no
Account to the kids, just the tray
Of sweets of all kinds, some large and some small
But of a variety to suit them all
Mrs Simpson, she stands there whilst they make up their minds
Which sweets to choose from the various kinds
"I'll take one of those, My, aint' they whoppers -
Oh no, not one of those, they're only gob stoppers!"

Mrs. Simpson stands waiting, her hands on the tray
And you'll hear her repeating "What do you want today?
Come on, make your minds up, I haven't all day
Get what you want, then pop off to play"

The kids get together, they push and they shove
Till she says to them "Oh, do stop it Love
Get your sweets, some chewing gum or a liquorice stick
I really don't care, so long as you're quick
But while you are choosing what sort or which kind
There's a lot of my customers waiting behind
So give me your answers, and call it a day
My arms are fair aching with holding this Tray".

Tess Whitlock

Untitled

I'm right here with you
If you look up into the sky at night
You'll see me
And I'll be watching you
Jewels of the sky
We all become one
Birds of the night
One thousand eyes
Against black satin
The biggest jewel is waiting to take us
Creeping up on us like some beautiful dream
So peaceful
Unheard by ears that don't understand.

S. Winterbourne

Time!

What is Time?
Is it yours - or is it mine?
Is it used well, or wasted?
Was love tested, or just tasted!
Did we use it well last week, last year . . .
Were we happy or did time shed a tear?
There's too much to do, to see
To live a commitment, or to be free?
Whatever the choice might be,
Time wasted is a sin.
Go out and make life win.
For Time is such a precious thing.

Jane A. Webber

Unemployed

When your luck has hit zero and you feel really down
You've no food and your giro's not due
You sit slumped in your chair with a permanent frown
It's an effort just to make a fresh brew

Your brains are in turmoil what the heck can you do
And life feels a complete waste of time
Better go to the Social and stand in the queue
If you don't you'll not get a dime

Because you are desperate you ask for a sub
But the request is answered with scorn
It's just tough if you're broke and clean out of grub
They don't care if you're sad and alone

With head bent down low against driving sleet
You cannot believe what you see
A tenner has blown just down at your feet
Off to Safeways now smiling with glee.

Elsie Watson

The Joy Of A Dream

A dream is a gift that we all possess,
It can be used very little
Or to great excess.
You can travel the world
And to places beyond,
You can stay where you are
And snooze all night long.
Age is no problem
Whether naught or till late,
A dream is a quest
Where there is no set date.
They can't all be happy
Or sweet or come true,
But there's never no harm done
And the cost,
Just to you!

C.R. Whitworth

Time Was

Time is like liquid, though measured in stone,
It's stiffening clouds interred in our bones,
The breathing of music,
The stain on the Sun, so Time runs:

Time is a light, a flame, in the dark,
Hidden in rings, in trees in the park,
Beginning again, never reaching an end
The pendulum frozen, still:

Time is what happened, when God let out breath;
Time is silenced, forever, by death,
Yet is whispered, in murmurs,
That could smash open rocks,

For time, always hunted, by mad, panting, clocks,
Is a sly and a wild and a cunning, Old Fox!

Richard Westall

Legacies
(After reading of teenage gangs)

There are indications that man was
contemporary with the latter part of the ice age

Primeval man, born in a cave squeezed courage through a block of ice;
the hacking flint that was his food, necessity, was all he had -

But boys whose present is the past curse necessity with feuds -
the last obscurity of fear streaked with a courage that is worse

And immune as angels vaunt a name, tradition seeping through the blood;
tradition, ravenous as love, straining on the thing it made

Until even the mountain in the glen sends, shivering, its ancient fame
and the name it has focused on is on these walls they call their own.

And Cain, staring down from Cain, is the last tragic hero left,
and the blind unreason of the blind twists the instinct with the mind

And sinister as hope, sustains the fatal glamour of the brave -
whose helpless girls who cannot lie stand motionless behind their eyes.

Donald Ward

Love Is All

We have been together for many years,
Sharing the sunshine laughter and tears,
Giving each other all the love from our hearts,
From day one we have never been apart,
We took our vowels on that special day,
And have been very happy in our own way,
We both have taken all in our stride,
Not letting things worry us just let them ride,
The secret is you have all, and a true companion,
It's not all high living or sparkling diamonds,
When we are old and grey and the body tired,
We can look back at all we have admired,
Things we loved to do together and share,
In love understanding, we both cared,
L   is love and laughter
O   is the orchestra playing,
V   is chapter and verse,
E   is eternity.

Teresa Walker

Alone

I hate myself
I'm all on my own
I'm lost in my own head
I want to run away
Where can I go?
I'm like a volcano
I'm going to explode
Oh, what shall I do?
I'm
ALL
CLOSED
UP!

Gemma Woodall (Age 9)

When Death Comes

Here I lay inside my box a light aside my head
The boots I wear upon my feet smell as though I'm dead.

The places I go the things I see all happen in my brain
Too much longer in this box and I shall go insane.

It's smelly it's grotty it's not where I should be
Maybe somewhere different out there alone with thee.

Two curtains drawn and dark moves in to shadow out the light
Try and try to keep awake I always lose the fight.

Under cover deep down low I try to get away
But every time I open up it's a shiny bright new day.

One day soon will be a different tale, as you shall soon discover
Because my friends the story ends with a heart wrenching shudder.

You grasp your pain only in vain as the light leaves your eyes
Your heart does stop and then you drop and lose all mortal ties.

D.S. Welburn

The Farmer

Well the truth is I'm a Farmer,
I know you say not one of those,
But I'm not a stuck up one,
I'm one that wears old clothes.

I'm the one that has no holidays
My wife says "Lets fly around"
I say "Not blooming likely girl"
I'll keep my feet on the ground.

I'm the one that gets the kids to work
And when they come for their pay
I say "I've got no money kids
But the farm will be yours one day".

I go down to the pub each night
And we have a lot of laughs
People buy me lots of pints
I pay them back with halves.

A Farmer has to be careful
In case he hits hard times
I'm worth two million on paper
But would like some cash for writing rhymes.

Charles Seymour Wheatley

Spring Breeze

The sparrow soars high above,
Breathing in the first spring breeze
Washed over land from the sea,
Moving across fields, through trees,

Lifting up a butterfly
And drawing downwards a hawk
That caught the scent of rabbits,
By a quarry full of chalk.

The surge of air keeps running
The bird's prey follows suit,
Knocking stones into the lake,
Where fish into shadows shoot.

Ripples on the flat surface;
Their maker hurries on past,
Over a farm, a town, a
City until, there, at last:

It spies its home, the ocean,
Waiting with waves open wide.
Racing now, it leaves the shore,
To play again with the tide.

Claire Watson

Confused

Lost wishes and dazed dreams
Do you know where I am
For I'm here there and everywhere
Trying not to bleed
This life and world where people are in need

Times of sorrow times of joy
Sometimes emotion is devoid
As I'm sitting here alone
Like a dog without a bone
Longing for a lady to change this heart of stone

Letting go of things unknown
Should one live with seeds already sown
If I get lost where is my guide
To rid the sorrow and show me pride
As this sea of fate
Twists and turns my heart
Would it stop me from falling apart
So I can walk tall in this brand new start

G.D. Watkins

Wild Influence

Just yesterday I strolled the heath,
some magic stirred my being.
An urgency awakened the
poet within me, bringing
words bubbling to the surface,
eloquence dictating
an eagerness to steer the pen,
in lyrical creation.

Now I mope in emptiness,
within the quiet of my dwelling,
gone the highland quickening,
the jostle and the clamouring.
My pen denied the formula,
leans starved of inspiration,
impotent without the spur,
devoid of motivation.

Tomorrow's dawning I must seek
the moorland stimulus,
tread a rough scenario,
a rugged impetus.
And breathe the vital influence,
a wild country tuition,
my hand to guide and gratify,
a literary ambition.

Ivy Wood

Silence

An Inspirational verse for those afraid to be alone

Have you ever stopped and listened to the silence and what it means
When you are sitting all alone
Time to reflect your thoughts of long ago
When your life was shared by others
Maybe it was not that perfect
But it was all you had - and all you knew
You did not think you would grow old and grey alone -
With the silence of your thoughts
But in your reflection, in your silence if you really listen to your inner self
You will know you are not alone
For God loves all his children - and are you not one of those?
So keep your silence close to the core of your very being
And God will surely share your time with you in the silence.

God Bless You

Margaret Wallis

478

Thanksgiving

Each year at the close of the harvests
Our American cousins celebrate Thanksgiving.
All over the nation families meet up
And share a great feast as a sign of achievement.

In Britain our Christmas and New Year celebrations
Nurture this theme: the importance of family.
We meet up or telephone, eager for contact,
A reaffirmation of our part in our family.

The feast of Thanksgiving is about more than the family.
It celebrates providence, hardship and effort;
Survival despite difficulty achieved through co-operation,
An acknowledgement of what a family achieves.

Each day we can celebrate as groups or individuals.
Those without families must not feel excluded.
We are totally free to celebrate our efforts
And mark those achievements we see as praiseworthy.

A spirit of Thanksgiving can bind us together,
Both families and individuals can find serenity.
Use Thanksgiving in your life to effect transformation.
And really find out what it means to be human.

Let us give thanks for the process of being,
The daily experience of hardship and kinship.
The celebration must take place deep within us,
Complete affirmation of what it means to be human.

Anne-Marie Whitwell

Requiem To Love

Anyone who loved like us that lasted all those years
Who shared so many memories, with joy and many tears
And though I loved you truly I'm not ashamed to grieve
But think of you with love and joy because I believe
You are only just a prayer away. If only I could see
God's promises, eternal life promised to you and me.
I can feel you in the blustering winds, the gentle summer rain,
I can feel you in the music which I listen to with pain.
But the knowledge of the joy it gave forever will remain.
I hear you calling in the day and near me in the night,
If only I could talk to you, but you are out of sight.
I must keep ever busy and live my life each day,
Until the Saviour calls me, until I hear him say.
Your work on earth is over, come rest with me today
And then with my beloved forever will I stay

Dorothy Webster

Willow Cottage

The cottage stood uncared for
in the glow of the evening light,
neglected rambling roses,
with pansies just out of sight.
A tumbledown old shed
with tools of a dying trade,
willow canes all strewn about
baskets lying unmade.
Wonder why the owner left
in hurried disarray
could it possibly be the things he could see
that would cause him such dismay.
For instance, the tiny little men
who watched from the shelves above
or the fluttering of gossamer wings,
watched by the cooing dove.
Just maybe, it was the the laughter of gnomes
as they sang and danced in the night
or the Fairy Queen, as she held court
now and then, soaring up in flight.
Whatever it was, there's nothing to fear
nothing to harm anyone here.
Just the sigh of the wind, in the willow trees
and whispering voices in the evening breeze.

Mairearad Wilson

Lost Love

You can take away
The photographs
Bracelets and the rings

You can leave aside
The time that lapsed
All because of things

One thing that can't
Be taken
Try! Try! as you may

The dreams and hopes
Of all the things
That should have been today

Peggy Woodley

Springtime

Melting ice from trees that seem to cry
Swollen rivers hurrying to the sea pass by
Daffodils and crocus in abundance everywhere
Lambs that skip and bleat in springtimes morning air.

Skylarks hover high in cloudless skies of blue
Oh I love spring's awakening don't you.
When trees and shrubs begin to bloom.
To lift sad face of winter's gloom

The scent of spring so fills my head
And hedgehogs appear from leafy bed
Birds chorus now is singing loud
For winter's lost its shivery shroud.

R. Willis

Love Your Neighbour

Man still abuses this globe, although God gave
His precious son Jesus, the world to save.
Greediness has besmirched His lovely creation.
Countryside desecrated by filthy pollution,
Population explosion, and sad war-orphaned children;
Religions forgotten, nations no longer brethren.
Sex, a true confirmation of real devotion;
Its sleazy side without love's deep emotion
Leads to abuse, rape, murder and violence.
Such occurences must never be treated with tolerance.
Love is friendship, neighbourliness and fun
In a lovely world of snow, rain and sun.
Watch the glowing faces of a couple in love
As they stroll arm-in-arm along a beautiful cove,
A mother's smile when she holds her new-born child,
And Man's love for animals, domestic and wild.
The little deeds of unrequested aid
To others who are sad, lonely or afraid,
Shine out like a diamond in God's heavenly crown
Which makes Him reluctant all us sinners to disown.
Forgive us, Dear Lord, our many sins, we pray
And give us yet another lovely day,

On this Planet called Earth

Annette E. Weston

A Longing For Peace

"The Bastards have done it again",
Was the cry yelled out that night,
A phone call and a speeding car
That sped right out of sight
The message was, "A bomb somewhere"
But where? Nobody knows
We've got to find that evil thing
We must before it blows
Suddenly a blast is heard,
The stillness of the night is blurred,
"A house has gone", was that fateful cry,
For some poor innocent souls,
No life! No love! No dreams!
Only to die.

John Webb

That Humour

That humour
born of desperation
and sustained by boredom
served us well.
Not laughing really,
we choked on drops of acid.
It was not mirth that shook our frames
but the cold, dry wind
blown from an emptiness inside of us
that is otherwise expressed
by a scream.

Gareth Williams

481

Dowdy Dressing Gowns

There you were this picture of desire
Dressed to kill
Made up to the nines
I as a moth to a flame
Powerless

Unusually you took to me
And we went to your place
For some hanky panky
And a cup of tea

Still to this day I cannot understand
Why the most glamourous of women
Back in their nest with a new man
Who for all they know
Just might
Be Mr. Right
Or even if it is just a one-night stand
Thrust their feet into scruffy old slippers
And wrap themselves around
In dowdy dressing gowns

David Michael Walsh

My Birth

At last I've escaped the
dreaded womb.
Where for the last nine
months I've been entombed.
I wrestled and stretched
and strutted my stuff, but
there comes a time when
enough is enough!!!

But don't think I'm coming
out head first, boy oh boy
I'm in reverse.
Now I'm here to scream and
shout, bet you're sorry you
let me out!!!!

Gillan Worth

Christmas Book

I have a list of folks I know all written in a book
And every year when Christmas comes, I go and take a look
And that is when I realise that these names are all a part,
Not of the book they are written in but of our very hearts.
For each name stands for someone who has crossed my path sometime
And in the meeting they've become the rhythm in the rhyme
And while it sounds fantastic for me to make this claim
I really feel that I'm composed of each remembered name
And while you may not be aware of each remembered link
Just meeting you has changed my life a lot more than you think.
For once I've met somebody the years cannot erase
The memory of a pleasant word or a friendly face.
So never think my Christmas cards are just a mere routine
Of names upon a Christmas list forgotten in between,
For when I send a Christmas card that is addressed to you
Its 'cause you're on the list of folks that I'm indebted to
And every year when Christmas comes I realise anew
A great gift life can offer is meeting folks like you.
So may the Christmas spirit that ever more endures
Leave the richest blessing in the hearts of you my friend and yours.

Lucy Florence Woodhouse

Exams

What's happening to me, I'm trapped and cannot explain,
I'm panicking inside, and feeling insane.
I've got to hide, a corner I must find,
Can't rid this pain overtaking my mind.

Demons dodging, chanting and screaming,
No concentration, stomach heaving,
Hopelessly tired, knotted and sick,
Got to calm down and restore my wits.

Overcome I can, and will follow my dream,
And cut through the nerve always hindering me.

I'm really very strong, and talented I know,
Gifted in music, just too shy to show.

I enjoy my guitar, love it so much,
It fills up my heart, and keeps me in touch,
With all aspects of life, its qualities fulfilling,
It's fun, exciting, dynamic and soothing,
It enhances the highs, and lessens the lows,
And can always be relied on, to help moods unfold.

I will face my problem, and believe in myself,
And answer my own plea, cry to no one for help.

My sense of humour I've got to revive,
I know it's the key, that will help me to ride,
The exam performance I have got to get through,
And give it my all, and to me it will prove.

Loraine Woodward

Space

I set off in the sky,
It was so high,
Lots of shooting stars,
Shooting at me.

Bang! A space ship landed,
Out popped an alien,
I felt so scared,
There were lots of different planets.

On my way back,
I went to Mars,
It was a bit cold,
I felt unhappy living in space,
When I got home I felt SICK!

Stacey Wolsey (Age 10)

No Strings Attached

Family is a spiritual, cultural parachute -
a high flying banner of fabric
suspending me in my descent to the grave

Cutting the strings makes me free to be me
but I would lose sight of all
that makes me what I am

Dirty linen, exotic silk . . .
some handle easier than others
in the wind

I must respect the fabric of my family
in spite of imperfections
or
suffer indignity
the humiliationo
of a dead-weight mangled parachute
dragging me down.

April Wood

When Times Are Hard . . . .

When times are hard and friends are scarce
When everything seems wrong
When moods are dark and smiles are few
When days and nights are long
When hearts are sore and heads unclear
When souls are in distress
When dark clouds threaten, stars don't shine
And everything's a mess
When tears are shed and hands are wrung
When feelings run too high
When colours fade, when all is grey
When all you do is cry
When questions seem unending
But answers never come
When minds and senses scream aloud
But hearts and souls are numb
When nothing that means anything will ever be the same
I know that help is always there
I simply call Your name

Anne Wright

The Eight-Fifteen

At first I thought it might be a bird,
Then I saw it was only a lonely feather or
Two, down by the railway-line. I paused, I
Saw two minute feet clinging to murky metalwork.
Dead - I suppose - I hope, I said as I made
Out a pale, abandoned beak. But
One foot stuck at a gripping angle,
Oh dear! and was that pale beak
Raising itself to the gentle rain to wash
Its parched throat - such a slow
Movement of its head I still thought, hoped
It was dead and yet, the rain washed
Clear a dusty eye - perhaps its prayer
Would deserve reply.
From the bank I heard a blackbird cry
And again the head, slowly nodded, the beak
Too parched to speak, please, it mimed,
I'm here, it seemed to say -
        Only the train came and
        Shook its life away.

Robert Wynn-Davies

Ugh

I don't know what's happening to me
Can't believe how things seem to be
Growing up, is that what it's called?
I'm cracking up, that's all.

I don't find kids TV funny anymore
I read books and stare at the floor
I want to wake up early every day
I want to throw my toys away.

I don't know what's happening to me
I watch all the adverts I see
Growing up, is that what it's called?
That's getting crippled and bald.

I want the posters down off my wall
I want to read poetry, not play ball
I watch documentaries on TV
What the hell is happening to me?

I want to have baths and early nights
I want to eat healthy so my skin gets nice
I want to get everything cleared away
Kids TV wasn't funny today.
Kids TV wasn't funny today . . .

Donna Wright

The Masterpiece

The great canvas of the sky
Painted by a hand unseen
Memorable in its beauty,
Azure blue summer sky,
Billowing frothy clouds
Dance in a frenzy of
Whirling pirouettes
Like whipped cream upon a
Strawberry trifle,
Ever changing as seasons pass,
Stormy grey,
Wildly exaggerated
Glorious in its magnificence,
Sunsets that set the sky afire
Clouds caught up in the inferno
Dance wildly across the canvas stage,
Gently yielding to the velvety night,
Where a thousand myriad lanterns
Hang suspended like precious
Sparkling diamonds
O'er the firmament,
A feast of optical delight,
What hand could have
Fashioned such a masterpiece.

Yvonne Wright

Caught Live

Think of the slow music.
Gradually waning yet winding,
Like a disappearing mound.
The end pulls all in; the banter begins.

As blackness departs, like a quick dawn,
The energetic lights nag the brain.
Pressure pushing into the arena,
Waiting for several explosions.

Flowing further into the set,
The river widening, gathering more speed.
Brightness reaches all pockets,
Seats feel weight release.

Off. Darkness descends again.
Appreciative sounds echo, permeating wide walls.
Sudden flash. Deflecting, appearing to all,
Ten-thousand faces.

Christopher J. Wogan

Just Memories

Though years may leave them poor in health
In other ways there's so much wealth,
The memories of the years gone by,
Sometimes a laugh, perhaps a cry.

A photograph can bring such joy
Look! That's our Jimmy when a boy
And that ones me on that river cruise,
My long black dress and low heeled shoes.

Things moved slowly in those days
Yet so much happier in many ways,
Patience and love was the family scene
Today, alas, it's just a dream.

With neighbours there in times of strain
There were no thoughts of personal gain
Trust, was always to the fore
It's all gone now, for evermore.

R.J. Woodward

Choral Bells

Ten thousand snowdrops small and bright
Spread a carpet gleaming white.
Glistening in the morning glow;
They paint the wood, as driven snow.
Choral bells on slender stem
Tremble, like the slim Aspen;
Nodding in the chilly breeze
That sallies through the gaps in trees.
Joy and cheer to all they bring
With fragrant whisperings of Spring.
Each year are picked these tiny flowers,
From their peaceful wooded bowers;
Bunched and wrapped in ivy vine;
Bound together with garden twine;
Then laid with care in full display,
Loving gifts for Mother's Day!
This tender flower, in graceful ease
Will always bloom beneath the trees -
Till folk of future time decide
To build a road through woodland ride!

Patricia Woodley

Blindness!!!

Keeper of my "constant" night,
Expose the "manhole" of life's light,
That I may become replete of this lovely day!!

Spin worlds "kaleidoscopic" Joseph's coat someone -
Making patterns of delight!!

Gain strength "twilight" eyes,
That I may see the "sequinned" play . . . .
As soft winds jostle tired leaves,
And nods praying heads of pregnant grain!!

Or on this day I may laugh at the fireball grimace
As dirty sheep-clouds trespass on his domain!!

To have sweet child plait me a headband of flowers
I've only known by smell,
Or rose-buds kissed with dew!!

Keeper of my "constant" night . . . .
Expose the "manhole" of life's light . . . .

That I, may blossom too!!

Thomas A. Woodley

A Wry Comment On Democracy Today?

We learn in school that when we vote, it's such a simple task,
We put a cross against the bloke, who does all that we ask.
One man one vote, that is the way, for a government that's fair,
To rule the roost, and have a say, for people everywhere.

That is, of course, if things go right, and everything is equal.
Sadly we're in sorry plight, a poor misguided people
A mandate is being given out, to those whose cause is muted
OF THE PEOPLE? there's no doubt, once their VOTES are counted.

BY THE PEOPLE? there's the rub, because we're ruled by Party
The one that wins is at the hub, of all that's clean (or dirty)
FOR THE PEOPLE? then tell me why, and who, we think we're kidding
As, palms outstretched, our rulers vie, for shares in the highest bidding.

F.J. Wrighton

Family Love

I dearly loved my Mum and Dad
And think of all the fun I had
With sister Audrey and sister Joan
There was lots of love within our home.

My dear old gran, we all called "Nan"
Was always there to hold our hand
And Mum was there to cook our food
Such tasty dishes and oh so good.

I left all this in my late 'teens
Something happened which changed the scene
A war arose and I went to sea
How sad it was that this had to be

Many times I thought of home
As on treacherous seas I had to roam
But peace arrived and home I came
To my family's love - yes once again.

J.Thomas Wright

Life's Enigma

Everyone who's been born must die.
Like everyone, I wonder why.
Some believe they're born again
They know not how or where or when.
Some believe God calls them home
Never more to grieve or mourn,
Where love and happiness abound
And only joy and peace are found.
Some believe there is a hell
Where the really bad must dwell.
Some believe this is the end
No more of you and me, my friend.
I do not know I cannot tell
Which I think is just as well.
The answer we must wait to find
When we leave this world behind.

Gladys E. Yates

487

Interlude

There are boundaries that border any storm
Lines existing where the rain
Does not dissolve
But hangs like a lace curtain

I found one once in late spring
Along a country lane
One side of the road bone dry
The other pouring rain
Cascading . . . . .
And me dancing on the edge
Like a latter-day Gene Kelly
Or a young mans eye
On the hemline of a dress
So tangible . . . . . .
Like that sudden summer rain in the playground
That kicked up asphalt dust
So dry you could taste it
Like the graphite flavour
Of those long redundant ink wells

Paul Wood

Bullying

Oh! sir it was only a joke,
I only gave that fat lad a poke.
You girl why do you stare,
All I did was pull your hair.
Let's get him he's on his break,
See how much punching he'll take.
Squeeze his arm make him yell,
It's okay he won't tell.
Oh! look at him his face looks funny,
Come on let's see if he's got any money.
I do have teachers who really care,
But try and tell them if you dare.
I know I'll get it the following day,
In the toilets or playground they'll make me pay.
Why are people so cruel and unkind,
I know it's not something in my mind.
I may be different in shape or size,
Or frizzy hair and different eyes.
But we have feelings that still count,
So think next time before you hit out.

Linda Woodhouse

488

Dad

Introduce catheter to urethra.
Idiosyncratic oxygen cylinders,
Like those second-hand Singers and Morris Cowleys
Before the war.

Medicines,
Names contents instructions for use
In English.

Nurses white male yes
Nurses black female no
Concerning these things.

Shuffle cut deal a request of cards
Back to younger days,
But she declines his invitation.

Sense now the moment when
Distance between him and his lemon drink
Has become a bridge too far.

Fear in bright bright eyes.
Last handshake firm.
Last debtor's gasp: give me some money.
What did money really mean to him?

Journey's end is domestic hallway.
Dressing-gown and slippers remains.
Sudden sobbing of a mother's boy,
Boy's wife responding: yes yes.

Peter Wybrew

New Life

What are you feeling as you sway in the breeze
Are you glad of the raindrops now falling with ease
Are you tired after fighting your way to that height
Are your arms feeling heavy and knowing their plight
Will you sigh as your burden gets blown by the storm
Out of your arms to help newness to form
A rest for the winter, a time to rejoice
A conserving of life's forces, a need to give voice
To burst forth with newness, a fountains fine spray
Freshness and joyful, gone all feelings of dismay.

June Woodward Martin

Ode To A Teenage Daughter

Oh daughter of mine, you're so many things
On a good day, an angel with wings.
A mother's help, my very best friend,
Oh! mum I'm broke, have you a fiver to lend.

Those tete-a-tete's at night on my bed.
When all your worries, you know, can be said,
I'm much too fat, I don't like my hair.
Why can't I find a nice boy anywhere?

Then there are the days when you grow horns.
Never a less fortunate girl has been born.
Your mum doesn't care, she hasn't a clue
Can't tidy my room, I've got things to do.

Your music's too loud and so are your clothes,
You look like a tart, in make up that glows.
Your skirt is too short your hair is too long,
Go back twenty years, that's my mother's song.

We have our ups, then we come down.
I love you when you smile or when you frown.
I'll always be there, whatever you do,
Because I'm your mum and your best friend too.

Janice Wright

Captive Heart

Capture my body and see if it bleeds;
Capture my history, capture my blood,
Capture my essence for the great and the good.

Keep me confined for longer than death,
Just tell the world of my final breath.
Capture my soul - lie if you must,
Watch as my image fades into dust.

You may take my freedom, you may take my name,
You may take my sanity but you MUST take the blame.
You may take the strength that keeps me alive,
You may take the love that helps me survive.
You may take my hearing, my sight and my touch,
You may take all the memories I treasure so much.
But when all the hills have turned ashen with doubt,
You will have taken everything except my heart.

Brian Wood

A Lost Soul

A poor old man in tattered clothes,
Walks aimlessly down the street.
People stare at him and say things like -
"He hasn't any shoes on his feet!"
But wait,
Hold on!
Have you ever considered that what you
Are doing is wrong!
He has a heart, he has two ears, two eyes,
He feels!
So he may not be handsome!
He may not be clean!
But he is still a person like you and me!
Apart from the fact he has no home,
No-one to turn to when he's alone,
A poor old man with an unclean face,
Trying to keep up with the world and its pace,
So next time please don't judge him,
By the way he looks or how he lives
He is a person like you and me and like everybody is in this world,
They deserve to be treated equally!

J.S. Young (Age 15)

Ghostly

Midnight has stuck and silence fills the air,
Those who stay in this place should beware,
I slowly appear through the wall,
And rattle keys in doors as I walk along the hall,
My long white shroud drags along the ground,
As I wail and let out my awesome sound,
My face is ugly, pale, and white,
And I haunt all through this place at night,
Many have come and done their best,
To put my tormented spirit down to rest,
But those who have looked upon my face,
Screamed out loud and fled from this place,
For hundreds of years I have walked,
Through these halls and corridors,
Passed through the walls and doors,
I have moaned and groaned,
As through this place I have roamed,
I have frightened people out of their wits,
Blew out candles and smashed things to bits,
But always comes the breaking of the dawn,
When I shall once more disappear back through the wall.

Allan John Young

My Inheritance

I have treasures within my heart I hold,
They sparkle like diamonds and glisten like the gold,
For they are priceless memories of the ones I have loved so dear,
Safely stored inside me to keep them always near,
They are the gifts my loved ones have bequeathed to me,
No richer inheritance could there ever be,
These wonderful memories spread over so many years,
The happiness we shared as well as times of tears,
Oh so many times I go down that memory lane,
Wishing they were still here, so we could have those happy times again,
When we were all together so much we took for granted.
Never did we realise each day a memory seed we planted.

Ruth Zardecki

The Angler's Wish

An old and tired fisherman lay dying in his bed
Surrounded by his family wet cheeked with eyes of red
"Do not grieve or weep for me" the man to them did say
"I've lived my life, I've loved, I've laughed, I've watched the break of day
You've filled my days with pleasure and life's been good to me
I've watched you grow from childhood my spirit lives in thee
My time is short before I go please heed my final wish
That you scatter please my ashes at the river where I fish
Then if you need to speak with me you'll know where I'll reside
At peace beside the river in beloved countryside"
With that the old man closed his eyes and very gently died
I'll swear he was already there down by the riverside

Leonard Young

My Blessing To All

May there be hope closely beside you
Walking your way in the path of the year
May there be kindness to carry the lantern
While faith lights your weary footsteps
In the ways that you fear
Zest for your leisure and joy for your spirit
Mornings of fragrance and twilight of peace
And what the year robs you of time youth and beauty
May it refund you in sweet joys and peace

E.M. Young

The Death Of Mrs Beeton

The clever lady editress came fourth time to childbed.
Her first two sons no longer lived; they had already fled.
A friendless, year-old, third-born boy alone remained alive;
It was the end of January in eighteen sixty-five.

The dear lady and her husband had wished this child to be
A play-mate for their third-born child; a lonely boy was he.
The magazines; the recipes; the patterns for a dress;
Now for a time were set aside for family happiness.

A boy was born: the mother well, at first presumed to be.
But on the day that followed a high temperature had she.
Puerperal fever claimed her: she succumbed within a week.
Her inconsolable husband in vain his wife did seek.

She lay in bed untouched, one hand upon the coverlet.
She seemed as real as life itself, yet free of all its fret.
Closing the door he took her hand, her slender fingers counted:
Each gentle squeeze past times awoke; and so his sadness mounted.

He stood beside her inert form, his future now uncertain.
Across the glad years of their love her death had drawn a curtain.
What of the problems in their business, without her at his side?
What of the ladies' publications, without her hand to guide?

That lifeless, chilly hand he held. He gently placed it on the bed.
Her hand has lost its cunning, came the thought within his head.
Gifted editorial partner, loyal to the very end of life;
Usque ad finem, he wrote, in final tribute to his wife.

Brian Young

False Suicidal Thoughts

I don't want to die thinking about you
It wouldn't work.
I would have to say that you still bothered me.
In the very moment before I hit the rocks,
I still need you.

I am on this cliff now most of the time
Waiting for that instant second.
Waiting and waiting.

Maybe jumping will be better tomorrow.

Paul Yussarian

BIOGRAPHIES
OF
POETS

ADAMS, OLIVE NEWTON: [b] 21/7/1920 Durham; [p] Frederick & Elizabeth Fatkin; [m] Married; [ch] Malcolm and Alan; [ed] Grammar School; [occ] Retired Civil Servant; [activ] I write and perform mostly humourous monologues and sketches to entertain at over 60's clubs, nursing and residential homes as a member of a group "The Starlight Entertainers". We got together at the "Age Concern" centre in Newcastle, MEA House; [pub writ] Two poems. I have only previously entered three competitions; "In a life of the usual ups and downs I have found that laughter really is the finest medicine. The warm handclasp of a lonely or sick old person to whose face you have brought a smile is a rich and rewarding experience, the greatest antidote to worrying about oneself."

ALEXANDER, MONTY: [b] 30/5/43 Lisburn, Northern Ireland; [p] Hugh & Agnes Alexander; [m] Married to Elizabeth Verner; [ch] Claire, Ruth, Stuart, Catherine & Phillip; [ed] Purdys Burn Village School, Botanic Primary School and Orange's Academy, Belfast; [pub writ] Sunlight & Shadows 1995, Passages of Time 1996, Church Gazettes etc.; "Paint a picture in words for the blind to see."

ANDERSON, AUDREY V.: [b] 12/09/39 Harrogate; [p] Gilbert & Doris James; [m] Married 1959 to Roy Anderson; [ch] Michael J. Anderson & Julie V. Darley; [ed] King James Grammar School, Knaresborough, N. Yorks 1950-1955; [occ] Retired Building Society Customer Services Asst.; "It has given me great pleasure, over the past forty years, writing poems and letters for my family and friends. Whatever the occasion, good or bad, happy or sad they have been written from the heart, Following in the footsteps of my late paternal grandmother."

ARMES, ANDREW: [b] 06/05/73 Reading; [p] Roy & Wilhelmina; [m] Single; [ed] Yateley

Comp. Warwick University, Warwick Business School; [occ] Manager; [awards] Psychology Degree, Business Masters. University rowing champion coxless pairs; [activ] Young Enterprise Volunteer; "Never take life too seriously and discover what is most important to you as soon as you can. I believe in being healthy in body and mind and always being able to laugh, especially at yourself."

ASHA-AKRAM, NOREEN: [b] 24/10/82 Huddersfield; [p] Akram & Zubida; [ed] Birkby Infants, Birkby Juniors and Fartown High, Huddersfield; "I like to express myself in my poetry. I have found that by using your imagination we can create any atmosphere or feeling we desire!!"

ASHBY, JENNIFER: [b] 18/07/57 Surrey; [p] Edred & Moira Tims; [m] Married 1984 to Paul; [ch] Katherine, Stephanie & Gregory; [ed] Howard of Effingham Co. Sec. School, Exeter University; [occ] Housewife; [awards] BA Hons. Degree in Geography; [activ] Chair of local Playschool, on Village Hall Committee, Sunday School Teacher; "I have been writing poems since I was 7, mostly on landscape or wistful themes. I haven't written much lately, however, as I'm busy with 3 children and various aspects of village life (I've been Chair of a playgroup twice)."

AYLAND, JOYCE: [b] 05/07/41 London; [m] Married; [ch] Jill, Tony, Brian, Bobby & Mark; [ed] Secondary Modern; [occ] School Escort; [awards] Medal for Disabled Sports events. Diploma for creative writing; [activ] Basingstoke Baptist Church; [pub writ] Poems in local paper, about 12 a year. Poems published in 8 books in a year; "I like to write about every day situations, the third world, funny things, in fact anything to cheer people up and give people encouragement in my poems."

BAILEY, JACQUELINE MARIE: [b] 08/07/64 Leicestershire; [p] Allen & Annette Ridgway; [m] Married; [ch] Emma & Edward; [ed] Local Colleges and Further Education Colleges; [occ] Civil Servant; [awards] Award in computing and sports. Poetry Award of Excellence; [pub writ] Wrote dance show pieces, 3 poems published now!; "I love to be creative and enjoy writing and painting, it gives me and my family a lot of pleasure. I love the great outdoors enjoying walking, cycling, caravaning and sports. I find inspiration everywhere in life's unpredictable web of fortune and while out and about exploring, I never go anywhere without my pad in hand for writing or sketching. This poem I dedicate to my family for all the great seaside holidays we have had together and the many we have to come. My heart is at the seaside I love the sea and its shores, this poem represents the humourous sides of the seaside holiday."

BARR, JEAN: [b] 08/09/48 Hull; [p] Dora & Arthur (Dec'd) Hirons; [m] Married to Reginald in 1993; [ch] Carl, Michelle, Clare, Kirsty, Richard and Toni; [ed] Villa Place Junior, Bean Street, Flinton High School For Girls; [occ] Carer for Disabled Husband; [pub writ] One certificate from International Library of Poetry for outstanding achievement; [pub writ] "Memories Down The Road", "Football", "To The Bone"; "I was born on Hessle Road into a very large family. Times were very hard, we were considered poor, but that has never been a handicap for me. It's inspired me."

BECKETT, SHIRLEY M. TEMPLE: [b] 16/06/37 Widnes, Cheshire; [p] Thomas Temple & Lilian Bradshaw; [m] Divorced; [ch] Keith, David, & Wayne; [ed] Saint Beads Junior School, Fairfield Secondary School, Widnes; [occ] Artist, Poet, Voluntary Work; [awards] Top of Art Class for four years.Window Dresser, Department Store, age 16. Trained Butcheress at 15, Grocery Co-Op at 17. Won BBC "Names The Same" 1954; [pub writ] Ten poems in books, three publishers, four in local paper; "To have my own book of poems. I've written 100 in the past few years. It's a gift. I've done poetry readings, I did not realise how much my poems meant to people who are stressed, they stop me in the street telling me they often read them. Knowing how much they, apart from friends and family appreciate my work makes the effort to keep writing worthwhile."

BERRIE, DAVID THOMAS: [b] 07/08/89 Gravesend; [p] Janet and Thomas Berrie; [ed] St. Joseph's R.C. School, Northfleet, Kent; [activ] Boys Brigade Member; "I enjoy writing words down. I want to be a palaeontologist, poet and author when I'm older. I've written several poems for fun already."

BETH: [b] 17/11/51 Horsforth, Leeds; [m] Married to Ken; [ch] Helen & Hannah; [ed] Aireborough Grammar School and Pudsey Technical College; [occ] Housewife; [awards] Recently completed training as a reader in the C. of E.; [activ] Member of All Saints Church Otley; [pub writ] Various poems published in anthologies in the past 12 months, plus short articles in Church magazine; "Being a Christian is central to all that I am and do and this is reflected in my writing. I enjoy expressing myself and my thoughts on life through my poetry. Being published is a bonus!"

BILLINGHAM, TONY RAYMOND: [b] 19/12/35 Pleck, Walsall; [p] Fredrick & Elsie Billingham; [m] Married to Evelyn Billingham 1955; [ch] Julie, Mark, Paul & Steven; [occ] Caretaker, Chuckery T.M.C. Walsall;

BINKS, JANE MARIE: [b] 26/12/70 Hull; [p] R.A. Binks & Mrs. M.T. Aspin; [m] Single; [ed] Mersey Junior School, Hull, David Lister High, Hull, Andrew Marvell Sixth Form, Hull; [occ] Accommodation Resource Officer; [awards] QARANC (Queen Alexandra's Royal Army Nursing Corps) completed 3yr training, exemplary grade; [activ] Queen's Silver Jubilee Trust; "I have learned that 'Life is not a rehearsal' (finally at 26 yrs) and any experiences good or bad should be seen as guidance in moving forward in life. Life is a great test of strength and character this I know for definite."

BIRD, ANN LAVINIA: (Pen Name Remus Poll) [b] 05/30 Chorlton-Cum-Hardy; [m] Married Derek 1954; [ch] Carole, Alan and David, Grandchildren James & Samantha; [occ] Retired; [career] Textile Design, General Nursing; [pub writ] Support letters to newspapers!; "Keeping a joyful attitude to life, while trying in my small way to help people suffering the injustices which life brings to many."

BLACKBURN, DEBBIE: [b] 20/10/70 Hull; [p] Andrew & Eileen Munn; [m] Married to Andy in 1992; [ch] Danielle Alicia aged 3 and Isaac Jacob aged 2; [ed] Greatfield High School; [occ] Housewife and mother; [awards] Childcare, floristry, retailing and first aid and dancing awards, and City & Guilds Certificates; [activ] Blood donor, Great Ormand Street Hospitals (Tooth Fairy), Hull's New Theatre, cinema and fine wine and good food are favourites of mine; [pub writ] Poetry in local newspapers; "Take every day as it comes and make it a good one, you don't know what you've got till it's gone. I like people to take me as I am or not at all, I'd like to dedicate my poem to my children, my mum, my husband and Joanne Smith who sadly died of leukemia."

BLACKWELL, DAVE: [b] 08/03/77 Dartford; [m] Single; [ed] Nwk College of Technology, Performing Arts. Work Experience Programmer; (occ) Trainee Programmer; [awards] BTEC National Diploma in Performing Arts; [activ] Weight Training, Programming (Computer), Writing and Acting; [pub writ] Five poems published, one with a magazine and four in individual books; "I dedicate this to those who pushed me and believed in my poetry."

BLOW, GARY: [b] 24/10/72 Derby; [p] Mari & David Blow; [m] Single; [ed] St. Hughs C of E; [occ] Presenter/Entertainer; [awards] Certificate of Merit for my work in The Channel 4 Documentary "Seasiders"; [pub writ] Currently writing an autobiography on the life of a self made entertainer; "Too many people have an opinion on how you should run your life, but I feel as long as I can find a right blend of happiness in work, love and home, I will always be happy. As my late Grandad once told me "Never grow old with regrets!" He didn't, neither will I."

BOZZONI, BEVERLEY: [b] 13/02/57 Leicestershire; [p] John Smith & Dorothy Crutchley; [m] Married; [ch] Sadie, Lindsey, Craig, Shaun & Marc-Ross; [ed] Lutterworth Grammar School; [occ] Housewife; "I wrote poetry for my own pleasure until my family encouraged me to enter this poetry competition."

BRADFORD, MARY: [b] 20/01/50 Cirencester; [p] Arthur & Rosamond Rimes; [m] Divorced; [ch] Carl; [ed] Chipping Norton Comprehensive; [occ] Reflexologist; [awards] M.B.R.A. (Reflexology) N.L.P. (Neuro-Linguistic Programming); [pub writ] This is the first; "I feel that the most important objective in life is to discover and come to terms with our unique selves. Writing is my way of achieving that."

BRADLEY, TRACY: [b] 10/01/78 Dartford; [p] Philip & Joan Bradley; [m] Single; [ed] Dartford West High School for Girls; [occ] Clerical Officer; [awards] NVQ 2 Travel & Tourism. Netball Trophys. I won an award for outstanding sales when I worked for Going Places Travel Agency; [activ] Play for a local netball team; "This is a dream come true to have one of my poems published - but this is not for me - it is for my Grandad, Ronald William

Foster. His memory is for ever in my heart."

BRIDGEMAN, J.H.: [b] 16/07/15 Twenty; [p] John William & Rose Ann; [m] Widowed; [ch] John Edmund Noel & Shirley Rosemary; [ed] Bourne Fen Elementary, left school at age 13½ years and worked on a farm; [occ] Retired; [occ] Head Herdsman, won many prizes at Royal Show; [activ] Member of Bourne Urban Council 9 years. Mayor of Bourne 1952-1953. (Age Concern Trustee Bourne Butterfield Centre); [pub writ] "The Last Smile", "When I Was A Boy" and "Old Age"; "I started writing poetry after my wife died in 1992. It was a gift from God which my wife's death revealed. My first poem "That Last Smile" was given to me by my wife just before she died."

BRIGGS, EILEEN: [b] 13/08/35 Bracknell; [p] Winifred & Leslie Langley; [m] Married; [ch] Julie & Philip; [ed] Bullbrook C. of E. School; [occ] Secretary/Housewife; [activ] Holy Trinity Church Charity Work; [pub writ] Local paper and magazines; "Poems are about life. Happy times and sad times."

BROWNBILL, JEAN: [b] 12/08/38 St. Helens; [p] Edna & George Dixon; [m] Married; [ch] Michelle, Colette, Tracy, Steven, David & Gregory; [ed] Whistow High, British & European College of Preventative Medicine; [occ] Masseuse; [awards] Diplomas in Anatomy, Physiology and Therapeutic Massage also Reike Master; [activ] Volunteer Healer at Healing Centre in Chester; [pub writ] Even though I have been writing poems for years I have never submitted anything for publication before; "Writing is therapeutic for me. I pour out all my feelings in my poems and find I'm a much calmer and more tolerant person as a result."

CANNABY, CHRIS: [b] 24/05/80 Coventry; [p] Sue & Keith; [m] Single; [ed] Twycross House School where I am taking English, Biology and Geography at "A" Level; "I have found that as long as one treats life like a game, one can survive. Any hint at seriousness can result in a serious illness."

CARPENTER, ROGER: 04/01/54 Cambridge; [p] Peggy & Terry; [m] Divorced; [ch] Daniel & Amy; [ed] Secondary Modern, GCSE in English Language, English Literature and Art; [activ] Voluntary work for Oxfam Member of R.S.P.C.A.; [pub writ] Several poems in various publications; "I began writing poetry seriously while in prison. Mostly on the subject of my own personal experiences i.e. lost love marriage breakdown, no access to my children. I find it therapeutic and a release for pent up emotions!"

CHALONER, JUDITH ELIZABETH: [b] 12/12/52 Heswall; [p] Edith & Arthur Chrimes; [m] Single; [ed] Pensby Secondary School; [occ] Receptionist; [activ] Clwyd Badger Group; "Dedicated to my parents Edie & Arthur sadly missed. Special thanks to Bill & Jean Edge (Cilcain) for their love and support, also my dear cousin Carol Hill (Yorkshire)."

CHARLTON, LYNNE: [b] 02/06/50 Ilkeston; [m] Married; [ed] Michael House School; [occ] Housewife; [awards] Swimming certificates including Life Savers Badge 3. Poetic awards, 1 Eistedfod Certificate; [activ] Member of 5 fan clubs and Hilltop Assemblies of God Church; [pub writ] 10 poems. Write ups in 2 fan club magazines and mentioned in D.C.F. letter; "I like giving friends and the public something to read, for their enjoyment and to give much pleasure to many people."

CHEERS, NATALIE: [b] 10/02/84 Liverpool; [p] Kath & John Cheers; [ed] Student in year 8 at Woolston High School Warrington; [pub writ] Book and film reviews and short articles in local and children's newspapers; "I believe that poetry is more than creative writing. It is a powerful connection between reality and fantasy and a strong method of self-expression."

CLARE, JEFFREY JOSEPH: [b] 17/05/38 Walsall; [p] Frances Ann & Frank; [m] Married; [ch] David, Philip & Stephen; [ed] Secondary Modern; [occ] Crane Driver; [pub writ] "The Beauty of Belief Beloved", "The River" and "Thoughts of God Mother"; "I try to make my poetry picture all aspects of life, and take great pleasure in being able to transfer my thoughts to verse and perhaps by doing so bring enjoyment to other people."

CLARK, JOAN: 21/08/24 Liverpool; [p] Frank & Olive Leeson (Dec'd); [m] Widow; [ch] David, Lucinda, Paul & Joanne; [ed] Convent Grammar School; [occ] Retired; [awards] SRN & Health Visitor; [activ] Life Membership - International Society of Poets; [pub writ] "The Brooch" - A Historical Romance. My pen name "Evelyn Sefton". 10 poems in anthologies; "In my retirement, at last I have time to express my feelings in poems and stories. I feel honoured to have some in print."

CLARKE, TOM: [b] 25/09/50 Wath-Upon-Dearne; [p] Sheila & Thomas; [m] Single; [ed] 3 Years at The Royal Academy of Music, London (1968-71). One year at Manchester Teacher Training College (1971-72); [occ] Musical Director; [awards] Associate of The Royal Academy Of Music (A.R.A.M.) 1993. [activ] Member of The Royal Society Of Musicians of Great Britain; [pub writ] Piano pieces of children's musicals; "Poetry is about the decline of the countryside and man's relationship with God, the soul and nature."

CLEGG, MARGARET: 14/02/26 Garstang; [p] James & Dora Carter; [m] Married [ch] Janice & Martin;[ed] Left School at 14 years . Pilling Church of England School; [occ] Retired; [awards] Member of Lancashire Federation of Women's Institutes; [activ] Member of the Mother's Union And W.I.; [pub writ] Poem in Church magazine; "If someone hasn't a smile, give them one of yours."

COCKERTON-AIRY, SUSAN: [b] 13/01/59 Nairobi/Kenya; [p] Michael & Jennifer; [m] Married Paul 1994; [ch] Bunny; [ed] St. Andrews, Turi, Kenya, Hatherop Castle School, Glos.; [occ] Picture Restorer; [awards] 2 Italian Government Scholarships to study restoration in Italy. Included on the conservation register of the Museums and Galleries Commission; [activ] Christian. Member of the Tots Club, Long Compton, with Bunny; "Painting is the Queen of the Arts, but poetry is the music of the soul."

COGHER-ADAMS, KAREN: [b] 05/10/62 Newton Abbot, Devon; [p] Michael & Anna-Marie Cogher; [m] Married; [ch] Georgina & Francesca; [ed] Grammar School; [occ] Housewife & Mother; [awards] Diploma in Counselling Skills. Typing Skills; [pub writ] "Suffering Apple" Anchor Books; "The pen is mightier than the sword! I find writing poetry a fantastic outlet also reading the bible and learning about Jehova God's wonderful promises."

CORRY, S.: 30/11/69 Weston-Super-Mare; [m] Single; [occ] Self-Employed; [activ] National Trust; [pub writ] This is my second poem to be published; "My only ambition in life is to be happy and writing poetry helps me achieve this."

COULSON, FRANCES: 28/05/60 Glasgow; [p] John & Agnes Woodside; [m] Married; [ch] Danielle Elizabeth Coulson; [ed] Crainhill School, Glasgow; [occ] Housewife; [awards] Volunteer Cancer Association. Carer people with learning difficulties. Aromatherapy, still learning; [activ] Caring for people that need me; [pub writ] Nothing so far keep trying; "The poems I write are the result of meeting people who are emotionally scared. I have this great feeling of empathy so I express it by putting pen to paper."

COWPERTHWAITE, MARIA: 06/12/61 Stoke Poges, Bucks; [p] William & Georgine Neaves; [m] Married; [ch] David Kash and Alex Gareth; [ed] Newtown High School, Newtown, Powys, Wales; [occ] Housewife & Valet; [awards] City and Guilds in Cake Decorating; "I am dyslexic and to have one of my poems printed is a dream come true. I enjoy writing poems and short stories. It gives my family pleasure to read what I have written about them all."

CRANE, MARK: 27/06/78 Leicester; [m] Single; [ed] Earl Shilton Community College; [occ] Student; [awards] Four 'A' Levels Ten G.C.S.E.'s; Recognition of Honour from the Guildhall School of Music and Drama; "Writing poetry for me is a form of meditation. This particular poem was written from an empathetical stance. I am most inspired when travelling, which I believe to be the key to understanding the world. I learnt a great deal from a very good teacher and friend Pauline Walker."

CRON, HUGH: 09/06/67 Ayrshire; [m] Married to Gwen; [ed] Mainholm Academy; [occ] Unemployed; [pub writ] Various anthologies both here and in the U.S.A. Also on the internet with examples of my poetry. "I'm a realistic pessimist with delusions of optimism, the said optimism being my writing. For Gwen who's got even more to put up with!"

CROSBIE, ANGELA E.: 03/03/58 Whiston, Lancs. [m] Married to Gary in June 1990; [ch] Son from previous marriage; [ed] Prescot Girls Grammar School and Mabel Fletcher Technical College; [occ] Housewife and Homemaker; [awards] Awards and qualifications in music including Grade VIII Distinction for voice; [activ] Former member of The Royal Liverpool Philharmonic Choir (RLPC); "I try to make the most of each day, treat the world kindly and value happiness, peace and my husband. I take baby-steps through troubled times, find writing a joy and therapeutic. If it brings others pleasure then I'm more than thrilled."

CUNNINGHAM, THOMAS WALTER: [b] 02/06/37 Ireland; [p] Bernard & Moya; [m] Divorced; [ch] Kane, Carl & Dean; [ed] Secondary School; [occ] Retired; [pub writ] "The Old Bent Teak" published by Poetry Institute Of The British Isles Ltd.; "Still trying to understand the human condition."

DARBYSHIRE, GRAEME LIAM: [b] 28/03/87 Wigan; [p] Susan & Eric and brother Simon; [ed] Student at Marsh Green School,

Wigan; "I like to write silly limericks. I like to draw and make animated models out of plasticine and clay."

DARKE, JANE: [b] 12/11/70 Huntingdon; [ed] Stamford High School; [awards] Graduate Diploma in Music at Colchester Institute; "I love music poetry is the natural progression from music because of the rhythms used. I am concerned with the future of civilisation and mans' physical and spiritual plight. Poetry is the most concise means of personal expression for me."

DAVIES, JANET M.: (Pen Name Janet Coulthard) [b] 10/09/37 Sevenoaks; [p] Floss & Walter Coulthard; [m] Married to Robert; [ch] Carolyn Jane & Jeremy Robin; [ed] St. George's Secondary School, Ramsgate. School of Nursing, Rhyl, N. Wales; [occ] Retired Nurse; [awards] School Prizes, Nursing Certificates and Gardening Prize; [pub writ] One letter in National Magazine; "My priorities in life are fairness and justice. I deplore violence and ugly-ness. In my garden I can surround myself with beauty. Through writing I can portray my ideals."

DAVIES, JUNE: [b] 27/01/42 Parkgate; [p] George (Dec'd) & Irene Terry; [m] Married; [ch] Gary, Maxine, Ian & James; [ed] Rawmarsh Secondary Modern, Rotherham Technical College; [occ] Retired; [awards] RSA Typing III RSA, 120 w.p.m. Shorthand and RSA English II; "Our family are close and we spend time together. I often think of poems and from now on will keep pen and paper handy!"

DAVIS, MARILYN ANNE: [b] 04/02/44 Redditch; [p] Lesley & George; [m] Married; [ch] Samantha Lesley Jones; [ed] Alcester Grammar School; [occ] Housewife & Retired Driving Instructress; [awards] Approved Driving Instructor (ADI). Diploma in Driving Instruction (Dip DI). 8 'O' Levels in 1960; [activ] Voluntary help local College, people with literacy difficulties. Also visited prisoners for a short time in Hewell Grange Open Prison; [pub writ] Poem entitled "Voyage of Recovery" in Amateur Poetry Book entitled "Closet Poems"; "I started writing extensively in 1993 following surgery for removal of a brain tumour. My first poem was "Rebirth", a statement of how I felt about me after brain surgery. "Voyage of Recovery" was about subsequent months. I suppose the trauma triggered something within me."

DAWSON, DOROTHY: [b] 21/03/39 York; [p] Wallace & Rose Jones; [m] Married to Clive 1967; [ch] Mark; [ed] Mill Mount Grammar

School for Girls York; [occ] P/T Sales Assistant; [awards] Dale Carnegie Laboratory Class Certificate 1994; [activ] Member of York Speakers Club and a Committee Member; [pub writ] Poems and letters in local newspapers; "I think we never stop learning and the only barrier to self achievement is the one we create ourselves."

DELDAY, DOUGLAS: [b] 04/05/29 Kirkwall; [p] John & Isabel; [m] Widower; [ch] Elenor, Vivienne, Stuart, James, Sharon, Louise, Stephen & Jeanette; [ed] Kirkwall Grammar School, Orkney Islands; [occ] Retired; [awards] Editors Choice Award National Library of Poetry USA 1994. P.I.B.I. Award of Excellence 1995/96; [pub writ] Other poems, letters to press etc. ISBN 0-9699334.3.C, 185786316X, 1857862295; "Retirement gives me ample time to put words on paper. If people read my work, then I am happy. My aim would be to have my own book of verse published."

DOBSON, PHYLLIS VALERIE: [b] 09/07/28 Cumbria; [p] Graham; [m] Married; [ch] Susan & Shirley; [ed] Secondary School; [occ] Retired H/W; [awards] Qualified Nurse. Top sales in country as a cosmetics manager; [activ] Raise money for charities; [pub writ] Poems in magazines and newspapers, one read on radio; "To write words of love and encouragement and meaningful happenings in this changing world, where you, my friends can feel the pain, the peace or the joy in the depths of your heart."

DUNN, ELEANOR: [b] Birkenhead; [p] Charles & May Brandes; [m] Married; [ch] David, Jaymie and Paul; [ed] Prenton Secondary School, Mersey Park School, Laird School of Art; [occ] Housewife (Poetess); [awards] Song writing 3 awards, 3 awards for Poetry. Small awards for various stories. Published 35 poems in magazines etc.; [activ] Member of Poetic License Poetry Cafe One Eyed City Poets. Live Performances on radio. clubs etc. Fund raiser for our writers workshop; [pub writ] 35 Poems, 2 short stories, 1 poem published in Ohio U.S.A. Various writings in small magazines and papers; "I am a workaholic as far as writing poetry stories etc are concerned. I get much satisfaction from my poetry and like to pass on my thoughts to people through my work."

DUNNE, MARY: [b] 11/01/26 Liverpool; [p] Robert & Bridget Davies; {m] Married to John; [ch] Paul, Angela & Brian; [ed] Our Lady's of Reconciliation, Liverpool; [occ] Senior Citizen; [pub writ] Have had poetry published in Scotland, Wales and England; "John and I spent

20 years in Scotland before retiring to Wales four years ago. I lived here in Wales during World War II working on the land with the WLA."

EVANS, ELAINE M.: [b] 10/12/66 Coventry; [p] Betty & Dennis Walker; [m] Married 27/07/96; [ch] Mathew; [ed] Lyng Hall Comprehensive, Coventry Technical College; [occ] Senior Laboratory Technician; [awards] BTEC Diploma in Science; [activ] Depression Alliance Support Group Leader; [pub writ] Two poems as result of competition entries (one under my maiden name); "What goes around comes around is my philosophy. Writing poetry is a form of therapy. It is 2-dimensional and non-judgmental, a good form of release."

FERRY, KIRSTIN: [b] 18/01/64 Kirby-Muxloe, Leics.; [p] Hazel & Peter Ferry; [m] Single; [ed] Huron Heights S.S., Seneca College in Newmarket, Ontario, Canada; [occ] Computer Operator; [awards] Certificates in photography and desk top publishing; "I have found that to be content in one's life and later in someone else's, one must first find themselves, know themselves."

FISHER, NORA: [b] 31/01/23 [m] Widow; [ch] Betty and Joyce; [ed] State education; [occ] Housewife; "I am widowed and live alone in a council bungalow. I have two married daughters who blessed me with eight grandchildren and seven great grandchildren. I read a lot and I like to write, I have been on my own for eleven years. I had a perfect marriage which is my pride and joy."

FOX, JILL: [b] 02/05/40 Kemsing, Sevenoaks; [p] Harry & Ivy Fisher; [m] Divorced; [ch] Susan & Nicholas; [ed] Secondary School; [occ] Civil Servant;[pub writ] "Me" to be published in book called International Library of Poetry; "My poems reflect my life, and although often sad they are the "magical" part of me."

GEORGE, LOUISE: [b] 17/06/57 Norwich; [p] Jill & David George; [m] Divorced; [ch] Henry, Lucy & James; [ed] Queen Elizabeth Girls' Grammar, Carmarthen, St. Godrics College, London; [occ] Farm Secretary; [activ] Parachute jump for charity, B.T. Swimathon, charity fun runs etc! Love amateur dramatics, keep fit, creative writing, listening to music; [pub writ] None before!; "Being a single working parent of three teenagers, I am very busy and find relaxation in exercise and writing! I enjoy the children and their friends and helping them in all their activities."

GIGGINS, LESLEY: [b] 02/09/49 Dartford; [p] Cyril & Joan Bennett; [m] Married in 1977 to Roger; [ch] Paul, Antony & Catherine; [ed] Dartford Girls Grammar School; [occ] Full time mother; [awards] GCE's in English Language, Mathematics, Geography, Needlework & Scripture; [activ] Regular Church-goer confirmed Christian; [pub writ] Various poems in mixed-author collections during the past three years; "Writing poetry gives me great pleasure. To know it is appreciated by others is a bonus."

GRANT, PAMELA ANN: [b] 29/08/67 Birmingham; [p] Margaret & Brian Knight; [m] Divorced; [ch] Daniel and Charlotte; [ed] The Leys High School Redditch; [occ] Housewife; "This is my first attempt at poetry so to have my poem published is a great achievement. Thank you!"

GRAY, JUDITH: [b] 04/07/80 Cambridge; [p] David & Lyn Gray; [m] Single; [ed] Bottisham Village College, Currently at Cambridge Regional College; [occ] Student; [awards] 9 GCSE's Bronze & Silver Duke of Edinburgh Awards; [activ] Member of a local darts team; "I enjoy spending time with family and friends as this helps me get to grips with different thoughts and feelings. I am inspired by loved ones, so to be able to write such meaningful poetry."

GREENE, JAMES: [b] 08/06/51 Motherwell; [p] Patrick & Elizabeth; [m] Single; [ch] Louise; [ed] Secondary School; [occ] Unemployed; [awards] Dr. of Metaphysics; [activ] Member of Labour Party; [pub writ] "Howling Wind", International LIbrary of Poets; "I belong to Greenpeace, IFAW, WWF. I am a pacifist and CND supporter."

HALL, BARNEY: [b] 15/02/86 Southend-on-Sea, Essex; [p] Jackie & Sean Skirrow Hall; [ed] St. Helens School, Westcliff, Essex, Holmfirth Junior School; "I think that writing poems is very enjoyable and factual for me, and will help me express myself for when I grow up. I think if you work hard at school you get good rewards."

HALL, JOY: [b] 20/05/30 Somersham; [p] Milly & Percy Barlow; [m] Widow; [ch] Enid, Vivienne and Colin; [ed] Slepe Hall, St. Ives, Huntingdon Private School For Girls; [occ] Retired; [activ] Bingo caller and helper at Windsor Court Somersham. Member of Ivy Leaf Club, St. Ives and Somersham British Legion; [pub writ] First poem published in 1995, this is the ninth book out with one of my poems in each; "I write from the heart and give pleasure to others."

HANCOX, GRAHAM: [b] 20/12/47 Workington; [p] Marguerette Hancox; [m] Single; [ed] Workington Newlands School; [occ] Tarmacadam Machine Operator; [awards] City & Guilds in Road and Highway Reinstatement; [pub writ] Poem in firms magazine; "I have never sent a poem away before, I usually just write for my own satisfaction but if I can give pleasure to other readers then it's a bonus. You needn't be special to voice your thoughts. Just write what you feel."

HARDING, JOYCE: [b] 1952 Lincolnshire; [m] Married 1974; [ch] 5 children (2 boys and 3 girls); [ed] Left school age 15 without any qualifications; [occ] Partner in business with my husband; "I enjoy gardening, reading and being with my family."

HART, BRYAN: [b] 03/08/22 Bradford-on-Avon, Wiltshire; [p] Barlow & Doris Hart; [m] Married Doris Turner in 1946; [ch] Stephen & David;

HATCH, PAULINE: [b] 06/04/51 Warrington; [p] Gerald & Edna Higham; [m] Divorced; [ch] Anthony, Sheila, Gail & Carl; [ed] Woolston High School, Gainsborough Secretarial College; [occ] Stores cashier; [awards] 2 Typing Diplomas, ULCI Pitman Shorthand; [activ] Elected Treasurer of Hollinfare Women's Club, Rixton; "I count my blessings that I have led a very eventful life and met such a lot of very fascinating people."

HELLEWELL, BARBARA: [b] 06/03/40 Huddersfield; [p] Isabella & Lewis Jebson (Dec'd); [m] Married; [ch] Mark and Anne; [ed] Skelmanthorpe Secondary Modern School, Scissett and Huddersfield Technical College; [occ] Housewife; [awards] Poetry Award of Excellence Certificate. Special Commendation Certificate. Editor's Choice Award Certificate; [activ] Huddersfield 'Examiner' Travel Circle; [pub writ] 30 poems published in 47 books plus second prize local competition and newspaper. 4 poems broadcast on regional radio 'Write On' programme; "My other interest is playing the Yamaha P.S.R. 400 keyboard. It took me a year to learn as it is a different technique to playing a piano which I learnt in earlier years."

HENDERSON, JIM: [b] 12/03/45 Flintshire; [p] William & Doris Henderson; [m] Married 1970 to Jean; [ch] Robert & Andrew; [ed] Richard Gwyn Secondary School, Flint; [occ] Unemployed; [awards] Trained helpline Operator, Basic Computer Skills; [activ] Volunteer Community car scheme for disabled and elderly; [pub writ] Poems published in various anthologies, two collections published locally; "I like to express myself through my writing, I find my voluntary work very rewarding and like to meet people."

HESLOP, JANET: [b] 09/06/52 Hull; [p] Philip & Joan Addison; [m] Divorced (twice); [ch] Davin Alexander Addison Kemp & Daniel Philip Joseph Kemp; [ed] 10 G.C.S.E.'s and 5 'A' Levels. Studying for a BA Degree; [occ] Student; [pub writ] Poems published, "To Granny Yates", "All This And More", "Talk", "All Senses Cry", "Separation" and "Desertion"; "My friends are my support and I truly believe in them. I have hope for the future and know all will be well."

HEWITT, ELIZABETH BELL: [b] 11/07/32; [p] Thomas & Ethel Brown; [m] Widow; [ch] Cheryll; [ed] Pittington County School; [occ] Retired; [pub writ] One poem by Poetry in Print; "Born in a small village in County Durham. Reader of all types of books. Lived in various parts of the United Kingdon even a croft in the Scottish Highlands."

HINCHEY, DENNIS MICHAEL: [b] 06/07/46 Cardiff; [p] William & Emily Hinchey; [m] Married to Sylvia and now lives in West Wales; [ch] Helen, Carrie, Victoria & Ruth; [ed] Secondary Modern, Followed by Llandaff College 5 years Apprenticeship; [occ] Retired Police Officer (HG); [awards] City & Guilds Mech. & Eng. Commended 4 times for bravery and life saving; [activ] Chairman local NSPCC Committee and helping school children on road safety aged 5 - 11 years at Primary School level. Also story teller to local children in street and for many years Youth Club volunteer; [pub writ] None, first attempt ever!; "Dearly wish I had taken time out for further education in the past and request "Globally" that all peoples be treated equally."

HOBBS, LAURA: [b] 24/10/78 Gravesend, Kent; [p] John & Sheila Hobbs; [m] Single; [ed] Gravesend Grammar School For Girls, Gravesend, Kent; [occ] Student; [awards] Violin - Grade 8, Pianoforte - Grade 6. National Pool Lifeguard Award. Class 5 Gymnastics Coaching Award; [activ] Gravesham Youth Music. Istead Rise Sports Acrobatics Club. Gravesend and Northfleet Swimming Club; "I wrote "The Fox" in year 8 to express my anti-blood sports views. After taking my A-Levels this summer, I will follow a sports degree at University, and hope to pursue a career in sports instruction."

HOULT, LINDA: [b] 08/02/53 Hampstead; [p] Les & Olive Whittaker; [m] Divorced; [ch]

Jonathan & Adam; [ed] Dixie Grammar School, Market Bosworth. Hinckley College; [awards] Various 'O' Levels; [activ] Dance Certificates & Medals (R.A.D.) Brown belt in Wado Ryu Karate; [pub writ] April '78 "My pregnancy" 'Parents' National Magazine. Various Letters and odes in local newspapers. "No One Knows", Passages of Time Anthology; "I find writing and drawing satisfies the creative in me and gives me the greatest sense of achievement. In the past, I have used poetry as a therapeutic channel to heal myself and help others."

HOWELL, MAUREEN: [b] 09/12/40 Haslemere; [p] Violet & (The late) George Morris; [m] Divorced; [ch] Karen, Lee, Jacqui & Ann; [ed] Secondary; [occ] Classroom Assistant. Ex Barclays Staff London; "Surprised and pleased on receiving your letter."

HOWIE, JOHN (JACK): [b] 03/07/20 Antrim, N.I.; [p] Isobel & John Howie; [m] Widower; [ch] John Jeffrey Howie; [ed] Elementary, Mech. Eng. Course Larne Technical School; [occ] Retired Mech. Engineer; [awards] Engineering Certificates with Distinction. Top Eng. Suggestion Award Michelin Tyre Co. 1979. Eng. works Manager; [activ] Church Member, Active life member ballroom dancing, music steward of charity, Clay shooting; [pub writ] Short stories Belfast Telegraph. Poem in 'Sunlight and Shadows' PIBI, Poem in 'Passages of Time' Poetry in Print; "Poetry writing gives me lasting friendship and inspiration which is most rewarding. My thanks and congratulations to PIBI and PIP for publishing poets work worldwide."

HULL, MARIE-LOUISE: [b] 11/11/70 Penzance, Cornwall; [p] Fiona & Ronald; [m] Married; [ed] Hayle Comprehensive School, High Lanes, Hayle, Cornwall; [occ] Salesperson; [awards] Secretarial & Business Qualifications; [pub writ] "Crippling Companion" and "Stephen's Success" this competition; "Look after the one you love."

HUNT, ANTHONY G.: [b] 24/09/65 Camberwell, London; [p] Don & Phyllis Hunt; [m] Single; [ed] University of Keele B.Soc.Sc (Hons), Politics & Economics, MA (Diplomatic Studies); [occ] Civil Servant; [awards] Licensed Radio Amateur, City & Guilds Amateur Radio Certificate; [activ] Bromley Town Church, Radio Society of Great Britain, Musicians Union, Royal British Legion; [pub writ] "In the East" in Between The Lines (ISBN 1857314239), "The Aching Man" in Stirred Not Shaken (ISBN 1857316762), "Ghost Glen" in Poetry Now South East 1997 and "In The West" in Passages of Time (ISBN 0-9528964-0-0); "I like to see myself as an observer and try to paint what I see with words. If, by doing this I can bring pleasure to one person, it is all worthwhile. Hold on to what you know is right - your beliefs are your strongest anchor."

JACKSON, KARAN ELLEN-MARY: [b] 23/07/64 Devises; [p] John & Carol Jackson; [m] Divorced; [ed] HREOD Burna Swindon, Wiltshire; [occ] Repair Technician on P.C.B.; [pub writ] One poem in "Passages of Time"; "My poetry is a personal diary of my life, written most often in times of stress or extreme happiness. The times which inspire me most, when others can read what I've written and relate to it I realise that I'm not alone in life's trials, tribulations and exaltations."

JAMES, GORDON A.: [b] 14/09/43 Cardiff; [m] Married Carol in 1979; [ed] Cathays High School, Cardiff. Exhibition Scholarship to University College, Cardiff in Welsh & French; [occ] Retired Teacher (Welsh Language); [awards] B.A.(Wales) in Modern Languages, Diploma in Russian Language (Extra-Mural). Teacher 1967-95 (Early Retirement!); [activ] Has taught Welsh to adults in various evening classes; [pub writ] 25 poems in various anthologies, won School Bardic Chair with an ode in Welsh; "I find rhyme particularly suitable for humourous poetry. I also use the Welsh 'Cynghanedd' (Rhyme & Alliteration) in English occasionally. I write mostly in English these days!"

JOLLEY, ALWYN: [b] 29/03/30 Warrington; [p] Stanley & Ellen W. Jolley; [m] Single; [ed] Bewsey High, Warrington; [occ] Retired; [awards] A.I.S.T. Swimming Certificate (Associate Member of the Institute of Swimming Teachers); [activ] Compassion in World Farming; [pub writ] "The Message From The Burning Bush" and "First Impressions, poetry books. Single poems in local newspaper and anthologies; "In gratitude to the Spirit of Grace whose underlying love eased the passage of loved ones from life and who inspired my first attempt at the afore-mentioned book. I also find satisfaction in trying to express my interpretation of His will."

JONES, ALISON: 22/06/73 Greenwich; [p] Ken & Joan; [ch] Katherine & Samuel; [ed] Christ Church C of E Primary. The John Roan School, Blackheath; [occ] Housewife; [pub writ] "Please Write Soon". Anthology "Gone But Not Forgotten"; "This poem is dedicated to my dear Katie & Sam. I love you both dearly. Thank you for being part of my life."

JONES, RUTH IRENE: [b] 10/06/31 Somerset; [p] Clifford & Irene Phillips; [m] Married; [ch] Ian and two Grandsons; [ed] Village School East Brent Nr. Weston-Super-Mare; [occ] Retired; [pub writ] One poem published by The International Library of Poetry. Two poems printed by Poetry Today (Llangollen); "I started writing at age of 45 years. I enjoy putting my thoughts in to verse. For me or my friends."

JORDAN, BRIAN EDWARD: [b] 15/12/39 Willen Hall; [p] Joe & Marjorie; [m] Married in 1961 to Marjorie Meeson; [ch] Christine & Susan; [ed] Edward Shelley High School, Walsall. Walsall & Wolverhampton Technical Colleges; [occ] Retired Engineer/Teacher; [awards] Engineering Degree; [pub writ] Technical Book Reviews;

KEECH, MARIAN: (Pen Names Martinella Brooks and Agnes Mae) [b] 31/08/38 Southampton; [m] Divorced; [ch] Richard,Grandchildren Kariss and Hayley; [ed] St. Josephs R.C. School Southampton; [occ] Carer/Writer; [awards] Diploma The Academy Of Children's Writers; [activ] Writing, Photography, Environment Issues; [pub writ] Arrow Books Anthologies. "Millenniums Child" in Out of the Chasel, "Bliss" in Red Hot Lovers, "Children of Dunblane" in Back to the Future, "The Way of Things" in The World About Us, "Adam" in Treasured Memories, "No Brighter Light" in Heroes And Villians, "Peace" in Days Gone By, "Oh Lucky Man" in Bundles of Joy, "Wishing" in World of Words, "Wondering" in Special Memories all 1996/97. Poetry Today, "Rainbow Lady" in Sands of Time, "Groovy" in Whispering Winds 1996/97. Arrival Press, "Snow" in Poets Premier, "Lost Love" in Is This Love 1996/97. International Library of Poetry "Sorrow" and "Embers" in A Lasting Calm 1997, "Jewels of the Imagination" 97. "Sorrow" in book and on audio tape. Poem "Embers" Publishers Choice Award. Hilton House Publishers "Peace" in Flowers of the Field (Special Commendation Award) 1997. I have also been runner up and short listed several times for my short stores and poetry in the UK and USA; "I get my inspiration mainly from every day life and the environment and a lot of my work reflects Man's Inhumanity to Man."

KENNEDY, MARY: [b] 31/05/43 Glasgow; [p] Fred & Carol Stoddart; [m] Married to Gilbert (37 years); [ch] Drew, Ian & David; [ed] Kinning Park Primary, Lambhill Secondary, Vale of Seven Academy; [occ] Hospital Domestic; [awards] Adult Open Learning Course, English Comm 3 & 4. Passed Intro to

Computers; [activ] Creative Writing, knitting, poems (writing); [pub writ] Poems in local magazine. 12 Poems including 2 in PIBI; "When I reached 50 I decided to do English Highers, I missed out on having married very young. I have 5 lovely grandchildren who give me the inspiration for my writing."

KENT, APRIL LOUISE: [b] 26/04/80 Worcestershire; [p] John & Linda Kent; [m] Single; [ed] North Bromsgrove High School, Sixth Form, Bromsgrove, Worcestershire; [occ] Student; [awards] 6 G.C.S.E. passes, received a pass in Intro, Grade 1 and 2 in Electronic Piano. Received a 'Very Good Pass' in an English Speaking Board Course. A medal from Avoncroft Art Exhibition for 'Best School Artist 1996'; [activ] Volunteer at Stroke Association, Member of local 'Technics Music School For Piano'; [pub writ] Poems in School Magazine; "Expression through words has always interested me; Poetry seems the best way to achieve this. Everything I feel, I try to put into words, either on paper or verbally . . . It's how I choose to cope with anything life has to throw at me!"

KETTLE, CAROLE DIANE: [b] 12/12/42 Kirby Muxloe, Leics.; [p] Enoch & Florence Crane; [m] Married; [ch] Debbie, Diane, Denise & Darna; [ed] South Wigston High School, Anstey Martin High School, Hinckley Technical College; [occ] Housewife; [awards] R.S.A. & Pitmans in Shorthand & Typewriting. College of Preceptors:- Religious Knowledge, Art, and Needlework; [activ] Heart-Link; [pub writ] "Seasons", International Soc. of Poets. (Summer) International Society of Poets. Between A Laugh & A Tear. Editor's Choice Award; "I find in poetry a release for pent up emotions. A lot of my poetry reflects my depressive state when my last daughter left home. I now enjoy writing in verse on many subjects."

KING, BRIAN JOHN: [b] 08/11/49 Langley Park; [p] Ronald & Dorothy King; [m] Married; [ch] Peter, Amy and Philippa; [ed] Secondary Modern School Education; [occ] Retired Police Officer; "I have experienced some horrific sights, as a result of my chosen profession, that have saddened me greatly. However, these have been outweighed by the lighter, humourous moments. I am an emotional person and am affected deeply by injustice, however caused. I take great pleasure from "People Watching" and get "Tickled" at the mannerisms and idiosyncrasies of ordinary people. I take great pleasure in relating these observations in the form of poems."

LAW, LINDA J.: [b] 03/04/52 Liverpool; [p]

Edith & Max Morris; [m] Divorced; [ch] Linda & Hayley Law; [ed] Yew Tree Comprehensive, Liverpool; [occ] Housewife; [awards] Hairdresser, Photographer; [activ] Ex School Governor. Volunteer at local school; [pub writ] Include two poems published in the last two anthologies; "I have always enjoyed writing and expressing my feelings through poetry. I also do a lot of painting which reflects a great deal of emotional feelings. With two teenage daughters around both my poetry and paintings are very varied. I also think children can give both pleasure and sadness, but lots and lots of inspiration."

LEA-MORRIS, SUSAN E.: [b] 04/08/47 Walsall; [p] Ron & Betty Morris; [m] Divorced; [ch] Gavin, Jacquline, Leigh & Louise (Daley); [ed] National C. of E. Bloxwich Walsall; [occ] Retired; [awards] Local garden competition; [activ] Bloxwich pen pushers; {pub writ] Poems International Library of Poetry; "Poetry Now" magazine and Poetic Enlightenment from the Midlands; "I believe one should never give up in anything one wants to achieve. Always keep trying. My garden is my inspiration."

LINSCOTT, JUNE: [b] 07/01/47 London; [m] Married; [ch] Barnaby; [occ] Nursery Teacher in Public School; [activ] I love playing tennis and help at vacation bible school annually; [pub writ] Poem in Anchor Poets 1997. Short stories (children's) in local newspaper; "I am a Baptist. I love putting my thoughts and feelings into verse. Most satisfying."

LIVINGSTONE, JONATHON: [b] 22/04/80 Walsall; [m] Single; [ed] I am studying 'A' Levels in Sociology, English Lit and Geography. I am passionate about early 19th Cenury Poetry, which is found in the English 'A' Level Course; [activ] I am looking to join an institution which enables one to express ideas in the form of creative writing and poetry. I enjoy athletics and creative writing; [pub writ] I have written a number of poems, which are yet to be published; "'Brothers and Sisters' was written following a rage contained argument with my sister. I have discovered that emotions are best conveyed in written form. Writing enables one to escape from the routine of life, and enter a world where words are a powerful tool. Having a poem published excites one greatly."

LOFT, PAUL SHAMAN: [b] 14/06/61 Dartford; [p] Leonard & Barbara Loft; [m] Divorced; [ch] Ricky Lee Loft; [ed] The Downs School For Boys, Dartford; [occ] Artist and Craftsman; [awards] On the International Squad for Judo (1975-79); [activ] Conservation work throughout Kent; "I appreciate life and all its facets deeply. My writing is an expression of my strongest hopes and fears, loves and hates. I hope any readers will gain some understanding and sympathy for issues that lie close to my heart."

LOWE, NORMAN: [b] 15/04/29 Manchester; [p] May & Albert Lowe; [m] Married to Madge; [ch] Cynthia, David, Graham, Gordon, Sandra, Carol & Darren; [ed] Basic left school at 14 years old; [occ] Retired G.P.O. Engineer; [pub writ] "Metre", "Who", "Festive Snow", "Holy Star", "Effort", "Delight" and "Present Time"; "I have written poetry for most of my life on and off, but earning a living is most time consuming with little time for much else. I am now retired so I can write to my hearts content."

MARTIN, NICOLA: [b] 04/10/58 Leicester; [p] Rita & Keith Pollard; [m] Widowed; [ch] Liam, Ryan & Louise; [ed] Selby Secondary, Peterborough Regional College; [occ] Housewife/Mother; [awards] 'A' Level Politics & Law; [activ] Member of Catholic Church; [pub writ] Poems entitled 'Life' and 'Hope'; "I have had an eventful and emotional life. This has helped tremendously in my ability to write poetry. I find writing a much easier and pleasurable way to communicate with others as often it takes time for me to say what I feel."

MEADOWS, MARGARET: [b] 27/03/37 Coventry; [p] Florence & Eric Harris; [m] Married; [ch] Tracey & Karen; [ed] Grammar School; [occ] Semi retired/Part Time Proof Reader; [activ] WI Deputy President; [pub writ] 5 Poems and small articles in local paper; "I find poetry writing to be therapeutic and I like to express feelings. I am a voluntary charity worker and attend a creative writing course. Blood donor."

MERRIMAN, SHEILA: [b] 11/12/36 Redditch; [p] Harold & Ada Crump; [m] Married; [ch] Wendy Ann, Neil Andrew & Trudi Alison; [ed] Bridge St. Girls School, Redditch; [occ] Retired; [pub writ] One poem published in "The International Library of Poetry"; "I have been writing poetry for two years, for my own pleasure, I also enjoy reading, knitting, swimming, and crosswords."

McDONALD, NATASHA: [b] 11/07/79 Germany; [p] Alex & Olivia McDonald; [m] Single; [ed] Archbishop Holgate's School, York Sixth Form College; [occ] Student; [pub writ] Three poems published in various anthologies; "If one person enjoys a poem that I have written, I forget that many other people may not enjoy it.

I also feel that trying to touch people through writing is very worthwhile. People that I may never see, know my words, know my thoughts."

McENEANEY, CASSIE: [b] 10/05/86 Egham; [p] Daughter of Ross McEneaney and Kim; [ed] St. Cuthberts Catholic School, Egham, Surrey; [occ] Student; "This poem is dedicated to all the families who lost their children in the Dunblane massacre, and who touched my heart as a child myself."

McINTYRE, DENISE: [b] 17/08/45 Hull; [p] Alexander & Nora McAndrew; [m] George McIntyre; [ch] Paul, Michele & Darron; [ed] Paisley Street School, Hull; [occ] Housewife; [awards] 7061 City and Guilds in Catering; "After bouts of ill health I could not work. My grandchildren came along to enrich my life and inspired me to write poetry."

McMAHON, JOSEPH: [b] 21/12/88 York; [p] Marie & Denis McMahon; [ed] St. Wilfrids R.C. Primary School, York; "Enjoys cycling, swimming, writing stories and drawing townscapes. Members of fit kids gym club and an alter boy at English Martyrs Church."

MOATE, LESLIE: [b] 22/05/20; [p] William & Pat; [m] Widower; [ch] Barry; [occ] Manager Furniture Shop; [activ] Chairman of Haverhill Chamber of Commerce Traders 3 years. President of Haverhill Chamber of Commerce 3 years. Made Life member when I retired; "Retired at age of 64 to look after my sick wife Freda. She had a stroke on 30th April 1996 (our wedding anniversary). Had a second stroke on 6th August 1996, later died in Newmarket Hospital on 6th November 1996, married for 55 years. I found writing poems about Freda and my feelings good therapy. Some of my poems have been put on computer at Newmarket Hospital which I hope will help patients and carers."

MOGGACH-CHRYSTAL, CHRISTINA: [b] 05/10/32 Huntly; [p] Ernest & Mary Smith; [m] Divorced; [ch] Thomas, William & Joshua; [ed] Gordon Secondary School, Huntly, Aberdeenshire; [occ] Housewife; [pub writ] One poem published in the anthology, Island Moods And Reflections; "I love poetry. Poetry was one of my favourite subjects at school. I never dreamed that one day one of my own compositions would be considered good enough to be published. My thanks to the P.I.B.I. for that. I also write short stories."

MURDOCK, ANDREA: [b] 27/09/75 Belfast; [p] Andrew & Isobell; [m] Single; [ed]

Cairnmartin Community High School, Belfast Institute; [occ] Chef; [awards] Catering and Hospitality Levels one and two; [pub writ] Two poems "So Great The Love" and "The Place I Love To Call Home"; "I view life as an open book but the book is not yet completed for I believe I control my own destiny. There is no greater power on earth than the power of love."

MURPHY, DIANE: [b] 17/04/64 Walsall; [p] Gerard & Anne Dilger; [m] Married to Shaun in 1985; [ch] Dean; [ed] St. Thomas Moore Roman Catholic School, Willenhall, West Midlands; [occ] Housewife; "The Poetry I write reflects my thoughts and outlook on life. I am delighted to have my first poem published and hope to write many more, as it gives me great satisfaction."

MURRELL, TRACY: [b] 27/06/70 London; [p] Sylvia & Roy Murrell; [m] Single; [ed] Saffron Walden County High School; [occ] Secretary; [pub writ] Poem entitled "You" published in "Poetry Now" last year; "Had my first poem published at the age of 10 and I've been writing poetry ever since. I find it easier to express my thoughts and feelings in a poem."

NASH, BARBARA ANN: [b] 12/04/46 Evesham; [p] Ken & Barbara Shepherd; [m] Married; [ch] David, Pauline & Sara; [ed] Prince Henry's Grammar School, Evesham; [occ] Housewife; "I try to put my inner feelings into my poetry. I am a very new writer."

NAZREEN, SAIMA: [b] 27/12/78 Pakistan; [p] Ashiq & Riaz Hussain; [m] Single; [ed] Alumwell Comprehensive School, Walsall; [occ] Student; [activ] Volunteer helping the elderly, run by The Walsall 'Befriending Project'; [pub writ] This will be my first published piece; "Personally, I feel that true poetry comes from the heart which is why I wrote 'This World'. It displays how I view the world and how I have been treated by it. This has been my sole inspiration. I hope that other people can relate to what I write."

NEIL, DOROTHY: [b] Cardiff; [p] Thomas & Dorothy; [ed] Lady Margaret High School, Cardiff; [occ] Retired Shipping Clerk; [awards] From Her Majesty The Queen's Lady in Waiting a letter of thanks from Buckingham Palace, on behalf of H.M. The Queen, for a poem which I wrote for the occasion of her 70th birthday. [activ] Member of an art group. Studying French, other interests: music and cats; [pub writ] Ninety poems published since 1992 in various anthologies; Also some in magazines and news papers; "I have found that being tenacious

in the face of adversity has paid dividends. My best poems are written in times of stress. Writing poetry has been very therapeutic and successful."

NEWPORT, MARGARET A.: [b] 15/04/22 West Ham; [p] John & Daisy Rees; [m] Married; [ch] David & Margot; [ed] Brentwood High School, Art School, Commercial College; [occ] Housewife; [awards] Wrote plays for a group of GFS girls; [activ] Parish Councillor, School Governor, Ex Secretary of local W.I., Ex Secretary of Play Area, Secretary of over 60's Club; [pub writ] A study of the village of Hinton Charterhouse for W.I. Village book; "I report on W.I. meetings for magazine and press. I aim to be a useful member of the village community."

NORMAN, PHYLLIS IRENE ESMÉ: [b] 24/01/21 Aldeburgh, Suffolk; [m] Married to John, 1942; [ch] Michael, Anthony, Jeremy, Jonathan; [occ] Clergy wife and the many and varied things that entailed!; [awards] Personal Secretary to L & N.E. Railway Company's Chief Legal Advisor, followed by Personal Secretary to Consultant Psychiatrist and group of Medical Officers; [pub writ] Poem "Aldeburgh Martello Tower" in Sunlight & Shadows, 1996; "Deep regret at the abolition of discipline for our children, which has cost this country millions of pounds and resulted in untold stress to our teachers. It did me good, not harm, and we are denying this loving care to our children."

ORRITT, RICHARD: [b] 18/11/09 Nantyr, Glynceiriog; [p] Henry & Elen Orritt; [m] Widower; [ch] Glasnant (Deceased) and Gwyneth; [ed] Nantyr Council School, Glynceiriog, North Wales; [occ] Retired; [activ] A life long member of Nantyr Presbyterian Chapel and Elder for 51 years; [pub writ] Hymns and poems in local chapel and village magazines. 2 hymns published, one in 1979/80 and one in 1969/70 in annual publications for singing festivals throughout Wales in Presbyterian and Wesleyan Chapels; "I have won countless prizes for my poetry throughout Wales and have one full size oak chair and seven small ones which take pride of place in my home."

OSBORNE, KIRSTIE: [b] 30/10/87 Rugby; [p] Phillip & Caroline Osborne and sister Laura; [ed] St. Andrews Benn Primary School; [pub writ] "Colours" in Sunlight & Shadows; "Kirstie wrote this poem while in Mr. Seed's class. She really enjoys reading and writing poetry. Kirstie has recently successfully completed her swimming survival Stage 1."

OWRAMENKO, MARIANNA: [b] 31/05/54 Manchester; [p] Dmytro and Winifred Owramenko; [m] Single; [ed] Sedgley Park College, Manchester; [occ] Residential Social Worker; [awards] Teacher training certificate; [pub writ] "The Other Side of the Mirror", Anthology of Verse; "Poetry is an expression of life."

PAGET, ALMA: [b] 24/02/22 Stamford; [p] Elsie & Harold Aldridge; [m] Widow; [ch] Patricia Anne Newton; [ed] KGGS & Bedford College; [occ] School Teacher at Haberdashers Aske, Elstree; [awards] 2nd in International Needlework Comp. Editor's Choice Award in International Library of Poetry etc. [activ] Art Society, W.E.A., Chorals. Play the violin, Member of St. John's Church; [pub writ] Poetry in "Voices On The Wind" "Awaken To A Dream" and 10 small anthologies; "I adore writing poetry short stories but painting being my 'true love' sold many and collected many. Exhibited Lincoln Usher Gallery in the past and Nottingham Castle etc."

PALMER, JEAN: [b] 15/10/51 Isleworth; [p] Gordon & Phyllis Palmer; [m] Single; [ed] Kneller Girls School, Twickenham; [occ] Collator; [activ] Blood Donor for the last three years I have walked the London Strollerthone for Children In Need; [pub writ] A poem in a magazine called 'War Time' and two others in books; "I try to help others and try to make people laugh, which I am happy to say I quite often do."

PALMER CHAMARETTE, DR. N.: [b] 08/08/04 Romford, Essex; [p] Arthur & Mary Chamarette; [m] Widower; [ch] David & Michael; [ed] London Hospital & Manchester M.D.B.S., D.P.M. M.R.C. Psych.; [occ] Retired Consultant Psychiatrist; [awards] Physician Psychiatrist to Home Office; [activ] Life member of British Red Cross; [pub writ] Nursing Mirror London "Dream In Therapy". Caducus. "Poisoning by Methyl Chloride" Hong Kong; "Not equipped by natural intelligence to accept spiritual intangibles therefore asked for "The Free Gift" of spiritual truth and understanding."

PANZER, OLIVE: [b] 16/09/21 Brighton; [p] Mary & Vernon Churchill-Simmonds; [m] Divorced; [ch] Susan & Janet. Grandchildren Charles, Richard & Adrian; [ed] French Speaking Convent (Matrix) Notre Dame De Lourdes; [occ] Retired; [awards] Served War: W.A.A.F. to rank of Flight Officer Technical Equipment. Trained in London as beautician.; [activ] Voluntary secretary to Conservative Party 1958. Asst. Parish Secretary 1960-1994. 1

year in Dubai/R.C St. Augustine's 74-75. Member of Royal Tunbridge Wells Art Society (Water Colours). Hon. Asst. Secretary to Executive Committee, Women's Royal Air Force M.O.D. (Air) 1991-93. Pianist, gardening, flower pressing. Dog breeder, King Charles Cavalier Spaniels; "My experience in the R.A.F. in World War 2 totally changed my life. The responsibilities at such a young age placed a heavy burden on me. It was a great honour to receive the Kings Commission and to serve ones country. I have carried that honour all my life and hope I have been worthy of it."

PARKER, ALLAN CLAYTON: [b] 23/05/10 Keighley West Riding; [p] Thompson Dean Parker and Fanny Parker; [m] Married; [ch] Alistair Cameron, Joan Dorothy; [ed] Church School, Keighley Grammar; [occ] Retired Eng Buyer; "I am a grandfather and a great grandfather. My hobbies are listening to music (classical). Listening to cricket match commentaries. Unfortunately I lost my sight when 70 so this has hindered my poetry writing but have a small collection."

PARKES, DENNIS: [b] 04/03/19 Springfield Dudley; [p] James & Edith Elizabeth Parkes; [m] Single; [ed] Compulsory State Education 5-14 years; [occ] Retired; [pub writ] Poems at Arrival Press and Poetry Now, Peterborough. Hilton Publishers, Norwich and International LIbrary of Poetry, Kent; "Sometimes I write few verses to reflect little light on my old school teachers of the 1920's and 30's. Schooldays are most important days of our lives. Poetry harms no-one. Since world began poetry was good, is now and will always be."

POOL, JOHN: [b] 24/04/87 Sidcup, Kent; [p] John and Sue Pool; [ed] Prep School, Merton Court, Sidcup, Kent. Passed entrance exam to Eltham College 1997; "I enjoy swimming, playing the piano and football."

POTTS, ELIZABETH: [b] 11/07/70 Blackburn; [p] Henry & Jean Potts; [m] single; [ed] Wilmslow County High School; [occ] Self employed cleaner; [awards] CPVE Caring for people; [activ] Caithness Paper Weight Collector's Club; "I've been writing poetry ever since I was at school. It's wonderful to know it is not wasted time."

PRICE, CONSTANCE MARY: [b] 11/04/44 Colme; [p] Arthur & Clara Clements; [m] Married; [ch] Anne; [ed] Primet Colne then St. Rofes Special School, Stroud; [occ] Housewife; [awards] Level 3 in English at Nelson College; "I love writing poetry as a hobby but my ambition is to see one in print."

PROSSER, JACQUELYN: [b] 25/08/47 London; [m] Married Brian in 1966; [ch] Tony & Wendy; [ed] Grammar School in London and Art College; [occ] Re-canes antique furniture; [activ] Voluntary work helping in two local schools with art and craft; "I have found much pleasure can be gained from writing and it seems to put my previous experiences into perspective and helps me to move on in my life."

REID, ELIZABETH MARY: [b] 16/08/29 Crick; [p] Mary & Jack Collinson; [m] Divorced; [ch] Stephen John, Christine Patricia; [ed] C. of E. [occ] Retired; [awards] Editor's Choice Outstanding Achievement in Poetry International Society of Poets; [activ] Help at school with children; [pub writ] "Motorway Fog Madness" published in Poetry Now, also 2 poems to be printed by International Society of Poets; "I love all nature all the seasons simply being alive to feel each different day emerge and each different sunset set."

REVELL, VICTORIA MARGARET: [b] 29/04/52 Yorkshire; [p] Jean & Peter Mellonie; [m] Married; [ed] Hull High School for Girls, Tranby Croft, and Hull College of Art & Design; [occ] Ex Civil Servant (20 years), part-time Hygiene Officer; [awards] First Leisure plc Customer Care Certificate in Advanced Technical Skills; [activ] Volunteer Carer & Member of British Diabetic Association; [pub writ] Poems in quarterly civil service magazine, called "Manorisms". "My love of words, expression and feeling keeps my mind in a positive balance ensuring 'The Feel Good Factor of Life'. I have a stronger and more considerate personality. I have also discovered a great happiness by expressing my thoughts with the written word through my poems."

RICHARDSON, J.R.: [b]19/08/21 Wensleydale; [p] Septimus & Rachel; [m] Married Ella Metcalfe 1942; [ch] Brenda & Maureen; [ed] Primary; [occ] Retired farmer; [awards] Constant attention to the job in hand brought ample reward; [activ] Associate member of St. Oswalds Church tower bell ringers. Bowling Club member; [pub writ] Poems, "Time Oh Time", "Tides of Love" (2) "Tree of Humanity" (2) "Joy of Christmas", "Phantom Thoughts", and "Life is a River"; "My poem "Ash Tree", each stanza is dedicated to persons known, the 3rd stanza to ladies of our poetry group, Pat, Sue, Penny and Jill, for use of their homes each week and their words of poetry like rustling leaves sweet symphony make."

RICHARDSON, VIVIENNE YVONNE: [b] 31/05/46 Ashton-U-Lyne; [p] Edward & Dorothy Richardson; [m] Divorced; [ch] Yvonne, Joanne & Richard; [ed] St. John's C. of E. Mossley, Ashton-U-Lyne, Lancs; [occ] Accounts Assistant; "I have loved writing since I was eleven years old. I feel relaxed when writing, who knows one day that 'book'."

ROBERTS, JUNE HILARY: [b] 11/06/50 Huddersfield; [p] Norman & Freda Brook; [m] Married to Ian; [ch] Kenney and Angela; [ed] Educated at Huddersfield Technical College in Office Management and Business Studies; [occ] School Technician & Catering Manager; [awards] Certificates in Shorthand Typing, English and Music. Plus City And Guilds Foundation Course in Literacy; [activ] A member of Holme Valley Choir and a support Teacher of Adult Literacy; [pub writ] Three Poems published with Arrival Press Publication; "I have a keen interest and enthusiasm in English and Music. My natural flair for writing, developed through the medium of poetry has enhanced my creativity. I believe in the importance of true love and friendship."

ROBINSON, PATRICIA: [b] 08/03/42 Willingham-By-Stow; [p] Joe & Madge Kieran; [m] Married Trevor in 1961; [ch] Dean; [ed] St. Mary's R.C. Brigg; [occ] Housewife; [activ] Knitting Club Member. Line Dance Member. Like travel; [pub writ] Local evening paper; "I do my best in all I do, help others if I can, like to write poems about nature and life."

ROKYCKYJ, MARIAN: [b] 04/02/33 Hull; [p] Tom & Doris Louis; [m] Married; [ch] Michael, Peter, Sonia, Ann & Kevin; [ed] Left School at 14; [occ] Retired Dressmaker; "I often write poetry but this is the first time I have ever bothered to enter one in a competition."

ROSENTHAL, S.: [b] 21/11/29 Birmingham; [p] Betty & Harrey; [m] Married; [ch] Sydney; [ed] Public School, University; [occ] Retired; "Currently writing a book on business ideas."

ROWLEY LANGFORD, CHRIS: [b] 20/02/40 Battersea London; [p] Henry & Mabel Langford; [m] Married to Michael Rowley; [ch] Kate Jessica Eleanor Stafford; [ed] Grammar School, College, Camberwell Art School to Intermediate Level; [occ] Retired from teaching/local artist in watercolour/ink/oil/acrylic; [awards] Associate of Essex Institute of Higher Education. 2 Certificates of Further Professional Study Camb. Institute of Education (C.I.C.F.P.S.); [activ] Governor of local Primary School, WRVS member, RSA counselling skills certificate - Voluntary worker for M.E. Association telephone help line; [pub writ] Poems: "Time Share" Feb '96, "Autumn Air" '95 "Playground Tradition" '96 "Just By The Nature Reserve" '96; "For me poetry is a way to distil my thoughts and feelings. I like to communicate with people and poetry offers a line of communication to those I don't know personally."

ROY, PRESLEY MICHAEL: [b] 20/04/28 London, England; [ed] Upton Grammar, Berkshire. Newland Park College, Buckinghamshire, Hornsey College Of Art, London; [occ] Professional Artist; [awards] Teachers Certificate Art Advanced Level (Distinction), Reading University. Post Graduate Diploma in Art Education, London University. Mexico City Diploma Poetry/Visual International Bienal; [activ] "Distinguished Life Member" of International Society of Poets (USA); [pub writ] "The Role of The Art Teacher" (1976, UK), "The Art Lark" (1992 UK), Poetry verses in numerous anthologies, UK. (With 'Editor's Choice' Awards) from National Library of Poetry, USA); "My poems "Poetry Reading With Wine '97" is written with a sense of fun, for the most festive season of the year. For maximum appreciation/declamation of its rendering, several glasses (before and after) of "best fruits of the vine" is highly recommended."

SADLER, MARGARET: [b] Morley; [p] Clifford & Alice Sykes; [ch] Elise; [occ] Retired; [awards] Former Nurse, Pinderfields General Hospital, Wakefield and Care Assistant, Morley; [pub writ] Poetry, Local Newspaper; "I began writing poetry after the passing of my dear Mother. The inspiration I contribute to my grandfather Hedley Sykes who used to write poetry for the local newspaper."

SCOWCROFT, MARGERY: [b] 14/03/14 Wilmslow; [p] Mr.& Mrs. T. Davies; [m] Married; [ch] Roderick Ian; [ed] Kings School, Macclesfield; [occ] Traffic Control Manager; [activ] Westley Guild, Widows Club, Monday Club. Hobbies, playing my organ and my piano; [pub writ] "Comfort", Poetry Institute of the British Isles. "Faith, Hope & Love", Arrival Press, Peterborough; "I am enjoying my retirement, my life is now music and poetry and lots of friends."

SHARP, ALEXANDER: [b] 25/07/67 Surrey; [p] Roland & Janet Sharp; [m] Single; [ed] BSc. Cybernetics & Control Engineering, Reading University; [occ] Engineer; [awards] Radio Amateurs Exam; [activ] Radio Society of Great Britain; [pub writ] Academic Paper in Engineering Journal, 1 other poem in "Passages of Time"; "I dedicate this poem to my brother Nicholas who has just emerged from a difficult period in his life."

SHEPHERD, RUTH: [b] 01/04/83 Rotherham; [p] Alan & Irene Shepherd; [ed] Penistone Grammar School; [occ] Student; [activ] Guides, Help at Brownies, Dance, Creative Writing, Volley Ball; "I enjoy creative writing and I am a keen animal lover. I am aiming to be a vet and to enjoy my life."

SHORT-WINDSOR, JANET: [b] 09/11/33 Brighton; [p] Kathleen & Sydney Short; [m] Divorced; [ch] Stephen Philip and two grandchildren, Emma and Laura; [ed] Wistons Private School, Brighton; [occ] Retired Library/Tourist Officer; [awards] 2nd Prize 3 short stories. Won Prize and free holiday for story about my memories of VE Day; [activ] Assistant Sec. of Hailsham Choral Society. Sussex Singers. Sussex Opera & Ballet Society. Hastings Opera. Canford Summer School of Music. Eastbourne Sinfonia Choir. St. Bede's School Choir; [pub writ] 3 Short stories, Story about VE Day; "Ballet Dancer (on points) Ice Skating (several years ago). Still enjoy singing and barn dancing. Wrote words and music to a lullaby for my son when he was small, also a Xmas carol, set to music by a friend. Appeared in film "Half A sixpence". Still writing and hope it brings pleasure to others as it does to me as well as my music. A very soothing and relaxing pastime."

SIMPKINS, JOAN ELSIE: [b] 17/10/18 Burton-On-Trent; [p] William & Elsie Kirkland; [m] Widow; [ch] Barry & Pauline; [ed] Secondary School; [occ] Retired Security Officer; [activ] Member of British Legion; [pub writ] "Crucifixion", "Second World War", "Tell Me Why", "Four Seasons"; "I have always loved poetry, but did nothing serious until the loss of my husband, also a crossword and jigsaw addict. Love my dog and two budgies."

SIMPSON, KEITH JOHN: [b] 20/09/50 Birmingham; [p] Richard & Irene Simpson; [m] Married Karen Simpson in 1988; [ch] Sarah, Katie & Gemma; [ed] Lyndon High School, Hall Green College; [occ] Engineer; [awards] City & guild of London in Craftsmanship. Football Medals; [activ] British Legion; [pub writ] Short articles in magazines (National) and newspapers. Poems in various anthologies; "Tolerance is the key. Getting up tight with people only hurts yourself. My tension is released through my writing. Money cannot buy happiness."

SMITH, REGINALD PETER: [b] 30/10/39 York; [p] Reginald & Mary; [m] Married; [ch] Maria Jane; [ed] Manor School, York. University College, Scarborough. BA Open University (1982); [occ] School Teacher; [awards] Qualified Swimming Instructor (A.I.S.T.) Scarborough Swimming Club; [activ] Chairman Scouts & Guides 1st Scalby, Scarborough; [pub writ] 16 poems in various anthologies "Anchor Books" and "Poetry In Print" Ltd.; "I view poetry as a concise art form in which one paints, in words, emotions, expressions and experiences."

SONDH, JATINDER: [b] 07/05/83 Gravesend, Kent; [p] Sukhchain & Surinder Sondh; [ed] Year 9 Student at Secondary School. St. Georges C.E.; [activ] Member of Saint Georges Dance Club, St. Georges Drama Club and St. Georges Writer's Club; [pub writ] None but many unpublished short novels and poems; "I believe that the human "emotion" is the most special yet hardest to express. My writing helps me to express my feelings to life and helps others to achieve this."

SPENCER, GRAHAM: [b] 04/02/51 York; [p] Peter & Sylvia Spencer; [m] Married to Susan Wood in 1973; [ch] Scott & Lisa; [ed] York School of Art; [occ] Interior Decorator; [awards] Undertaken Commissions for the National Trust, Castle Howard, Yorkshire Television, Forte's, Crayke Castle etc.; "I like to put down a picture of life's rich characters onto paper with words, so that you can see them looking back at you from the page."

STEWART, MICHAEL: [b] 26/12/47 Leigh, Lancs; [p] William Henry & Annie; [m] Married 7/4/84; [ch] James Michael, Thomas Alexander, Lian; [ed] Bedford High School, Leigh, Wigan and Leigh College, University College Salford, Salford College;[occ] Lecturer, Isle of Man College; [awards] City & Guilds, CPD, Cert. Ed., HNC subjects, TDLB Full Awards, NWRAC, AIBSU; [activ] Leigh Rangers/Miners ARLFC. Warrington Anglers; [pub writ] Church magazines, short stories, newsletters, anthologies; "Life is about people, without people there can be no life. To my wife Patricia, Aunty Edith, Jethro, Clarrice, Richard, Carl , Philipa and People X."

SWIFT, JESMOND: [b] 08/06/32 Queensborough; [p] Edith & James Booth; [m] Married Derek Swift 15/8/53; [ch] Christopher & Judith; [ed] Gravesend Grammar School For Girls, Avery Hill College, Eltham; [occ] Retired School Teacher; [awards] Teaching Certificate; [activ] Tangent Club, Inner Wheel; [pub writ]

Poem Inner Wheel Magazine; "I have always written poetry for my own, and I hope, others pleasure."

SYDENHAM, JOANNE L.: [b] 29/01/89 Huntingdon; [p] Steve & Vanessa, Sisters Natasha, Nicola and Lianne and brother Stephen; [ed] Stukeley Meadows Primary School, Huntingdon; [awards] Swimming and Gymnastics awards; "I like writing poetry and I am very good at English writing."

SYGRAVE, ROSEMARY A.V.: [b] Perth, Scotland; [p] Rose & (The Late) Henry C. Sygrave; [m] Divorced; [ch] Christopher, Candy, Robin, Ronald & Adrian (Menzies); [ed] Perth Junior Academy, Goodlyburn J.S. School, Perth High School; [awards] 2 Certificates/Awards of excellence for poems. Short listed in National Competition; [pub writ] Almost 40 of my poems published in various anthologies and 10 in other publications. 1 short story; "I write from my heart, into lines of verse, which help me to start - ease times of distress."

THOMAS, BETTY: [b] 28/06/28 Rawmarsh; [p] Cyril & Edith Hatfield; [m] Widow; [ch] Linda; [ed] Rawmarsh Secondary Modern; [occ] Retired Factory Worker; "I wrote this poem along with another 10 years ago when I was feeling very low in spirit and it gave me a tranquil feeling so I locked it away thinking no-one else would see it except myself.You will never know how happy and thrilled you've made me by selecting my poem to publish. Thank you so much."

THOMPSON, JOHN ANTHONY ROW-LAND: [b] 24/10/24 Manchester; [p] Ruth & John; [m] Married; [ch] John & Susan; [ed] Manchester Grammar School. BSc. (Econ); [occ] Retired; [activ] Golf Club; "The computer, bought for my 70th birthday, was from my wife and children to keep my mind active in my dotage. They did not realise what a pandora's box they had opened."

THORN, JOHN: [b] 02/10/23 Chagford, Devon; [p] Reginald & Lilian; [m] Married to Eve (51½ years); [ch] Hilary & David; [ed] Chagford Elementary School (Dartmoor), Totnes Grammar School. St. John's College York. St. Aidan's Theological College Birkenhead. Many Literary & Teaching Courses. Since retiring, many creative writing courses, beginning in 1986. Wilberforce 6th Form College (1994-1996); [occ] Retired Teacher; [awards] Diploma in the Education of Handicapped Children (Hull) 1970. Certificate Modern Literary & Historical Studies (Hull

University) 1983 GCSE Fine Art Grade B 1995; [activ] September 1942, entered RN, as a rating, served in Combined OPS - invasions of Sicily, Salerno & Normandy. Secretary, Scarborough Young Liberals 1948-1951. 1955 Anglican layreader until 1970. Lost faith. Returned to Church as worshipper in 1993. Now joining Roman Catholic Church. [pub writ] Nothing worth speaking of; "As a child, I was raised to be a Plymouth Brother. Since 1938, in a rough and tumble way, I have sought "The Truth", in as many senses of the word, as my intellect, imagination and life experience would allow.

TILL, CATHERINE JEAN: [b] 03/02/32 Middlesbrough; [b] Alex and Ethel Davies; [m] Married; [ch] Steven & Elaine; [ed] Elementary, Cargo Fleet High School For Girls; [occ] Housewife; [pub writ] A few Letters to Newspapers & Magazines;

TUCKER, DOROTHY: [b] 23/03/61 Kingston, Jamaica; [p] Henry and Ena Tucker; [ed] University of North London, Institute of Education, London; [occ] Teacher; [activ] Member of a Baptist Church and choir member; "I find pleasure in expressing thoughts, feelings and memories through songs and poetry. When the thought of eventually approaching and passing through the door of death comes to mind, I find rest in knowing that my eternal destiny lies in the hands of one who is wiser than I."

TUNSTALL, BARBARA: [b] Walsall; [m] Married; [ch] Pamela and Teresa; [ed] Secondary Modern School. Walsall West Midlands; [occ] Retired Midwife; [awards] Gold Medal. Sister Dora Centenary, Walsall. Local Heroine; [pub writ] Two anthologies, plus two Christian Poetry Anthologies; "Working in a caring profession has been a reward for me, my life is still caring, fulfiling the needs of others. Writing and reading poetry is inspiring for me."

TURNER, JOHN: [b] 15/10/38 Rotherham; [p] Thomas & Alice (Deceased); [m] Married to Brenda; [ed] Secondary Modern (Park Street); [occ] Retired; [activ] Church (Pentecostal) committed Christian . Sponsor child in Brazil; "I try to look not only at my own needs but also the needs of others, social injustice is my pet "hate". I love to see people happy it ought to be more contagious these days. Poetry helps me to express my innermost thoughts on all issues concerning the heart."

VIGUS, EMMA: [b] 17/10/74 Hertfordshire; [p] Richard & Catherine Vigus; [m] Single; [ed] Chancellors School, Cranfield University; [occ] Student; [awards] Studying for a BSc (Hons)

Degree in Business Management and the Environment; [activ] I enjoy socialising, theatre, cinema and horse-riding; "Passion feeds the mind and the pen."

VINALL-BURNETT, MARGARET: [b] 03/10/13 Haslemere, Surrey; [p] Arthur & Frances Bennyworth; [m] Widow (twice); [ch] Nancy, Albert, Carolina, Rosalind, Robert, Dorothy, Jeffrey & Kenneth; [ed] Cross-in-Hand Village School, Heathfield Surrey; [occ] Retired Cook; [awards] Member International Society of Poets; [activ] Disabled Association Access etc. Roehampton Hospital London; [pub writ] "Disabled Meg" and "Something to Say" Devon & Dorset. Poetry Now (2) PIBI 1995-96. Anchor Books (9) I.S.P. 1996 (2); "I lost a leg at Hastard 1942. Married Robert Burnett 1945. Stalag 383 POW he died in 1975. I have family in Australia."

WALLER, WILLIAM GEORGE: [b] 08/06/15 Portsmouth; [p] William Charles & Sarah Elizabeth; [m] Married; [ch] Terence Christopher & Margaret Jane; [ed] Barton Peveril Grammar School, Eastleigh 1925-1933 Southampton University 1933-36; [occ] Headmaster, Retired; [awards] BA Honours Degree, London Ext Diploma in Education Cambridge; [activ] Ex President Romsey Rotary Club, President Romsey Blind Club. Former Principal Further Education Centre; [pub writ] Sunshine & Shadow 1990; "Married Margaret (Peg) childhood sweetheart 1938. Founder Headmaster, Romsey Community School. Forced to retire on becoming blind. Now composes on tape recorder."

WASSELL, ANNETTE R.M.: [b] 09/07/64 Walsall; [p] Hazel Yvonne Beecroft; [m] Married; [ch] One daughter, Rhianne Alanah Wassell; [ed] Aldridge Comprehensive School; [occ] Clerk-Typist at Social Services Dept.; [pub writ] Poem entitled "Nuclear Holocaust" included on recorded album by "The Sears"; "During early 80's I was a "Performing Poet", a memorable experience which would never have happened without the love, support and encouragement of friends - especially Claire Taylor, my family and husband Andrew."

WAY, OLWEN: [b] 30/03/23 Lahore, Pakistan; [p] Garrett; [m] Widowed; [ch] Mary, Gregory, James Radegunde and Gabrielle; [ed] Perse Cambridge and Prep School Bexhill; [occ] Teaching, Nursing; [awards] Competed with 5 children in Pony Club and show events. Breeder and owner of Welsh Cobs I found success in the show ring; [activ] After the Second World War I ran a Thoroughbred Stud outside Newmarket with my husband. Member of Poetry group in Cambridge; [pub writ] Various poems published over the years and was for a time an editor on a poetry magazine; "An increasing awareness of the need for the relevance of poetry in making some sense of our world."

WELLER, THERESA LOUISE: [b] 31/08/70 Walsall West Midlands; [p] Brian Weller and Shirley Spinks; [m] Single; [ch] Lyndon Weller and Leon Weller; [ed] Bluecoa C. Of E. Comprehensive School; [occ] Housewife; [awards] Blood Doner; "I find that poetry enables me to put my feelings into words. I wish to thank a close friend of mine for giving me the encouragement to be honest with myself and to share with others this talented gift that God has blessed me with."

WESTALL, RICHARD: [b] 13/07/52 Southampton; [p] Myrtle & Norman Westall; [m] Married to Wendy in 1983; [ed] Park House School (Newbury), South Berks College of Further Education; [occ] Presently unemployed due to being disabled by M.E.; [activ] Founder/Leader of a Day-Centre for the Homeless (Newbury); [pub writ] Seven Poems including "Time Was" in various anthologies (1992-1997); "I am a Christian (And Socialist); I also suffer from M.E. (Chronic Fatigue Syndrome): These factors influence my poetry. I admire Stephen Spender and T.S. Eliot amongst others."

WHITE, SHONA: [b] 09/06/26 London; [p] Gretta & Harrold Bridger; [m] Widowed; [ch] Steven, Grant & Marissa; [ed] Lewisham Prendercast School & Bromley Grammar School, Kent; [occ] Retired Medical Secretary; [awards] Teacher of English to Foreign Students; [activ] Bridge, Ex-Rotarian Nigeria, Jamaica & Malawi. Animal Welfare; [pub writ] Articles in Medical Magazines, Autocar, Top Gear, and Poetry Publications. Local newspapers; "My life has been so varied as my husband's work took him to Iran and Africa (16 years) with much tragedy (Widowed twice) and three children. My release from stress is thro' "writing"."

WHITLOCK, TERESA: [b] 14/09/12 Preston; [p] Richard & Eleanor; [m] Widow of Managing Director of Whitlock Heating Co.; [ch] Fred, Brian, Judith & Maureen; [ed] Local School Gained Scholarship 11 plus etc.; [occ] Retired; [awards] Publicans daughter also learned to weave in cotton trade to help with War Effort; [activ] Langridge Women's Institute President for seven years (Now retired). Drama, floral art, are my hobbies also writing; [pub writ] 5 poems;

"I try to keep a good sense of humour and be friendly to people and help my family as much as I can."

WILLIAMS, CHRISTINE: [b] 14/12/50 Warrington; [p] George & Lillian Warburton; [m] Married to Ken Williams; [ch] Tracey Anne and Debbie Jane; [ed] Bewsey Secondary Modern School; [occ] Housewife;

WILLIAMSON, WILLIAM THOMAS: Pen Name Bill Williamson [b] 09/02/19 Dover, Kent; [p] Arthur & Winifred Williamson; [m] Single; [ed] Christ Church Secondary; [occ] Retired Interior Decorator of Period Property; [pub writ] First Poem Pending; "I get great satisfaction from writing poetry and short stories. It enables me to express my true feelings as I have been disabled for several years."

WILSON, JAMES ANDREW: [b] 17/02/38 Cardenden; [p] Gordon & Isabella; [m] Married to Helen on 13/10/56; [ch] Gordon, Janice, Peter, Helen, Margaret & June; [ed] Auchterderran Junior Secondary; [occ] Retired Miner; [awards] Colliery Deputy, Scafield Colliery, Kirkcaldy, Fife, Scotland; [activ] Charity Work (Singing), Golf, Angling; [pub writ] First attempt at poetry. Numerous other unpublished poems; "Since retiring and having time on my hands I now have time to express oneself thro poetry on life and losses of the friends I have known, and the world in general."

WILSON, MARGARET: [b] 03/04/31 Hull; [p] Elsie & Harry Poskitt; [m] Divorced; [ch] Linda Littlefair; [ed] Fifth Avenue High School, Hull; [occ] Nurse for 27 years; [awards] I have reached Grade 6 in Practical and Musical Theory (piano). 5 years study since retirement; [activ] I am a member of the Royal College of Nursing; "I like to keep active physically and mentally and to help others whenever I can. I have also composed music for my poem, and other poems. I practice Tai-Chi for relaxation."

WOODHOUSE, LUCY FLORENCE: [b] 05/11/03 Ham Farm Ramsdell; [p] Henry and Annie Rowell; [m] Widow; [ch] Nine Girls and two boys; [ed] Ramsdell Village School; [occ] Retired; [pub writ] Poems published in Basingstoke Gazette; "I love the country because it gives me so much inspiration and enjoy giving other people pleasure, through my writing."

WOODLEY, PEGGY: [b] 06/06/49 Leicester; [p] William & Cassie Pritchard; [m] Married; [ch] Asa John Bailey Tomkins; [ed] Heathfield High School, Earl Shilton, Leics. Hinckley

Grammar. North Warwickshire College of Art; [occ] Artist - Poet (Antiques field); [awards] Fashion Photographic Model/Beautician/Regent Academy of fine Arts "Antiques Course"; [activ] Foster parent to "Guide Dogs For The Blind Association."; "Through always living a full happy life, helping others caring for our world I've learnt through my poetry to share all my experience openly with others, to give others pleasure, filled with thought."

WOODLEY, THOMAS ALFRED: [b] 16/11/22 Llanbradach; [p] Frank & Edith; [m] Single; [ed] Ponllanfraith Elementary School; [occ] Retired Railwayman; [awards] War Medals; [pub writ] 3 poems Poetry in Print; "There is nothing better to cool ones head than to experience cool grass at ones feet!!"

WRIGHT, JANICE: [b] Accrington; [p] Marjorie & James Fell; [m] Married; [ch] Lisa and Jamie; [ed] St. Katharine's College of

Education, Liverpool; [occ] Headteacher; [awards] Teaching qualifications. Primary Management. First Aid; [activ] Methodist Church. Most of my time taken up with school activities; [pub writ] Never tried before, but have written plays in verse for school; "I enjoy everything to do with words and rhyme. I write to relax."

YOUNG, JUSTINE: [b] 24/04/81 Dunkerton, Bath ; [p] Sally Irene and Micheal John; [ed] Bath College; [occ] Student; [awards] Aids poetry competition. Emergency aid and several certificates for mime at midsummer-set; [activ] Charity - sending boxes of things e.g. clothes to poor people in Bosnia; [pub writ] Local newspaper, Bath Chronicle; "I have found poetry a good resource of expressing my feelings, views and opinions. I hope this is shown in my work. I strive to achieve the best in life, but I know happiness is the true fulfilment."

INDEX OF POETS